Michael Psellos on Literature and Art

Michael Psellos in Translation

Miniature portrait of Michael Psellos and his pupil Michael Doukas, Ms Pantokrator 234, fol. 254 (12th century). © Holy Monastery of Pantokrator, Mount Athos. Used with permission.

Michael Psellos on Literature and Art

A Byzantine Perspective on Aesthetics

edited by
CHARLES BARBER
and **STRATIS PAPAIOANNOU**

University of Notre Dame Press

Notre Dame, Indiana

University of Notre Dame Press
Notre Dame, Indiana 46556
www.undpress.nd.edu

Published in the United States of America

Library of Congress Cataloging-in-Publication Data

Names: Psellus, Michael, author. | Barber, Charles, 1964– editor.
Title: Michael Psellos on literature and art : a Byzantine perspective on aesthetics / edited by Charles Barber and Stratis Papaioannou.
Description: Notre Dame : University of Notre Dame Press, 2017. | Series: Michael Psellos in translation | Includes bibliographical references and index. |
Identifiers: LCCN 2017001226 (print) | LCCN 2017016284 (ebook) | ISBN 9780268100506 (pdf) | ISBN 9780268100513 (epub) | ISBN 9780268100483 (hardcover : alk. paper) | ISBN 0268100489 (hardcover : alk. paper) | ISBN 9780268100490 (pbk. : alk. paper) | ISBN 0268100497 (pbk. : alk. paper)
Subjects: LCSH: Aesthetics, Byzantine. | Art—Philosophy. | Literature—Philosophy.
Classification: LCC BH137 (ebook) | LCC BH137 .P7413 2017 (print) | DDC 801/.9—dc23
LC record available at https://lccn.loc.gov/2017001226

∞ *This paper meets the requirements of ANSI/NISO Z39.48-1992 (Permanence of Paper).*

Contents

Note to the Reader

The present volume is the third in the project *Michael Psellos in Translation*, following two earlier works: *Mothers and Sons, Fathers and Daughters: The Byzantine Family of Michael Psellos,* edited by Anthony Kaldellis (2006) and *Psellos and the Patriarchs: Letters and Funeral Orations for Keroullarios, Leichoudes, and Xiphilinos,* translated by Anthony Kaldellis and Ioannis Polemis (2015). Like those volumes, this one too is the result of a collaborative effort. It is divided into two parts, the first devoted to Psellos' literary theory and the second to his visual aesthetics; Stratis Papaioannou was responsible for the review and writing of Part 1, and Charles Barber for Part 2; the names of the two editors or those of further contributors have been further identified in the chapters.

We have neither followed nor imposed absolute rules for the rendition of Psellos' demanding Greek into English, though we have generally attempted to err on the side of the literal meaning. We have also tried to create some consistency in the translation of recurrent rhetorical terms. The most important and common among these are cited also in their original Greek form within square brackets [ ], and have been gathered in a "List of Rhetorical Terms" at the end of the book. When necessary, though rarely, Greek terms have been simply transliterated and explained with a footnote.

Square brackets are used also for line and page numbers as well as for necessary explanatory remarks or simply supplementary words for the sake of clarification. Angle brackets < > have been employed either (a) to indicate words that have been added by editors of the Greek originals in places where a lacuna in the text has been identified or (b) to include words and phrases that were deemed necessary to complete the meaning in English.

The names of most Byzantine persons have been transliterated into English, thus: Psellos and not Psellus, Ioannes Sikeliotes and not John of Sicily, and so forth.

Acknowledgments

We would like to thank the many contributors to this volume for their efficiency and patience, the two anonymous reviewers who provided much useful commentary, as well as Stephen Little, our editor at the University of Notre Dame Press, for supporting this project; Matthew Dowd undertook the copyediting of the book and we are grateful for his exemplary work. The editors would also like to thank the Center for Hellenic Studies for allowing us to include in this volume slightly revised versions of Elizabeth A. Fisher's introductions to and translations of Psellos' *Encomium for Kyr Symeon Metaphrastes* and his *Discourse on the Miracle that Occurred in the Blachernai Church*, which are also available at: http://chs.harvard.edu/wa/pageR?tn=ArticleWrapper&bdc=12&mn=5478.

Stratis Papaioannou would also like to thank: Dr. Byron MacDougal who, with utmost care, precision, and adeptness, reviewed the English as well as the translations of Part 1; the Classics Department at Brown University for generously funding the project; David Konstan, who commented on the translation of several passages, and Ioannes Polemis, who read the critical edition of the *Letters*, as both offered precious suggestions; and Charis Messis, who, with his usual wisdom, discussed the contents of the book at various stages of its creation.

Charles Barber would like to thank: the University of Notre Dame and Princeton University for the sabbatical leaves that made work on this project possible.

Abbreviations

Psellos' Texts

Chronographia edited by D.R. Reinsch, *Michaelis Pselli Chronographia.* 2 vols. Berlin: De Gruyter, 2014.

Concise Answers to Various Questions edited by L.G. Westerink, *Michael Psellus, De omnifaria doctrina.* Utrecht: J.L. Beijers, 1948.

Concise History edited by W.J. Aerts, *Michaelis Pselli Historia Syntomos.* Corpus Fontium Historiae Byzantinae. Series Berolinensis 30. Berlin: De Gruyter, 1990.

Criscuolo 1990 edited by U. Criscuolo, *Michele Psello, Epistola a Giovanni Xifilino.* Byzantina et Neo-Hellenica Neapolitana 1. Naples: Bibliopolis, 1973; new ed., 1990.

Discourse Improvised . . . about the Style of the Theologian edited by (a) P. Levy, *Michael Psellus: De Gregorii Theologi charactere iudicium, accedit eiusdem de Ioannis Chrisostomi charactere iudicium ineditum*, 46–63. Diss. Straßburg; Leipzig: R. Noske, 1912. (b) A. Mayer, "Psellos' Rede über den rhetorischen Charakter des Gregorios von Nazianz." *Byzantinische Zeitschrift* 20 (1911): 27–100, at 48–60. Both editions are cited: the paragraph number refers to the paragraph divisions in Levy's edition, while the numbers refer to the lines in Mayer's edition.

Encomium for his Mother edited by U. Criscuolo, *Michele Psello: Autobiografia; encomio per la madre.* Naples: D'Auria, 1989.

G Letters: edited by P. Gautier, "Quelques lettres de Psellos inédites ou déjà éditées." *Revue des Études Byzantines* 44 (1986): 111–97, at 126–97.

K-D Letters: edited by E. Kurtz and F. Drexl, *Michael Psellus: Scripta minora magnam partem adhuc inedita II, Epistulae.* Orbis romanus, biblioteca del testi medievali a cura dell' Università cattolica del Sacro cuore 5.2. Milan: Società editrice "Vita e pensiero," 1941

K-D I Various texts: edited by E. Kurtz and F. Drexl, *Michael Psellus: Scripta minora magnam partem adhuc inedita I, Orationes et dissertationes.* Orbis romanus, biblioteca del testi medievali a cura dell' Università cattolica del Sacro cuore 5.1. Milan: Società editrice "Vita e pensiero," 1936.

Maltese Letters: edited by E. V. Maltese, "Epistole inedite di Michele Psello." *Studi Italiani di Filologia Classica* III 5 (1987): 82–98 and 214–23; 6 (1988) 110–34.

On John Chrysostom edited by P. Levy, *Michael Psellus: De Gregorii Theologi charactere iudicium, accedit eiusdem de Ioannis Chrisostomi charactere iudicium ineditum*, 92–98. Diss. Straßburg; Leipzig: R. Noske, 1912.

On the Different Types of Style of Certain Writings edited by J. F. Boissonade, *Michael Psellus de operatione daemonum cum notis Gaulmini: Accedunt inedita opuscula Pselli*, 48–52. Nürnberg, 1838. Repr. Amsterdam: A. M. Hakkert, 1964.

Or. for. edited by G. T. Dennis, *Michael Psellus: Orationes Forenses et Acta.* Stuttgart: Teubner, 1994.

Or. fun. I edited by I. Polemis, *Michael Psellus: Orationes Funebres,* vol. 1. Berlin: De Gruyter, 2014.

Or. hag. edited by E. A. Fisher, *Michael Psellus: Orationes Hagiographicae.* Stuttgart: Teubner, 1994.

Or. min. edited by A. R. Littlewood, *Michael Psellus: Oratoria Minora.* Leipzig: Teubner, 1985.

Or. pan. edited by G.T. Dennis, *Michael Psellus: Orationes Panegyricae.* Stuttgart: Teubner, 1993.

Phil. min. I edited by J.M. Duffy, *Michael Psellus: Philosophica Minora* I. Stuttgart: Teubner, 1992.

Phil. min. II edited by D.J. O'Meara, *Michael Psellus: Philosophica Minora* II. Leipzig: Teubner, 1989.

Poem. edited by L.G. Westerink, *Michael Psellus: Poemata.* Stuttgart: Teubner, 1992.

S Letters: edited by K.N. Sathas, Μεσαιωνικὴ Βιβλιοθήκη*:* Συλλογὴ ἀνεκδότων μνημείων τῆς Ἑλληνικῆς ἱστορίας*, V;* Μιχαὴλ Ψελλοῦ ἱστορικοὶ λόγοι, ἐπιστολαὶ καὶ ἄλλα ἀνέκδοτα, 219–523. Venice: Phoinix, 1876 = Paris: Libraires-Éditeurs, 1876. Repr. Athens: Γρηγοριάδης, 1972.

Sathas IV and V Various texts (excluding the letters), edited by K.N. Sathas, Μεσαιωνικὴ Βιβλιοθήκη: Συλλογὴ ἀνεκδότων μνημείων τῆς Ἑλληνικῆς ἱστορίας IV; Μιχαὴλ Ψελλοῦ ἑκατονταετηρὶς Βυζαντινῆς ἱστορίας *(976–1077).* Venice: Phoinix, 1874; and Μεσαιωνικὴ Βιβλιοθήκη: Συλλογὴ ἀνεκδότων μνημείων τῆς Ἑλληνικῆς ἱστορίας, V; Μιχαὴλ Ψελλοῦ ἱστορικοὶ λόγοι, ἐπιστολαὶ καὶ ἄλλα ἀνέκδοτα. Venice: Phoinix, 1876.

Theol. I edited by P. Gautier, *Michael Psellus: Theologica* I. Leipzig: Teubner, 1989.

Theol. II edited by L.G. Westerink and J.M. Duffy, *Michael Psellus: Theologica* II. Munich: K.G. Saur, 2002.

To One Asking "Who Wrote Verse Better, Euripides Or Pisides?" edited by A. Dyck, *Michael Psellus, The Essays on Euripides and George of Pisidia and on Heliodorus and Achilles Tatius*, 40–50. Vienna: Verlag der Österreichischen Akademie der Wissenschaften, 1986.

What Is the Difference between the Texts Whose Plots Concern Charikleia and Leukippe? edited by A. Dyck, *Michael Psellus, The Essays on Euripides and George of Pisidia and on Heliodorus and Achilles Tatius*, 90–98. Vienna: Verlag der Österreichischen Akademie der Wissenschaften, 1986.

Other Commonly Cited Works

BHG F. Halkin. *Bibliotheca hagiographica graeca*, with an *Auctarium* and a *Novum Auctarium,* 5 vols. Brussels: Société des Bollandistes, 1957–84.

Lampe G. W. H. Lampe. *A Patristic Greek Lexicon.* Oxford: Oxford University Press, 1961–68.

LSJ H. G. Liddell and R. Scott, eds. *A Greek-English Lexicon*, 8th ed. (Oxford, 1897); rev. 9th ed., H. S. Jones, R. McKenzie, et al. (1925–40); supplements by E. A. Barber et al. (1968) and R. Renehan (1975, 1982); with a revised supplement (1996).

ODB A. P. Kazhdan, ed., *The Oxford Dictionary of Byzantium.* New York: Oxford University Press, 1991.

For all other abbreviations, we have followed the *ODB.*

General Introduction

Stratis Papaioannou

Though Michael Psellos is a towering figure in the history of Byzantine letters, his theoretical and critical reflections on literature and art are little known beyond a circle of specialists. Modern readers know Psellos primarily for his *Chronographia*, a history of eleventh-century Byzantine emperors and their reigns, an international Byzantine "best seller" with its fourteen translations into modern languages since 1874.[1] Yet Psellos also excelled in describing as well as prescribing practices, rules, created objects, and creative subjects of literary discourse and visual culture. The present volume introduces precisely this aspect of Psellian writing to a wider public. The aim is to illustrate an important chapter in the history of Greek literary and art criticism, and thence to contribute to the history of premodern aesthetics.

To this purpose, we have gathered together thirty Psellian texts, all of which are translated—some partly, but most in their entirety—into English; in the case of a group of Psellian letters, a new edition of the Greek original is also offered. The majority of the works are translated for the first time in any modern language, and several of them have found their first sustained discussion here. We have grouped them in two separate sections, which roughly correspond to two areas of theoretical reflection that are associated with the modern terms of "literature" and "art." What these terms mean in a Byzantine

1. See Moore 2005: 445–57 for the bibliography of studies and translations (until the year ca. 2000); recent new edition by Reinsch 2014.

context, and for Psellos specifically, is explained in the relevant introductions to the two sections. In these introductions, the reader will also find general discussions of what kinds of texts we have selected and where these texts belong within Psellos' oeuvre as well as within the wider Byzantine tradition in terms of content, context, and literary form.

What are presented in this book are indeed two different collections brought together (somewhat deceptively, we might acknowledge) under the headings of literature and art. Modern readers are accustomed to link these two fields to each other as they consider them (along with other activities such as theater and music) as parallel and related expressions of human creativity and leisurely entertainment, pleasure, and pastime—in other words, the modern commonsense understanding of *aesthetic* experience.

The actual Byzantine connection is somewhat different. All the essays fit the requirements—and indeed several of them represent exquisite specimens—of what in Byzantium would have been regarded as rhetoric and philosophy, ῥητορική and φιλοσοφία. The two terms denoted, respectively, high discursive style and high discursive knowledge, representing the apex of Byzantine education and erudition. Together, the two disciplines covered almost all aspects of linguistic expression and learning in Byzantium. And they were "high" both because of the specialized training they required and because of their perceived social status. Though not all Byzantine professional rhetors/philosophers could hope to enjoy high social and economic benefits, acquaintance with rhetoric and philosophy as practices was frequently a prerequisite for high social distinction.

The selected texts in both sections also converge in their concern for *aesthetic* experience, in the more literal meaning of *sensuous* perception of material form. They intersect, that is, in their emphasis on the creation, manipulation, experience, and understanding of what may be termed cultured sense perception, whether in words or in images. As such, these texts display views, attitudes, and ultimately *tastes* regarding what is thought to be beautiful as well as moral, appealing as well as mentally and psychologically effective in texts and artistic objects.[2]

The underlying theory of literary and visual taste, the theory of aesthetics, that is—by which word we do not mean here any systematized theory or

2. See further Papaioannou 2013: 29–50 (on rhetoric and philosophy) and passim.

neatly defined separate field of thought—is not Psellos' alone. As is perhaps always the case with aesthetics, his aesthetic too addresses a set of expectations that are indebted both to earlier traditions of writing and thinking about literature and art as well as to contemporary ideas and practices—in this case, those of the Constantinopolitan social elite to which Psellos belonged. The details of this nexus of intellectual tradition and eleventh-century Constantinopolitan social and intellectual aristocracy will be illuminated by the collection of texts and the discussions that follow below.

Michael Psellos (1018–1078)

One of the most prolific and popular medieval Greek authors, Psellos has been regarded as everything from a typical Byzantine courtier to a protagonist in the history of Byzantine culture. A total of 1176 titles (among them 500 letters as well as 163 spurious works) are attributed to him in impressively numerous manuscripts, and an immense modern bibliography deals with his life and works.[3]

He was born to a middle-class family in the Constantinopolitan suburb Ta Narsou, at a time when Constantinople, and the empire ruled by its imperial court, had reached a peak in economic, political, military, and cultural impact on the Mediterranean, Balkan, and wider European and Middle Eastern worlds. His surname, perhaps a personal designation, denotes someone who "lisps." Starting at the age of five, he began his education in grammar, orthography, and Homeric poetry. At eleven, he continued with rhetoric and then philosophy, studying together with future friends under several teachers (including Ioannes Mauropous, another notable intellectual figure of the century). This education provided entry to provincial administration and then imperial bureaucracy. By 1041, Psellos became secretary in the imperial court—an untitled poem can be set in this context (*Poem.* 16). Around 1043, he came to the

3. This outline of Psellos' biography follows closely Papaioannou 2013: 4–14, which contains further references and bibliography. See further Volk 1990: 1–48; Ljubarskij 2001=2004; Kaldellis 2006: 1–28; and Karpozilos 2009: 59–75. See also the biography offered in Reinsch 2014: ix–xvi. See also Kaldellis 1999; Barber and Jenkins 2006; Lauritzen 2013; and Pappioannou 2013 (a modern Greek, updated version is in preparation). All Psellian ergo-graphy and bibliography before 2000 is gathered in Moore 2005.

attention of emperor Konstantinos IX Monomachos (1042–1055)—two of his earliest texts are an encomium for Monomachos, occasioned by the failed revolt of Georgios Maniakes (1043; *Or. pan.* 2) and a funeral poem for Monomachos' mistress Maria Skleraina (*Poem.* 17; ca. 1045).

Under Monomachos' patronage, Psellos' career blossomed, his wealth increased, and his social network was enlarged. From this time on, his primary function was that of teacher, public orator, and impromptu court advisor and mediator. He remained an unofficial court "secretary" drafting documents and operating on behalf of an increasingly large number of associates and clients (as is evident from a number of his letters).

For his teaching, he was given a new title created especially for him, likely around 1045: ὕπατος τῶν φιλοσόφων. The term translates as the "consul of the philosophers" and indicates something like "the chief of the teachers" who taught in essentially private schools, supported partly by the state. Psellos prided himself on this title as well as on his international fame as a teacher; for example, he attracted students of southern Italian (Ioannes Italos; see *Or. min.* 18 and 19) and Georgian descent (Ioane Petric'i). He also tutored the nephews of the patriarch Michael Keroularios (1005/1010–1059) with whom Psellos had a turbulent relationship (see Kaldellis and Polemis 2015: 11–22, 37–128), and, later, taught Theophylaktos Hephaistos (1055–1107), the future archbishop of Ochrid.

Things changed in the 1050s, both in Psellos' private and public life. His biological daughter Styliane died around 1052; a good marriage for his adoptive daughter Euphemia fell through, likely in 1053; and his mother, Theodote, died in late 1054 (the relevant texts are translated in Kaldellis 2006). Along with friends (such as Mauropous), he also fell out of favor with Monomachos. He was "forced" to become a monk at a monastery in Bithynia, changing his lay baptismal name Konstantinos (or Konstas for short) to a monastic one, Michael.

He quickly returned to Constantinople in 1055 and would remain there until his death, continuing to work as a teacher, speaker, and advisor, but apparently without the luster of his Monomachos years— even if he accrued more titles (*proedros, prôtoproedros,* and *hypertimos*). His association with the imperial family of the Doukai provided the most significant context for his literary and social activity during this period. The son of Konstantinos X Doukas and Eudokia Makrembolitissa, the future emperor Michael VII

(1071–1078), was his student—their relationship is commemorated in the only portrait of Psellos we possess from a late twelfth- or early thirteenth-century manuscript (Athos, Pantokratoros 234, f. 254r). After various ups and downs in his political influence, Psellos likely died in 1078—if we are to accept information reported in Michael Attaleiates' *History* (though the issue is far from settled).[4]

Apart from official documents and a large number of letters of recommendation and intervention, his oeuvre may be divided (though the division is often lost in the texts themselves, as already noted above) into what he termed insistently (a) ῥητορική and (b) φιλοσοφία: the former referring to literarily wrought works for public performance or private communication and the latter designating texts for the purposes of teaching that took the form of poems, letters, lectures, compilation of excerpts, and essays. These texts usually addressed a circle of close friends, associates, students, and patrons that he acquired throughout his career. The most important of these were the following: the emperors Konstantinos IX Monomachos and Michael VII Doukas, the *kaisar* Ioannes Doukas (?–ca. 1088; thirty-seven of Psellos' letters are addressed to him, as well as a funeral oration for his wife, Eirene: K-D I 21 dated to the mid-1060s), and Konstantinos, the nephew of Keroularios (seventeen letters; *Or. min.* 31; *Or. for.* 5; see also the very lengthy hagiographical oration on Michael Keroularios: *Or. fun.* 1 with Kaldellis and Polemis 2015: 49–128).

Psellos taught everything from basic grammar, Homeric poetry, and Aristotelian logic to Hermogenian rhetoric and Neoplatonic philosophy, and wrote on nearly every subject (from medicine to law and from vernacular expressions to occult sciences)—most of these texts are gathered in *Theol.* I and II, *Phil. min.* I and II, and *Or. min.*, and several of these are translated below. Psellos aggressively expanded the curriculum, in terms of both method and the authoritative texts that were to be studied, commented upon, and revised. His most important contribution in this respect is the use of pre-Byzantine rhetorical aesthetics and Neoplatonic hermeneutics (especially those of Proklos, 410/412–485) for the interpretation of the rhetoric and theology of

4. Reinsch (2014: xvi) perhaps too readily accepts that Psellos must have died in 1076.

Gregory of Nazianzos (329/330–ca. 390), to whom Psellos devoted numerous texts; three of them are included in the present volume (*Discourse Improvised . . . about the Style of the Theologian*; *Theol.* I 19 and 98).

For Monomachos, Psellos composed instructional poems in fifteen-syllable *politikos* verse (*Poems* 1, 2, 3, 4, 6) and a first redaction of his relatively popular *Concise Answers to Various Questions* (= *De Omnifaria Doctrina*). For Michael VII, he wrote several more instructional pieces (*Poem* 7 on rhetoric is translated in this volume), revised several of the earlier poems and the earlier *Concise Answers*, and wrote the *Historia Syntomos*, a compendium of biographical vignettes of Roman rulers from Romulus to Basil II with a decidedly Roman perspective on the history of the empire.

His rhetorical production includes: several encomia for emperors (most importantly Monomachos: *Or. pan.* 1-7; S 115); a rather peculiar mixture of a legal document combined with panegyrical speech pertaining to the so-called Usual Miracle in Blachernai (*Or. hag.* 4, written in July 1075—also in the present volume); funeral orations—notable among them are two lengthy pieces on Konstantinos Leichoudes (*Or. fun.* 2) and Ioannes Xiphilinos (*Or. fun.* 3), both completed after August 1075 (translated in Kaldellis and Polemis 2015); lengthy and rhetorically elaborate letters (five of them in the present collection); short playful pieces (e.g., an *Encomium of Wine*: *Or. min.* 30); several texts of self-defense, including an invective poem against a monk Iakobos in the form of a hymnographical *kanôn* (*Poem* 22); hagiographical texts in the mode of Symeon Metaphrastes; and, of course, the texts on literary and visual aesthetics presented below.[5]

Somewhere between rhetoric and instruction, encomium and classicizing history lies his most renowned text: the *Chronographia,* which is primarily a history of a series of Byzantine emperors from Basil II to Michael VII. In its present, incomplete form, the text ends with the description of Ioannes Doukas who was clearly an (if not *the*) addressee of the work in its last version. Yet, the *Chronographia* was written and revised in stages (the earliest evidence points to 1057) for a small, though fluid, group of addressees (particularly members of the Doukas family). Though it survives in essentially one manuscript (Paris, BNF, gr. 1712; twelfth century), this brilliantly textured

5. Psellos also wrote icon-epigrams, though none survives (except perhaps *Poem.* 33); cf. K-D 211, translated as *Letter One* in this volume.

narrative exerted influence in twelfth-century historiography and has been Psellos' most popular text among modern scholars.[6]

Psellos' texts (including the *spuria*) are transmitted in approximately 765 manuscripts; about a third of these manuscripts date from the twelfth through to the fourteenth century. However, the transmission is uneven. We do not possess a collection of his works that dates to his lifetime or reflects his editorial choices. And only a few texts circulated in a somewhat wide number of manuscripts (works of popularizing knowledge, such as some of his *Poems*).[7] The rhetorical works—often highly self-referential, with an emphasis on aesthetic pleasure, emotion (*pathos*), and Hellenism—survive in relatively few manuscripts. Nevertheless, these texts reached an influential audience among the educated elite during the twelfth century (the princess and historian Anna Komnene, 1083–ca. 1150–55, is important in this respect) and then again in the late thirteenth century. The three most important Psellos manuscripts betray these later Byzantine readers: Florence, Bibl. Med. Laur., Plut. gr. 57.40 (early twelfth century); Paris, BNF, gr. 1182 (likely commissioned by Eustathios of Thessalonike in the late twelfth century), and Vatican, BAV, gr. 672 (late thirteenth century, before July 1293; for this date cf. Pérez Martín 2012: 171; the manuscript was produced perhaps in the circle of the rhetor Manuel Holobolos—on this see below pp. 222 and 231n33)—they are also the primary witnesses for the texts of our collection.

Psellos' most important modern readers/editors were Leo Allatius (Chios 1586–Rome 1669) and Konstantinos Sathas (Athens 1842–Paris 1914), followed by a host of scholars who worked on the protean and prolific Psellos. It is in their footsteps that we offer the present book.

6. For the immediate audience and reception of the *Chronographia,* see Reinsch 2013; see further the introduction to the new edition in Reinsch 2014: xvi–xxxii.

7. His *Poem* 1, on the inscriptions of the Psalms, survives in the earliest dated manuscript with Psellian works: Harvard MS Gr. 3, a psalter dated to 1105—Psellos' poem in ff. 1r–7v: Στίχοι πολιτικοὶ τοῦ μακαριωτάτου ὑπερτίμου τοῦ Ψελλοῦ ἑφερμηνευτικοὶ τῶν ἐπιγραμμάτων τῶν ψαλμῶν. On this manuscript, see Kavrus-Hoffmann 2010a: 82–102.

PART ONE

On Literature: Rhetoric and Λόγοι

Introduction to Part One

Stratis Papaioannou

Texts and Contexts

The fifteen texts that follow comprise the full corpus of Psellian works that provide theoretical reflections on literary discourse in a sustained fashion. Together, they offer a good introduction not only to Psellos' literary aesthetics, but also to Byzantine rhetorical theory in general.

We begin with a series of five introductory summaries and collections of excerpts that deal with technical matters of rhetorical style, all of which are based on pre-Byzantine, Greco-Roman handbooks of rhetoric. The first two review the most important such handbook in Byzantium: Hermogenes' *Art of Rhetoric*.[1] The third text summarizes Dionysios of Halikarnassos' popular *On Composition,* while the fourth is based on a less common text, Longinos' *Art of Rhetoric*. The fifth, titled *On Tragedy,* deals with a somewhat marginal topic in middle Byzantine literary theory, ancient drama, reviving again earlier, antiquarian material.

Essays of rhetorical criticism devoted to specific authors and literary texts come next. The first two, *On the Different Styles of Certain Writings*

1. This is the Byzantine title given to four treatises attributed to Hermogenes (second c. CE): *On Issues* (Περὶ στάσεων), *On Invention* (Περὶ εὑρέσεως), *On Forms* (Περὶ ἰδεῶν), and *On the Method of Force* (Περὶ μεθόδου δεινότητος); in Byzantine manuscripts, these treatises were usually prefaced by Aphthonios' *Preliminary Exercises* (Προγυμνάσματα. fourth c. CE), forming a unified manual. Interestingly, at least as far as we can tell, Psellos did not write on Aphthonios. Cf. further below pp. 16–17, 21.

(text no. 6) and *The Styles of Gregory the Theologian, Basil the Great, Chrysostom, and Gregory of Nyssa* (no. 7), examine swiftly and comprehensively a large number of earlier authors and provide us with a brief panorama of the Byzantine rhetorical canon. The texts numbered 8 and 10 focus with greater detail on Gregory of Nazianzos and John Chrysostom respectively, the two most important authors of the Byzantine canon; these two authors alone, it should be remembered, are preserved in what is the largest group (in numbers; though excluding lectionaries) among the manuscripts that survive from the middle Byzantine period. Texts 11 and 12 are comparisons of major texts/authors with regard to versification (Euripides vs. the Byzantine poet Georgios Pisides) and romantic narrative (the novels of Achilleus Tatios and Heliodoros).

Three further sections (9, 13, 14) complete the collection. These are somewhat *sui generis* in the history of Byzantine literary criticism and rhetorical theory. The first, no. 9, consists of two lectures that Psellos delivered in front of his students. Both texts deal with specific phrases from Gregory of Nazianzos' *Orations*. The primary focus of such Psellian lectures, of which a large number have survived, was philosophical interpretation of the theological content of Gregory's speeches. Nevertheless, Psellos often departs from his main task and comments on the style of Gregory's rhetoric. The two lectures translated below are exceptional in devoting most of their space to precisely such rhetorical analysis.

Text 13 is in essence a hagiographical encomium that praises the sanctity of Symeon Logothetes or Metaphrastes, an author who flourished during the second half of the tenth century and who is mostly known for his *Menologion*. The latter was an immense and remarkably popular collection of earlier saints' *Lives*, the majority of which were rewritten by Metaphrastes and his team in a rhetorical fashion. Unlike other Byzantine hagiographical eulogies, Psellos' evaluation of Symeon focuses again on Symeon's rhetoric and his exceptional narrative skills. It thus promotes a saint who is saintly first and foremost on account of his literary achievement.[2]

The *Encomium for the Monk Ioannes Kroustoulas* (no. 14) is the most singular text in the present collection, though thanks to its theme it forms a pair with the eulogy of Symeon that precedes it. Addressing a small audience of

2. On this point, see Papaioannou 2013: 158–62.

friends, the *Encomium* describes in effusive learnedness the recital of an accomplished contemporary public reader by the name of Ioannes Kroustoulas in the Constantinopolitan church of Theotokos in the Chalkoprateia neighborhood. Psellos recounts and elaborates on the reading techniques of the apparently famous monk who recited—indeed performed (as Psellos suggests)—narrative texts from the *Menologion,* most likely that of Symeon Metaphrastes. This is the single detailed description that we possess about an activity that was rather common in middle Byzantine urban as well as monastic churches.

As we move from summaries and collections of excerpts to applied rhetorical theory and criticism, different aspects of Psellos' approach to literary aesthetics become evident. This variation is occasioned both by different functions and different contexts or audiences. The former group of texts contains succinct compilations of teaching notes that were produced in the context of Psellos' instruction—either of individual tutees or larger groups. Here, Psellos works as a compiler who rearranges earlier material for his students, and possibly also for his own use as teacher. Somewhat similar is the function of several texts in the second group, though here Psellos puts forth material that he has digested and rewritten according to his own individual tastes and preferences. Lastly, the two *Encomia* on Symeon and Kroustoulas reflect Psellos' role not so much as a teacher but as an intellectual who writes for colleagues, friends, and associates. For them, Psellos creates an image of himself as the most knowledgeable and eloquent voice of their (as he suggests) *shared* aesthetics by capitalizing on and indeed superseding all the principles of rhetorical skill elaborated in the previous set of texts.

Though most of the actual details of addressee, date, location, immediate circulation, and publication are forever lost to us (for each text, see the relevant introductions), we can plausibly imagine these texts being read or heard, individually or in small groups, primarily by Psellos' students and then also by his close friends and colleagues. As we can deduce from a variety of indications, the students were the sons or nephews of the middle and high Constantinopolitan and perhaps also provincial aristocracy who came to study with him. They often remained his "disciples" when they progressed in their careers and joined a second, more intimate circle of friends and colleagues, people who, like Psellos, prided themselves on advanced literacy and learnedness.[3]

These initial readers but also (quite likely) Psellos himself lie behind the relatively few manuscripts that preserve the texts included in the present volume. Though no eleventh-century, that is, contemporary manuscript survives, the collections that these students, associates, and possibly Psellos created during his lifetime were inherited and then rearranged and copied by twelfth-century readers, often descendants of families contemporary to Psellos.[4] The two most important manuscripts in this respect are: Florence, Bibl. Med. Laur., Plut. *gr.* 57.40 (**L**) (early twelfth century) and Paris, BNF, gr. 1182 (**P**) (late twelfth century). From their arrangement we can decipher *collections* of lectures as well as of essays preserved as such.[5]

Before placing Psellos' texts in the wider discursive tradition to which they belong, it should be noted that the series of texts on rhetorical theory translated below does not cover every single Psellian utterance on literature. Such comments can be found in a much wider set of Psellian writings. We find, for instance, several relevant side-remarks in his *Chronographia,* his public lectures and orations, and his private correspondence—on, for instance, the value of digressions in historiographical narrative (*Chronographia* 6.70), the notion of rhetor as creator (*Epitaphios in Honor of . . . Xiphilinos*; *Or. fun.* 3.22.58–95),

3. It is not the place here to examine either Constantinopolitan school life or Psellos' networks of students and friends in any detail; see Bernard 2014: passim with relevant discussions and the earlier bibliography.

4. See the discussion in Papaioannou 2013: 250–67.

5. These collections include several of the fifteen texts translated below as well as many of the texts in the second part of this volume that deal with visual aesthetics. More specifically, the "educational" texts are gathered together in folios 101r–168r of **L** (several more are dispersed in ff. 202v–283v) and also, though not in the same sequence, in **P**, especially in quires 5 to 17 and 21 to 29 (= ff. 258r–319v, 1r–32v, and 42r–108v). This sequence of the folios in **P** may seem out of order. However, the quires of the ms. have been rearranged some time after the creation of the ms., and several of them have been lost. In its original ordering, the relevant folios, 258r–319v, 1r–32v, and 42r–108v correspond respectively to the following, complete, quires: 5 to 13, 14 to 17, and 21 to 29; see Gautier 1986: 58. Quires numbered 35–36 and 38–43 in the manuscript (= 151v–188v) contain further texts from Psellos' teaching activity, though they are not grouped together as consistently as in the earlier quires, but are intermixed with other kinds of texts that belong to Psellos' activity as performer/rhetor (speeches, funeral orations, etc.).

or the distinction between oral communication and writing (*Letter* S 11).[6] Such passages are so numerous that if we were to include all of them, this volume would grow to unyielding proportions.

Relevant also are an important number of Psellian essays and treatises on the preparatory discursive sciences of grammar and logic or the science of music, a field related to aesthetics.[7] We also encounter several allegorical, that is, philosophical and theological, readings of literary texts—such as Psellos' allegories on Homer (*Phil. min.* I 42–47).[8] Though these texts are to some extent pertinent to the ideas and reading practices associated with the phenomenon of discourse, they too have been omitted from this volume. As will be explained below, the principle of selection has been to include only those Psellian writings that are preoccupied with discourse as "literature" and neither regulate aspects of discursive knowledge in general nor dissect literary texts and forms for the purpose of elaborating philosophical theories (as is the case with Psellos' texts in the allegorical mode).

The Tradition

As readers proceed through this collection, they will increasingly encounter the resounding voice of Psellos who introduces his own aesthetics rather than merely reproducing or complying with expectations determined by tradition. Indeed, as will become apparent, a defining feature of the texts that follow is

6. See Papaioannou 2010 on *Chronographia* 6.70; Papaioannou 2013: 79–80 on the *Epitaphios* of Xiphilinos; and Papaioannou 2004 as well as Messis and Papaioannou, forthcoming, on S 11. See also the side-remarks in Psellos' treatise on a phrase from "everyday speech" (ed. Sathas V 537–41; cf. Moore 2005: 398–99) about five different types of style that people imitate (those of epic poetry, tragedy, comedy, satyr play, and Aesopic fables) and about the "magnificent" diction of Menander as opposed to the rather "vulgar and mad after women" style of Aristophanes (Sathas V 538.12–23).

7. For listing and bibliography, see Moore 2005: 397–401, 410–11 (six works pertaining to matters of grammar, such as etymology and metrics); also 478–81 (on *Poem* 6, a very popular verse introduction on grammar); see also 404 (item 1011) for an unpublished essay "Περὶ ἐγκωμίου συνθήκης"; 232–52 (numerous works on logic); and 312–13 (one text on music).

8. Moore 2005: 266–71; cf. Cesaretti 1991: 29–123. For other Psellian exercises in allegorical interpretation, see the works listed in Moore 2005: 264–65, 271–72, 397–99.

the degree in which Psellos inserts himself in his own writing. Simultaneously and perhaps paradoxically, as we transition from summaries and collections of excerpts to Psellian essays and reach the last text, the encomium of Kroustoulas, which happens to be also the most individual of all—in form, content, and execution—the density and complexity of references and allusions to earlier texts increases.

Psellos' relation to the earlier tradition of literary aesthetics is thus intricate. From a certain perspective, the corpus of texts in this volume is representative of the wider Byzantine tradition of literary theory—which Psellos apparently knew well. This tradition was based on three late antique/early Byzantine registers of discursive thought:

(a) rhetorical handbooks—dominant among them was the aforementioned *Art of Rhetoric* of Hermogenes (second c. CE), prefaced by Aphthonios' *Preliminary Exercises* (Προγυμνάσματα) (fourth c. CE)—commentaries on Hermogenes and Aphthonios, and shorter technical treatises;
(b) Neoplatonic (third–sixth c. CE) commentaries on Plato's dialogues, which combined stylistic analysis with philosophical hermeneutics; and
(c) scholia, often in the form of marginal notes, on classical and postclassical rhetorical texts (from Homer—who, for Byzantine readers, belonged to the rhetorical tradition—to Demosthenes, and from Ailios Aristeides to Gregory of Nazianzos).[9]

During the middle Byzantine period preceding Psellos, this earlier tradition was expanded in at least two significant ways. The first was the application of Hellenic rhetorical theory to the reading of Christian rhetorical practice and, especially, the promotion of Gregory of Nazianzos' *Orations* (partly in place of Demosthenes) as the best model for the explication of Hermogenian aesthetics.[10] The second was the rediscovery of alternative theoretical models beyond Aphthonios and Hermogenes for the understanding of discur-

9. On these different forms of discursive science in Byzantium, see S. Papaioannou, forthcoming, "Aesthetics." See also Hoffmann 2006, Agapitos 2008, and Conley 2009.

10. In Ioannes Sikeliotes' outstanding commentary of Hermogenes' *On Forms*, passages from Gregory's *Orations* consistently replace examples from Demosthenes (Walz 1834: 80–504); cf. Conley 2003 and Papaioannou 2013: 56–63.

sive phenomena; this is evident, for example, in tenth-century manuscripts that preserve such rhetoricians as Dionysios of Halikarnassos.[11]

Psellos' summaries of Hermogenes and Dionysios, his promotion of Gregory of Nazianzos as the ideal rhetor, his Neoplatonic readings of Gregory's theology, and his readings in a wide array of texts that included earlier material that had previously been relegated to obscurity are thus well explained in view of the immediate Byzantine tradition. After all, Psellos engaged directly with the extensive Byzantine exegetical work on the corpora, for instance, of Hermogenes and Gregory of Nazianzos.[12]

Yet Psellos also departs from the tradition, both by omission and by expansion. Certain earlier types of literary theoretical reflections are absent from his writings. For instance, Psellos does not write detailed commentaries on any canonical text—either of rhetorical theory or of rhetorical practice. This was an activity that seemed to characterize all other Byzantine professional rhetoricians like himself—from Ioannes of Sardeis (ninth c.) and Ioannes Geometres (tenth c.) to Ioannes Tzetzes (twelfth c.), Eustathios of Thessalonike (twelfth c.), and Maximos Planoudes (late thirteenth–early fourteenth c.). Nor does he deal with the mere basics—there is no engagement with Aphthonios, for instance. Psellos, that is, does not get to the nitty-gritty of other Byzantine teachers; and he is no philologist, in the narrow sense of the word.

Simultaneously, Psellos outdoes tradition. Though earlier writers, like Patriarch Photios (ninth c.), Arethas (tenth c.), or Ioannes Sikeliotes (ca. 1000) were well-versed in both Neoplatonic philosophy and Greco-Roman rhetorical theory, no one combined them as creatively as we will observe Psellos doing in his texts that follow. Furthermore, though earlier writers too (especially Photios) were not preoccupied exclusively with distant, "ancient" models of rhetoric but also displayed their interests in contemporary literature, no one engaged with recent rhetorical production like Psellos does—especially with respect to Symeon Metaphrastes. Finally, no one articulates as poignantly as Psellos an aesthetics of discourse that does not submit the pleasure of reading and the creativity of stylistic form to either moral or ontological constraints. At that, Psellos comes very close to expressing a purely *literary* understanding of discourse.

11. See, e.g., Aujac 1974.

12. See *Theol.* II 6 164–74 (on Greg. Naz. *Or.* 2.13). On his attitude toward exegetes of Gregory, see pp. 151–52 below.

Literature

But what is "literature" and "literary" in the essays that follow? As is perhaps clear from all the aforementioned, literature signifies something different than merely that type of writing that capitalizes on formal or imaginative creativity, in poetry and fiction, and serves primarily the needs of pleasure and entertainment.[13] The prescription of patterns for public declamation (mostly judicial and advisory speech-making) and of rhetorical virtues such as "clarity" and "force"—the pillars of the Hermogenian system of thought—are not among the chief features of modern literary theory, if they feature at all. Nor would sermons and narrative that praise ideal models of Christian behavior and expand on theological concepts (such as the works of Gregory of Nazianzos and Symeon Metaphrastes) be categorized as literature in a modern bookshop, let alone be considered the apex of literary production.

The terms that Psellos—and his tradition—use for literature are telling in themselves: rhetoric and discourses, ῥητορική and λόγοι. Both cover a much wider spectrum of texts that only to a small extent overlaps with modern "literature." Rhetoric refers to a type of style or a register of language (in terms of syntax, composition, and vocabulary) that can be used for all kinds of discourse—including those that capitalize on stylistics and aim primarily at entertainment. *Logoi* include any text that may be informed by rhetoric and elaborates some form of knowledge—from history and (religious) biography to philosophy and science.

Yet these terms, rhetoric especially, *do* also converge with what we understand as literature. First of all, like literature today, rhetoric and "discourses" usually required advanced literacy and access to education and, moreover, designated activities, skills, and knowledge that carried social meaning. They were, that is, cultural capital available to and controlled by a professional and sometimes social elite, and pursued by those who wished to access or influence the Byzantine ruling elite by means of that cultural capital. More importantly for our purposes here, rhetoric like literature today was often linked with discourse and texts that were solely focused on *aesthetics* (style, form, and pleasure) rather than, as would be proper for *logoi* in general, ethics and learning. In theoretical reflections about rhetoric and discourses—

13. See Todorov 1973.

which is what the texts of this volume essentially are—we detect precisely an attempt, whether conscious or unconscious, to defend, explain, and even, in Psellos' case, *promote* this aesthetic dimension of rhetorical *logoi* and thus to pronounce purely literary theory.

In the introductions to the texts that follow, we have highlighted the various ways in which this Psellian approach is sought; nevertheless, two major aspects can be mentioned here.[14] The first pertains to Psellos' emphasis on the emotive nature and power of discourse, on how, that is, discourse expresses the author's emotions, represents the emotive worlds of characters, and incites affect—in Greek πάθος—in readers and listeners. This maximization of emotion, rather than its control, corroborates a general trend in Psellian thought, which is the avoidance of introducing moral principles in aesthetic judgment. Unlike many of his predecessors and many comparable contemporaries in neighboring cultures (writing in Latin or Arabic),[15] Psellos is rarely concerned with delimiting *ethical* writing and *ethical* reading. Instead, beauty and pleasure, form and performance, materiality and emotionality usually take precedence in his rhetorical theory.

The second aspect relates to Psellos' view of the production of discourse or "authorship"—to put it in a single term that does not, however, exist in either classical or Byzantine Greek.[16] Through a series of asides, comments, and sustained statements, Psellos identifies the rhetor as the individual, autonomous, and primary agent of discourse, the one who *creates* discursive form without the intervention of divine inspiration or, even, the oppression of rhetorical tradition. And, while the author is configured as creator—and not merely as an imitator of God, nature, or model rhetors—his discourse is not reduced to mere expression of his character, emotions, or ideas. Rather, Psellos also stresses the performative and theatrical nature of the discursive game and thus envisions an author who can also become an actor of many masks in his own writing, a *literary* author, that is.

14. For a more detailed account with references and relevant bibliography, see Papaioannou 2013: 27–128. For earlier approaches, see Ljubarskij 1975 and 2001: 348–68 and 509–11 (= 2004: 197–217 and 379–82), as well as Milovanović 1979.

15. See Papaioannou 2013: 91.

16. On the subject, see now Pizzone 2014.

1 *Synopsis of the Rhetorical Forms*, based on Hermogenes' *On Forms*

Translated with introduction and notes by Stratis Papaioannou

Introduction

The *Synopsis of the Rhetorical Forms* is presented as a letter addressed to an anonymous student. It survives in Psellos' main manuscript, the late twelfth-century Paris, BNF, gr. 1182, but has been preserved also anonymously in a post-Byzantine manuscript, Moscow, GIM, Sin. gr. 303 (sixteenth–seventeenth c.), and its apograph.[1] In the Paris manuscript, the text is placed together with Psellos' summary of Dionysios of Halikarnassos' *On Composition* (*On Literary Composition*: this volume, Part 1, no. 3), along with a few other similar treatises that derive likely from Psellos' teaching activity. Followed in the present volume by a longer piece (*Poem* 7) below, the *Synopsis* has been set first in our collection because together the two pieces provide a concise introduction to Hermogenes' corpus, the fundamental handbook of high rhetorical theory in Byzantium.

There is, in fact, nothing particularly Psellian about this short text. Similar summaries of Hermogenes' *On Forms,* produced by teachers of rhetoric, circulated in Byzantine manuscripts before and after Psellos. The earliest version of such a summary has been re-edited recently by Michel Patillon in his

1. Moore 2005: 403–4.

monumental new edition of the Hermogenian work (Patillon 2008–12: 4:235–54: *Synopses of the On Forms*). Patillon located the composition of the anonymous *Synopsis* in the context of the original unification of the Hermogenian corpus—or the *Art of Rhetoric* as the Byzantines referred to it—during the course of the fifth century and, in its later middle Byzantine version, during the ninth century. As is well known, the corpus included, in this sequence, the following five "principal" works: Aphthonios' *Preliminary Exercises* (Προγυμνάσματα) and four treatises attributed (the second and fourth wrongly) to Hermogenes, *On Issues* (Περὶ στάσεων), *On Invention* (Περὶ εὑρέσεως), *On Forms* (Περὶ ἰδεῶν), and *On the Method of Force* (Περὶ μεθόδου δεινότητος).[2] Simultaneously, as Patillon argues, the corpus was rounded off with introductions and summaries that systematized Hermogenes' complex system of rhetorical-theoretical thought. It thus included such anonymous texts as a *Preface to the Art of Rhetoric* or the *Synopses of the On Forms* as well as a few other brief treatises.[3] The anonymous *Synopsis,* which serves as a model for the Psellian work, is first attested in manuscripts of the tenth century. From the same context, we also possess a lengthy commentary of *On Forms* by Ioannes Sikeliotes, a teacher and rhetorician, active around the year 1000.[4] At the end of each chapter devoted to each of the Hermogenian *Forms*, Sikeliotes provides a concise summary, titled Σύνοψις;[5] if we were to put together all these summaries by Sikeliotes, they would create a similar review to that offered by Psellos.

Following these models, Psellos' letter arranges the system of Hermogenes' stylistic virtues or, what we might call, effects of style in the following way. The seven basic *Forms* [ἰδέαι] are presented in this order:

(1) Clarity [σαφήνεια] and its two subcategories: Purity [καθαρότης] and Distinctness [εὐκρίνεια]
(2) Grandeur [μέγεθος] which is divided into Solemnity [σεμνότης], Asperity [τραχύτης], Vehemence [σφοδρότης], Brilliance [λαμπρότης], Vigor [ἀκμή], and Amplification [περιβολή]
(3) Beauty [κάλλος]

2. For a discussion of the contents of the Hermogenian texts, see the introduction to the next essay by Jeffrey Walker in this volume; for Aphthonios, see Kennedy 2003 and, especially, Patillon 2008–12, vol. 1.

3. Patillon 2008–12: 1:v–xxxiii.

4. On Sikeliotes, see now Papaioannou 2015 with further bibliography.

5. Sikeliotes, *Comm.* 173.7f., 203.13f., 249.25f., etc.

(4) Rapidity [γοργότης]
(5) Sincerity [ἀληθινὸς λόγος] and its subcategory, Sternness [βαρύτης]
(6) Character [ἦθος] and its own subdivisions: Simplicity [ἀφέλεια]; Sweetness [γλυκύτης]; Pungency [δριμύτης]; and Moderation [ἐπιείκεια]
(7) Force [δεινότης], the culmination of all the virtues

The order differs slightly from the sequence of the Forms in Hermogenes' treatise (and its original *Synopses*), where Character follows Rapidity—perhaps a result of sloppy review on Psellos' part. Following Hermogenes, each of these Forms are then dissected according to eight categories (notably the last four deal primarily with what we might call prose rhythm):

(1) Thoughts [ἐννοίας]: content appropriate for each style
(2) Method [μέθοδος]: modes of presentation, arrangement, composition, and narrative
(3) Diction [λέξις]: choice of words and expressions
(4) Figures [σχήματα]: particular stylistic devices[6]
(5) Cola [κῶλα]: clauses; that is, semantic units of about seven to ten syllables
(6) Composition [συνθήκη]: arrangement of words within sentences
(7) Cadence [ἀνάπαυσις]: the ending of phrases and sentences
(8) Rhythm [ῥυθμός]: the rhythmical patterning of entire sentences

Here too, our treatise is not as rigorous as similar texts. Psellos leaves out a great deal of information. Occasionally, he (or the later scribes) makes mistakes (see, e.g., note 13 below). Yet the treatise serves its purpose. The interested student could acquire a quick review of the basic Hermogenian categories or, better said, a basic reference to the study of the Hermogenian magnum opus, since Psellos' text—just like the next text in our collection (*Poem.* 7)—presupposes an extensive and direct engagement with Hermogenes' *On Forms* (and, one might add, detailed *commentaries* of it).

Editions and translations. The text has not yet been edited on the basis of all the existing manuscripts. The two earlier editions, based on different testimonies,

6. On Byzantine theory of rhetorical "figures" see now Valiavitcharska, forthcoming.

have been employed here, since they complement each other (Walz 1833 and Bake 1849: 147–50; numbers in square brackets indicate pages in the latter's edition). I have also consulted the Russian translation (Miller 1975: 158–60). For convenience, I have added in parentheses the corresponding paragraphs in Hermogenes' work that Psellos summarizes. The descriptions of subcategories of the major Forms have been indented. Finally, annotation has been rather selective. The interested reader should consult the detailed notes offered by Patillon's recent edition of *On Forms* (2012) and also the comments included with the following text translated in the present volume (especially lines 353–517). It should be noted that I have followed Patillon's translation and thus departed greatly from Wooten's (1987) often problematic English rendering of *On Forms.*

Synopsis of the Rhetorical Forms

Translation in collaboration with Christopher M. Geadrities

As you requested, I am writing this letter to you so as to offer a most concise summary, an art in miniature,[1] of the rhetorical forms. Let me begin with the first things first.

Clarity [σαφήνεια; *On Forms* 1.2[2]]

Clarity, since it is a general type [γένος],[3] is divided into two forms: Purity [καθαρότητα] and Distinctness [εὐκρίνειαν].

Purity [καθαρότης; 1.3]

Purity contains thoughts [ἐννοίας] which are entirely ordinary and in no way profound [1.3.1–3]. Method [μέθοδον]: plain narration of the subject matter that admits nothing extraneous [1.3.4-8]. Diction [λέξιν]: without figurative expressions, but with rather ordinary words [1.3.9]. Figure [σχῆμα]: the simple sentence [τὸ κατ' ὀρθότητα][4] [1.3.10–16]. Cola [κῶλα]: short, resembling *kom-*

1. Τεχνύδριον: a handbook. See also the discussion in the next essay of this volume.

2. Subsequent citations omit the title of Hermogenes' treatise; all citations are from the edition of Patillon 2012.

3. In the Aristotelian sense of *genus*.

4. As opposed to the oblique construction (πλαγιασμός), which involves the presence of a genitive absolute, subordination, etc.

mata [1.3.17].[5] Composition [συνθήκην]: indifferent to hiatus [1.3.18–21]. Cadence [ἀνάπαυσιν]: iambic, trochaic, and with similar metrical ending [1.3.22–25].

Distinctness [εὐκρίνεια; 1.4]

Distinctness has those thoughts that announce their subject and lead the speech back to its starting point; those that formulate the arrangement of the topics that will be discussed; and those that provide a transition from one topic to another [1.4.4-7]. Method: presenting the subjects in natural order [1.4.8-9]. Figures: grouping topics together; also separating them and enumerating them [1.4.11-16]. Diction, cola, composition, cadence, and rhythm [ῥυθμόν]: the same as those used in Purity [1.4.11-17].

Grandeur [μέγεθος; 1.5]

Grandeur is divided into Solemnity [σεμνότητα], Asperity [τραχύτητα], Vehemence [σφοδρότητα], Brilliance [λαμπρότητα], Vigor [ἀκμήν], and Amplification [περιβολήν].

Solemnity [σεμνότης; 1.6]

The thoughts of Solemnity are (a) those that concern God,[6] when spoken of as God; (b) those that concern divine matters—for example, the seasons, and the revolution of the universe; (c) those notions or such matters that are divine by nature, but are encountered primarily in human affairs—for example, the

5. For the distinction of the longer unit of a colon (containing seven to ten syllables) from the shorter unit of the *komma* (up to six syllables), see "Hermogenes," *On Invention* 4.4: τὸ μὲν ἀπὸ τεττάρων καὶ πέντε συλλαβῶν μέχρι τῶν ἓξ κόμμα ἐστὶν τὸ δὲ ὑπὲρ τὰς ἑπτὰ καὶ ὀκτὼ καὶ δέκα καὶ ἐγγίζον ἤδη τῷ τριμέτρῳ καὶ μέχρι τοῦ ἡρωικοῦ προχωροῦν κῶλον γίνεται. An anonymous Byzantine commentary (which survives, among other mss., in the eleventh-c. Paris, BNF, gr. 2977, an important collection of rhetorical theory), suggests larger figures, perhaps reflecting middle Byzantine practice: *komma*, up to nine syllables or three words; colon, seven to sixteen syllables or "more than three words" (Anonymous, *Prolegomena to a Comm. on Hermogenes' On Invention* 822.12–823.5, ed. Walz 7.2). Cf. Valiavitcharska 2013: 111.

6. Rather than "gods" as in Hermogenes and also the original *Synopses*.

soul, justice, self-restraint, and other similar things; **[155]** (d) those thoughts that concern great and noble <human> deeds [1.6.1–11]. Methods: commanding declarations given without hesitation; also allegories[7] [1.6.12–15]. Diction: words that are extensive[8] [1.6.16–23]. Figures: the simple sentence and the insertion of personal judgments [ἐπικρίσεις] [1.6.24–29]. Cola: rather short [1.6.30]. Composition: with hiatus; dactylic, anapestic, and spondaic [1.6.31–34]. Cadence: such that it makes the speech spondaic or dactylic, but without metrical ending [1.6.35–37].

Asperity [τραχύτης; 1.7]

Asperity includes such thoughts as those used by persons of inferior status when they censure superiors [1.7.5–12]. Method: to censure openly [1.7.13]. Diction: both the metaphorical and the inherently harsh[9] [1.7.14–15]. Figures: commands, questions, refutation [1.7.16–18]. Cola: rather short and more like *kommata* [1.7.19]. Composition: with hiatus, without rhythm, and irregular [1.7.20–21].

Vehemence [σφοδρότης; 1.8]

Vehemence contains thoughts that censure and refute persons of inferior status [1.8.1–4]. Method: directness [1.8.5]. Diction: the sort that invents words according to the subject matter [1.8.6]. Figure: *apostrophe*[10] and pejorative statements [1.8.7–9]. Cola: *kommata* and rather the sort that pause after individual words [1.8.10]. Composition, cadence, and rhythm: the same as those of Asperity [1.8.11].

Brilliance [λαμπρότης; 1.9]

Brilliance contains those thoughts that make the speaker full of confidence, or, rather, they are the sort of thoughts in which he is confident [1.9.4–6].

7. This is the only instance where Hermogenes refers to "allegory," by which he seems to indicate metaphors and images applied to divine persons or matters.

8. They require, that is, a wide open mouth in their pronunciation; Hermogenes notes that such words are especially those that include the phonemes α and ω.

9. By which Hermogenes seems to mean repetition or excessive presence of voiceless plosive consonants in particular (π, τ, κ).

10. Direct questions, addressed to the opponent.

Method: speaking without hesitation and relating illustrious deeds in a more illustrious fashion [1.9.4–10]. Diction: solemn [1.9.11]. Figures: direct denials, lack of connectives [ἀσύνδετον], subordination [πλαγιασμόν], employment of detached phrases [ἀποστάσεις] [1.9.12–17]. Use of long cola [1.9.18]. The rest is like that used in Solemnity.

Vigor [ἀκμή; 1.10]

The thoughts and methods of Vigor are the same as those of Asperity and Vehemence, while its figures, cola, composition, cadence, and rhythm are like those used in Brilliance.

Amplification [περιβολή; 1.11]

The thoughts characteristic of Amplification admit something extraneous to the argument **[156]**, or add the genus to the species, or add something which is undefined to that which is defined, or add the whole to the part. They also include speaking about the matter in a way that is not plain, inverting the order of affairs, and using parenthetical statements [1.11.3–14]. The following are rather a matter of method: the inversion of the order of facts, the parenthetical statement, the expansion made in reference to quality, and the placing of the confirmations of a statement before the statement [1.11.15–21]. There is no diction characteristic of Amplification, unless someone would say that it is synonymous expressions [1.11.22–28]. Figures: enumeration, the enumerative figure [τὸ ἀπαριθμητικόν], the introduction of arguments in order of importance, suppositions, partition, subordination, run-on constructions, employment of detached phrases, copulative constructions involving negation, the inclusion of many thoughts in one sentence, or the insertion of parenthetical statements [1.11.29–59].

Beauty [κάλλος; 1.12]

The form of Beauty is indivisible. It does not have its own characteristic thoughts or method. Figures: clauses with an equal number of syllables [παρισώσεις], repetition of a word at the beginning of a colon [αἱ κατὰ κῶλα ἐπαναφοραί], counterturn [ἀντιστροφή],[11] climax [κλῖμαξ],[12] negations, the division of paired thoughts, *hyperbaton,*[13] novel expressions, and repetition of a word in different forms [1.12.11–39]. Cola: rather long[14] [1.11.40–44]. Composition does not admit hiatus [1.11.45–47].

Rapidity [γοργότης; 2.1]

The form of Rapidity is also indivisible. It does not have its own characteristic thoughts, but its method is the use of rapid objections [2.1.4–6]. Figures: incidental remarks by insertion,[15] run-on constructions, lack of connectives in sequence of *kommata*, swift variation, and rapid[16] interweaving [συμπλοκαί] [2.1.7–29]. Composition: without hiatus [2.1.32–34]. Cadence: ends in a trochee, and is not stable [2.1.35].

Sincerity [ἀληθινὸς λόγος; 2.7]

Sincerity is also indivisible. Thoughts: simple and moderate. Method: the expression of indignation and the other emotions, without revealing in advance whatever[17] might be employed, and without maintaining their sequence

11. For this figure, that involves the repetition of the same word in the same position of the subsequent colon; see the definition of Ioannes Sikeliotes (*Comm.* 335.17–24): ἀντιστροφὴ γὰρ λέγεται ἢ διὰ τὸ στρέφειν τὸν ῥήτορα τὴν αὐτὴν λέξιν ἐν τῷ αὐτῷ τόπῳ τοῦ δευτέρου κώλου· ἢ διὰ τὸ ὥσπερ ἀντιπρόσωπα ἀλλήλων εἶναι τὰ αὐτὰ σχήματα· ἔχει δὲ καὶ τοῦτο τὸ σχῆμα ὁ Θεολόγος· "καίτοι, κἂν εἰ τοῦτο ἦν, οὔπω δῆλον ὥσπερ Ἑλληνικὸν ἦν" [*Against Julian* = *Or.* 4.103]· καὶ "εἴπερ τοῖς συνθέτοις τὸ εἶναι μόνον συνθέτοις" [*On the Theophany* = *Or.* 38.7], καὶ "Ἀβραὰμ οὐκ ἔγνω ἡμᾶς· καὶ Ἰσραὴλ οὐκ ἐπέγνω ἡμᾶς" [*Farewell Speech*= *Or.* 42. 3].

12. Hermogenes' example of this rare figure is Demosthenes, *On the Crown* = *Or.* 18.179: οὐκ εἶπον μὲν ταῦτα, οὐκ ἔγραψα δέ· οὐδ' ἔγραψα μέν, οὐκ ἐπρέσβευσα δέ· οὐδ' ἐπρέσβευσα μέν, οὐκ ἔπεισα δέ.

13. For this figure, see now Chiron 2010.

14. Emending here μικρότερα to μακρότερα, following the text of Hermogenes.

15. Reading ἐξ ἐπεμβολῆς ὑποστροφή instead of ἐξ ἐπιστροφῆς ἐπεμβολή; cf. Anonymous, *Synopses of the On Forms* 10.5 (with Patillon's relevant critical apparatus).

16. Emending here τραχεῖαι to ταχεῖαι, following the text of Hermogenes.

17. Reading ὅ,τι instead of ὅτι. We would like to thank one of the reviewers for this correction.

[2.7.4–27]. Diction: harsh [2.7.28–31]. Figures: piteous appeals, sudden outbursts, apostrophe, and insertion of personal judgments [2.7.32–44]. Composition, cadence, and rhythm: like those found in Vehemence; in piteous appeals **[157]**, however, these should be simple [2.7.45].

Sternness [βαρύτης; 2.8]

Sternness is not a style that is observed in and of itself, rather it comprises Simplicity [ἀφελείας], Moderation [ἐπιεικείας], and other forms related to Character [ἠθικῶν]. Thoughts: reproachful [2.8.1–2]. Method: the use of irony [2.8.3–14]. Figure: hesitation when discussing things that are agreed upon [2.8.15–16]. Sternness does not include the other six parts,[18] but rather obtains them from the forms related to Character [2.8.19].

Forms related to Character [ἠθικαὶ ἰδέαι; 2.2]

Simplicity [ἀφέλεια; 2.3]

Simplicity is one of the forms related to Character. Thoughts: those of naïve characters,[19] or irrational animals and plants [2.3.1–16]. Methods: those used in Purity as well as redundancy with respect to the division into parts [2.3.17–18]. Diction: idiomatic expressions—for example: "to brother [ἀδελφίζειν]"[20] [2.3.19–20]. Figures and cola: those used in Purity [2.3.21]. Composition: rather simple and loose [λελυμένη] [2.3.22]. Cadence: stable [βεβηκυῖα] [2.3.23].

Sweetness [γλυκύτης; 2.4]

Sweetness is separate from Simplicity. Thoughts: mythical, those close to mythical narratives, things that please our senses, and those that add rational intent to things that have no free will [2.4.1–18]. Methods: those of Purity

18. I.e.: diction, figures (in Hermogenes the "hesitation . . ." is included in the discussion of method), cola, composition, cadence, and rhythm.

19. Among whom, Hermogenes (2.3.4) includes infants, women, rustic farmers, and simple-minded harmless people.

20. Isocrates, *Aeginiticus* 30.

[2.4.19]. Diction: simple and rather poetic [2.4.20–30]. Figures: those of Purity [2.4.31]. Composition: avoids hiatus [2.4.32]. Cadence: that of Solemnity—that is, stable. Rhythm: like that of Simplicity [2.4.33].

Pungency [δριμύτης: 2.5]

Pungency is also separate from Simplicity. Thoughts: superficially profound [2.5.1]; whenever a word indicates a concept literally even though it is not its proper meaning [2.5.2–8]; the use of words that sound similar [2.5.9–10]; the use of puns [τὸ ἐκ παρονομασίας] [2.5.11–12]; and when we add more metaphorical expressions after having used a metaphor [2.5.13–15].

Moderation [ἐπιείκεια: 2.6]

Moderation belongs also to the category of Character. Thought: showing oneself at a disadvantage willingly, and granting some advantage to one's opponent [2.6.1–7]. Method: not speaking vehemently against your opponent [2.6.8–23]. The rest: as in Purity and Simplicity [2.6.24].

Force [δεινότης: 2.9]

This too is an indivisible form.[21] Thoughts: the paradoxical, the profound, the powerful **[158]**, and all of those that create Grandeur. Method: the sort that is appropriate for all such thoughts as well as any that produce Grandeur. Methods in discourse that is not Forceful, but appears to be such:[22] those characteristic of Simplicity and Character. Diction [of Forceful discourse that both is and appears to be such]: very dignified and metaphorical. In the discourse that does not seem to be Forceful, but is such: the diction is simple and according to character [2.9.29–33]. The form of Force, which seems to be forceful but is not, has the most power with respect to its diction [2.9.34–37]. The figures, cola, composition, cadence, and rhythm [of Forceful discourse that both is and appears to be such] are like those found in Grandeur.

21. Following his model (Anonymous, *Synopses of the On Forms*), Psellos focuses on the various aspects of Forceful discourse "that both is *and* appears to be such" [2.9.18–28], but adds features of Forceful discourse "that is, but does not appear to be such" [2.9.29–33], and of Forceful discourse "that is not, but appears to be such" [2.9.34–37].

22. Following here the edition in Walz.

2 *Synopsis of Rhetoric in Verses*, based on the Hermogenian Corpus

Translated with introduction and notes by Jeffrey Walker

Introduction

Michael Psellos' poem *Synopsis of Rhetoric in Verses* (Σύνοψις τῆς ῥητορικῆς διὰ στίχων) was probably composed sometime between 1060 and 1067, for the young emperor-to-be Michael VII Doukas. The manuscripts say that its companion-poem, a synopsis of "grammar" (literacy and literature: *Poem.* 6), was written "to the most pious Emperor, lord Michael Doukas, at the command of his father and Emperor, so that with sweetness and contentment he would bear his lessons"; and the *Synopsis* is billed as written "to the same Emperor." Within the poem itself, the recipient is repeatedly addressed as στεφηφόρε, δέσποτα, and ἄναξ (crownbearer, lord, master), but no name appears.

It is possible that Psellos has reworked material composed much earlier for Constantine IX Monomachos, the emperor who first raised him from obscurity and made him "Consul of the Philosophers" (see Westerink 1992: 80). As he says in the *Chronographia*, during the 1040s he entertained Constantine with lessons in philosophy and metaphysics, and when the imperial patron grew fatigued with such abstruse matters, "I took up the rhetorical lyre, charmed him with its word-harmonies and rhythms, and led him toward another kind of excellence" with lessons in the rhetorical resources for both style and argument (*Chronographia* 6.197). Psellos concludes the *Synopsis of Rhetoric in Verses* by declaring it "full of sweetness, full of charm, / sweet-speaking, sweet-voiced, and unusually sweet-singing" (ll. 543–44). If this poem is not a reworking of the earlier material presented to Constantine IX, it seems to have been written in the same (or a similar) "charming" and entertaining style.

Psellos' synopses of both grammar and rhetoric, as well as a third didactic poem apparently also for Michael Doukas, *Synopsis of the Laws* (*Poem.* 8), are composed in *politikoi stichoi*, a Byzantine term that scholars normally translate as "political verse," though "public verse" might be better. (The adjective *politikos* can be translated as political, civic, public, communal, common, of the city.) Political verse was the basic medium of popular (or "folk") Greek poetry from medieval to modern times; it was recited and sung in taverns, and scrawled as graffiti in the streets of Constantinople; it was used in popular religious poetry, notably the hymns of Symeon the New Theologian at the turn of the eleventh century; and, in Byzantine high society from the eleventh century on, it became an important medium as well for poetry presented to imperial audiences, especially didactic and civic-ceremonial poetry. The rules of political verse were fairly simple: each line consisted of fifteen syllables, broken into two half-lines of eight and seven syllables respectively, usually with a caesura (a brief pause) between them. Within this two-part line, the rhythm of stressed and unstressed syllables was fairly flexible, though there generally was a major stress on the next to last syllable of the line (perhaps with a rising tone). There was no rhyme, and no set stanzaic structure: the poet composed line-by-line. Political verse was so different from the ancient, classical forms of Greek poetry, and seemingly so loose, that Byzantine scholars were sometimes undecided whether it was really "poetry" at all, or subliterary poetry, or a kind of rhythmic prose. It was the "modern poetry" of Psellos' day. (For further discussion, see Lauxtermann 1999, Jeffreys 1974, and Beaton 1980; see also Bernard 2014: 243–51 with a discussion of Psellos' poems in political verse.)

The "sweet" and charming qualities of Byzantine political verse often do not come through in English translation (without making the English sound bizarre), so it may be helpful to provide a brief snippet, in transliteration, from the *Synopsis* in its original Greek. Here are the poem's first three lines (try reading them aloud, with emphasis on the stress-accents):

Εἰ μάθοις τῆς ῥητορικῆς / τὴν τέχνην, στεφηφόρε,
ἕξεις καὶ λόγου δύναμιν, / ἕξεις καὶ γλώττης χάριν,
ἕξεις καὶ πιθανότητα / τῶν ἐπιχειρημάτων.

In the translation presented in the following pages, this comes out as:

If you learn the art of rhetoric, crownbearer,
you'll be an able speaker, and you'll have a graceful tongue,
and you'll have the most persuasive epicheiremes (arguments).

The translation here partially (if imperfectly) reflects the rhythmic and figural texture of the original, but even a partial reflection frequently is not possible in reasonably "natural"-sounding English. It will help to keep in mind, as you read, that Psellos is in fact writing *verse* with a lively, rhythmic, richly figured style. (In the Greek lines quoted here, one can find anaphora, polysyndeton, isocolon, and perhaps chiasmus.) At its worst, political verse could take on the hippity-hoppity, repetitive feel of greeting-card doggerel. At its best, it could clip along with the verve, variety, expressiveness, and charm of (say) the best poetry of an Alexander Pope (or, I suppose, good hip-hop lyrics). Psellos handles it fairly well. It is not difficult to imagine that young Michael Doukas would have been "charmed" enough to "bear his lessons" with "sweetness and contentment," and would have enjoyed listening to, and perhaps reciting, the verses of Psellos' poems on grammar, on rhetoric, and on the laws.

One should not assume, however, that Psellos is writing the same kind of poem as Pope's famous *Essay on Criticism*—though the *Synopsis* is indeed an "essay" of sorts in verse. As the title indicates, Psellos is writing a *synopsis*, an overview, of the material that Michael was supposed to be cheerfully learning in his "lessons" in rhetoric. In essence, the *Synopsis* is a rapid, compressed summary of the contents of the so-called Hermogenian corpus, a collection of rhetorical treatises attributed to the second-century rhetorician Hermogenes of Tarsos (on which see also above p. 21 in this volume).

Psellos surveys four of the five treatises attributed to Hermogenes, in the standard order: *On Issues* (1 volume), *On Invention* (4 volumes), *On Forms* (2 volumes), and *On the Method of Force* (1 volume). *On Issues* is concerned with the identification and analysis of the question at issue in a dispute (the στάσις, the precise point of disagreement), and the use of selected "headings" or topics appropriate to the different kinds of issues to generate relevant arguments; *On Invention* is concerned with methods for handling the standard parts of an oration (preface, narration, and proofs), with the fourth volume devoted to figures of speech; *On Forms* is an "advanced" treatise concerned with the detailed analysis of particular stylistic qualities (such as clarity, dignity, vehemence, rapidity); and *On the Method of Force* is, perhaps, a "capstone" treatise (or it was understood as such) on various methods for speaking "forcefully"—that is, with δεινότητα, a hard-to-translate term that basically means "awesomeness" (or "terrifying-ness"), and in late-classical rhetoric generally means something like stunning skillfulness, impressiveness, and virtuosity. In Byzantine rhetorical terminology, moreover, δεινότης is identified with disguised, double, or allusive meaning, or what Psellos calls "paradoxes and profundities" (l. 507; see Kustas 1973).

Of these four Hermogenian treatises, only two are recognized by modern scholars as actually written by Hermogenes: *On Issues* and *On Forms*. The others were added at some point in late antiquity or the early middle ages, perhaps to substitute for actual Hermogenian treatises that had been lost, or perhaps by simple misidentification, or both (Kennedy 2005: xiii–xv, 201–3). Whatever the facts of authorship may be, in Psellos' day all four treatises were believed to have been written by Hermogenes and to comprise the complete, basic course of rhetorical instruction. In the notes to the following translation of the *Synopsis*, the unknown author (or authors) of *On Invention* and *On the Method of Force* is referred to as "Hermogenes" (with quotation marks), while the author of the genuine treatises is referred to as Hermogenes (without quotation marks).

The Hermogenian corpus, from *On Issues* through *On the Method of Force*, amounts to 429 pages in the standard earlier modern edition (Rabe 1913; see now Patillon 2008–12). Psellos reduces it all to 545 lines of verse, which run a mere twenty pages in Westerink's 1992 edition (the text on which this translation is based)—equivalent to perhaps ten pages of prose. So the *Synopsis* is very compressed indeed. This raises a question about how it was meant to be used. In fact, Psellos' rendition of the Hermogenian lore is at times so compressed, so elliptical, that one can scarcely grasp what he is talking about unless one is familiar *already* with the Hermogenian source. This observation suggests that the "synopsis" is meant as a "reminder" (ὑπόμνημα), a set of review-notes set to verse for ease of memorization and review: a pleasant way for young Michael Doukas to recall his lessons. One might infer, then, that the lessons would have been first presented in duller and more detailed form. But that idea does not square so well with a notion that Psellos composed his verse synopses of grammar, rhetoric, and law to beguile the imperial student into "bearing his lessons" with good cheer.

It seems unlikely that Michael Doukas would have read the Hermogenian texts themselves, or would have patiently sat through a "reading" or even a detailed exposition of their contents. Psellos' "portrait" of Michael, at the end of the *Chronographia*, presents him as a shallow dilettante and moral weakling (while pretending to praise him; see the discussion of "figured problems" at ll. 345–47). Aside from Michael's weakness as a student, moreover, the Hermogenian texts are notoriously reader-unfriendly, even for professional scholars (although, apparently, ancient rhetoricians found Hermogenes more serviceable for teaching than his competitors; Heath 2004: 44). It is arguable that the Hermogenian texts were never meant, in the first place, to be read by students, and that they were meant, rather, as a technical resource for the rhetoric-teacher. There are, for example, passages where it is quite clear that Hermogenes is addressing himself to professional teachers, and talking *about* but not *to* the student. The Hermogenian texts provided an exposition of terms and concepts to be used in guiding students through their declamation exercises—practice-orations composed in response to the fictive scenarios or "cases" (ὑποθέσεις) given in set "problems" (προβλήματα)—as well as rhetorical-critical study of the canonic orators and writers that students were encouraged to take as models for imitation. But declamation was the central, crucial activity: in declamation, the student would put all of his rhetorical knowledge together and actualize it in discourse-creation and performance. (The Greek word for declamation, μελέτη, means "practice, exercise, rehearsal.") Ultimately, the student's ability to declaim, and beyond that to perform in actual public discourse, was more important than his ability to recite rhetorical precepts—though he could, of course, use the precepts to reflect on his own (and others') performances.

Psellos closes the *Synopsis* (l. 545) with a reference to "profiting" from "speaking playfully," παίζων λογικῶς, which could also be rendered (more literally) as "playing discursively, rationally, argumentatively"—in other words, playing "games" of speechmaking and debate. He also says the "profit" in this "play" will be aided by (or even derive from) the τεχνύδριον he has provided (l. 541): a "mini-art," an "art in miniature." This suggests that the *Synopsis* is a brief version and "reminder" of the things that Psellos has been saying to Michael in conjunction with his "playful" speaking exercises.

He also says, in mid-synopsis, "Take the overview from me, and then forthrightly ask your questions, / and I will tell you the solution of the problem: / then you will not wonder, lord, at the writer's art, / if you have a quick survey of the whole" (ll. 287–90; presumably the "writer" is Hermogenes). Here the "overview" (σύνοψις) stands forth as an "abbreviated" version of, and replacement for, the whole "art" (τέχνη) embodied in the Hermogenian corpus; and where the "abbreviated" mini-art needs filling out, Michael must ask his questions, "wonder" about things, and receive more detailed explanations. If Michael was attentive, there must have been many questions; but if he was not, perhaps he was entertained anyway by the sprightly music of a sometimes-incomprehensible (for him) piece of poetry.

However the text was originally meant to be used, modern readers who are not familiar with the Hermogenian treatises—and few are—may frequently find Psellos' brief renditions too elliptical, too obscure for comfort and may wish to "ask [their] questions" too. For this reason the translation has been annotated fairly copiously with additional explanations. There are also notes that indicate which Hermogenian book and chapter Psellos is referring to, and some that address problems of translation. Readers who wish to undertake a more detailed comparison of Psellos' treatments with the Hermogenian originals now have a full set of English translations available—Heath 1995 (*On Issues*), Wooten 1987 (*On Forms*), and Kennedy 2005 (*On Invention* and *On the Method of Force*); see also Patillon 2008–12 (French translation with detailed commentary of the entire corpus).

This is not the place for a detailed comparison of Psellos with Hermogenes, but the notes do indicate what seem to be occasional divergences, exclusions, modifications, additions, or confusions. A careful examination of what Psellos includes, leaves out, changes, or expands will show that the *Synopsis* is not a mere summary, but an interpretation and adaptation of its source. On one hand, for example, in his treatment of *On Issues* Psellos more or less omits Hermogenes' sometimes-maniacally detailed discussions of the "division" of each issue into "heads" of argument (which comprises about two-thirds of the text), while focusing more on the general outline of the theory (the subject of the opening two chapters). On the other hand, he omits mention of virtually no chapter from *On Invention*, which at four volumes is by far the longest Hermogenian treatise, and he adds some non-Hermogenian examples from patristic sources (Basil the Great, Gregory of Nazianzos, and John Chrysostom)—which either are his own additions or a reflection of Byzantine teaching practice in his day. His treatment of *On Forms* is accurate and fairly detailed, though he adds no new examples; at one point (l. 475), he finds Hermogenes' treatment of one variant of the "subtle" style dubious. He treats *On the Method of Force* very sketchily. And so forth. One can derive a picture from such details of what Psellos and his contemporaries found more or less useful and more or less intelligible in Hermogenian rhetorical theory. He seems interested in the general idea of στάσις, but not so much the details of Hermogenes' system; he is very much engaged with teaching how to handle the parts of an oration; he is interested in advanced stylistic criticism (something that shows up elsewhere, in his critical essays); and he passes along a few pointers for speaking deftly, selecting about half of what the Hermogenian text discusses.

Editions and translations. The translation that follows uses the Greek text of Westerink 1992, based on all eight available manuscripts (including Paris, BNF, gr. 1182; Moore 2005: 482); numbers in square brackets indicate verse numbers in that edition. I have tried to render it line-by-line as much as possible, so that the line numbers of the translation generally correspond to the line numbers in Westerink. (Psellos does, in fact, generally treat the political-verse line as a unit of meaning, and as a unit of composition.) In addition I have generally followed Westerink's "paragraph" divisions, again for ease of matching the translation to the Greek original. I have added, as "signposts" in the right-hand margin, the titles of the Hermogenian books where Psellos begins to take them up as well as the Greek term of the Hermogenian "forms." I have generally rendered technical terms in English equivalents, while preserving the Greek term in brackets (e.g., [ὑπολήψεις] for "prejudgments"); the exceptions are terms that have already been absorbed into the English technical vocabulary of rhetoric and are fairly familiar (e.g., metaphor, enthymeme, epicheireme). In the notes, all citations of the Hermogenian source are to the edition of Patillon.

Synopsis of Rhetoric in Similar [i.e., Political] Verses to the Same Emperor

If you learn the art of rhetoric,[1] crownbearer,
you'll be an able speaker,[2] and you'll have a graceful tongue,
and you'll have the most persuasive epicheiremes.[3]
The art surveys political questions,[4] ***On Issues* [I. 4]**
and a political question, according to the technographer,[5]

1. τῆς ῥητορικῆς τὴν τέχνην: *technê*, "art," signifies either a body of techniques/principles for methodically accomplishing a goal (as in the "arts" of sculpture, music, navigation, engineering, politics, etc.), or—particularly in the case of rhetoric—a *handbook* that offers a systematic exposition of the art's principles (cf. Latin *ars*). In what follows I will generally render *technê* as "art." "Art of rhetoric" here also indicates specifically the Hermogenian corpus.

2. ἕξεις καὶ λόγου δύναμιν: literally "you will have power of speech"; reading *δύναμιν* here as "power, capacity, ability, faculty." The "power" of discourse is a commonplace in earlier rhetoric; see, e.g., the introductory statements in Dionysios of Halikarnassos' *Roman Antiquities* 1.1.3, Diodoros of Sicily's *Library of History* 1.2.5, and, especially, Hermogenes' *On Forms* 1.1. Cf. also Aristotle, *Rhetoric* 1.2.1.

3. ἐπιχείρημα: in rhetorical theory, an argumentative movement composed of linked subarguments and amplifications (compare the *sorites* in logic, composed of linked syllogisms). See note 60, below.

4. Literally, "it is a *theôros* of political *zêtêmata*." Θεωρός seems to echo the Aristotelian definition of rhetoric as "a faculty of observing (δύναμις τοῦ θεωρεῖν) in any given case the available means of persuasion" (*Rhetoric* 1.2.1); thus θεωρός can be understood here as "observer" in the sense of a "surveyor" of the rhetorical resources available for any given "question." Ζήτημα is a technical term in Hermogenes, signifying the political or civic "question" (or "inquiry") with which the rhetor is concerned in a particular case.

5. "the writer of the τέχνη": i.e., Hermogenes.

is a doubtful matter that is arguable and divisible[6] on both sides,
according to the customs and laws of cities,
concerning the just, the good, and the advantageous.
Indeed the kinds [εἴδη] of rhetoric are just these three—
judicial [δικανικὸν], advisory [συμβουλή], and panegyrical [πανήγυρις]—
for the end of judicial rhetoric is the just,
of panegyrical [πανηγυρικοῦ] the good, and of advisory the advantageous.[7]
A disputable question, my lord, is given
no limit by the art (for that is a matter of law);
but the art establishes the point in question at any time.[8]
Questions differ in their potential,
for they bear greater and lesser persons [πρόσωπα] and actions [πράγματα].[9]
Often they are inconclusive in either respect,
and then the power of the rhetor is revealed,[10]
when he takes up a case that is weak in either way
and by the power of reasoning strengthens it and prevails.[11]

6. Μερική: "divisible" into parts, i.e., the particular "headings" of invention that Hermogenes prescribes for different stases (types of issues, such as fact, definition, or quality).

7. These are, of course, the standard three "species"/genres of classical rhetoric. Aristotle's *Rhetoric* calls them *δικανικόν* ("judicial" discourse); συμβουλευτικόν or δημηγορικόν ("advisory" or "public" discourse, i.e., on questions of policy or action); and ἐπιδεικτικόν ("display"); later rhetorical handbooks tend to prefer the term πανηγυρικόν to ἐπιδεικτικόν (cf. Lauxtermann 1998; also Papaioannou 2013a: 103–13). Modern English translations of these terms (reflecting Latin influence) frequently render them as forensic, deliberative, and epideictic; I have tried to stay closer to the original sense of the Greek and to Byzantine usage.

8. The point here is that the art of rhetoric itself prescribes no predetermined end (or outcome) to the process of disputation, but it identifies the precise point in dispute, the στάσις, and supplies a series of positions for the arguers on opposing sides; the process of disputation can in principle go on indefinitely, but in a trial the ending is set by trial procedure.

9. Technical terms in *On Issues*, denoting the "persons" (historical figures such as "Demosthenes," stock characters such as "rich man," etc.) and the "actions" (or "facts") laid down in the set problems for declamation exercises.

10. I am rendering ῥήτωρ "untranslated" as rhetor, since it can mean either "orator" (or "speaker" or "writer") or "rhetorician" (a teacher of rhetoric).

11. I.e., the given facts in a well-formed declamation problem (persons, actions, circumstances) are normally insufficient in themselves to determine the outcome of the case, so that success will depend on the inventional and argumentational powers of the rhetor. A very similar notion is expressed by an anonymous scholar preserved in mss. from the tenth c. and later: rhetorical training consists, he says, of "disputable and evenly

There are also many ill-formed problems,
which are ill-balanced or even prejudiced in nature;[12]
and there are, moreover, those that are by nature wholly invalid,
as they are one-sided or ultimately insoluble.[13]
Questions are valid,[14] are brought to trial, and are declaimed on
when they involve both a person and an action that admits of judgment,
and that gives rise to persuasive arguments on either side.

Altogether, lord, there are thirteen
issues [στάσεις], as they are called, from the disputation
of rhetors using persuasive epicheiremes.[15]

The first of these is conjecture: this is, master,
an examination that substantiates what is the case from a clear sign,
or from particular suspicions about a person.[16]

---

balanced problems for the reason that whenever one side of the case is argued with greater strength, the power of the speaker is revealed, and not of the problem itself, which furnishes either side of the case with equal strength" (Walz 1834: 49). This idea is not found in Hermogenes, though one might argue that it is implicit.

12. Hermogenes recognizes three kinds of faulty (yet arguable) declamation problems: the "ill-balanced" (ἑτερορρεπής), the "ill-formed" (κακόπλαστα, e.g., proposing a historical scenario that is contrary to fact), and the "prejudiced" (προειλημμένη, cf. *On Issues* 1.24). Psellos, however, seems to consider the ill-balanced and the prejudiced as types of the ill-formed.

13. Ἀσύστατα: literally "without cohesion, indeterminate, unformed"; Hermogenes deploys this term to mean "invalid" declamation problems that are not capable of producing a determinate issue, and thus are of no use for declamation exercises. Hermogenes identifies eight types of "invalid" issues (*On Issues* 1.14–21), of which Psellos mentions two. (The "one-sided" differs from the "ill-balanced" and "prejudiced," above, as it has no arguments at all on one side.) In the next three lines Psellos paraphrases Hermogenes' criteria for distinguishing coherent or "valid" problems (1.13). It is worth noting that he is here moving through the Hermogenian material in backwards order.

14. I.e., forming a coherent or determinate issue to be argued.

15. Introducing a review of Hermogenes' synopsis-chapter (*On Issues* 2). This etymology from "disputation [τὸ στασιάζειν]" is not Hermogenian. The thirteen *issues* that follow are: (1) conjecture [στοχασμός], (2) definition [ὅρος], (3) practical deliberation [πραγματική], (4) counterplea [ἀντίληψις], (5) counterstance [ἀντίστασις], (6) countercharge [ἀντέγκλημα], (7) shift of issue [μετάστασις], (8) forgiveness [συγγνώμη], (9) letter [ῥητόν] and intent [διάνοια], (10) rhetorical syllogism [συλλογισμὸν ῥητορικόν], (11) conflict of law [ἀντινομία], (12) ambiguity [ἀμφιβολία], and (13) objection [μετάληψις].

16. This line (34) is an exact quote from Hermogenes (*On Issues* 2.1.5 ap. crit.; Patillon treats it as an interpolation); it seems to suggest the headings of "motive and capacity"

The second is definition, as it is called:
an examination of the name for an action.[17]
The third is practical deliberation: it investigates what should be done,
from which it receives its name, crownbearer.[18]
The fourth is counterplea, on grounds of non-liability,
when a forceful accusation demands accountability for some act.[19]
The fifth, in turn, is counterstance: here the defendant
grants the charge that has been brought against him,
and sets against it some good outcome from the very thing that he has done.
If [sixth] someone admits to having committed murder,
he shows that the victim himself deserved it:
he frames a countercharge, and countercharges justly.
If [seventh] he can aptly place the blame on someone else
(if something is to be punished), it is a shift of issue;
but [eighth] if he is without defense, the issue is forgiveness.
If [ninth] a punishable act is connected with law,[20]
and one side puts forth the letter of the law
while the other sagely takes the law by its intentions,
the issue is letter and intent.
If [tenth] some act resists assimilation to the letter of the law,
then one works up a rhetorical syllogism:
this is a comparison of the uncodified to the codified.[21]

in developing arguments about the likelihood that a person committed an alleged act. What Psellos makes less than clear is that "conjecture" involves questions of fact, and inquiry into the kinds of proof by which claims about fact can be substantiated—an ἔλεγχος οὐσιοποιός, a process of "examination establishing what is."

17. E.g., if it is established that someone killed someone (the question of fact), one may dispute whether the killing was murder, justifiable homicide, an accident, etc. (the question of definition). Psellos (like Hermogenes) is thinking of the defendant, who will seek to put a favorable name on the act he is charged with.

18. I.e., the name of this issue, πραγματική, derives from τὸ πρακτέον, "what should be done"—cf. πρᾶγμα, "action, business" (the main concern of political deliberation).

19. I.e., "counterplea" arises when a defendant admits to an action but denies that it was wrong or that he has any legal liability. This is the first of a set of issues (4–8) discussed by Hermogenes under the general heading of "judicial discourse" (δικαιολογία), all of which arise from the position taken by the defendant.

20. Psellos here transitions to the "legal" issues (9–12), which are concerned with the interpretation of laws.

21. This issue deals with extension of a law to novel situations that it was not originally written for (or that it does not directly mention), by "inference" (συλλογισμὸν)

If [eleventh] there is a controversy involving two or more laws
and it is a question of selecting not many but one of them,
naturally the issue is conflict of law.

But [twelfth] ambiguity is an issue that proceeds
from the prosody of accent or the parsing of words.[22]

If [thirteenth] there is controversy whether any judgment should be made,[23]
the issue is objection, which you divide as follows,
for codified and uncodified kinds of this occur:
call the codified kind [ἔγγραφον] a complete legal exclusion,
possessing the strength and power of argument from law;
and call the uncodified kind [ἄγραφον] non-legal, for it does not cite law,
but is more rational.[24] In fact two issues,
practical deliberation and objection, as the art says,[25]
in a certain way lie between the rational issues and the legal ones,
not as unified wholes, but as composed of elements from both.[26]

---

from certain features of the act in question to analogous acts explicitly covered by the law (see Hermogenes *On Issues* 2.11; and Heath 1995: 34, who renders this issue as "assimilation"). Psellos' "rhetorical syllogism" may echo Aristotle's definition of the enthymeme (*Rhetoric* 1.2.8).

22. Psellos has in mind ambiguities in the meanings of written laws, arising from differences in meaning determined by pitch-accent (in words otherwise spelled or pronounced the same) or from different possible ways of parsing a word or phrase.

23. This thirteenth issue constitutes a fourth main type of position, alongside conjecture (στοχασμός), definition (ὅρος), and quality (ποιότης, with its "rational" and "legal" subdivisions); it has to do, in essence, with whether the matter in question can reasonably be brought to trial at all or should simply be dismissed (or, perhaps, transferred to a different venue).

24. The distinction here is between "objection" founded on the charge of παραγραφὴ ("outside/against what is written")—an argument that the case falls outside of written law, or that the charge itself or the procedure is illegal—and "objection" founded on appeals to principles not explicitly encoded in written law, such as notions of appropriate venue or whether there is a prima facie basis for a trial (or a debate). This distinction further corresponds to the division (in Hermogenes) between the "rational" and "legal" subdivisions of the "qualitative" issues—the "rational" issues (3–8) involving the qualitative judgment of an act (in terms of considerations of justice, moral defensibility, mitigating circumstances, etc.), and the "legal" issues (9–12) involving the interpretation of written laws.

25. The remark that follows does not explicitly appear in the Hermogenian text (as we now have it), though it is inferrable from it (see the following note).

26. That is, they may draw on both "rational" and "legal" topics. As Heath's (1995) analysis of Hermogenes' *On Issues* shows, Hermogenes treats the different issues as

Each of the abovementioned issues
is called by both special [ἰδικοῖς] and generic [γενικοῖς] names:
each is split up into both special and common [κοινοῖς] heads, in a certain way,
of which some belong particularly to the prosecution,
and some to the defense, while the common topics belong to both.

Again, according to another division, the subject-matter of the issues
is in a certain way divided into types, since a speech has genre,
and it is minutely subdivided, with no gap permitted.[27]

That is the theory of issues, lord.
Next you should be told as well about prefaces, ***On Invention* 1 [l. 81]**
and the invention of the rest of the speech, and figures.[28]

A speech composed with art, master,
has both body and soul, both head and feet:
the thought is its soul, the diction is its body,
the introductory matter is its head, and the epilogue is its feet.

Indeed there are many topics of prefaces,
but Hermogenes writes in his treatise of just four kinds.

[First, the topic] from prejudgment of persons and actions:
one should, with respect to prejudgment of the matter at hand,
compose prefaces that give thanks or express regret.[29]

---

drawing on overlapping sets of "heads" and topics. Psellos seems here to be recognizing that point, if only glancingly.

27. This short, highly general segment on the subdivision of each issue into headings and topics (ll. 72–79) represents the latter two thirds of Hermogenes' *On Issues* (chapters 3–12), in which the "division" and handling of each issue is discussed in detail; Psellos has explicitly "covered" only Hermogenes' introductory discussion (chaps. 1–2). Psellos' mention of an "other division" appears to invoke the Aristotelian notion of ἴδια and κοινὰ from the *Rhetoric,* especially Aristotle's treatment of the ἴδια belonging to the advisory, epideictic, and judicial species/genres in book 1—though this account does not really square well with the treatment of topics in Hermogenian issue-theory.

28. Psellos here begins his overview of the four books of the Pseudo-Hermogenian treatise *On Invention*; Book 1 is concerned primarily with the "invention" of prefaces; the other books are concerned with "the rest of the speech, and figures."

29. The topic of ὑπόληψις, "prejudgment" (*On Invention* 1.1; "supposition," Kennedy 2005: 5; "préjugé," Patillon), involves opening with a *response* to existing attitudes toward "the matter at hand," or in other words the givens of the case: insofar as they can be regarded as good or bad, the speaker can open with expressions of thanks or grieving.

[Second,] from division:[30] this is such,
master, that when two crimes have been committed,
and each of them is to be judged and punished,
we divide and compose a preface such as this:
if this person is to be punished even for one of these crimes,
how much should he be chastised on account of both?
And likewise for the second and third types,
master, of this topic of the preface:
division from prejudgment and from considerations of time.[31]
Again, the art establishes a third topic of prefaces,
which it designates as "from abundance,"[32]
as when accusing someone of murder I add
that I could accuse him of sacrilege as well—
a greater and worse crime than the first.
The fourth topic of prefaces is from the occasion [τοῦ καιροῦ],
as when one claims in public proceedings that what is sought
has come to pass already in events that have transpired.[33]
A whole preface consists of these four parts:
opening, elaboration, proposition,
and finally the closing, which completes the preface.[34]

30. In *On Invention* 1.2 "division (ἐκ διαιρέσεως)" appears as "subdivision (ἐξ ὑποδιαιρέσεως) ("subordination," Kennedy 2005: 17)," of which "Hermogenes" recognizes the three types mentioned here. The idea is to amplify the seriousness of the matter in question by invoking "subdivisions" or subsidiary considerations.

31. All three types of "division" involve cases with multiple misdeeds; the second involves repeat malefactors whose known bad past can be discussed, and the third looks to "time" as it involves repeat malefactors who should be dealt with "once and for all," so that their crimes will no longer be repeated.

32. ἐκ *περιουσίας*: *On Invention* 1.3 (Patillon: "*a fortiori*"; Kennedy 2005: 23: "superfluity"). The idea is that the speaker *could* indict the accused for an even greater crime than he actually is charged with.

33. *On Invention* 1.4.

34. πρότασις, κατασκευή, ἀξίωσις, βάσεως: *On Invention* 1.5. "Hermogenes"' third term is ἀπόδοσις, "which is an ἀξίωσις." Ἀξίωσις seems to signify an evaluative statement, or an announcement of the speaker's central claim. "Hermogenes" says that the "more political" (as opposed to "panegyrical") kind of preface may consist of a "plain ἀξίωσις," i.e., a simple announcement of the proposition the speaker intends to argue for (106–7). Κατασκευή, which (as a rhetorical term) usually signifies "confirmation" or "proof," here seems to signify any sort of supporting statement, development, or elaboration. See Kennedy 2005: 9n9; 27nn40, 44.

A preface is adequately amplified
by doubling a word, or doubling a colon.[35]
The four parts may be illustrated with an example, thus:[36]
"What memorial of martyrs would be satisfactory, for one who loves martyrs?"
This is the opening of the speech. Next observe the other parts:
"For the honoring of martyrdom is an act of goodwill to the Lord."[37]
This clearly is an elaboration of the opening.
"With speech, therefore, honor him who has been martyred."[38]
This clearly is the proposition. Next see the closing:
". . . so that you yourself would willingly become a martyr."[39]
It is called a closing, since it is a final part
in which the whole preface seems to come to rest,[40]
and also an elaboration of the proposition,
which we do to venture an additional remark as we embark—
concerning which, I shall teach you the progression of the speech.[41]
And that is a brief art of prefaces for you. ***On Invention* 2 [l. 127]**
When you are going to bring your speech to the narration [διήγησιν],

35. On the definition of a colon, see above, p. 25n5.

36. The example that follows is not, of course, from "Hermogenes": Psellos quotes from Basil the Great's very popular *On the Forty Martyrs of Sebasteia*, though not with complete accuracy (see below). For the original see *Homily* 19 (PG 31, 508–25 [508b1–4 and 6–7]), read on the martyrs' feast day, March 9 of the Byzantine calendar.

37. Psellos compresses Basil's statement, which in its full form is (roughly), "for the honor paid by fellow-servants to the good bears proof of our goodwill to our common Lord" (PG 31, 508b2–4).

38. Again, Psellos loosely paraphrases Basil's language: "With sincerity call blessed him who has borne martyrdom" (PG 31, 508b6–7).

39. Here Psellos actually expands Basil's briefer phrase, "so that you would voluntarily die a martyr" (PG 31, 508b7), which is a continuation of the preceding line. The only locution in common to both Psellos' and Basil's versions is τῇ προαιρέσει, "voluntarily" ("by choice").

40. βαίνειν ἔοικε, literally "seems to walk on," with a notion of the preface coming to rest sententiously (with "panegyrical" flourishes) in its βάσις. Cf. the perfective senses of βαίνειν as "stand" (or "stand on a base"); and the senses of βάσις as a "step, measured movement, rhythmical close," and also "base" or "pedestal."

41. According to "Hermogenes" (106–7), the βάσις takes on a panegyrical or "epiphonematic" function when it gives a reason for the proposition (ἀξίωσις). An ἐπιφώνημα, in rhetoric, is a sententious "added remark" used to finish off a passage with a flourish. Psellos conceives this as a flourish performed as a speaker completes his preface and "embarks on" or "goes into" the body of the speech.

consider from what you shall derive the preliminary statement [προκατάστασιν]:[42]
it is the preliminary part of a narrative,
in essence a pre-narrative of things from beginning to end.[43]
It truly would be artless if, without preliminaries,
you immediately began the narrative itself.
The subject of immigration, for example, takes preliminaries;
likewise the proposal and repeal of laws. Indeed the majority
of cases [ὑποθέσεων] take preliminaries too.[44]
For such narratives you should undertake a prelude,
and may it be your preliminary statement, artfully composed.

When you have set forth the preliminary statement, state the narrative.[45]
It is, in style, both ample and varied:
it is not confined by set rules of speech,
but is amplified with many cola and lines of thought.
And if indeed you wish to recast it
in different locutions, with varied words,
embellish and interpose, first, what must be done,
then the reason for it, then what has been left undone,
and then the reason for that, in those four steps.[46]

42. "Hermogenes" defines προκατάστασις as a προδιήγησις, a "pre-narrative" before the narrative proper; the chapter-title given in the manuscripts (perhaps a later addition) also refers to the διήγησις as a κατάστασις, a "setting down" of the given facts a particular case is about (108–9); see Kennedy 2005: 35n55. Psellos now turns to the second book of *On Invention*, which is concerned primarily with the handling of narrative (2.1).

43. "Things from beginning to end," τὰ ἀπ' ἀρχῆς εἰς τέλος, is a standard topic of invention for narration (i.e., "the sequence of events"). The προκατάστασις is a brief preliminary overview of the matters to be related in more detail by the narrative proper.

44. A rapid gesture toward the following two chapters of *On Invention*—2.2, "On immigration, and invention in these matters"; and 2.3, "On introduction of laws"—and possibly (and more generally) the next several chapters as well, which take up war and peace (2.4), impiety and murder (2.5), and crimes against the state (2.6). The term ὑπόθεσις was a technical term for a specific "case" (as in a declamation exercise), as opposed to a θέσις or "general proposition" for philosophical debate.

45. Psellos here turns to the subject-matter of *On Invention* 2.7, "On narration."

46. "Reason" here is αἰτία (cause), not justification. Psellos only partially reflects (and seems more rigid than) the procedure suggested in *On Invention* 2.7. "Hermogenes" recommends that every statement in the narrative be "extended" to three or four cola that reiterate and embellish the idea—and that the narrative ideally should state "what has been done," the reason (αἰτία) for it, "what has not been done," the reason for that,

Know the three modes of narration, crownbearer: the simple [ἁπλοῦς],
the argued [ἐγκατάσκευος],[47] and the highly wrought [ἐνδιάσκευος].
When the facts are many and complex,
and have inherent strengths and subtleties on both sides,[48]
narrate, lord, not argumentatively but simply.
There is an example of this in Demosthenes:
"We went out to Panactus two years ago,
and the sons of Ariston were billeted with us;
soon they were abusive in full view of everyone,
and they were violent and struck [us] and broke the chamberpots."[49]
But if the narrative in brief is very forceful,
narrate it with argument, expanding it with reasons;[50]
and if it is both brief and also very clear,

and also rational "calculations" (λογισμοί, e.g., "if this were the case, then . . ."). Psellos' notion of "interposing" these things reflects "Hermogenes'" illustration, which discusses (1) thing not done + reason; (2) thing done + reason; (3) thing not done again + reason; etc.—all treated "in many and varied cola."

47. "argued," Kennedy 2005: 55; "with confirmation" (*avec confirmation*, Patillon), in line with the common rhetorical use of the term κατασκευή to mean "confirmation" of a proposition. Here the *ἐγκατάσκευος* mode of narration is linked with the statement of a "reason" in the sense of a cause (αἰτία) of a given fact; as a statement of the reason why something happened, it is more an elaboration or explanation than a proof.

48. "Hermogenes" speaks here of "many and varied" facts that "weigh against the opponent and help our case" (2.7.17); Psellos seems to be thinking still of evenly balanced declamation problems.

49. The example here, as in *On Invention* 2.7.20, is drawn from Demosthenes' *Against Conon* (34), in which Demosthenes says he will narrate the facts as briefly as possible; but the situation represented here by Psellos only vaguely resembles that of Demosthenes' narrative (or "Hermogenes'" version of it). Demosthenes and his friends suffered affronts from the sons of Conon, and Ariston is only briefly mentioned later in the speech; likewise, Conon's sons abused first the slaves of Demosthenes and his companions—beating them, emptying chamber-pots on them, and urinating on them—and then they assaulted Demosthenes and his companions themselves. Psellos appears to be quoting from (vague) memory to a student who has not actually read Demosthenes' speech, or he is misquoting "Hermogenes"—who, for that matter, does not quote Demosthenes accurately either. ("Hermogenes" has the sons of Conon urinating on Demosthenes and his friends and breaking chamber-pots over their heads.)

50. I.e., when the facts comprising the narrative are brief and forceful (favorable for one's case), the speaker may elaborate "argumentatively" with discussions of "reasons" (αἰτίαι, causes) for what happened.

elaborate it boldly, in highly wrought ways.
And what is highly wrought [ἐνδιάσκευον]? An ornate style.
And here a poetic example should be given you:
"First they drew back [the victim's head], cut the throat and flayed the skin,
then butchered out the thighs and covered them with savory fat,
and carefully roasted them and drew them off [the fire]."[51]
A second example should be given to you too,
an extremely clever one from the *Funeral Oration* of the Theologian:
"They lunge and shout, they send a cloud of dust on high,
they sit and hold the reins, they lash the air,
they yoke and immediately re-yoke [their horses] in some way." [52]
And when the master of sophistomania[53] says "on high,"
then adds the cause—that they are many and young[54]—
he has briefly given you an argued exposition.

The preconfirmation (for this must be mentioned too) ***On Invention* 3 [l. 175]**
is called the preliminary part of confirmation;[55]
and this also should be taught to you with examples,
not from the Demosthenic writings, but from those of the Theologian.
For this masterful philosopher and rhetor,
when impelled to confirm God's monarchy,
set forth all three heads of his argument:
"There are," he said, "three ancient doctrines concerning God:
anarchy, polyarchy, and finally monarchy."[56]

51. *Iliad* 1.459–60, 466; 2.422–23, 429; and elsewhere (this is a formula). This example—an approximate quote in political verse, not Homer's hexameters—apparently is "highly wrought" because of its use (in Greek) of archaic poetic diction and a higher than usual density of schematic figures (most notably asyndeton, homoioteleuton, parisosis, and paromoiosis, not to mention poetic meter). Neither this nor the following example are taken from "Hermogenes'" *On Invention.*

52. Cf. Gregory Nazianzos, *Funeral Oration for Basil the Great* = *Or.* 43.15.

53. ὁ πάνσοφος τὴν σοφιστομανίαν, more literally "the man all-wise at sophistomania" (also from *Or.* 43.15).

54. πλῆθος καὶ νέοι, loosely paraphrasing Gregory's τῶν νέων οἱ πλεῖστοι.

55. Psellos is now moving to the subject-matter of *On Invention* 3, which deals with methods of κατασκευή, "confirmation/proof" of one's case; προκατασκευή, "preconfirmation," is the subject-matter of 3.2. Preconfirmation, like the "preliminary statement" (προκατάστασις) of a narrative, is in essence what modern handbooks call a "forecast" statement of what is to come in a particular section of a discourse.

56. Gregory Nazianzos, *On the Son* = *Or.* 29.2.

The presentation of these three headings, then,
is a preconfirmation artistically set forth.
There is, too, a kind of rebuttal called "forcible,"[57]
when we take up our opponents' strongest argument
and turn it against them, as though demonstrated by themselves,
as Chrysostom did in his *Philogonios*.[58]
When he was introducing his argument on the mysteries,
he barred the unrepentant from coming to communion,
as some maintained that they would not
submit to communion every day, but only once a year.
The masterful teacher, he of the tongue called golden,
forcefully replied, "this itself is a grievous error,
since you neither purify yourself nor make progress toward complete purification
when you partake of the holy mysteries just one time."
In a speech, the heading [κεφάλαιον] of the case
is introduced either by us or our opponents,
the latter of which requires a wholly artistic and embellished rebuttal.[59]
It is introduced artistically in "four-wheeled" fashion,
with the proposition and support, a counterproposition,
and an oppositional rebuttal from the counterproposition.
The proposition introduces the support,
and the support is the opponent's argument,

57. Βίαιον: *On Invention* 3.5 (though it is the third chapter, according to the text of "Hermogenes" and followed here by Psellos). It seems odd, to the modern mind, to move directly to "rebuttal" from "preconfirmation" without taking up "confirmation" itself. However, since the Hermogenian *On Issues* generally treats the actual arguments in a case as arising from the *denial* of an accusation, and generally organizes its issue-system around the positions of *defense*, it may in fact be logical to think of the "confirmation" (or "proof") of a case as starting from λύσις, "rebuttal" (or, more literally, "release, loosening, undoing" of the charge). It is also possible that Psellos is taking λύσις in the more general sense of a "solution" to a problem (i.e., "loosening" or "untying" a knot).

58. In what follows, Psellos "quotes" very loosely from John Chrysostom's *On the Blessed Philogonios* (PG 48 755.21–23). For an English translation of the passage, see Harkins 1982: 180–81 (*Homily* 6.35).

59. *On Invention* 3.4. Here Psellos (with "Hermogenes") continues the theme of refutative (or defensive) strategies as the starting-points of "confirmation"; what follows is a technique for developing "headings" of argument introduced by the opponent.

while the counterproposition is a promise of rebuttal,
after which the rebuttal arises from epicheiremes.
The epicheireme confirms the rebuttal,
and elaboration [ἐργασία] is a function of epicheiremes,
just as the enthymeme is, in turn, [a function] of elaboration,
and the epenthymemes of proenthymemes.[60]
From manner, person, time, place, and cause—
but primarily from the facts themselves, for in them lies the subject-matter,[61]
the elaboration gathers the preliminary arguments
and is fortified with illustration and examples,
and comparisons of lessers, greaters, equals, and opposites.
The natural form of enthymemes is drawn
from every circumstance by means of comparisons;
the epenthymeme is a doubled enthymeme.[62]
You must use objections [ἐνστάσει] and counter-rejoinders [ἀντιπαραστάσει]
in all cases,[63] for they are serviceable in their way,

60. Psellos is jumping around in the Hermogenian chapters on epicheiremes, enthymemes, and ἐργασία (*On Invention* 3.5–9). "Hermogenes," having taught that λύσις is "confirmed" by epicheiremes, says that ἐργασία "confirms" (or "elaborates," κατασκευάζει) the epicheireme, and that the enthymeme "confirms" (κατασκευάζει again) the ἐργασία (3.8.151). The epicheireme, in the loosest sense an "argument," is commonly conceived in rhetorical treatises as a five-step movement consisting of "a proposition, supporting reason, proof of the reason, embellishment, and conclusion" (Kennedy 2005: 85). An enthymeme is a stylistically pointed summing-up of a claim and its proof, often functioning as a "cap" to a passage of discussion (such as an ἐργασία consisting of examples, or, even, a bundle of subordinate enthymemes), and is often stated in antithetical form (see below); thus the supporting-reason-plus-proof part of an epicheireme can be understood as an enthymeme in itself, and an ἐργασία can be understood to be summed up, "confirmed," or *completed* by an enthymeme also, so that the epicheireme can be understood as being composed of enthymematic parts. An "epenthymeme" is an additional enthymeme added as a supplement (or embellishment) to a preceding ("pro") enthymeme (3.9.152).

61. Ὕλη, "wood," or raw material, i.e., to be carved or worked upon (*On Invention* 3.6.2). Psellos seems to differ from "Hermogenes," who seems to have in mind something like the Aristotelian notion of "material cause."

62. See n. 60. The "epenthymeme" is an enthymeme "added onto" ("epi") an enthymeme.

63. *On Invention* 3.4. The "objection" or ἔνστασις is in essence a denial of some proposition, thereby putting it ἐν στάσει (in dispute); the "counter-rejoinder" or ἀντιπαράστασις answers the opponent's counterstatement to the objection, at which point the issue becomes more precise.

but the objection is more confrontational,
and introduces denial and rebuttal of the act in question,
while the counter-rejoinder is more subtle.
Thus, if someone should say, "You were not required to kill,"
he has taken up a counterstance [ἀντίστασιν] that rejects the act;[64]
but if someone says, "It may have been necessary, but not in such a manner,"
he has spoken a counter-rejoinder, a more moderate rebuttal.
But what should be brought first to questions in dispute
is impossible to say; judge this according to your reason.
However, a counter-rejoinder smooths the way.[65]

The so-called "from a beginning until its end"
is the most essential heading of them all,[66]
and it is elaborated in different ways—
not with circumstantial details, but with various partitions, extended periods
delivered in a single breath [πνεύμασι], and tightly-woven periods.[67]
Each subdivision accomplishes a characterization,

64. This is, apparently, counterstance functioning as an ἔνστασις, "objecting" to a claim that the defendant had acted in self-defense.

65. The interesting points here—which seem to be Psellos' additions—are that ἀντιπαράστασις is preferable to flat ἔνστασις and that one does not begin a process of argumentation by flatfootedly declaring one's thesis (the sort of thing commonly recommended in modern textbooks). Rather, one first engages with an opponent's position, establishing the precise issue to be resolved through ἀντιπαράστασις, and then unfolding a *lusis* by means of epicheiremes, each elaborated with ἐργασία and enthymemes.

66. Τὰ δ' ἀπ' ἀρχῆς λεγόμενα μέχρις αὐτοῦ τοῦ τέλους: *On Invention* 3.10.154–58. "Hermogenes" calls it ἀπ' ἀρχῆς ἄχρι τέλους, "from beginning to end." Psellos' version of the name suggests that this topic has to do with a sequence of events treated as an entelechial unfolding from an originating event [ἀρχή] to its logical or necessary outcome [αὐτὸ τὸ τέλος]. It has relevance for practical deliberation, which tries to project the probable results of a proposed action, as well as for any discourse, including the narration of a judicial discourse, or history, where one would need to narrate a rationally coherent sequence of events and represent characters, very much in the manner of an Aristotelian plot; thus a discussion of style and prosôpopoiïa comes into play.

67. I.e., one does not elaborate this heading by adding more circumstantial details, but by breaking it into numerous small parts, which can be done (says "Hermogenes") with various figures, and by using complex sentence-structures. In rhetorical terms, a "period delivered in a single breath" (πνεῦμα) is a unit of oratorical prose rhythm. Composition by πνεῦμα lends itself to a paratactic, "additive" style. A period (περίοδος) is, of course, a "periodic" (hypotactic/cumulative as opposed to paratactic/additive) sentence. Both πνεῦμα and περίοδος are discussed as "figures" in *On Invention* 4.3, 4.4.

and finishes artistically with a supposition.[68]
In a practical deliberation, this so-called heading
of "from a beginning until its end" is difficult to refute;
use the headings of objection mainly.[69]

The arrangement of epicheiremes, lord,
is of two kinds: demonstrative [ἀποδεικτική] and panegyrical
[πανηγυρικωτέρα].[70]
The former is judicial, and requires
an especially contestatory style of civic discourse;
the latter is altogether beautiful and brilliant, and colors the discourse.
If, then, a speech includes both kinds of arrangement,
save the more brilliant kind for last.

"Definition, counterdefinition, ratiocination and rebuttal
are four names, but with two functions,"[71]
for ratiocination and definition derive their power from the same things,
as do counterdefinition and rebuttal of ratiocination.
When the speech is setting forth the subject-matter,
the ratiocination itself and its rebuttal
follow from the matter and come after it,
while definition and counterdefinition come first.[72]

68. Πλαστόν: a fictive epicheireme added at the end of a "beginning-to-end" sequence, as a striking way of rounding out the facts (*On Invention* 3.11). "Hermogenes" does not suggest, as Psellos seems to, that a πλαστόν should be added to *every* subdivision. Psellos seems to be thinking of the uses of "beginning-to-end" in history-writing or poetry, and of the "cuttings" as scenes with characters making speeches.

69. *On Invention* 3.12. "Objection," μετάληψις, is not a topic of invention but the general *issue* of arguing for dismissal or transference of a proceeding; it functions here as a means of dismissing an opponent's version of the facts (his story "from beginning to end") as prima facie improbable or inadmissible or otherwise defective (e.g., there are no witnesses or other evidence to confirm the story).

70. *On Invention* 3.13.

71. *On Invention* 3.14. This is a quotation of the opening sentence of the chapter, slightly rearranged to fit the meter of "political verse."

72. Psellos' compression makes the point here somewhat murky. The idea is that counterdefinition [ἀνθορισμὸς] follows from definition [ὅρος], and rebuttal from ratiocination; that definition/counterdefinition (of the established facts, actions) necessarily precedes rebuttal/ratiocination [λύσις/συλλογισμός]; and that all of this requires a prior narration of the facts. "Hermogenes" suggests that definition and ratiocination, on one hand, can be confirmed by "the same epicheiremes," while, on the other, counterdefinition and rebuttal can likewise be confirmed by "the same epicheiremes" appropriate to them (3.14; Kennedy 2005: 124–25).

Learn, as well, the embellishment [διασκευὴν] of the problem,[73]
for vivid representation of the action is subtle,
as I said before concerning narrative.
Here the rhetor must aim at probability.
Even if embellishment is possible twice, or often,
it should not be used indiscriminately, but should be managed economically,
so that you won't be thought vulgar for using it all the time.
But if you wish to bring it into a speech at a certain point,
you can derive a pretext for discussion from a single word:
for example, if you say "find me so great a number,"
it is available to your argument, lord, from history.[74]
The first figure of speech is opposition [ἀντίθετον], ***On Invention* 4 [l. 269]**
which provides you with a twofold line of thought:[75]
from a question of fact in its natural form
it takes the opposite thought to its completion.
For example, "it is day, for if it were not day . . .
then it is day."[76] That is the figure of opposition.
The period [περίοδος] is a key to epicheiremes,[77]
bundling together copious thoughts and figures,
and their overall conception, with accurate art.

73. *On Invention* 3.15. The "problem" [πρόβλημα] is the set-problem for a declamation exercise. What Psellos and "Hermogenes" have in mind are quasi-digressive amplifications on particular points, chiefly in the form of narratives drawn from history (when they are relevant), and that "embellish" the bare facts with vivid, emotive, poetic, or exaggerated (but still credible) description. This was typically treated in ancient handbooks as a function of epilogues, though the epilogue proper is not treated (or even mentioned) by "Hermogenes" (Kennedy 2005: 127).

74. A very elliptical rendition of an example from "Hermogenes" (3.15), where discussion (in a declamation) of the sacrifice of 300 prisoners calls up a further discussion of the 300 Spartans who died at Thermopylae, which is then employed as a "commonplace" to embellish the vivid description of the sacrifice and to heighten the sense of outrage. The "single word" that provides the pretext is "300."

75. *On Invention* 4.1–2. Psellos now turns to the subject-matter of book 4, which is concerned with figures of speech.

76. Again Psellos gives an elliptical rendition of "Hermogenes'" example. As "Hermogenes" gives it, it is: "*Since it is day, that must be done.* This is the action in question. And the opposite of this is, *For if it was not day, but night, perhaps it should not be done; but since it is day, it is appropriate to do it*" (4.2). As Kennedy notes (2005: 141n207), this is a standard example in ancient (especially Stoic) logic; Psellos apparently regards it as familiar enough to be merely mentioned in abbreviated form.

77. *On Invention* 4.3.

Various declensions make up a period,
but the vocative delivered in a single breath is not the place for one:[78]
[for example,] "O, you—what name could anyone properly call you by?"[79]
He [Demosthenes] has not bundled it, but strung it out, so it's not a period.
There are many types of periods, master.
There is the monocolon, and the double too,
and there's the tricolon as well, and the quadruple.[80]
A period can also take chiasmus,[81] or be inverted in some way.
The examples of all this are clear.[82]
Take the overview from me, and then forthrightly ask your questions,
and I will tell you the solution of the problem:
then you will not wonder, lord, at the writer's art,
if you have a quick survey of the whole.

There is also the figure of the rhetorical period delivered in one breath:[83]
it is a composition of speech completing a whole thought
in cola [κῶλα] and phrases [κόμματα] smaller than cola.
The hexasyllabic or briefer phrase
is counted the same as a poetic measure,
while anything above a trimeter up to a heroic verse
is considered a straight, extended colon.

There are two types of artistic periods delivered in a single breath:
either you take one thought and variously ring the changes on it
in cola and phrases; or you take many different thoughts
and elaborate each one in phrases and cola.

Vigor of speech [ἀκμὴ λόγου] (for you must learn this too) is
a quick change of figures within a period delivered in a single breath;
but there is also a vigor of thoughts [ἀκμὴ νοημάτων],

78. *On Invention* 4.4–5, on "a period delivered in a single breath" (πνεῦμα) and its "extension" (τάσις), are both glancingly alluded to here, and discussed more fully below. Psellos is here echoing "Hermogenes'" language (at 4.3).

79. Demosthenes 18.22 (*On The Crown*), as quoted (accurately) by "Hermogenes" (4.3).

80. That is, periods composed of single, double, triple, and quadruple cola.

81. The figure of "crossover" parallelism, e.g., "fair is foul and foul is fair"; the name derives from the Greek letter χ.

82. I.e., in "Hermogenes."

83. *On Invention* 4.4.

when, having filled out a thought with a period delivered in a single breath,
you slip unnoticed into another, and thence another.[84]

The dilemma [διλήμματον] is a striking figure of speech:[85]
when, having split a question into two alternatives,
each of which is a trap,[86] you ask your opponents to reply,
either you render them unable to speak,
or else they rashly speak and you defeat them.

Echo [παρήχησις] is the figure of similar words
that sound the same, lord, with different meanings,
as when Xenophon said, "He persuades [πείθει] Peithias."[87]

The circle [κύκλος] is rounded off, if someone puts the same pronoun,
or another part of speech, at the beginning and end [of a construction].[88]

There are two types of additional remark [ἐπιφωνήματος].[89]
The first is a statement interjected from outside the subject at hand,
by which you take up a sort of accompaniment,[90]
and venture cautiously an additional commentary.
A brief Homeric example should be mentioned:
"And together with Euros, Notos roused and rushed headlong,
and stormy Zephyr, and sky-born Boreas,
and they covered with clouds the land and sea alike;

84. Ἀκμή, usually translated as "florescence" or "vigor" (as a stylistic term), literally means "zenith" or "culminating point"; "Hermogenes" seems to think of it, in vigor of speech, as a process of varying the figural constructions employed in the "extension" of a single idea in a single *pneuma* (i.e., ringing the changes on a single idea); and, in vigor of thought, as a process of building to a climactic statement by moving "unnoticed" from one idea to another, as one moves from one *pneuma* to another, while seeming to reiterate the same idea. The notion of an "extended *pneuma*" glancingly alludes to *On Invention* 4.5, on τάσις (a "chapter" consisting of a single brief paragraph).

85. *On Invention* 4.6. "Striking" here translates δριμύς, more literally "sharp, piercing, keen, shrewd."

86. Ἀμφίκρημνον, literally "having cliffs all around," or in other words "hemmed in on all sides."

87. *On Invention* 4.7. Πείθει τὸν Πειθίαν is a pun on "the Pythian," an epithet of Apollo. "Figure" in line 312 translates κάλλος, literally "beauty," which Psellos repeats from "Hermogenes," and which Kennedy (2005: 173) renders as "ornament."

88. *On Invention* 4.8.

89. *On Invention* 4.9. As noted above, an ἐπιφώνημα is a sententious "added remark" used to finish off a passage with a flourish.

90. ἐπᾴδων, literally "sing along to."

and down from heaven rushed the night."[91] This last item
is an additional remark brought in from outside the subject,
alien yet legitimate (as you may wish to understand),
venturing to derive the night from heaven.[92]
Some recognize a second [type of] additional remark,
when, having extended in varied cola a period delivered in a single breath,
one adds a colon that pulls everything together,
as in Homer's elegant description of Ajax,
which recapitulates everything with a single colon:
"One evil after another was hammered on."[93]
A third [type of] additional remark is quite acceptable if you bring in
metaphorical expressions from what has been said earlier
and properly apply them to make comparisons.

A metaphor [τροπὴ] is the use of a common word
for both the presented fact and something else that is introduced.[94]

Dignified language [σεμνὸς λόγος] beautifies a name with a name:[95]
for if you call a prostitute a courtesan,[96] you transform her;
you dignify what she is called by artfully translating it.

But if some wholly artless statement has not been properly prepared for,
call it bad taste [κακόζηλον] for what is fitting in a speech.[97]

91. *Odyssey* 5.295–96 (Psellos' ll. 322–23), and 293–94 (ll. 324–25); describing the east, south, west, and north winds respectively, when stirred up by Poseidon. Psellos modifies Homer's lines to fit the meter of political verse—and follows "Hermogenes" in "quoting" them out of order for the sake of illustrating ἐπιφώνημα.

92. "Alien" because "night" is not properly part of a description of the winds; "legitimate" as a supplement because it, like them, is part of a description of the darkening sky. Kennedy (2005: 175n256) considers this example in "Hermogenes" to be unilluminating; Psellos likewise seems to be struggling to explain it.

93. *Iliad* 16.111.

94. *On Invention* 4.10; "Hermogenes'" point is that a "trope" is a word "which can be applied in common to the subject and a subject brought in from elsewhere" (4.10; Kennedy 2005: 179). Psellos' highly compressed rendition of this idea makes it fairly obscure.

95. *On Invention* 4.11.

96. That is, call a πόρνη a ἑταίρα.

97. *On Invention* 4.12. Κακόζηλον, more literally, means "bad imitation" or tasteless emulation of γενικώτατος λόγος, "most proper speech" or speech most suitable to its kind (or genre).

There is also a figured kind of problem [πρόβλημα τῶν ἐσχηματισμένων],
either by implication, indirection, or opposition,
and implication is more rhetorical by far.[98]

Comparative problems absolutely must be described for you.
In conjecture, and in motive and capacity, it is easy:
what the "I" and the "you" have ascribed to motive
easily produce a comparison for you, crownbearer.[99]

And that is the end of the *Invention* for you.

There also is a third study of the incandescent art, ***On Forms* [l. 353]**
which is called the *Forms,* namely the particular shapes of discourse,
by which the speeches of rhetors are distinguished.[100]
Each form consists of eight components:
the first is the thought; next is the diction;
third is the figure of speech;
and fourth is the method of thought[101] —
after which there are the cola, and then the remaining three,
the cadence, the composition, and finally the rhythm.
Each form is divided into these components.

98. *On Invention* 4.13. "Figured problems" are cases for declamation exercises in which the ostensible subject of the speech is actually a cover for something else. In the "by implication" type (κατ' ἔμφασιν) the speaker hints at things that cannot be spoken openly (i.e., because they are too shameful or too politically dangerous); in the "by indirection" type (κατὰ πλάγιον) the speaker's arguments lead to different conclusions than those they are ostensibly proving; and in the "by opposite" type (κατ' ἐναντίον) the speaker says the opposite of what he means. Kennedy (2005: 189–93) translates these types as "by implication," "deflected," and "by the opposite"; Patillon renders them as "by allusion" (*par allusifs*), "by indirection" (*par indirects*), and "by the contrary" (*par le contraire*).

99. *On Invention* 4.14: προβλήματα συγκριτικά, "comparative problems" (i.e., for declamation exercises) involve the weighing of alternatives, usually at the *issue* of conjecture or definition; "motive and capacity" are subheads of conjecture.

100. Psellos is now taking up Hermogenes' *On Forms.* It is noteworthy that Psellos sees the Περὶ Ἰδεῶν as a τέχνη for the "study" (μάθημα) and "characterization" (χαρακτηρίζονται)—the critical description and, simultaneously, the identification—of orators' styles. See the closing paragraphs of *On Forms* (2.12.34–37). For relevant chapters in Hermogenes' work along with the Greek terms for each form, see the previous essay in this volume.

101. Hermogenes explains the "method" as the "figure of thought" (σχῆμα . . . τῆς ἐννοίας; *Forms* 1.1.32) through which the "thought" is expressed—such as apostrophe, ratiocination, personification, rhetorical question, etc.

The first three principal forms that are distinguished[102]
are called clarity, grandeur, and beauty;
and the opposite of the clear is the obscure,
grandeur has meanness as its opposite,
and the slovenly is contrary to the beautified.
The next four forms that are individually laid out are
rapidity, of which the opposite is the supine,
and character, sincerity, and force.
Clarity is divided into these two parts: **Σαφήνεια [l. 371]**
into purity, as I say, and distinctness:
the opposite of the former is amplification,
and of the latter, confusion, which is a fault.
Grandeur is divided into these six forms: **Μέγεθος [l. 375]**
solemnity, asperity, and brilliance third,[103]
and vigor, vehemence, and amplification sixth.
There are four forms in the division of character: **Ἦθος [l. 378]**
moderation, simplicity, sincerity, and sternness.[104]
Character is never viewed as just itself,
but is composed from simplicity and moderation,
while from moderation spring pungency and sweetness.[105]
The thought of purity is the common and customary; **Καθαρότης [l. 383]**
the method is a straightforward setting forth of facts;
the diction is clear and not metaphorical, and follows normal usage;
the figuration is the simple sentence;
the cola are short and bring each thought to completion;
the composition is unconcerned with hiatus;
and the cadence is an iambic sort of phrasing.

102. Psellos here introduces Hermogenes' seven main forms: Clarity, Grandeur, Beauty, Rapidity, Character, Sincerity, and Force. Clarity, Grandeur, Character, and Sincerity (or Truthfulness) have subtypes, while all of these forms together, when combined with supreme skill, yield "Force = δεινότης" (which might also be rendered as "stunning virtuosity" or, more literally, as "awesomeness").

103. Psellos here begins to depart slightly from the order of Hermogenes' chapters.

104. Psellos here differs from Hermogenes, who makes the subtypes of Character Simplicity, Sweetness, Pungency, and Moderation, and makes Sternness a subtype of Sincerity.

105. Psellos here seems to grasp one of the key insights of Hermogenes' *On Forms*: stylistic types are recognized as variably composed from overlapping (or blended) sets of features and subtypes.

The thoughts of distinctness fall under two heads; **Εὐκρίνεια [l. 390]**
those that sum up, and refer the discourse back
to a starting point, and, conversely,
those that elegantly give shape to what will come.[106]
The method is putting forth facts in natural order,
the opposed positions first and rebuttals second;
the figuration is that of groupings, partition [μερισμός], or arrangement [τάξις];
and the diction, cola, rhythm, cadence, and composition
are such as also belong to the sister-types of purity.

The thoughts of solemnity are about gods and things divine; **Σεμνότης [l. 399]**
the methods are commanding and confident declarations,
especially allegorical statements that ward off nearly everyone;
the diction is broad and beautiful, and fills the mouth;
the figuration is the simple sentence; the cola are cut short;
the composition allows for all sorts of hiatus,
and is dactylic, spondaic, and anapestic;
and the cadence uses spondees and dactyls,
from which it arrives at a familiar and fitting rhythm.

The thought of asperity is the censure **Τραχύτης [l. 408]**
of greater persons, unexpectedly;[107]
the method is not to soften the listener artfully,
but to be undisguised and uncomplicated;
the diction is harsh in itself, and also metaphorical;
the figures are imperious and highly refutative;
and the cola are brief, and the composition is non-rhythmical.

The thought of vehemence is the refutation of lessers; **Σφοδρότης [l. 415]**
the method is unhesitating; the diction inventive of new words;
the figuration is apostrophic; the cola are generally trisyllabic;
the composition frequently clashes vowels together;
and the rest is the same as asperity, and differs in no way.

106. Hermogenes (1.4.2) says, "It is the function of distinctness to determine what aspects of the case the judges should consider first and what they should consider second and to make that clear to them" (Wooten 1987: 14).

107. Hermogenes' point is that the censure should occur as an "unexpected" outburst or departure from the speaker's (ostensibly) planned remarks.

The thoughts of brilliance are wholly brilliant in nature, **Λαμπρότης [l. 420]**
the kind that are confident and frank;[108]
the diction is that of a swelling solemnity;
the figuration includes direct denial, lack of connectives,
subordination and employment of detached phrases, which is more artistic;[109]
and the cadence, rhythm, and composition are solemn.

The thoughts and methods of vigor are like **Ἀκμή [l. 426]**
those of asperity and vehemence;
the figuration is that of brilliance; the cola those of vehemence;
and the cadence, the rhythm, and also the composition
are those of brilliance too.

Amplification has no characteristic diction, as rhetors say, **Περιβολή [l. 431]**
unless someone wants to argue for synonymous expressions.
The figures are those that generate variations on a thought:
subordination, partition, putting the point,[110]
supposition, and run-on constructions.[111]
There are no other specific features of the abundant style.

Beauty has no characteristic thought or method, **Κάλλος [l. 437]**
but its figures are many and varied:
all clauses with an equal number of syllables [παρισώσεις],

108. "Confident and frank" expression is the method of brilliance, according to Hermogenes (1.9).

109. Ἀπόστασις, as a rhetorical term, indicates "setting-off" in the sense of breaking off a sentence and starting an independent colon (where one might otherwise choose to subordinate it in a periodic construction).

110. Τὸ κατὰ τὴν κρίσιν, "what is under judgment" (?); this does not appear in Hermogenes, and seems to be a muddle for what Hermogenes calls τὸ κατὰ ἄρσιν καὶ θέσιν (1.11.53), which Wooten (1987: 52) translates as "negation and affirmation," but which in *metrical* terminology means "upbeat and downbeat" (the raising and lowering of the foot in keeping time), or the short and long syllables composing a metrical foot. Hermogenes may be adapting the notions of *arsis* and *thesis* metaphorically to indicate "upbeat" and "downbeat" iterations of the same idea, which he illustrates with this example from Demosthenes (*On the False Embassy* 12): "not as one who would sell your interests [etc.] . . . but as one who would keep watch on the others."

111. "Run-on" (or perhaps "add-on") constructions involve the addition of phrases and cola that expand a sentence with circumstantial details. Hermogenes' example (1.11.41) is "Since there was no longer any meeting of the Assembly because of their being used up already . . ." and the rest of the long sentence that follows (in Demosthenes, *False Embassy* 154).

repetition in cola (but not in *kommata*),
counterturns, climax, *hyperbaton*,
novel expressions, repetition of a word in varied cases, and attractive negations.[112]
The cola are somewhat long; the composition avoids hiatus.

No one will discover the thought of rapidity either, **Γοργότης [l. 444]**
and its proper method is unlike the others:[113]
it uses a quick succession of replies.
The figures of rapidity are the "run-on" construction,
lack of connectives, quick variation,
linked repetitions [ἀναστροφαί], interruptions [ἐπιστροφαί],[114] and interweaving;
the composition should avoid hiatus;
the cadence is trochaic and never stately.

The thoughts of simplicity are completely accessible, **Ἀφέλεια [l. 452]**
wholly unaffected, even childlike;
the method is redundancy, especially with division into parts;[115]
the diction includes idiomatic expressions, such as "to brother";[116]
the cola are those of purity; the composition is relaxed;
the cadence is steady; and the rhythm likewise.

The thoughts of sweetness are mainly the mythical, **Γλυκύτης [l. 458]**
or those that give rise to narratives resembling myths,
things that please the senses, and the assignment of rational intent
to things that lack it, for that is altogether sweet.[117]
The method is that of purity; the diction that of simplicity;
the figuration that of purity, and likewise beauty;
the composition avoids hiatus, and is almost metrical;
the cadence is that of solemnity; and the rhythm is that of simplicity.

112. εὐειδεῖς ἀναιρέσεις: what Hermogenes calls affirmation by double negatives (1.12.38).

113. Hermogenes says rapidity has only one method, which resembles "cleverness and pungency" but is not the same (2.1.4).

114. Psellos' rendition of what Hermogenes calls ὑποστροφή, "incidental remark" (2.1.8).

115. That is, accumulation of superfluous or redundant details (pleonasm), by substituting for a general concept its component parts, e.g., instead of "harvesters and others who work for hire," "harvesters and diggers and binders and shepherds and herdsmen" (2.3.13).

116. Isocrates, *Aegineticus* 30.

117. As when (as Hermogenes points out, 2.4.13) Socrates in the *Phaedrus* says the trees outside the city have no wish to teach him anything. The remark that "this is altogether sweet" is Psellos' addition.

The thoughts of pungency are superficially profound: **Δριμύτης [l. 466]**
the method is not to bring flashy cleverness into your discourse,
but to write complex and wondrous things in the simplest way.
There is a second kind of pungency, in diction,
which is proper usage that is properly not proper:
for properly dogs are "philanthropists,"
for they love [*philousi*] humans [*anthrôpon*], but also not properly,
since philanthropy has another meaning;
so what is conveyed through the same diction
is pungent in a certain way—if indeed the technographer thinks so.[118]
Another type of pungency is the pun;[119]
and another is sequenced substitution,
which leads from a hard trope to a harder.[120]
The thought of moderation is willingly to claim less
than one could, **Ἐπιείκεια [l. 479]**
and to be charitable to an opponent and grant him some point,
and to say that you have entered the lawcourt by necessity;
the method is to play down one's rights,
and not to make vehement declarations against one's opponents in court;
the diction and the rest are like simplicity.
The thoughts of sincerity and spontaneity **Ἀληθὴς καὶ ἐνδιάθετος λόγος [l. 485]**
are those of simplicity, moderation, and indignation in some way.
Indignation is the method for such thought—
when the purpose of what is said is not complaining—
with the use of emotional outbursts, oaths, fear and distress,
wishing, anger and astonishment that have not been indicated in advance,

118. This example, which derives from Hermogenes (2.5.4), is hard to square with the notion, above, of pungency as *not* clever contrivance but "deep" things said in a simple way; Psellos, for his part, appears to have some difficulty with it. Hermogenes seems to have had in mind the double entendre, or the superficially simple but polyvalent locution.

119. Specifically, παρονομασία is the type of pun in which a word is used (repeated) in both its "proper" sense and a figurative sense (or, simply, in different senses).

120. Τὸ κατ' ἀκολουθίαν, lit. "following, sequence, analogy," rhetorically is substitution between words that can be thought to imply each other (e.g., "fire" and "light"). Hermogenes' idea is that ἀκολουθία progresses from a less strange or difficult metaphor to a "harder" one, thus making it seem less strange (than if it had been directly introduced without preparation); 2.5.13.

and counter-proposition not connected to the rebuttal,
and the assertion of thoughts without preparation
and without coherent sequence in the progression of ideas.[121]
The diction is that of piteously spoken asperity,
purity, simplicity, and especially sweetness;
and the figuration is that of the vehement and repetitive type of style:
apostrophe, deictics [τὸ δεικτικόν], artful perplexity,
doubtfulness, personal judgments, and self-correction.
The cola, cadence, rhythm, and composition
are all those of vehemence and simplicity.

The thoughts of sternness—should someone be vexed **Βαρύτης [l. 501]**
by enumerating good deeds and, perhaps, acts of ingratitude—
are those that reproach those who have shown ingratitude,
especially by dwelling on the good things that resulted.
The method is that of subtle ironies addressed to enemies.
There is no other special feature of sternness besides these two.

The thoughts of force are paradoxes and profundities; **Δεινότης [l. 507]**
the diction is dignified and highly figured;
the figuration, cola, rhythm, cadence, and composition
are (among the forms enumerated) those of solemnity, vigor,
brilliance, and amplification.

Let civic discourse be adorned in every way,[122] **Πολιτικὸς λόγος [l. 512]**
and let it have these forms in particular:
character, sincerity, amplification,[123]
rapidity, clarity, asperity, vigor,
solemnity, brilliance, and force of method,[124]
which I will overview for you, as in one heading.

121. The general point here is that the complaint should seem to emerge spontaneously, not by premeditated design, in a speech ostensibly devoted to other purposes—and that it should express itself in what seems to be an unplanned, "disordered" way.

122. *On Forms* 2.10, on the use of the forms in πολιτικὸς λόγος, "civic (political, public) discourse." Psellos omits the last two chapters (2.11–12), on "pure civic" (ἁπλὸς πολιτικὸς) and "pure panegyrical" (ἁπλὸς πανηγυρικὸς) discourse.

123. Psellos here employs περιβεβλημένον, "amplified, expanded, cast-around, circumlocutory," as an apparent synonym for Hermogenes' term.

124. Δεινότητα μεθόδου: this seems different from the title of the final book in the Hermogenian corpus, *On the Method of Force* (Περὶ μεθόδου δεινότητος), and suggests an interpretation of it as a treatise on "forceful method" rather than the "forceful style"

Unfamiliar diction has three methods ***On the Method of Force* [l. 518]**
of inventing obscure ideas, [which are]
foreign words, technical terms, or legal terms;[125]
mistakes in diction are corruptions and improper usages;[126]
we should use the same word
whenever there is one word that suits the facts;[127]
there is an abundance of both diction and thought,
of diction by dwelling on something, and of thought by arguments;[128]
for presumptuous and rash thoughts in a speech
there are two remedies and excuses,
acknowledgment of rashness and a brief insertion;[129]
you should artistically pass over something in a speech
to increase suspicion about what clearly has been left unsaid;[130]
a timely circumlocution is not without art;[131]
understand that repetition occurs for the sake of
teaching something, or firmness of manner;[132]

---

in general, though l. 540 refers to μέθοδοι δεινότητος ἰδέας, "methods of the form of force." On this Hermogenian treatise—which bears little resemblance to the treatment of Force outlined by Hermogenes in *On Forms*—see Kennedy 2005: 201–3. It may not have been written originally as a treatise on Force, and looks like something of a miscellany on figures of discourse (perhaps, however, suggesting "method"). In the exposition that follows, Psellos touches on only some of this book's thirty-eight chapters, mostly those from its first half, and very cursorily at that.

125. *Method* 2.

126. *Method* 3: φθορὰ καὶ ἀκυρία.

127. *Method* 4.

128. *Method* 5: κατὰ διατριβὴν . . . κατ' ἐνθυμήσεις. "Hermogenes" mentions two methods each for abundance (περιττότης) of diction and thought: for diction, "dwelling" and "fullness" (πλῆθος); and for thought, "supplemental argumentations" (ἐπενθυμήσεις) and the insertion of "general statements" (καθολικοί λόγοι).

129. ὁμολόγημα βραχεῖά τε προσθήκη: i.e., insertion of a qualification or an "as it were"; *Method* 6.

130. τεχνικὴ παράλειψις: i.e., mentioning something by saying that you won't discuss it, or conspicuously leaving it out; *Method* 7.

131. *Method* 8.

132. *Method* 9. "Hermogenes" mentions three functions for ἐπανάληψις (repetition, resumption): "teaching (or explaining) something" (διδασκαλία πράγματος); "recommendation or attack on a person" (προσώπου σύστασις ἢ διαβολή); and "firmness of

the figure of interrogation cannot be denied;[133]
equivalencies, inversions, feigned improvisation,
amplification then proof, speaking opposites,
praising oneself when it is acceptable in the speech,
the use of verses by quotation and adaptation,
and artfully speaking in tragic style in prose—
all these are methods of force.[134]

Well then, may this synopsis of the art be an art in miniature for you:
a lesson easily taken in, concise and brief,
full of sweetness, full of charm,
sweet-speaking, sweet-voiced, and unusually sweet-singing,
so that even when speaking playfully[135] you shall profit from the discourse.

---

character" (ἤθους βεβαίωσις), which Kennedy (2005: 219) renders as "strengthening characterization." Psellos reduces these to two, in essence by collapsing the second and third into one, which he calls βέβαιος τρόπος, "firmness of manner," which arguably is a defensible simplification based on "Hermogenes'" examples.

133. *Method* 10. Πεῦσις, "interrogation," is in essence the "rhetorical question."

134. A very rapid gallop across *Method* 13 (on ἴσα σχήματα, equal figures), 14 (ὑπερβατόν, inversion), 17 (προσποίησις, feigning spontaneity), 18 (αὔξησις and ἀπόδειξις, amplification and proof in judicial speeches), 22 (τὸ λέγειν ἐναντία, saying the opposite of what one means), 25 (τὸ ἐπαινεῖν ἑαυτόν, praising oneself without giving offense), 30 (χρῆσις ἐπῶν ἐν πεζῷ λόγῳ, the use of verses in prose), and 33 (τὸ τραγικῶς λέγειν, speaking tragically).

135. Παίζων λογικῶς: more literally "playing discursively (or argumentatively)"; Psellos may mean composition and declamation exercises.

3 *On Literary Composition*, based on Dionysios of Halikarnassos' *On Composition*

Translated with introduction and notes
by Antony Littlewood

Introduction

This short work is in answer to a correspondent who had enquired about varieties of verbal expression. Although he is called "most learned" by Psellos, we have no way of knowing whether this superlative adjective was used as flattery to a social superior or in jocular manner to an inferior, possibly even a student. That it was not meant literally is made clear by the elementary nature of the piece.

Psellos' own contribution to this opusculum is small, since fully two-thirds are taken from the treatise on the arrangement of words and euphony, the *On Composition,* written by the Greek rhetor and historian Dionysios of Halikarnassos sometime in the first half of the first century CE.[1] Many of Psellos' opuscula are excerpted from older authorities, for example, much of

1. Περὶ συνθέσεως ὀνομάτων, lit. *On the Arrangement of Words,* commonly known by its Latin title *De Compositione Verborum.* On Dionysios, see Bonner 1939 with de Jonge 2008 and Wiater 2011.

the *Concise Answers to Various Questions*[2] (addressed, in its final version, to Michael VII Doukas) on topics ranging from religion to the natural sciences, and also some of his philosophical works. These are often successful, being on quite specific subjects such as the still unedited opusculum on the meaning of the name Caesar,[3] which is largely dependent upon John the Lydian. Here, however, while Dionysios' original, despite many difficulties of interpretation, is a thorough and coherent treatise, Psellos' excerpts—even with his own introduction, connecting passages, and conclusion—are not a summary of Dionysios but rather a collection of often disjointed excerpts,[4] which do not extend to Dionysios' important section on levels of style. The recipient of the present opusculum will have received little aid in an attempt to improve his rhetorical powers; but Psellos did at least use a highly reputable source and one already cited by major figures of the Second Sophistic and beyond such as Hermogenes and Syrianos (Aujac 1974). That Dionysios' treatise was known in Byzantium before Psellos' time is shown by the fact that two copies of it were made within the century anterior to his birth.[5]

Attitudes in both antiquity and the Byzantine period towards what is today considered as plagiarism varied in respect to "literary" and "scholarly" works. For the first it must be remembered that Memory (Μνημοσύνη) was the mother of the Muses, namely, that every author aimed to build upon the achievements of his predecessors. Thus improvement on and refinement of preexisting works were the desiderata, naked originality often an unnatural vice. As most literature was written both by and for a literary elite, authors expected their auditors/readers to recognize quotations and reminiscences of familiar passages and to appreciate any new variations; and it would spoil the

2. Or, in its alternative Greek title, Διδασκαλία Παντοδαπή, often known by its Latin title *De Omnifaria Doctrina*; its survival in no fewer than 150 mss. attests to its popularity, although many mss. contain only fragments, and the majority are of either late- or post-Byzantine date.

3. In Vatican, BAV, gr. 672, fol. 272r–v (and its apograph, Vat. gr. 1900, fol. 401v–402r).

4. For an analysis of this see Aujac 1975: 268–72. On Psellos' methods of working in general, see O'Meara 1989: 55–56, 59–60.

5. Paris, BNF, gr. 1741 (on which see below p. 75n2) and Florence, Bibl. Med. Laur., Plut. gr. 59.15, both the best and the earliest surviving mss. of the work.

artistry, as well perhaps as the intellectual challenge, to insert the names of sources.[6] A distinction was, nonetheless, drawn between imitation (μίμησις) and downright theft (κλοπή), and charges of plagiarism were made, the earliest by the comedian Aristophanes who complained that in the *Marikas* his rival Eupolis had "turned my own *Knights* inside out" (*Clouds* 553–54), while ancient treatises "On Theft" are known to have existed.[7] Far greater latitude was allowed to scholarly "plagiarism." Material from earlier works was used, paraphrased, abridged, excerpted, and copied. Except to disagree, sources were rarely mentioned. Aristotle was the first to give credit to others, and gradually his example was followed, sometimes with lists of authors prefacing a new work (the best known is probably that of Pliny the Elder for his great *Historia Naturalis*). Psellos' selection, copying, review, and rewriting of Dionysios' work are thus nothing strange in their Byzantine context.

Psellos' opusculum is intended to be of benefit to a writer of either prose or verse. In this connection it must be remembered that eleventh-century Byzantium was a very oral society, most "literature" being appreciated when read aloud. Hence Psellos' (and Dionysios') emphasis upon sound, including rhythm (an important element of prose as well as of verse). Psellos begins by stating bluntly that "the most important part of rhetoric" is knowing how to create "varieties of verbal expression." He then distinguishes, with mention of ancient exemplars, between the pleasing and the beautiful before listing the elements that provide one or the other or both. The most important is "appropriateness" (to both subject-matter and nature of composition). Also useful are variety of rhythms and accentuation of syllables. This leads him to consider the pronunciation of individual letters of the alphabet and the resultant combination in syllables. He ends by stating that "the careful orator" must be consistent in how he expresses each individual emotion.

Editions and translations. Psellos' opusculum is preserved all told in seven manuscripts, of which the best is the Psellian Paris., BNF, gr. 1182 (late twelfth c.).

6. For evidence of the compelling need in Byzantium for varying quotations see Littlewood 1988.

7. Porphyry even made a list of these that is preserved in Eusebios, *Praep. Evang.* 10.3.12. In a letter written a century after Psellos, Ioannes Tzetzes (*Ep* 42; ed. Leone) accuses his addressee of thieving both his own commentary on Lykophron's *Alexandra* and also a friend's funeral oration, in the latter case by cobbling together extracts.

Four other manuscripts are from the sixteenth, one from the sixteenth to seventeenth, and one from the eighteenth centuries (a copy of a surviving earlier manuscript). The two pre-Psellan manuscripts of Dionysios' treatise confirm the accuracy of Paris. gr. 1182, from which the opusculum has been twice edited, by Walz (1833: 598–601) and, with discussion, by Aujac (1975); see further Moore 2005: 403, where also bibliography and earlier translations may be found.

Phrases in quotation marks indicate passages that either are quoted directly from Dionysios' treatise or repeat with minor changes in order or form or simply paraphrase Dionysios' wording; for a precise juxtaposition of the two texts, see Aujac's edition—the numbers in brackets below indicate sections in this latter edition.

On Literary Composition[1]

[1] You enquired, most learned <sir>, what is, at any rate, unpleasant and rough and how many other varieties there are of verbal expression. Know, then, that changing arrangement of words [συνθήκη τῶν ὀνομάτων][2] creates such differences. This is the most important element of rhetoric.

[2] "The subjects of this great science" are the knowledge of how to harmonize the constituent parts of a speech, the alteration of the harmonized elements into whatever form one wants[3] and, third, the understanding of "what modification is needed of the matters used—I mean subtraction, addition, and alteration—and the implementation of these suitably [οἰκείως] for future need."

[3] "There are two most important things at which those who compose verse and prose ought to aim—pleasure [ἡδονή] and beauty [τὸ καλόν]—for the ear desires both these things. There are some literary styles that are pleasingly but not beautifully composed," and again others that are "beautifully but not pleasingly composed. Now the style of Thucydides and that of Antiphon of Rhamnus are outstanding for their beauty, but they are not pleasing to the ear." On the other hand those who have described the style of the writings "of Xenophon the Socratic granted him pleasing literary composition but cer-

1. Περὶ συνθήκης τῶν τοῦ λόγου μερῶν, i.e., literally, *On the Arrangement of the Parts of Discourse*. The Greek word λόγος can mean, among many other things, both speech and word, and Psellos in this opusculum does indeed deal with letters, the component parts of words.

2. What Psellos means is changing the choosing and putting together of individual words and their constituent parts. The phrase evokes the precise title of Dionysios of Halikarnassos' treatise; see n. 1 of the introduction to this text.

3. Πρὸς ὃ βούλοιτο τις, for this Psellian addition, see Papaioannou 2013: 81.

tainly not beautiful. The style of Herodotus, however, has both these qualities, for it is both pleasing and beautiful."

"These are the four most important elements" of such composition—I am speaking of that which combines the pleasure and beauty—"melody, rhythm, variety [μεταβολή], and the appropriateness [τὸ πρέπον] that goes closely with those. **[4]** Indeed the ear is first pleased by beautiful melodies, second by rhythms, third by variations, and in all these by the appropriate." Before these[4] "let us under pleasure list elegance [ὥρα], grace [χάρις], euphony [εὐστομία], sweetness [γλυκύτης], persuasiveness [τὸ πιθανόν], and such like; and under beauty, magnificence [μεγαλοπρέπεια], sternness [βάρος], gravity [ὄγκος], solemnity [σεμνολογία], magnitude [μέγεθος], dignity [ἀξίωμα], and qualities like these."

[5] Not only does melodiousness "in song and on instruments" possess "melody and variety," but so do "words"; for in these too "the ear is charmed by the melodies, is carried away by the rhythms, welcomes variations, and desires what is suitable [οἰκεῖον] to it";[5] and "the melody of dialogue" is a sort of "distinction" between the baritone and oxytone accentuation of different syllables.[6] **[6]** And since the repetition of these very things is tedious and brings satiety, the changes of patterns—I mean linguistic patterns—create unceasing pleasure for auditors. **[7]** "Nevertheless I think that in every instance one must consider the opportune moment [καιρόν];[7] for this is the best measure of pleasure and unpleasantness."

4. Psellos' previous sentence is a rough version of one that comes a few lines *later* in Dionysios' treatise. Do the words πρὸ δὲ τούτων mean that Psellos realized this but did not wish to cross out the sentence and write it again lower down?

5. Psellos, following Dionysios, uses here the word οἰκεῖον, which may be no more than a stylistic variation on the earlier πρέπον (translated by "appropriate"), but may perhaps emphasize more what is inherently its character.

6. Unlike in Byzantine and modern Greek where all accents (the most recent Greek types show only the acute and this only on polysyllabic words) uniformly express a stress or an ictus, in ancient Greek the accents, first added visually probably in Alexandria ca. 200 BCE for foreigners learning to speak the language, indicated pitch, the acute probably a rise of about a spoken fifth (of not more than three and a half tones) above other syllables, and the grave a falling accent (of no more than one tone according to Psellos' source Dionysios, who gives further details, including the pronunciation of the combined [circumflex] accent [*Comp.* 40.17–42.14]). The most thorough and recent work on Greek accents is Probert 2006, but for discussion of pronunciation of accents see Allen 1987: 116–24.

7. In rhetorical theory, καιρός became closely associated with πρέπον and οἰκεῖον. On *kairos*, see Kinneavy 1986.

[8] "Just as there is a pleasant type of diction, so there is also a noble one; and just as there is an elegant rhythm, so there is also another that is solemn." Then, second, you <can have> beauty in harmonious diction, which gives rise to the pleasing as well. The prime "cause" of composition being beautiful or pleasing is "the nature of the letters and the force of the syllables, of which the words are woven." **[9]** There is to be sure not one single nature of so-called letters,[8] and, to avoid touching on the distinctions mentioned by the grammarians, each letter is produced by a different configuration of the tongue and by the teeth and the lips. Now some <letters> are prolonged by the breath, others are shortened; some open the mouth more, others "less"; **[10]** some "press the sound downwards around the base of the tongue,[9] others upwards"; some "make the mouth round and compress the lips," and "for these the breath strikes its blow at the edge of the mouth";[10] **[11]** others have a different configuration in pronunciation. It would be superfluous to speak at length about such matters;[11] but if you, whenever you like, on your own at your leisure[12] softly pronounce each of the elements,[13] you would more accurately know for which the tongue is not employed while the lips are closed or open, when also the tongue makes some movement and in which direction the sound of each element goes or changes and from which point; **[12]** for some are pronounced "at the tip of the lips,"[14] others "with the tongue being pressed against the top of the mouth near the upper teeth and then being made by the breath to vibrate,"[15] and some are given utterance "when the tongue rises to the palate near the throat and the wind-pipe sounds in response to the breath,"[16] while others <are given utterance> in another way.[17]

8. The Greek here could mean also "of letters when they are spoken aloud."
9. Dionysios is here (51.16–17) speaking of the letter η.
10. Dionysios is here (52.2–4) speaking of the letter ω.
11. Dionysios, who in this section draws upon the Alexandrian grammarian Dionysios of Thrace (ca. 170–ca. 90 BCE), is more painstaking than Psellos, devoting a few pages to the subject (50.12–57.8). Psellos is not, however, completely honest for, although he omits some of the vowels and all the semivowels (ζ, λ, μ, ν, χ, ρ, σ, and ψ) dealt with by Dionysios, he does proceed to quote in a shortened version the latter's pronunciation of the nine voiceless consonants.
12. The words ἐπὶ σχολῆς may mean "for an exercise."
13. I.e., letters, although Dionysios mentions (50.1–11) that some grammarians distinguish between the two words.
14. I.e., the labials, β, π, and φ.
15. I.e., the dentals, δ, θ, and τ.
16. I.e., the palatals, γ, κ, and χ.
17. I.e., the semi-vowels (see above n. 11).

"It is indeed from letters possessing such properties that are formed what are called syllables."[18] **[13]** And "it is absolutely necessary that the syllable formed from such elements keep both the individual property of each and the combined <property> of all of them, which comes about from their combination and juxtaposition. From them there come about both soft and hard sounds, smooth and rough, those that produce a sensation of sweetness on the ear and those that produce a sensation of bitterness, those that are astringent, those that are relaxing, and those that create every other mood."[19] **[14]** The cola too <created> by the syllables and the periods <created> by the cola are of the same kind and possess the same arrangement and divergence.

[15] "The writers of dithyrambs used to change the modes also, composing in the Dorian, Phrygian, and Lydian <modes> in the same song;[20] varied the melodies, making them sometimes enharmonic, sometimes chromatic, sometimes diatonic;[21] and in rhythms showed independence with great freedom."

[16] As for us, we do not use the same type of composition when we are disturbed by different emotions. The careful orator must fit what is appropriate to each state of the soul, and neither create a difference in his words for the same emotion nor produce the same order and composition for different <emotions>.

Such is the gist of the art of composition and such the variety and power possessed by this aspect of rhetoric.[22]

18. Dionysios, unlike Psellos, has indeed described the properties of all the letters in each category.

19. Dionysios adds the adjective "physical."

20. Psellos has here skipped many pages in Dionysios and turned to musical modes (which differed from each in a way similar to that of major and minor scales today). This short passage on dithyrambs fits logically into Dionysios' discussion of variety of meters and melodies in the different types of poetry, but in this opusculum it bears little relationship with what preceded or with Psellos' own conclusion.

21. These are the three "genera" of the tetrachord, of which the diatonic was subdivided into two "colors" and the chromatic into three, thus giving six different sequences of intervals within a tetrachord (unlike in standard modern Western music, which employs only whole tones and semitones, ancient Greek music employed intervals of a ¼, ⅓, ⅜, ½, ¾, 1, 1 ¼, 1 ½, 1 ¾, 1 ⅚, and 2 tones).

22. Obedient to rhetorical ring-composition Psellos ends with a repetition, though employing for the most part different vocabulary, of his opening.

I wish to record my gratitude to Anthony Kaldellis for valuable comments on both introduction and translation; to Stratis Papaioannou for his percipient and meticulous editing; and to an anonymous reader for a few sapient observations.

4 *On Rhetoric*, based on Longinos' *Art of Rhetoric*

Translated with introduction and notes by Stratis Papaioannou

Introduction

In *On Rhetoric*, Psellos offers excerpts, after minor edition, revision, and commentary, from a text titled the *Art of Rhetoric* (ed. Patillon and Brisson 2001; fr. 48). The original work is attributed to the third-century Neoplatonist philosopher and rhetorician Longinos, a man of Syrian origin, contemporary and rival of Plotinos, and celebrated teacher in Athens—the philosopher Porphyry was one of his pupils. Once famous for his wide learning (a sentiment still echoed in Psellos' view of him), Longinos has had a fragile afterlife. His many works—philosophical, rhetorical, philological—have survived only in fragments, the lengthiest of which is indeed his treatise on rhetoric.[1]

Along the lines of his source, Psellos' brief collection of excerpts focuses on judicial discourse (δικανικός λόγος), on forms and techniques of forensic

1. See Patillon and Brisson 2001 and Heath 2002; see also the relevant *Suda* entry (lamda.645). Psellos refers frequently to Longinos: see *Or. min.* 8.194; K-D 28 (36.7); *Theol.* I 56.7–9 (reproduced in Patillon and Brisson 2001 as Longinos' fragment 37B); 75.117–26 (fragment 24B); 98.30–40 (fragment 41). Ioannes Sikeliotes too references Longinos, yet not his *Rhetoric* (see Patillon and Brisson 2001: fr. 53, 56, and 59). It seems highly unlikely that Psellos knew the famous *On the Sublime* attributed (also) to Longinos in its single Byzantine manuscript (the late tenth-c. Paris, BNF, gr. 2036).

rhetoric. Psellos first surveys the structure of a speech, identifying the goal of the preface, narrative, proof, and peroration, and offering some remarks about the latter two parts. Then he deals with specific devices of style and argumentation. This section includes a brief but significant digression on oratorical delivery. The conclusion discusses Longinos' model rhetors (in this order): Aeschines, Plato, Herodotus, Thucydides, Isocrates, Lysias, and Demosthenes.

Like the *Synopsis* of Hermogenes' *On Forms* or his summary of Dionysios of Halikarnassos' *On Composition*, Psellos' *On Rhetoric* too should be regarded as a teacher's reading notes on an earlier rhetorical manual, which are then put together (not altogether smoothly) and presented to a student. The recent editors of our treatise have discussed in great detail how Psellos' text compares to what survives from Longinos' work. There is no need to repeat their work here (Patillon and Brisson 2001: 58–111). Since their focus, however, was to recover Longinos' original work, it is important in this introduction to highlight the Psellian perspective, by noting variations that seem to reveal middle Byzantine sensibilities.

Since the Hellenistic period at least, ancient rhetorical training included five components, a set of tasks expected of the skilled rhetor: invention (εὕρεσις—*inventio* in Latin rhetoric), disposition (οἰκονομία/διοίκησις/τάξις—*dispositio*), style/diction (λέξις—*elocutio*), delivery (ὑπόκρισις—*pronuntiatio* or *actio*), and memory (μνήμη—*memoria*). Longinos' original treatise reflects this approach, even though it is unclear if the surviving final section on "memory," which accompanies the treatise in its basic testimony, belonged to the original work or not.[2] This ancient structure of rhetorical training is obscured in Psellos' text. Though he mentions λέξις and ὑπόκρισις, he does not clarify for his reader that these are part of an original five-part sequence. Moreover, he has excluded any discussion either of arrangement or of

2. Patillon and Brisson print it as an independent appendix and consider it a separate work. The relevant manuscript is the famous mid-tenth-c. Paris, BNF, gr. 1741, which contains various rhetorical treatises including Dionysios of Halikarnassos' *On Composition*, Ps.-Demetrios' *On Style*, Menandros' *On Epideictic Speeches*, as well as Aristotle's *Rhetoric* and *Poetics*. For the ms. see Harlfinger and Reinsch 1970, Aujac 1978: 29–34, Irigoin 1997: 171–82, and Patillon and Brisson 2001: 100–107; also Kavrus-Hoffmann 2010b.

memory and, in general, has reduced greatly the original text.[3] This may be a matter of chance and random selection. Yet the absence of any discussion of (specifically) memory techniques seems to reflect the overall indifference about this subject among middle and, then, late Byzantine teachers of rhetoric. Perhaps influenced by Hermogenes, medieval Greek rhetoricians discuss little this aspect of a rhetor's skills in their manuals.[4]

The other two Psellian departures are brief but significant. The first pertains to his discussion of delivery, ὑπόκρισις. Though he reduces significantly the Longinian exposition on the matter, Psellos amplifies a point implicit in Longinos: while proffering Longinos' notion that delivery persuades by "deception" rather than logical necessity, Psellos suggests that oral delivery is "the best" or "the most beautiful thing [τὸ κάλλιστον]" in rhetoric.[5] This notion was to be repeated by Psellos' student, Ioannes Italos in his own treatise on rhetoric; indeed, Italos seems to acknowledge directly his teacher regarding this point.[6]

The second Psellian deviation (and the only explicit one in the text) is his disagreement with Longinos' critique of Plato's style. "He (i.e., Longinos) . . . blames . . . Plato for his inartistic mixture of the rhetorical forms and the bulkiness, too poetic, of his prose style," Psellos writes. He immediately adds: "This is not my view, but the words of the rhetor." As is obvious from many other Psellian statements, several of which are included in this volume, Plato was for Psellos an unquestionable authority of thought *as well as* style (com-

3. Only 439 lines (in the recent edition) survive of Longinos' original work, which was certainly longer; Psellos' text occupies 111 lines.

4. Indeed, the *On Memory* which follows Longinos' *Art of Rhetoric* in the Paris ms. is perhaps the single *rhetorical* treatise on memory that is transmitted in Byzantine manuscripts. This is in sharp contrast with the fate of the subject in medieval Latin rhetorical theory; cf. Carruthers 1998 with Messis 2006: 107–11 (for a Byzantine perspective on memory in general).

5. Ancient rhetoric saw delivery as a most *powerful* element; cf. Aristotle, *Rhetoric* 1403b21–1404a35, and Longinos, *Art of Rhetoric* 373 (δύναται δὲ μέγιστον εἰς πίστιν . . .). Furthermore, Longinos defines delivery as "performance of what is *truthfully* represented by each rhetor: the characters, emotions, dispositions of the body, and intonation of the voice appropriate to the underlying subjects: μίμησις τῶν κατ' ἀλήθειαν ἑκάστῳ παρισταμένων ἠθῶν καὶ παθῶν καὶ διάθεσεων σώματός τε καὶ τόνου φωνῆς προσφόρου τοῖς ὑποκειμένοις πράγμασι" (370–72; following here the main ms. contra the edition of Patillon and Brisson). This is a definition that Psellos interestingly omits.

6. See Conley 2004: 425–26.

parable only to Gregory of Nazianzos).[7] This view and also his critique of Longinos on this specific point seem to derive from the Neoplatonist, i.e., Proklean, tradition to which Psellos subscribed. Perhaps this same tradition occasioned Psellos' interest in Longinos' *Rhetoric* in the first place.[8]

Editions and translations. The text for this translation is from Patillon and Brisson 2001: 208–12 (fr. 49); numbers in square brackets indicate line numbers from that edition. For several earlier editions, see Moore 2005: 402–3, which also includes a presentation of the manuscript tradition. All six manuscripts are post-Byzantine. They seem to derive from a common archetype where our text was preserved along with a few other Psellian texts of similar educational purpose, including rhetorical essays (texts 3 and 6 from part 1 of this volume). In two of the manuscripts, the treatise is transmitted anonymously. Following Patillon and Brisson's edition, I have set in quotation marks all the passages that are, or are presented as, direct quotes from Longinos.[9]

7. Similar views also in *On the Different Styles of Certain Writings* and *Theol.* I 98 on Greg. Naz. *Or.* 43.1—see pp. 102 and 161–62 below; cf. *Theol.* I 88.74–75 (on Greg. Naz. *Or.* 38.8), where Gregory is said to be an "imitator" of Plato's allusive description of the soul in the *Phaedrus.*

8. See Longinos' fragments 19, 21, 24–37, in Patillon and Brisson 2001, all from Proklos' *Comm. on the Timaeus*, a text that Psellos knew well and quoted often, including two relevant passages on Longinos: *Theol.* I 56.7–9 (reproduced as fragment 37B); 75.117–26 (fragment 24B). See also *Theol.* I 98.30–40 (fragment 41), where Psellos presents a very critical view of Longinos' reading of Plato's *Phaedrus*; the full text of *Theol.* I 98 is included in chapter nine of this present collection. Psellos cites from Longinos' *Art of Rhetoric* also at the beginning of his *The Styles of Gregory the Theologian, Basil the Great, Chrysostom, and Gregory of Nyssa,* translated later in this volume.

9. In their Greek text, the editors set in italics passages that survive in the preserved part of Longinos' *Rhetoric*, while they enclose in quotation marks these same passages along with the parts that Psellos announces with words like "he says," etc. Since we do not possess the full original text, there is some uncertainty as to what actually belongs to Psellos' rephrasing or opinion.

On Rhetoric

[1–5] The *Rhetoric* by Hermogenes of Tarsos is also fine. How could it not be? It is, after all, the most comprehensive treatment of every aspect of this art. Yet, in comparison, also the *Rhetoric* of Longinos, the best of critics, is not inferior.[1] Indeed, for readers, he is even easier to understand.

[6–12] He begins straightaway with the prefaces [προοιμίων], and explains to everyone the stylistic virtues appropriate for each rhetorical method. He says: "The work of the preface is to create gentle disposition, good-will <toward the speaker>, attentiveness, and readiness to learn; narrative shows the facts; the work of proof is to persuade why the facts are thus; peroration amplifies, reminds, and urges the listener to vote according to our wishes."

[13–21] "The main points [κεφάλαια]," Longinos continues, "are a species [εἶδος]: just like the copies of certain images or statues, what one says about them is composed in accordance with a model. The instruments [ὄργανα] are the various plausibilities [εἰκότα]; and parts of the latter are the probable indications [σημεῖα], demonstrable proofs [τεκμήρια], testimonies obtained under torture, witnesses, laws, decrees, contracts, proclamations, and the like." All these are with respect to their *genus* plausibilities, but with respect to their species they are also elements of proof [στοιχεῖον], as I mentioned. "Let us call 'probable indications,'" he says, "what can demonstrate past events, 'plausibilities' what demonstrates the future course of events, and 'demonstrable proofs' what are undeniable facts."

1. Longinos is known as the κριτικός; e.g., *Suda* lambda.645, and Psellos, *On the "In the Beginning was the Word"* (John 1:1) = *Theol.* I 75.117.

[21–33] He calls "enthymeme" [ἐνθύμημα] a rhetor's syllogism, which sometimes may lack a conclusion and/or proposition; this enthymeme can be demonstrative, refutative, gnomic, or serve as a model. If it includes an example, then it is a complete argument. For a fully developed enthymeme is the one that is complete in all respects. The general parts of logical elaboration [κατασκευῆς] are two: the enthymeme and the example [παράδειγμα]. The latter proceeds from similarity to similarity and from what is known to what is unknown; the former offers a summary of the examples—for in enthymemes the speech curtails the many dispersed examples; it is for this reason that mentioning examples is like an explication of enthymemes.

[34–39] "Examination," he says, "of the fortunes, professions, lineage, wealth, manners," and the like, "that accompany persons or matters is most effective for the purpose of invention [εὕρεσιν]." And later: "Before these, there should be the presentation of the paramount, seminal points regarding the subject matter as well as the application of these paramount, general, and most basic points to the specifics."

[40–49] "The function and task of perorations [ἐπιλόγων]," he says, "is to remind <the audience> through recapitulations what has been said previously and to augment what has been agreed, making it stronger or weaker, through partition of the subject-matter and by juxtaposition of similar points and their opposites." Also: "The nature of perorations is that of prefaces in reverse; for often the same approach fits both one's preface and one's exhortation of the judges in the peroration." Also: "In a preface, one must introduce the arrangement of the main parts and announce the manner of their demonstration, while the peroration contains augmentations [αὐξήσεις] and reminders of what has already been said."

[50–59] Additions and removals often pattern a speech. Allegory too brings novelty to it; "overused, washed out expressions that have been used a million times create boredom." Novel syntax as well as "moods, voices, and alterations in the tense of the verb" excite the listener. "Therefore, one should say: 'ἀμφὶ σοῦ λέγομεν [I speak concerning you]' and 'χάριν σήν [for your sake],' 'θαυμάζω σου [I admire you]' and 'καταφρονῶ σε [I disdain you],' 'θάρρει τούτους [you should take courage in them],' 'ὡς εἰδεῖεν θεοὶ [as the gods might know],' 'ἀνύσασιν ἄν [they would have accomplished],' and similar expressions."

[60–65] "Not the least important part of rhetoric is that which deals with diction [λέξεως]; for" beautiful words "are like the 'light' of meanings and arguments." "There is no advantage to acumen and sharpness in judgment, division, and examination of ideas and chains of reasoning, if you do not match thoughts with the best diction."

[66–72] "The period [περίοδος] is a type of enthymeme articulated in well-ordered rhythms, and with cola and sections that are symmetrical in length."[2] "Preventive treatment,[3] abrupt interruption of a sentence, designed omission,[4] and irony[5] are enthymemes and techniques of argumentation for the sake of persuasiveness and species of the proof. They could also be considered as parts of the demonstration [ἀποδείξεως] based on emotion [παθητικῆς] and on character [ἠθικῆς] that are appropriate for the virtue of delivery."

[73–76] Indeed, delivery [ὑπόκρισις] is the best thing in the art of rhetoric.[6] For "it does not lead by pressure, like proof and demonstration do, but rather lures and compels the judge's view to adopt the standpoint of the speaker."

[77–86] "You should refine your speech," he says, "and plait it as if with bands, colors of flowers, and every shade of paint. You should use polished and rounded style in the proofs at law courts, but a more solemn diction in advisory speeches. As for the oration that is to be displayed in theaters and aims to captivate the viewers, it is strongly recommended that it be composed with precision and spoken using all kinds of beauty; in this case too you must employ moderation and love of beauty without extravagance.[7] Exaggerated embellishment so as to please the ears of the listeners is just flattery, while solemn expression, if supplemented with moderate pleasure, never creates surfeit."

2. Longinos (*Art of Rhetoric* 336–41) defines the various sentence units (such as *komma,* colon, and section [περικοπή]) in the following way: ἔστιν οὖν τὸ μὲν κόμμα ἐκ δυοῖν λέξεων ἢ τριῶν, τὸ δὲ κῶλον διπλάσιον ἢ κατὰ τοῦτο, καθάπερ διττῶν ἄρθρων μετέχον . . . ἡ δὲ περικοπὴ ἐκ δύο κώλων καὶ τριῶν ἐστι κατὰ λόγον τῶν εἰρημένων μερῶν καὶ αὐτὴ συντιθεμένη.

3. Προδιόρθωσις: for this term, cf. "Hermogenes," *On Invention* 4.12.

4. For these two figures of ἀποσιώπησις and παράλειψις (*reticentia* and *praeteritio* in Latin respectively), cf. "Hermogenes," *On the Method of Force* 7; on ἀποσιώπησις, see also Hermogenes, *On Forms* 2.7.36 = *On True Speech.*

5. On this figure, see Alexander, *On Figures* 18: "Εἰρωνεία δέ ἐστι λόγος προσποιούμενος τὸ ἐναντίον λέγειν."

6. Cf. the discussion in the introduction above.

7. An echo of Thucydides, *History* 2.40 (φιλοκαλοῦμεν μετ᾽ εὐτελείας)?

[87–90] "Whether it is about something good or something bad, a subject matter," he says, "is amplified in two ways: either by partition <of its main points> or by comparison." "To speak in a civic fashion [πολιτικῶς] is to adorn the speech with persuasive and, to the extent possible, demonstrative [ἀποδεικτικοῖς] enthymemes."

[91–93] "We are able," he says, "to argue either side of a dispute, both because we can hold opposite opinions about the same matter, and because the good are somewhat similar to the bad."

[94–99] "Plausibilities [εἰκότα]," he writes, "are generally admitted [ἔνδοξοι][8] statements about things that usually happen; from these, we derive the enthymemes, the demonstrations, the proofs, and the ratiocinations about the main points of our investigation. A probable indication [σημεῖον] is something done or experienced from which we surmise whether what we investigate has happened or not."

[100–111] The rhetor proposes seven men who are best in every stylistic virtue and who can adorn our rhetorical expression [φράσιν]: two from the Socratic philosophers, namely Aeschines and Plato; two from those who composed history, Herodotus and Thucydides; and three among the so-called rhetors, namely Isocrates, Lysias, and Demosthenes. He regards as flawless in every discursive genre five among them. However, he blames Thucydides for his dense and overwrought style and Plato for his inartistic mixture of the rhetorical forms and the bulkiness, too poetic, of his prose style—this is not my view, but the words of the rhetor [i.e., Longinos].[9]

8. For this Aristotelian concept, see, e.g., *Topics* 100b21 and *Rhetoric* 1355a17.
9. For Psellos' preference for Plato, see the introduction above.

5 *On Tragedy*

Translated with introduction and notes
by Stratis Papaioannou

Introduction

The *On Tragedy*, *Περὶ τραγῳδίας*, is yet another collection/edition of excerpts attributed to Psellos, though in this case the identification of either its Psellian authorship or its original source is on less secure footing. Regarding the question of authorship, we can only rely on the indirect testimony of the single manuscript that preserves the short treatise: the Oxford, Bodleian Library, Baroccianus 131, a rhetoro-philosophical collection of mostly eleventh- and twelfth-century texts, written by several scribes over a long period during the second half of the thirteenth century.[1] Though anonymous in its inscription, the *On Tragedy* is included in a section of the manuscript (397v–446v, written by scribe A; the *On Tragedy* on ff. 415r–v) that contains, albeit anonymously, several Psellian writings as well as notes and excerpts from a variety of texts that seem to originate in Psellos' milieu and, possibly, Psellos himself.[2] Additionally, some Psellian echoes are present in the introductory phrases and also elsewhere in the text.[3] This evidence is perhaps sufficient (though not conclu-

1. For the ms., see Wilson 1978; also Pérez Martín 2012: 168–73 and Papaioannou 2013: 256–57, 263.

2. Pontikos (1992: xv–xl) questions, unjustifiably in my view, the attribution to Psellos of most of these texts; in this respect, see Duffy 1992, texts 4, 17, 20–28, 33, 37, 40, and 55.

3. See the notes to the translation below.

sive) to regard Psellos as the likely excerptor and compiler of *On Tragedy*—at least this is the assumption of this translation.[4]

As with other comparable Psellian texts, we rarely hear Psellos' voice directly. Rather, the text reproduces in fragmented form either an earlier essay that was itself a collection of excerpts or, equally plausibly, passages from several ancient treatises related to the topic of Athenian fifth-century drama. Exactly which essay or essays Psellos read in order to create his short exposé on tragedy is unclear. Since no single direct source has been identified thus far, the question must remain unanswered.[5]

Perhaps more important is the question of who would be interested in creating this collection and making this particular selection of excerpts; this was an undertaking that obviously required some effort—especially if, as is likely, he culled from several different texts. The response might lie in the expansive attitude toward philosophical and philological knowledge promoted by Psellos. Ancient theater is, after all, no random piece of learned culture for Psellos, as is evident from his engagement with Euripidean drama in the essay *To One Asking "Who Wrote Verse Better, Euripides or Pisides?"* (number 11 in this present collection).[6] In general, Psellos' interests in performance and rhetorical theatrics could easily provide yet another motivation to work on the *On Tragedy*.[7]

Because of its antiquarian subject, the *On Tragedy* has attracted an attention that is unusual—in comparison to that devoted to the other Psellian rhetorotheoretical treatises—though again the focus has been the recovery of ancient

4. The most recent editor (Perusino 1993: 16–17) seems inclined to assign the text to an anonymous compiler, yet her argument that this text reveals an unscrupulous (and thus un-Psellian) editor is rather unconvincing, given the existence of many similar texts by Psellos; most important among the latter is the *Concise History*, which contains some "factual" errors that have entered Psellos' text most likely from his sources.

5. Glucker 1968 argues that the author of the treatise is Psellos, who is paraphrasing a late peripatetic treatise (perhaps as late as Themistios).

6. Similarities between these two texts reinforce the attribution to Psellos; cf. also Perusino 1993: 15.

7. Apart from the essay on Euripides, see text 14 of this present collection: Psellos' *Encomium for the Monk Ioannes Kroustoulas Who Read Aloud at the Holy Soros*. See also the brief comments in Psellos' treatise on a phrase from "everyday speech" (ed. Sathas V 537–41; cf. Moore 2005: 398–99) about the diction of Aeschylus, Sophocles, Euripides, Aristophanes, and Menander (Sathas V 538.12–23).

sources and knowledge, rather than the importance of this text in the immediate context of its production and circulation.[8] The concentrated interest is perhaps justified, since this peculiar text transmits a certain post-classical understanding of ancient tragedy that has left only faint and muddled traces in other late antique and medieval texts. This understanding originated in Aristotle's *Poetics*, yet it also expanded, and, ultimately (to the extent we are able to judge it) transformed the Aristotelian framework.

As far as one can tell, post-classical philosophical and rhetorical thought produced several Aristotelianizing treatments of ancient drama, tragedy in particular. It is not the place here to provide a full list—the topic still deserves comprehensive treatment.[9] What interests us is that no such treatise survives before we reach Psellos' essay and then a similar work of twelfth-century Constantinopolitan philology, Ioannes Tzetzes' *On Tragic Poetry* (written ca. 1140; Pace 2011). Perhaps due to the gradual disappearance of actual performance of classical Greek drama in Roman and then Byzantine theater entertainment (when mime acting and pantomime dancing dominated the stage),[10] earlier thinking about classical drama was reduced to antiquarian knowledge, circulating only in the limited context of advanced education and display of learnedness. More importantly, this thinking was dispersed in a variety of discourses dealing with wider subjects, such as music, philology (scholia, lexicography, and metrics), philosophy, and rhetoric.

For late antique and medieval philologists, that is, there existed no single authoritative text on ancient drama (hence also the relative neglect of Aristotle's *Poetics*, which survives essentially in two Byzantine manuscripts), but rather a wider, unsystematized discourse about it.[11] The field is complex and

8. For the earlier bibliography, see Moore 2005: 401–2; see also Porter 2010: 109–12 for a more recent discussion, focusing on the "polemical stance" to Aristotle in the treatise.

9. Three examples, documented in the sources, may be mentioned here: Athenaios (*Deipnosophistae* 14.40) quotes from an *On Tragedy* by Douris (ca. 340–ca. 270 BCE); Stephanos of Byzantion (sixth c.; *Ethnika* 349.1–3) refers to a certain Istros (possibly third c. BCE) who wrote a "book" *On Tragedy*; and, according to the *Suda* (phi.422), Philostratos the Elder (second/third c. CE) wrote an *On Tragedy* in three books (along with forty-three tragedies and fourteen comedies). None of these works is preserved.

10. See Webb 2008.

11. The two Byzantine mss. of the *Poetics*: (a) the important mid-tenth c. Paris, BNF, gr. 1741, already mentioned earlier (see p. 75n2 above); and (b) Florence, Bibl. Riccardiana, gr. 46, mid-twelfth c. in the milieu of the famous scribe Ioannikios (cf. Baldi 2011). For a recent new edition of the *Poetics*, where also the Syriac and Arabic evidence is adduced, see Tarán and Gutas 2012.

includes everything from the Neoplatonic reception of Aristotelian and, of course, Platonic thought on ancient drama, to scholia on the texts of ancient dramatists, to occasional comments on tragedy and comedy in grammatical theory (especially, Dionysios of Thrace and his Byzantine commentators) and, even, Hermogenian rhetorical theory (despite its general neglect on theatrical discourse). This wider field was known to Psellos. More specifically, the *On Tragedy* contains references to the following texts: the pseudo-Plutarchean *On Music,* Hephaistion's *Handbook on Meters* and Pollux' *Onomasticon*—both second-century texts, well-attested among Byzantine manuscripts—and encyclopedic compilations such as the *Suda,* itself based on dictionaries, biographical works, and scholia to classical literature. They all point to Roman–Greek discursive science, as almost all else in Byzantine "scientific" thought.

The notions that are given prominence in this first Byzantine text on tragedy deserve a few further remarks. Notably, our text does not offer any straightforward, comprehensive definition of tragedy along the lines of Aristotle's famous ἔστιν οὖν τραγῳδία μίμησις πράξεως. We hear nothing, for example, about tragedy's purpose, its τέλος. Psellos and his sources are focused on the *what* and, primarily, the *how* of tragic drama.

In both respects, the *On Tragedy* deviates from Aristotle. As far as tragic mode/practice is concerned, the un-Aristotelianism is immediately apparent by the extensive focus on meter, music, and—the most un-Aristotelian of all elements (cf. *Poetics* 1450b15–20)—spectacle;[12] and, it should be added, all topics are treated in a manner that suggests late classical practice of tragic performance and composition.[13]

The beginning of the text supplies also some thoughts on the what, the *subject,* of tragedy. It is instructive to compare directly the relevant Aristotelian views on the matter with those of Psellos. Here is Aristotle's *Poetics*:

> ἔστιν οὖν τραγῳδία μίμησις πράξεως σπουδαίας καὶ τελείας μέγεθος ἐχούσης . . . δι' ἐλέου καὶ φόβου περαίνουσα τὴν τῶν τοιούτων παθημάτων κάθαρσιν. (1449b24–8)

12. See Porter 2010: 109–12.
13. Perusino's commentary is especially useful in this respect.

> . . . ἡ γὰρ τραγῳδία μίμησίς ἐστιν οὐκ ἀνθρώπων ἀλλὰ πράξεων καὶ βίου . . . οὔκουν ὅπως τὰ ἤθη μιμήσωνται πράττουσιν, ἀλλὰ τὰ ἤθη συμπεριλαμβάνουσιν διὰ τὰς πράξεις. (1450a16–22)
> . . . δεῖ τὴν σύνθεσιν εἶναι τῆς καλλίστης τραγῳδίας . . φοβερῶν καὶ ἐλεεινῶν εἶναι μιμητικήν. (1452b31–33)
>
> ———
>
> Tragedy, then, is representation of an action that is elevated, complete, and of magnitude . . . and through pity and fear accomplishing the purification of such emotions [παθημάτων].
> . . . because tragedy is representation not of persons but of actions and life . . . so it is not in order to provide representation of character that the agents act; rather, their characters are included for the sake of their actions.
> . . . the structure of the finest tragedy should be . . . representing fearful and pitiable events.[14]

And here is Psellos (sections 1 and 2 below):

> Ἡ τραγῳδία . . . ὑποκείμενα μὲν ἔχει, ἃ δὴ καὶ μιμεῖται, πάθη τε καὶ πράξεις, ὁποῖα τὰ ἑκάτερα. . . . Τὰ δὲ πάθη μᾶλλον μιμεῖται ἢ τὰς πράξεις· τὸ γὰρ πρωταγωνιστοῦν ἐν πᾶσι τοῖς τραγικοῖς δράμασι τὸ πάθος ἐστί. Μιμεῖται δὲ ἡ τραγῳδία καὶ τὸ καλούμενον ἦθος, καὶ μάλιστα ἐν τοῖς στασίμοις ᾄσμασιν, ἐν οἷς καὶ αἱ ἀποφάσεις ἠθικαὶ καὶ γνωμολογίαι καὶ ἐπιτιμήσεις. Μιμεῖται δὲ καὶ τῶν ἀψύχων πολλά. Ἡ δὲ πρᾶξις δυσμιμητοτέρα τοῦ πάθους. Οὐ τὰς τυχούσας δὲ πράξεις ἡ τραγῳδία μιμεῖται, ἀλλ' ὅσα ἡρωϊκῶν καὶ πρακτικῶν ἠθῶν εἰσιν οἰκεῖα καὶ μεγαλοψύχων, καὶ μάλιστα ἐὰν τελευτῶσιν εἰς πάθη.
>
> ———
>
> Tragedy . . . has as its subjects those things that it also represents [μιμεῖται]: *pathê* and actions, whatever each might be. . . . Tragedy represents *pathê* more than actions; for in all tragic dramas, *pathos* is the protagonist. Tragedy also represents the so-called character [ἦθος]—especially during *stasima,* where one also finds declarations that display character, maxims, and expressions of censure. Additionally, it represents many inanimate things. Action is more difficult to represent than *pathos.* Tragedy does not represent ordinary actions, but only those that belong to characters who are he-

14. Translation by Haliwell (1995), slightly modified.

roic, dedicated to action, and high-spirited, and especially those actions that end in *pathê.*

The most glaring difference between the two definitions is the elevation of *pathos*—which, in this context, may denote both suffering and, as I would like to argue, emotion—to the most important object of tragic representation, or mimesis. For Aristotle, *pathos,* as emotion, is located in the reception of tragedy, and signifies the feelings aroused and then cleansed or released by tragedy in the audience. This was a rather strategic move on the part of Aristotle who could thus avoid the Platonic anxiety regarding poetry as the means to represent, reenact, and, ultimately, induce *pathê,* that is, passions—a notion propagated most famously in book 10 of the *Republic.*[15]

It is true that representation of *pathos* as suffering may be implied by Aristotle's later clarification in the *Poetics* that the actions imitated in a tragedy should be "fearful and pitiable"—this idea is echoed in Psellos' text.[16] Psellos also makes a concession that points to Aristotle's definition: he too claims that action is more difficult to represent than *pathos.* Nevertheless, the emphasis placed on the representation of *pathos* is unparalleled in Aristotle, who actually relegates such representation to the activity of dancers, and thus to spectacular mimesis, unrelated to the essence of tragedy.[17]

The background of the Psellian approach is provided by other definitions of tragedy that circulated in post-classical and Byzantine philological and philosophical discourse. As in *On Tragedy,* references to the imitation of *pathos* as well as (another un-Aristotelian element) of êthos, as "heroic character," are customary. Here is a more or less complete list of these post-classical and Byzantine definitions of tragedy:

15. See especially 606d1–7. On ancient approaches to the representation of *pathos,* see further Gill 1984.

16. See also Aristotle's definition of *pathos,* here in the meaning of suffering, as a "component" of the plot (μῦθος) (1452b11–13): πάθος δέ ἐστι πρᾶξις φθαρτικὴ ἢ ὀδυνηρά, οἷον οἵ τε ἐν τῷ φανερῷ θάνατοι καὶ αἱ περιωδυνίαι καὶ τρώσεις καὶ ὅσα τοιαῦτα ("suffering is a destructive or painful action, such as public deaths, physical agony, wounding, and the like"). Cf. also Porter 2010: 110n161.

17. 1447a26–28: ἡ τῶν ὀρχηστῶν (καὶ γὰρ οὗτοι διὰ τῶν σχηματιζομένων ῥυθμῶν μιμοῦνται καὶ ἤθη καὶ πάθη καὶ πράξεις) ("the art of dancers—since they too, through rhythms translated into movements, *represent characters, emotions, and actions*").

- "representation [μίμησις] of the lives, words, and sufferings [παθῶν] of heroes"[18]
- "poetry in verse for the sake of song contest dedicated to the terrible sufferings [δεινοπαθείᾳ] of persons and actions"[19]
- "narration [διήγησις] of the sufferings of heroes"[20]
- "reporting [ἀπαγγελτική] actions full of suffering"[21]
- "representation of characters, actions, and sufferings [παθημάτων]"[22]
- "representation of characters [ἠθῶν] and emotions/sufferings [παθῶν]"[23]

Compared to these definitions, what we encounter in Psellos' text is a further promotion of *pathos* as both suffering and emotion as *the* characteristic aspect of tragedy.[24] This is a sentiment that, as far as I can tell, is expressed only once more in the Greek tradition: in another Psellian text, his *To One Asking "Who Wrote Verse Better, Euripides Or Pisides?"* (40–41). There, we read that "*pathos* is the ultimate subject of tragic poetry = τὸ τελεώτατον κεφάλαιον τῆς τραγικῆς ποιήσεως τὸ πάθος ἐστί." Here, the term πάθος is to be under-

18. Commentaries on Dionysios of Thrace's *Art of Grammar* 2: *Scholia Marciana,* Hilgard 1901: 306.6–8: Τραγῳδία ἐστὶ βίων καὶ λόγων ἡρωϊκῶν καὶ παθῶν μίμησις ἔχουσα μυστήρια καὶ σεμνότητα πλοκήν τέ τινα τῶν κατὰ μέρος. Cf. Melampous the Grammarian (or Diomedes), *Comm. on the Art of Dionysios of Thrace,* 17.15–18.12. Also, see Psellos, *On Grammar* = *Poem.* 6.206: ἡρωϊκὴ γὰρ μέστωσις ἐστὶν ἡ τραγῳδία (a strange definition; a likely rendering: "tragedy is the filling up <with emotion> of heroes").

19. *Scholia* on Plato's *Republic* 394c2 (ed. Greene 1938): τραγῳδία ἐστὶ ποίησις ἔμμετρος πρὸς ἅμιλλαν ᾠδῆς ἐπὶ δεινοπαθείᾳ προσώπων τε καὶ πραγμάτων γιγνομένη, καθ' ἣν τῷ νικήσαντι τράγος ἔπαθλον ἐδίδοτο, ἐξ οὗ καὶ τὸ ὄνομα ἔσχεν.

20. *Etymologicum Gudianum,* ed. Sturz 1818: 358.18–19: κωμῳδία γὰρ ἔστι βιωτικῶν πραγμάτων διήγησις· τραγῳδία δὲ ἡρωικῶν παθῶν.

21. *Suda* tau.900: ἡ τραγῳδία ἐμπαθῶν πραγμάτων ἀπαγγελτική. From the *Scholia* to Aristophanes' *Acharnians* 9a.

22. Ioannes Tzetzes, *On Tragic Poetry* 184–85: ἄκουε λοιπόν, τί τέλος τραγῳδίας / μίμησις ἠθῶν, πράξεων, παθημάτων.

23. *Scholia* on Demosthenes' *Or.* 2, 135b.2–3: καὶ γὰρ ἡ τραγῳδία μίμησίς ἐστιν ἠθῶν καὶ παθῶν.

24. In fact, a few variations of the above definitions do not mention *pathos. Scholia Londinensia,* Hilgard 1901: 452.13–14: Τραγῳδία δέ ἐστι βίων καὶ λόγων ἡρωϊκῶν μίμησις ἔχουσα σεμνότητα μετ' ἐπιπλοκῆς τινος. And later 475.1–3: Τραγῳδία ἐστὶ βίων τε καὶ λόγων ἡρωϊκῶν ἔμμετρος μίμησις ἔχουσα σεμνότητα μετὰ πλοκῆς τινος. *Etymologicum Magnum,* ed. Gaisford 1848: 763.58–764.1: βίων τε καὶ λόγων ἡρωϊκῶν μίμησις.

stood more in the sense of "emotion," since, in the preceding lines, Psellos discusses (and praises) Euripides' ability to represent both the character and the emotions of persons enacted in his plays (lines 38–40). This prioritization of *pathos* exists despite or regardless of Platonic anxieties against the representation of *pathos*/emotion/passion, a commonplace in late antique Neoplatonic discourse with which Psellos was certainly familiar.[25]

Since we do not possess his original source, it is impossible to tell whether this is a Psellian innovation or not. Yet it undoubtedly points both to a concept favored by Psellos—his valuation of emotive discourse[26]—and to a certain post-classical rhetoricization of the understanding of ancient tragedy.[27] By the latter, I mean that, even though the source and vocabulary of Psellos in this text derive from ancient *poetics*, his approach reflects Byzantine theories of *rhetorical* discourse that provided the overarching framework for the discussion also of poetry (whether epic or drama).[28]

The definition of tragedy in Psellos and in the aforementioned post-classical texts bears similarities, for instance, to the common and more widely known definition of the rhetorical exercise of êthopoiia (speech-in-character) as "representation [μίμησις] of the character of an underlying person," one of whose three types is the "pathetic" that "shows emotion [πάθος] in every respect" (Aphthonios, *Progymnasmata* 34.2–3 and 35.1–10). Also, the reference to character as being expressed primarily through "declarations that display character, maxims [γνωμολογίαι], and expressions of censure" is reminiscent of the Byzantine rhetorical appetite for memorable statements that express one's intention, γνώμη.[29] Finally the peculiar reference to tragedy's imitation

25. See, e.g., Proklos, *Comm. on the Republic* 2.89.2–4: εἰ οὖν ἡ ποιητικὴ μιμητικὴ παθῶν ἐστιν, ἡ μιμητικὴ τῶν παθῶν αὔξει τὸ παθητικόν. Cf., earlier, Plutarch, *How Should the Young Listen to Poetry* 26a–b.

26. See Papaioannou 2013: 109–13, 116–17, and 195–200.

27. Cf. Agapitos 1998.

28. Cf. the alternative definition of tragedy in the *Commentaries* on Dionysios of Thrace's *Art of Grammar* 2, where tragedy is defined as "funerary poetry": *Scholia Marciana*, Hilgard 1901: 306.30–32: Τραγῳδία ποίησίς ἐστιν ἐπιτάφιος τῶν τραγικῶν, [τοῦ τε Μενάνδρου,] τοῦ Σοφοκλέους, τοῦ Αἰσχύλου, τοῦ Εὐριπίδου καὶ ἑτέρων τοιούτων. Cf. also *Scholia Vaticana*, Hilgard 1901: 172.17–18: Τραγῳδία ποίησίς ἐστιν.

29. For this, see *Chronographia* 7.168 and *What is the Difference between the Texts Whose Plots Concern Charikleia and Leukippe?* 62–63—if we were to look for examples in Psellos alone.

also of "inanimate things," which has troubled commentators,[30] has its parallel in rhetorical theory: it is rhetorical discourse that occasionally "imitates/represents/mimics birds and inanimate things = ὄρνεις μιμεῖται καὶ ἄψυχα" (Ioannes Sikeliotes, *Comm.* 172.29–30).

It is in this juncture of Byzantine rhetoric with ancient poetics that we must place the import of Psellos' *On Tragedy.*

Editions and translations. The edition used is Perusino's (1993), who offers also a translation in Italian and detailed commentary; I have followed his section numbering. For earlier editions and translations, see Moore 2005: 401–2. Since the text seems to gather disparate notes and definitions and should thus not be read as a continuous exposition, I have introduced more paragraphs than the available editions. I have also left certain technical Greek terms transliterated.

30. Browning (1963: 73) notes that the statement is "puzzling and without parallel"; Perusino (1993: 45–46) cites some possibilities from Pollux and scholia.

On Tragedy

[1] Tragedy, about which you inquired,[1] has as its subjects[2] those things that it also represents [μιμεῖται]: *pathê*[3] and actions, whatever each might be.

The means by which it represents are: plot, thought [διάνοια], diction, meter, rhythm, melody [μέλος], and, in addition to these, the types of spectacle [ὄψεις]: staging, settings [τόποι],[4] and movements and gestures [κινήσεις]—provided, respectively, by the stage-producer, the sponsor, and the actor.[5]

1. This introductory phrase is very common in Psellian letter treatises.

2. Ordinary Aristotelian/Neoplatonic terminology. Cf. Psellos, *Explanation about the Manners of Philosophy* = *Phil. min.* I 49.82–85 (from Elias, *Prolegomena of Philosophy* 5.19–23): Λαμβάνεται τοίνυν πᾶς ὁρισμὸς ἢ ἐκ τοῦ ὑποκειμένου ἢ ἐκ τοῦ τέλους ἢ ἐκ τοῦ συναμφοτέρου· πᾶσα γὰρ τέχνη καὶ ἐπιστήμη ἔχει ὑποκείμενον, ἔχει καὶ τέλος, καὶ ὑποκείμενον μὲν περὶ ὃ καταγίνεται, τέλος δὲ ὃ ποιῆσαι προτίθεται.

3. Since it is impossible to tell if, in the text, the term πάθος has as its primary meaning "emotion" or "suffering/misfortune," I chose to leave it untranslated. Cf. the discussion above.

4. For *topos*, cf. the *Suda* entries on "stage" and "side-scene": Σκηνή ἐστιν ἡ μέση θύρα τοῦ θεάτρου. Παρασκήνια δὲ τὰ ἔνθεν καὶ ἔνθεν τῆς μέσης θύρας. ἵνα δὲ σαφέστερον εἴπω, μετὰ τὴν σκηνὴν εὐθὺς καὶ τὰ παρασκήνια ἡ ὀρχήστρα. αὕτη δὲ ἔστιν ὁ τόπος, ὁ ἐκ σανίδων ἔχων τὸ ἔδαφος· ἀφ' οὗ θεατρίζουσιν οἱ μῖμοι. ἔστι μετὰ τὴν ὀρχήστραν βωμὸς τοῦ Διονύσου· ὃ καλεῖται θυμέλη παρὰ τὸ θύειν, μετὰ δὲ τὴν θυμέλην ἡ κονίστρα, τουτέστι τὸ κάτω ἔδαφος τοῦ θεάτρου (*Suda* sigma.569); ἔοικε παρασκήνια καλεῖσθαι ὁ παρὰ τὴν σκηνὴν ἀποδεδειγμένος τόπος ταῖς εἰς τὸν ἀγῶνα παρασκευαῖς (*Suda* pi.436). Browning (1963: 72) suggests that *topoi* indicate here such things as "the revolving περίακτοι or other visible signs of locality such as the *parodoi*, as opposed to the stage buildings"; this reading fits the later occurrence of *topos* in our text (section 10).

5. A significant variation of the list offered by Aristotle; Porter 2010: 110. Cf. *Poetics* 1450a7–12, where only diction and song are indicated as "means," along with

The sections of a tragedy are: prologue, episode, *exodos*, choral song, on-stage singing by the actors.[6]

The parts of the chorus' song are: entrance ode [πάροδος], *stasimon*,[7] *emmeleia*, *kommos*, exit ode [ἔξοδος].[8]

[2] Tragedy represents *pathê* more than actions; for in all tragic dramas, *pathos* is the protagonist.[9]

Tragedy also represents the so-called character [ἦθος]—especially during *stasima,* where one also finds declarations that display character, maxims [γνωμολογίαι], and expressions of censure.

Additionally, it represents many inanimate things.

Action is more difficult to represent than *pathos.* Tragedy does not represent ordinary actions, but only those that belong to characters who are heroic, dedicated to action, and high-spirited, and especially those actions that end in *pathê*. For many actions are fine and serious, but also *un*-tragic.[10]

---

spectacle [*opsis*, in the singular], which is considered a "mode": "Every tragedy, therefore, must have six components, which give it its quality, namely, plot, character, diction, thought, spectacle, and song [μελοποιία]. Two of the components constitute the means of mimesis, one its mode, and three its objects [i.e., plot, character, and thought]." Perusino (1993: 40–41) divides differently Psellos' passage: according to her, the stage-producer (σκηνοποιός) is responsible for both the "staging" and the "settings," while the sponsor (χορηγός) and the actor (ὑποκριτής) are responsible for the movements and gestures of the chorus and the actors respectively.

6. Cf. *Poetics* 1452b14–18 where, however, a basic fourfold division is offered first; this does not include on-stage singing (ἀπὸ σκηνῆς), which is, nevertheless, mentioned by Aristotle in the immediate vicinity of the initial definition (verses 18 and 25). See also Psellos, *To One Asking "Who Wrote Verse Better, Euripides or Pisides?"* 46 (cf. Perusino 1993: 42): καὶ ἄλλο μέν ἐστι τὸ ἐπὶ σκηνῆς, <ἄλλο δὲ τὸ> χορικόν.

7. Literally: a "stationary ode."

8. Cf. below section 4 with *Poetics* 1452b23–25: "*Parodos* is the first complete utterance of the chorus; *stasimon* is a choral song without anapestic and trochaic rhythms; *kommos* is a lamentation shared between chorus and actors." This second, choral *exodos* is different from the one mentioned earlier and that, in Aristotle's definition (1452b21-2), indicates: "that whole portion of a tragedy *after* the final choral song." *Emmeleia* here (and also in section 4; cf. Perusino 1993: 43) seems to indicate choral song *within* an "episode"; later on in the treatise (section 11) it indicates "tragic dance."

9. See the discussion in the introduction above, from which it is important to repeat here the similar Psellian statement in *To One Asking "Who Wrote Verse Better, Euripides or Pisides?"* 40–41 (cf. Perusino 1993: 44–45): ἐπεὶ καὶ τὸ τελεώτατον κεφάλαιον τῆς τραγικῆς ποιήσεως τὸ πάθος ἐστί.

10. ἀτράγῳδοι: a reading/correction of Browning; cf. *Poetics* 1452b34–1453a1.

[3] In tragedies, the first part is complication [δέσις] and the second is resolution [λύσις],[11] or change that results from the passing of time, often with the intervention of some divinity.[12]

The so-called *ekkyklêma* is required[13] by the *drama* so that events within the house may become visible.[14]

The *drama* includes a messenger, an announcer,[15] and a lookout.[16]

Some characters are introduced onto the stage with theatrical machines, upon which both gods and some heroes appear.[17]

In tragedies, there can be one or two choruses; the latter is termed *dichoria*.[18]

[4] Tragic poetry is divided in two modes: the so-called choral and the on-stage; each of these is further divided in song [ᾠδὴν] and speech [λέξιν].[19]

11. *Poetics* 1455b24.

12. Δαιμόνιον: also a "demon" in Byzantine parlance.

13. In Greek: αἴτημα. Browning (1963: 73) notes that there is "no exact parallel" to this usage; Perusino offers a somewhat inexact parallel in Plato (1993: 48); but for a Byzantine similar usage, see Eustathios, *Parekbolai on the Iliad* 3.824.21: κατὰ τὸ αἴτημα τοῦ μύθου.

14. Cf. Pollux, *Onomasticon* 4.128: καὶ τὸ μὲν ἐκκύκλημα ἐπὶ ξύλων ὑψηλὸν βάθρον, ᾧ ἐπίκειται θρόνος· δείκνυσι δὲ τὰ ὑπὸ σκηνὴν ἐν ταῖς οἰκίαις ἀπόρρητα πραχθέντα. See also Photios, *Lexikon,* epsilon.418: "ἐκκύκλημα καὶ ἐκκύκληθρον· μηχάνημα ὑπότροχον, ἐφ' οὗ ἐδείκνυτο τὰ ἐν τῇ σκηνῇ."

15. The difference between "ἄγγελος" and "ἐξάγγελος" is discussed often in Byzantine dictionaries. Cf., e.g., Georgios Choiroboskos, *Epimerismoi on the Psalms* 85.15-7: Τί διαφέρει ἄγγελος αὐτάγγελος καὶ ἐξάγγελος; Διαφέρει· ἄγγελος μὲν γὰρ λέγεται ὁ τὰς ἀγγελίας ἄγων, ἐξάγγελος δὲ, ὁ ἔξω τὰς ἀγγελίας ἄγων. Or Hesychios, *Lexikon, epsilon*.3488: ἐξάγγελος· ἄγγελος, ὁ τὰ ἔσω γεγονότα τοῖς ἔξω ἀγγέλλων.

16. For these terms, see the notes in Pace 2011: 102–6 and 121–22.

17. "The reference is to the so-called θεολογεῖον" (Browning 1963: 73).

18. Pollux, *Onomasticon* 4.107: παιδικὸς χορός, ἀνδρικός, κωμικός, τραγικός. καὶ ἡμιχόριον δὲ καὶ διχορία καὶ ἀντιχόρια. ἔοικε δὲ ταὐτὸν εἶναι ταυτὶ τὰ τρία ὀνόματα· ὁπόταν γὰρ ὁ χορὸς εἰς δύο μέρη τμηθῇ, τὸ μὲν πρᾶγμα καλεῖται διχορία, ἑκατέρα δ' ἡ μοῖρα ἡμιχόριον, ἃ δ' ἀντᾴδουσιν, ἀντιχόρια. Also Hesychios, *Lexikon* delta.2022: διχοριάζειν· ἐν δύο χοροῖς ᾄδειν.

19. The information tersely offered in this section is treated in similar discourse but in much more detail in Tzetzes' *On Tragic Poetry.* As is clear from Tzetzes' discussion, choral parts that include speech refer to dialogue between the leader of the chorus and the actor(s), or introductory statements that announce the arrival of a character; similarly, song "on-stage" seems to refer to solo singing, duets, or even trios by the actors; see Perusino 1993: 50–54.

Of the spoken part, some is metric (e.g., iambic and trochaic) and some is periodic (e.g., anapestic and iambic). The prologue, episodes, and *exodos* all belong to the metric portion.

Choral song is divided in five parts: entrance ode, *stasimon, emmeleia, kommos*, and exit ode.

Kommos is agitated and intense lament.[20]

[5] Ancient musical composition [μελοποιία] for tragedy employed the pure enharmonic genus and a mixture of the enharmonic and the diatonic;[21] no tragedian seems to have used the chromatic genus until Euripides—for the moral nature of this genus is effeminate [μαλακόν].[22]

As far as modes [τόνων] are concerned, ancient tragedy employed mostly the Doric and the Mixolydian—the former because it is proper to solemnity; the Mixolydian because it contributes to lamentation. It also uses what were then referred to as the "relaxed" harmonies: the Ionian and the relaxed Lydian.[23] Sophocles was the first to make use of the Phrygian and the Lydian; and he employed the Phrygian in a more dithyrambic fashion.[24] The Hypophrygian and the Hypodorian were rare, since they are more appropriate for the dithyramb—the first to introduce the Hypodorian and the Hypophrygian modes into tragedy was Agathon.[25] The Lydian is indeed more akin to the style of the *kithara*.

The ancients used scales of narrow range. Euripides was the first to use scales of extended range;[26] this type of musical composition was called by the

20. Aristotle (see n. 8 above) offers a different definition of the *kommos*. No medieval dictionary defines the term in the precise words used here.

21. For the three *genera* of ancient music (diatonic, chromatican, and enharmonic), see p. 73n21 above.

22. Plutarch (*Quest. Conv.* 654d–e) credits Agathon as the first to use the chromatic genus; see Pickard-Cambridge 1968: 322–23; see also the discussion in Browning 1963: 74–75 and Perusino 1993: 59–60.

23. For these modes, cf. "Plutarch," *On Music* 1136a–1137a with Browning 1963: 75 and Perusino 1993: 60–61. On the "relaxed" harmonies, see Plato, *Republic* 1290a with Browning 1963: 75.

24. For this information, see Aristoxenos, *Fragmenta* 79 = *Life of Sophocles* 23: φησὶ δὲ Ἀριστόξενος ὡς πρῶτος τῶν Ἀθήνηθεν ποιητῶν (sc. Σοφοκλῆς) τὴν Φρυγίαν μελοποιίαν εἰς τὰ ἴδια ᾄσματα παρέλαβε καὶ τοῦ διθυραμβικοῦ τρόπου κατέμιξεν. As Browning notes (1963: 75), "there is no parallel to the statement that Sophocles employed the Lydian" (whatever is meant by the latter term).

25. Cf. Aristotle, *Problemata* 920a8–10 and 922b10–27 with Pickard-Cambridge 1968: 323.

26. Πολυχορδία: literally, the use of many strings in the *lyra*.

ancient music theorists "bored through and through."[27] In general, Euripides pursued many more modes and tonalities[28] than his predecessors;[29] he also used appropriate rhythms: both the single and double bacchius[30] and the lesser ionic,[31] and occasionally the *proceleusmatic*.[32]

[6] In tragedy, speech must not be subordinated to the melody and the rhythm.[33] Rather, it should prevail and be handled skillfully.

Excessive "spinning around"[34] is inappropriate for tragedy and its dignity.

[7] Tragic songs comprise the strophe (also called *periodos*[35]) and the antistrophe.[36]

27. Ἀνάτρητος: Browning (1963: 77) suggests that this term carried negative connotations and might be related to ancient derogatory descriptions of the style of "new" tragedy (namely, Agathon, Timotheos, Euripides).

28. Reading –χροιά (in its musical sense of "nuance of scale") as the stem behind the text's "πολυ-χρούστερος." Browning (1963: 76) suggests "χρόαι (i.e. sub-species of melodic genera)."

29. Cf. also *To One Asking "Who Wrote Verse Better, Euripides or Pisides?"* 38 on Euripides' being "παντοδαπὸν τῇ ποιήσει γινόμενον."

30. LSJ: "a metrical foot of three syllables."

31. For the definition of this, see Hephaistion, *Handbook on Meters* 37.9–39.22.

32. LSJ: "a foot consisting of four short syllables." For all these terms, see further the discussion in Browning 1963: 77–78.

33. This notion exists already in Plato; cf. *Republic* 398d8–9: τήν γε ἁρμονίαν καὶ ῥυθμὸν ἀκολουθεῖν δεῖ τῷ λόγῳ. See Browning 1963: 78.

34. Ἐνδινεύεσθαι: "convoluted expression"? A very rare word attested only in Theocritus, *Idyll* 15.82, and Longos, *Daphnis and Chloe* 1.23.2; see also the note in Perusino 1993: 73–74.

35. Cf. Dionysios of Halikarnassos, *Demosthenes* 50: κατὰ περίοδον, ἣν καλοῦσιν <οἱ> μουσικοὶ στροφήν with Browning 1963: 78 and Perusino 1993: 74–75. Following a scholion on Hephaistion that defines *periodos* as "a section comprising different cola," Browning places the meaning of *periodos* within traditional *rhetorical* semantics (a similar definition, e.g., in Longinos, *Art of Rhetoric = Fragment* 48.347–49); scholia on Aeschylos, Aristophanes, and Sophocles recommend a different definition: *periodos* is a type of metrical colon that combines iambics with trochees (see, e.g., Byzantine *Scholia on Oedipus Rex* 649; Longo 1971). The term is used again by Psellos in his essay on Euripides and Pisides (lines 119–21): ὡς ἐν χορῷ, βαβαί, τῆς τῶν χειρῶν ἀντεπιβολῆς καὶ τοῦ κύκλου καὶ τῆς ἑλίξεως καὶ τῆς περιόδου καὶ τοῦ ἐπῳδοῦ καὶ τῆς στροφῆς καὶ τῆς ἀντιστροφῆς. See also p. 184 below.

36. This section covers material discussed in Hephaistion's *On Poems* and *Introduction to Metrics,* two Byzantine recensions of apparently the same work, used by Byzantine philologists in their explication of ancient meters; cf. Browning 1963: 78–79 (Browning speculates that the last part of the section on the change of structure in choral songs reflects "a fragment of Hephaestion independent of the two surviving recensions of the *De poematibus*").

Some of the songs are without an antistrophe,[37] while others contain one.

Of the antistrophic ones, some are with a single strophe, others are called *epodic*.[38] In dramatic plays, there exists both *proodic* and *mesodic* strophes.[39]

Commonly, of all the antistrophic songs, some are simple, others show change in structure. This change may go either from a single strophe to another single strophe, from an *epodic* to an *epodic*, from a single strophe to an *epodic* one, or the reverse.

[8] In reference to the tragic meter, the account is simple. In tragedy, most employ only two meters: the iambic <trimeter> and the trochaic tetrameter.

The anapestic tetrameter was used only by Phrynichos, the ancient.[40]

[9] There exist also other songs and meters classified under tragedy, for example, the *mesaulion*, the *epiphthegma,* the *anaboêma,* the rhythmical anapest.[41]

Mesaulia are short musical instrumental pieces[42] between songs.[43]

Epiphthegmata[44] are used mostly in satyr plays; but they exist also in tragedies.

37. Μακρά: cf. Aristotle, *Problemata* 918b13–16 with Browning 1963: 78.

38. Literally an "after-song."

39. These terms that indicate multiple strophes of different form or content are defined by Hephaistion (*On Poems* 66.24–67.15) in the following way: Ἐπῳδικὰ δέ ἐστιν, ἐν οἷς συστήμασιν ὁμοίοις ἀνόμοιόν τι ἐπιφέρεται. . . . Προῳδικὰ δέ ἐστιν, ἐν οἷς τὸ ἀνόμοιον προτέτακται τῶν ὁμοίων. Μεσῳδικὰ δὲ ἐν οἷς περιέχει μὲν τὰ ὅμοια, μέσον δὲ τὸ ἀνόμοιον τέτακται.

40. This information about Phrynichos (sixth–fifth c. BCE) is offered only in our text. In the *Suda* (phi.762), Phrynichos is regarded as the inventor of the "tetrameter" (Browning 1963: 79), which is also credited, however, to Aristophanes (alpha.3932; also tau.395). Browning speculates that since anapestic tetrameters were common in comedy, "the statement could only be made by someone who distinguished between the two Phrynichi [the tragedian and the comedian, who are often conflated], *i.e.* a writer of respectable antiquity. A fuller version of Hephaestion seems a likely source."

41. The section again echoes Hephaistion, but seems to reflect a fuller version; cf. Browning 1963: 79.

42. Κρουμάτια: most likely played by the ancient pipe (αὐλός).

43. Browning (1963: 79) cites Eustathios (*Parekbolai on the Iliad* 3.251.9–10) as the only parallel to this; however, see also Photios, *Lexikon,* delta.479: Διαύλιον· τὸ μεταξὺ τῆς ᾠδῆς αὐλούμενον. λέγεται καὶ μεσαύλιον. For further references (Aristeides Quintilianos, scholia on Aristophanes, and Hesychios), see Perusino 1993: 81.

44. Namely, shout, interjection, or, as Perusino suggests (1993: 82), refrain.

The *anaboêma*[45] belongs rather to the category of singing; it is something between song and recitation.[46]

Sometimes tragedians compose anapests, both for the chorus and for the actors on stage.[47] These fill all the roles of messenger and, in *parodoi,* they are placed before the songs.[48]

[10] *Korônis* is a sign that indicates the end of a section: when the actors exit the stage and leave the chorus alone; when they reenter; whenever the setting must change; or the setting and the chorus; or the entire plot; also at the beginning and end of an episode.[49]

Regarding the songs: some are set on stage, others are performed by the chorus.

[11] Of the actors, no one ever danced in a tragedy—dancing belonged exclusively to the chorus.

And later on:[50] The form of tragic dancing is the so-called *emmeleia,* just as in satyr plays it is the *sikinnis* and in comedy the so-called *kordax*.[51]

45. "A cry *extra metrum*"? So, Browning 1963: 80. See also the discussion in Perusino 1993: 83.

46. Καταλογῆς: Browning cites Hesychios, *Lexikon,* kappa.1244, which defines καταλογή as the recitation of songs without music: τὸ τὰ ᾄσματα μὴ ὑπὸ μέλει λέγειν. Related is also the term παρακαταλογή (e.g., in Aristotle, *Problemata* 918a10), which denotes "recitative, melodramatic delivery" (LSJ).

47. Following here Perusino's edition who at this point adopts a suggestion made by Glucker 1968: 270.

48. For this problematic passage, see Browning 1963: 80.

49. This presentation of the philological (more specifically: *colometric*) sign of *koronis* reflects Hephaistion's discussion in his *On Signs.* See Browning 1963: 80 and Perusino 1993: 85–87.

50. Here, we hear the voice of the excerptor. Perusino 1993: 16n5 reads this as perhaps an indication that Psellos is citing a single source; however, this may apply simply to this part of the text.

51. *Emmeleia* (not an Aristotelian term) is explained simply as a "tragic dance" in the *Suda* (epsilon.971–72). Pollux' *Onomasticon* 4.99 relates *emmeleia,* as in our text, to the comic *kordax* and the *sikinnis* of satyr plays. The phrasing of the text is closest to Aristoxenos' *On Tragic Dance,* fragment 104, Psellos' likely source in this section here; see Browning 1963: 81 and Perusino 1993: 87–88. See also Eustathios of Thessalonike, *Parekbolai on the Iliad* 4.272.8–16, where all the relevant ancient references are collected: Ἰστέον δὲ καὶ ὡς ἐκ τοῦ «μολπῆς ἐξάρχοντες ἐδίνευον» ἐρρέθη παρὰ τοῖς ὕστερον εἶδός τι ὀρχήσεως ἐμμέλεια. φησὶ γοῦν Παυσανίας, ὅτι ὄρχησίς τις ἦν τραγικὴ λεγομένη ἐμμέλεια. Αἴλιος δὲ Διονύσιός φησι καὶ αὐτός, ὅτι ἐμμέλεια τραγικὴ ὄρχησις, ὥσπερ ἡ κωμικὴ κόρδαξ καὶ ἡ σατυρικὴ σίκιννις. ἐκαλεῖτο δέ, φησίν, ἐμμέλεια καὶ τὸ

The form of this dancing was solemn and dignified, having long pauses in between movements.

[12] The tragic choruses used to sing the entrance odes with utmost solemnity, accompanied by the pipes—the best pipers used to play for them: one would play the chromatic *periodos*, another the enharmonic, and another the diatonic.

Euripides and Sophocles used the *kithara* in their tragedies.[52]

Sophocles also used the *lyra* in his *Thamyris*.[53]

ὑπὸ τὴν τραγικὴν ὄρχησιν ᾀδόμενον αὔλημα. ὁ δὲ Παυσανίας λέγει καί, ὅτι ὀρχήσεως εἶδος καὶ ὁ ξιφισμὸς καὶ σχῆμα ἐμμελείας, ὅθεν ἀποξιφίσαι τὸ ἐξορχήσασθαι, ὥσπερ καὶ ἀποφοιτᾶν παρὰ Λυσίᾳ τὸ παύσασθαι φοιτῶντα, ὅ ἐστι μανθάνοντα. Finally, *emmeleia* occupies much of Tzetzes' attention in his *On Tragic Poetry*; cf. Pace 2011.

52. For Euripides, see a similar sentiment in *To One Asking "Who Wrote Verse Better, Euripides or Pisides?"* 86–90 (cf. Perusino 1993: 90–91): [Εὐρι]πίδῃ δὲ τούτων μὲν [ἧτ]τ̣ο̣ν ἐμέλησεν, ἐπραγματεύσατο δὲ πλέον ἐκείνου περί τε τ̣[ὴν με]λοποιΐαν, φημὶ δὴ τὴν [ἐν λ]ό̣γοι̣[ς], καὶ τὴν χρῆσιν ταύτης καὶ τὰς τρεῖς ταύτας τῶν καλλίστων ἐ̣π̣ι̣στημῶν, μουσικήν τε κ̣α̣ὶ̣ ῥ̣υθμικὴν κ̣α̣ὶ̣ [μετ]ρικήν, ὥ̣σ̣περ α[ὐλοὺς καὶ] κ̣ιθάρας καὶ λύρας ταῖς οἰκείαις συναγαγὼν ὑποθέσεσι.

53. Cf. *Life of Sophocles* 24–25 (Radt 1977: 29–40). For the instruments mentioned here, see further Pickard-Cambridge 1968: 163–65.

6 *On the Different Styles of Certain Writings*

A Rhetor's Canon

Translated with introduction and notes by Stratis Papaioannou

Introduction

Though we can infer prevalent canons for rhetorical education—through the surviving manuscripts and relevant scholiastic activity—we encounter relatively few explicit and concise statements by Byzantine writers about which authors belonged in the canon and why they were considered models for emulation in the context of Byzantine education. Psellos' *On the Different Styles of Certain Writings, Περὶ χαρακτήρων συγγραμμάτων τινῶν,* is one such rare statement.[1] The text is presented in the usual Psellian manner, in first-person perspective, that is. Psellos surveys swiftly a series of classical and post-classical

1. Two other examples: Photios, *Letter* 207 to Amphilochios of Ikonion (on models of letter-writing); and the late thirteenth-c. *On the Four Parts of the Perfect Speech* (Hörandner 2012), which lists models for various genres—it should be noted that this later rhetorical canon belongs to the Psellian tradition; cf. Papaioannou 2013: 264–65. Photios' *Bibliothêkê,* a massive collection of book reviews, also offers a "canon" of authors, yet only through cumulative, unsystematized statements about style. Regarding the notion of the canon, very useful are the remarks in Hexter 2012 (dealing with medieval Latinity).

authors and texts; or rather he surveys their "χαρακτῆρες" which, as he acknowledges, he has read, used, and emulated in his own writings. By the term "χαρακτήρ," Psellos refers to individual, unique, subjective style *as well as* to an objectified mode of particular expression that can serve as a model and thus be imitated by others.

These authors, texts, and "styles"—twelve in total—are divided in two tiers: the "Muses," namely, "serious," content-oriented rhetoric, and the "Graces," playful, entertaining discourse.[2] The Muses include the following "books" (in our chronological order): Thucydides, Lysias, Plato, Isocrates, Demosthenes, Plutarch, Ailios Aristeides, and Gregory of Nazianzos.[3] Among the Graces, Psellos lists (again in our chronological order): "the book of Leukippe" (i.e., Achilleus Tatios), Lucian, Philostratos, and "the book of Charikleia" (i.e., Heliodoros).[4]

Though the list does not exhaust all the authors and texts that Psellos considered models of style, it is rather representative in its selection, arrangement, and presentation as it refracts the ideology of middle Byzantine learnedness through the lenses of a professional rhetor. Psellos chooses to present his canon as a set of subjective choices. Nevertheless, none of the names that he lists are unique or unfamiliar in the context of middle Byzantine high discursive culture. The surviving middle Byzantine manuscripts, contemporary philological work—recorded both in these manuscripts and in collections such as Photios' *Bibliothêkê* or the *Suda*—and allusions embedded in middle Byzantine rhetorical production itself confirm each and every one of Psellos' choices.[5]

2. The association of the Muses with elevated learning is a commonplace; indicative, e.g., is the relevant *Suda* entry (mu.1291): Μοῦσα: ἡ γνῶσις . . . ἁπάσης παιδείας αὕτη τυγχάνει αἰτία . . . εἰσὶ δὲ πᾶσαι ἐννέα: Κλειώ, Εὐτέρπη, Θάλεια, Μελπομένη, Τερψιχόρη, Ἐρατώ, Πολύμνια, Οὐρανία, Καλλιόπη. πολλὰς δὲ τὰς Μούσας ὑπὸ τῶν θεολόγων παραδεδόσθαι, διότι πολὺ τὸ ποικίλον ἔχει τὰ μαθήματα καὶ παιδεύματα, καὶ πρὸς πᾶσαν χρῆσιν οἰκεῖον.

3. Implicitly, the list includes also Homer, since Psellos mentions Calliope, the muse of epic poetry; however, he does not discuss Homeric style as he does with regard to the other authors of the list.

4. It is important that Psellos speaks repeatedly of "books (βιβλία)," evoking perhaps relevant practices in Byzantine book culture where the works of a single author were often collected in one book, and where, additionally, fictional narrative texts circulated under the name of the main character of the story; for this, see Papaioannou 2014b.

5. Much of this is surveyed in Papaioannou 2013, part 1, where also the earlier bibliography. For various aspects, see further Hunger et al. 1961, Lemerle 1971, Pöhlmann 1994–2003, and, for a brief overview, Gaul 2010. Both Photios' *Bibliothêkê* and the *Suda*

The origins of these choices are pre-Byzantine. The basic classical core for this list reproduces the canon of names (Homer, Thucydides, Lysias, Plato, Isocrates, Demosthenes, along with a few others) assembled in the last chapters of Hermogenes' *On Forms*, which provided the most important canon for Byzantine rhetoricians such as Psellos.[6] This earlier canon has been expanded in order to include Greek writing of the Imperial Period (Plutarch and Ailios Aristeides; Achilleus Tatios, Lucian, Philostratos, and Heliodoros) as well as one Christian rhetor, Gregory of Nazianzos—all well-established favorites in middle Byzantine high rhetorical culture.[7]

It is in this last choice that Psellos' own predilections begin to come in the foreground. Three among these stand out.

(a) Elsewhere, Psellos may present additional Christian authors as models of style—most importantly in three essays included in the present volume, where Basil of Caesarea, Gregory of Nyssa, John Chrysostom, and Symeon Metaphrastes are celebrated for their discourse, rhetorical style, and philosophical content.[8] However, though in these other essays Psellos seems to satisfy the expectations of his learned Christian audience, in reality only Gregory of Nazianzos has left a deep imprint in Psellos' own rhetoric and philosophical thinking, as can be seen both by the numerous allusions to Gregory and the essays/lectures devoted to his orations. Psellos' actual models, as evident by his own texts, are mostly non-Christian: whether "serious" (especially Plato and Demosthenes) or "playful" (all four names in his list of "Graces"). This is not to say that we should discover some sort of anti-Christian/pagan worldview in Psellos. Rather, what is at work is Psellos' preference for a certain type of high rhetoric; and, in this regard, only Gregory of Nazianzos qualified among the Christian writers included in the middle Byzantine canon.[9]

---

contain entries on or references to almost all the authors listed by Psellos: for the *Bibliothêkê,* specifically, see cod. 262 (Lysias), 159 (Isocrates), 265 (Demosthenes), 245 (Plutarch), 246–48 (Ailios Aristeides), 86 (Achilleus Tatios), 128 (Lucian), 44 and 241 (Philostratos), and 73 (Heliodoros). For Photios and the ten Attic orators specifically, see Smith 1992.

6. *On Civic Discourse* = *On Forms* 2.10; *On the Simply Civic Discourse* = *On Forms* 2.11; *On the Simply Panegyrical Discourse* = *On Forms* 2.12.

7. Already in Photios; cf. Bompaire 1981.

8. *The Styles of Gregory the Theologian, Basil the Great, Chrysostom, and Gregory of Nyssa*; *On Saint John Chrysostom*; *Encomium for Kyr Symeon Metaphrastes.*

9. For all this, see Papaioannou 2013 passim.

(b) A second departure is targeted against the rhetorical canon of the Imperial Period. Unlike the tradition of rhetorical thought to which Hermogenes belonged, especially as expressed in a prominent predecessor, Dionysios of Halikarnassos, Psellos places Plato above all other classical authors.[10] This is a sentiment that Psellos articulated repeatedly, as we saw already in the essay on rhetoric excerpted from Longinos.[11] In this respect, Psellos seems indebted to Neoplatonic hermeneutics, especially Proklos, who, in his commentary on the *Republic* for instance, presented Plato as the summit of ideal style.

(c) There is also a third Psellian deviation that pertains to his admission that playful writing—Lucian, Philostratos, and the two ancient novels—is important for the creation of one's own style. As is well known, these types of texts remained nearly invisible in post-classical and late antique rhetorical theoretical discourse that formed the basis for middle and late Byzantine rhetorical education. There are no mentions of the novels or Lucianic and Philostratean discourse in contemporary rhetorical theory. These authors and texts first surface in theoretical writing only centuries later, in Photios' *Bibliothêkê* and then the scholia in middle Byzantine manuscripts. But even then, the references are enveloped in explicit reservations about the moral or ideological dangers that these texts posed for a Byzantine Christian audience.[12] Psellos perhaps reflects some of this same discontent when he argues that one should read and imitate these texts only after he has studied the Muses well. Yet, in his case, the source of the discontent is not ethics or dogma, but rather a certain rhetorical morality that requires that one covers the basics, that is, the "serious" style, first. And even in expressing his disapproval of contemporary Byzantine rhetors who indulged only in playful style, Psellos concedes that he too at first began to engage in rhetoric in the wrong order, starting first with the Graces.

Ultimately, even if playful, entertaining rhetoric should be reserved for the beautification of a discourse that is serious in its substance, Psellos propa-

10. See especially Dionysios of Halikarnassos, *On Demosthenes* 23, 25–26, and 32 where a critique of Plato's style in juxtaposition to Demosthenes, the undoubted favorite of this tradition.

11. See pp. 17 and 19 above.

12. See especially the reception of Lucian, on which see Russo 2011 where also the earlier bibliography.

gates in this essay two primary, typically Psellian, virtues/methods: mixture and variation.[13] The ideal rhetor cannot but mix the Muses with the Graces, and also constantly vary his style. In this way, χάρις, whose complex semantics—as grace, charm, appeal, and, in the plural, the Graces[14]—are maximally exploited, proves to be a *sine qua non* of ideal style and the ideal rhetor: Gregory of Nazianzos and his double, Psellos himself.

Editions and translations. The text used for this translation is Boissonade 1838: 48–52 (the numbers in brackets indicate pages from this edition); for the six manuscripts, which preserve the text (most important among them the Paris gr. 1182), editions, translations, and studies, see Moore 2005: 409.

13. See Papaioannou 2013: 100–103.

14. The minor goddesses of Greek mythology: Peitho/Persuasion, Aglaea/Splendor, and Euphro<sy>ne/Mirth—as listed in the relevant *Suda* entry: chi.123; a variation from the ancient list of Aglaea, Euphrosyne, and Thalia ("Good Cheer").

On the Different Styles of Certain Writings

Those who read the book of Leukippe and that of Charikleia, and any other book of delight and charming graces [χάριτας], such as the writings of Philostratos of Lemnos and whatever Lucian produced in a spirit of indolent playfulness, seem to me as if they had set out to build a house, but before raising and positioning walls and columns, laying the foundations, and completing the roof, they already wish to adorn the house with paintings, mosaics, and all other decoration. To the majority of people, those who work in this way seem rather successful. **[49]** Indeed, as it seems to me, some of them have even tried their hands on writing minor texts; these are turgid in diction[1] and, from the very first line, immediately thunder and leap with intensity; but then they quickly fade away, just like a flash of lightning.

In short letters and brief addresses, this manner of reading [ἀναγνώσεως] has some effect; in such texts, the handling of the parts of the text is on a small scale and the naive listener is content with conspicuous charms [χάρισι] and the fine flowers of diction.[2] In extensive writings, however, and where discourse

1. For this expression (φλεγμαίνοντα τοῖς ὀνόμασιν), see Synesios, *Letter* 5.101–2 to his brother Euoptios (perhaps Synesios' most popular letter in Byzantium, if we judge from allusions to it) and *On Dreams* 14.14–15 (on a negative type of diction that is to be avoided) with Philostratos, *Life of Apollonios* 1.17 (on Apollonios' avoidance of such a style; the phrase is repeated in Photios' *Bibliothêkê* 241 331b29–30 and in the *Suda* delta.1030 and kappa.912) and it is commented upon in the Byzantine scholia (most likely by Arethas) on Philostratos' text (Kayser 1844: 179). See Levy 1912: 41 and also pp. 129 and 173 below.

2. Or "of words" = "τῶν λέξεων" which is the variant in Escorial, gr. 220 (Φ III 1); see Criscuolo 1976: 59.

must take many forms and render the power of the creator[3] known, the flowery spring of these men's diction, which fills one's ears with honey, falls short.[4] Not every form [ἰδέα] is about charms [χαρίτων]. Rather, just as it is necessary to make certain parts of the speech pleasurable, so also one needs to render others with asperity; just as it is necessary to speak with solemnity, so also one needs to speak with more simplicity;[5] and, just as it is necessary to intensify the meaning, to build it up, and add density to it, so also one needs to relax and resolve it.

The correct handling of discourse is a matter of variation [ποικίλον τι χρῆμα]. And it proceeds in reverse order, if compared to ritual initiation. There, the preparatory ceremonies and the besprinkling with lustral water come first, and then follows the entrance to the innermost sanctuary; there, it is necessary to carry the torch first as a worshiper, and then perform the sacrifice as a priest.[6] If someone, however, might wish to become a perfect competitor in flawless rhetoric [τεχνικοῦ λόγου], then he must occupy himself first with the beehive and only then go to the flowers.

At first, I too approached the matter in this way: I flew around those kinds of books **[50]** from which I could only collect and pick dew, patina, and flower.[7]

3. τοῦ δημιουργοῦντος τὴν δύναμιν.

4. For the expression "filling one's ears with honey (καταμελιττούσης τὴν ἀκοήν)," cf. Synesios, *Dion* 2.3, and p. 132 below.

5. Allusions to the Hermogenian Forms of sweetness (γλυκύτης), asperity (τραχύτης), solemnity (σεμνότης), and simplicity (ἀφέλεια).

6. Similar metaphors with similar wording ("preparatory ceremonies and the besprinkling with lustral water" = "τὰ προτέλεια καὶ τὰ περιρραντήρια") are employed in the introductory section of a commentary to Porphyry's *Eisagoge* and Aristotle's *Categories,* attributed to a late sixth-c. Christian Neoplatonist by the name of either Elias or David, to describe the various steps in philosophical curriculum that lead from elementary instruction in logic to the perfect learning of "theology" through the middle levels of ethics ("περιρραντηρίοις") and then physics ("προτελείοις"); *Commentary on the Ten Categories of Philosophy* 121.5–19.

7. The image of the bee as a proper reader is reminiscent of Plutarch, *On Listening to Lectures* 41e–42b, and *How the Young Man Should Study Poetry* 30c–d, 32e–f, with Xenofontos 2013: 127–34 and, ultimately, Plato, *Republic* 365a (I thank Byron MacDougall for this reference). The most immediate, Byzantine echo is Basil of Caesarea's *Address to Young Men as to How They Might Benefit from Pagan Learning* 4.36–51; cf. also. Unlike Basil's or, also, Plutarch's moralizing approach, however, Psellos is not interested in the ability of the bee to disregard what is pleasing in a flower, in order to collect only what is useful. Psellos wishes to collect pleasure and exterior charm; it is only that this must be done in the right order. The reference to "patina" (correcting πίννα to πίνος) joined with "flower (ἄνθος)" echoes a passage from Dionysios of Halikarnassos' *On Demosthenes* (5), on the style of Plato.

But when my labor started to move towards my goal, I was not even able to run a short race in that way, and I was out of breath immediately after the starting line. So I took a different route, superior and with greater legitimacy. I let the Graces slip out of my hands and busied myself with the Muses, neglecting none of them, neither the one that governs prose nor Calliope herself.[8] Among such books, Demosthenes, Isocrates, Aristeides, and Thucydides were most valuable to me. In this list, I included Plato's dialogues, all of Plutarch, whatever has been found of Lysias, and our own theologian Gregory, whom I consider the ultimate summit of excellence in seriousness [σπουδῆς] as well as charming Graces [χαρίτων].

From Demosthenes, I collected his fullness of meaning and intensity in each and every topic and the perfect handling [οἰκονομία] of the parts of a speech. From Isocrates, his natural expression,[9] his mature grace,[10] and the use of common words. From Aristeides, the pleasure that, unnoticeably, envelops his force [δεινότης], the precision of his arguments, and his most productive construction of elaborations and enthymemes.[11] From Thucydides, his innovative tongue and the dense accumulation of thoughts; also the fact that his writing, though misshapen, is full of intellect; and the composition that does not pursue novelties;[12] **[51]** and the varied form of his thoughts. Plutarch traversed for me all charms of diction and every periodic and harmonious thought; he also enchanted me, both when he narrates with simplicity, and,

8. Calliope is the Muse of heroic poetry, the muse of Homer. The reference to Clio, the Muse who "governs prose" or, literally, "loose [λελυμένης] diction," seems to echo Dionysios of Halikarnassos' praise of Lysias for being like a "poet," though with a diction "freed from meter" (*On Lysias* 3.36–41; elsewhere, Psellos cites directly from this essay of Dionysios: see *Letter* 17.41–46, Maltese). For the juxtaposition of Muses to the Graces, see the introduction above.

9. Against Dionysios of Halikarnassos who explicitly argues that Isocrates does not show the "natural and simple" manner of composition as Lysias; cf. *On Isocrates* 2 with Hörandner 1995–96: 341. This is a feature that Psellos also associates with John Chrysostom; see p. 168 below.

10. Psellos associates "elderliness" with "instruction" (cf. *Chronographia* 7.169: on Michael VII Doukas), both virtues associated with Isocrates in Hermogenes' *On the Simply Civic Discourse* = *On Forms* 2.11.9.

11. Psellos borrows these terms from "Hermogenes," *On Invention* 3.5–9.

12. In this phrase, Psellos seems to appreciate innovation at the level of diction ("innovative tongue"), but not at the level of syntax/composition ("composition that does not pursue novelties") and, as we read later on in the same text, content: "*without* . . . falling into novelties in *thought*."

alternatively, when he expresses meaning in varied ways. I used Lysias' arts as merchandise for every discursive transaction. Above all, however, the Muse, lyre, Grace, trumpet, and thundering voice of the Theologian satisfied me in the stead of anyone else's eloquence.

Whenever I wanted to conceal and amass density of meaning in my writing, Thucydides' speeches sufficed for me. For the arrangement and rhetorical organization of a speech, I would use Demosthenes' arts as my model. The Isocratic style was sufficient for me to express a subject in a natural fashion, without speaking in paradoxes and thus falling into novelties in thought. As for Plato, he is divine, but also difficult to imitate; whatever he appears to approach with ease because of his clarity, was lofty and steep for me. Indeed, those who compare the man to the writings of Lysias and Thucydides and then attempt to make him follow in their steps seem to me to have read him wrongly.[13] If Gregory, great in both virtue and eloquence, did not challenge Plato in both respects, I would grant to the latter the position of being beyond, so to speak, comparison with any other philosopher and rhetor, as far as discourse is concerned.

After I had obtained enough from these men, **[52]** I needed to add also charming grace [χάριτος] to discursive grandeur. It is then that I collected for my complete equipment also books like those of Charikleia and Leukippe and any other similar book. And if indeed I might also say something about myself: I am inferior to the stylistic virtue and power of all of these authors. My discourse, however, is varied and adorned [ποικίλλεται] by all of them and their individual contributions blend into a single form. I am one from many; yet if someone reads my books, many from one might appear.

13. Psellos may have in mind Dionysios of Halikarnassos and his criticism of Plato's style; see especially *On Demosthenes* 23, 25–26, and 32.

7 *The Styles of Gregory the Theologian, Basil the Great, Chrysostom, and Gregory of Nyssa*

Translated with introduction and notes
by Stratis Papaioannou

Introduction

The following essay expands the rhetorical canon presented in *On the Different Styles of Certain Writings,* perhaps to the point of contradiction, since this essay insists on the superiority of several Christian rhetors, and not just Gregory of Nazianzos. But such "contradictions" are only for modern eyes; there is, after all, no unified system in Psellos' rhetorical canon. In the essay translated below, Psellos uses Dionysios of Halikarnassos and elements of Hermogenian theory, in order to elevate the three Cappadocian Fathers—Gregory of Nazianzos, Basil of Caesarea, and Basil's brother, Gregory of Nyssa—along with John Chrysostom into masters of rhetoric that could function, indeed supplant, classical and postclassical authors as models of style.[1]

One important concern of Psellos in *The Styles* is to strike a delicate balance. This is his main point: though the earlier, pagan—for which Psellos

1. This task is explored more extensively by Psellos in the two, lengthier essays devoted to Gregory of Nazianzos' and Chrysostom's style, also included in this present volume.

uses the typical Byzantine term Ἕλληνες ("Greek")[2]—authors provided the horizon through which the rhetorical eloquence of the Christian rhetors can be appreciated, explained, and understood, Psellos' Gregory and his peers did not actually *imitate* their non-Christian predecessors. The argument is thus twofold and coheres not only with a desire to elevate the Byzantine tradition against the classical one, but also with Psellos' own preoccupation with unique individuality. He thus claims (a) that the Christians are perfect rhetors according to (though *not* because of) the measures of the Greek *art* of rhetoric and (b) that, simultaneously, they are perfect by *nature,* by their own individual skill and talent.

The latter part of the argument is notable in that it does not mention what could have been the obvious and simple difference between Christian and pagan writers, namely, that the Christians are divinely inspired—as, for instance, Photios had asserted earlier and Ioannes Mauropous implied in Psellos' own time.[3] Psellos, that is, does not retreat to theological views—even if he calls Gregory the "Theologian" and Chrysostom the "Golden Lyre of the Spirit" and praises Gregory of Nyssa for his interpretation of the scripture. Rather, it is rhetorical aesthetics that matters here, the aesthetics whose basis was primarily the Roman Greek canon of orators and rhetorical virtues (e.g., Dionysios of Halicarnassos' views of Demosthenes and Lysias). Furthermore, in its beginning, the essay is punctuated by some appropriations of the Demosthenic, self-representational voice, while it is concluded with a typical gesture, by returning to Psellos himself who expresses the wish that he too can be a rhetor whose discourse channels the virtues of all four fathers.

Typical is also the extensive space devoted again to Gregory of Nazianzos in this essay. Indeed, the image of Gregory as an ingenious author/actor is enlarged here in ways not found elsewhere in Psellos' writings. Gregory is likened to a lion who possesses not only a leonine, virile nature but also the performative/imitative/mimicking skills of monkeys and can thus adopt the character, style, and voice of different personas.[4]

The essay is addressed to an anonymous "most learned brother." He could be possibly identified with one of Psellos' closest students and friends,

2. For the problems associated with the term "pagan," adopted in my translation below, see Cameron 2011.

3. See Papaioannou 2013: 71–74.

4. See Papaioannou 2013: 122–24 for a discussion.

Konstantinos, the nephew of the patriarch Keroularios, if we take into account the fact that in its earliest manuscript, the Florence, Bibl. Med. Laur., Plut. gr. 57.40 (late eleventh or early twelfth c.; abbreviated as **L**), our text follows a letter to Konstantinos (G 21).

Editions and translations. The text is from Boissonade 1838: 124–31 (the numbers in brackets indicate these pages), though I have consulted also the Laurentianus manuscript. For the six manuscripts, as well as editions, translations, and a few studies, see Moore 2005: 406–7.

The Styles of Gregory the Theologian, Basil the Great, Chrysostom, and Gregory of Nyssa

Most learned brother,[1] you asked who and how many of those belonging to our philosophy sculpted their discourse according to the art of rhetoric, and if they are indeed worthy to compete with the likes of Lysias and Demosthenes in their logical elaborations by reference to facts, in their persuasiveness with the use of character, in their choice and arrangement of words, as well as in their use of rhetorical ornamentation and theatrical figures.[2]

1. The word "brother" is absent in **L**.

2. ταῖς τε πραγματικαῖς κατασκευαῖς καὶ ταῖς ἠθικαῖς πιθανότησι, καὶ τῇ τῶν ὀνομάτων ἐκλογῇ καὶ συνθήκῃ, ἔτι μὴν τοῖς ἐπιθέτοις κόσμοις καὶ τοῖς θεατρικοῖς σχήμασι (using the punctuation of **L**). Psellos employs here a passage from Longinos' *Art of Rhetoric* 184–88 (Patillon and Brisson 2001; fr. 48): . . . εἰ μὴ συντείναις τῇ βελτίστῃ λέξει τὰ νοήματα, καὶ ῥυθμοῖς χρήσῃ πρεπωδεστάτοις ἐκλέξει τε καὶ θέσει τῶν ὀνομάτων καὶ [πλήθει] ῥημάτων. πολλὰ γὰρ τὰ κηλοῦντα τὸν ἀκροατὴν ἄνευ τῆς διανοίας καὶ τῆς πραγματικῆς κατασκευῆς καὶ τῆς ἠθικῆς πιθανότητος. The phrase τῇ τῶν ὀνομάτων ἐκλογῇ καὶ συνθήκῃ evokes also terminology from Dionysios of Halikarnassos' *On Composition*. From Dionysios further derives Psellos' addition of ἐπίθετοι κόσμοι and θεατρικὰ σχήματα, common phrases in, e.g., Dionysios' *On Demosthenes*: 1 (rhetorical ornaments), 18 (both phrases), and 25 (theatrical figures). *On Demosthenes* 18, specifically, bears resemblance to Psellos' phrasing above: οὐχ ἅπαντα δέ γε τὰ πράγματα τὴν αὐτὴν ἀπαιτεῖ διάλεκτον, ἀλλ' ἔστιν ὥσπερ σώμασι πρέπουσά τις ἐσθής, οὕτως καὶ νοήμασιν ἁρμόττουσά τις ὀνομασία. τὸ δ' ἐκ παντὸς ἡδύνειν τὰς ἀκοὰς εὐφώνων τε καὶ μαλακῶν ὀνομάτων ἐκλογῇ καὶ πάντα ἀξιοῦν εἰς εὐρύθμους κατακλείειν περιόδων ἁρμονίας καὶ διὰ τῶν θεατρικῶν σχημάτων καλλωπίζειν τὸν λόγον οὐκ ἦν πανταχῇ χρήσιμον.

Well, in answer to your inquiry, I say that **[125]** our circle[3] of authors who zealously strived for eloquence is large. Of the entire chorus, I place four in the lead: the trumpet of theology, Gregory; his friend, the Great Basil; the one who shared with Basil the same parents, Gregory; and the Golden Lyre of the Spirit. Each of them, on his own, could stand comparison with any pagan sophist you like. It is not that they are superior to every pagan writer in every respect. Rather, in certain aspects, each of them can compete with the best of the pagans; in other aspects, they might lag behind (one must speak the truth); but, in most instances, they would outstrip their opponents.

Indeed, I will not make the same mistake as those judges of the two sides who, following their own whim, did not cast their vote according to each rhetor's proper measure, but, just as they despised the belief of the pagans, so also they detested their discourse. They thus set themselves against the pagans and, purposefully siding with their own, turned the pagan writers away as foreign. I will not do that; I am not that deluded.[4] Rather, since they too possess discursive authority and have contributed a great portion, either by the art of rhetoric itself or through discursive powers unknown to that art, I will set up the contest appropriately, ranking each against his proper opponent; and then I will cast my vote—with only the following as my premise:[5] whatever Demosthenes is for the opposing side, I mean the pagans, this is what the Theologian Gregory is for us.

Gregory the Theologian

From the three genres of rhetoric, Demosthenes is most **[126]** accomplished in judicial rhetoric and, compared to the rest, most forceful [δεινότατος] in

3. κύκλος: the term is reminiscent of Philostratos, *Lives of the Sophists* 2.32.

4. οὐ δὴ ποιήσω τοῦτο ἐγώ· οὐχ οὕτω τετύφωμαι. From Demosthenes, *On the Crown* 11.4–5: οὐ δὴ ποιήσω τοῦτο· οὐχ οὕτω τετύφωμαι. Psellos uses the same phrase also in K-D 186 and in *To Those Who Argue that Man Is Not Good by Nature (An Essay in Improvised Fashion)* = *Phil. min.* II 17 (82.22; the references are not cited by the editors). For the importance of this Demosthenic text (promoted also by Hermogenes' *On Forms*) for Psellian self-representation, see Papaioannou 2013: 133, 147, and 167.

5. τοσοῦτον ὑπειπών. Again from Demosthenes, *On the Crown* 60, a passage also discussed in Dionysios of Halikarnassos' *On Demosthenes* 14 as well as Hermogenes' *On Vigor* = *On Forms* 1.10.8, and a phrase repeated elsewhere by Psellos: *On the Psalms, Their Inscriptions, etc. to the Emperor Kyr Michael Doukas* = *Theol.* II 1.30–31 and *Phil. min.* I 36.628 (neither referenced by the editor).

advisory speeches. Whenever he chooses to proclaim panegyrics, however, he is inferior compared both to himself and to the others. By contrast, Gregory not only outdid Demosthenes' eloquence [γλῶτταν] in the panegyrical form, but, in this regard, even a heavenly trumpet (if there were such a thing) could not raise its sound in competition with him.[6] As for the contests at court and those speeches where he offers advice, Gregory is capable of competing with Demosthenes. In these kinds of speech, Demosthenes' tongue [γλῶττα] at first froths with the great stream of his invective, but then seems to lose its steam and his breath wanes. As Gregory, however, advances in the contests, his discourse peaks and the conclusion of his invective is like a torrent against the person whom he censures. Moreover, he varies his agonistic discourse with alterations and metaphors; some parts he closes with shorter periods, others he opens with a period delivered in a single breath.[7]

Gregory sculpted his own discourse after the model of every Attic muse. He is fashioned, however, mostly after Aristeides,[8] and he seems to have emulated this man more than anyone else—with the difference that Aristeides' tongue thunders but does not cast bolts of lightning: he confuses every ear with his arguments, no less than Pericles upset Greece;[9] with the way he handles argumentation, he exhausts his listeners and makes everyone wish that the rhetor's voice would stop. Gregory's tongue never exhausts anyone: his eloquence in words, his well-arranged[10] **[127]** composition, and his ornate figures never let any listener tear himself away from pleasure.

Many times, Gregory's texts are filled with Lysias' eloquence, especially when he chooses to use prefaces characterized by simplicity [ἀφελῶς]—not because he curtails the grandeur [μέγεθος] of the speech purposefully, but because he is such, so to speak, by practice and nature.

Often, he eludes everyone in imitating also Thucydides' style: he moves away from common language most swiftly, but, after torturing the syntax for a short while and troubling the ears of his listeners, he is again restored back to his own style.

6. For the importance of Gregory's excellence in *panegyrical* discourse, see Papaioannou 2013: 103–24; see p. 120 below.

7. πνεῦμα: from "Hermogenes," *On Invention* 4.4; see p. 51 above.

8. That is, Aelios Aristeides.

9. Cf. Aristophanes, *Acharnians* 530–31; the phrase also in Diodoros of Sicily, *Library of History* 12.40.6 and Julian, *Letters* 31 (To Proairesios).

10. διηρμοσμένη **L**: διηρημένη Boissonade.

Whenever he pursues a solemn style [σεμνὴν φράσιν], he draws from the source of Isocrates: from there he obtains the streams of this form, but does not pour them out from an equal outlet; rather, he compresses and rounds them off,[11] "tightening the pipe" (as he himself says),[12] and not letting the stream of discourse flow without control.

Gregory adopts also the muses of Herodotus, but does not lose himself in petty detail as Herodotus does; rather, Gregory renders the muses authoritative and solemn.

Just because Gregory has been fashioned from many rhetors does not mean that the influence of each is separated into distinct parts of his speeches. Rather, just as mixed colors create a new form, different from them and, in some cases, better than the originals themselves, so also the color of Gregory's discourse is adorned by countless colors, yet it is something different, and far superior to them. For the extremities are not always better than the middle, but in some cases the latter rules over the combination of both extremes.

[128] His discourse, I argue, is not an aggregate of foreign and disparate elements. Rather, it is both uniform in nature, like the rose rising from the womb of the earth along with its natural color, and also multiform, if one were able to divide the color (as if it were some kind of mixture) into different tones and shades from which one might artistically reproduce it.

Let us therefore suppose a lion were to appear, who, while keeping his[13] virile brow and never descending from his dignified rank, could attune himself to the character and figure of other beasts and imitate them all, just as we see monkeys at the ready to imitate both those inferior and superior. The divine Gregory would be exactly such a creature. His discourse is everything that the lion is by nature: dignified, formidable, imposing, and all but unapproachable to the many. But then again, he also imitates the sound of every beast and transforms himself into the form, character, figure of each, while weaving his own roar into each new voice.[14] By contrast, each among the

11. Qualities that Dionysios of Halikarnassos attributes to Lysias as opposed to Isocrates; *On Isocrates* 11; cf. *On Lysias* 13.

12. Gregory of Nazianzos, *On the Son* = *Or.* 29.1: ἵν' εὐσύνοπτα γένηται τὰ λεγόμενα . . . καὶ μὴ τῷ μήκει τοῦ λόγου διαχεθῇ τὰ νοούμενα, καθάπερ ὕδωρ οὐ σωλῆνι σφιγγόμενον, ἀλλὰ κατὰ πεδίου χεόμενον καὶ λυόμενον.

13. I keep here the gender of the Greek. The lion's "maleness" is especially important as in the Greek it is juxtaposed with the "monkeys" for whom Psellos uses the feminine article.

14. Cf. Papaioannou 2013: 122–24.

pagan rhetors adapted himself to a single form of discourse (whether lofty, middle, or plain)[15] and is fashioned by that alone.

Such, then, is Gregory's discourse. And he can compete against every rhetor—including those not mentioned above. For rhetors who came later took after those mentioned; and in the case of rhetors who preceded them, the images were better than the prototypes.

Basil the Great

The Great Basil, just as he disregards all earthly matters, so also seems to dismiss **[129]** the artificial ornaments of rhetoric.[16] He wishes to be himself some kind of rhetorical manual; yet his texts are not fashioned after the art of rhetoric. He has read the rhetors, indeed all of them; and he drew from them the power of the speech-writing style.[17] Still, in this respect, he superseded them by far. Since he chose to not misuse discourse,[18] he does not strive much for force according to methods.[19] His discourse is unaffected; it thunders artlessly, as if from the clouds, obscuring every other voice.

15. This theory of three main types of style (χαρακτήρ or, alternatively, λέξις), the lofty/elevated/grand (ὑψηλός/ή), the plain (ἰσχνός/ή—Psellos uses this traditional term in *On John Chrysostom* 9; here, he writes: ψιλός), and the one in between them (ὁ μεταξύ τούτων), i.e., the mixed or composite (μικτή, σύνθετος), or, as Psellos calls it, the middle (μέσος) style, derives ultimately from Dionysios of Halikarnassos (*On Demosthenes* 1–7, also 33–34, and passim) who, influenced by the Peripatetic preference for "the mean" (μεσότης), identified this third type as the best; cf. de Jonge 2008: 35 and 258 with further bibliography; Psellos' terminology is reflected also in the *Suda* (chi.94), that cites Markellinos (fourth c. CE?), *Life of Thucydides* 39: Χαρακτῆρες λόγων φραστικῶν ὑψηλός, ἰσχνός, μέσος. Cf. also Ioannes Doxapatres, *Rhetorical Homilies on Aphthonios' Progymnasmata* 141.9–15: χαρακτῆρες δέ εἰσι τρεῖς, ἁδρός, ταπεινός, μέσος· ἁδρὸς μὲν οὖν ἐστιν ὁ κομπηρὰς ἔχων λέξεις, νοῦν δὲ ταπεινόν, ὡς ἔχει τὰ τοῦ Λυκόφρονος· ταπεινὸς δὲ ὁ νοῦν μὲν ἔχων ὑψηλόν, λέξεις δὲ ταπεινάς, ὡς τὰ τοῦ θεολόγου· μέσος δὲ ὁ μήτε νοῦν ὑψηλὸν ἔχων μήτε λέξεις κομπηράς, ἀλλ' ἀμφότερα μέτρια, οἷά εἰσιν ὡς ἐπὶ τὸ πλεῖστον τὰ τοῦ Χρυσοστόμου. For the rather fluid conception of the three levels of style in Byzantium, see Ševčenko 1981.

16. τῶν ἐπιθέτων τῆς τέχνης κόσμων: see n. 2 above.

17. λογογραφικὴ ἰδέα: for this collocation, explained as discursive "expression" (ἑρμηνεία), cf. Ammonios, *Comm. on Aristotle's On Interpretation* 4.27–5.1.

18. Cf. Plato, *Gorgias* 483a: κακουργεῖς ἐν τοῖς λόγοις. The same phrase in *Theol.* I 98.47 (on Greg. Naz. *Or.* 43.1; translated below p. 162).

19. An allusion to the title of "Hermogenes'" *Method of Force*.

The way he handles breath is like Demosthenes (just to give you an image of it; for his does not in fact imitate him); indeed, Basil's way is unrivaled, if one were to set their speeches in comparison.

His form of argumentation could be described following Aristeides' model; however, if one were to listen both of them, he would either be immediately worn out by the rhetor or turn to someone's else's voice, while he would find increasingly more pleasure in the thunder of Basil's speeches and would start dancing to their echo.

Gregory of Nyssa

Such is also Gregory, his brother. Indeed, I know of no other rhetor who is more grandiloquent than these two. Yet, what Gregory of Nyssa is to the other rhetors, so is the Great Basil to him. For his brother's tongue is like a flute compared to the trumpet of Basil; but compared to Demosthenes, Aristeides, and their likes, one would call Gregory a trumpet. **[130]** He is much inferior to Basil in panegyrics. When he wishes to unveil the divine oracles and the hidden truths of scripture, however, he stands on his own, having nothing to fear next to Basil; if you compare them in this, you would not grant Basil the victory in every respect.

John Chrysostom

John of the Golden Tongue, though divine in virtue and beyond compare, has not neglected discourse, just as he neglected everything else. Rather, he is a true icon of rhetoric.[20]

His speeches are composed of every form and he is a great master of the civic discourse [πολιτικοῦ λόγου] and handles each of the genres of rhetoric with skill. He knows well the voices of opposition;[21] he knows well also the beauty of the panegyrical style.

He is also shaped in various ways in his advisory speeches, not using the art of rhetoric as some kind of canon for this effect, but rather becoming himself a canon of this form for others.

20. τῆς τέχνης . . . ἄγαλμα.
21. That is, judicial rhetoric.

He does not imitate Lysias, the rhetor; but his discourse is fashioned after Lysias' eloquence—except that the latter is simpler, while John is more forceful and brilliant [λαμπρότερος]. He does not elevate his speech through metaphors, allegories, and circumlocutions, nor through bacchic and dithyrambic words,[22] but through his harmonious composition and the dignity [ἀξίωμα] of his style.

As for me, I would dearly love to proclaim panegyrics like the Theologian Gregory, speak brilliantly like the Great Basil, interpret the divine sayings like Gregory of Nyssa, and, like the Golden Lyre of the Spirit, have his stature in advisory speeches, **[131]** while sweetening my discourse with simple and ineffable charms.

22. From Philostratos, *Lives of the Sophists* 1.19 (on Niketes of Smyrna): ὑπόβακχος δὲ καὶ διθυραμβώδης.

8 An Encomium of Gregory of Nazianzos' Style

Translated with introduction and notes by Stratis Papaioannou

Introduction

The *Discourse Improvised to the Bestarchês Pothos Who Asked Him to Write about the Style of the Theologian* is, arguably, a manifesto of Psellian discursive aesthetics, indeed a manifesto of learnedness for the middle Byzantine educated elite in general. Addressed to a member of the Constantinopolitan low aristocracy, it surveys in exquisite rhetoric the style of *the* model author of the early Byzantine past, Gregory of Nazianzos.

Its layered, yet also extravagant eloquence frustrated modern commentators, quick to discover what they thought was merely a confused compilation of earlier rhetorical theory.[1] The essay is certainly different from the systematic Aristotle, or from Dionysios of Halikarnassos and Hermogenes who tested theories with examples. Yet amidst its encomiastic tone, and following an old tradition that aligned rhetorical aesthetics with philosophical metaphysics, Psellos' essay pursues a series of remarkable innovations in the context of premodern Greek discursive theory, perhaps of medieval literary theory altogether: the notion of the author as creator (especially: §§ 1–5, 15 and 23–25), authorial versatility and the implication that the author is like an actor, per-

1. Cf. Mayer 1911: 60–61.

forming characters and their emotions in his texts (§§ 37–46 and 55–57), and the promotion of readerly pleasure and material beauty rather than moral benefit or learning (§§ 6–24). These innovations are easy to miss, both by the way that they are hidden behind an eclectic selection of allusions and quotations to earlier rhetorical and philosophical theory, and by the way they expand on little studied aspects of middle Byzantine rhetorical aesthetics.[2]

In his usual strategy, Psellos hides behind the mask of tradition. Dionysios of Halikarnassos is his most immediate front—a choice in itself remarkable, given the prevalence of Hermogenes in contemporary rhetorical instruction. Along with Dionysios and his *Demosthenes*, the following are also important for this Psellian text: Synesios of Kyrene's *Dion,* some Hermogenes, and, to a lesser extent, Philostratos' *Lives of the Sophists*. Moreover, Psellos has incorporated in this essay Neoplatonic philosophical frameworks and, in key moments, ancient novelistic discourse. As expected in an essay about style, the rhetoricians provided Psellos with the vocabulary to describe Gregory's diction, composition, and stylistic virtues. The Neoplatonists (especially Proklos), however, allowed Psellos to further articulate his view of the ontology of discourse: the innovative idea that ideal style is neither inspired by God (as some Byzantine authors had claimed) nor a product of imitation coupled with personal study and talent (as rhetorical manuals insisted), but is effectively a creation out of nothing by an individual genius—a modern notion before modernity. In its turn, the novelistic discourse gave Psellos the means to express the sensuality, in fact eroticism, that characterizes the interaction between reader and author, or rather between reader and literary language—a postmodern view before postmodernism.[3]

Even the use of earlier rhetorical theory is manipulated to fit new arguments. On the surface, the main message is unambiguous, yet perhaps unsurprising and thus perhaps of little importance due to its ideological weight in a Byzantine context: Gregory is by far superior to any earlier author of the rhetorical canon. Similarly, Plato is used as the most important ancient figure for the sake of comparison, since, for Psellos and his audience, Gregory was first and foremost a *philosopher*, not just a rhetor. When getting to the details, however, Psellos permits himself much freedom, especially towards the tradition of Dionysios, Hermogenes, and the latter's Byzantine commentators who,

2. It is not the place here to tease all this out. For a full analysis, see Papaioannou 2013, chaps. 2 and 3. See also the notes to the translation below.

3. Notably, Psellos presents himself as a *reader* of Gregory, rather than as a listener.

in the century preceding Psellos, had applied Hermogenian theory to explain and promote Gregory's rhetoric.[4] Unlike his predecessors, Psellos renders Gregory a master of primarily panegyrical discourse, the λόγος πανηγυρικός. This was the kind of discourse that Hermogenian thought (as well as Dionysian and, ultimately, Aristotelian/Platonic theory) associated with language and composition that maximized theatrics and artistic display and aimed mostly at pleasure—with Homer as the ultimate example of it. This earlier tradition preferred what in Hermogenes is termed civic, "political" discourse (λόγος πολιτικός): the judicial and advisory rhetoric that focused on persuasion and served the needs and ethics of the *polis*.[5]

It is not, of course, that Gregory lacks in "political" discourse, which in this essay is synonymous with rhetoric in general. In Psellos' view, Gregory remains "ethical" in all the Byzantine senses of the word: morally upright, instructing morality to his audience, and representing good character in his rhetoric. He also provides knowledge—indeed universal knowledge, not just *theological* knowledge (§§ 26–33). But for Psellos, Gregory incorporates also what in earlier writing—notably in the speeches of Gregory of Nazianzos himself—was considered consistently inferior and, sometimes, reprehensible and dangerous: the rhetorical theatrics of panegyrical discourse.

These views, which are created through an accumulation of images, metaphors, and allusions, and a manipulation of technical jargon, address a specific audience. Pothos, the immediate addressee, was a student and later friend of Psellos, the son of an earlier acquaintance, who held the military office of *megas droungarios*. Tutored by Psellos, Pothos had a career as tax collector and provincial judge, and accordingly increased his social and material capital.[6] The *Discourse . . . on the Style of the Theologian* was written for Pothos at an un-

4. Especially in the Ioannes Sikeliotes' *Commentary* on Hermogenes' *On Forms*; see Conley 2003 and Bady 2010.

5. See further Papaioannou 2013: 103–13.

6. A *patrikios*, Pothos, commissioned a ten-volume copy of the *Menologion* of Metaphrastes, of which one volume, the *Patmensis* 245 dated to 1057 and covering the month of January, survives today; Komines 1968: 5–6. Apart from the *Discourse . . . on the Style of the Theologian,* several other texts addressed to Pothos by Psellos have been preserved: another essay titled *To the Bestarchês Pothos Who Asked Who Is beyond Encomia* (*Or. min.* 15; it follows the *Discourse* in Paris gr. 1182) as well as twenty-five letters (in some of these, Pothos is addressed as *magistros*, a title higher than that of *bestarchês*).

known date.[7] It provided him and, we might suppose, a wider circle of friends, students, and associates, since such texts circulated beyond the immediate addressee, a thorough yet concise justification of high rhetoric.

The *Discourse* thus produced a double effect. On the one hand, by identifying high rhetoric with Gregory of Nazianzos, Psellos expressed an ideology of learnedness and an aesthetics of urbanity that was to be shared by, and, simultaneously, became obligatory for, the Constantinopolitan elite; the image of Gregory's style as a precious artistic object that parallels the likely conspicuous consumption of Pothos (§§ 6–24) is the most potent expression of this ideology and aesthetics. On the other hand, the essay provided the ideal pretext for Psellos' claim that he could offer the best instruction as well as discursive entertainment to this elite. For, ultimately, as with most of the texts in the present volume, and also in most of the texts that served as Psellos' model in this essay (most notably Synesios' *Dion*), behind the author's ideal writer (i.e., Gregory) lay the author's (i.e., Psellos') own self-portrait.

To the extent that we can judge, the text was successful. It survives in thirteen manuscripts, a large number for Psellos and texts of this kind. Among these manuscripts, we find not only Psellian collections (such as the Paris, gr. 1182), but also a manuscript of Gregory of Nazianzos' works, which suggests that for some readers Psellos' became a useful appendix to the rhetorical corpus of the church father. This manuscript is the Vatican, BAV, Palatinus gr. 402, an expensive parchment book. In the late eleventh-century, the full corpus of Gregory's *Orations* along with marginal notes, Ioannes Geometres' scholia to *Orations* 1 and 45, as well as Geometres' *Encomium* for Gregory were copied in the Palatinus. Sometime later, likely during the twelfth century, another quire

7. Two pieces of evidence suggest that the essay was written late in Psellos' career, perhaps in the 1060s or early 1070s: (a) in one of his lectures on Gregory of Nazianzos, which date likely in the 1050s (*Theol.* I 98.133–34; see p. 166 below), Psellos announces that, in the future, he plans to write a comprehensive essay on Gregory's style; and (b) in four of its transmitting mss. (the earliest among them: Venice, Bibl. Naz. Marc., gr. 524, late thirteenth c.), the *Discourse* is followed by Psellos' letter S 86, a text of learned instruction addressed to Konstantinos, the nephew of the Patriarch Keroularios. Since most of the letters to Konstantinos date to the 1060s and 1070s and since mss. often retain some chronological order within their Psellian collections, perhaps the *Discourse* is to be set in the same period.

was added with the life of Gregory by Gregory the presbyter and Psellos' *Discourse* (ff. 380v–387v).[8]

The text proceeds in the following order. Psellos introduces Gregory as the ultimate model of rhetoric (§§ 1–7), while addressing an issue common in prefaces to rhetorical treatises: the origin of ideal discourse—Hermogenes' *On Forms* but also earlier texts such as Isocrates' *Against the Sophists*, Aristotle's *Poetics*, and Longinos' *On Sublimity* are good examples of the practice of starting with this issue. Then Psellos turns to a detailed discussion of Gregory's word selection and word arrangement (§§ 8–25), which is followed by a digression on the varied content of Gregory's discourse (§§ 26–33). Gregory's treatment of the three genres of rhetoric (deliberative, judicial, and, especially, panegyrical: §§ 33–34) is discussed next, along with some general remarks on Gregory's paradoxically lucid obscurity, his mixture of stylistic virtues (i.e., the Hermogenian forms), and his figurative style (§§ 47–54). Psellos concludes with a brief review and an epilogue addressed to Pothos (§§ 56–57).

Editions and translations. The Greek text used is that of Levy 1912, but the Mayer 1911 edition has also been taken into consideration—in brackets, I give the paragraph number as divided in Levy, followed by the line numbers from Mayer. For further editions and translations, see Moore 2005: 404–5.

The notes below do not comment on every single technical term and much of the annotation repeats information presented and discussed in Papaioannou 2013 passim. Levy and Mayer provide more detailed commentary, though they have missed several references (especially those to Neoplatonic discourse) and sometimes identified doubtful allusions.[9] For the reader's convenience, titles of sections have been added.

I would like to thank Alessandra Bucossi, Elizabeth Fisher, Nadezhda Kavrus-Hoffman, Manolis Patedakis, Alice-Mary Talbot, and especially Börje Bydén for a long afternoon session in the fall of 2007, when an early draft of the following translation was discussed.

8. See Tacchi-Venturi 1893 with Sajdak 1914: 91–95 and Mossay and Hoffmann 1996: 185–87. For the ms. transmission of Psellos' *Discourse* on the style of Gregory, see further Mayer 1911: 30–47 and, for a better review, Levy 1912: 1–21; cf. also the list in Moore 2005: 405–6.

9. For example, Mayer (1911: 74) discovers some echoes of the rhetorician Demetrios in Psellos.

Discourse Improvised by the Hypertimos Psellos, Addressed to the Bestarchês Pothos, Who Requested of Him to Write about the Style of the Theologian[1]

Introduction

[§ 1; 1–5] My dearest Pothos, do not be amazed that I have reduced the number of sophists and philosophers and attempted to limit the entire art and power of discourse to a single man, while the rhetors before me identified the individual style of each sophist and philosopher (those attentive to language) with a view to general elegance of expression.[2] **[§ 2; 5–18]** Those rhetors had

1. The reference to supposed improvisation is common in Byzantium; see, e.g., Cavallo 2006: 61–62; for the addressee of the text, see the introduction above.

2. For the expression "power [δύναμις] of discourse," cf. Gregory of Nazianzos, *Funeral Oration for Basil of Caesarea* = *Or.* 43.1 together with the introductions to Dionysios of Halikarnassos' *Roman Antiquities* (1.1.3) and Diodoros of Sicily's *Library of History* (1.2.5). For the distinction between sophists and philosophers, see Synesios, *Dion* 1 with Philostratos, *Lives of the Sophists* 479–84; see also Gregory of Nazianzos, *Or.* 43.14 (on the presence of the best rhetors and philosophers in Athens) and *On Himself and to Those Who Claim that It Was He Who Wanted the See of Constantinople* = *Or.* 36.12 (with a negative connotation). The phrase "elegance of expression [τὸν τῆς ἑρμηνείας . . . ὡραϊσμόν]" is reminiscent of the beginning of Dionysios of Halikarnassos' *On Composition* (1) where Dionysios refers to the love for discursive beauty that

not seen all the virtues of <diction and> action gathered in a single man, but had observed different virtues in different authors; and still they did not wish to provide a half-finished evaluation of style, but, rather, a complete and comprehensive one.[3] They thus collected different contributions from different authors to obtain the generic form. From Plato, for example, they gathered his dialogical phrasing; from the Socratic Aeschines they took his melodious composition; from Thucydides his sublimity and loftiness of thought; from Herodotus his all-harmonious rhythm; from Isocrates his adaptability in epideictic and panegyrical speeches; from Demosthenes his bitterness in judicial contests as well as his intellect and fullness of grandiloquence[4] and breath; from the Asianic Polemon, Herodes of Marathon, the Ephesian Lollianos, and the others who excelled in discourse, they gathered that quality particular to each one's own person and nature.[5]

[§ 3; 18–26] I, by contrast, was more fortunate than they were. I witnessed a man who was above all others, the man whose name is synonymous with theology—I mean Gregory. In his own texts, he mixed the outstanding features of each one of those authors in a more exact fashion. The result: he does not

---

characterizes the impulsive yet inexperienced youth: "ἐπτόηται γὰρ ἅπασα νέου ψυχὴ περὶ τὸν τῆς ἑρμηνείας ὡραϊσμόν."

3. ἐβούλοντο δὲ μὴ ἡμιτελῆ τὴν κρίσιν τοῦ χαρακτῆρος εἰσενεγκεῖν, ἀλλὰ τελείαν καὶ ἀπηρτισμένην. Cf. Dionysios of Halikarnassos, *On Demosthenes* 8.13–14: ἡμιέργους τινὰς ἅπαντας οἰόμενος εἶναι καὶ ἀτελεῖς.

4. μεγαλοφωνία: cf. Psellos, *Theol.* I 68.130 (on Greg. Naz. *Or.* 39.12; the term is applied again on Gregory) with Gregory of Nazianzos, *Funeral Oration for Basil* = *Or.* 43.1, 68, and 76 and *Letter* 46 (all references to Basil of Caesarea), and also Proklos, *Comm. on the Timaeus* 1.62.15 (on Socrates). Nowhere, as far as I can tell, is the term explicitly associated with Demosthenes.

5. In mentioning the various authors that preceded Gregory, Psellos combines several Roman Greek lists of canonical authors with a special debt to Dionysios of Halikarnassos as well as Hermogenes (to these two Psellos owes: Plato, Aeschines, Thucydides, Herodotus, Isocrates, Demosthenes) and Philostratos (from whom: Aeschines, Polemon [ca. 90–144 CE], Herodes Attikos [ca. 101–177 CE], Lollianos [second c. CE]); see further Mayer 1911: 64–71. Psellos consciously downplays here the primacy of Demosthenes actually evident in both Dionysios and Hermogenes. Acknowledging Demosthenes' primacy in previous rhetorical theory would have undermined Psellos' assertion that he is the first to focus on a singular author in order to define generic style. Elsewhere, Psellos admits that he follows Hermogenes in this respect; cf. *In Support of the Nomophylax [=Ioannes Xiphilinos] against Ophrydas* = *Or. for.* 3.279–82 and *On the Theologian's Phrase: "even though you ought <to reap> the opposite fruit through the opposite"* = *Theol.* I 19.81–84 (on Greg. Naz. *Or.* 40.24).

seem to have collected these features in emulation of them.[6] Rather, he himself became through his own will an archetypal image of discursive charm [ἀρχέτυπον λογικῆς χάριτος ἄγαλμα].[7] Therefore, setting aside the others' forms of discourse, I chose to describe to you the style only of him and to dedicate this study to no one else but you; even though, as you know, many have urged me to do so. Having promised this long ago, I am now honored to present it to you.

[§ 4; 27–38] That great man had received the first principles of philosophy from on high, by lifting his mind up toward the incorporeal and divine forms and taking a portion of the streams of knowledge from that unitary source.[8] One might then suppose that he also seized the beauty and power of his discourse in an ineffable way from some heavenly source and mixed it with his writings according to harmonies of a superior music. This would be a novel idea,[9] and one would then have to add to the heavenly sources, which have already been enumerated, a source also for discourse.[10] From this source, then, in addition to the others, Gregory drew his fill and poured the rivers of his discursive charm over us.

6. μὴ . . . κατὰ ζῆλον ἐκείνων. Cf. Dionysios of Halikarnassos, *On Demosthenes* 8.13–14: ἑνὸς μὲν οὐθενὸς ἠξίωσε γενέσθαι ζηλωτὴς οὔτε χαρακτῆρος οὔτε ἀνδρός ("he did not deem it worthy to emulate any style or any man"). Psellos claims a similar status for John Chrysostom, who, though late in the history of rhetoric, did not imitate others (*On John Chrysostom* § 3–5; see text 10 in this collection).

7. ἀρχέτυπον ἄγαλμα: cf. Heliodoros, *Aethiopian Tale* 2.33.3 (on the beauty of the main female protagonist, Charikleia, who, "just like an archetypal image, attracted every eye and every mind"). Psellos alludes to the same phrase also in *Theol.* I 48.32–43 (on Greg. Naz. *Or.* 40.2). λογικὴ χάρις: before Psellos, the expression usually indicates the "divine gift of reason"; so, e.g., Gregory of Nyssa, *On the Creation of Man* 144.33–34, and, later, Photios, *Amphilochia* 149.13–14. After Psellos, the term often indicates "discursive charm"; see, e.g., Psellos' student Theophylaktos (*Letters* 28.17–18). In general, the Greek term χάρις is translated throughout as charm (a common notion in non-Christian aesthetic vocabulary: see, e.g., Dionysios of Halikarnassos, *On Demosthenes* 13.9), except when Psellos is clearly alluding to Christian "grace."

8. ἑνιαῖα πηγή: cf. Proklos, *Platonic Theology* 5.118.4 and *Comm. on the Timaeus* 1.446.30 with Photios, *Amphilochia* 181.114–16 (on the holy Trinity).

9. "Idea" translates here "νόημα," the reading of the mss. adopted by Mayer (1911); Levy (1912) proposes (perhaps correctly) "νᾶμα" (stream, spring).

10. In middle Byzantine writing, we encounter the idea that rhetoric, as form and style distinct from content, originates directly from God. The earliest attestation of such a notion is found in Photios, who argues the superiority of Paul's discursive "wisdom, power, and force" over that of the ancient rhetors; the origin of this superior rhetorical style (and not just content) is divine "grace" (*Letter* 165; cf. Kustas 1961–62 and 1962; Afinogenov 1995). Comparable ideas are encountered in the eleventh century; cf. Ioannes

If however nothing but the divine exists in heaven and all the other kinds of beauty are imitations of those heavenly things and flow from first principles in the soul or in nature,[11] even so this amazing man appears to have obtained what is beyond nature. **[§ 5; 38–45]** For Gregory achieved what no one had ever achieved by himself, not even with regard to particular virtues. Without emulating the ancients, he opened up each and every stream from a source within himself,[12] channeled them into one discursive set of pipes, turned the multitude into one, attached the highest to the middle and this in turn to the lowest,[13] then struck up a spiritual tune and sang

---

Doxapatres, *Rhetorical Homilies on Aphthonios' Progymnasmata* 83.1–93.15 (ed. Rabe); and Ioannes Mauropous, *Discourse on the Three Holy Fathers and Teachers* 108, 113, 115, 116; Mauropous' *Poem* 22.

11. By "first principles in the soul or in nature (ψυχικαί καὶ φυσικαὶ ἀρχαί)" Psellos refers to two distinct ontological levels within a Neoplatonic hierarchical chain of existence. According to this view, existence is layered in a series of ontological strata that begin in God and proceed downwards in the following order: mind, the soul, nature, body, and, finally, matter. The upper three layers, from mind to nature, are regarded as secondary causes of motion and, hence, each is seen as partially the origin of the layer immediately inferior to it—thus Psellos can speak, in the cited passage, of the "soul" or "nature" as "first principles." Psellos returns recurrently to this hierarchical scheme; see, e.g., the order of presentation in his *Concise Answers to Various Questions*: God (discussed in chapters 1–20), νοῦς (21–29), ψυχή (30–56; with four appendices 194–97), φύσις (57), and then topics relating to the body and matter (58–193). For the Neoplatonic tradition: Siorvanes 1996: part 3 (with a focus on Proklos). Psellos presents here a hypothesis that he seems to regard as unlikely; cf. Psellos, *On Eternity* 2–12 (ed. Westerink 1948: Appendix 2) on the absence of discourse in the heavenly, extra-temporal realm.

12. οἰκεία πηγή: a Proklean expression; see, e.g., *Comm. on the Timaeus* 1.319.3–9. For the metaphor of "opening up the streams," cf. also Psellos, *Chronographia* 6.42 (here on himself reopening the streams of philosophy) and, also, Gregory, *On Himself and to Those Who Claim that It Was He Who Wanted the See of Constantinople* = *Or.* 36.2 (also in the first person)—I thank Byron MacDougall for this reference.

13. Cf. Synesios' image of the perfect "philosopher" who turns "the multitude into one" and like Apollo sings "his sacred and ineffable melody" (*Dion* 5.1; with Levy 1912: 40); Psellos cites this very passage also in his *Monody in Honor of the Prôtosynkellos and Metropolitan of Ephesos Kyr Nikephoros* (K-D I 206–10; at 208.6–9). The image is also reminiscent of Plato, *Republic* 443c9–e2 where Socrates is describing the truly just man who "masters and orders himself, comes to peace with himself, and harmonizes these three principles [the three parts of the soul], as if literally the three notes: the lowest, the highest, and the middle"; cf. also Proklos (*Comm. on the Republic* 2.4.15–20), who employs the musical metaphor in order to describe the cosmic Chorus-leader who unites all with his "divine harmony."

during his life such a melody as not even the swan sings, when, as the story goes, it is about to migrate toward its own god.[14] With all this, Gregory out-voiced nature.[15]

[§ 6; 46–53] As for myself, whenever I read him—and I do this often, initially for the sake of philosophy but soon after for entertainment—I am filled with indescribable beauty and charm. On numerous occasions, I even abandon what I have been studying and, leaving behind the intended meaning of his theology and spirited away in my senses, I enjoy spring in the rose-gardens of his words. Realizing that I have been carried away, I adore my ravisher and cover him with kisses.[16] If I am forced to return from the phrasing to

14. On the metaphor of the swan's song see Plato's *Phaedo* 84e–85a with Levy 1912: 25 and Gregory of Nazianzos, *On His Verses* 54–57 (= *Carm.* II.1.39 = *PG* 37 1333.6–9; on himself as an old man singing his swan song) with *On Theology* = *Or.* 28.24 and *Letter* 114. See also Olympiodoros, *Comm. on the First Alcibiades* 2.29–31, 83–86 and 155–62, Anonymous, *Prolegomena to Platonic Philosophy* 1.20-38, and *Suda*'s entry on Plato (pi.1707), on anecdotal stories that identified Plato with the swan (Apollo's sacred bird) and his song; cf. Riginos 1976: 9–38. Psellos is well aware of the Neoplatonic association of Plato with Apollonian genealogy; cf. *Theol.* I 106.110–13 (on Greg. Naz. *Or.* 31.5), *Phil. min.* I 46.49 and *Phil. min.* II 19 p. 89.15–16. In one of his letters, Psellos suggests that the Platonic metaphor of the "swan's song" might apply to himself (S 176 to Aristenos, Bourtzes, and Iasites; 454.21–25).

15. Psellos uses the same image in order to describe the activity of God's creation of the world; see *Theol.* I 90.66–76 (on Greg. Naz. *Or.* 38.11). See also Psellos' *Theol.* I 69 (on Greg. Naz. *Or.* 39.13); in lines 84–94, Psellos demarcates the difference between human and divine nature in Christ: "being superior to fate, the incorporeal element is by nature superior also to nature and is rather God, who not only *out-voiced* nature, but is also himself its creator." See also *Theol.* I 7.9 (on David as a writer), *Letter* 105 (K-D 134.14–15; on Ioannes Mauropous and his ascetic practice). The reference to "out-voicing" (ὑπερφωνεῖν) might echo the beginning of Philostratos' *Lives of the Sophists* (1.484.5), a passage quoted also in Synesios' *Dion* (1.8).

16. The passage follows Byzantine "erotic" discourse. Cf. Gregory of Nazianzos, *Poem* 1.2.10; also Symeon the New Theologian, *Hymn* 24.146–54 (with Gregory of Nazianzos, *Or.* 24.9) and *Ethical Discourses* 6.21633, on "being robbed" by the senses. Cf. Prokopios of Gaza, *Declamation* 2.74–97 for an erotic scene in a "rose-garden" with Plutarch's *Amatorius* 770b that criticizes the inconsistent boy-lovers who, like soldiers, "pass the spring of the year in regions that are lush and blooming and then decamp as though from a hostile country." The expression "to cover someone with kisses" is used in the first person rarely; cf. Achilleus Tatios, *Leukippe and Kleitophon* 2.7.5 and 2.9.3; Symeon the New Theologian, *Hymn* 18.115–17; and Eumathios Makrembolites, *The Story of Hysmine and Hysminias* 3.7, 4.21, 5.11, 7.3, 9.18.

the meaning, I feel pain because I am enraptured no longer, and I lament the addition as though it were a privation.[17]

[§ 7; 53–61] The beauty of his speech is not like the one practiced by the more coarse among the sophists. Theirs is a matter of display and theater,[18] which might charm someone once, but make him grow edgy on a second encounter; for without having smoothed the edges of their lips, they ventured upon their writings with audacity rather than art.[19] Gregory's beauty, however, is not like that (far from it!). His is like the harmonious beauty of music.

Word Selection and Composition

I shall speak more plainly and, simultaneously, in more technical terms, by disentangling what is complicated so that you might obtain a better understanding with examples from simple things. **[§ 8; 61–72]** Words, my son, lie scattered about, just like (one might say) unarranged stones: different pieces lie next to one another without adding up to form a composite image nor arranged one by one into different groups according to their various characteristics. Some words are bulky;[20] they fill the jaws or, rather, strike the surrounding air and crash upon the ears of the listeners; then they raise noise within the labyrinthine ear-passages and astound the soul—I speak metaphorically in order to present you with a more vivid image. Others are smooth and even in nature,[21] without being entirely mellifluous or attractive to the ear. Finally, there are those in the middle, tuned to harmonious principles so that they neither raise noise nor offer pleasure. You might liken other words to

17. Psellos records a similar reaction, while gazing at an icon; K-D 211 (to Konstantinos, the nephew of the Patriarch Keroularios), 248.12–17—the entire letter is translated on pp. 359–60 below.

18. Cf. again Gregory of Nazianzos on his own rhetoric in *On Himself and to Those Who Claim that It Was He Who Wanted the See of Constantinople* = *Or.* 36.3—I thank again Byron MacDougall for this reference.

19. The images of improper rhetoric stem from Philostratos' *Lives of the Sophists*, but Psellos evokes them through Synesios' reading of Philostratos; cf. *On Dreams* 14.17–18 (on "smoothing") and *Dion* 3.7 (on sophistic "audacity") with the discussion in Levy 1912: 41 and 68–69.

20. εὔογκος: a term occasionally used in rhetorical theory; see, e.g., Anonymous (twelfth c.), *Comm. on Aristotle's Rhetoric* 186.6–12.

21. The combination "smooth" (λεῖος) with "even" (ὁμαλός) ultimately derives from Plato's *Timaeus* (67b), echoed in much Neoplatonic diction.

bright green stones, others to bright red stones,[22] others to stones that gleam from within,[23] and others to stones with rough surfaces.

[§ 9; 72–84] These words lie everywhere, though not all in the same place. It is the most mercantile of souls that usually collect them. Some travel to them by sea, others by land. Some import those beautiful stones from Africa, others from Europe, and others still from elsewhere. When naked, human souls are without difference; yet when they take on a body they become varied and, due to that instrument, they alter with respect to their appetites.[24] Therefore, some have come out to the land of Havilah and have acquired the "green stone" (as the Bible says somewhere) in exchange for much zeal and struggle.[25] Others have desired the stone that has the color of the air. Others have pursued the fiery stone. Still others have fallen in love with ruby.[26] Finally, the base multitude have placed on top of their headstone, like some kind of device, a minor form collected from whatever material lay at hand.

[§ 10; 85–97] That great man, however, "bought" the "highly precious pearl," since he became (in his own words) "a wholesale merchant."[27] And since it was necessary to bind it in gold and set it amidst precious stones,[28] he felt, as it were, no shame[29] at combining it with diversely colored and brilliant stones (rather than with the basest ones) and binding it with that gold stone from Suphir[30] (rather than with the worthless gold). Therefore—let me stop

22. τὰ δὲ (ὀνόματα ἀπεικάσαις ἂν) φλεγμαίνουσι (λίθοις): echoes Synesios, *Letter* 5.101–2; see p. 104 above.

23. Cf. Heliodoros, *Aethiopian Tale* 2.30.3; Levy 1912: 69.

24. The notions of the body as an "instrument" (ὄργανον) of the soul and of the differentiation of human souls according to the different bodies to which they are attached stem originally from Plato (cf. *Timaeus* 41d–42d) and are common in Byzantine philosophical discourse; for a discussion relevant to Psellos' argument here, see Proklos, *The Elements of Theology* 209.

25. Genesis 2:11–12.

26. This rare reference to ruby (παντάρβη) derives most likely from Heliodoros, *Aethiopian Tale* 8.11 and 10.14; cf. Mayer 1911: 73n4.

27. Matthew 13:45 with Gregory of Nazianzos, *Or.* 6.5 and 19.1.

28. Possibly an echo of Heliodoros, *Aethiopian Tale* 10.32.4, where, at the conclusion of the novel, the male protagonist Theagenes is crowned with a "gold crown with inlaid stones."

29. Ἀπερυθριάζω is a strongly negative word in Byzantine tradition; cf., e.g., *Suda* alpha.2204 with John Chrysostom, *In Matthaeum*, *PG* 57.426.59–61. Psellos is once proud to "put away any shame" while displaying the best of his discourse; see *Letter* 7.3–8 (Gautier).

30. Isaiah 13:12.

my excessively figurative speech—Gregory collected for the composition of his discourse those words that are round in their shape and spherical,[31] neither aimlessly extended nor overflowing,[32] but both pleasing and charming in their forms and solid as well as light in their consistency.[33] His words are unlike those collected by Thucydides the son of Oloros, Niketes from Smyrna, or Skopelianos, but rather such as those gathered by Lysias from Athens, Isocrates, Demosthenes, Aeschines the Socratic, and Plato himself.[34]

[§ 11; 97–105] I omit the various Sopatroi or Phoenixes and all the others who usurped the name "sophist" by the refuse of their words.[35] I also omit the others whom I enumerated as having excelled in their word selection—I did praise them but only in comparison with other rhetors, since in reality not even they were entirely faultless in their collection of words. In fact, they seem to me like Morning Stars, Mercuries, and the other planets, when compared to the rest of the heavenly bodies: they may be more luminous than the other sophists, yet when the sun rises over them they simply fade after rising in the early morning and traversing fifteen degrees.[36]

[§ 12; 106–12] In this respect, those who lived before the times of the Theologian and evaluated the style of individual rhetors were fortunate. Thus, I do not blame Dionysios, who ranked Lysias and Demosthenes first, nor The-

31. Cf. Ps.-Dionysios of Halikarnassos, *Art of Rhetoric* 10 = *On the Mistakes in Declamations* (on "round and spherical" prefaces); the pseudonymous *Art* is the first text included in the mid-tenth c. Paris., BNF, gr. 1741 (on which see pp. 75n2 above); the text dates likely to the early second c.; Heath 2003.

32. This last term (περιρρέοντα) is regarded as a fault in Isocrates' style by Dionysios of Halikarnassos (*Demosthenes* 18).

33. The juxtaposed combination of the words "solid (εὐπαγὴς)" and "light (κοῦφος)" exists only in Philostratos' *Heroikos* (673.10-28) in an eroticized description of the naked body of a young man.

34. Niketes and Skopelianos are Roman Greek rhetors, discussed in Philostratos, *Lives of the Sophists* 1.19 and 1.21; cf. Mayer 1911: 74. Psellos mentions these two rhetors (along with Aeschines and Plato) again in his *Praise of Italos* = *Or.* 19.81–85. The two rhetors are mentioned also by Michael Italikos in his *Discourse Spoken in Improvised Fashion to the Queen Lady Eirene Doukaina* = *Or.* 15 (Gautier 1972: 147.3–6), a likely Psellian influence.

35. τοῦ τῶν σοφιστῶν ὀνόματος ἐπεβάτευσαν: from Synesios, *Dion* 1.9 (cf. Levy 1912: 40). Phoenix is discussed in Philostratos (*Lives of the Sophists* 2.22); Sopatros, a fourth-century figure, is mentioned in Eunapios, *Lives of the Sophists* 6.2–3 (cf. Mayer 1911: 75).

36. For this description from ancient astronomy, cf., e.g., Proklos, *Comm. on Plato's Timaeus* 3.125.9–11.

ophrastos the colleague of Aristotle, nor Chrysippos the philosopher,[37] nor Longinos the critic, nor Philostratos from Lemnos who extolled many a certain Lesbonax, Hermokrates, Eudoxos, and Dion, and others who lived before them and excelled over others.[38] **[§ 13; 112–25]** Gregory, the great one, had not yet descended from heaven to arrive in this world. Or, rather, while standing in heaven, Gregory had not yet taken up his trumpet of discourse, widened his mouth, or filled the trumpet with his breath, attracting to his sound, with his grandiloquence, not only the living but also raising from the dead those natures buried in their bodies and bringing them back to life. If Eunapios, who lived after Gregory, or any other later pagan described the style of others but did not include Gregory, I wonder whether they confused his writings with those of others.[39] And if a certain Philostorgios counted Gregory among the best, claiming that the rhythm [βάσιν] of Gregory's speeches is greater than that of the rest, I am also not happy with that testimony.[40] Heaven with its beauty and grandeur is by itself sufficient to astonish every soul, even if no one praises it.[41] **[§ 14; 126–37]** As for me, I have chosen now to describe the style of the man not in order to add anything to him but in order to remove your soul from fragmenting divisions and direct it toward one concord of beauty, charm, and power.

37. It is rather unlikely Psellos knew directly the literary critical works of Theophrastos, Aristotle's student, or of Chrysippos. Dionysios of Halikarnassos names both authors in his rhetorical treatises, and it is perhaps because of this that the two names appear in Psellos' list. Mayer (1911: 76–77) suggests as Psellos' source the now-lost second book of Dionysios of Halikarnassos' *On Ancient Rhetors*.

38. Philostratos mentions Hermokrates, Eudoxos, and Dio, but not Lesbonax; that name and its association with the ridiculing of Roman Greek rhetoric Psellos might have adopted from Lucian's *On Dance* (69); see Mayer 1911: 78 with Arethas, *Scholia on Lucian* (45.69). Lesbonax is also mentioned in Photios (*Bibliothêkê* 74 52a22–23) and in the *Suda* (lamba.307).

39. On Eunapios of Sardeis, see Penella 2000.

40. Psellos' most likely source for Philostorgios is to be found in the *Suda*'s entry on Basil of Caesarea: beta.150, regarding Gregory's as well as Basil of Caesarea's superior rhythm (βάσις). Philostorgios, a late fourth-/early fifth-century church historian, wrote a continuation of Eusebios' ecclesiastical history that survives only in fragments due to Philostorgios' bad repute in Byzantium. Photios devotes one of his reviews in the *Bibliothêkê* to Philostorgios, making note of how the historian, though a heretic, admitted to Gregory of Nazianzos' high level of "learning" (*Bibliothêkê* 40 at 8b33–36).

41. For the expression "heaven with its beauty and grandeur," see Gregory of Nazianzos, *Or.* 40.41, where the expression is applied to the Trinity.

The admirable Gregory selects the parts of speech in the manner I presented. One will not find even a single word, when separating it from the rest, that is not mellifluous, well-proportioned, harmonious—I am referring to the harmony that derives from the letters, the one that the eminent Dionysios also studied[42]—florid, well-resonating, eloquent, filling one's ears with honey.[43] He then composes his first composition—let the discussion of other features wait: the arranging of *kommata* and cola, the constituent parts of every period and units delivered in a single breath[44]—in an extremely well-proportioned manner that no one who has not read Gregory could imagine even if the reader were to conjure up in his mind whatever composition he might wish. **[§ 15; 138–48]** The philosophers argue that only two things are unimaginable: intellect and God.[45] All else remains within our purview: that which concerns the substance of the soul is only dimly comprehensible, while nature and bodies subordinate to nature are more manifest.[46] Gregory's composition is like the intellect and God as it too falls beyond and outside our imagination.[47]

Do not think that what I said is just words.[48] With simply a collection of the most beautiful words, one is not prepared for eloquence. Take the case of a builder: he would not consider merely his collection of building materials enough for the most beautiful shape of a house.[49] Collected materials need

42. For an example of Dionysios' praise of harmony, especially lexical harmony, see *On Composition* 22.56–195 (on a verse from Pindar).

43. For the expression "filling one's ears with honey," see Synesios, *Dion* 2.3 (Levy 1912: 41; Mayer 1911: 85n1). See also above in *Styles of Certain Writings* (p. 105).

44. Psellos speaks here of short and longer syntactical units (κόμμα, κῶλον, περίοδος, and πνεῦμα) whose discussion is to follow that of the basic arrangement of words.

45. Cf. Psellos, *Theol.* I 12.113–18 (on Kosmas the Melodos, *Kanôn on Holy Thursday, PG* 98 481b), where Psellos attributes this notion to Plato (cf. *Sophist* 264a1–7) and Porphyry.

46. See n. 11 above.

47. Cf. Gregory of Nazianzos, *On the Theophany* = *Or.* 38.7, an elaborate description of divinity where we read of God's essence as "extending beyond [ὑπερεκπίπτειν] conception" and providing "images [φαντασίας]" impossible to capture; these phrases are cited verbatim in Psellos, *Concise Answers to Various Questions* 15 (a chapter on "Who is God") and alluded to in his *Oration on the Annunciation* = *Or. hag.* 2.12–14 (Christ's immaculate conception).

48. A very similar phrase in Synesios, *Letter* 43.35–36; cf. Levy 1912: 41.

49. The metaphor of the builder stems from Dionysios of Halikarnassos, *On Composition* 6; cf. Levy 1912: 75.

also perfect composition, if indeed beauty is not a matter of collection but of connection.[50]

[§ 16; 148–62] And I know that, being passionate about sensual beauty, you often weave around a desired body some forehead ornament, a neckpiece, or a band.[51] Let me then use your example for my essay. Among the pearls in your collection, I don't think that all are massive and round; and the same could be said of your clear gems or your green gems. Let us assume then that some of them are transparent and beautiful in both color and shape, but others lack brilliance or are even eroded, as if by brine,[52] and they have veins, while others have deep open fractures, and still others are small and do not illumine the artist's creation at all. If the one who restores the ornament's beauty has not studied the arrangement of material, he might cause additional blemish not only to those stones lacking brilliance, but even to the transparent ones by placing them helter-skelter, or by not hiding the faulty ones, or by arranging the string of jewels askew, or by not placing the cones and round stones by themselves, or by not measuring, or by not arranging the stones by triangles and rectangles, or by interchanging the shapes at random.

[§ 17; 164–73] Let us suppose that someone who knew how to join elements together were to take different parts, most of which had little value in themselves. He would then arrange them aptly and fittingly and mix them one next to another in proper proportions. In some places, he would increase the larger parts with the smaller ones. In other places, he would enforce adornment upon the most insignificant stones through the greater gems. Through mediating distances he would render similar what is different, while working a perfect concord through the dissimilarity of the materials before him. Not only will you not deny my example, but, I know, you will approve of it. For if you do not accept it, Pheidias will prove you wrong. Having made the body of

50. The imperfect "connection" is used here in order to keep Psellos' rhyming wordplay "συλλογή . . . ἁρμογή." The phrase echoes Dionysios of Halikarnassos, who in his introduction to the *On Composition* makes a similar case about the primacy of composition over word-choice (chaps. 3–5); cf. also *On Demosthenes* 51.

51. Cf. *Chronographia* 6.57 (on Monomachos sending gifts to his "beloved" Maria Skleraina). Speaking of a *desired* body, Psellos toys here with the name of his addressee, *Pothos*, i.e., *Desire*; cf. Levy 1912: 29.

52. A Platonic metaphor; cf. *Phaedo* 110a with Levy 1912: 75.

Aphrodite with gold, he attached some kind of dark stone in order to represent her eyes.[53]

[§ 18; 173–80] You would not let the jeweler whittle away at a sapphire nor chip off bits from a piece of jasper, nor would he be able to add anything to them either. Yet the artist of discourse can both reduce and remove parts through coalescences[54] as well as amplify others through certain additions, or even remake others into manifold figurations through allegories.[55] Those ignorant of this science have gained nothing by hunting beautiful words; they have arranged them without taste and thus rendered their delivery unpleasant. **[§ 19; 180–87]** Lysias, Isocrates, Demosthenes, and, especially, Herodotus took common and current words, then arranged them properly, and thus surpassed the grandiloquence of the rest. As for this great father, he has treated word-harmony with great care and, in comparison to others, quite exceptionally. In some places in his speeches, Gregory created such great eloquence through varied mixtures of simple words, words without any grandeur, that no one else has contributed to the art even with novel words.[56]

[§ 20; 187–98] I am unable to capture the ways by which he happens to produce such extraordinary beauty; I can only make guesses by experiencing it and without the involvement of reasoning.[57] For whenever I think I have

53. Psellos is likely referring to the statue of Aphrodite *Ourania*, which Pheidias made for the Eleians, according to Pausanias (6.25.1). The reference to Pheidias' insetting of dark-stone eyes is unique, not attested in any other ancient source; for a possible influence see Plato, *Hippias major* 290a–d where a discussion of Pheidias' making of the eyes of Athena not of gold but from stone—has Psellos replaced Athena with the more erotic Aphrodite? Another possible influence could be Plato, *Republic* 420c–e where Socrates argues that, though an inferior color, black applied to the eyes of a statue contributes to its overall beauty. For the statue of Aphrodite at Elis and its few and brief descriptions see Lapatin 2001: 90–95; Lapatin knows Psellos' passage from Keil and, wrongly, doubts Psellos' authorship.

54. On "coalescence" (συναλιφή), the joining of two syllables into one, either by synaeresis, crasis, or elision, in order to avoid hiatus, see, e.g., Dionysios of Halikarnassos, *On Composition* 6.22.

55. On allegory and discursive variation, see Longinos, *Art of Rhetoric* 258–64.

56. The paragraph alludes to several passages from Dionysios of Halikarnassos' essays on Demosthenes, Lysias, Isocrates, as well as his *On Composition*; cf. Levy 1912: 76–77.

57. Cf. Dionysios of Halikarnassos, *On Lysias* 11.4–11 on how certain aspects of aesthetic appearance can only be captured by sense-experience (αἴσθησις) and not reason (λόγος).

captured his ways and I ascertain that his beauty streams forth from them, I see other sources from which his stream of charm pours. Regardless whether he binds the discourse together or if he sets it apart and dissolves its harmony,[58] whether he rounds it off with periods or if he stretches it out through periods delivered in a single breath, whether he ends in anapaestic rhythms or if he measures discourse in ionic dipodias,[59] whether he condenses the thought so as to create tetrameters or if he extends it into hexameters; whatever he does, he assails me with charm from all sides, more charm than either the morning star or the evening star emits.

[§ 21; 198–203] Lysias' beauty is like the beauty of lilies or that which dwells in violets or envelops the bloom of narcissus: Lysias merely pleases the ear, just as these flowers merely please the eye; his beauty does not open for itself the doors of the soul. The round and well-turned quality of his words is hollow and superficial.[60] If someone presses it again and again with his lips, it collapses. **[§ 22; 203–13]** Demosthenes' beauty is dispersed in isolated places and, wherever found, is short and fragmented (I do not need to speak now about those who defend him). Isocrates' beauty is more visible, yet excessively diffuse and uncongealed. Plato's is appealing yet not well mixed, while Herodotus' is more eloquent than that of others but quickly changes course and retreats. As for that of Dio, I would not compare it to that of Plato, as Philostratos from Lemnos declares;[61] yes, his beauty is full of charming words and through variation renders the listener vigorous,[62] but it is neither rounded nor cohesive, as it is loose and without periods.[63]

58. In the sentence that begins here, Psellos enumerates (rather abstractly) aspects of prose rhythm that evoke many similar discussions of (primarily Demosthenic) style in Hermogenes' *On Forms*; cf. Patillon 2008–12: 4:liii–lxi.

59. I.e., in a repeated sequence of two long and two short syllables: – – v v | – – v v; cf., e.g., Hermogenes, *On Forms* 1.6.32.

60. Cf. Plato's *Phaedrus* 234–35 where Socrates is depicted as being temporarily ecstatic by Lysias' rhetoric and "rounded" diction.

61. Philostratos, *Lives of the Sophists* 1.7: βλέπων δὲ πρὸς τὴν Δημοσθένους ἠχὼ καὶ Πλάτωνος, ᾗ, καθάπερ αἱ μαγάδες τοῖς ὀργάνοις, προσηχεῖ ὁ Δίων τὸ ἑαυτοῦ ἴδιον.

62. ἀκμαῖον τὸν ἀκροατὴν δίδωσιν: possibly from erotic discourse; cf. Achilleus Tatius, *Leukippe and Klitophon* 2.37.8 (on the *akmê* of the erotic act) or 1.3.3 (on the *akmê* of passion). Ἀκμὴ (vigor) is an important Hermogenian form (*On Forms* 1.10), used regularly in rhetorical theory; cf. Synesios, *Dion* 3.6.

63. For the adapted borrowings from Synesios' *Dion* and Menander the Rhetor; see Mayer 1911: 89–90.

[§ 23; 214–24] The beauty, however, of our Theologian's speech is, firstly, similar to itself throughout. If you begin reading his texts in the natural order, whatever comes next will seem better spoken and sweeter to you. If you wish to go backwards, you will end up with the same conclusion, as if the same author is both similar and dissimilar in an identical fashion. For he becomes better whether he moves forwards or backwards.[64] Then, having tuned his creations as if to a lyre, he envelops everything in rhythm—not the licentious rhythm that many among the rhetors have used, but the most self-restrained one.[65] He also does not complete his discourse with uniform cadences,[66] but he varies its endings. He is indeed poetically metrical as much as is possible, yet he never appears to depart from prose; and whatever type of prose he chooses, he is still adorned with metrical rhythm.

[§ 24; 224–34] Furthermore, Gregory continuously varies his use of meaning by transposition and alters his diction toward what is more pleasurable. He handles philosophical thoughts in more rhetorical fashion [πολιτικῶς] and rhetorical [πολιτικάς] thoughts more philosophically. While he appears not to attend to rhetoric, his discourse is replete with rhetorical bloom. So it seems to me that, having absorbed once and for all the entire stream of the art of rhetoric, and on the one hand having watered his mind with this, while on the other having himself opened a living and sweet source from his own soul, he did not produce his speeches by looking at a model, but was himself an archetypal stylistic model for himself. Hence, whatever he might say is immediately and artlessly rhetorical, even if he does not deliberately pursue such a thing.

[§ 25; 234–41] Unlike the many who do not anticipate the theme of a speech by their own thinking, Gregory arranges[67] his speeches like the god who according to Plato created the forms:[68] having first divided into segments

64. For this passage and its application of Christian ontological models to the author as creator, see Papaioannou 2013: 82–83.

65. Cf. Philostratos, *Lives of the Sophists* 2.20 (on Apollonios of Athens).

66. Along with thought, method, diction, figures, cola, composition, and rhythm, cadence (the conclusion of cola) was a principle category of style in Hermogenes' *On Forms*; see the introduction to text 1 of this collection.

67. οἰκονομεῖ: Psellos plays here with the double connotation of this verb; the rhetorical notion of arrangement (οἰκονομία) in terms of content (πραγματικός τόπος) (cf. especially Dionysios of Halikarnassos, *On Demosthenes* 51; see also *On Lysias* 14 with Mayer 1911: 90) and the Christian notion of divine "economy," God's dispensation and ordering of creation.

68. For the middle Platonic and Neoplatonic origin of this notion and a discussion of Psellos' sources, see Papaioannou 2013: 74–87.

and completed the speech according to thought, he then proceeds with expression.[69] Therefore, even his improvised speech is premeditated. In a brief moment, Gregory has foreseen everything; almost "outside of Time," his mind runs through the text, leaving some elements out while judging others appropriate, and then his obliging tongue reveals what has been produced to the listeners.[70]

Digression on Content

[§ 26; 242–53] Gregory did not actually set philosophy and rhetoric apart in reality, as he did nominally. Rather, while lavishing philosophy with the eloquence and grandiloquence of words, he governs the rhetorical tongue by the bridle of his mind. He thus proclaims sublime and obscure teachings floridly as if they are beautiful roses. Simultaneously, he graciously grants sublime discourse to humble topics, those that proceed through stories [ἱστοριῶν][71] or events, and elevates them into allegories. Hence, occasionally he does not spare common appellations, but he includes in his speech many a Martha, Mary, Peter, and Simon;[72] sometimes they unfold according to deeper contemplative meaning [θεωρίαν] and sometimes appear to remain at the level of narrative [ἱστορίας].[73] Through a deed mentioned for the sake of advice something else is implicitly signified and, as the mind is suspended in its contemplation, imagining what lies beneath to be something different, it recognizes the humble as sublime.

69. "Dividing" (τέμνειν) and "completing" (ἀπαρτίζειν) derive from the Hermogenian terminology of versification; cf. Ioannes Sikeliotes, *Comm.* 496.32–497.2.

70. These statements should be read in the strong sense of a Creator who thinks of the world before creation, rather than in the narrower Neoplatonic sense of God thinking of the eternal world "outside of Time"; see Philo *On the Creation* 26–29 and 164–65 as opposed to Porphyry, *History of Philosophy* 18.15–21 or Julian, *On the Emperor Sun, to Salustius* 43.3–7, where the Neoplatonic view is articulated. This ontology of discourse is set also in the framework of rhetorical theory; see Mayer 1911: 90.

71. ἱστορία refers here to relatively short narratives that may be memorable or may require allegorical interpretation; for the different meanings of the term, see Papaioannou 2014a.

72. Cf. Gregory, *On Holy Easter* = *Or.* 45.24; with the discussion and correction of the passage by Mayer (1911: 91).

73. θεωρία is typically juxtaposed to ἱστορία in Byzantine biblical hermeneutics; cf. Gregory of Nyssa's *Life of Moses*.

[§ 27; 254–63] His discourse is embellished not only with what the art of rhetoric supplies. It is also adorned by every science and story [ἱστορίας]: of barbarians and of Greeks, old sayings, maxims from the stage of satyr plays, stories from Aesop, lyric songs, poetic elaboration, all kinds of verses from Sappho, Archilochos, Anakreon,[74] the Orphics, Pythagoras,[75] doctrines from the Peripatos, what was philosophized in the Stoa and the various schools, whatever many a Pyrrhon reserved judgment upon, whatever the dogmatics asserted,[76] what the followers of Heraclitus did not perceive, what Zenon and Melissos expressed in paradoxes,[77] what Aristotle affirmed and Plato proposed—in short, teachings gleaned from every way the world has been understood and explained.[78] **[§ 28; 263–66]** In addition to these, his texts are full also of geography: how parts of the elements in some climates have been transformed, how islands appeared by themselves. There is simply nothing that he has read and then forgotten.

[§ 29; 266–73] He is also knowledgeable in mathematics like no one else is. He knows about the courses and movements of stars, including those that wander, those that are fixed, and those that descend and ascend through measurable intervals. He knows what is obliquity and what is latitude, double orbits, orderly progression, whatever is not in agreement with what has been discovered to date but nevertheless is confirmed by analogy, the natures of numbers, and principle generations of numbers, the exactness of geometry, the commensurability of music expressible in numbers.[79] **[§ 30; 274–80]** Yet he does not adduce these in his speeches nor does he imitate Plutarch, the author of the *Parallel Lives*, who untimely adorns rhetorical [πολιτικάς] themes with examples from music and geometry. Gregory may pass over

74. Sappho and Anakreon are listed together by Dionysios of Halikarnassos as models of the panegyrical/theatrical type of harmony in composition; *On Demosthenes* 40.

75. Cf. Ps.-Nonnos, *Commentaries* on Greg. Naz. *Or.* 4 (*Against Julian*): *historia* 78 (on the Orphics); *historia* 17 (on the Pythagoreans).

76. References to the opposing philosophical schools of the Sceptics (Pyrrhon of Elis [c. 365–275 BCE] was the founder) and the Dogmatists; Sextus Empiricus (the only Pyrrhonist philosopher whose work survived in Byzantine mss.) wrote Πρὸς δογματικούς (*Against the Dogmatists*).

77. Major exponents of the pre-platonic Eleatic school. Cf. Ps.-Nonnos, *Commentaries* on Greg. Naz. *Or.* 4 (*Against Julian*): *historia* 29 (a reference to Zeno).

78. See further Levy 1912: 80–81 on Psellos' listing of philosophical schools.

79. For this paragraph, see Levy 1912: 81.

an approaching mathematical thought; if ever he is obliged indeed to make mention of it, he handles it in a rhetorical fashion [πολιτικῶς] and he expresses it without resorting to mathematical terminology; the majority of the listeners do not recognize this difference and thus do not realize that his thought is mathematical.

[§ 31; 280–88] As for true hypotheses or generally held hypotheses,[80] he presents them better than Plato. For Plato either conceals the latter or is burdensome by extending the former for too long. By contrast, the great father applies discursive variation to logical demonstration and creates unceasing pleasure, even when he extends it. When he engages in dialectic, he neither conceals nor becomes bombastic nor makes convoluted statements. When he questions his opponent and has the upper hand, as far as possible (for he is confident in how he will resolve the argument) Gregory supplies him with direct answers and thus removes the fault inherent in the dialectic discussion through the difference in his own utterances.[81]

[§ 32; 288–95] He knows well the natures of beings both in the manner of narrative and in the manner of separable as well as inseparable principles.[82] After these, he proceeds to discourse about incorporeal beings; this is a knowledge he does possess yet he does not make a show of it—in this respect, Gregory imitates his Paul in every case for, as I believe, he too was at some point raised up to heaven and heard inexpressible things which he holds to himself.[83] He tests his skill in arguments about divine providence and

80. ἀληθεῖς ὑποθέσεις καὶ ἐνδόξους: Mayer (1911: 92), followed by Levy (1912: 81), thought that Psellos is referring to the rhetorical notion of "reputable" subjects (e.g., about divine matters; cf. Hermogenes, *On Forms* 1.9); however, Psellos is thinking here of logic and dialectics (cf. Aristotle, *Topics*, passim, with the definition of ἔνδοξα in the *Suda*: epsilon.1182), another science that he ascribes to Gregory.

81. Psellos is likely referring to passages like *Or.* 27.8 (*First Theological Oration, Against the Eunomians*), where Gregory constructs an imaginary opponent, asks questions of him, and then supplies him with convenient answers. I thank Byron MacDougall for this reference.

82. The vocabulary here derives from Neoplatonic ontology; for other applications of these categories in Psellos, see *Concise Answers to Various Questions* 44 ("On the Soul") or *Various Collected Passages* <from Philoponos' *On Aristotle's "On the Soul"*> = *Phil. min.* II 13, p. 32.30–33.2.

83. Niketas Stethatos (*Refuting Letter to Gregory the Sophist* =*Letters* 6.8) makes the same argument about Basil of Caesarea, referencing Gregory of Nazianzos' *Epitaphios in Honor of Basil of Caesarea* = *Or.* 43.70, the passage that perhaps has inspired Psellos here as well.

judgment wherever he is obliged to, still he offers only as much as he knows that the listeners can receive, while he leaves the rest in the heavenly treasures. **[§ 33; 296–303]** After these, he approaches theology, being everywhere "in line with the rule."[84] He does not dare anything novel, like many do.[85] He knows well the knowable monad and what is beyond being and intellect and life,[86] nevertheless he acknowledges being and life and posits an intellect from whom the things of this world proceed. Rarely and then addressing only a few people, he uses more elevated concepts; some times, he posits them by staying close to the literal meaning [ἱστορίαν], at other times, he abandons it; on many occasions, he adapts those concepts that join the many into the single harmony of the Spirit.

Gregory and the Three Genres of Rhetoric

[§ 34; 304–8] My present discourse, however, is not about these matters. For I did not compose my essay in order to show that the man is a philosopher, but in order to display how he varies his rhetoric with every discursive form and learning.

Gregory is attuned to the three genres of rhetorical art as no other.[87] **[§ 35; 308–14]** He advises by weaving censure with admonitions and by smoothing it with different methods of presentation.[88] He practices judicial discourse in mellifluous and piercing voice; for his movement[89] has pulses and hissings

84. See Gal. 6:16 and Phil. 3:16.

85. νεανιεύεται: "to act in a bold, youthful, and thus immature manner" when attempting theology is reproached by Gregory of Nazianzos (*Syntaktêrios* = *Or.* 42.18), but affirmed when Gregory himself inserts daring self-representational metaphors (*Or.* 42.2).

86. Again terms of Neoplatonic ontology (cf. Proklos, *Elements of Theology* 115); cf. Psellos' *Proof of Christ's Incarnation,* a letter to the sultan Malik-Shah on behalf of Michael VII Doukas (ca. 1073 or 1074) = *Theol.* II 3.147.

87. Following Hermogenes' division, Psellos will go on to speak about Gregory's advisory, judicial, and panegyrical rhetoric.

88. ταῖς μεθόδοις: in the Hermogenian sense of μέθοδος, the manner of presenting a subject matter (thought, idea, or topic), one of the primary elements (στοιχεῖον) of discourse; Hermogenes, *On Forms* 1.1.18.

89. κίνησις: perhaps an allusion to the rhetorical term, related to the Hermogenian Form of vivacity (γοργότης) (Hermogenes, *On Forms* 2.11.5, on Hyperides); but could it be, rather, that Psellos here refers to body motions or gestures?

and the intensity of his breath makes frequently excited leaps.[90] When he advises, he resembles a stream of oil that flows silently and enters into the soul calmly.[91] When he fights against his opponents, he resembles brimstone and storms and the fiery bursts of clouds.[92] **[§ 36; 314–19]** His words are subject to variation in both genres. As for the rhythms, at times they are mellifluous and full of harmony, at times harsh and striking. Never does he abandon philosophical thoughts, but sows them everywhere in his speeches so as to intensify what is smooth or relax what is intense.

[§ 37; 320–24] Gregory is most accomplished in panegyrical discourse.[93] One might compare his other types of speeches to the likes of an Isocrates, Plato, or Demosthenes, yet no one stands the test against him in panegyrical discourse.[94] Indeed, this genre is much more difficult than the other ones. **[§ 38; 324–31]** This is why Demosthenes and any other rhetor before or after him have been proven most varied and productive in judicial and advisory rhetoric, but every single one of them—to a greater or lesser degree—have failed in the panegyrical form. Plato is beautiful when he posits the forms in the *Parmenides,* when he discusses manifold beauty in the *Phaedrus,* or when he philosophizes about the soul in the *Phaedo*; yet he is not of such quality when composing the *Funeral Oration*.[95]

90. "Hissing" sounds are perhaps inappropriate in this context; such sounds belong to the practice of magic or Greek tragedy performances, as Plotinos (cf. *Enneads* 2.9.14) and Eustathios of Thessalonike (*Parekbolai on the Iliad* 3.96.1–4) attest respectively. Nor is "leaping" appropriate; in Gregory of Nazianzos, this activity is assigned to the inappropriate world of spectacles (*Epitaphios in Honor of Basil* = *Or.* 43.15) or, at least, to that inferior type of discourse, *panegyrical* discourse (*Against Julian I* = *Or.* 4.7).

91. A common metaphor in Psellos; cf., e.g., *Chronographia* 7.180 (on Ioannes Doukas). Directly from Plato, *Theaetetus* 144b5 or, more likely, indirectly through Dionysios of Halikarnassos, *On Demosthenes* 20.

92. For an explanation of these natural phenomena see, e.g., Psellos, *Phil. min.* I 19.135ff.

93. For the importance of Gregory's excellence in *panegyrical* discourse, see Papaioannou 2013: 103–24; see also p. 120 above.

94. For a similar statement, cf. Sikeliotes, *Comm.* 292.2–293.11 (though Sikeliotes does not proceed with Psellos' emphasis on Gregory's *panegyrikos logos*).

95. The critique of Plato's *Menexenus* stems from Dionysios of Halikarnassos, *On Composition* 23–30 (cf. Mayer 1911: 92–93) and contrasts Synesios' view (*Dion* 1.13). For a more general critique of Plato, see Dionysios of Halikarnassos, *On Demosthenes* 23–32 (with de Jonge 2008: 264–67), though Psellos has reversed the argument: while Dionysios finds Plato too panegyrical, Psellos finds him not panegyrical enough.

[§ 39; 331–38] In his speech against the false witnesses of Stephanos, in indicting Aeschines for his dishonest embassy, in defending himself for the golden crown, in setting forth his speeches on Olynthus, in inveighing against Philip,[96] Demosthenes closely resembles an Olympian trumpet, richly executing his discourse and concluding his arguments as he wills. But when he dares to perform a panegyric for those who fell in the war, he becomes a different man, but not like Arkeisios did.[97] **[§ 40; 338–41]** Thucydides is profound in thought especially in his various speeches, piling up and layering ideas upon ideas; yet he too, when singing the *Funeral Oration,* alters his form and falls beneath his potential.[98]

[§ 41; 342–52] The great Gregory, as if being the very first to invent this genre of rhetoric and then, using his form as a model, apply it to the entire art, has brought the genre to a perfection that cannot be superseded. With thunder and lightning like the Zeus of the myths, Gregory enters in his prefaces immediately with paradoxical and continuous thoughts, with indescribable beauties and inexpressible charm, with flowers of words and variations of figures, astounding the listener and making him now to marvel, then clap, break out in dance to the rhythm, or experience *pathos* along with what is narrated. Then Gregory proceeds and, if he so wills, reviews quickly the entire subject, returns to the beginning instantly, and expounds on the main topics.

[§ 42; 352–58] Sometimes, he includes several prefaces, whenever he is forced to prefigure certain things; at other times, he considers even just one preface to be sufficient.[99] Sometimes, he starts *in medias res*, then in-

96. Titles of various Demosthenic speeches. With the phrase "defending himself," Psellos refers to the rhetorical genre of ἀπολογία, to which Demosthenes' *On the Crown* belonged.

97. Psellos alludes here to the legend that Odysseus' grandfather Arkeisios was the product of an alteration from animal to human form, since his mother, originally a bear (in Greek, ἄρκτος), was transformed into a woman upon her conception of a son from Odysseus' great-grandfather, Kephalos (cf. *Etym. Magn.* 144.22 with Mayer 1911: 93n1). If I am reading the metaphor correctly, Psellos suggests that Demosthenes alters with a negative effect; rather than moving like Arkeisios from an inferior to a superior form, Demosthenes loses in stature. Psellos' criticizes here Demosthenes' *Epitaphios,* which was considered by Dionysios of Halikarnassos as spurious (*On Demosthenes* 44.16–26).

98. Psellos' criticism of Thucydides' *Funeral Oration* is nontraditional, contrasting again with Synesios' view (*Dion* 1.13); cf. Mayer 1911: 93.

99. For the introduction of several prefaces, see Anonymous, *Prolegomena to a Comm. on Hermogenes' On Invention* 70.10–71.29. See also p. 172 below on John Chrysostom.

stantly gives up the attempt, and goes back up to the first subject. Stringing topics together as if but for a moment, he handles them according to his own will. Fashioning and remaking them as if they were supple wax, he kneads them with his fingers so as to refashion and change them into versatile figures.[100]

[§ 43; 359–67] By certain arts that he himself has invented, Gregory articulates and disarticulates his discourse; he both composes and dissolves it. Through divisions and sections, he renders the shortest parts lengthy, while he folds and gathers together into recapitulating summaries what is extensive and long.[101] His detached phrases are original and unusual, while his enlivening narratives are prolific.[102] While expressing solemn subjects in a solemn manner, he does not deprive subjects of different quality from a similar diction. Nowhere does Gregory depict a character without assuming his voice.[103] Rather, everywhere he is vivid [ἐναργής] and assimilated to his subjects.[104] He is both vigorous and animated [ἔμψυχος].[105] By his transformations, he

100. The metaphor of discourse as "wax easily fashionable" goes back to Plato; see *Republic* 588d1–2 with *Suda* kappa.1537 and pi.1693 where the expression is recorded as proverbial. There is a passage remarkably similar to Psellos expression in Cicero, *de Oratore* III 177: "sicut mollissimam ceram ad nostrum arbitrium formamus et fingimus = we form and mold [words] like soft wax to our own will"; on Cicero's theory of language in *De Oratore,* see Dugan 2005: 75–171 and, especially, 268–69 on Cicero's view of the fluidity of speech. Apart from speech itself, Psellos regards also the human voice of a performing reader as "more easily fashionable than wax"; see *Or.* 37.316 on the reader Ioannes Kroustoulas (see p. 238 below).

101. For the expression "recapitulating summaries," see Dionysios of Halikarnassos, *Roman Antiquities* 1.5 with Psellos, *Charikleia and Leukippe* 103–4.

102. ἀπο-στάσεις ("detached phrases"; cf. Hermogenes, *On Brilliance* = *On Forms* 1.9.12–17) and ὑπο-στάσεις ("substantiating narratives"; *On Amplification* = *On Forms* 1.11.50) are different types of figures (σχήματα); the latter term carries the connotation of rendering something visible (cf. the notion of *enargeia* and the comment by Mayer 1911: 95–96). Psellos' wordplay has remained untranslated here.

103. ἀνηθοποίητος: this term as well as the entire passage echo Dionysios of Halikarnassos description of Lysias' skill in *êthopoiia* (*On Lysias* 7–8 and 13); see the discussion in Papaioannou 2013: 109–13. For this term specifically, see Zucker 1963.

104. On ἐνάργεια, see Papaioannou 2011.

105. The last concept refers to animated performance of character, rather than sincere spontaneity in the Hermogenian sense of ἔμψυχος λόγος, *On Forms* 2.7: *On True Speech.* Cf. Psellos' *Letter* to Nikephoros Keroularios (M 17.26–52) where he associates ἐμψυχία with his own rhetoric and juxtaposes it to the inferior ἠθοποιΐα that Dionysios of Halikarnassos praised in reference to Lysias (citing the passage from Dionysios' *Lysias,* 7–8 and 13, mentioned above, note 103).

invents more novel points of departure.[106] **[§ 44; 367–72]** He weaves together and harmonizes suspended thoughts with those that are complete and established, thereby creating a connection between thoughts that are scattered.[107] He adorns his narratives with various preludes as if with flowers. Then, through the distributions of parts, fictions, embellishments, and personifications, he makes these narratives the kind that leave his listeners and readers always wanting more.[108] **[§ 45; 372–79]** Gregory, a man of such majesty, immediately assumes whatever persona happens to be introduced in his speech.[109] He changes himself and adopts the emotion [*πάθος*] of the one who is speaking: at times he wets his eyes with tears; at times he is full of cheer and wears a wreath of victory, leading the procession, shining on a chariot with gold-studded bridle (if it so happens);[110] and at times he complains, implores, breaks down in lamentations.[111] Yet everywhere, there remain his grandiloquence[112] and the weightiness of his discourse, his natural grandeur and unembellished beauty.

106. ὁρμάς: Psellos likely refers to opportunities for speech (as in ἀφ-ορμάς), rather than emotional responses or "impulses."

107. For this technique, which Psellos knows from Dionysios of Halikarnassos, see Mayer 1911: 95.

108. μερισμοῖς, πλάσεσι, διασκευαῖς, and προσωποποιΐαις, all figures that aim to produce the effect of enargeia (cf. Mayer 1911: 96). Psellos' reference to "narrations" (διηγήσεις) suggests that Psellos is discussing in this paragraph Gregory's stylistic treatment of the second part of a speech, the one that follows the introductory part that Psellos treated in the previous paragraph. This structure is reminiscent of the order in which Dionysios of Halikarnassos discusses Demosthenes' or Lysias' structuring of discourse into preface (προοίμιον), narrations (διηγήσεις), proofs (πίστεις), and peroration (ἐπίλογος) (see *On Demosthenes* 45.21–36 and more extensively *On Lysias* 16–19) as well as "Hermogenes'" *On Invention* (chapter one: προοίμιον; two: διήγησις or κατάστασις = statement; three: κατασκευή = confirmation or proof). Psellos will complete this structure toward the end of his essay.

109. εὐθὺς τοιοῦτός ἐστιν ὁ τοσοῦτος: the same wordplay in a letter that Psellos received from his friend and teacher Mauropous; Ioannes Mauropous, *Letter* 33.4–5: πρὸς τοιούτους [i.e., Mauropous] καὶ ὁ τοσοῦτος [i.e., Psellos].

110. For the expression "gold-studded bridle," see Dionysios of Halikarnassos, *Roman Antiquities* 8.67.9 with Flavius Josephus, *Jewish Antiquities* 11.35.

111. The verbs that Psellos uses allude to female emotional reactions or effeminate behavior; see, e.g., *Etymologicum Gudianum,* pi.477.51–57 (ed. Sturz).

112. μεγαληγορία: along with dignity, a stylistic that Dionysios of Halikarnassos associates with Demosthenes' advisory rhetoric (*On Demosthenes* 45.38–40) as well as with the lofty style of Thucydides (here along with the virtue of force; *On Thucydides* 27).

[§ 46; 379–85] I know, of course, that this kind of style[113] by nature lacks displays of emotion and figures of speech;[114] for this reason, only the rhetor who speaks naturally and nowhere makes his speeches overwrought succeeds in the style that displays character [τῷ ἠθικῷ]. . . . [There is here a gap in the text, where Psellos presumably discussed the opposite kind of rhetor, successful in the *pathêtikos* style, the one that displays emotion.] These two, however, partially succeed and partially fail. By contrast, the Father joined what is incompatible,[115] escaped the failures of both types of rhetor, and simultaneously exceeded "by an entire cubit and a hand" the successful points of each.[116]

General Remarks: On Obscurity, Mixture of the (Hermogenian) Forms, and Figurative Style

[§ 47; 385–94] Since he did not write an explanatory treatise, he left his writings to be interpreted. For (and this is the most admirable thing) Gregory is both more clear in his diction than anyone else and, simultaneously, unclear to almost everyone. I am not referring to those passages where he shows theology in inexpressible words nor where he hints to us at some more sophisticated

113. *Namely*, the style defined by magniloquence, etc.

114. ἀπαθής and ἀσχημάτιστος: notably, also characteristics of the divine nature in Christian theology; cf., e.g., Gregory of Nazianzos, *Or.* 28.7 (on figurelessness) and 28.11 (on *apatheia*).

115. From Synesios, *Against Andronikos, to the Bishops* = *Letter* 41.270–71: πολιτικὴν ἀρετὴν ἱερωσύνῃ συνάπτειν συγκλώθειν ἐστὶ τὰ ἀσύγκλωστα.

116. A cubit equals six palms, each one of which equals the width of four fingers. Psellos' view of the combination of the ethical and pathetic style echoes Dionysios of Halikarnassos' view of Demosthenes' combination of the plain (exemplified by Lysias) and grand (exemplified by Thucydides) styles; see Dionysios of Halikarnassos, *On Demosthenes* 8.11–28 on Demosthenes' "mixed" style (including the mixture of "ethical" with "pathetic" *lexis*) with *On Demosthenes* 1 and 2 on Thucydides and Lysias and *On Lysias* 8 again on Lysias' unembellished artlessness and naturalness. However, Psellos has somewhat altered the understanding of these styles. Following an Aristotelian line of thought (cf. Gill 1984), "ethical" and "pathetic" are associated by Dionysios primarily with the kinds of effect that the two forms produce to their audience, namely, steadfast character or relaxation through the former, cognitive or emotional intensity through the latter (cf. *On Demosthenes* 22: where Dionysios' describes his "ethical" reaction to Isocrates' rhetoric and his "pathetic" response to Demosthenes' speeches). For a fuller discussion of this important innovation of Psellos, see Papaioannou 2013: 111–13.

dogma.[117] I am also leaving aside his allegories in stories [ἐν ἱστορίαις]. These would require another essay, a superior and more elevated examination. Rather, in those passages where Gregory handles meaning rhetorically and is pure in his phrasing and lucid in his words, he is incomprehensible to his readers.[118] What I argue here is not what the majority thinks. **[§ 48; 394–98]** For Aristotle too is difficult to understand with respect to his diction, and Aristeides the rhetor is also difficult to construe and interpret thanks to a peculiar quality of his phrasing; Plutarch too is similar in his moral treatises. Yet that which I perceive in the great Gregory is different. **[§ 49; 398–03]** Even though he could clarify his statements, Aristotle intentionally obscures them, and stores much in a single word. Aristeides delivers his words just like oracles in prophecies by removing those words that he ought to include to clarify his meaning. And the philosopher Plutarch is difficult to comprehend not because of his discursive composition, but, rather, when he mixes various philosophical views. **[§ 50; 403–11]** By contrast, though Gregory does not over-dogmatize, and though he always takes care to be clear, nevertheless there is no one who is not puzzled by his writings. (Hence, scores upon scores have composed various exegetical books on his works as if on manuals of art; I too have added my own explanations of many difficult passages, improvising, as you know, off-the-cuff responses to the questions.) In those subjects too that require improvisation about a general proposition, Gregory is most productive and inventive, as is apparent especially in his advisory speeches.[119]

[§ 51; 411–19] Gregory mixes the forms [ἰδέας] unlike Plato who mixes them only in part of his texts; unlike Lysias who neglects most of them; unlike Demosthenes who is one man in his public speeches and another in his private ones;[120] unlike Isocrates who in every instance over-embellishes his ut-

117. For this expression, see Gregory of Nyssa, *Comm. on the Song of Songs* 6.121.6 or 6.457.17; Psellos summarized this text of Gregory in verse form (the lengthy *Poem* 2).

118. For whiteness as a metaphor for discursive clarity, see Mayer 1911: 97n3.

119. "Productive" also for the reader; cf. Proklos, *Comm. on the Parmenides* 690.34–35 who speaks of Socrates' "most productive *aporias.*" On the "subjects that require improvisation about a general proposition (θετικαὶ ὑποθέσεις)," see Philostratos, *Lives of the Sophists* 576.17–19 with Mayer 1911: 98n2.

120. Cf. Hermogenes, *On Forms* 2.9.13–14 (though the sentiment there is a positive one; see next note).

terances and takes pleasure in similar beginnings and endings; and unlike Aristeides who everywhere pursues force in diction and seeks praise for his novelty of composition.[121] Gregory, rather, mixes the discursive forms like those who join harmonies together according to arithmetical principles using everywhere his own mixtures. **[§ 52; 419–24]** He is powerful in his ethical mode,[122] vigorous in his concise mode.[123] He is everywhere more extravagant in his solemn and brilliant mode, while he never abandons the method of force. He projects amplification within reason, ever guided by the exigencies of the moment, and checks that same amplification with his limpidity, while never departing from clarity.

[§ 53; 425–30] He has arranged many of his speeches so as to yield two meanings, the one apparent, the other hidden. Gregory intends the hidden meaning, yet he lavishly develops the passage that hides it, so that he can display as much as he wants and still elude examination. His words are ambiguous, so that they are capable of both meanings. His discourse proceeds figuratively and does not lack irony. **[§ 54; 430–35]** When he complains about his many sufferings, without seeming to do so he crafts this emotion with such art that most people sense what he means but does not express. When he does not dare to touch upon ineffable dogmas lest he lay himself open to criticism from his audience, he follows closely the literal level of the story while allegorizing it discretely. In certain occasions, he also elaborates on what is hidden, when what is allegorized is inapproachable.

121. On the prehistory of the various views (primarily from Dionysios of Halikarnassos and Hermogenes) listed here see Mayer 1911: 98–99 and Levy 1912: 87–89. The most notable case is that of Demosthenes, who is presented by Hermogenes as the ideal rhetor precisely because, in displaying his *force,* he "is another in private speeches, another in public ones, and yet again different in the Philippic public speeches, different in the advisory ones, but everywhere he employs force" (*On Forms* 2.9.13–14). Psellos strategically leaves out the last part of Hermogenes' statement, for he wishes to attribute the fundamental quality of *force* to Gregory (as he will add immediately it is Gregory who "never abandons the method of force").

122. I.e., pursuing the Hermogenian form of character (ἦθος).

123. Conciseness is related to the Hermogenian form of rapidity (γοργότης). The rest of this section parades a series of further Hermogenian forms.

Final Review and Conclusion

[§ 55; 436–41] Gregory captivates the ear in every way: both when he begins his speech immediately with a preface and when he commences without a formal introduction, namely, simply and without method as the art dictates, or, as it seems to me, both quite artistically and, to put it this way, by his own will and design. In proofs, he can achieve anything he wishes, and he is particularly strong in the elaboration of his arguments. He does not present, however, all of his arguments, but whichever ones happen to be called for by the occasion. **[§ 56; 441–49]** While being of many forms in his manner of treating a topic, he is similar to himself throughout his discourse and, yet again, dissimilar: he never abandons his art and, simultaneously, he alters himself exactly in those instances where he does not abandon art.[124] Thus, while the thoughts of his prefaces are more powerful and deep, he transforms himself into greater variety when he proceeds to the main theme. Then again, when he touches upon the matters at hand, he is vivid and true. When he handles the final statements of a point he is accurate and brief. And when he wishes to complete his speech, his phrasing is loosened and relaxed, and he makes use of every thought at his disposal in order to make his meaning clear.[125]

[§ 57; 450–54] Yet this present essay is for me just the beginning of speaking (even if I know that even what has been said thus far will satiate your soul). Therefore, for now, feast as much as possible on this preliminary initiation into my essays about the Great one.[126] When this is sufficiently digested, I shall contribute the rest of the feast.

124. For this passage, with its ingenious combination of Neoplatonic with rhetorical thought, and its rather unique praise of the mixture of similarity (ὁμοιότης) with dissimilarity (ἀνομοιότης), see Papaioannou 2013: 119–21.

125. πᾶσαν ἔννοιαν πρὸς τὴν νόησιν προκαλούμενος. The phrase could, alternatively, be translated as follows: "he summons the entire cognitive faculty [of his reader] to an understanding of his [Gregory's] meaning"; cf. Proklos, *Comm. on the Parmenides* 833.19–21: Ὁ μὲν οὖν Παρμενίδης μαιευόμενος τὸν Σωκράτη, καὶ προκαλούμενος τὰς ἐν αὐτῷ περὶ τούτων ἐννοίας.

126. Gregory too describes himself as someone who provides a "feast," a ἑστιάτωρ (*On the Theophany* = *Or.* 38.6; the passage was commented by Ioannes Mauropous: *Letter* 17.84-85).

9 Two Lectures on Gregory of Nazianzos

Theol. I 19 (on *Or.* 40.24) and 98 (on *Or.* 43.1)

Translated with introduction and notes
by Stratis Papaioannou

Introduction

The following two texts derive from Psellos' work as a teacher in advanced learning. They belong to the lectures as well as essays (letters or, sometimes, lectures addressed to a single pupil) gathered together in Paris, BNF, gr. 1182 (**P**) and the earlier Florence, Bibl. Med. Laur., Plut. gr. 57.40 (**L**).[1] The first of the texts, attested in **P**, is titled *On the Theologian's Phrase: "even though you ought <to reap> the opposite fruit through the opposite"* (*Theol.* I 19) and addresses an unnamed student. The second, attested in both **P** and **L**, is titled *On the Phrase: "Among all [people], there exists no one for whom this among all [things will not be found to be the case]"* (*Theol.* I 98) and is directed towards a larger audience, also without any reference to named individuals.[2]

We have already seen aspects of Psellos' teaching through revised excerpts from earlier treatises, such as his *Synopsis of Rhetoric*, or through essays, such as the *Discourse Improvised . . . about the Style of the Theologian*,

1. See p. 14 in this volume.

2. For all the manunscripts that transmit the two lectures, three for *Theol.* I 19 and, impressively, nine for *Theol.* I 98, see Moore 2005: 168 and 172–73 respectively.

composed so as to examine a specific topic from Psellos' perspective. The series of lectures/letters to which the two following texts belong, however, allow us to catch Psellos the teacher in action as we observe him engaged in another type of instruction, this one based on text-exegesis.

The 116 texts edited in Gautier's *Theologica*, volume I (to which we may add several from *Theologica,* volume II, edited by Westerink and Duffy), present a rather cohesive group. All texts are of more or less similar length, and as lectures would have lasted about an hour—often on the same subject, sometimes interrupted by a break and continued on another day (see, e.g., *Theol.* I 7 and 8 or *Theol.* I 85.95–105). Psellos' audience had apparently completed the early stages of education, since they seem to have been already exposed to rhetorical theory (see, e.g., *Theol.* I 98, trans. below) and Aristotelian logic (see, e.g., *Theol.* I 71.106 or 76.11), and were being introduced to higher philosophical studies, devoted precisely to the exegesis of what we may call "canonical" texts (the Bible, Gregory of Nazianzos, and others).

Usually incited by a question from his students, Psellos zooms in on a brief passage that he tackles as a master interpreter by using a variety of skills and methods. Psellos may paraphrase a passage,[3] and may employ manuscript collation (e.g., *Theol.* I 19), prose metrics (e.g., I 69 and 73), Aristotelian and Neoplatonic logic (e.g., I 3 and 107), rhetorical theory (e.g., I 27.144–47), patristic exegesis (e.g., I 108), and, most importantly, Neoplatonic hermeneutics (usually Proklos).[4]

Most of the passages receiving commentary come either from the Bible (both the Old and New Testaments)[5] or, in their majority, the *Orations* of

3. What he calls παραφράζειν or μεταποίησις. See *Theol.* I 71.3–6 and 29–30: ἡμεῖς δ', ἐπεὶ δοκεῖ τὰ ῥητὰ καὶ ἀσάφειαν τινὰ ἔχειν διὰ τὴν τῶν νοημάτων συστροφήν, πρὶν ἢ κατὰ μέρος αὐτὰ ἐξηγήσασθαι καὶ τὰς αἰτίας εἰπεῖν δι' ἃς ἕκαστον λέγεται, παραφράσομεν, εἰ δοκεῖ, πρὸς τὸ σαφέστερον, ἵνα τέως τὴν ἐπιπόλαιον διάνοιαν τῶν ῥημάτων γνόντες, οὕτω δὴ καὶ τοῦ βάθους τῶν νοημάτων ἐπήβολοι γένοισθε . . . Τοιαύτη μὲν ὡς ἐφικτὸν ἡ τῶν θεολογικῶν τούτων ῥητῶν πρὸς τὸ σαφέστερον μεταποίησις.

4. From Proklos and Neoplatonic hermeneutics derive the interpretative approaches that Psellos calls "ethical," "dialectical," "natural," and "theological"; compare Psellos, *Theol.* I 54.109–23 with, e.g., Proklos, *Comm. on the Parmenides* 913.14ff. and *Comm. on the Timaeus* 1.117.19. For Neoplatonic commentaries, see Hoffmann 2006, where also further bibliography.

5. This is especially the case in essays included in *Theol.* II.

Gregory of Nazianzos, Psellos' answer to the Neoplatonists' Plato. But there are also other texts from the Byzantine canon: the liturgy attributed to John Chrysostom (*Theol.* I 13), the seventh-century *Klimax* of Ioannes (*Theol.* I 30), and the hymns attributed to John of Damascus (*Theol.* I 11) and his adoptive brother Kosmas of Jerusalem (*Theol.* I 12), both authors of the eighth century. Through a close reading of these texts, Psellos imparts not only theology but also an array of methods and sources; indeed, sometimes it seems that the Christian texts that are commented upon are often just an excuse to instruct students in earlier, Greco-Roman modes of thinking.[6]

Though certain authors are predominant (such as Proklos, whom Psellos regards as his most important model),[7] Psellos' sources are impressively diverse: from Plotinos to Chaldean Oracles and Hermes Trismegistos, from Ailios Aristeides to Origen, from Basil of Caesarea and Gregory of Nyssa to the corpus attributed to Dionysios the Areopagite and Maximos the Confessor (with whom he does not fear to disagree sometimes: *Theol.* I 59.168–70), to the more recent John of Damascus and Andreas of Crete; in the case of the latter two, Psellos engages in source criticism, pointing how they have "stolen" ideas from earlier fathers (*Theol.* I 65.71 and 59.186–95).[8] Psellos also

6. At one moment, Psellos himself acknowledges this preoccupation with earlier, non-Christian thinking and defends his approach, adopted, as he claims, for the sake of the students' learning and not for the display of his own knowledge (*Theol.* I 51.99–104): ἐγὼ δὲ οὐκ ἀγνοῶ ὅτι ἐκ περιττοῦ πολλὰ τοῖς θεολογικοῖς ἐπεισκυκλῶ ῥητοῖς, ἀλλ' οὔτε φανητιῶν τοῦτο ποιῶ οὐδὲ πολυμαθείας δόξαν θηρώμενος, ἀλλ' ἵν' ὑμεῖς, ὧν τοῖς βιβλίοις μὴ ἐντυγχάνετε, τούτους ἐνταῦθα γινώσκοιτε οἵτινές τέ εἰσι καὶ ἃ ξυγγεγράφασι· βούλομαι γὰρ τελέους ὑμᾶς ἐκ τελέων εἶναι καὶ μὴ τοῖς καιριωτάτοις ἐλλείποντας μέρεσιν.

7. *Theol.* I 54.118–23: οἷς δὲ δεῖ ἐπεξηγεῖσθαι ῥῆσίν τινα προκειμένην, πειρᾶσθαι καὶ ἠθικὰς ἐπάγειν πίστεις καὶ φυσικὰς καὶ θεολογικάς. οὕτω καὶ Πρόκλος ποιεῖ τὸν Τίμαιον ἐξηγούμενος· ὁ μὲν γὰρ Πορφύριος εἰς τὰ ἠθικὰ μόνα καθήκοντα τὸν λόγον ἑλᾷ, Ἰάμβλιχος δὲ θεολογικῶς μόνον ἐφερμηνεύει τὸ προτεθέν, ἀλλ' ὁ μὲν Πρόκλος παντοδαπὸς ταῖς ἐξηγήσεσι γίνεται.

8. The latter passage is worth quoting in full (*Theol.* I 59.186–95): καὶ μάρτυς τῷ λόγῳ ὁ τῆς Νύσσης φωστὴρ Γρηγόριος· περὶ γὰρ τοῦ κυριακοῦ σώματος λέγων ἐπάγει ταυτί· σῶμα . . . ἰδιότητος. τοῦτο δὲ ὁ τῆς Κρήτης Ἀνδρέας κεκλοφὼς ὡς οἰκεῖον ἐν τῷ περὶ Λαζάρου λόγῳ ἐξεφώνησεν. ὅθεν καὶ πρῶτον ἐγὼ ἐκεῖσε τὸ ῥητὸν ἀναγνούς, ἐθαύμασα ὅπως πρὸς τὸν ἄλλον αὐτοῦ χαρακτῆρα μετήλλακται, καὶ ἐμοὶ ἔμπνους ἐκεῖσε γενέσθαι ἔδοξεν· ὡς δ' ὕστερον εὗρον τοῦ λόγου τὸν πατέρα, ἐκεῖνον μὲν οὐ πάνυ τι ᾐτιασάμην χρυσοῦν κεκλοφότα ἱμάτιον, ἑαυτὸν δὲ ἀπεδεξάμην, τὸν Σκύθην ἐγνωκότα μετὰ τοῦ κάνδυος.

acknowledges that he has consulted earlier commentaries (e.g., in *Theol.* I 10) and criticizes teachers and exegetes from a recent past, such as Ioannes Sikeliotes and Ioannes Geometres.[9]

Equally impressive is Psellos' teaching approach. Psellos interacts with his students, asks questions, invites them to improve their study, speaks with passion about his own interests and work, and lures his audience. Sometimes, he turns against ancient opponents: in *Theol.* I 3, Psellos reproaches Eunomios, the Cappadocians' main opponent, directly (lines 44–67). Or he stages a fictive trial: in *Theol.* I 14 (96–151), Psellos impersonates "God" and "man," who, using Paradise as their court room, present their cases in front of a supposed judge, who, however, remains "beyond conception" (since "who can judge God?"; line 100).

Ultimately, he sketches images of himself and of his students. As he claims, he proceeds slowly, reining in his students' hunger for learning as they rush like "horses hard to bridle," and he offers them proper intellectual food: a "discursive feast . . . filled neither with spices nor with Attic lingo nor with overwrought sophistic concepts, but with the summit of divine thoughts and theologies" (*Theol.* I 85.95–105).[10] As for his students, they "throw him, like a Jonah but without having committed a sin, into a deep sea of concepts and dogmas"; he struggles to "come to the surface," but cannot find a safe harbor, while they continue to sail on calm waters; "I am tied down by 'eternal bars' [Jonah 2:7]," Psellos writes, ". . . and I do not know if the beast will . . . release me too (like Jonah) from the storm, as I

9. *Theol.* I 47.80–100: Psellos opposes Sikeliotes for his criticisms of Ioannes Geometres (though he still regards Geometres "quite burdensome and faulty"); in Psellos' view, though a "sophist" in reality, Sikeliotes titled himself a "philosopher" and attacked also such prestigious "sophists" as Synesios, Libanios, and Prokopios. On Sikeliotes, see further Papaioannou 2015.

10. Ἔχετε οὖν, ὦ παῖδες, τὴν τῶν ἀμφιβαλλομένων ἐπίλυσιν. καὶ οἶδα μὲν ὅτι πρὸς τὸ ἐφεξῆς τοῦ λόγου σφαδάζοντες, ὥσπερ ἵπποι δυσήνιοι ὅλῳ ποδὶ πρὸς ἐκεῖνο φερόμενοι, δυσχερῶς ἀνακόπτεσθε. ἀλλ' ἐγώ, οἷόν τινι χαλινῷ τῇ σιωπῇ τὸ πρόθυμον ὑμῶν καταρτύων καὶ μὴ πάντῃ σφυγμοὺς καὶ κινήσεις ἀτόπους περὶ τὰ ὀρεκτὰ βουλόμενος ὑμᾶς ἔχειν, ἀλλ' ἀφαιρεῖν ἐθέλων τῆς ψυχῆς τὴν περὶ τοὺς λόγους λιχνείαν, σήμερον μὲν τὴν περὶ ἐκεῖνο θοίνην ὑμῶν ἀφαιρήσομαι, αὔριον δέ, εἴ γε θεὸς ἐθέλει, τὴν περὶ ἐκεῖνο λογικὴν τράπεζαν παραθήσομαι, οὐ καρυκείας γέμουσαν οὐδ' Ἀττικῶν γλωττισμάτων οὐδὲ κατατέχνων καὶ σοφιστικῶν νοημάτων, ἀλλ' ἐννοιῶν θείων καὶ θεολογιῶν ἀκρότητος, ἧς μόνος οὗτος, ὥς ἔμοιγε δοκεῖ, ὁ μέγας πατὴρ ἐπεβάτευσεν.

have been thrown into the sea not by some lot, but for my intense love for you—. . . τῷ δι' ὑμᾶς ἔρωτι" (*Theol.* I 76.159–70).[11]

It is in this context that the following two texts should be set. We may regard both as lectures—though it is impossible to tell if the *Theol.* I 19, addressed to a single "you" (lines 2–3), is in fact simply a letter, or a lecture then repackaged as a letter, or (perhaps more likely) a lecture occasioned by the question of a single student. In any case, both texts explain difficult sentences from two among Gregory of Nazianzos' so-called sixteen "Liturgical Homilies": *Oration on the Holy Baptism = Or.* 40.24 and the preface to the *Funeral Oration for Basil the Great = Or.* 43.1.[12] Both texts use the techniques described above: philology, logic, and Neoplatonic exegesis. They have been included in the present volume, however, because here Psellos temporarily abandons close reading and offers general remarks about Gregory's rhetorical style, articulating several notions that pertain to literary aesthetics.

In *Theol.* I 19, after treating the Gregorian passage by means of philology and logic, Psellos goes on to portray Gregory's discourse as an exquisite artistic object, fashioned by a creative genius, and then concludes by recording his own reaction as a reader of Gregory. For this personal expression, Psellos employs but also refashions Gregory's own words borrowed from the latter's reaction as a reader of his friend Basil of Caesarea (from the *Funeral Oration for Basil the Great = Or.* 43.67).

11. Ὁρᾶτε εἰς οἷόν με βυθὸν νοημάτων κατηγάγετε καὶ οἵῳ πελάγει δογμάτων, ὥσπερ τὸν Ἰωνᾶν, μηδὲν ἡμαρτηκότα ἀπερρίψατε, ὡς μικροῦ δεῖν καὶ κήτους συλληφθῆναι γαστρί; ὅθεν ζητῶ μὲν ἀνανήξασθαι, οὐκ ἔχω δὲ ὅπως τὴν ἐπικειμένην ἀπώσομαι θάλασσαν ἢ τίσι 'λιμέσι' προσορμίσω 'εὐδίοις'· ἅπαντα γάρ μοι ἀλίμενα καταφαίνεται καὶ πανταχοῦ 'πέτραι προβλήτιδες', τινὲς δὲ καὶ ὕφαλοι βραχεῖ καλυπτόμεναι ὕδατι. καὶ ὑμεῖς μέν, ἐπειδή με ἅπαξ ἐκρημνίσατε κατὰ τοῦ βυθοῦ, τὸ ἱστίον πετάσαντες ἐπὶ λειοκυμονούσης πλεῖτε θαλάσσης· ἐγὼ δὲ ἤδη καὶ 'σχισμαῖς ὀρῶν' προσέρριμμαι καὶ ποταμοῖς ἀεννάοις μεμέρισμαι καὶ 'μοχλοῖς αἰωνίοις' καταδεδέσμημαι· ὧν δὴ ῥυσθῆναι ἐπεύχομαι μέν, οὐκ οἶδα δὲ εἰ κἀμὲ τὸ θηρίον ἐξαγάγοι καὶ ἀπαλλάξει τοῦ κλύδωνος, οὐ κλήρῳ βληθέντα εἰς θάλασσαν, ἀλλὰ τῷ δι' ὑμᾶς ἔρωτι.

12. Gregory's sixteen "Liturgical Homilies" are *Orations* 1, 11, 14, 15, 16, 19, 21, 24, 38, 39, 40, 41, 42, 43, 44, 45 of the modern editions (though not arranged in this order in the Byzantine manuscripts). These *Orations* were selected, sometime during the tenth century, as sermons to be read at significant feasts of the Byzantine church calendar; see Somers-Auwers 2002.

Theol. I 98 discusses a notoriously difficult sentence, excised by modern editors as a gloss, from the preface of Gregory's *Funeral Oration.* Not only was this a very popular speech in Byzantium, but also its proem and this very phrase attracted attention by Byzantine readers and teachers of rhetoric.[13] Here, like a typical teacher perhaps, Psellos at the beginning seems to forget the question posed by his students. Instead, he gives a long excursus on his ideal author, Plato. Only then can he turn to the single author who superseded Plato, namely Gregory, and his difficult phrase, which is then explained through theories of proper rhetorical argumentation as well as notions of rhetorical metrics and rhythm.[14] Psellos concludes again with a general description of Gregory as a rhetor in comparison to the ancients. Though the latter are unable to match Gregory in any respect, their aura still determines the lecture; at some point, Psellos collapses the Constantinopolitan present with the glorious Athenian past: "Are you not afraid," he asks his students, who had shown incompetence in comprehending Gregory, "that some Athenian might indict you for wickedness and refer you to the supreme court of Areopagos?" (lines 49–51).

Editions and translations. Both texts are edited in *Theol.* I, texts no. 19 and 98 (numbers in brackets indicate line numbers from that edition); for bibliography and information on the manuscripts, see the relevant entries in Moore 2005: 168 and 172–73. At the beginning of the first lecture, the manuscript is damaged; I have indicated the gaps with ". . .", and Gautier's restorations in angle brackets; my own explanatory additions are in square brackets. For a recent discussion of the second lecture (*Theol.* I 98), see Bossina and Fatti 2004.

13. See, e.g., Ioannes Sikeliotes, *Comm.* 239.14–15, 242.1–2, 313.1–5, 373.24–26, and 456.9–11; Anonymous (twelfth c.), *Comm. on Aristotle's Rhetoric* 197.31–33; Gregorios Pardos, *Comm. on Hermogenes' On the Method of Force* 1116.26–30; and Eustathios, *Preface on his Comm. on Pindar* 12. The relatively large number of manuscripts (nine) that preserve this particular Psellian lecture is also telling.

14. For this passage and its importance for Byzantine theories of prose rhythm see Hörandner 1995: 289–90.

38.[1] On the Theologian's Phrase: "even though you ought <to reap> the opposite fruit through the opposite"[2]

[1–13] I too was often troubled by this phrase of the Theologian, about which you raised a sensible question . . . <"and you will be famished> in the midst of such abundance of goodness, though you ought to reap the opposite fruit through the opposite: <a harvest through assiduous effort,> and refreshment through the fountain."[3] At first, it seemed to me . . . thought; for as the words of science say: by the similar <one may comprehend the similar, yet not the contrary with the> contrary.[4] How could one comprehend the incorporeal, while in the body, or the irrational by using reasoning . . .? How could one understand whiteness by means of blackness . . .? Based on this, Plato too <asserted that> matter <is known through "bastard> reasoning."[5] . . . such a thing that it [*i.e.,* matter] is, so that we might understand it while being in this [*i.e.* the body]; for how could formless disgrace[6] be perceived by an essence

1. This is the number assigned to this piece in the collection of Psellos' lectures in **P**.

2. δέον τὰ ἐναντία τῷ ἐναντίῳ καρποῦσθαι: *Oration on the Holy Baptism* = *Or.* 40.24; for the full phrase, see the next note.

3. καὶ λιμώξεις ἐν τοσούτῳ πλούτῳ τῆς ἀγαθότητος· δέον τὰ ἐναντία τῷ ἐναντίῳ καρποῦσθαι, τῷ ἀόκνῳ τὸν ἄμητον, καὶ τῇ πηγῇ τὴν ἀνάψυξιν.

4. Cf. Aristotle, *On the Soul* 405b15: φασὶ γὰρ γινώσκεσθαι τὸ ὅμοιον τῷ ὁμοίῳ.

5. Plato, *Timaeus* 52b2: λογισμῷ τινι νόθῳ—a common place in Neoplatonic writing (cf. also Symeon Seth, *Synopsis of Physics*, 4.56 = *On Matter*).

6. ἀνείδεον αἶσχος: Gregory of Nazianzos, *On Human Nature* = *Poem* 1.2.14.35, where Gregory is describing the "flesh." Cf. also Psellos, *Theol.* I 104.64–67 (on Greg.

that has acquired form? Matter is thus comprehended by "bastard reasoning," since we grasp the qualities that matter does not possess, through those that belong to form [εἶδος], matter's opposite.

[13–19] How could this great father then claim that someone could "reap the opposite fruit through the opposite"? And when he offers an example to his own words, he elucidates it in a rather strange way: how are "assiduous effort" and "harvest," "fountain" and "refreshment," opposites? Indeed, these are so far from being "opposites" that they are actually "dear" and "mutually agreeable."[7] Those things that are opposite to each other are opposed, by nature, diametrically; not only are "fountain" and "refreshment" *not* separated from each other, but they even coincide.

[20–27] Following such logic, in the past I used to obelize the passage—an *obelos* is a critical sign of rejection of a spurious passage, indicated with an oblique line.[8] But then I was persuaded to preserve it by examining other manuscript copies that had the same phrase. Therefore, I started investigating how it could be that the great Father could say such a thing. Slowly approaching the form of the thought, I discovered the stratagem of his intention. Not philosophically, but rather rhetorically, he avoided certain phrases, while adopting others. The style of this phrase is very artistic, but its meaning is philosophical, based on rigorous knowledge.

[27–39] "And you will be famished," he says, "in the midst of such abundance of goodness, though you ought to reap the opposite fruit through the opposite: a harvest through assiduous effort, and refreshment through the fountain." The sense of the passage follows logic. With respect to the way that they are separate and come to being from each other or (to be more precise) after each other, opposites do not refrain from being opposites; yet with respect to the way they are uttered in a sentence, opposites happen to be relatives;[9] for an opposite is opposite to an opposite thing. Thus, when the Father

---

Naz. *Or.* 21.2): ἡ μὲν οὖν ὕλη εὐμισητότατον πέφυκεν· ἄμορφος γὰρ πάντῃ οὖσα καὶ ἀνείδεος ὡς αἶσχος ταῖς ἀνθρωπίναις μισεῖται ψυχαῖς. τὸ δὲ σῶμα εἰδοποιηθὲν κάλλους τε φαντασίαν παρέχει καὶ συμμετρίαν ἀρίστην, καὶ διὰ τοῦτο περιέπεται παρ' ἡμῶν καὶ ἀσπάζεται.

7. Cf. Plato, *Theaetetus* 146a7; a common pairing, e.g., in Proklos.

8. For this and other such critical signs, as used by Byzantine philologists, see Chrysostallis 2012.

9. Cf. Aristotle, *Categories* II, 6a–b.

said that "even though you ought to reap the opposite fruit through the opposite," he hinted at an opposition towards something, such as, for instance, virtue is opposite to evil[10] and, again, punishment and enjoyment: through virtue (which is opposite to evil) we reap the fruit of enjoyment (which is opposite to punishment). In the same way, through assiduous effort too (which is opposite to idleness), we reap the fruit of harvest (which is opposite to unfruitfulness), and, through the fountain (opposite to aridity), we reap the fruit of refreshment (whose opposite is exhaustion).

[40–48] My explanation does not examine now in detail the nature of opposites, nor does it define precisely how these are separate from other kinds of contrast (this would require a lengthy treatise),[11] but I have taken this matter into consideration only to the extent that it might help the present example—I defer a more precise treatment for another occasion. For I am not presently ignorant that most philosophers posit evil to be a privation, condemning it to nonexistence.[12] Yet even Plato and Aristotle, who define evil in this way, often include it among the opposites.[13] Gregory's injunction to not "be famished in the midst of such abundance of goodness" alludes to such a meaning.

[49–56] You see what wealth has been stored in this brief phrase? Such is this great man. While others wrote either in a philosophical way, but without charm, or composed rhetorical pieces, yet devoid of philosophical meaning, he has blended both in such an admirable fashion so that neither is harmed by the other and that each receives from the other its inherent benefit: by the delight of his expression, the depth of his meaning is sweetened, while from the grandeur of his thoughts, the embellished diction is adorned.

[56–69] His discourse does not resemble the sculptural art of Kalamis but that of Daidalos and Polykleitos. The former worked his craft upon whatever materials lay at hand, while the latter two would not deem it worthy to display the exactness of forms in any other material than that which came from Athens. Such is also the statue [ἄγαλμα] of the Father. Its material is quite brilliant and transparent, emitting Attic brightness: the words are graceful,

10. Cf. Aristotle, *Categories* II, 6b.15–16.

11. For such a treatment, see Aristotle's *Categories* II.

12. Cf. Plato, *Timaeus* 30a2–3 with Psellos, *Concise Answers to Various Questions* 96–97.

13. *Theaetetus* 176a6; Aristotle, *Categories* II, 13b36.

solemnity is dignified, and everything is heroic.[14] Its form [εἶδος]—which is the philosophical intellect [νοῦς]—is so[15] gently attached to matter and breathes animation [ἐμψυχίαν] into it in such a manner that the statue seems to be alive and to resemble, in a manner of speaking, the "god-like statue."[16] Daidalos' statues may have appeared to be moving[17] and Polykleitos' Zeus too perhaps was made not standing on both feet, but in contrapposto,[18] yet the discursive images of the father do not themselves move but force their viewer into motion.

[70–80] Whenever I, myself, encounter either grandeur of meaning, or beauty of diction, or perfect composition of the parts of speech, or his rhythm and appropriateness, or his allure and charm joined with his precision, and dignity mixed with clarity, I often become ecstatic like the possessed; I am

14. The comparison to ancient sculptors alludes directly to a passage in Dionysios of Halikarnassos where Isocrates is compared to Lysias (*On Isocrates* 3.33–45). Dionysios juxtaposes Isocrates' "more sublime and . . . dignified expression," "the great sublimity of his construction, belonging more to the nature of heroes rather than humans," and compares his "rhetoric" that resembles "the art of Polykleitos and Pheidias in its solemnity, grandness of art, and dignity" to Lysias' superior "charm" in diction that, "because of its fineness and charm, is like the art of Kalamis and Kallimachos."

15. Gautier reads the manuscript's "ὅτω" as "ὅτῳ," which, however, makes little sense; if corrected into "οὕτω," the word anticipates the "οὕτως" of the following phrase. The same correction has been proposed by Ioannes Polemis; see I. Polemis 1991: 306–7.

16. Psellos joins various registers of discourse in this passage. εἶδος, juxtaposed to "matter": a Neoplatonic notion of Aristotelian origin; compare Aristotle, *On the Soul,* passim with, e.g., Ioannes Philoponos' *Commentary,* passim. νοῦς: Proklos, *Comm. on the Timaios*, passim; also *Comm. on the Republic* 2.212.20–26 (on the divine demiurge creating the ἄγαλμα of the world). ἐμψυχία: for this Stoic/Epicurean term and its adoption and subsequent transformation by Neoplatonists into the notion of "embodied soul," which derives but is separate from the transcendent, immortal soul, see Karamanolis 2007. "God-like statue = θεοείκελον ἄγαλμα": a description of Adam, created and animated by God; Anastasios of Sinai, *Hexaemeron* 10.749–50 and *Suda* alpha.425; cf. Clement of Alexandria, *Protreptikos* 12.121. For the metaphor of the sculptor who enlivens his statue, see the rare instance, in Lucian(?), *Encomium of Demosthenes* 14: μόνος γέ τοι τῶν ῥητόρων, ὡς ὁ Λεωσθένης ἐτόλμησεν εἰπεῖν, ἔμψυχον καὶ σφυρήλατον παρεῖχεν τὸν λόγον. For this entire passage, see futher Papaioannou 2013: 83–85.

17. For Daidalos and his animate statue-making, cf. Steiner 2001: 44–50, 139, and passim. On the Attic style of Daidalos' statues, see Philostratos, *Eikones* 1.16.1.

18. Polykleitos is not known for a Zeus, but for his *Doryphoros*. Following imperial rhetoric (Galen, Lucian, Plutarch), middle Byzantine rhetors often reference Polykleitos (along with Pheidias) as a master sculptor. For ancient *testimonia* on Polykleitos, see Overbeck 1868: 166–75.

filled with divinely inspired motion. If someone happens to approach me at that moment, as if "having drunk from a spirit of divination," I breathe out oracles and begin to sing prophetically from his *theological* tripod. "The prophetess sat near the vault" and, filled by some invisible spirit, would either whirl her eyes, or shake her hair, or toss her head about.[19] Filled with his ethereal and pure thought, "*I* am altered in a divine alteration" and become better in nature than I am now.[20]

[81–93] If some measure of life should be stored for me and I rework the art of rhetoric as I see fit—since in my opinion it has not yet been perfected—I will imitate Hermogenes in only this one respect: I will tailor the power of the art to one single model.[21] And, leaving aside Plato and Demosthenes, I will create a precise exposition of rhetoric using only Gregory. I will demonstrate that Demosthenes cultivated only the civic kind of speeches, and even this not to perfection (for Demosthenes is deficient in the panegyrical type of discourse, as much as he is advanced in other genres); and Plato, who engaged in the genre of dialogue and developed it according to his power, is tepid not only when he does philosophy but also when he treats his thought in a rhetorical fashion. This great father, however, surpassed Demosthenes in civic discourse, and Plato in philosophy, or, rather, surpassed Demosthenes in thought and Plato in diction. Having defeated both of them, he obtained the victory against everyone.

19. The phrases in quotation marks come from Proklos' lost work on the Chaldean Oracles as cited in Psellos' *Accusation* of the Patriarch Keroularios: *Or. for.* 1.311–21; cf. *Theol* I 74.77–82. See also Menandros, *On Epideictic Speeches* 19–25: ἐξαγγελεῖς δὲ σαυτοῦ πάθος, οἷον ὡς ἐν ὑποδείγματι, . . . πλάσας τοιοῦτον λόγον, ὅτι Ἀπόλλων πολὺς ἦν θεσπίζων περὶ τοὺς τρίποδας καὶ καταλαβὼν Κασταλίαν καὶ τοὺς Δελφοὺς ἐπλήρου τὴν προφῆτιν μαντικοῦ πνεύματος. See Papaioannou 2013: 93–94.

20. Gregory of Nazianzos, *Funeral Oration for Basil of Caesarea* (*Or.* 43.67); Gregory's phrase is used in a similar context as Psellos by Niketas David Paphlagon in his *Encomium in Honor of Gregory* (25.36–26.40).

21. Cf. Psellos, *In Support of the Nomophylax <=Ioannes Xiphilinos> against Ophrydas* = *Or. for.* 3.279–82 and *Theol.* I 19.81–84 (on Greg. Naz. *Or.* 40.24).

On the Phrase: “Among all [people], there exists no one for whom this among all [things will not be found to be the case]”[1]

[1–21] It is no surprise that you, philosophers who know clarity in an expression, are confused by complex rhetorical periods.[2] Just as philosophical concepts are inaccessible to rhetors, so too rhetorical twists and subtleties are as it were unapproachable to philosophers. I wanted you to come to know both abilities well so that philosophical meaning would be dressed in rhetorical diction and your form of discourse would be beautiful in its entirety: with respect to both visible and intelligible beauty. However, the comprehension of “true being” has lured you toward the discovery of nature and the perfection of theology and has kept you away from the art of sophistry. It is necessary, therefore, that I—someone well versed in both disciplines, having mixed them in musical harmony, so that I rhetoricize philosophically and philosophize artistically—

1. Following here the Greek title as transmitted in the earlier ms., Florence, Bibl. Med. Laur., Plut. gr. 57.40 (and also in Vienna, ÖNB, theol. gr. 160, thirteenth c.), according to which Psellos’ speech is about Gregory’s “ἐπ’ οὐδενὸς οὖν τῶν ἁπάντων οὐκ ἔστιν ἐφ’ ὅτῳ οὐχὶ τῶν ἁπάντων,” which I translate here in agreement with Psellos’ interpretation offered in this lecture. Gautier has preferred the version of Paris, BNF, gr. 1182, perhaps considering (wrongly) this manuscript as the earlier testimony. According to the Paris ms., the speech is about the sentence that immediately precedes in Gregory’s *Funeral Oration for Basil the Great* = *Or.* 43.1: Ὧν γὰρ τοὺς ἐπαίνους, οἶδα τούτων σαφῶς καὶ τὰς ἐπιδόσεις (“if I know the praises of something, I also know clearly its growth,” translated again in agreement with Psellos’ interpretation).

2. For a definition of περίοδος, see “Hermogenes,” *On Invention* 4.3.

must expound the arts of rhetoric to you. I must explain how those who have reached the pinnacle of this art leave some things unspoken in their texts while elsewhere adding redundancies. For I am not envious of those who follow Gorgias and Polus;[3] and I admired neither the eloquence of Polemon, uttering his words with a "whistling sound" without displaying philosophical character [ἦθος], nor Herodes' sweetness adapted to the height of philosophy.[4] Rather, I belong to the group of Dion, Favorinos, and Leon of Byzantion: whichever of their subjects you examine, you will find it philosophical yet pronounced with charm—skillfully, that is, and with beautiful words.[5]

[22–43] I wish to parade my discourse also next to the art of Plato and emulate his rhetoric. And definitely my case proves the fable about the turtle to be true as I compare myself and compete with a horse, beautiful, virile, enormous, really a matter of poetry, stamping over the plains.[6] Away with them, those Aristeideses and Dionysii, and anyone else who has bad-mouthed Plato regarding his word selection![7] In my view, this man—alone among men of

3. This disparaging of Gorgias and his student Polus is a commonplace among philosophical readings of rhetoric (cf. Stephanos Skylitzes, *Comm. on Aristotle's Rhetoric* 268.22–28); it goes back to Plato's *Gorgias*. Hermogenes regards both rhetors (or "sophists," as he calls them) as the representative examples of those who pursue that inferior style which *appears to be*, but *is actually not* "forceful" (*On Force* = *On Forms* 2.9.34).

4. The statements about Polemon (ca. 90–144 CE) and Herodes Attikos (ca. 101–77 CE) echo Philostratos, *Lives of the Sophists* 2.15 (on Polemon's "whistling sound"; cited also in Anna Komnene, *Alexiad* 14.7.4) and 2.18 (on Herodes' "sweet treatment of thoughts").

5. "whichever . . . skillfully" is taken almost verbatim from the introduction to Synesios' *Dion* (1.5): ὧν ἥντινα ἂν λάβῃς ὑπόθεσιν, φιλόσοφός ἐστι μετακεχειρισμένη σοφιστικῶς, τοῦτ' ἔστι λαμυρῶς ἀπηγγελμένη καὶ δεξιῶς (cf. Psellos: ὧν ἥντινα ἂν λάβῃς ὑπόθεσιν, φιλόσοφός ἐστι λαμυρῶς ἀπηγγελμένη, τουτέστι δεξιῶς καὶ μετ' ὀνομάτων καλῶν). In his text, Synesios criticizes Philostratos' evaluation of Dio Chrysostom. Psellos is aware of Philostratos' original text as well: Synesios (1.2) places Dio with Plato's student, Leon of Byzantion; Philostratos places him with Leon, but also with his contemporary Favorinos (*Lives of the Sophists* 1.2 [Leon], 7 [Dio], 8 [Favorinos]).

6. πεδίων κροαίνοντι: Homer, *Iliad* 6.507, a metaphor that Gregory of Nazianzos applies to himself in the *Funeral Oration for Basil* = *Or.* 43.24 (I thank Byron MacDougall for this reference). For the fable about the turtle and its competition with the horse, see Libanios, *Progymnasmata* 1, *Fable* 2; according to the fable, the turtle wins the race due to its diligence.

7. Cf. Ailios Aristeides, *To Plato, on Rhetoric* and *To Platon, In Support of the Four* (see further Flinterman 2000–2001; Milazzo 2002); and Dionysios of Halikarnassos, *On Demosthenes* 23, 25–26, and 32 with his *On Composition* 25. This defense of Plato against the rhetoricians is a common place in Psellos; see above pp. 76–77.

the ages—treads the summits of both philosophy and rhetoric, neither parading himself next to someone else nor allowing anyone else to imitate him. Indeed, I pour wide laughter[8] on Longinos when he compares Lysias' letter on eros with Plato's artful speeches on the same subject and claims that he is ashamed of the man [Plato] because he appears inferior to the rhetor.[9] "Based on which knowledge or trained skill," I would say to him, "are you, most excellent one,[10] measuring the arts of Plato? Or which capability do you possess that is superior to his, so as to be able to understand in what regard the man is deficient and in what he is abundant? Don't you hear Proklos, the truly great philosopher, saying loud and clear that if the Greek gods wanted to compose writings or rhetorical speeches they would compose them following the harmony and composition of Plato?[11] Nevertheless, you, together with Aristeides and Dionysios of Halikarnassos, wait for me for another occasion when I will put on my discursive gear and take up a war against you in support of Plato."

[43–51] This is what I would say and claim: no one, absolutely no man, can compete with Plato—with the exception of Gregory, great in theology, whose phrase "among all, there exists no one for whom this among all [things will not be found to be the case]" you pose for examination today. And to you I would say that you abuse the text, even though you happen to be students of philosophy. For not only do you confuse the various concepts, but you also cut the words themselves from their context [συμφράσεως]. Are you not afraid that some Athenian might indict you for wickedness and refer you to the supreme court of Areopagos?

[52–68] What do I mean? I mean that you should not pose the question regarding this passage starting from that point. Rather, you should begin with

8. A learned expression that Psellos uses also elsewhere (*Chronographia* 5.20); the *Suda* cites Simokattes' letters (*Letter* 61.15–16) for an example (gamma.116): Γέλως πλατύς· ὁ δὲ Πέρσης ἐς τοσοῦτον ἐληλάκει φρυάγματος ὡς γέλωτα τῶν ἀγγελλόντων καταχέειν πλατύν. Σιμοκάτης φησί.

9. This phrase has been included in the fragments of Longinos; Patillon and Brisson 2001: fr. 41. Lysias' speech in Plato's *Phaedrus* (230e6–234c5) is designated as a "letter" by the fifth-century Alexandrian Neoplatonist Hermeias, whose commentary on the *Phaedrus* Psellos knew.

10. ὦ βέλτιστε: a common (and rather polemical) form of address in Plato; see, e.g., *Apology* 24e1.

11. I could not locate an exact parallel for this statement. In his *Comm. on the Timaeus* 1.60.1–11, cited by Gautier, Proklos parallels Plato's making of the *Republic* with the "divine creation/poetry [ποίησις]" of the divine "demiurge [δημιουργός]."

the phrase "if I know the praises of something, I also know clearly its growth." For the phrase "among all, there exists no one for whom this among all [things will not be found to be the case]" is part of that other period testing the validity of a universal statement through the particulars. That great man had clarified in advance, as if in a prefatory statement,[12] and set three things on account of which it behooved him to deliver the encomium of his companion: himself, those who praise virtue, and discourse itself.[13] He takes these one by one, tackles them rhetorically, and elaborates them. After going through what pertained to his own person and examining perfectly the first topic, he came to the second one, which was the "exhortation" of the listeners "toward virtue" (for "when the righteous is praised," as someone said [Proverbs 29:2], "people will rejoice," in divine, that is, joy and the pleasure), which listeners enact through deeds and thus assimilate themselves to the praised one. Then he confirms this partial proposition, by adding[14] in a solemn, universal, and categorical fashion this period: "if I know the praises of something, I also know clearly its growth."

[69–92] The meaning of this period is the following. Virtues and vices, arts and artlessness, abilities and inabilities, accept neither increase nor decrease in themselves as they are. For justice and piety, injustice and impiety, philosophical ability and a-philosophical, so to speak, inability, exist on their own, always, and we say that these increase or decrease with respect to the lives of those who strive after them. Virtue, for instance, is increased with the golden race according to Hesiod, while it decreases with the silver one and now even more with the iron one.[15] As the one is increased or decreased, the other, as if on a scale, is definitely raised up or lowered down. For this increase and decrease, the Greeks blame the weavings of the stars and Fate. *We* attribute the inclination toward the one or the other to the self-movement and authority of intention; this is strengthened especially when either this or that is praised. For when virtue is extolled, everyone is inclined and aims toward

12. προκατασκευή: for this term, see "Hermogenes," *On Invention* 3.2: ἔργον δὲ αὐτῆς τὸ προεκτίθεσθαι τὰ κεφάλαια καὶ τὰ ζητήματα, οἷς περιπλακεὶς ὁ λόγος συμπληρώσει τὴν ὑπόθεσιν.

13. Cf. Gregory, *Or.* 43.1: Οὐκ οἶδα δὲ εἰς ὅ τι ἂν ἄλλο χρησαίμην τοῖς λόγοις μὴ νῦν χρησάμενος. ἢ ὅ τί ποτ' ἂν μᾶλλον ἢ ἐμαυτῷ χαρισαίμην ἢ τοῖς ἀρετῆς ἐπαινέταις ἢ τοῖς λόγοις αὐτοῖς, ἢ τὸν ἄνδρα τοῦτον θαυμάσας.

14. Reading "ἐπήγαγεν" (**L** and **w**) instead of "ἐξήγαγεν" (**P**).

15. Hesiod, *Works and Days* 109–26, 127–42, and 174–201.

it; and when vice is praised, again many run to it. When rhetoric is honored, everyone becomes a sophist and a rhetor. When philosophy is appreciated, everyone offers proofs and syllogisms. Sicilians are all tyrannical (especially Philistos) because both Dionysii chose to be tyrants rather than kings. And when Plato converted the younger Dionysios to philosophy leading him away from tyranny, again everyone became a geometer drawing shapes and the court was full of dust.[16] Then again, when Dionysios changed his mind and became ill-disposed toward Plato, all became ignorant of geometry, praising immediately tyranny and serving the tyrant.[17]

[93–98] "If I know the praises of something, I also know clearly its growth," that is to say, those things grow that are crowned with praises. The word "clearly" of the second colon is not redundant, but is said by the great Gregory so that the rhythmical harmony of the sentence is preserved. For the rhetor should not have added superfluous syllables to the subsequent *komma* of the period.[18]

[98–108] Having proclaimed this period so solemnly, Gregory confirms it again by induction, not by listing specific people by name, but by indicating this through the phrase "among all, there exists no one." "My statement," he says, "that every praised thing receives growth and increase is so powerful that its truth can be seen if we consider any single person": when virtue is praised, he is a worker of virtue, but when vice is the subject of hymns, the same individual is a worker of vice; now a worker of philosophy, the same man is at another time a worker of rhetoric. For, he says, "among all, there exists no one" person "for whom this among all" things will not be found to be the case: increase and growth of praised and revered things. For the first "among all" refers to persons, while the second to things.

[109–30] The thought is complete in itself with respect to its power and rhetorical zeal. It is wholly compact and Aristeidian, missing words, and hence seeming to be confused or, rather, truncated abruptly and cut in half. Such phrasing is rather intellectual, befitting philosophers, and very Platonic

16. The image of geometers drawing figures in the sand or dust is possibly reminiscent of Socrates in Plato's *Meno* 82a7–85c; I owe Byron MacDougall this reference.

17. The passage on the Sicilians' fickleness is taken from Plutarch, *Dion* 13 and *How to Distinguish a Flatterer from a Friend* 78d.

18. Cf. Hörandner 1995: 289–90 on these statements pertaining to prose rhythm.

on account of the contraction of its thought—just as those texts in which there is much elucidation are corporeal and with material dimensions.[19] For this reason, Plato too is verbose and thorough in his *Gorgias* but rather abstruse and compact in the *Parmenides*. Such is also Plotinos and the great Proklos who wrote an elementary introduction to the theologian [Plato].[20] Before their time so also was Aristotle, who in his intellectual overview of the types of the soul is extremely dense and condenses his thoughts to narrow breadth, but who is exceedingly pleasant, elucidating, and celebrated for the beauty of his words, when discussing the nature of animals. Indeed, in my view, Demosthenes and Aristeides created their rhetorical speeches in imitation of that man [Aristotle].[21] Aristeides, however, defied the harmony of the art of rhetoric comprising all types of voice; he is therefore of a single form, tiresome, and, in most cases, obscure in his diction. Demosthenes, by contrast, is a Parrhasios when working on Hermes and a Myron when working on the heifer:[22] having attuned himself to every art and also to the disposition and capacity of his audience, at one time he is eloquent with his noisy words resounding, at another he furrows the brows of his speeches and he is mostly sulky like Heraclitus; sometimes he is barren and abstruse, at other times, he

19. For this opposition ("intellectual" vs. "corporeal" and "with material dimensions"), often applied to the distinction between soul and body, see, e.g., Proklos, *Comm. on the Timaeus* 3.324.25ff.

20. A reference to Proklos' *Elements of Theology*.

21. Though perhaps not echoed by Psellos here, it should be noted that Dionysios of Halikarnassos refutes the idea of some of his contemporaries that Demosthenes achieved his superb rhetoric by following the tenets of Aristotle's *Rhetoric*. "It was not the rhetor that received from the philosopher the arts according to which he constructed those admirable speeches of his, but rather Aristotle wrote these arts by citing the works of Demosthenes and the other rhetors" (*To Ammaeus* 12.66–71).

22. Psellos writes "τοκάδα," which literally translates as either "mothered" or "mothering" and which could be any animal, including humans. Myron was most famous for his heifer, a favorite topic for epigrammatists, as thirty-six epigrams, e.g., in the *Palatine Anthology* attest; cf. also Tzetzes and Prokopios and, for the references, see Overbeck 1868: 103–7. On Parrhasios and his Hermes, see Overbeck 1868: 323, where a single reference from Themistios, Psellos' likely source here. The passage is worth quoting: ὥσπερ, οἶμαι, φασὶ τὸν Παρράσιον, ὅτι γράφειν τὸν Ἑρμῆν ἐγχειρήσας τὴν ἑαυτοῦ μορφὴν τῷ πίνακι ἐγκατέθετο καὶ ἐξαπατᾷ τοὺς ἀνθρώπους τὸ ἐπίγραμμα τῆς εἰκόνος. οἴονται γὰρ ὅτι Παρράσιος ἑαυτὸν ἐτίμησέ τε καὶ ἐκύδηνε τῷ ἀναθήματι, πόρρω ὄντες τῆς τοῦ ζωγράφου σοφίας, ὃς ἵνα φύγῃ ἀπειροκαλίαν τε καὶ φιλαυτίαν, ἀλλοτρίῳ ὀνόματι εἰς τὴν γραφὴν κατεχρήσατο (*To the Emperor Constantius, that the King Is Especially a Philosopher, or a Speech of Thanksgiving* 29c–d).

is palatable and sumptuous; now loose in his phrasing, then convoluted by the varied manner of his articulation.

[131–34] The great theologian Gregory has left all these behind, like an eagle flying above jackdaws.[23] I make this argument now, without offering any proof. At the appropriate occasion, and if God keeps me well, I will provide a clear, full inquiry.

23. The juxtaposition of eagles and jackdaws is common in Gregory; see, e.g., *Letters* 178 and 224; see also *De Vita sua* 1680–81 (where Gregory calls his opponents "jackdaws"); I thank Rebecca Falcasantos and Byron MacDougall for these references.

10 *On Saint John Chrysostom*

Translated with introduction and notes
by Stratis Papaioannou

Introduction

Like the *Discourse Improvised . . . about the Style of the Theologian*, Psellos' essay on John Chrysostom titled *Εἰς τὸν ἅγιον Χρυσόστομον* is an encomium of a Christian orator, described in the terms of traditional rhetorical theory. The primary source for Psellos is again Dionysios of Halikarnassos, to whom some Hermogenian theory has been added. Indeed, one might claim that just as Dionysios had his two favorites, first Demosthenes but then also Lysias, and composed essays on the style of both, so also Psellos repeats the ancient rhetorician's arrangement of the rhetorical canon by writing on Gregory of Nazianzos but then also on Chrysostom.

That Chrysostom is somewhat inferior to Gregory for Psellos, like Dionysios' Lysias was to his Demosthenes, is clear both by the shorter encomium devoted to Chrysostom and, in general, by how rarely Psellos refers to him or alludes to his texts.[1] This slight neglect of Chrysostom is partly remedied by this essay, which not only completes Psellos' implied (self?-)image as a new Dionysios, but also satisfies expectations that would have been typical among

1. As we saw above, Chrysostom is included in Psellos' rhetorical canon presented in *The Styles of Gregory the Theologian, Basil the Great, Chrysostom, and Gregory of Nyssa*. But there is little more of Chrysostom in Psellos. For two rare instances, see *Theol.* I 29.125–34 and 72.2–9 with no discussion, however, of John's style.

his audience. John with the "Golden Tongue" was, after all, famous precisely for his eloquence. His prominence in middle Byzantine book culture is undeniable: a very large number of manuscripts circulating with his texts,[2] many hagiographical narratives and encomia devoted to him,[3] and, of course, his immense influence on Byzantine homiletics.[4]

Psellos pays tribute to these expectations by presenting Chrysostom as an ideal rhetor, whose most important feature seems to be his natural, unembellished expression, maximized by his transparent clarity (§§ 3–5, 9–10, 16–19, 23)—his equivalent to Lysias' "vividness" as praised by Dionysios of Halikarnassos (*On Lysias* 7). Other features suggest Psellos' own predilections. The importance of variation in both style and narrative (§§ 6–7, 15, 22–26), the reference to the representation of both character and emotion (§ 26), and his authorial individuality and autonomy (§§ 5 and 11) betray this Psellian self-reflection in Chrysostom's style. Like his Gregory, Chrysostom too, though comparable to the ancient rhetors according to *their* standards, is said to have created his style without imitating them (§ 5). Mimesis thus proves, yet again for Psellos, inferior to originality.

Editions and translations. The text of the translation is from the old but good edition of Levy 1912 (his paragraph numbering is indicated in brackets). Levy based his work on the two manuscripts that preserve the text: the Psellian Paris, gr. 1182 as well as an early fifteenth-century rhetorical collection, *Oxford, Bodleian Library, Auct.* T.1.11 [Misc. 189], where, after Plato's *Gorgias* and a series of orations by Aelios Aristeides and Isocrates, the following Psellian texts on Christian rhetoric are included: the *Discourse Improvised . . . about the Style of the Theologian, The Styles of Gregory the Theologian, Basil the Great, Chrysostom, and Gregory of Nyssa,* the essay on Chrysostom, and the *Encomium for Kyr Symeon Metaphrastes.*

For an important discussion of Psellos' essay, see Hörandner 1995–96. See also the entry in Moore (2005: 406).

2. Cf. *Codices Chrysostomici Graeci*; see also Haidacher 1902, for a popular tenth-c. anthology of Chrysostom excerpts made by Theodoros Daphnopates.

3. For the latter, see, e.g., *BHG* 870–83h; Psellos' text is no. 881m.

4. See, e.g., Bonis 1937b: 12 on the influence of Chrysostom on Ioannes Xiphilinos, a nephew of Psellos' friend, the Patriarch Ioannes Xiphilinos. For Chrysostom's reception in general, see also Wallraff and Brändle 2008.

On Saint John Chrysostom

(Translation in collaboration with Christopher M. Geadrities)

[§ 1] To John—golden in soul and tongue, our own native Demosthenes and Plato—most men usually attribute all heavenly graces, with the exception of the following two: first, that he dealt with sinners more gently than others; and, second, that he did not compose his speeches in a rhetorical fashion—not due to lack of skill but rather out of contempt for the methods of rhetoric, since he is nowhere evasive but instead pronounces everything in a straightforward manner.

[§ 2] Without an intention to contest those who speak this way as if they speak about good qualities, it seems best to me to let their former argument pass—I mean that he is too mild. However, against those who do not think of his skill as I do, I can make a sufficient argument regarding his rhetorical method, his mixing of the forms, and his overall disposition and perfection when it comes to speeches. Just because he has made his art neither apparent nor perceptible to the many, it does not follow that he should be deprived of praises for rhetorical skill. Rather, exactly because he handles the art of discourse in a hidden and philosophical manner, he ought to be crowned with a resplendent crown in front of the entire world, as if in a great theater.[1]

[§ 3] I assert that there is not one kind of rhetoric, but two, at the very least. The one is spectacular [θεατρική] and ostentatious, while the other is inaccessible to most people. The former is adorned with artificial ornaments

1. A metaphor common in Chrysostom himself; see, e.g., *On the Statues* 4.4 = *PG* 49 64.54.

and charm, decked out with figures of speech and rhyming words, as well as sections and periods with matching beginnings and ends.[2] The other kind of rhetoric pays little attention to such things. Instead, it adopts natural expression and is a straighforward conveyor of content. **[§ 4]** Since there are two kinds of rhetoric, some of the rhetors have preferred, so to speak, the licentious and crazed rhetoric, while others have honored the modest and decorous one.[3]

[§ 5] Among the followers of the latter rhetoric, the great father ranks first. For I know that if someone wished to describe the style of those rhetors of natural expression, he would pass over Lysias and Isaeus, as well as Plato, Dio Chrysostom, and all those who pursued the simple and ethical style [ἰδέα],[4] and would place John as the model for instruction in this style. Indeed if John had preceded the others in time, I would say that he is the original form of the style [τὴν ἰδέαν τοῦ χαρακτῆρος] found in their speeches. Since, however, he received the care of rhetoric succeeding those men, I would still not call him their imitator; rather, I would show that he practiced the same art as they and then clearly surpassed by far those who preceded him.

[§ 6] Concerning his rhetorical power, what am I to say except how acclaimed his works are even by those who do not know him?[5] While treating the same subject in many speeches, he appears different by the way he invents, arranges, and handles his thoughts; and neither does he take recourse to always the same thoughts in his prefaces nor does he set forth his narrations with mere variations of familiar themes. **[§ 7]** He offers proof upon proof with the best discursive economy. I know that some have attributed this also to

2. "Section (περικοπή)" is a unit larger than a colon and smaller than a period; cf. Longinos, *Art of Rhetoric* 339–46. For the fullest discussion of periods and cola (from a Byzantine perspective), see "Hermogenes," *On Invention* 4.3.

3. The distinction of two kinds of rhetoric echoes a similar distinction in Dionysios of Halikarnassos' programmatic statements in his *On Ancient Rhetors.*

4. ἀφελῆ . . . καὶ ἠθικήν: A quotation from Dionysios of Halikarnassos' *On Isaeus* 3, where this style is attributed to Lysias. The usage of the term ἰδέα instead of Dionysios' λέξις may echo also the two closely related Hermogenian *forms* of simplicity (ἀφέλεια) and character (ἦθος).

5. In this section, Psellos deals briefly with Chrysostom's invention (εὕρεσις) and discursive economy (οἰκονομία—organization/management/arrangement) of rhetorical content ("thought": ἔννοια) in the three main parts of a speech: preface (προοίμιον), narration (διήγησις), and proof (πίστις); these are discussed, among other places, in the first three books of "Hermogenes," *On Invention.*

Lysias the rhetor, but there is a great difference: John fashions different speeches out of the same subjects; in the case of Lysias, it is the varying circumstances of his topics that make his speeches different.[6]

[§ 8] Thus, with regard to his rhetorical power, I do not think that any of the earlier rhetors is equal to the great father. When it comes to his rhetorical skill, composition, and mixing of the forms, he could be compared to many others; still, he would appear to have attained something better with regards to those aspects for which each of those earlier orators was successful.

[§ 9] Given that there are three styles, namely the lofty, the middle, and the plain, he is neither weighty and bombastic in his composition, nor altogether common and trivial in his diction; rather, he aims especially for clarity.[7] **[§ 10]** He does not complete his periods without restraint, diffusely, and without a plan, but rather tightens their stream as one would the flow of water with a pipe—not a pipe that is curved and circuitous, but rather the sort that is spacious and simple.[8] This part—I mean that the sentences return upon themselves as if in full circle—few of the sophists have accomplished successfully. I believe that Lysias and Demosthenes have done so, but Demosthenes in a sophistical and bitter manner, while Lysias in a simpler though too compact way. By contrast, our father treated both simplicity with artistry and his artistic skill with the utmost simplicity.

[§ 11] He launches into his subject matters sometimes by immediately laying hold of his topic and at other times holding it suspended at a distance. This, in my view, is not a defect of his discourse but rather the highest virtue, especially whenever a digression occurs purposefully. This sort of thing is less esteemed in judicial oratory, yet for many reasons it is fitting for the

6. For a praise of Lysias' rhetorical "power" manifested in the various parts of a (judicial) speech, see Dionysios of Halikarnassos, *On Lysias* 16–19.

7. For the three-level theory of style, see p. 115n15 above. Psellos seems to imply that Chrysostom is following the middle style, though the emphasis on clarity places him also within the field of the plain style, whose best exponent was Lysias, according to Dionysios of Halikarnassos' original theory of the three types of styles; cf. *On Demosthenes* 2.

8. Levy's addition of the verb "ἐγχεῖ" at the end of this sentence seems unnecessary. The image of the pipe, in which words are "tightened like water," stems from Gregory of Nazianzos (*On the Son* = *Or.* 29.1) and is common in Psellos; see p. 114 above.

teacher who does not compose his speeches with the clock in mind but arranges his interpretations according to his own will. **[§ 12]** Neither when Chrysostom speaks about his topic at the onset nor when he approaches it obliquely does he ever appear to be doing something that lacks skill. In the former cases, he ascends by moving downwards; in the latter, he leads his speech downwards by elevating it.[9]

[§ 13] He handles the prefaces in all sorts of ways and clearly achieves the manner appropriate to a teacher in addition to introducing every thought fitting for a preface.[10] Either he reprimands his listeners, using speech like a spur for the arousal of interest into what he introduces; or he shows at first consideration for his audience and predisposes the minds of the lazier listeners, drawing their attention. Then, as soon as he has offered a cure and a supportive crutch, he sparks forth like lightning, balancing his speech by loosening the reins and, simultaneously, restraining that part of the soul that is difficult to bridle. Occasionally, he even praises the listeners, so that he might captivate them and incline them toward a similar zeal; using the praises as a loan, he then requests multiplied interest. **[§ 14]** If a preface seems sufficient for the subject matter, he moves on. If it seems to be hanging, however, he adds, unnoticeably, another preface. The two prefaces then seem as one, though each is divided according to its own thoughts.[11]

9. With this obscure and paradoxically structured sentence about Chrysostom's process of logical/rhetorical argumentation, Psellos perhaps wishes to present Chrysostom's ability to both elevate his subjects (as well as his audiences) and, simultaneously, render them comprehensible.

10. For various ways of handling the preface (προοίμιον) of a speech, see the first chapter of "Hermogenes," *On Invention* along with its Byzantine commentaries; cf., e.g., Ioannes Doxapatres, *Prolegomena* to his *Comm. on Hermogenes' On Invention* 363.5–22. For the concept of the "manner appropriate to a teacher," see Ioannes Sikeliotes, *Prolegomena* 407.20–26 with Ioannes Doxapatres, *Prolegomena* to his *Comm. on Hermogenes' On Invention* 372.20–29 (ed. Rabe) where a fourfold division is introduced: διαιρετικός, ὁριστικός, ἀποδεικτικός, and ἀναλυτικός. For "thoughts fitting to a preface," see Ioannes Doxapatres, *Rhetorical Homilies on Aphthonios' Progymnasmata* 134.1–3 (ed. Rabe) (on the *progymnasmata* as preparatory for such thoughts) and Psellos, *Epitaphios in Honor of the Most-Blessed Patriarch, Kyr Ioannes Xiphilinos, Or. fun.* 3.22.65–66 (on Xiphilinos' skill in composing *prooimia*) with *Discourse Improvised . . . about the Style of the Theologian* §§ 41–43: 342–58 (on Gregory of Nazianzos) and pp. 43–45 above.

11. For employing two prefaces, see Anonymous, *Prolegomena to a Comm. on Hermogenes' On Invention* 70.10–23 (ed. Walz, vol. 7) where an example from Demosthenes' third *Olynthiac* is adduced. See above p. 142 on Gregory of Nazianzos.

[§ 15] When he narrates,[12] he is neither verbose nor does he use turgid words[13] or conclude the narration too quickly. Rather, having offered an exposition of the subject matter part-by-part, he adorns it with various additional narratives [ἐπεισοδίοις]; having added some of those, he then immediately returns the speech to its main subject; and then, after proceeding and interrupting again the sequence, he quickly rounds this part off and concludes it. The device originates, I think, in Herodotus, except that Herodotus renders the secondary task superior to his main work and makes the additions greater than the parts to which these are added,[14] while Chrysostom, after a brief digression, makes a turn and comes back.

[§ 16] Whenever he explains a biblical phrase, whether pertaining to doctrine or to the narrative, he reveals and clarifies the meaning to his listeners in many ways, both gathering all kind of narrative [ἱστορίαν] and disclosing matters of doctrine.[15] His discourse then arrives at character, capturing every notion for the remedy of his listeners' souls.[16] **[§ 17]** He is also willing to treat matters allegorically; he adjusts his speech, however, according to his audience. Having opened his mouth enough so as to show to the more educated ones that he speaks from the pulpit and the innermost sanctuary, for the most part he sets everything within a discussion of character and a precise examination of virtues—though now is not the time to discuss these matters.

[§ 18] Let my discourse instead trace the father's rhetorical art. For just because he uses his speech in an unpretentious manner, this does not mean that he does not care for method. Rather, while for others method consists in embellishing topics and speaking forcefully, for him method is style that is unconstrained and pure.[17] Art and method do not depend upon convoluted speech, but on that

12. Having discussed prefaces (προοίμια), Psellos moves to a discussion of the second part of a speech: narration, διήγησις.

13. For this Philostratean/Synesian expression (φλεγμαίνουσιν ὀνόμασιν), see pp. 104 and 129 above.

14. Cf. Dionysios of Halikarnassos, *Epistle to Pompeius Geminus* 11–14, who seems to praise Herodotus' digressions; Photios (*Bibliothêkê* 60 19b.19–25) is somewhat critical of this feature in Herodotus.

15. For the term ἱστορία see p. 137 above.

16. Cf. 2 Cor. 10:5.

17. ἐν τῷ ἀπολύτῳ καὶ καθαρῷ χαρακτῆρι. Photios (*Bibliothêkê* 5 3b.13–15) makes a similar remark on Sophronios of Jerusalem: Ἀφοριστικῷ δὲ κέχρηται χαρακτῆρι, καὶ ὡς ἐπίπαν ἀπόλυτός ἐστιν αὐτῷ καὶ ἀσύνδετος ὁ λόγος, οὐκ ἄχαρις δέ, ἀλλὰ καὶ λογικοῖς ἐπιχειρήμασι περιηνθισμένος. The notion derives likely from Aphthonios who

discourse that is assimilated to the subject matter and fitting for the occasion. Indeed, this very thing—namely, to appear not to speak according to method but to do so intentionally—is, itself, a matter of method and rhetorical art.[18]

[§ 19] For instance, by presenting certain affected and strange meters in many of his plays, Euripides of Phlyeia received the bad reputation of ill expression among many philologists.[19] Thucydides has similarly been blamed for adding one bombastic figure upon the other, while he should have loosened the density of his diction.[20] By contrast, the one with the golden tongue refines his speeches in his own soul as if in a melting furnace and thus displays all his words as pure and transparent. His phrasing is neither full of rhetorical figures nor of neologisms and periods, but, rather, his words are common, his composition is unpretentious, and the dignity of his discourse is lofty and rises to the sky.

[§ 20] He invents his arguments not according to technical rules, but in a natural fashion and then handles and arranges them very methodically. He lays out all the sections first and then distributes the thoughts belonging to each; or, alternatively, he proceeds by completing one section at a time, rendering simultaneously his subjects and their elaboration. When he attempts to prove something, he does not introduce as many arguments as the art of rhetoric might demand, but only as many as seem sufficient to his purpose. He either sets forth these arguments, having first announced and enumerated them in advance, or he presents them unexpectedly and spontaneously. **[§ 21]** As he advances, his speech becomes more vigorous and more brilliant, because his spirit does not fade, but rises more fervently. He is not like a land breeze that ends quickly, but, like a gentle zephyr, he bursts into the souls of his listeners without causing any pain.

[§ 22] His discourse is a mixture of all the forms and no one could say that, though adorned by this or that form, it is missing this one or that one.[21]

---

prescribes an ἀπόλυτος style for the *progymnasma* of speech-in-character or êthopoiia (*Progymnasmata* 35.11–45): "Ἐργάσῃ δὲ τὴν ἠθοποιίαν χαρακτῆρι σαφεῖ, συντόμῳ, ἀνθηρῷ, ἀπολύτῳ, ἀπηλλαγμένῳ πάσης πλοκῆς τε καὶ σχήματος." Cf. the relevant commentary by Ioannes of Sardeis (pp. 208–9).

18. Cf. Hermogenes, *On Forms* 2.9.29–33 (on discourse that is forceful but does not appear to be so).

19. For Euripides' supposed Phlyeiasian origin, cf. *Suda* phi.550 and note in Dyck 1986: 53.

20. For this assessment of Thucydides, see Hörandner 1995–96: 342–43.

21. Psellos will go on to discuss various Hermogenian forms, starting with clarity (σαφήνεια).

Rather, he is clear like no other. **[§ 23]** Wherever purity falls by the wayside, he restores it by adding distinctness with various methods: he enumerates, divides, recapitulates, or concludes rapidly.[22] It would follow that such a discourse would have neither sternness nor dignity. Nevertheless, his discourse is raised from the earth to the sky, accumulating grandeur by gradual progression and becoming suspended on high. Or, rather, he is immediately such. I often compared him to air, namely, a body that is thin, fine, transparent, reaching toward the ether. For his discourse too is transparent such that one might compare it, rather than air, to . . .[23] and leading every soul to astonishment by the grandeur. **[§ 24]** His thoughts are solemn yet with civic character, and his diction is pure and resplendent, while he divides most of his arguments with *kommata* that are easy to take in at a glance. In some cases, he is adorned with brilliance, gazing all around himself, like a peacock,[24] and delighting in that he begat spiritual children by his instruction in the gospel.[25] In other instances, he adds *kommata* upon *kommata*, thus completing his thoughts at length. **[§ 25]** He possesses moderation more than anyone else, yet he often reprimands his audience while employing vehemence. His rhythms acquire passion and his spirit shows the same symptoms. This becomes his art; for the passion is not natural but adopted for the sake of the audience's needs.[26] He uses vigor for his thoughts and displays only as much amplification as might not hurt the ear. For he applies this amplification to one section of the speech only in order to explain what has preceded. **[§ 26]** Which other rhetor is so accomplished in character? Who is more powerful in emotion? Who can apply irony as well as he does? Is there anyone who has taken more care for precision in words? No one; far from it!

[§ 27] For these reasons, I would chastise anyone who denies the man the art of discourse, in which he has partaken more than those who have followed strictly the rules of rhetoric in their writings.

22. For these methods appropriate to the form of distinctness (εὐκρίνεια), see pp. 25 and 59 above.

23. There is a gap here in the text; Levy follows Keil and adds "τῷ αἰθέρι," an unconvincing conjecture.

24. For this metaphor, see Gregory of Nazianzos, *On Theology* = *Or.* 28.24 and *Against the Vanity of Women* = *Poem* 1.2.29.77–86 (ed. Knecht 1972; cf. pp. 78–79).

25. Cf. 1 Cor. 4:15; cf. John Chrysostom, *Fourth Homily on the Second Epistle to the Thessalonians* = *PG* 62 492.30–47.

26. For this phrase, see the remarks in Hörandner 1995–96: 343n41.

11 *To One Asking "Who Wrote Verse Better, Euripides or Pisides?"*

Translated with introduction and notes
by Antony Littlewood

Introduction

The idea of comparing an Attic tragedian from the fifth century BCE with a Byzantine iambic poet of historical and theological subjects from the seventh century CE has been deprecated in harsh language by most modern scholars who have commented on this opusculum by Psellos. It would not, however, have appeared in any way bizarre to a Byzantine, for both were writers in verse on, generally, lofty themes. The fact that one was a dramatist, although recognized, was hardly an obstacle to a comparison since plays were not performed in Byzantium but merely read like other poetry. Also, for all the lip-service paid to literary genres by Byzantine writers,[1] there had been an increasing breakdown in generic distinctions since the late Roman period when the influence of rhetoric in the Second Sophistic permeated not only prose but also every kind of poetry.[2] Consequently all poetry could be enjoyed

1. A more valid categorization of Byzantine literature, and one that crosses the borders of the traditional genres, would be that of humor, eroticism, subversion, etc. (see Littlewood 2005, esp. 142–43).

2. Whereas in antiquity perhaps only Aristotle gained distinction as a writer of both prose and verse (Cicero's opinion of himself as the greatest prose-writer and poet of his age earned mockery), many Byzantine authors, including Psellos, moved easily from one to the other.

for its rhetorical beauty—and therefore could also be compared. Moreover, Psellos' main discussion is of meter, and both Euripides and Pisides (the latter almost exclusively) wrote iambics.

Whoever wrote the title (almost certainly not Psellos himself) assumed that this piece, like so many of the author's opuscula, was written in answer to a question. If so, the questioner was probably merely one of his pupils.[3] The work, in the form of a σύγκρισις ("comparison") so beloved by the rhetoricians, is not one of Psellos' more thoughtful productions. It owes much to Hermogenes and Dionysios of Halikarnassos, and has marks of haste, such as at times a not entirely coherent jumping from one subject to another, too frequent repetition of the same word, and simple parading of technical terms.

The main points of interest in the work today are Psellos' awareness of changes in rhythmic patterns over a long period of time and of the move from quantitative to accentual verse, his appreciation of different styles of speech for different characters (and consequent criticism of Odysseus' defeat by Hecuba) in Euripides, and his realization that *Prometheus Bound* is different from the other plays ascribed to Aeschylus.[4]

The final answer in the work as to poetic superiority is, unfortunately, unclear owing to the mutilated condition of the manuscript at that point. Although Psellos devotes more attention to Euripides, the victor was perhaps Georgios Pisides, a conclusion that was valid if the main purpose of the work was to determine which poet was a better metrical model for the composition of iambic verse.

Editions and translations. The opusculum is preserved in Vatican, BAV, Barberinianus gr. 240, a manuscript of the late thirteenth century that is both written in a notoriously difficult hand and badly damaged. Extracts were copied from it in the seventeenth century by the Greek-Italian humanist Leo Allatius (Leone Allacci), and survive in codex Vallicellianus 166 and codex Vallicellianus 206, the latter of which contains also a partial translation into Latin. These are of some use since the Barberinianus manuscript has deteriorated in the last three hundred years (it is now completely protected in nylon sheathing), but Allatius' transcriptions are not always reliable. The first publication of the whole text is that of Colonna 1953. In 1986 Dyck re-edited the work,

3. Dyck points out the elementary nature of such material as who the Phrygians were and what a solecism is.

4. See also pp. 19 and 82–90 above.

furnishing it with a commentary and an English translation;[5] for further editions and bibliography, see Moore 2005: 407–9. The present translation follows Dyck's text except where otherwise noted—numbers in brackets indicate line numbers from Dyck's edition.[6] Words contained within angle brackets indicate restorations for either a lacuna in the Barberinianus or a word so badly damaged there that it can no longer be read with confidence. Words contained within square brackets are simply additions to make the meaning clearer.

5. The lines specifically concerning Euripides have been more recently edited by Kannicht 2004: 117–18. Wilson translated a few lines into English and made a few comments on the piece (1983: 178–79).

6. Of the reviews of Dyck's edition I have found most useful those of D. A. Christides (*Hellenika* 37 [1986]: 371–77), E. V. Maltese (*Maia*, n.s. 39 [1987]: 169–71) and especially U. Criscuolo (*Byzantinische Zeitschrift* 81 [1988]: 56–58). The most detailed discussions of the text are Kambylis 1994 for the opening lines (Dyck 3–11) and 2006 for the remainder of the opusculum.

The Same [i.e., Psellos], To One Asking "Who Wrote Verse Better, Euripides or Pisides?"

[3–11] The tragedian Euripides of Phlyeia and Georgios <of Pisidia>, who wrote in the iambic meter more accurately than the many others who used it,[1] are "both spearmen"[2] in meter and poetry. <Since they made the>[3] same verbal utterance very much alike, so to speak, it is hard to see what distinction there is between them and which is superior to the other. <If>, however, <someone>[4] has a notable <knowledge> of both <arts>, the metric and the rhythmic, that is lofty and theoretical understanding concerning meters and feet, it is not very difficult to find some difference between the two and to grant the prize of victory to one over the other.

1. I accept Criscuolo's supplement of χρησαμένους rather than Dyck's ἑπομένους ("followed").

2. Reading "ἄμφω μὲν αἰχμη[τά]," following Kambylis' (1994) suggestion. Cf. Homer, *Iliad* 7.281 (a formula often quoted in Byzantine texts, including Psellos—see his *Encomium in Honor of the Most-blessed Kyr Konstantinos Leichoudes, Patriarch of Constantinople,* Sathas IV 393.12–13).

3. I translate Criscuolo's restoration of a plural verb rather than Dyck's singular (whose subject would be Pisides).

4. Psellos here most probably refers to himself. In the *Encomium for His Mother* (1723–30) he claims that he was attracted to music, "grew up with it and have appropriated it as my own," examining not only "types of . . . meters" but also "the essence of its rhythms" (translated Kaldellis 2006: 100).

[12–32] Let us by all means preface this point to our account—that meters and rhythms over the years <have taken on> innumerable variations. The heroic meter[5] does not nowadays keep its ancient dignity nor take its place among the most exact meters; but the ithyphallic meters[6] and <iambic> combinations are mixed with the dactylic and spondaic, nor does the iambic meter obviously possess the same pauses, rhythms, and composition as earlier examples, but is now more theatrical [θεατρικώτερον] and has as it were become shameless on the stage as it leaps beyond every <metrical unit> and flies beyond every rhythm, the single thing to be emulated now being what leaps out of the meter rather than the iambic beat.[7] Tragic poetry, however, adorned with various rhythms and embracing manifold meters <does not completely> dance out or overleap its subject matter, but there are times when it aims for mellifluous sounds, chooses a rhythmic structure based on feet, and welcomes metrical combinations of words, whereas when the poet so fancies it turns from the [customary] pitch [of the voice] and completely alters the rhythm. At times the rhythm is snatched away, but at others it walks upon a trisyllabic or tetrasyllabic <metrical> base. And when rhetorical speech is expressed with beauty[8]—I mean the form [ἰδέᾳ]—it somehow makes rhythmical . . . more musical rhythms;[9] when in other forms [ἰδέαις] it is above all rough,[10] <I mean> it makes meters <rough> and roughens the hearing.

[33–44] At all events Euripides, who had a very exact knowledge of poetry like no one else—unless someone prefer Sophocles to him—<is admirable for

5. The dactylic hexameter used from the time of Homer for epic, but not restricted to that genre. Pisides revolutionarily chose iambic trimeters for his epics heroizing the emperor Herakleios.

6. The ithyphallic meter (-˘-˘- -) was so called from its use in the Dionysiac phallus-carrying (φαλλαγωγία), which Aristotle affirms to be the origin of comedy. It is a form of iambic (or, with the suppression of the first syllable, trochaic) syncopation and is frequently found in the dactylo-epitrites of drama.

7. I accept here Haslam's (in the editions' app. crit.) οὐδ᾽ ἰαμβόκροτον for Allatius' reading of καὶ ἰαμβόκροτον in what is now a lacuna in the ms. The translation of this exceedingly rare word I owe to my colleague C. G. Brown.

8. Hermogenes' form of κάλλος.

9. Perhaps "rhythms more musical"; the lacuna makes the choice uncertain and the meaning of the sentence rather unclear.

10. This translates Criscuolo's restoration of ἐντραχύς ἐστι rather than Dyck's ἐντραχ[ύν]ει ("roughens"); Kambylis (2006) suggests ἐκτραχύνει. The passage alludes to the Hermogenian form of τραχύτης.

his variety and ability to imitate everything;[11] and> sometimes you will find <the same Euripides preserving the form> of dithyrambs and also <striving for something new>,[12] and sometimes <being master of> other graceful and serious forms, adorning himself with choriambs[13] and becoming poetically highly versatile,[14] a master at delineating characters when character must assume a grave aspect, and again a master in expressing emotions [παθητικώτατον] when sufferers' emotions [πάθη] <seethe>,[15] since emotion [πάθος] is the ultimate subject of tragic poetry.[16] This is the distinction between the two forms of speaking, the tragic and the comic, namely that emotion [πάθος] <is the foundation> of the one, laughter and charm for the most part of the other.

[44–54] The parts of tragedy are many in respect to not only the stage but also to all the acting and the composition. Singing [by actors] on stage is one thing,[17] that of the chorus <another>, a parascenium [side-scene] one thing, a proscenium another,[18] episodes one thing, preludes another, messengers speak one way, Phrygians, a barbarian horde, another, and captive women or another <kind> of chorus (again speak differently). All meters[19] are not appropriate to all [roles], but the poet must call up a female song and imitate a barbarian character, make his Greek extremely idiomatic and devise dialogue appropriate to the characters presented. For this reason the words and meters are different and divergent for each group and the meters are not congruous with each other.

[54–64] Now Sophocles' and Aeschylus' thoughts are more profound and their verbal resources more stately, and, while they do not always have grace

11. On this, see Papaioannou 2013: 116.

12. 12. On this crux see Kambylis (2006). In any case the general sense must be as in the translation.

13. A choriamb (-˘ ˘-) is often associated with iambics.

14. On Psellos' fondness for this word (παντοδαπός) see Duffy and Papaioannou 2003: 225–26.

15. Colonna (1953) asserts that he read ὑποκυμαίνει where there is now a lacuna in the ms.

16. See also p. 19 above with Psellos' treatise *On Tragedy* (pp. 82–98).

17. For "on-stage singing," see relevant statements in Psellos' *On Tragedy* (pp. 92–93 and 97–98 above).

18. This translates Haslam's emendation ἕτερον μὲν τὸ παρασκήνιον, ἕτερον δὲ τὸ προσκήνιον. The ms. reads ἕτερον δὲ τὸ ἑτεροσκήνιον ("and the second scene another").

19. I translate Christides' πάντα τὰ for Dyck's πάντων <ταὐ>τὰ ("the same <meters . . . to all actions> of all <characters>").

and euphonious rhythms, their words are for the most part more stately and so to speak very decorous. So, in respect to *Prometheus Bound* <Aeschylus> deviates a little from his proper character,[20] and, through taking <excessive> delight in pure iambics and tiny words that beguile the ear, he treats his subject in too delicate a manner, since for his other dramatic subjects, especially when he portrays the house of Darius,[21] he is in general wonderfully forceful and hard to describe, and one would not understand his divine visions without being as it were an initiate.

[64–93] Euripides, on the other hand, the author of eighty or even more plays,[22] is everywhere statuesque and graceful not only in the grace of his language but also in the passions themselves. Frequently he reduced the Athenians to tears by his apt timing, for they fancied that what they saw was actually happening.[23] When he brought on Orestes mad, after offering a suitable preface about the affairs of Tantalos, and then continued to [Orestes'] sister Electra and those neighborhood women who had gathered to see and gaze at Orestes, Euripides has Electra say "with silent foot";[24] but Orestes is made to stay where he stood while the women, in response to Electra's words "Be silent, do not make a din, let there be no din!"[25] unrolled a dance for each other, uttered their lines to the music, and, not bothering whether they ought to have pronounced their words with a rising pitch, sang in different wise.[26] In this way is Euripides careful everywhere in rhythmic speech, verbal eloquence, and appropriateness of rhythm. He simply brings into his own poems the whole art of music and even the tempi themselves, nor do his speeches lack

20. Although since antiquity *Prometheus Bound* has been transmitted as one of the seven surviving plays ascribed to Aeschylus, Psellos anticipates in part the consensus of modern scholarship that attributes the play to another tragedian (possibly Euphorion).

21. In *Persians.*

22. The *Suda* reports that according to some authorities Euripides wrote ninety-two plays, of which seventy-seven were extant in the time of the original composition of the information contained in the relevant entry (epsilon.3695).

23. ᾤοντο γὰρ τὰ λεγόμενα ὁρᾶν ὡς γινόμενα: a reference to the rhetorical virtue of ἐνάργεια, vividness; cf. Papaioannou 2011.

24. *Orestes* 136.

25. This is an inaccurate remembrance of *Orestes* 140–41. The text may be corrupt, but it is difficult to see how an anacolouthon (not unknown in Psellos' oeuvre) could have been avoided.

26. That is, the pitch-accent of spoken Greek gave way to the demands of the melody.

pitch-intervals or foreign words.[27] The man has taken much thought over variety in other matters too, for he varies[28] <meters> and language and, <as much as he can>, diversifies his phraseology. The man <overlooks> neither plots <nor characterization, although in these matters the tragedies of Sophocles> were elaborated and worked on more than others. Euripides was less concerned with these matters, but gave more elaboration to musical composition, I mean in his words, and to its use and to those three of the most beautiful arts, music, rhythm and meter, bringing into his own plots as it were <oboes[29]>, kitharas, and lyres.[30] <When there was need> to speak like barbarians he imitates their language in such a way[31] that the same man [Euripides] appears both to speak perfect Greek and to commit solecisms in the most precise way, <for> to speak with barbarian vocabulary contrary to Attic is solecistic.

[93–99] There are times when Euripides strays from what is appropriate and gives in to the power of his eloquence rather than to the requirements of poetry. For instance, when he sets Hecuba against Odysseus,[32] a hero of noble birth and master of eloquence, he puts her above him, bestowing upon her the prize of honor. He works on Odysseus' declamation not without charm, but makes him inferior to the female captive. What, however, is a fault in Euripides is an achievement for others, but the precision of his language and the power of his knowledge demand the best from everybody.

[100–110] Such is Euripides. The sage from Pisidia, I think of lesser Antioch,[33] is not a poet of hexameters[34] but aimed at the iambic meter

27. γλωττημάτων, West's restoration, can mean also "obsolete words." At any rate they would be unusual words not familiar to his audience.

28. I have here followed the punctuation of (and addition of δὲ by) Kambylis (2006).

29. I have translated Colonna's restoration of αὐλούς, a word usually translated as "flute," although this reed instrument was quite unlike the modern transverse flute, being closest to the oboe (but without its keys) among modern instruments. The medieval and Renaissance shawm is an even closer parallel.

30. Properly the kithara is a box-lyre (with sides distinct from front and back), the lyra a bowl-lyre. See also Psellos' *On Tragedy* (p. 98 above).

31. Following Kambylis 2006: 140–41.

32. *Hecuba* 216–437.

33. Of the numerous Antiochs this is the one north of Pisidia in Phrygia Paroreios, the modern Yalvaç. Psellos is the sole source for the birthplace of Georgios Pisides.

34. Ninety such lines, however, are attributed to him by Sternbach 1893: 38–54.

only—I mean the <ancient and uniform type>—and, since he exerted himself principally with this he in no way varies characters . . ., and neither dramatic construction nor varied. . . . He composes his iambics very rhythmically and in a euphonious way, not minutely dividing the iamb into many parts but being satisfied at times with only three.[35] His <diction[36]> is on every occasion unforced as if he is thinking up neither the concepts nor the words but rather reading them[37] as they lay before [his eyes]. All his words are pure Greek and combine the euphonious with the elevated.

[110–32] If he were to handle a metaphor, whether one of the playful and graceful type or one of the solemn, he puts forth in language what he has thought and makes it appropriate in such a way that he appears not to spoil the other subject from which he set out for his own subject.[38] So, having mentioned a disease in his work, he immediately wheels in the whole art of medicine, sparing no <causes> or the things with which diseases are treated. If he hangs a cord from heaven and attaches to it certain powers, then immediately the rope and the attachments, both those at the top and those at the very bottom of that slack chain,[39] [become evident]. If he gathers together the Seasons and hastens them on as in a dance—ah, gracious me! —the intertwining of hands, the circle, the whirling around, the small units of motion,[40] the epode, the strophe, the antistrophe,[41] the pause,[42] the movement! If he chooses to make his words theatrical and says that his gathering of the Seasons is a four-

35. A reference to twelve-syllable verses with only three words, a practice much more common in Psellos' poetry than that of Pisides—on this, see Hörandner 1995: 286–88.

36. Allatius read ἡ ἁρμονία ("harmony") in the lacuna restored by Dyck as ἡ φράσις ("diction").

37. Retaining ταῦτα from the ms.

38. I.e., the application of his metaphor or simile is true to the original image.

39. Psellos varies his vocabulary, referring to the same cord by three different words in a single sentence. Although he is thinking of the opening of Pisides' *Contra Severum*, part of his description depends more upon a famous passage in Homer (*Iliad* 8.19–20).

40. Τῆς περιόδου probably refers to the metrical units (translated into movements in the dance) larger than feet and often corresponding to a line or half-line of choral lyric as written on the modern page. The word can also mean simply an orbit or revolution, much the same as the earlier "circle" (τοῦ κύκλου).

41. One would expect the order to be strophe, antistrophe, epode.

42. The words καὶ τοῦ ἡσύχου were excised already by Allatius, but may be correct.

horse chariot, how much does he say about charioteers and the best style of chariot-driving, how much about yokes, wheels, and hubs, what wheel-naves[43] and felloes, cheek-pieces and snortings he has! His <language> gets down to even the finest points of the science and to matters that even those who have worked systematically at the science would not mention. If he were to set phalanxes against each other, you would find there the entire cavalry and infantry arrays, the spear-men, the javelin-men, the archers, the sworn band, the <captain>, the leader of the rearguard, the comrades on the flanks, the rear-rank men. His verses leap forth as if from a sling, <vigorously> expressing his purpose together with the feet and meter.

[133–38] If you were to compare the Pisidian meters and rhythms with the tragic <poetry>, I mean that of Euripides, . . .[44] of diction and seeing the blood from the earth . . . the superiority over the poet; for I do not know if anyone <knows how> to write iambic verse more finely, just as no-one [would know] how to <write epic> [more finely], if he had not made his heroic lines few[45] and easily countable.

43. χοινικίδες ("hubs") and πλῆμναι ("wheel-naves") may be virtual synonyms or may perhaps refer to different mechanisms. In one of the two principal types the wheel turned on a "stub"-axle, being prevented from falling off by a lynch-pin, in the other the wheel was fixed to a rotating axle which itself turned within a bearing mounted beneath the chassis. In either case Psellos is just parading his knowledge of technical terms.

44. After the letters ἥττ there is a small lacuna followed by probably ἐκείνου and then ca. thirty-five missing letters. ἥττ suggests either the comparative adjective ἥττων ("worse") or some form of the verb ἡττῶμαι ("be worsted by"), both of which normally are followed by a genitive as found here in the pronoun. Although ἐκεῖνος usually, but not always, refers to the last named, which would suggest a victory for Euripides, the word γὰρ ("for") in the final section, which is surely in praise of Pisides, introduces an explanation of what has gone before. This would suggest a victory for Pisides, but the lengthy lacuna makes a final decision impossible (see above, p. 177). For a different reconstruction, see Kambylis 2006: 147–49.

45. Dyck gives the usual meaning of "short" for βραχεῖς, which may be correct, but, as Maltese points out, in later Greek the word frequently means "few," and Psellos is fond of pleonasm.

I am grateful to Stratis Papaioannou for his percipient and meticulous editing of this opusculum.

12 A Comparison of the Novels of Heliodoros and Achilleus Tatios

Translated with introduction and notes
by Antony Littlewood

Introduction

Psellos provides most of the little literary criticism surviving from Byzantium between the magisterial book reviews of the great scholar Photios in the second half of the ninth century and the comments of the intellectual Theodore Metochites in the early fourteenth century. The present work is his only comparison of two pagan productions. That he chose romantic novels is interesting in that after the third or fourth century none had been written by the time of Psellos' death, exciting adventure stories having been provided by Saints' *Lives*, which have many similarities with the romances.[1]

The two romances are Heliodoros' *Ethiopian Tale* (about Charikleia and Theagenes) and Achilleus Tatios' *Leukippe and Kleitophon*. Both authors had been given fictitious Christian careers, indicating continued reading of them but discomfort at their overt sexuality, and had been discussed by Photios, who liked the linguistic style but expressed reservations about the moral tone of Achilleus Tatios (*cod.* 87) and praised more warmly the language of He-

1. Writers could later even interpret romances as allegories of the hero's successful search for God.

liodoros (*cod.* 73). During the revival of the composition of romances in the twelfth century Eumathios Makrembolites took Achilleus Tatios as his model, Niketas Eugenianos made much use of Heliodoros, and Theodoros Prodromos had clearly read both.

As befitted a rhetorician, Psellos' preoccupation is with beauty of diction (his innumerable ways of expressing it tax the translator), and he is consequently concerned, as had been Photios, with the utility of the two works for writers of his own time. He does, nonetheless, go to considerable length to defend the morality of Heliodoros, perhaps because of attacks in some circles (he suggests at the beginning that there was contemporary debate in Constantinople). His most percipient observation, for which there is no surviving precedent, is for the structure of the *Ethiopian Tale*, which he likens to a snake hiding its head in its coils. In accordance with his own revolutionary interest as a historian in the importance of personality, he has some interesting remarks about the depiction of Charikleia. While he prefers Heliodoros to Achilleus Tatios, his essay does have many marks of a double encomium. That he takes Heliodoros as the earlier writer was the common belief until a second-century papyrus containing a fragment of Leukippe and Kleitophon was published in 1938.

Editions and translations. Psellos' treatise is preserved in two independent and famous late thirteenth-century collections of the author's works, Vatican, BAV, Barberinianus gr. 240 and Vatican, BAV, gr. 672. There are four apographs of the latter. The text that I have used is that of Dyck 1986, which edition is accompanied by introduction, English translation, and commentary. An earlier English translation was provided in Wilson 1983: 174–76. For further bibliography, see Moore 2005: 409–10. Bracketed numbers in bold indicate line numbers in Dyck's edition.

What Is the Difference between the Texts Whose Plots Concern Charikleia and Leukippe?

[3–13] I know that many among even the extremely well-educated disagree over these two romantic compositions that deal respectively with Charikleia and Leukippe, girls of both refined beauty [τὸ εἶδος ἀστεῖαι] and exceptionally superior character [ἦθος].[1] Some say that the composition about Charikleia gains a unanimous victory over the romantic treatment of Leukippe, while others to the contrary say rather that the former is inferior to the latter. Being familiar with both and having carefully examined their diction and thought, I side with none of those who have made such a judgment and have flatly spoken out against either girl; in my view each composition is in different respects superior and inferior to the other, although that about Charikleia is on the whole the better.

[14–28] The beauty of the story about her is neither excessively embellished and theatrical nor of a truth exaggeratedly Attic[2] and highflown, but it is distinguished by its elevated tone. It is lacking in neither charm nor what is

1. I cannot reproduce the pun on "beauty" and "character," Psellos' words for which (εἶδος and ἦθος), though spelled very differently were pronounced almost exactly the same (the only difference is that the central consonants are respectively voiced and unvoiced).

2. I read here Wilson's suggestion of ὑπεραττικόν for the simple ἀττικόν in the mss. since Psellos is unlikely to have adversely criticized normal Attic style, in which indeed he writes this treatise (and most other of his works).

conducive to pleasure, but has the bloom of dainty and suitably graceful vocabulary and through a variety of figures of speech and novelty of diction in composition has been raised to a higher level. It has been composed very elegantly, given life by flashes of amazing ideas and founded upon the arts of Isocrates and Demosthenes, for the underlying theme appears to be controlled in advance and any contradiction is immediately reconciled with it.[3] Initially a reader may consider much material superfluous, but, as the narrative progresses, he will marvel at the writer's tight organization: the very beginning of the work is like a curled-up snake, for these creatures hide their head within their coils while thrusting forward the rest of their body, and the book, as though assigning the introduction of the plot to the middle where it has slipped, makes its middle a beginning.[4]

[29–35] The tale luxuriates in flowers of every grace. It gives pleasure through its author's diction and fine use of language, and is beautiful through its loftiness of phraseology and because it gives the illusion of being composed to a large extent in elevated metrical style.[5] It is adorned too with additional stories that breathe, as someone might say, the charms of Aphrodite. It has linguistic elegance, a style of composition that, being poetic but yet not wearisome,[6] fills the avid ear with honey, a coherent organization, and, by virtue of its linguistic beauty, an as it were heroic quality diffused over all.

[36–43] As to what I know most people criticize (I mean in regard to Charikleia), that the author does not have her speak in a womanly or feminine way but, contrary to the rules of rhetoric, makes her utterance rise to a more sophisticated tone, this I for my part cannot praise sufficiently, for the writer has not introduced an ordinary type of girl but an initiate of the Pythian [i.e., Apollo], wherefore most of her laments are oracular, and she, inspired like

3. To try to make sense of the passage I have followed Dyck in translating τὸ ὑποτρέχον as "the underlying theme," a meaning unattested elsewhere but perhaps possible since the two elements of the word signify respectively "under" and "running"; Wilson, however, choosing an attested though rare meaning, translates as "interruptions to the narrative," which must be parallel to his "conflicting element" (my "any contradiction"), thus leaving "with it" ambiguous. The text may be corrupt.

4. For this, see further Agapitos 1998.

5. The Greek could conceivably mean "in a suitable degree of elevation," as Dyck translates it.

6. φορτικόν, i.e., with exaggerated and self-aggrandizing display of the author's skill (cf. Papaioannou 2013: 132), or, alternatively, "without vulgarity," as Dyck takes it.

prophetesses in ecstasy, is wholly the product of the tripod's cauldron [i.e., the Delphic Oracle]. The author also treats the other characters very appropriately.

[44–53] As to the unseemly aspects of the plot, which one could not cover up, he has shown by the decent manner of his narrative that they are good when spoken though bad when acted out. Thus he clears even the old man Kalasiris of the blame for pimping, a thing scarcely credible before our author by the subtle complexity of his skill rebuts the apparent accusation. More remarkably in so voluptuous and so languorous a novel he has preserved the firmness and, as it were, stubbornness of self-control, for having once drawn Charikleia's soul to love he has preserved it from that of Aphrodite Pandemos [i.e., vulgar lust][7] since even in defeat it has not shaken off its propriety.

[54–65] I note that the book touches also upon learned matters, for there are introduced subjects from the physical sciences, coining of maxims, theological discussions, and even material concerning the revolving sphere, and the book does not shy away from the fortunes generated by that last[8] —witness the commands of Kronos that Kalasiris endeavored to escape by means of certain secret words. I think, to speak in pagan terms, that not all aspects[9] came together for this one thing; but the work is not very different from the public speeches of Demosthenes with the Bacchic thyrsus[10] and consequent inspiration. The book also takes thought for whoever encounters it in that it refreshes him by means of variety, unusual phraseology, parenthetic interludes, and all manner of changes [in plots]. It includes maxims as fine as I have ever met, and, to speak briefly, is a blend of elegance and grace possessing a sweetness and beauty that one could find nowhere else.

[66–77] The book concerning Leukippe is, I believe, created in imitation of Charikleia's.[11] Yet the painter[12] did not transfer all the aspects of the original work to his own style, but, although he is wanting in other respects, he is

7. Πάνδημος ("Of All the People") was a cult title of Aphrodite in Athens. The *locus classicus* is Plato, *Symposium* 180d–181c.

8. This obscure phrase (which, like the following, Wilson refrains from translating) clearly refers to astrology.

9. In translating σχήματα as "aspects" I follow Dyck in taking this clause to refer still to astrology, whereas Wilson, translating "figures" and punctuating with a following comma, clearly links it with the following comment on linguistic style.

10. This is the ivy- and vine-clad wand capped by a pinecone carried by Dionysian devotees. Dionysos was considered the god of poetic ecstasy.

11. See the introduction to this opusculum.

12. ὁ ζωγράφος λόγος, literally "the painting discourse/reason/mind," an allusion to Gregory of Nazianzos' *Or.* 11.2. Dyck, wrongly, strikes out λόγος as a gloss.

sweeter in his expression than his predecessor. Since he gives no heed to grandeur, he is clearer because he falls short [in grandeur] and sweeter for his diction, which is very much that of the common people and in every way theatrical.[13] Now most ears[14] are not fond of literature because it babbles away, but delight deeply in the pleasures afforded by words if these pour into them. Although in certain passages he wishes to stand straight upright, he is like those who suffer from gout, since he quickly forgets the high-pitched strain[15] and is bound by his customary habits. He consequently seems for the most part vulgar in expression and to shoot somewhat wide of Attic correctness of diction.

[77–95] The book lacks vigor in its subjects and boldness in its introduction of them, but it treats facts naturally, preserves a chronological sequence and approves of clarity, preferring the tongue to the mind and the normal to the novel. When [the author] rises to oratory he is tested severely in his skill since he is indifferent to force [δεινότητος] and its method,[16] although he does take thought for beauty of composition and does not forget his habitual nature. He produces marvels and novelties in events, for he cuts open the lovely maiden, buries her, and again brings her back from the recesses of Hades — and elsewhere he effects other such events. These things are taken from his model [Heliodoros' romance]. He is, however, negligent in the relations of his lovers, and his tongue betrays his character. By elaborating what in accordance with rhetoric ought to be mentioned briefly and putting before one's view, as it were, what one would close one's eyes to if one saw them accidentally, he shows ignorance of the rules of rhetoric; and because of the pleasure of elegant language he continually makes his meaning indecent. He even tears apart the nature of the couple's erotic relationship and rapidly alters the lover's state before returning him to how he was; and he has only the one good thought—that time knows how to wither even the heights of love.

13. Here I follow the interpretation of Dyck. Wilson clearly suspected the omission of a negative before the second adjective of the received text, δημοτικωτάτην οὖσαν καὶ θεατρικωτάτην, in translating (with a query) "very ordinary and altogether unpretentious."

14. It must not be forgotten that most reading, even if by oneself in private, was done aloud, thus permitting readers to hear the beauty of the sounds of the words.

15. Here there is an untranslatable paronomasia. Psellos means merely that the author wishes, but fails, to be elevated. ὀρθοῦσθαι means "rise upright," while τοῦ ὀρθίου νόμου refers to "high-pitched melody." The next sentence continues the wordplay with ὀρθοεπείας ("correctness of diction").

16. An allusion to the pseudo-Hermogenian work Περὶ μεθόδου δεινότητος.

[96–101] To sum everything up, I admire the book about Charikleia both for its ideas and its appropriate language, and I have found it worthy of praise throughout. As for that about Leukippe I think that it will suffice a rhetorician in the dearth of another narrative, so that, if he were to wish to embellish certain parts of his own works with flowery graces drawn therefrom, he may take from a source readily available whatever has contributed to its ornamental beauty.

[102–4] There, my friend, you have the difference between the books in brief but with many important points. I have not dealt with matters in detail but have summarily characterized their styles for you.[17]

17. I am grateful to Anthony Kaldellis for reading over both introduction and translation and for making valuable suggestions, and to Stratis Papaioannou for his perceptive editorial work.

13 *Encomium for Kyr Symeon Metaphrastes*

Translated with introduction and notes
by Elizabeth A. Fisher

Introduction

"The literary commemoration of the saints is the last chapter of the works that confirm the Gospel message" (220–22).[1] In these few words, Psellos illuminates the significance of hagiography in Byzantium and suggests the reason for the high regard enjoyed by Symeon Metaphrastes in Psellos' own time and in later periods as well.[2] The ten-volume collection of 148 saints' lives formed under Symeon's direction in the late tenth century became an integral part of the Byzantine liturgy. The enduring interest in Symeon's great work is apparent from the fact that some 850 manuscripts and fragments copied between the eleventh and eighteenth centuries preserve parts of it.[3] Because Psellos reasonably assumed that his audience of educated Byzantine readers would

1. Parenthetical references in this introduction refer to lines of the Greek text. Another version of this introduction furnished with the Greek text in citations such as the one above is available at http://chs.harvard.edu/wa/pageR?tn=ArticleWrapper&bdc=12&mn=5478. A slightly different version of the translation that follows may be found there.

2. Modern scholars, however, typically fault the loss or suppression of authentic and more ancient texts in favor of Symeon's homogenized and polished versions.

3. Patterson Ševčenko 1990: 1.

immediately recognize Symeon's name and the nature of his literary achievement, a brief description of the Metaphrastic menologion will equip the modern reader of Psellos' encomium with some approximation of a contemporary Byzantine reader's frame of reference.

Psellos states that Symeon undertook his great project at the request of an unnamed emperor (331–33). Two other eleventh-century sources note that Symeon became known for his menologion circa 980, early in the reign of Basil II (976–1025),[4] that is, approximately a century before Psellos composed Symeon's encomium. Arranged chronologically beginning with the start of the ecclesiastical year in September, a menologion presents a narrative for each liturgical feast day to be read aloud during the service of *orthros* on the saint's commemoration day. To assemble his unique and innovative collection, Symeon adopted and adapted existing narratives of the lives of martyrs and ascetics, correcting factual errors, applying proven rhetorical techniques to engage his audience, and rephrasing (or "metaphrasing") the humble diction of the original texts at a uniform and elevated stylistic level. He replaced their simple sentence structures, colloquial vocabulary, and loose grammatical constructions with the polished "Attic" literary style cultivated by the Byzantine educational system and characteristic of classical and patristic literature (280–95).[5] As Psellos observes of Symeon, "He completely transforms the style without altering the substance <of the original>, but he corrects what was amiss in its forms <of expression>; he does not invent the contents but he alters the manner of diction" (288–91). His texts offered an alternative to older versions written in a style that seemed ridiculously rustic to Symeon's learned contemporaries (184–86).

Symeon apparently did not complete the Metaphrastic menologion. The majority of its entries belong to the months between September and January, with the result that readings for the later part of the church year needed to be supplemented from other sources. Ioannes Xiphilinos completed such a sup-

4. Høgel 2002a: 66–69. Høgel's thorough and well-documented study examines in detail the topics of scholarly controversy surrounding Symeon's life and the Metaphrastic menologion itself. On Metaphrastes' biography, see also the recent entry at Lilie, Ludwig, Pratsch, and Zielke 2013: 228–33 (Symeon #27504) as well as Papaioannou 2017.

5. For a description of the "Attic" style imposed upon older texts by Symeon, see Ševčenko 1981: 298–303.

plement during the reign of Alexios I Komnenos (1081–1118), approximately a century after Symeon himself worked.[6]

A variety of evidence indicates that the Metaphrastic menologion rapidly gained currency both in Constantinople and beyond in the course of the eleventh century. Its provision of a hagiographic text—in some cases quite lengthy—to be read each day is particularly appropriate for the life of a monastic community.[7] In fact, the typikon of the Monastery of Euergetis (1054) specifically designates the Metaphrastic menologion as the source of each day's reading during the daybreak service of *orthros*; long readings could be divided into segments.[8] Also in the second half of the century, some thirty separate illustrated editions of the ten-volume set were produced for the wealthy, who perhaps intended to donate such a precious item to a monastery or church.[9] Palaeographical details and iconographical features of these deluxe menologia suggest that they were produced by scribes and illuminators connected with the imperial court.[10] Members of the intellectual elite in Constantinople can be identified as owners of copies (e.g., the founder of the Euergetis Monastery, Kyr Paul; the imperial official Eustathios Boilas; the historian Michael Attaleiates; et al.).[11] Moreover, the Metaphrastic menologion traveled far afield from the imperial court and elite of Constantinople. In the late eleventh century, the prolific translator Eprem Mtsire produced a Georgian version accompanied by an intriguing preface entitled "Brief Reminiscence on Symeon Logothetes and the Story of Those Responsible for the Translation of the Present Readings."[12]

Psellos' encomium is an important source for reconstructing Symeon's biography, but by no means the only source. After 987 and before circa 1007, Symeon's close friend and confidant Nikephoros Ouranos composed a poem lamenting the death of the great hagiographer but providing little information about his life beyond the observation that the two shared unspecified troubles in life.[13] Eprem's preface to the Georgian translation of the Metaphrastic

6. Patterson Ševčenko 1990: 6.
7. Høgel 2002a: 224.
8. Patterson Ševčenko 1990: 3–4.
9. Patterson Ševčenko 1990: 204; Høgel 2003: 224–26.
10. Høgel 2003: 227.
11. Patterson Ševčenko 1990: 4.
12. Cited by Høgel 2002a: 69; for information on Eprem's career and translations, see *ODB* s.v. "Ep'rem Mcire."
13. Høgel 2002a: 64–65.

menologion and a brief biographical note on Symeon by the fifteenth-century bishop and theologian Markos Eugenikos (ca. 1394–1445) also provide unique data, but it must be assessed carefully. Some anecdotes appear to be legendary, while other information may simply be incorrect. Because Symeon shared his name and some aspects of his career with several other prominent individuals of the tenth century, isolating details of his biography from theirs is a difficult task.[14] In the following account of Symeon's career, I have adopted a minimalist approach, including only information generally accepted by modern scholars.

Symeon evidently attained prominence at the imperial court of Byzantium under several emperors of the mid-tenth century CE. Born to a wealthy family in Constantinople, he began his career at court as a secretary in the imperial chancery, perhaps under Romanos II (959–63), and eventually rose to the office of λογοθέτης τοῦ δρόμου (or "Chief of Imperial Communications")[15] at some point during the reign of Nikephoros Phokas (963–69), of Ioannes Tzimiskes (969–76), or of Basil II (976–1025). By 975 he had also received the honorific title of μάγιστρος; two seals of "Symeon *magistros* and *logothetês*" survive from the 970's or 980's.[16] At this point in his career Symeon complied with the imperial request to compose his menologion. For unknown reasons, he never completed this task. An intriguing and perhaps legendary tale preserved by Eprem Mtsire claims that Basil II took great offense at a statement recorded in Symeon's *Life of Theoktiste* (November 10) that the good fortune of Byzantium perished with the emperor Leo VI (886–912); reacting to this statement, Basil II dismissed Symeon in disgrace, stopped work on the Metaphrastic menologion, prohibited its public reading, and ordered all copies of it destroyed.[17] Sometime after the termination of his menologion project, Symeon died, perhaps spending the final years of his life as a monk. His death evidently occurred on November 28 sometime after

14. *ODB* s.v. "Symeon Logothete." Høgel 2002a: 62–76 evaluates the medieval sources for Symeon's career and examines (76–87) biographical data that scholars sometimes assign to him on less than solid ground. More recently Wahlgren 2006: 3–8 leaves open the question of whether Symeon Metaphrastes may be identified with the tenth-century chronicler known as Symeon Logothete.

15. Høgel 2002a: 64–74. For a description of this important office, see *ODB* s.v. "Logothetes tou Dromou."

16. Oikonomides 1973: 323–25.

17. Høgel 2002a: 69, 128n4.

987,[18] when Nikephoros Ouranos returned to Constantinople and could have composed his poem lamenting the death of Symeon. Travelers and pilgrims visited Symeon's grave in the fourteenth and fifteenth centuries at the Church of the Virgin Hodegetria in Constantinople near the imperial palace.[19]

Psellos begins his encomium by sketching Symeon's early career (1–155) and then turns his attention to Symeon's great achievement, the menologion (156–375). He assesses the significance of the menologion at length and provides a unique description of the process that enabled Symeon to produce it. According to Psellos (though the relevant passage is rather obscure), Symeon perhaps dictated an oral version of a *vita* to scribes who recorded it in stenography, then passed the stenographic text to others who transcribed it and submitted the transcription to final redactors for correction against Symeon's original dictation (333–41); constrained by the magnitude of the project, Symeon apparently entrusted the final version of a text to these redactors, while he himself continued the massive task of composing each metaphrasis orally.[20] Modern scholars examining the metaphrastic lives have further refined Psellos' description of Symeon's methods. Of the 148 lives in the menologion, 120 conform to the pattern Psellos outlines.[21] In the case of the remaining lives, Symeon admitted some fourteen to eighteen texts into his collection without alteration, either because they were already written in an acceptably "Attic" style (e.g., Jan. 14, *On the Monks of Sinai and Raithos*, originally attributed to Neilos of Ankyra) or because the existing old version enjoyed the status of a classic that could not be changed or improved (e.g., Jan. 17, *Life of Antony* by Athanasios of Alexandria).[22] Symeon also created eight new texts by combining two or more written and oral sources into something different from any one of them (e.g., Sept. 1, *Symeon Stylites*).[23] To a large number of texts in his collection, Symeon added his own preface composed in a standardized form.

18. Symeon's feast day was eventually transferred from November 28 to November 8. Patterson Ševčenko 1990: 2.

19. Høgel 2002a: 61, 72–73.

20. Høgel 2002a: 93–94 interprets Psellos' somewhat cryptic account of Symeon's working methods; he revised his interpretation in Høgel 2003: 222, as well as in Høgel 2002b: 30. For a full discussion of this passage and its interpretation, see note 39 to the translation.

21. Høgel 2002a: 96–102 compares several "metaphrased" texts with the older texts Symeon adapted.

22. Høgel 2002a: 92–93.

23. Høgel 2002a: 102–9.

In these prefaces, Symeon emphasized the utility and pleasure to be gained by reading the heroic deeds of martyrs and ascetics but avoided any reference to himself or to his own times; occasionally, he inserted brief comments upon his sources.[24] Psellos specifically commends Symeon's prologues as models of clarity, brevity, and organization: "For the prologues to <Symeon's> discourses straightaway engage with their subject matter, and he proceeds in short order to declare his intention for the work clearly" (276–79).

Although conceding that some hyper-sophisticated critics considered Symeon's level of diction and literary style insufficiently learned (230–42), Psellos defends Symeon's style as generally accessible ("Although he knows many levels of speech, he uses the <one> that suits both a scholarly and a general audience alike, and he satisfied both groups at once," 257–61) and appropriate to his purpose: "I do not know anyone among them all who fit his style more exactly to the works he elected to compose" (270–71). Rather wistfully, Psellos then contrasts Symeon's appeal and influence as a writer with his own (322–29):

> I therefore admire <Symeon> for the beauty and grace <of his language> no less than for the usefulness of his subject matter; although I have written many <works> on many <subjects>, my writings would not stimulate <in others> such a desire to rival and imitate <them>. <My writings> will perhaps seem very desirable to men of letters, <who> will admire them because of their diction and their varied <rhetorical> figures. The majority of people, however, will scorn <my works> because <most people> do not have any interest in <philosophical> inquiries and inexpressibly <profound> thoughts.

Psellos' *Encomium for Symeon* is indeed a work that would please even the most learned and rhetorically accomplished of Byzantine readers. His diction is Attic at a level of sophistication beyond that attained by Symeon, and his narrative includes learned allusions to classical literature, ancient civilization, and scientific topics. Although a translation into readable English cannot convey the full effect of Psellos' complex sentences and elaborate Attic constructions,[25] various literary devices are apparent even in translation. The first two

24. Høgel 2002a: 141–45.

25. For example, the first paragraph of the encomium consists of twenty-nine lines and three sentences; I have broken it into two paragraphs and six sentences in the English translation.

paragraphs of the encomium contain both similes and metaphors, feature frequent hyperbole, and conclude with an indirect reference to a historical figure.

An educated Byzantine reader attuned to the rhetorical tradition might well have recognized frequent allusions to popular rhetorical treatises in Psellos' encomium. Psellos casually alludes to classical works like the anonymous *Art of Rhetoric* attributed to Dionysios of Halikarnassos and to the late antique texts standard in Byzantine rhetorical education written by Hermogenes and his successors; he also refers to the rhetorical commentaries of the relatively obscure eleventh-century author Ioannes Sikeliotes. The format of the *Encomium for Symeon Metaphrastes* follows the pattern prescribed by standard rhetorical handbooks, first providing a prologue to set his subject in context, then systematically covering the topics recommended by ps.-Hermogenes (*Progymnasmata* 7; trans. Kennedy 2003: 82) as appropriate for an encomium: the subject's nationality and family, remarkable aspects of his birth, nurture and education (15–74), his noble character and his qualities of mind (75–129), the nature of his relationships with others (130–55), his career and notable achievements (110–55 and 184–375), and finally his death and any noteworthy events following upon it (376–92). Psellos moves skillfully among these topics traditional in an encomium, expanding his discussion of Symeon's career and achievements to analyze the literary and stylistic features of his menologion and to detail the process of its composition.

The tone of Psellos' narrative shifts from that of an encomiast to that of a hagiographer as he nears the close of his text, for Psellos attributes the qualities of Symeon's holy subjects to Symeon himself: "He sets a martyr's constancy and an ascetic's endurance as two courses <of action> for himself and runs in both races not with the swiftness of his feet but with the agility of his thinking" (310–13). Psellos then deems Symeon worthy of a heavenly reward, comparing his writings to those of authors "who exert their efforts in discoursing about the Gospel and who interpret the <profound> depths of the Word; their goals are the same, and they begin from similar <motives>. If the goal of their undertakings is in both cases the salvation of souls, how do their motivations not stand on equal <footing> one with another and <how would> their writings <not> be measured against the same standard or, to express my <view on the matter, how> will they <not> inherit equal <portions of glory>?" (359–65).

In closing Psellos applies a *topos* of hagiography to his virtuous secular subject and describes Symeon's joyful ascent to heaven at the conclusion of his life on earth,[26] noting the miraculous fragrance that suffused his gravesite[27] until it was desecrated by the intrusion of a second corpse (376–83). Psellos ends his encomium with a prayer to Symeon, treating his illustrious subject as a veritable saint before God (383–92):

> <O Symeon>, whom I consider the best and most eloquent of men, this miracle of yours (i.e., the gravesite's fragrance) reveals abundantly your purity and holiness after your other <accomplishments> brought <you> to utter perfection in virtue. May you be gracious unto me if I have not accurately expressed your virtue in its entirety nor apportioned to you the praise and honor <flowing> from all your noble <traits>. Do not regard me in anger for what I have failed to mention, but may you hold me in memory for what I have written, if any memory of <those> here <on earth> exists for the purified souls in God's image that belong to <those of> you <now in heaven>.

Among the *topoi* of traditional hagiography is the closing invocation of a saint like that offered by Psellos.[28] Psellos' prayer to Symeon concludes with the concern that his work may be an inadequate expression of Symeon's great virtues; such a tone of self-doubt is most uncharacteristic of Psellos' literary persona but completely consistent with the *topos* of modesty found in the epilogue to a saint's life.[29]

26. Høgel 2004: 193.

27. The "odor of sanctity" frequently marks a saint's blessed death and sanctified corpse; for a discussion of its significance, see S. Harvey 2006: 220–28. A few examples will provide a context for Psellos' application of the hagiographical *topos* here. "Stooping to look into the tomb, they saw the blessed woman lying intact, and smelled the fragrance that issued forth" (Laiou 1996: 269); "magnificent perfumes and incense . . . could not match the fragrance that issued from her skin. . . . [T]here they solemnly buried her, the corpse emitting the same, nay a much more wonderful fragrance" (Rosenqvist 1986: 110–11); and finally, "as when someone sleeps happily and his face is illuminated from wondrous drowsiness, even to this time Basil is there illuminated with the same glory and emitting such sweetness of fragrance, lying intact and whole and totally uncorrupted" (Sullivan, Talbot, and McGrath 2014: 677–78). I am grateful to Denis Sullivan for these citations. Further instances of this *topos* are available from the Dumbarton Oaks Database of Byzantine Hagiography under the word "euodia." See http://www.doaks.org/research/byzantine/resources/hagiography-database.

28. Pratsch 2005: 351–53.

29. For a general discussion of the *topos* of modesty, see Pratsch 2005: 341–42.

Since Byzantium had no formal process of canonization until the thirteenth century, this encomium represents a practical step towards claiming for Symeon the status of saint.[30] Psellos contributed further towards gaining recognition for Symeon as an Orthodox saint by composing for him an *akolouthia* (*Poem.* 23), a liturgical office to be used in celebrating a saint's feast day.

Although neither Psellos' encomium nor his *akolouthia* for Symeon can be dated even approximately within Psellos' long career, his literary activities on behalf of Symeon coincide with the period of extraordinarily productive interest in the Metaphrastic menologion during the second half of the eleventh century. Nancy Ševčenko suggests that Psellos' appreciative presentation of Symeon as a skillful literary stylist may have inspired the enthusiasm of elite circles in Constantinople for the illustrated Metaphrastic menologion, while Høgel wonders if Psellos received an imperial commission to compose his encomium for some unattested public celebration of Symeon's work organized by an emperor.[31] These suggestions are not mutually exclusive, and I would like to add a third consideration that might have encouraged Psellos to compose his *Encomium for Symeon.*

Psellos apparently identified strongly with his subject. As already noted, he compared his own literary accomplishments with Symeon's in the course of evaluating the prose style of the Metaphrastic menologion. Psellos also observes that Symeon possessed a rare gift for combining equal expertise in rhetoric and in philosophy (52–74), thus winning admiration and acceptance among both philosophers and rhetoricians. As already noted, Psellos' encomium demonstrates that he, too, is adept at rhetoric; he also establishes his credentials as a philosopher by integrating vocabulary from classical—and especially from Neoplatonic—works of philosophy throughout his discussion of Symeon and his writings.

Aspects of Psellos' life and work resemble Symeon's, for both gained fame for their secular activities as intellectuals closely connected with the imperial court, but neither undertook the life of an ascetic nor embarked upon

30. At the time of Psellos, saints were not officially canonized but rather informally recognized through various popular manifestations of devotion: veneration of their gravesites and relics, prayers offered to them, liturgical commemoration of their feast days, creation of a biography celebrating their holy deeds and miracles, or incorporation of their images on icons and in churches. See *ODB* s.v. "Canonization."

31. Patterson Ševčenko 1990: 4 and Høgel 2002a: 156.

a career in the ecclesiastical hierarchy; however, both Psellos and Symeon may be associated with the monastic life during a period of disfavor at the imperial court. Although Psellos concentrated his literary efforts upon secular subjects, among his numerous and varied writings is an elaborate contribution to hagiography, the area of Symeon's expertise. Psellos' *Life of St. Auxentios*, a saint not included in the Metaphrastic menologion, is lengthy, rhetorically ambitious, and innovative in some historical details; in composing it, Psellos observed the techniques he commends in Symeon's work.[32] Alexander Kazhdan has noted that Psellos adjusted aspects of Auxentios' biography to resemble Psellos' own circumstances.[33] Anthony Kaldellis has observed that in his *Encomium for his Mother* Psellos attempts to portray her as both a saint and a martyr, virtually canonizing her, and "effectively appropriates her sanctity for himself."[34] It has recently been suggested that the anonymous *Encomium of John the Baptist* as well as four additional encomia of saints (Panteleemon, Kallinikos, Laurentios, and Prokopios) are also compositions by Psellos in emulation of Symeon's achievement.[35]

As Høgel has remarked, the parallels between Symeon's career and Psellos' are numerous and significant.[36] Psellos claims particular familiarity with the emperors Constantine X Doukas (1059–67), Romanos IV Diogenes (1068–71), and Michael VII Doukas (1071–78). Did Psellos present this encomium to one of them with the hope of portraying himself as the new Symeon?[37] Is Psellos' *Encomium for Symeon* part of an even more ambitious program to secure a place among the saints for a scholar and man of affairs like Symeon—and like Psellos himself?

Editions and translations. The text used for this translation is *Or. hag.* 7 (pages 269–88; bracketed numbers indicate a range of lines in the Greek text); see also the entry in Moore 2005: 364–65. Words in angle brackets indicate words and phrases that are implied rather than stated in the Greek text.

32. Text published in Fisher 1994: 1–94. For a discussion of the rhetorical aspects of this work, see Fisher 2006.

33. Kazhdan 1983; discussed by Høgel 2004: 192–93.

34. Kaldellis 2006: 30, 33–34.

35. Papaioannou 2013: 50n79.

36. Høgel 2004: 193.

37. I am indebted to Stratis Papaioannou for this stimulating suggestion. See also p. 12 above.

Encomium for Kyr Symeon Metaphrastes[1]

[1–15] In proposing to praise Symeon, great in his conduct and in his discourse,[2] <and to praise> his reputation and his success, bright and widely proclaimed throughout all the world, I do not know what words to use about him nor what to say of all <that I could> in order to present an adequate panegyric. For <he was> a man not only adorned with discourse and possessed of an intellect most adept at creating ideas and a tongue like the flow of the Nile—<though> not periodically nor at great intervals, but daily increasing by thousands of cubits and issuing in a flood at the most appropriate moment—but <he was> also <a man> ennobled in the admixture of his character traits,[3] in

1. Psellos applies the honorific title κῦρ ("sir") to his subject, not presuming simply to name him, and adds the epithet traditionally attached to him that identifies his activity in producing elegant paraphrases ("metaphrases") of texts originally written in a style unacceptable to the audience. This practice served to elevate humble texts or simplify overly ornate ones.

2. Commendation of a man for how he lived and how he spoke (ἐν βίῳ καὶ λόγῳ) originated in Aristotle's *Nicomachean Ethics* (1127a24, 1128b2) and was adopted by such varied Greek authors as Athanasios the Theologian (fourth century CE), John of Damascus (seventh–eighth century CE), Ioannes the Confessor and Theodoros Stoudites (both eighth–ninth century CE) and Psellos.

3. "Admixture of character traits" (τὴν ἀπὸ τῶν ἠθῶν κράσιν), i.e., "temperament," is a phrase favored by the anonymous second-century author of the *Art of Rhetoric* attributed to Dionysios of Halikarnassos; see Heath 2003: 81, 94. This anonymous author used the phrase four times in chapters 10 and 11; it occurs often in Psellos' writings.

his assemblage of all virtues, and in providing a pattern for those who wish to emulate a great man's prudent way of life.[4]

[15–31] Constantinople blossomed with the life of this famous man in due season, as one might say, the foremost city <bringing forth> the foremost man, the fairest of cities <bringing forth> the guardian fairest to speak of. By giving him the gift of bearing him as her child and by honoring him with such an origin, she received in return from him the <privilege of> bringing forth such a one, who would suffice alone <and in himself> to give in return the fairest award to that <fairest> of cities. And because of that man her previous honor increased, becoming most magnificent; in times past she surpassed the other cities by as much beauty and greatness as a place in paradise <surpassed them> in extent and circumference. Subsequently, because of him and by <virtue of> the blossoming of his newborn virtues, she exceeded the other cities, so that even if <beauty and greatness> in adornment had not been her lot from the beginning, <even if > she had not been fortunate in <her> great founder <Constantine>, this wondrous offspring of hers would have been enough for her in respect to competing with other quite important cities and in respect to <establishing> her totally incomparable excellence, which is unrivalled.

[31–51] Even from the very moment of his birth, so to speak, and from <the time when> his full head of hair grew, he was like the whelps of lions, who show immediately their proud expression and the fullness of their manes.[5] Indeed, the flowers of his intelligence blossomed, his mind took deep root, and his intellect sparkled quite marvelously. Now in others, these qualities would be sufficient for them to be <considered> perfect, but in his case they were obviously the preliminary outline of a perfect nature. Just as some trees grow in accord with their nature with hardly any need of a cultivating hand and increase even more in beauty and size if they are watered a little, Symeon's nature was some such thing, straightaway advancing swiftly and straight up. Thus without any training he spoke with an orator's skill, while the depths of his soul produced philosophical concepts in abundance. When he examined carefully the discourses of the philosophers and gained from that study first principles as starting points for

4. μεγαλοπρεποῦς βίου καὶ σώφρονος: cf. Lucian (?), *Encomium of Demosthenes* 18: φύσεως μεγαλοπρεποῦς . . . βίου σώφρονος.

5. See Aristotle *History of Animals* 728b27.

finding what he sought,[6] he emerged suddenly, elevated on high and discovering the Sun from its rays or, so to speak, from the Sun he gazed at its rays. In the former case by means of a syllogistic argument he inferred the primary <cause> from its secondary <effects> and in the latter case he drew as a syllogistic conclusion <effects> secondary in nature from their primary causes.[7]

[52–74] Symeon knew that man's nature in its perfected state is adorned with these two things: that which comes from his intellect and that which flows from his tongue. <He recognized> that some of those wise men <who went> before us perfected the intellect through philosophy, while others refined their speech through rhetoric. With the exception of one or two, the rest showed an inclination towards one or the other of the two categories. For some, the tongue flooded like a river through constant dialectical argument, while for others the elevated contents of their own thoughts provided a <compelling> herald's summons, so that the latter group was all but devoid of speech and the former group lacked the higher <form of> intelligence. Symeon was midway between the two and became an agent to bond together those who until then stood at variance. And as if suspending his speech from the mooring cable of his intellect while stationing his intellect upon his words, he used rhetorical skill to guide[8] his <knowledge of> philosophy into a more pragmatic function plainer <to understand>, at the same time elevating his rhetorical skill by means of philosophy and commingling the two <disciplines> each with the other by <using> the attractions particular to each one. In a manner of speaking, he gave his intellect a voice and his tongue intelligence. Indeed, he presented philosophy with the persuasiveness of character

6. Psellos uses philosophical terminology to describe Symeon's study of Aristotelian first principles (ἀρχαί), adopting the language of the second-century-CE Aristotelian commentator Alexandros by adding, "for finding what he sought" (πρὸς τὴν τῶν ζητουμένων εὕρεσιν; e.g., *In Aristotelis Metaphysica commentaria* 143.13, 172.11).

7. Psellos uses the language of Aristotelian logic to describe deductive reasoning (i.e., perceiving the existence of a cause from its effects—συλλογιζόμενος) and inductive reasoning (i.e., perceiving from a cause the existence of its effects—συμπεραινόμενος). Aristotle designated these two types of argument deductive and inductive syllogisms (see *Prior Analytics* 24b18, 68b15).

8. Psellos displays his vast command of Greek vocabulary with the rare compound word προσεμβιβάζειν ("guide"), used once and apparently coined by the tenth-century Patriarch Nikolaos I Mystikos (*Letter* 32.307).

<in the rhetorical sense>[9] and practiced rhetoric with a mental profundity typical of philosophy. Because he accommodated himself equally to the two sorts <of discipline>, neither did philosophers despise <Symeon's> political subjects, upon seeing that they had a philosophical hue, nor did rhetoricians, mollified by <Symeon's> rhetorical practices, feel vexed at <his philosophical> knowledge.

[75–109] Accordingly, to all the cities he seemed to be some sort of beacon kindled from Byzantium, like a torch raised on high. In truth, the site <of Constantinople> was like some heavenly realm, sparkling with every sort of discourse. Through this one torchbearer, <the city> illuminated the entire inhabited world and in addition to her own luster cast a glittering light with another's radiance as well. <What was> yet more amazing and what would cause one to admire <Symeon> more was <the following>. While most people consider education as the basis for becoming rich—not in order to come into possession of <morally> better things, but to luxuriate in vanities through attending to these <matters>—Symeon who actually possessed noble birth, had acquired a good name from his family, and enjoyed extensive wealth—namely, precisely the things because of which one might avoid learning—nevertheless used the resources <gained> from worldly good fortune to study philosophy. Thereupon he emulated neither the more disengaged of those who practice philosophy nor the more pretentious of the rhetoricians. For the former group, stunned by philosophy's rays as if by boundless radiance, immediately squeeze their eyes shut and neither advance virtue into practical action, nor employ its principles with a truly noble spirit, nor assume the leadership of cities, nor take into public life what they have learned and present <it> to the general population; instead, like a harvest without fruit, they cultivate long beards[10] and assume sullen expressions. Then some of them run through the center of town and needlessly indulge in unrestrained public speech,[11] while others live in

9. μετὰ τῆς ἠθικῆς πιθανότητος: from Longinos' *Art of Rhetoric*, see p. 80 above. For the rhetorical notion of "character," see Papaioannou 2013: 68–69.

10. The well-known literary stereotype of a philosopher included a long beard and often a ragged cloak as well.

11. The phrase "unrestrained public speech" (ἡ ἄκρατος παρρησία) apparently originated with the anonymous author of the *Art of Rhetoric* (see chapter 11.8.13); perhaps Psellos refers to the famous third-century-BCE mathematician Archimedes, who reputedly demonstrated this quality by leaping from his bath and running naked into the streets shouting "Eureka!" after he solved a difficult problem. The Roman author Vitruvius is the earliest surviving source for this popular legend (Vitruvius, *De architectura* 9 pref. 9–12); I can find no Greek source for it.

barrels where they have shut themselves up;[12] others spend their whole lives examining <topics> through questions and answers,[13] and yet others conduct inquiries concerning natural science by contributing to <everyday> life useless <presentations of > contradictory arguments and wordy disputations.[14] The majority of rhetoricians undergo this same experience by claiming the sensible art <of rhetoric> as a basis for <exercises in> silliness, even when it is necessary to determine and expedite what is beneficial to cities; some of them devise their own, others use stock plausible inventions to add a tragic touch to life.[15]

[110–29] Symeon, however, was not like this—far from it! He did not adopt a different <style of> dress, nor compromise in any way his truly noble spirit, nor embarrass his family with any sort of silly novelties, nor offer a model of political subjects only to remodel it,[16] nor otherwise play the part of a <disreputable> sophist. Instead he employed his hereditary affection for honorable conduct as most useful raw material for accomplishing what is good and straightaway took the excellence <derived> from his studies as the basis both for true nobility of spirit and for brilliance. For as a special favorite of the emperors he was entrusted with the most honored assignments of all; <Symeon> received a position close to the imperial throne because of his keen intelligence and, due to his natural aptitude, also <held> an administrative post in government supervising public affairs. He initially received an appointment to the imperial chancery, privy to confidential resolutions and working with <imperial> advisors. When his trustworthy character in these <duties> made him well known, he undertook responsibilities in external affairs in addition to his duties in the palace, with the result that it was he who conveyed to the emperor messages from outsiders and <relayed> imperial

12. The famous fourth-century-BCE cynic philosopher Diogenes proverbially lived the simple life in a wine cask (CPG I 87.14).

13. Aristotle discusses dialectical argumentation (ἡ διαλεκτικὴ ἐρώτησις) in *De interpretatione* 20b22–30; Platonic dialogues like *Euthyphro* exemplify the process.

14. This stereotypical complaint against philosophers makes a famous ancient appearance in Aristophanes' comedy *The Clouds*, where Socrates conducts a fatuous philosophical inquiry over the broad-jumping and singing abilities of fleas (142–68).

15. σκηνὴν τῷ βίῳ ἐπετραγῴδησαν: cf. Psellos, *Letter to Xiphilinos* 1–3: Ἐμὸς ὁ Πλάτων, ἁγιώτατε καὶ σοφώτατε, ἐμός, ὦ γῆ καὶ ἥλιε, ἵνα τι καὶ αὐτὸς ἐπιτραγῳδήσω τῇ τοῦ λόγου σκηνῇ.

16. Psellos relishes the wordplay πλάσας/μεταπλάσας and uses it elsewhere in his writings (*Encomium for his Mother* 1774; *Chronographia* 4.37); the phrase originated in Plato's *Timaeus* 50a6.

<communications> to outsiders as well. He was, so to speak, the administration's precise <communications> link.[17]

[130–55] The sun in <the course of> its orbit sometimes <looks> upon others and sometimes upon us. In contrast Symeon was himself wholly attentive both to the emperor and to public affairs. Indeed, as our discourse described him earlier, he <was> multifaceted in nature, capable of formulating plans in advance and of accomplishing <them>. <He was able> to drive the barbarians farther from the territory belonging to the <heirs of the> Roman <Empire>, to prevail against them either through military expeditions or by means of artifice, to bring other countries into subjection,[18] and to adopt a ready stance regarding requirements of the moment for the matter at hand. <He> altered his behavior when it was necessary, devised new conduct when it was beneficial, and remained consistent whenever this seemed good. Moreover, the man was not devoid of graces [χαρίτων], but both his tongue and his wit were ready with suitable repartee in every endeavor. Although he was truly noble in dress, in demeanor, and even in the way he walked, he altered his behavior to <fit> the situation; because he was charming and agreeable, he immediately attracted everyone with his smile. His <helping> hand was generous because two <attributes>, his wealth and his inclination, extended it. His hand was <always> outstretched and open, and whoever wished drew liberally upon his <wealth> as if it flowed from a river. Such were the <qualities> of this great man, and he also took part in activities that typically assist our <Christian> faith, as was appropriate. They were . . .[19] but why should I not make more perfect use <of this kind> of narrative and promote <Symeon's> greatest achievement into a prominent position? Since I

17. Psellos describes Symeon's rise from chancery clerk to Logothetes of the Dromos allusively, in the manner admired by a rhetorically sophisticated audience in Byzantium. Symeon's position required him to coordinate all imperial chancery functions, including the collection of political information, arrangements for foreign embassies, and correspondence with foreign governments; see *ODB* s.v. "Logothetes tou Dromou." For a discussion of this passage, see Høgel 2002a: 67nn30, 31.

18. This passage is usually interpreted not in terms of Symeon's key role in diplomacy but rather as a claim by Psellos that Symeon actually participated in military campaigns, which seems very unlikely; for a full discussion of the issue, see Høgel 2002a: 67–68 with nn33, 34.

19. Psellos implies that he could, if he chose, say more about Symeon's pious activities, which perhaps involved generous financial contributions.

have <now> provided my narrative with a brief preliminary statement, I proceed to <my> chief purpose.[20]

[156–83] Distinguished indeed were the brave struggles of the martyrs against their enemies, whom they combated both overtly and covertly. Surely it is so! Their confrontational speech <was> brilliant and their convictions invincible—and <there was> their sacrifice of the <normal> conditions of life, their neglect of their natural <human needs>, their loss of amputated limbs, and finally their contempt for life. The ascetic life is no less lustrous than these <deeds>. For also in the <ascetic> life there is mortification of the flesh,[21] and <true> enjoyment <consists> in refusing to enjoy what one ought not enjoy; <in the ascetic life there is> rejection of the world, a bodily flight up to God, and resistance both to natural passions and to the worldly <temptations> flowing from evil spirits. For that very reason, both <the martyrs' and the ascetics'> styles of life, while glorious in the past, are also <glorious> again. However, until recently the way they lived on earth, or rather our recounting of their lives, was not recognized as brilliant, although accurate accounts of the <facts> of their martyrdom and of their ascetic practices are indeed preserved in the secret books that the angels will read out for the multitudes at the restitution <of all things>.[22] Moreover, before <the time of> the remarkable man <Symeon>, those who wrote of <the saints'> deeds here on earth by no means approximated their nobility of spirit. Instead, in some cases they gave erroneous reports of their <deeds>, while in other cases, because they were incapable of an appropriate presentation, they described their virtue as rude and paltry by failing to demonstrate nobility of thought,[23] or to employ attractive adornments of diction, or to describe accurately either the ferocity of <the saints'> persecutors or their shrewdness in answering when they gave <Christian> witness. <These

20. Psellos returns to the terminology of the anonymous *Art of Rhetoric* to describe his own rhetorical strategy in following his introduction with a preliminary statement to set the subject of the narrative in context (προκατάστασις). See Heath 1995: 157.

21. Psellos introduces a medical metaphor by using a rare phrase for "consumption of the flesh" (ἡ δαπάνη τῶν σαρκῶν) found only in the commentary on Hippocrates by the sixth-century writer Stephanos (*Commentary on Hippocrates' Prognosticon* I 5.37).

22. Psellos alludes to the book of life and the book of second death (see Revelation 20:12–15) that will be opened during the restitution of all things foretold by the prophets at the end of time (see Acts 3:21).

23. In the discussion of literary practice that follows, Psellos relies upon Hermogenian terminology.

earlier writers> also presented an adulterated version of the ascetics' practices by describing their earnest efforts without any artistry and seemingly with whatever <words> came to mind.

[184–206] For that reason, some had no patience for reading the annals <of their deeds> <because they were so> crude<ly written>, while others considered the accounts objects of derision.[24] Their awkward composition, incoherence of thought, and mediocre diction were harsh to the ear and repulsed rather than attracted <an audience>. Because of the authors <who wrote about them>, we habitually satirized the marvelous struggles and monumental victories of the servants of Christ. Although everyone complained loudly about the situation, those who had the ability to replace these <writings> with better <ones> lacked the will <to do it>, and those who had the will lacked the ability—some because of timidity of spirit, others because the enterprise was all engrossing and one man's lifetime would not be sufficient for it all. The marvelous Symeon did not feel the same as those who were stricken <by these difficulties>. He joined them as far as finding fault with the <accounts that were> written, then went farther and had the confidence for a daring project—or, rather, he succeeded in an undertaking where no one else had. For this reason, Symeon gained a reputation that was quite conspicuous among those held everywhere in high repute. He also dedicated to God the most beautiful things of all <when> he beautified and adorned the <spiritual> struggles and contests of the martyrs and the self-control and patient endurance of the ascetics;[25] because he offered devotion identical <to that of the martyrs and ascetics>, he received in return gratitude from everyone.

[207–29] For what could anyone compare with such an immense undertaking? What sort of compendium of ancient Greek lore or geodesy of the entire earth?[26] Were the accomplishments of the Persians and their predeces-

24. Ševčenko 1981: 298–303 cites this passage as an illustration of the "tyranny of high style" among Byzantine writers and readers; he notes Symeon's key role in elevating the genre of hagiography to an acceptable if not prestigious literary level.

25. Psellos repeats the association of "self-control" (ἐγκρατεία) and "patient endurance" (καρτερία) that originated in Aristotle's writings (see, for example *Nicomachean Ethics* 1145b8, 1150b1, 1152a4) and gained great popularity in Greek literature.

26. Psellos places Symeon in the company of classical authors by mentioning the lost works of two third-century-BCE scholars, Cleanthes of Assos, who wrote a compendium of Greek history entitled *Archaeology* (see Diogenes Laertios VII 174–75), and Eratosthenes of Kyrene, who calculated the circumference of the earth (see ODB s.v. "Eratosthenes").

sors the Babylonians as many? Were the later achievements in quite manly fashion by Alexander of Macedonia as great? These <accomplishments> are distinguished, especially <as recorded> by those who publish books of history in elegant language. While many are eager to read these books for the sake of <the skill with which> their authors composed them, the literary accounts that this noble man <Symeon> constructed for the martyrs and the ascetics demonstrate amplification appropriate to discourse and have a twofold objective—both <to inspire> imitation of their composition and <to encourage> imprinting of the self with saintly morality in the best way possible. I, however, might mention a third <consideration>, not inferior to these <other two>, but both more to the point and more elevating, <namely>, that the literary commemoration of the saints is the final chapter of the works that confirm the Gospel message. The fact that <Symeon> chose such subject matter for his writing is a most accurate testimonial to his sagacity; that he employed such content of thought and diction, at once clear and sublime, plausible, truthful, and natural, is also certain proof of his own wisdom and most of all an indication, one might suppose, <that he> attuned his usage <of words> to <particular > occasions and audiences.[27]

[230–65] Now to say something on this point and turn my argument in a more discursive direction—I am well aware that the works of <Symeon> are not given much serious attention by those who amplify their own speech more in the manner of the sophists, much less by those who spend their time in learned pursuits or in serious scientific inquiry; <they claim> that there is no notable mixture of forms[28] in his works, no obvious rhetorical figures in his discourses, no posing and solving of a problem in natural science, no geometrical proofs using technical terminology, no philosophical contents of thought to elevate the subject matter. Those learned individuals want everything written for exhibition, not for beneficial moral improvement. I, however, claim

27. In Psellos' time, Symeon's work was used both at the imperial court and in monastic communities (see Høgel 2002a: 150–54). Psellos' analysis of the significance of Symeon's stylistic choices uses widely popular Aristotelian terminology contrasting a certain proof (τεκμήριον) with a probable indication (σημεῖον); see Aristotle *Prior Analytics* 70b2–4.

28. Hermogenes commends rhetoric "with a mixture of forms" (τῇ μίξει τῶν ἰδεῶν) in his treatise *On Forms* (1.12.33 and 2.10.1 in reference to Demosthenes). The phrase recurs in the works of his commentators Syrianos (fifth century), Ioannes Sikeliotes and Ioannes Doxapatres (eleventh century), and Gregorios Pardos (eleventh–twelfth centuries).

that <Symeon's> works lack none of these <qualities>. Since in his view their utility is not as a sort of showpiece, he does not pack them with every example of every sort <of learning> right from their prologues. Instead, where his subject matter gives him an occasion, he uses <the techniques of> discourse to the extent necessary then returns to the objective he set for himself. For his discourse does not give attention to sophistic argumentation and forensic elegance, nor to a systematic treatment and observation of nature, nor indeed to the consideration of geometry or the even more esoteric discipline involving numbers. <Symeon> does not direct his attention to the movement of the heavens nor to <the question of> how the fixed portion of the universe relates to the planets, <which wander>; symphonic and homophonic chords are of no concern to him, nor were emmelic chords[29] <that occur> in addition to these. Therefore, he dismisses these <matters> as esoteric and makes use of them in some places when appropriate, but consistently holds to the truth and to an honest narrative. Although he knows many kinds of style, he uses the <one> that suits both a learned and a general audience alike, and he satisfied both groups at once. For with rhythmical <ornamentation> and with the beauty of his diction he attracted the learned listener and thoroughly entranced him in nets of <rhetorical> delights,[30] while he won over his popular audience with the clarity and freshness <of his diction>. He captivated both by being concise and persuasive.

[266–95] To avoid speaking less than the truth by disguising it, <I should mention that> I know many rhetorical styles of discourse that are better <than Symeon's>—I mean, <styles> belonging to more polished rhetoricians and <to> those who are beyond <the ability> of the majority to imitate with their resounding <mastery of> accent and rhythm[31]—but I do not know anyone among them all who fit his style more exactly to the works he elected to compose. But even if one of those individuals, extraordinary for his writing style

29. Psellos uses terminology drawn from ancient musical theory, a branch of mathematics; for an explanation of symphonic chords in harmonic intervals (σύμφωνοι), homophonic notes in unison and chords in octaves (σύμφωνοι), and emmelic chords that do not harmonize (ἐμμελεῖς), see Solomon 2000: 1:7. For a discussion of ancient musical theory, see West 1992: 218–53.

30. Psellos relished the phrase "nets of <rhetorical> delights," which he adopted from Longinus' fragmentary *Art of Rhetoric* (562.19) and used three times in his work.

31. Dionysios of Halikarnassos especially commended Demosthenes for his use of accent (τόνος) and of rhythm (ῥυθμός); see *On Demosthenes* 13.48–49 and 50.37.

and his <capacity for> reflection, had chosen such a project, in this respect he might have made the discourse more elaborate—but I do not mean more appropriate and more congenial to every audience. For the prologues to <Symeon's> discourses straightaway engage with their subject matter, and he proceeds in short order to declare his intention for the work clearly; in some <of his essays>, he summarizes the overall purpose of the discourse from the beginning, divides <it> up in parts, and adapts it to individual characters and circumstances. In all of them, <he maintains> the same rhetorical complexion in his discourse and a quality of expression that is consistent,[32] although he varies the delineation of characters subtly and, I might add, artfully. He does not alter the facts for the sake of his art, but in each case he interprets the particularity of the facts as they happened and <the particularity> of the individuals <involved>. He fixes his attention upon the older works as his models and does not deviate from them in order to avoid the appearance of creating something that is different from his original and <to avoid> violating it. He completely transforms the style without altering the substance <of the original>, but he corrects what was amiss in its forms <of expression>; he does not invent the contents, but he alters the manner of diction. His discourse is not confused or troubled by encountering irregularities in the narrative and deviations from its purpose; indeed, like the best of captains, when his ship is awash <in the sea>, he stands unperturbed at the tiller, plying it with utmost skill.

[296–329] There are <points> in his discourses where he even provides a geographical description of the homelands of <the saints> he is praising. He divides the entire earth into segments and focuses upon one of the sections, then clearly states something about its rivers and explains their sources in terms of natural features as well as <making some observations> about the advantageous physical setting of cities,[33] and <about> the <local> climate and harmonious <variation of> seasons, even if those who are in fact ill-disposed

32. Ioannes Sikeliotes applies the phrase "consistent quality of expression" (μία ποιότης) to rhetorical style in his *Comm.* 320.20. On Psellos and Sikeliotes, see p. 152 above, and also Papaioannou 2013: 29–127 passim.

33. Psellos' point applies to such passages as Symeon's remarks about St. Ioannikios ("His fatherland <was> the province of Bithynia and <his> village was called Marykaton, located at the northern portions of <Lake> Apollonias," PG 116, 37 A10–12) and about Daniel the Stylite ("this blessed <man's> fatherland, which lay between the Euphrates and Tigris rivers, is Mesopotamia, which comes by its name naturally," PG 116, 972 B1–5).

to hear <such things> do not listen to what he says. He handles the parts of a speech in a variety of ways, sometimes in a manner quite fit for a rhetorical contest and sometimes more mildly. Who would dispute with him over the charm of his narratives taken as a whole? Or over their composition? Or over the cadences of their rhythms? Or over the smooth adaptation of each successive <part> to all <the others>? I at any rate wish to contend on his behalf that he is not <pointlessly> verbose; I find that his discourses do not lack this <sort of> charm, but where they possess a <quality of> excess, in that abundance <of words there is> yet dignity and organization. He sets a martyr's constancy and an ascetic's endurance as two courses <of action> for himself and runs in both races not with the swiftness of his feet but with the agility of his thinking. Especially by running the ascetic's <race on> the double course he outdoes himself in vigor and becomes yet more fit for the competition.[34] <Symeon> certainly delights my ear when his discourse ascends a mountain or descends into a cave, sets one of his ascetic subjects beneath a pine or oak tree,[35] and imagines him eating plants and drinking from springs. For he adorns such narratives with locutions blooming with beauty and with colorful rose gardens of rhetorical figures. He presents the everyday events of the time as something the audience can picture rather than <simply> as something <the saint> did.[36] I therefore admire <Symeon> for the beauty and grace <of his language> no less than for the usefulness of his subject matter; although I have written many <works> on many <subjects>, my writings would not stimulate <in others> such a desire to rival and imitate <them>.[37] <My writings> will perhaps seem

34. Psellos compares Symeon's activities and those of his ascetic subjects to a footrace on a horseshoe-shaped track, adopting a metaphor for Christian life frequent in the New Testament (e.g., Hebrews 12:1–2).

35. Psellos embellishes this bucolic scene with a reference to the mountains and caves of Hebrews 11:38 and the pines and oaks familiar to his audience from Homer's famous description of the cave of the Cyclops (*Odyssey* 9.186).

36. Psellos commends Symeon's ability to link description (ἔκφρασις) of a subject or event with the quality that enabled an audience virtually to perceive it (ἐνάργεια). The four late antique texts of rhetorical exercises (*Progymnasmata*) regularly used in Byzantine education firmly established this link, repeating a standardized definition of *ekphrasis* in terms of *enargeia* (for example, Ps.-Hermogenes 16.11–12 in Rabe 1913, as well as Theon, Aphthonios, and Nikolaos). This standard definition originated in Aristotle's remarks about description in *Poetics* 1455a.22–26 and *Rhetoric* 1411b.24–25. For further discussion of this topic, see Dubel 1997: 252–57, Webb 1997: 229–30, and, for the Byzantine theory, Papaioannou 2011.

37. Psellos refers to Hermogenes' remarks to aspiring rhetors in *On Forms* 1.1.11.

very desirable to men of letters, <who> will admire them because of their diction and their varied <rhetorical> figures. The majority of people, however, will scorn <my works> because <most people> do not have any interest in <philosophical> inquiries and inexpressibly <profound> thoughts.

[330–49] People do indeed say that <Symeon> did not undertake the project as a hobby nor <simply> set it for himself, except to the extent that he was willing <to do it>. However, fervent appeals from the emperor moved him to undertake this <project>, as well as <appeals> from those who valued intelligent discourse. He had his preparations ready at hand and <had> a team of considerable size <composed> both of those who initially took down his dictation stenographically[38] and of those who subsequently transcribed it <in full>; each group <worked> in support of the other, one producing an initial <text>, the other a second <draft>. After them, the final redactors went over the written texts to compare them against the content intended <by Symeon> and to correct whatever <error> might have escaped the notice of those who drafted the texts, because <Symeon> could not possibly review the same <works> repeatedly <himself> due to their great number.[39] However, although his eagerness

38. For other examples of stenography in the middle Byzantine period, see Antonopoulou 1997: 101.

39. In this valuable but rather cryptic passage, Psellos provides an extraordinary insight into Symeon's scholarly methods and skill in oral composition, as well as a reference to the Byzantine use of shorthand stenography. My translation has benefited greatly from the French translation with valuable discussion and notes by Flusin and Paramelle 1984: 22–23 and from the English translation by Høgel, 2002a: 93–94. This important but difficult passage presents a mixture of technical and general vocabulary to describe a process apparently obvious to Psellos and his audience but puzzling to us. The verb ἐνσημαίνομαι used here is almost certainly a technical term referring to taking shorthand notes from dictation (Flusin and Paramelle 1984: 23n11). The sequence suggested by Flusin and Paramelle is dictation by Symeon (perhaps from "prepared notes," παρασκευή, 333), stenographic recording of Symeon's dictation, full transcription of the shorthand text, and final correction by redactors of any errors made in the process. Particularly vexing is the phrase describing the standard against which the redactors assessed the draft of the metaphrastic version (πρὸς τὴν προκειμένην—ὑποκειμένην in some manuscripts—διορθώσονται ἔννοιαν, 338–39), which I interpret as a reference to correction against the shorthand text taken down at Symeon's dictation (334–35); in contrast, Høgel translates "corrected according to its intended meaning" (presumably that intended by Symeon), and Flusin and Paramelle translate "rectifiassent d'après le sens du texte," which they explicate as *ad sensum*. The term παρασκευή is also problematic; Flusin and Paramelle translate it "preparatifs," while Høgel interprets it quite generally as "facilities at hand." I am grateful to Denis Sullivan for the opportunity to discuss this passage thoroughly on several occasions. For a different recent interpretation of the passage, see Wilson 2014.

for a <good> name was great and his attention <to the project> more than sufficient—or rather, exactly sufficient—for this <task>, even so the <harvest of> grain greatly surpassed the seeds sown, and the crop was such as never <before has been seen>, to this day. As a result, even if <Symeon> had applied himself to accomplish nothing else, and <even if> his other <achievements> taken together or individually were an insufficient basis for his renown, nevertheless the <fact that he> undertook such a labor and accomplished <it> with such exactitude in addition to <his other achievements is> reason in itself aside from anything else for an encomium <in praise> of the man.

[350–75] I at any rate do not consider it appropriate to compare Symeon's <literary> efforts with the writings of the learned <authors> of classical antiquity. What of it, if some of them composed Panathenaic <orations> and others wrote of the war between the Peloponnesian <allies> and the Athenians at an impressive <level of> diction?[40] <If> some took up the argument against the rhetors and others <argued> in favor of them?[41] Among <these authors>, extravagant erudition <was> conspicuous and remarkable, but <the capacity> to benefit <others was> puny and weak. I would never choose to match my contender against them, but if I might be indulged, I would place him on an equal <footing> with those who exert their efforts in discoursing about the Gospel and who interpret the <profound> depths of the Word; their goals are the same, and they begin from similar <motives>. If the goal of their undertakings is in both cases the salvation of souls, how do their motivations not stand on equal <footing> one with another and <how would> their writings <not> be measured against the same standard or, to express my <view on the matter, how> will they <not> inherit equal <portions of glory>? How many laurels for excellence would not have crowned this admirable man? Or, rather, how many would not have already adorned him for the <earthly> race

40. Psellos acknowledges the sophistication of his audience with learned allusions to the ancient Greek orators Isocrates (fourth century BCE) and Aelios Aristeides (second century CE), who composed "Panathenaic" orations, and to the late fifth-century-BCE historians Thucydides and Xenophon, who recorded the history of the Peloponnesian War.

41. Psellos refers to such classical authors as Antiphon, Lysias, and Demosthenes, whose orations on this controversial profession are now lost, although cited and admired by Byzantine commentators and grammarians; however, orations on this topic by Aelios Aristeides (second century CE) and by Libanios (fourth century CE) do survive.

he has run towards God and for the choral lyrics he performs[42] in the presence of those <saints> whose characters and lives here <on earth> he has recorded? He has indeed demonstrated even in his death what sort of life he endeavored to live, for eyewitnesses say that <Symeon> did not resemble one cut down <in life> nor severed <from it>, but he rather seemed liberated from some sort of bond as he reached with joyful acceptance towards the angels who conducted <him forward> and in some sense delivered himself into their hands so that he might depart swiftly from his body.

[376–92] Such was the manner of his death, and immediately everything filled with a fragrance <that persisted> not just for that moment nor until the third day <after his death>, but day after day thereafter, so long as the adornment <of the body> was laid up alone as a treasure in its tomb. The coffin would indeed have remained <thus>, spreading its perfume forever, had not certain persons committed such a criminal act as to place another body alongside <Symeon's>. At the very moment that <the corpse> fell against the great man, the fragrance stopped welling up. <O Symeon>, whom I consider the best and most eloquent of men, this miracle of yours reveals abundantly your purity and holiness after your other <accomplishments> brought <you> to utter perfection in virtue. May you be gracious unto me if I have not accurately expressed your virtue in its entirety nor apportioned to you the praise and honor <flowing> from all your noble <traits>. Do not regard me in anger for what I have failed to mention, but may you hold me in memory for what I have written, if any memory of <those> here <on earth> exists for the purified souls in God's image that belong to <those of> you <now in heaven>.[43]

42. Psellos uses vocabulary that suggests to the audience two famous classical competitions, the footraces in Panhellenic games and the contest in choral poetry at the Athenian Festival of Dionysos. Victors in both competitions were rewarded with crowns of laurel leaves.

43. I am grateful to Professor Ihor Ševčenko for sharing with me his unpublished translation of this difficult text and to Denis Sullivan and Stratis Papaioannou for advice and insights on its many challenges.

14 *Encomium for the Monk Ioannes Kroustoulas Who Read Aloud at the Holy Soros*

Translated with introduction and notes
by Stratis Papaioannou

Introduction

The *Encomium for the Monk Ioannes Kroustoulas* is a little known treasure among Psellos' texts.[1] It contains a rare description of what was a very common practice indeed in middle Byzantine Constantinople: the public recital of saints' *Lives* in monastic as well as urban churches, primarily during vigil or morning services. Though the directions of what was to be read and at which date as well as the actual texts, that is, the manuscripts, that were used for these recitals exist today in ample numbers, we lack any description of the reading itself—how it was done and by whom.[2] Psellos' text offers us precisely such a description, focusing on a skillful reader by the name of Ioannes

1. The information presented in this introduction is based on a forthcoming piece with detailed discussion and bibliography of Psellos' *Encomium* of Kroustoulas; see Papaioannou, in preparation.

2. For the evidence in middle Byzantine monastic *Typika*, especially that of the Evergetis monastery, cf. Jordan 2000–2005 and Jordan and Morris 2012. For the numerous manuscript *menologia* that survive from this period, and that were written precisely for the purpose of public reading, see the exhaustive survey in Ehrhard 1937–52.

Kroustoulas and a recital that took place at the church of the Virgin Mary in the Constantinopolitan neighborhood of the Chalkoprateia.

Built in the fifth century, the Chalkoprateia Virgin was a typical Constantinopolitan basilica, located not far from the Hagia Sophia. It was one of the most important churches in the city: the site of several annual celebrations and vigils, a station in many imperial processions, and the place where a renowned Constantinopolitan relic was stored, the Girdle of the Virgin, namely, the "Ἁγία Σορὸς" or "Holy Casket" of Psellos' text—the Greek name has been retained transliterated in the translation below.[3]

Ioannes Kroustoulas is not attested in any other contemporary source. Psellos' text refers to him as Ioannes *chartoularios.* He was thus a chancery officer either in the imperial or, more likely in this case, patriarchal administration.[4] His epithet, Kroustoulas, is mentioned only in the title of the earlier manuscript that transmits the text, Vatican, gr. 672, and indicates a likely family relation with another acquaintance of Psellos, a certain monk Elias.[5] Ioannes was also apparently a monk, as is indicated by the title of the second manuscript, Urbinatus gr. 134; additionally, in lines 65–66, Psellos speaks of a typically monastic garment that Ioannes wore during his reading. However this might be, he was associated with the small convent of Angouriou (lines 220–21), either a metochion of Saint Georgios of Mangana and located in the neighborhood of that monastery, itself an important eleventh-century urban foundation, or (perhaps less likely) another monastery of the same name on the Asiatic coast of the Bosporos.[6]

As we learn toward the end of the text (lines 450–60; see also line 34), the *Encomium* was addressed to two learned friends of Psellos, Kroustoulas himself (whom Psellos first met at the event in the Chalkoprateia) and an older friend (and possibly patron), a well-educated man and frequent interlocutor of

3. For the Virgin at Chalkoprateia, see Janin 1969: 237–42; see also Krausmüller 2011 and Hennessy 2012. Gautier (1980–82: 119, 122–23), followed by Littlewood (*Or. min.* 37, intro, p. 137), misread a reference in line 307 and wrongly claimed that the church in question is the Virgin of Ta Kyrou, which however did not house the Soros.

4. On the office of *chartoularios,* see Guilland 1976: XVIII.

5. See Gautier 1980–82: 121–22.

6. See Janin 1969: 9 and Janin 1975: 27–28 for these two monasteries respectively. In Patriarch Photios' letter collection, we find four letters (nos. 50, 74, 87, and 130) addressed to a certain eunuch Ioannes, patrikios and sakellarios κατὰ τοὺς Ἀγγουρίους; cf. Messis 2014: 216–17.

Psellos, whose name, nevertheless, he refrains from mentioning. The lavish praise that Psellos pours on both men renders this text first and foremost a document that enacts the preservation of an earlier friendship and narrates the creation of a new one, that with the famous reader Kroustoulas. What links Psellos with these two men is an exquisite learnedness, but also, it seems, a shared high social class, or at least the aspiration of belonging to one. Therefore, like almost all other texts in this anthology of translations, this text too is to be placed within the networks of social and cultural power of eleventh-century Constantinople.

The structure of the text is rather peculiar and does not follow any specific rules—those of a typical *enkômion,* for instance. Rather, it seems to reflect the relatively free flow of a narrative, filled with the extravagant praises and even more extravagant digressions that might have characterized the discussions among Psellos and his learned friends. Of course, this is an idealized, *written* version of such an interaction among the intellectual elite. As such, it is carefully embroidered with a dense web of explicit references and hidden allusions to an impressive array of earlier texts.

Psellos begins (lines 1–43) with a series of questions that trace his bewilderment as he enters the crowded church of the Holy Soros. We follow his quest as he gradually learns what the source of this large, excited crowd is: "Ioannes, the great in name, deed, and will," who is about to begin his lesson. Psellos is persuaded to enter and starts a lengthy description of Kroustoulas and his performance. This description, or rather praise, continues to the end of Psellos' lengthy encomium. The account is interlaced with numerous digressions on, for instance, the philosophical notion of the mind as wax (127–44), the division of "sciences" (210–20), as well as many others. Psellos is polemical against other critics of public recital (74–83) and includes a *psogos* of another reader, a bishop referred to as Taurenos (399–411). He is also self-promoting (see, e.g., 83–91)—indeed the usual Psellian "I" is, as elsewhere, ubiquitous.

Toward the middle of the text, Psellos places the praise in the mouths of unnamed men, ἄνδρας λογίους (194), whose authority on the matter is presented as being beyond doubt and who respond to Psellos' question as to the reason behind everyone's fascination with Kroustoulas. Their "speech" (lines 198–272) is so Psellian in nature that it is impossible to tell where it ends—

especially because Psellos does not clearly indicate when he switches back to his own voice.[7] Praise is also expressed through an additional dialogue that Psellos reports as taking place between him and another group of learned men (300–397)—this exchange is itself interrupted by a long digression that describes the intellectual discussions between Psellos and the second addressee of the *Encomium* of Kroustoulas (356–76). The text is thus artfully *dramatized,* reflecting the chats, gossips, exchanges of praise and blame, and, of course, the mixture of playful with serious intellectual conversation in Psellos' elite circles.

Psellos ends rather abruptly with the following remark: "My dearest and best of friends" (i.e., the unnamed second addressee of his text) "prevented me from moving forward with my writing, saying that I had written enough" (453–54). He then proceeds with a generous address (456–59) to both Kroustoulas and the "So-and-So" friend in order to conclude: "I now rejoice as well as I have found companions that cause me joy" (460).

As will be apparent from the footnotes, Psellos manages to parade nearly every aspect of his wide-ranging knowledge and discursive skills: from grammatical to musical theory, from Aristotelian logic to Platonic metaphysics, from Hermogenian rhetoric to Gregory of Nazianzos. Especially important are his multiple references to Neoplatonic commentaries of Aristotle and Plato (including a previously unnoticed reference to the *Introduction to Platonic Philosophy* by an anonymous Christian writer of the sixth century; lines 231–32). Particularly significant are also the numerous direct allusions to the corpus of the Jewish middle Platonist Philo; indeed, this Psellian encomium is among the few Byzantine texts to evoke so explicitly the authority of that pre-Byzantine biblical commentator and philosopher.[8]

Amidst this tour de force of Byzantine knowledge, the text, as noted above, constructs an image of the ideal reader and offers remarkable testimony of how saints' *Lives* were read aloud in Constantinopolitan churches (at least in the eleventh and twelfth centuries). This evidence deserves a full

7. Littlewood places the end much earlier at line 229, following Gautier who however also wonders if the end should be placed later, at line 272. In fact, one might argue that this excursus ends at line 293; the μετὰ ταῦτα of line 294 could thus refer not to the performance (as is translated below), but to the speech that had preceded.

8. Cf. Papaioannou 2013: 78.

analysis that cannot be offered here.[9] What must be highlighted nevertheless is how Psellos' aesthetics of performative reading coheres well with views that we have encountered earlier in this volume. Psellos, for instance, appreciates novelty and deviation from rules, and thus aesthetic autonomy; in his view, the individual skilled performer is beyond either prescription or description (lines 183–90). Also, emphasis is placed on the purely theatrical elements of Kroustoulas' delivery, the *aesthetics* of his supreme *hypokrisis* (passim)—as Psellos makes clear, its effect was not simply moral edification, but, even more so, entertainment and pleasure (198–210).[10]

As to the practice of reading aloud, it must also be noted here that Kroustoulas was one of several readers, or ἀναγνῶσται, who seem to have been involved in some sort of competition in reciting from the *menologion* (in this period, especially that of Symeon Metaphrastes presented in the previous text). As is evident from the *Encomium,* these competitive readers read aloud not only at the Chalkoprateia but in at least one additional important Constantinopolitan church, the Church of the Virgin in the *Ta Kyrou* neighborhood (lines 298–99), an institution associated rightly by Paul Magdalino with a lay fraternity whose primary activity was indeed the reading (and I would argue the composition) of ecclesiastical texts.[11]

The text survives essentially in two manuscripts: fully in Vatican, BAV, gr. 672, a manuscript with almost exclusively Psellos' corpus that dates to the late thirteenth century; and partially, in the late-fourteenth-century Vatican, Urbinatus gr. 134, an interesting rhetorical manuscript that contains among other things the twelfth-century verse romance *Drosilla and Charicles* by Niketas Eugenianos, as well as several Psellian texts, including the encomium for his mother, Theodote.[12] Two likely allusions by later authors, Niketas Choniates (1155/57–1217) and Manuel Holobolos (ca. 1245–1310/14), point to a highly intellectual readership.[13]

9. See further Papaioannou, in preparation.

10. Cf. Papaioannou 2013: 114–15.

11. Magdalino, forthcoming; I would like to thank Prof. Magdalino for sharing his article before publication.

12. Stornajolo 1895: 248–55. The scribe of our text is a certain Κρειονερίτης Φραγγόπουλος; see *RBG* 3A, p. 136.

13. See below, notes 86 and 31 respectively.

Editions and translations. The encomium is translated here for the first time. It has been edited twice, by Paul Gautier (with French summary: Gautier 1980–82) and by Antony Littlewood (*Or. min.* 37). The references and allusions to other authors have been significantly improved, though I have not indicated consistently discrepancy from the two editions in this respect. Numbers indicate lines in Littlewood's edition.

Encomium for the Monk Ioannes Kroustoulas Who Read Aloud at the Holy Soros

[1–18] What is this? As soon as I entered the church, I was bewildered. The sight was strange and uncommon. I have seen nothing like it before. My mind froze straightaway and, perplexed, I began asking the bystanders: "The Soros of the Virgin," I said, "always gathers a large crowd, but I have never before seen as many people as now. Her grace is infinite, but this crowd is beyond comprehension; Her succor is frequent, but this gathering of people equals the grains of sand; Her gifts exceed numbers, but this congregation is beyond perception. The noise, the shouts, the pushing and shoving, the crowding, the jostling, the reproaches, the bystanders melting and pressing together, all this commotion signals even fear for me. Has something unusual happened? Has anyone done something indecent and roused the crowd against him? Has someone opposed someone and created such a rally? For the masses love to rally for such fights, meddling in the affairs of others, setting themselves up as judges of the situation, and treating foreign matters as their own. Is the emperor here, or the empress or someone else on whose account the huge crowd has gathered?"

[18–33] While puzzling over this, others explained to me the reason for what was happening. It was none other than the fact that Ioannes, the great in name, deed, and will, whom they also called *chartoularios*, was set to do the reading. "It is for him that this crowd has gathered and most of the people have come. But you seem to be ignorant perhaps of what sort of man this is in prudence, wisdom, and virtue. If you were to find out, and come to listen to him speak, or came to talk with him, or just to meet him, you would bless the mother who gave birth to him and extol his father and pour eulogies on the man himself. He is—to give words to the matter—virile in character, beautiful in appearance, great in discourse, wisdom, nobility, and dignity, forthright in his soul, solemn in thought, charming in his speech, personable, compassionate, and generous (for this quality too should be listed among the virtues of the man); he possesses every goodness. But why am I saying all this?" he said. "Stay a little and you will see what I am bearing witness to."

[34–43] I was planning, dear men, to "sing my palinode"[1] and escape the gathered swarm, or, rather, like a stream making a circle, to turn around and exit from the point I had entered. After all, there was no single space left where I might stand to chant together with the many and give the customary respects. Every spot was filled: the tabernacle, the mercy seat, the veil, the temple, the side-scenes, the front hall, the entire space.[2] Thus rather than persuade, I was persuaded myself with that good persuasive force that saved me, and acquainted me with the man, and explained him more perfectly, and bound me in ineffable friendship. Pushing, and being pushed aside, I entered.

[44–53] It would have been proper to speak also about everything else that took place and create a detailed narrative; namely, one should convey what was said, indicate what happened, recall what was set forth, neglect no fact, such as the rhythmical movement, the joy, the exuberance, the solemn smiles, and only then lead the description to the man. But I love brevity—Aristotle the philosopher has taught me this.[3] So I will leave out most of what happened and, in imitation of the geometers, I will omit all exterior elements and will focus on the main aim of my subject alone; geometers too include in their books or theorems at hand only those elements that contribute to their main purpose, while disregarding everything else.[4]

1. A proverbial phrase, ultimately from Plato, *Phaedrus* 243b.

2. Psellos mixes here biblical (ἡ πρώτη σκηνή, τὸ ἱλαστήριον, τὸ καταπέτασμα) with classical vocabulary (ὁ ναός, τὰ παρασκήνια, οἱ πρόνεῳ), thus Old Testament ritual with Athenian theatrical terms.

3. From Neoplatonic commentaries (e.g., Olympiodoros, *Comm. on Aristotle's Categories* 27.25–26 and 31.6), rather than from Ps.-Aristotle, *Rhet. ad Alex.*, cited by Gautier and followed by Littlewood.

4. For a correction of the Greek text of this problematic sentence, see I. Polemis 1991: 314.

[54–61] Those who read before him had already left, and there is nothing for me to say about them, as I did not observe them. When he came in, with that wondrous walk, his usual and universal solemnity, with his eyes looking down, oh what charm! What unpretentiousness! What a smile hidden under his cheeks! What were those eyes gazing with calmness and clarity! What a look, what a gaze, what demeanor, and everything else, impossible to describe!

[61–73] Immediately, I recognized the man and the following small sign provided me with complete evidence. For, as soon as he stepped on the space from which he would read, he did not remain the same man. Nor did he retain the same solemn figure or the reserved, in every respect, manner. Rather, as if putting on the virility of a wild animal, he moved aside with his hand the monastic piece of clothing [ῥάκος] that we usually call *periauchenion*,[5] he took the candle and showed himself to be strong-willed—all but speaking with his body language, he offered a model for how a reader should act. He had not yet read the title of his text, and he had indicated everything. And, just as definitions represent for us the nature of things since they denote a genus and the constitutive differences,[6] so he too presented and revealed to us everything, as soon as he recited the heading.

[74–83] Now, some people consider the following as a display and unmistakable confirmation of a reader's skill, ignoring all other qualities—either because these people are perhaps uneducated and thus ignorant, or because they share the same temper. If someone knows how to shout loudly, so as to hunt wild beasts or wake up those sleeping, they give him the first prize immediately; they honor him, and consider him the leader of the chorus—a bad and rather dangerous judgment. It is as if one praises the instrument and extols the melody, is pleased by the playing and rejoices in the singing, but forgets to pay homage to the musician, while all grace is due to him and he should be considered as being beyond acclaim.

5. Literally, a collar; some kind of scarf, typical of monks. Cf. the relevant entry at L. Bender, M. Parani, B. Pitarakis, J.-M. Spieser, A. Vuilloud, *Artefacts and Raw Materials in Byzantine Archival Documents [Objets et matériaux dans les documents d'archives byzantins]*, available at http://www.unifr.ch/go/typika.

6. "definitions" = ὁρισμοί, "genus" = γένος, "constitutive differences" = συστατικαὶ διαφοραί: terms from Aristotelian logical treatises and their Neoplatonic commentaries (from Pophyry's *Eisagoge* to Arethas and Psellos), picked up also in grammatical and rhetorical treatises; see, e.g., Aristotle, *Topics* 101b.37 (on "definition") with Ioannes Sikeliotes, *Prolegomena* 418.8–10 (with wording similar to Psellos'): ἐπειδὴ γὰρ οἱ ὁρισμοὶ ἐκ γένους συνίστανται καὶ συστατικῶν διαφορῶν καὶ ἰδίων.

[83–91] But I do not judge and assess matters like they do. I am neither equal to the many nor do I inspect what is in front of me so as to gratify. I am neither fanned nor blown about with the wind, nor have I desired to say much while being discovered to be deficient in deeds. Rather, I was born and raised in discourse and I have honored education more than anything else. I acquire learning every day and I nurture my soul with texts before I feed my body. Many others agree and can bear witness to this aim of mine. In any case, my diligence and my relationship to them, so to speak, shows how I am.

[92–97] Indeed[7] one would be amazed by that person who recognizes this alone, namely, that man is a living thing, but is meanwhile ignorant of what sort of living thing man is and which are his other properties (and let me not add more examples of dumb people); or one would be amazed at that person who does not stretch his bow toward the target (as is expected of archers), nor makes an effort to shoot his arrows toward it, but emits them here and there and misses the mark.

[97–112] As far as I am concerned, I would say that someone is a reader if he has also examined the parts of speech with precision and has a detailed knowledge of the entire body of discourse—for Plato compared discourse also to a living thing, adding to it a head and arms and wisely granting it all other relevant features, which rhetoricians usually call prefaces, narrations, elaborations, rhythmical endings, perorations, embellishments, and arrangements.[8] I call a reader that man who masters the appropriate time for exhortation, the time for advice, and that for dissuasion; who knows when to oppose or when to offer a solution. A reader is that man who knows how to deliver panegyrics properly, is able to speak counterarguments in a judicial fashion; the one who knows how to punctuate correctly,[9] and turn a period or lengthen a colon, double a word and show amplification, and indicate the force of a preface and its references;[10] the one who knows how to express those phrases

7. Reading ἦ γὰρ, rather than ἢ γὰρ of the editions.

8. See Plato, *Phaedrus* 264c2–5, 266d7–8 evoked and elaborated in Hermogenes, *On Beauty* = *On Forms* 1.12.5–6 (see also *On Force* = *On Forms* 2.9.1), and then in echoes and commentaries of Hermogenes' passage and Plato's metaphor in various Byzantine rhetorical manuals; cf., e.g., Ioannes Sikeliotes, *Prolegomena* 398.2–401.22 for an amplified and particularly inspired example. See also Proklos, *Comm. on Plato's Parmenides* 658.34–659.23.

9. Cf. Dionysios of Halikarnassos, *On Composition* 26.

10. Several of these techniques are discussed in "Hermogenes," *On All Prefaces* = *On Invention* 1.5.

that share a similar ending[11] as well as those that are rapid, full of *kommata*, or *asyndeton*;[12] the one who knows how to conclude a *komma* if perhaps the text seems to be missing words,[13] such as copulative verbs and others that are often implied from the context,[14] and how to bring to rest the end of a sentence, or how to stage a proper delivery [τὰς ὑποκρίσεις], and how to aptly round off a thought.

[113–19] I saw this man to be such a reader. At one point, he would elevate the diction and exalt a thought; at another point, he would interpret the speech and arrange the words, while also dissolving the periods and bringing the cola to rest, and doing and performing everything else appropriately—as opposed to the ordinary person, who is called by everyone "a man of the common herd,"[15] who can string a long phrase together, but is entirely unable to parse it into predicate and subject, and these into syllables, and these into letters.

[120–44] When I saw the man, aiming my gaze upon him,[16] he often did not seem to me to be the same, even if he was the same. Like some Libyan wild creature,[17] he transformed and refashioned himself, altering his face into different forms, just as that famous Proteus would change into a variety of species—even though Proteus' transformations were not the same as his, nei-

11. Ἰσοκαταληξία: for this technique also known as *parison*, see "Hermogenes," *On the Method of Force* 16.

12. Figures pertaining to the form of rapidity (γοργότης); Hermogenes, *On Forms* 2.1.

13. Reading here διὰ τὰ λόγου ἴσως ἐλλείμματα instead of διὰ τοῦ λόγου ἴσως ἐλλείμματα.

14. For this phrase, see the correct reading proposed in I. Polemis 1991: 314.

15. Ἀγελαῖος: cf. Plato, *Politicus* 268a; see also the definition in the *Suda* (alpha.186 and 187): Ἀγέλαιος: προπαροξυτόνως μὲν ὁ ἀμαθής· Ἀγελαῖος δὲ ὁ ἐκ τῆς ἀγέλης. Ἀγελαῖος: ἰδιώτης. ἢ ὁ ἐν ἀγέλῃ διάγων. καὶ Ἀγελαίων, ἰδιωτῶν, ῥεμβωδῶν. τῶν ἀγελαίων ἔοικεν ἀνθρώπων εἶναι ὁ τοιοῦτος. ἀντὶ τοῦ εὐτελῶν. καὶ Ἀγελαίων, τῶν πολλῶν καὶ τυχόντων. εἴη δ' ἂν ἐκ μεταφορᾶς τῶν ἀγελαίων ζῴων ἢ ἀπὸ τῶν ἰχθύων, οὓς βόσκεσθαι ῥύδην καὶ ἀγεληδόν φασιν.

16. Ἀποσκοπεύσας: a word from Gregory of Nazianzos *Or.* 45.1? The relevant passage is discussed in Psellos' *Theol.* I 103.

17. A Byzantine proverb; cf. the *Suda* lambda.494: Λιβυκὸν θηρίον: οἷον ἐξηλλαγμένον. φασὶ γὰρ τὴν Λιβύην θηρία μὲν πολλὰ ἔχουσαν, ἄνυδρον δὲ οὖσαν, συνερχομένων δὲ παντοδαπῶν εἰς ἕνα πότον, εἶτα ἀλλήλοις ἐπιβαινόντων, ἐξηλλαγμένα καὶ σύμμικτα ἀποτελεῖν ζῷα. Cf. also Psellos, *Various Necessary Collected Passages* = *Phil. min.* I 55.483–84 (excerpting Alexandros of Aphrodisias): Τὰ Λιβυκὰ θηρία θέρους οὐ πίνει, ὅτι οὐκ ἔχει ὕδωρ, τοῦ δὲ χειμῶνος ἔχει· ὃ οὖν εἴθισται καὶ ποιεῖ.

ther their refashioning of their figure nor the dissimilarity of their action.[18] Ioannes' transformation happens to be a result of a soul that is easily impressible and of a personality that easily yields to all the best things. Indeed, our intellect (allow me to philosophize a bit) can partake in divine essence, just like melted wax.[19] If it is not captured and bound by the fetters of the body nor turns itself into a slave and captive without escape, but preserves its rank as master that is received from the divine (I mean its impalpability, uncircumscribability,[20] capacity to pervade everywhere through everything, and all other attributes that philosophical discourse mentions), then it adapts to everything that is good and is able to copy, whatever it wills. Philo metaphorically calls this intellect also a "fountain"[21] that rises from below and waters the entire face of the earth; he also says that it is a "heavenly plant," and he calls it an "inhabitant of paradise";[22] and it is only this mind that Philo honors with the condition of inspiration.[23] Now if I attributed Ioannes' ability (I refer to his ability to imitate easily[24]) to his soul and ascribed this extraordinary quality

18. The figure of Proteus (Homer, *Odyssey* 4.365ff.) has usually negative connotations in Greek writing; cf. Plato, *Ion* 541d; Philo, *Legatio ad Gaium* 80–81; and Gregory of Nazianzos, *Or.* 4.62 (on Julian who "was all and became all" like a chameleon, but also comparable to the "Aegyptian sophist" Proteus). For cases (as in Psellos) of a positive use of the metaphor of Proteus in a rhetorical context, see Dionysios of Halikarnassos, *On Demosthenes* 8.13–31; Philostratos, *Life of Apollonios* 1.4.4–1.5.1; Himerios *Or.* 68.63–70; Aristainetos, *Letter* 26 with Webb 1997: 137; and Geometres' *Ekphrasis of a Garden* = *Progymnasmata* 2:9.20–22 with the discussion of Demoen 2001 as well as Agapitos and Hinterberger 2006: 129–61, 194–95.

19. A favorite (Neo-)Platonic metaphor/image in Psellos; see Plato, *Theaetetus* 191c8–11, 194c4–d7 with Psellos, *In Support of the Nomophylax <=Ioannes Xiphilinos> against Ophrydas* = *Or. for.* 3.205–25: ὅπερ παίζων ὁ Πλάτων φησίν ὁ τῆς ψυχῆς κηρὸς αἴτιος· ἔστι γὰρ ἐν ἑκάστῳ κηρὸς ὥσπερ τύπους δεχόμενος τὰ μαθήματα. In the passage here, Psellos evokes specifically the usage of the metaphor in Philo, *On the Creation of the World according to Moses* 18 and 166 and *On Agriculture* 16 and 167. For another influence, see Synesios, *Dion* 18.4 with Psellos, *Discourse to the Emperor Kyr Konstantinos Monomachos* = *Or. pan.* 1.125–29.

20. For this term and its importance for Byzantine iconophile theology, see Parry 1996: 99–113.

21. *Allegory of the Sacred Laws* 1.28–30 and *On the Flight and Finding* 181–82.

22. *On Noah's Work as a Planter* 17 and 45–46; cf. Plato, *Timaeus* 90a2–8.

23. *Allegory of the Sacred Laws* 1.28.

24. Εὐμίμητον: this rare word appears also in Plato's *Republic* (605a5–6) with a passive meaning ("the condition of being easily imitated") and a negative connotation in the context of his critique on the so-called "mimetic" poet who is by nature (πέφυκε) inclined not toward the self-mastered (σῶφρον) but toward the irritable and varied

to it, this is also for a reason. For our nature moves first the body, while it is moved by the soul, and the soul by the mind, and the mind is led by God; therefore, whatever the mind might devise, he inscribes it on the tablet of the soul.[25] Therefore, as the philosophers claim that the one that sets in motion first is immovable, so also he (I mean that admirable and reverent man) is inimitable and incomparable in every respect.

[145–56] But let me return to where I left off. For even though the course of my speech has brought me to a different point, I return again to the matter at hand. So, I was looking at him with my gaze fixed, studying every detail; how he stretched out his hands, how he would start off, how he would perform, how he would shift his body, how he would change his spot; in every way, he retained his integrity in my eyes. Now he seemed like a soft breeze, then he was felt like a gentle wind. He would read long passages in one breath; he would use the right intonation. Often, he would employ a rough voice or his voice would become light like a feather and he would please the audience with mellifluous rhythms. He progressed in other parts with coordination, while in others he used unilateral combination,[26] and in still others he read without using any conjunction.[27] As for the cases, which by analogy the philosophers call the ends of words or syllables,[28] he delivered them in proper fashion.

(ποικίλον) *êthos*, which can be "easily imitated." In a similar fashion, Gregory of Nazianzos derides evil as something that "can be rather *easily imitated*" (*Poem* 1.1.13.720). The active meaning is encountered in Porphyry's *Hypomnêma* on the *Harmonika* of Ptolemaios (42.11–16), who attributes "varied figuration" (παντοῖος σχηματισμός), namely, the ability of the human tongue or mouth to "mimic" voices of animals or noises of things, to the "easily imitating" (εὐμίμητος) nature of the mind. Cf. also the use of the adverb εὐμιμήτως twice in the works of Maximos the Confessor (*PG* 91 12a and 1205A; cf. Lampe s.v.) in the positive sense of the ability of human nature to imitate the divine as it is its image.

25. Psellos returns recurrently to this Neoplatonic hierarchical scheme; see, e.g., the order of presentation in his *Concise Answers to Various Questions*: God (discussed in chapters 1–20), *nous* (21–29), *psychê* (30–56; with four appendices 194–97), *physis* (57), and then topics relating to the body and matter (58–193).

26. κατὰ μονομέρειαν: a term that is nowhere else used in this technical sense, as far as I know.

27. For a discussion of coordination and asyndeton, see Hermogenes' exposition on figures that should be used in the Form of rapidity (*On Forms* 2.1.12–20).

28. Unidentified reference.

[157–75] There is no one who has come here and heard the man and did not experience change in his soul and was not transformed into a good mood, regardless if earlier he was like rock, stone, or iron, or like a bloodthirsty and uncontrollable beast. Such was the charm dripping from his lips, so harmonious was his voice, in such a way he enchanted his listeners and cast a spell on those willing, that, even if someone (allow me to boast a little for the sake of the man) were to receive the tribulations of Odysseus, even such tribulations would fill his entire heart with joy. By the sweet melody of his voice he surpassed those so-called *oupiggoi,* which they say are a hymn to Artemis and Hippolytos,[29] as well as the melodious sounds of the Thracian Orpheus, the tunes from Kolophon,[30] and the beguiling songs[31] of the Sirens. He filled the souls as if with some sort of fomentation, healing drugs[32] for sick souls. It is impossible to know and it is rather not to be trusted whether Aelian writes the truth when he talks about some Polymnastos who charmed fiercely blowing winds, beguiling and calming them down, or smoothed the swelling sea with his singing.[33] I marveled and conveyed in writing so that lovers of discourse

29. Athenaios, *Philosophers at Dinner* 619b.

30. Most likely Polymnastos of Kolophon; cf. Hesychios *pi.*2891: Πολυμνήστ(ε)ιον ᾄδειν· εἶδός τι μελο[σ]ποιΐας τὸ Πολυμνήστ(ε)ιον. ἦν δὲ Κολοφώνιος μελοποιὸς ὁ Πολύμνηστος, εὐμελὴς πάνυ.

31. Κηλητήρια ᾄσματα: cf. the definition in the *Suda* (kappa.1507): θελκτικὰ μέλη. γράψαντας ἐς τοὺς ιβ΄ θεοὺς χρῆναι ταῦτα ᾄδεσθαι, οἱονεὶ τῶν παρόντων κακῶν κηλητήρια.

32. Παιώνεια φάρμακα: Aeschylus, *Agamemnon* 848. Cf. *Suda* pi.883: Παιώνειον: ῥίζης φάρμακον.

33. No such story is to be found in the surviving corpus of Aelian or anywhere else in Greek literature before Psellos. Nevertheless, the same story (as well as the list of earlier references in Psellos' passage) is evoked again in a similar context and in similar wording by the "rhetor of rhetors" Manuel Holobolos; *Encomium of Michael Palaiologos* 2: 91.34–39: μῦθος οὐκ ἄρα τὰ τῶν Σειρήνων, ὡς τοὺς αὐτῶν ἀκούοντας εἶχον καὶ ἄκοντας οἷον μεθεῖλκον πρὸς ἑαυτάς· οὐ λόγος ἄλλως τὸ τοῦ Ὀρφέως, ὡς καὶ οὗτος κρούμασι λυρικοῖς καὶ θῆρας ἔθελγε καὶ κινεῖσθαι λίθους παρέπειθεν· οὐδὲ τὸ ᾀδόμενον ἄπιστον, ὡς Πολύμναστος ᾄδων καὶ ἀνέμους ἐκήλει καὶ κατεμείλισσε θάλατταν. We have here clear evidence of a Byzantine reader of Psellos' text. Notably one of the two mss. of Psellos' encomium of Kroustoulas is the Vatican, BAV, gr. 672, produced precisely in the time (and, one might easily speculate, social context) of Holobolos, namely, the late thirteenth century. Inmaculada Pérez Martín has identified Holobolos or his circle as the likely context for the compilation of two other manuscripts with Psellian collections in the late thirteenth century, Vatican, BAV, Barberinianus gr. 240 and Oxford, Bodleian Library, Baroccianus 131; Pérez Martín 2012: 171–73.

too can marvel at the one whom I saw with my own eyes and at what I discovered after scrutiny (for I am no false judge of such matters; no one should ever think that!).

[176–83] The theory of discourse has placed definitions and rules for readers, as if to even out the paths and guide or lead them to the appropriate dwellings.[34] "You should read," it says, "tragedy like an ancient hero,[35] comedy like an everyday person,[36] elegies in shrilling manner,[37] epic with force,[38] lyric poetry in melody,[39] and laments in a downcast and wailing voice."[40] "Whatever is done without observing these rules," it adds, "both disgraces the virtues of the poets and"—along with other things—"renders the skills of the readers laughable."

[183–90] If the above indicates perfection and represents what the most prudent and learned men do, let me make a counterclaim as if blowing from an opposite direction: what kind of consideration and how much of it would that man deserve who has gathered together and observed all these rules like no one else, and daily explains them to those who are ignorant, and has invented new ways of reading, which surpass description, and whose deviations from the norm are even more appealing, whose discursive innovations are

34. Psellos will go on to cite Dionysios of Thrace, *Art of Grammar* 2, a text and a passage heavily commented upon in Byzantium (for various commentaries, see the edition in Hilgard 1901). Below, I have included the explanations from one such commentary by Melampous, an otherwise unknown (and of uncertain date) Byzantine grammarian. For Dionysios' text, see Kemp 1986.

35. Melampous the Grammarian (or Diomedes), *Comm. On the Art of Dionysios of Thrace*, ed. Hilgard 1901: 17.32–18.2: Ταύτην οὖν τὴν τραγῳδίαν φησὶν ὁ τεχνικὸς δεῖν ἡρωϊκῶς ἀναγινώσκειν, τουτέστι μεγάλῃ τῇ φωνῇ μετὰ πολλῆς σεμνότητος καὶ ὄγκου· δεῖ γὰρ ἡμᾶς τὰ τραγικὰ προφερομένους μιμεῖσθαι πάντα τρόπον τοὺς ἥρωας, καὶ μεγέθει σώματος καὶ λόγων ὑπερβολῇ.

36. Following here the text of Dionysios of Thrace, which reads βιωτικῶς, instead of Littlewood's and Gautier's Βοιωτικῶς. Cf. Melampous, *Comm.* 20.10–12: Ταύτην οὖν τὴν κωμῳδίαν δεῖ βιωτικῶς ἀναγινώσκειν, τουτέστιν ὡς ἐν τῷ βίῳ, μιμουμένους τὸ παρεισαγόμενον πρόσωπον καὶ τὴν ἐκείνου σχέσιν ἀναματτομένους.

37. Melampous, *Comm.* 21.2–5: «Λιγυρῶς», τουτέστιν ὀξυφώνως· ἡ γὰρ λύπη τῇ παρατροπῇ τῆς φωνῆς ἐκ τοῦ κλαυθμοῦ ὀξύτερά τινα παρεισάγει.

38. Melampous, *Comm.* 21.9–11: «εὐτόνως» ἀναγινώσκειν, τουτέστι συντόνῳ τῇ φωνῇ καὶ μὴ ἐκλελυμένῃ, ὡς καὶ ἡρώων ἀνδρῶν περιέχον ἱστορίας.

39. Melampous, *Comm.* 21.19–21: Ταύτην οὖν τὴν λυρικὴν ποίησιν δεῖ μετὰ μέλους ἀναγινώσκειν, εἰ καὶ μὴ παρελάβομεν μηδὲ ἀπομεμνήμεθα τὰ ἐκείνων μέλη.

40. Melampous, *Comm.* 21.22–23: «Οἴκτους» θρήνους, «ὑφειμένως» κεχαλασμένῃ τῇ φωνῇ, «γοερῶς» θρηνητικῶς.

savored by everyone, and whose interweaving of different styles is desired more than stylistic purity?

[191–98] Let others say other things about the man, even if it would be impossible—even with everyone expressing a view—to illustrate clearly his qualities and to represent the precise, the very truth. I saw then and there many men fixing their gaze upon him, learned men, belonging to those select few whom they call members of the synod and members of the senate. And I asked them what was the reason for their anxious behavior, that indescribable desire of theirs, since all of them hung, as it were, from the man and considered him their life. Again and again, I received from them the truth.

[198–210] They said: "If you want to find out exactly, if you are asking for a full recognition of what is happening and the unmediated absolute truth which knows how to not deceive the senses, well then no one among those present has come here (to say something rather bold) for the sake of spiritual grace or to reap spiritual fruits. Rather, they have come for this man that you see reading, offering pleasure. Just like someone who enters a meadow in bloom and sees there many and different flowers and fruits is delighted in his soul, often leaps with joy, and picks some of these, so also do we. Coming to this man, as if to some discursive paradise, each one of us returns again and again, acquiring as inviolable wealth, some his interpretation, others his method of delivery, others his reserved voice; one man acquires Ioannes' unexpected approach, another his spontaneity, one person his innovations, another his unusual technique, another his character and the transformation of speech.

[210–20] "The science beyond physics—I mean theology, the first science[41]—is like a commander of the other specialized methods and sciences. It appropriately distributes to each the principles that belong to it: to physics, that nothing derives from what is not;[42] to medicine, that opposites cure opposites;[43] to dialectics, that it is not possible to both affirm and deny something;[44] to arithmetics, another thing; to geometry, something else. Sometimes, theology provides also one common principle to all other sciences, for

41. See Psellos, *Various Collected Passages* = *Phil. min.* II 13 (37.32–38.13) with Steel 2005 on theology as the "first philosophy."

42. Aristotle, *Metaphysics* 11: 1063a24–26.

43. A very common statement, attributed to Hippocrates (*Of Flatus* 1).

44. Aristotle, *Posterior Analytics* 1: 77a.29–30.

example, that the good is desired by all[45]—for both the geometer and the mathematician and anyone who studies and practices some science would use this principle as his own.

[220–29] "The very same applies to this monk, the so-called Aggouriotes—if I should call him also by his epithet. To everyone here who has this or that understanding, he provides both the causes and the rhythms of speeches, both the repetitions of tropes and the detailed accounts of regular patterns,[46] as well as everything else—allow me to not mention the entire cluster of his good qualities, so as not to be flooded by them, as if by the streams of a river. Just as form [εἶδος] completes the essence of every being and when form is ruined then also the underlying essence is ruined,[47] in the same way when Ioannes does not lead them to the goal at hand, all these people that you see are lost.

[230–56] "Plato praises the method of logical division, the one that occurs through contradictory propositions;[48] no being, he says, can boast an escape of this method's powers.[49] But is not the following also a method of division, indeed the best of methods and the most fitting? I mean how he separates the parts of a speech and then again joins them appropriately. He displays the boldness of one character and then the most courageous response of another. In some places, he adds submissiveness to the character; in other places, he includes the opposite. This method too does not allow any such thing to escape without receiving an interpretation. At one moment, he will set the matter of the activity of the spirited element into motion,[50] which is also called 'the boiling of the blood in the region of the heart';[51] he will reproach the ty-

45. A common Neoplatonic notion; see, e.g., Ps.-Dionysios the Areopagite, *On Divine Names* 158.8–13.

46. Τοὺς κατ' ἀναλογίαν ἐκλογισμούς: the fifth part of the art of grammar, according to the definition of Dionysios of Thrace (*The Art of Grammar* 1).

47. A Neoplatonic notion in the tradition of commentaries of Aristotle; see, e.g., Simplikios, *Comm. on Aristotle's Categories* 101.12–21 or, especially, Ioannes Philoponos, *Comm. on Aristotle's Categories* 508.35–509.6 (cf. also below).

48. Cf. Aristotle, *On Interpretation* 22a39–b29.

49. This is actually not a quotation from Plato. Psellos evokes the sixth-century anonymous Christian Neoplatonist from whom we have an introduction to Plato; Anonymous, *Prolegomena to Platonic Philosophy* 23.7–11. Psellos was familiar with this text; cf. Papaioannou 2013: 73–74; cf. also below.

50. Namely, "anger"; cf. Nemesios, *On the Nature of Man* 16:74.8–9: ὁ θυμὸς ἐνέργεια μέν ἐστι τοῦ θυμοειδοῦς.

51. Nemesios, *On the Nature of Man* 20: 81.2; a common notion that derives from Aristotle, *On the Soul* 403a31.

rants, he will cancel their power, he will eliminate their force, he will reveal their weakness, he will indicate their shamelessness, he will narrate their defeat, he will fill the souls of the faithful with joy. At another moment, he will bring up the decision to impose the death penalty, he will declare the place of the martyrdom, he will describe the end. Then again he will lead the ascetic up on to the mountain, he will find a dwelling for him, he will feed him without any preparation, he will set a scanty table for him, and then he will conclude with his last song. He will render fittingly the high and the low pitch, he will express the sounds of unvarying pitch and those of varying pitch,[52] he will signal the parts of the harmony, he will convey the scales and the genera,[53] he will perform the intervals by his gestures. It is as if some grammarian would term the principles of discourse as phonemes [στοιχεῖα], syllables, words, nouns, verbs,[54] or a natural philosopher would term the principles of noncomposite bodies as matter, form, body without qualities, and four elements.[55] In the same manner, Ioannes too expresses one part as an interpretation, another as imitation, and he renders something as audacity, with another he shows moderation, or bravery, meekness, clemency, prohibition, or address. He assigns everything to its own place, and divides all else—so as not to mention everything one by one.

[257-272] "Who can explain the musical bridge that you carry within your breast, and the songs and chirpings that you carry on your tongue,[56] that all-harmonious melody, the pleasure that never ends, the ineffable method that cannot be surpassed? Begone Aeschylus and Stesichorus, who knew perhaps, as the story goes, to charm the many by their flutes, but lost their lives in a bad manner, the bywork of robbers' hands![57] Begone Kaphisias,[58]

52. Terms and notions from Ptolemy's *Harmonics.*

53. Namely the three genera of ancient and Byzantine music: the diatonic, the chromatic, and the enharmonic (see also p. 73n21 above).

54. Chapters in Dionysios of Thrace's *The Art of Grammar.*

55. All Aristotelian notions frequent in Neoplatonic commentaries; cf. Ioannes Philoponos, *Comm. on Aristotle's Categories*, passim.

56. "The musical bridge . . . within your breast," and the "songs and chirpings": Quotations from Gregory of Nazianzos, *On Theology* = *Or.* 28.24: τίς ὁ δοὺς τέττιγι τὴν ἐπὶ στήθους μαγάδα, καὶ τὰ ἐπὶ τῶν κλάδων ᾄσματά τε καὶ τερετίσματα. Psellos cites from the same paragraph from Gregory's oration in his letter G 7 to Ioannes Doukas.

57. This information derives from an entry in the *Suda* (epsilon.2681): Ἐπιτήδευμα: ἄσκησις, μάθησις. Ἱκανὸς ὄνομα, λῃστὴς τὸ ἐπιτήδευμα· ὃς ἀνεῖλεν Αἰσχύλον τὸν αὐλητὴν καὶ Στησίχορον τὸν κιθαρῳδόν.

58. Plutarch, *Pyrrhus* 8; Athenaeus, *Philosophers at Dinner* 538f and 629a–b.

Neoptolemos,[59] and the man from Rhegion, for whom, they say, when his string broke, a cicada came and sung his tune.[60] All of them are inferior to Ioannes, his melody, his beautiful voice, his soft song, his severe song, his moderate song, and everything else (for the man knows very well also that the *tonos* is a position of the voice without breadth,[61] that the *hypatê*[62] is the first and largest of the strings in a guitar, and that the medial [μέση] is precisely that, the middle one: as this latter one is stretched as if in the position of a center in relation to the highest strings and those middle ones that carry the same name, and in relation to the lowest strings and the very extremities). How much more inferior are they to Ioannes? As much as what is voiced by him is divine, piercing and sweet, and delights the soul, while those voiced by them are human, enfeebled, and entertain the body."

[273–86] Is not the following too a miracle more astonishing than the much celebrated ones? With these, he made some in his audience lament and, from their eyes, pour dire tears (what everyone quite appropriately calls messages of the soul[63]); others he made laugh and yield fully to the pleasures; others he brought to wailing. One of them, as Ioannes' words touched his soul, took off his garment and gave it to a pauper (for the church is not lacking any of these either); he chose to be naked for the sake of Christ and His reward that provides gifts in multiplied degree and bestows that kind of life that lasts forever. Indeed,

59. Diodoros of Sicily, *Library* 16.92.3: Νεοπτόλεμος ὁ τραγῳδός, πρωτεύων τῇ μεγαλοφωνίᾳ καὶ τῇ δόξῃ.

60. Psellos alludes to (but also misrepresents) a story from Greek mythography well known to Byzantine scholars: the competition between two guitar players, Ariston from Rhegion and Eunomos from Locri, with the latter winning with the help of a cicada. Cf. Gregory of Nazianzos, *Letter* 175, to Nikoboulos, and also Photios, *Bibliotheke* 186, on Conon's *Narratives* = 131b32-40. The story is best discussed in Antigonos, *Collection of Strange Stories* 1 (the text survives in a single ms., the famous, likely second half of the ninth c., Heidelberg, UB, Palat. gr. 398, 243v–261v): ἀφικομένων γὰρ εἰς Δελφοὺς κιθαρῳδῶν Ἀρίστωνος μὲν ἐκ Ῥηγίου, παρὰ δὲ Λοκρῶν Εὐνόμου . . . εὐημερήσαντος δ' οὖν τοῦ Ῥηγίνου ἐν τῷ ἀγῶνι ἐνίκησεν Εὔνομος ὁ Λοκρὸς παρὰ τοιαύτην αἰτίαν· ᾄδοντος αὐτοῦ μεταξὺ τέττιξ ἐπὶ τὴν λύραν ἐπιπτὰς ᾖδεν, ἡ δὲ πανήγυρις ἀνεβόησεν ἐπὶ τῷ γεγονότι καὶ ἐκέλευσεν ἐᾶν.

61. ὁ τόνος μὲν τόπος ἐστὶ τῆς φωνῆς ἀπλατής: verbatim from Kleonides, *Introduction to Harmonics* 1: τόνος δέ ἐστι τόπος τις τῆς φωνῆς δεκτικὸς συστήματος ἀπλατής.

62. The highest string, but with the lowest pitch.

63. Though the notion that tears are products of a grieving soul is commonplace, I could not locate an exact parallel to Psellos' statement here.

as I see it, simple, direct speech, though apt, has less power than the indirect, elaborate one. And this is opposite to the wound inflicted by a spear. While a spear wounds when thrown directly, but just grazes when it deviates from its target, speech is fixed in the very heart itself when it is discharged embellished by art, but it only reaches the ear when it is poured out artlessly.

[287–93] Is there such a person who witnessed Ioannes' impersonations of tyrants[64] and his voices and imitations of those opposing them and did not immediately smile or, to put it better, marvel and extol this man to the skies? You do not need me to jog your memory, if you have actually heard him mimic different languages, simulate the tongue of barbarians, include Armenian words,[65] and thus take a stand against the tyrant. As for those who have not experienced him, know that you are missing out on something truly great.

[294–99] Indeed, after Ioannes' performance there, I heard the reading also of some learned man who added much to the task.[66] But what do a bull

64. Cf. Anonymous (twelfth c.), *Comm. on Aristotle's Rhetoric* 220.19–27, 224.24–28 and the discussion in the introduction above: οἱ δὲ ἀναγνωστικοὶ . . . οὗτοι δέ εἰσιν ἐπιτήδειοι εἰς τὸ ἀναγινώσκειν οἱ ἀπομιμούμενοι τὰ πρόσωπα καὶ τὰ πράγματα ἐν τῷ ἀναγινώσκειν, καὶ εἰ μὲν τὸ πρόσωπόν ἐστι τυραννικὸν καὶ θυμούμενον, καὶ αὐτὸς ἀφίησι φωνὴν ἀγρίαν, εἰ δὲ ταπεινόν ἐστι τὸ πρόσωπον, καὶ ἡ φωνὴ αὐτοῦ ἐστιν ὑφειμένη· ὥσπερ ποιοῦσι καὶ οἱ τὰς μεταφράσεις ἀναγινώσκοντες ἐν τῇ Ἁγίᾳ Σορῷ. τοὺς γοῦν οὕτως ἀναγινώσκοντας τοὺς λόγους ἤτοι ὑποκριτικῶς καὶ μιμητικῶς ἀποδέχονται οἱ ἀκροαταί . . . ἔνθα δὲ δεῖ ὑποκρίσεως, ἐκεῖ ἡ ἀκρίβεια ἄπεστι καὶ ἡ τέχνη, χρεία δὲ μᾶλλον φωνῆς μεγάλης καὶ ποικίλης, ἵνα πῇ μὲν ὑποκρίνηται τὰς τυραννικὰς φωνάς, πῇ δὲ τὰς γυναικείας, πῇ δὲ τὰς ἀνειμένας, ὡς ἔστιν ἰδεῖν ὑποκρινομένους τοὺς ἐν τῇ Ἁγίᾳ Σορῷ ἀναγινώσκοντας. Gautier 1980–82: 120–21 misread this reference to "impersonations of tyrants" as a reference to the contemporary events of the rebel Leon Tornikes (1047–48).

65. Cf. Stephanos Skylitzes (twelfth c.), *Comm. on Aristotle's Rhetoric* 312.17–23 and the discussion in the introduction above: τῷ προσώπῳ ἐκείνῳ ὃ μιμεῖται διαλέξεως τινὰς φωνὰς ἐκείνῳ καταλλήλους συνθήσει, ὡς εἴ τις ἀναγινώσκων τὸ μαρτύριον τοῦ ἁγίου Εὐστρατίου καὶ ταῖς Ἀρμενίων φωναῖς μιμούμενος τὸν μέγαν Μαρδάριον χρήσαιτο, ὡς καὶ ὁ κωμικὸς τὸ τοῦ Σκύθου πρόσωπον ὑποκρινόμενος πολλὰ Σκυθικὰ καὶ βαρβαρικὰ εἶπεν, ἢ ἐὰν Ἀττικὸς ἀνὴρ λογογραφῶν πολλὰ τῆς Ἀτθίδος διαλεκτικὰ εἴπῃ· ἑρμήνευε γὰρ καὶ οὕτως.

66. Ἔγωγ' οὖν αὐτοῦ μετὰ ταῦτα καὶ μετά τινος λογίου ἀναγινώσκοντος ἤκουσα προσθήκην μεγάλην ἐπὶ τῷ πράγματι θήσαντος. This sentence, as edited in Littlewood, is syntactically awkward. I suggest that the phrase be corrected in this way: Ἔγωγ' οὖν αὐτοῦ μετὰ ταῦτα καὶ τινος λογίου ἀναγινώσκοντος ἤκουσα, προσθήκην μεγάλην ἐπὶ τῷ πράγματι θήσαντος. Namely, to (a) read "αὐτοῦ" as locative referring to the church at Chalkoprateia (Psellos has not mentioned any other location or occasion yet and is presumably still describing the original event); (b) remove the second "μετά" and take

and a dolphin have in common?[67] A negation and a positive statement? Destruction and generation? Material and intellectual things? Sophistry and wisdom? (Let me not add more examples, in reverence of learnedness.) Those who were there and the church of the Virgin of ta Kyrou know well.[68]

[300–311] At that point, some people also asked me that usual question and, perplexed, they wanted to know the cause; in response, I invented a teacher similar to them. "What," they said to me, "is this man, who possesses a voice sweeter than everything else, surpassing every lyre, outperforming the songs of cicadas, nightingales, swallows, and trumpets (so to speak), who has a character that can be easily fashioned to fit every role, and a tongue that is musical and truly sings beautifully, and an art that no one is able to describe?" And I, in turn, remembered appropriately that Platonic dictum; when Socrates was asking Timaeus "what is God?" he responded: "I know that he exists, but what he is I do not know. For I know that he is neither a body nor a color nor an angel nor any such creature but superior than them; yet what he is exactly I do not know."[69]

[311–17] So I too responded: "That this one is a human being, subject to the same definition as everyone else, I know quite well; what sort of features are the rest of his, I have no idea. For I can see a form that surpasses human nature, a gaze that is at one time cherubic, at another leonine, at another apelike, at another similar to a falcon; and then sometimes he leaps from joy, he is cheerful, he smiles, he even dances. His voice is suppler than wax and sometimes outdoes the trumpets of Nun. From where does all this come and how and from whom? I am bewildered.

[317–25] "Indeed, I would dare to say about him what they argue about the 'partial soul,' namely, that when it falls on earth, is overcome by oblivion,

---

"τινος λογίου" as the direct object of ἤκουσα—"λογίου" is sarcastic; (c) read "καὶ" as adding emphasis, rather than as conjunctive; and (d) reintroduce the comma after "ἤκουσα," as Gautier has it, apparently retaining the reading of the mss., so that the second participle would modify the first participle, and would not appear as being governed by "ἤκουσα."

67. Proverbial expression, attributed to Aelian, excerpted in the Suda (tau.556): Τί γὰρ δὴ δελφῖνι καὶ βοΐ φασι κοινὸν εἶναι, Σύλλᾳ τε καὶ φιλοσόφοις.

68. Apparently both men (or at least one of them) had performed also in the Church of the Virgin of ta Kyrou; see the discussion in the introduction above.

69. Plato, *Timaeus* 28c3–5; Psellos' reference is noted also in the margin of the ms. where the scribe has written "Πλάτωνος."

and then rushes to recollect its earlier existence, it becomes the subject sometimes of grammar, sometimes of medicine, and similarly of other arts—for it is set in a middle rank in relation to the entirely material things and those beings that are not such; whenever it is elevated from the bodies, no definition can encompass it; whenever it falls into matter and forgets, then a definition applies; and this is nothing strange.[70]

[325–37] "Whenever he is with us, engages in friendly conversation, chats about the usual things, provokes jokes, and pokes fun at others if he ever hears somebody say nonsense (for among his other qualities, he also despises those who dislike beauty[71]), he seems to be himself and not some other person. Yet whenever he might enter a church and approach the book, take a candle, and start his divine narration, he seems to be some other nature, different from human. For when he narrates the family origins of holy men, lists their ancestors, and describes their fatherland and their dwellings, whenever he sets up a comparison, asks questions, and applies proverbs and myths to a text, whenever he speaks eloquently, reveals the message of symbolic utterances, and often clarifies what is unclear, it is impossible to say what sort of man he is nor would anyone be able to ever figure out what to call him. He outshines every good and is proven to be beyond comparison."

[338–56] It is my custom to talk with learned men and never abandon their conversation. And they too know me, as I know them, and they often approach me and ask me about certain matters and receive the same interaction from me. So I chanced upon a man knowledgeable in every wisdom: he did not know this and that, while ignoring other things, nor did he walk the path of learning on one foot; rather, he was perfect in everything and through everything, and knew all things in a better way than the way in which the many know one thing. For the person who only knows one part but is ignorant of another part—and let me expand on this, perhaps superfluously, but indeed truthfully—he would definitely not be wise, but resemble a philosopher of

70. This whole passage is taken almost verbatim from Ammonios' (late fifth-/early sixth-c. Alexandria) Neoplatonic commentary on Aristotle's *Categories* (*Comm. on Aristotle's Categories* 36.22–37.20, a reference missed by the editors of Psellos' text). In Neoplatonic discourse, "partial soul" (as opposed to "universal soul") indicates a soul that is subject to time and death; cf., e.g., Proklos, *Comm. on the Timaeus* I 380.24–381.6.

71. μισόκαλος: here, not in the usual Byzantine sense of "hater of the good," often applied to the Devil or demons. Rather, Psellos uses the term as an opposite to "philokalos," a positive virtue of an urbane gentleman in his vocabulary; cf. Papaioannou 2013: 239.

physics who knows perhaps the essence of a subject thing but does not know its shape nor the principles of its existence, nor could he go beyond the bodies. Or if someone were to practice arithmetic but neglect other types of knowledge, he would not know the exact mean of mathematical proportions nor would he divide the numbers into flat and cubic[72] and know whenever these are properly called thus.[73] The same applies to the geometer, the one knowledgeable in music, the one who studies the forms of the stars, or the one who examines moral philosophy. As for the scientist of catoptrics or mechanics or whoever else is to be counted in the field of the quadrivium,[74] he would hardly know the subordinate subjects if he did not use for proof the superior premises.

[356–76] Yet this man (and he is so-and-so[75]) had traversed every path, as I discovered at that instance after much scrutiny. For as soon as I saw him speak eloquently, explain any subject that we chanced upon, elevate his diction to sublimity, and expand the various meanings better than those others who write about them, I was excited, I addressed philosophical questions, without noticing I touched on loftier matters, and I pursued the man from every direction, saying:[76] "What are the principles of being? What are the principles of the first statements and of the so-called immediate axioms? What is the division of intelligible essence? And how is some part of it essential, another intellectual, another imaginable, another subject to opinion? Can everything be defined? Can everything be proven, divided, analyzed? How do all the parts of the universe remain in harmony with each other according to some ineffable sympathy[77] and then again show antipathy[78] as if the entire

72. Namely, those that represent flat surfaces and those that represent bodies of three dimensions.

73. Common Byzantine mathematical jargon, explained, e.g., in the popular *Introduction to Arithmetic* by Nikomachos of Gerasa (first/second c. CE; ed. Hoche 1866).

74. Arithmetic, geometry, music, and astronomy.

75. Psellos does not offer this "learned" man's name.

76. Psellos will go on to list various terms, categories, and issues discussed in the context of a typically Neoplatonic curriculum, starting with Aristotelian logic (e.g., the term "immediate axiom" from the *Posterior Analytics*) and advancing to cosmology. These terms and questions are discussed in a variety of Aristotelian and Platonic texts as well as their Neoplatonic and Byzantine commentaries, well known to Psellos.

77. For this notion in Psellos, see Ierodiakonou 2006.

78. For the juxtaposition of συμπάθεια and ἀντιπάθεια, see, e.g., Proklos, *Comm. on the Timaeus* 1.301.3–22. See also S 188 (477.24–26).

universe happens to be one living organism?[79] And how did Plato first posit that the elements are bodies with geometrical surfaces, equating earth to a cube, water to a icosahedron, air to an octahedron, fire with the pyramid, the ether (or, as some argue,[80] the universe) with a dodecahedron, but then as if forgetting himself he ascribed to all of them entirely spherical bodies?"[81] And I put forward also other, more difficult subjects. What the many claim when they are better than some and boast about something, this I saw myself in this man: he knew everything better than each person knows their own name. But enough about all this.

[377–88] While we were still conversing, some other person interrupted our conference and returned our discussion to the man who is the subject of this speech. After some debate, a bishop (people know him as "Taurenos," but I will not explain now why) succeeded Ioannes as the protagonist of our exchange as some people there said: "That monk is great, but the fame of this bishop has captivated everyone's ears." We countered this idea and contended: "No one could be found who is superior to Ioannes. Yes, there is something better even than the good, but who could be declared superior to him?" The debate remained open at first, with much argument back and forth, and in no way could it be settled. I had not heard of this bishop before, but those who knew him fought hard on his behalf. In the end, the first prize was given to both—in open-ended disputes, they say, one must lean toward compassion.[82]

[388–97] Since we have learned how to be defeated honorably,[83] we did not claim anything more, except that when these two men are present no one else will stand up to read and that, while between white and black many colors could stake a claim (grey, red, and all the others) and between health and ill health what the doctors call neutral condition could take position (since recovery from an illness is neither health nor enacts what a healthy condition does),[84] no person

79. A common notion in Neoplatonic cosmology originating in Plato, *Timaeus* 30b7–8.

80. Cf. Ps.-Plutarch, *On the Philosophers' Doctrines about Nature* 2.6 (887b–c) or Eusebios, *Preparation for the Gospel* 15.37.5–6.

81. Again common notions in Neoplatonic cosmology originating in Plato, *Timaeus* 55a2–56b6.

82. Gregory of Nazianzos, *On Athanasios* = *Or.* 21.15.

83. Gregory of Nazianzos, *Apologêtikos* = *Or.* 2.103.

84. "Between white and black . . . condition does"; this long phrase does not allude to Aristotle and Galen (as cited in the Teubner edition), but is taken verbatim, though in

would willingly enter between these two men nor will anyone be able to open their mouth in front of them. But let me omit most of this discussion too.

[398–419] On the next day (I mean the next Friday), I heard also this bishop read—for word had spread to everyone that he had undertaken the reading. So I went, and I was able to put to shame the mistaken opinion of others and, by being there when this reader was there, to resolve the earlier debate. For the old bishop had an inarticulate voice and was similar to an all-devouring crow.[85] In some places (and let no one blame me in this case nor perhaps call me abusive or fond of scoffing), he did not even preserve the train of thoughts but he would rather deviate if he discovered something more interesting. And (not to present in detail the evil and wicked character of this man) he was so different from Ioannes as much as universal entities differ from partial ones, eternal beings from those subject to decay, and science from sense perception. And if some people resist and claim that this judgment is wrong and that we did not understand the man correctly, let them say as much nonsense as they wish. For uneducated men, even audacity is a right thing and cowardice has landed a spot on the left side. And if this man started as a reader first and thus attracted much attention by the many, well also when there is not light, shadow is a much-desired thing. Let us agree perhaps about his earlier fame and let this rumor stand. But, as we hear, Greece too once prospered, but the Macedonians deprived it of all its might; and Persians were thriving, but a single day destroyed that kingship; Egypt once breathed splendor, but like a cloud its good fortune departed. What is so strange then if earlier this bishop was successful but now another man has taken on the success?

[420–32] Indeed, I especially marvel also at this feature of the man. Though he is of this kind and possesses so many talents that he almost sur-

---

an incomplete way, from Ioannes Philoponos, *Comm. on Aristotle's Categories* 29.24–30 (cf. also above): ἔμμεσα δέ ἐστιν ἐναντία οἷον λευκὸν καὶ μέλαν, ὑγεία καὶ νόσος· ἔστι γὰρ μεταξὺ λευκοῦ καὶ μέλανος τὸ φαιὸν τὸ ἐρυθρὸν καὶ πάντα τὰ ἄλλα χρώματα, μεταξὺ δὲ ὑγείας καὶ νόσου τὸ παρὰ τοῖς ἰατροῖς λεγόμενον οὐδέτερον· τὰς γὰρ ἐκ νόσου ἀναλήψεις οὔτε ὑγείας εἶναί φασιν (οὐ γὰρ τὰ τῶν ὑγιαινόντων ἐνεργοῦσιν) οὔτε νόσους (τῆς γὰρ νοσοποιοῦ αἰτίας ἀπηλλαγμένοι εἰσὶν οἱ ἀναλαμβάνοντες)· οὐκοῦν μέσον τί ἐστι νόσου καὶ ὑγείας ἡ ἀνάληψις. Psellos has omitted this crucial last part, here in italics.

85. Cf. Aristotle, *The History of Animals* 593b12–14: Καὶ αἱ κορῶναι δὲ νέμονται ἁπτόμεναι τῶν ἐκπιπτόντων ζῴων· παμφάγον γάρ ἐστιν. For the circulation of Aristotle's text in Byzantium, see Berger 2005.

passes all mortals, he has never uttered any boasting remark, nor has reacted against anyone, nor have I ever heard him brag. Rather, just as it is said that those who know much claim that they are terribly ignorant,[86] so does he too daily and practices humility more than others practice boasting. Nor does he imitate the race of the Egyptians but the humility as well as gentleness of the meek Christ.[87] Nor has he ever uttered, like others have, the words of Alexander; as it is said,[88] when he assumed the rule of Europe and Asia, Alexander stood on a vantage point, looked all around him, and said to those present: "These parts and those parts are all mine." For Ioannes knows that to just appear to be something leads to the greatest inaction; and he persuades the listeners not by deceptive words, but by deeds, extending all-ensnaring flaxes[89] and captivating everyone with the good qualities in him.

[433–37] Nevertheless, let no one lose hope regarding greatness nor despair about excellence, fearing that he will never reach such a level since the man has surpassed everyone. Labor is the beginning of all good things, or, rather, the root of everything that is good is labor.[90] Let no one among us sleep, nor idle, nor neglect the good. Regarding this, I, myself, am both a giver and debtor.

[438–49] The human race never lacks God's gifts; but since He is unable to bear our great idleness, He estimates what he gives according to the power of those who receive it.[91] And if not everyone is apportioned the first place, let us not complain. For the good is rare, while the mass of the opposite qualities

86. A reference to Socrates (rather than Heraclitus as posited by Littlewood); cf. Anonymous, *Prolegomena to Platonic Philosophy* 10.43–50.

87. Mt. 11:29.

88. The story that follows is lifted from Philo, *On Cherubim* 63. The *Thesaurus Linguae Graecae* cites only one more instance of the story in Niketas Choniates who alludes to it in passing (*History* 480.3–4); is Choniates reading Psellos, rather than Philo? Quite likely so.

89. From Philo, *On Agriculture* 24, where the phrase appears with a positive meaning similarly to Psellos above; the phrase originates in Homer (cited by Gautier and Littlewood), who nevertheless uses it in the singular, with a negative meaning, and without the verb "τείνω" found in both Psellos and Philo.

90. Two quotes from Philo, *On the Sacrifice of Abel and Cain* 35 and 40, though Psellos does not employ, as Philo does, the term "virtue = ἀρετή" and thus evoke a moral connotation.

91. The entire sentence is lifted with slight alterations from Philo, *On the Posterity of Cain and His Exile* 145.

is beyond comprehension.[92] And the human race is threefold: some are of the earth, others from heaven, and others from God. The first are hunters of bodies; the second, artists and scientists; and the third, prophets and priests.[93] And the culmination of Seth's science did not become the beginning of many, but only of Noah, the just; and by Noah's perfection only Abraham was educated, while Abraham's utmost wisdom trained only Moses.[94] Therefore, the good does not belong to many; or, rather, the not good belongs to many, while only one person achieves the good and this only with difficulty.

[450–60] But I should conclude my speech, even if I want to say much more. My dearest and best of friends, the one who surpasses everyone in prudence, wisdom, and the power of discourse, and whom I desire more than anyone else, the So-and-so,[95] prevented me from moving forward with my writing, saying that I had written enough and against many a Hercules. And I am grateful to the Mother, full of grace, and I will offer Her the appropriate hymns and songs, because she joined me to these two men.[96] Rejoice So-and-so, the discursive lyre, the sweet-sounding trumpet, the mixing-bowl of learning, the inexhaustible sea. Rejoice you too, the monk, the instrument of the Spirit, the cicada of the Muses, who is never silent, but has somehow banished me for a long time from his song. I now rejoice as well as I have found companions that cause me joy.

92. From Philo: *The Allegories of the Sacred Laws* 1.102; cf. also *On the Migration of Abraham* 59.

93. Again from Philo, with small variation: *On the Giants* 60–61.

94. One last extensive quote from Philo: *On the Posterity of Cain and His Exile* 174.

95. As before, Psellos again does not offer us the name of this "learned" man and addressee of his text.

96. Psellos is thinking of the church of the Virgin in the Chalkoprateia.

PART TWO

Art and Aesthetics

Introduction to Part Two

Charles Barber

Within the extensive and rich corpus of Michael Psellos' writings, there are numerous and important discussions of images. These reflections are found in letters, in commentaries and paraphrases of philosophical works, and in hagiographic, judicial, rhetorical, as well as historical studies. While the sources are varied, they nonetheless provide an opportunity for us to examine how Psellos discusses works of art and also whether it is possible to identify the construction of an aesthetic attitude to art in the work of this crucial Byzantine philosopher. Of course, any discussion of "art" or "aesthetics" begs questions regarding the appropriateness of these terms for the visual culture of Byzantium.[1] Rather than addressing this broad and complex issue in this brief introductory essay, I will here focus on how these terms (or rather their Greek equivalents) make their appearance in Psellos' writings.[2]

The works gathered together and translated for this portion of our volume reveal a writer whose aesthetic response to works of art betrays a profound

1. Some of these issues can be found in Paul Kristeller's work and its legacy: Kristeller 1951, 1952. For a recent debate regarding this essay and for extensive references to its legacy, see Porter 2009a, Shiner 2009, and Porter 2009b. In light of these discussions one should now consult Porter 2010, which provides a rich model for rethinking the historical analysis of aesthetics in any period.

2. Discussions on Byzantine visual aesthetics include: Grabar 1945; Michelis 1955; Mathew 1964; Bychkov 1983, 2001; Karahan 2010; Tsakiridou 2013; Cantone and Pedone 2013; and Mariev and Stock 2013. The present essay can be considered a preliminary contribution to a larger project on Byzantine art and aesthetics.

interest and pleasure in the physical and sensible qualities of things, as well as an intellectual indifference towards and a desire to overcome these very qualities. It is a primarily visual aesthetic, one that is rooted in both Christian and Neoplatonic assumptions. As such, it is bound to the differences that inhere to the divisions that distinguish the sensible from the intelligible, the material from the spiritual, and the human from the divine. As we shall see, this aesthetic disposition leads Psellos to develop a consistent and hierarchal understanding of art that, even as it delights in human creativity, privileges a beauty and a subject that precedes and overwhelms the work of art.[3]

While the essays and letters gathered here cover a number of topics and approaches, it is possible to suggest that the key concerns in Psellos' visual aesthetics are summarized in the text presented here as *Letter Five*.[4] This was addressed to an unknown recipient. It appears to be a report on an encounter with a miraculous icon of the Mother of God in the monastery Ta Kathara (ἡ μονὴ τῶν Καθαρῶν). This letter is brief, but it nonetheless presents many of the facets of Psellos' views on art and its works. It tells us that Psellos claims to be a "most fastidious (ἀκριβέστατος)," perhaps exacting viewer of icons. Having introduced his perceptual engagement with the image, Psellos then leads us towards the necessity of this "visual sense (ἐκ τῶν ὀφθαλμῶν αἴσθησιν)" being surpassed. For the beauty that has here astonished Psellos does not come from his perception of the shape presented by the icon, which is a faithful imitation in color of the Mother of God's corporal nature, rather this "indescribable beauty (κάλλει ἀφάτῳ)" has disoriented Psellos, leading him to understand that beauty is not rendered by the visual and material shape found in the icon alone, but also requires a conceptual knowledge of the form (τὸ εἴδος) that lies behind the shape (τὴν μορφήν). This knowledge becomes known thanks to the miraculous activity of the Mother of God. She changes the nature of the icon, so that "divine-like beauty (τὸ θεοειδὲς . . . κάλλος)" can become visible there. Psellos thus leads us from an aesthetic or sensible perception of beauty to one that surpasses human visual perception and that is orchestrated by the

3. Much work remains to be done before Michael Psellos becomes a well-understood figure in intellectual history. For an important first step in discussing Psellos' visual aesthetics, see Cutler and Browning 1992. For an extended discussion of Psellos' writings on art see Barber 2007: 61–98. Note also Pentcheva 2010: 183–98. Some of the points raised in Barber 2007 are returned to in the present essay.

4. The letter can be found in chapter 23 of this volume; see pp. 374–76.

subject of the work of art. As such, it is an aesthetics that offers a model that differs distinctly from our modernist and representational modes of describing and responding to works of art. It is a perceptual mode that is governed by surprise and astonishment, as the normal condition of the thing seen has been miraculously overwhelmed by the subject that it re-presents.

This is an aesthetics that is rooted in the differential play of intelligible beauty and sensible perception. A framework for our understanding of how this play unfolds in Psellos' thought can be found in our first three selections: *On Perception and Perceptibles*, *On Beauty*, and *On Intelligible Beauty*.[5] These reveal a debt to both the Aristotelian and the Platonic traditions that is found throughout Psellos' writings and that betrays his adherence to a Late Antique conception of intellectual formation.[6] These texts show Psellos deploying both an Aristotelian account of the senses and Plotinian accounts of beauty to address aspects of human perception and intellection. Although very different in their perspectives, these essays establish themes that recur throughout Psellos' discussion of works of art. For example, in *On Perception and Perceptibles* Psellos follows Aristotle and Alexander of Aphrodisias in rendering a non-tactile account of human vision. As such, sight finds its cause in the subject of vision. It is the thing seen that moves the transparent medium (air) and that becomes manifest as a color impression upon the transparent and watery medium that is the eye. It is this emphasis upon the thing seen, on movement, change, and color, that echoes throughout Psellos' other texts and that underpins his accounts of human vision. In contrast, Psellos' discussions of Plotinos' notions of beauty allow him to construct a non-sensible account of an intelligible beauty. In these essays, Psellos examines the supernatural Beauty that descends from Intellect. His concern is, therefore, with that beauty that may reside in things but that, ultimately, has its origin in Intellect. It is a beauty that is not of this world, even if it may descend and become manifest in this world. An echo of this is to be found in *Letter Five*, where the Mother of the God "descends into knowledge only so much that, while her shape is not known, she astounds the viewer (εἰς γνῶσιν καταβᾶσα ὅσον μὴ

5. For an extensive analysis of these texts see Mariev 2013: 149–77. I would like to extend my thanks to Sergei Mariev for sharing his important work on beauty in Byzantium with me.

6. Kaldellis 2006: 29–110 offers a useful introduction to the intellectual background of Michael Psellos.

γινώσκεσθαι τὴν μορφήν, ἀλλ' ἐκπλήττειν τὸν θεατήν)." As such, Psellos grants control over the descent into knowledge to the Mother of God herself. It is she who polices how she is to be perceived, only becoming wholly manifest when a miraculous event that she determines temporarily overcomes the division between heaven and earth, the intelligible and the sensible. Psellos thus shows an engagement with quite distinct aesthetic legacies,[7] one determined by a human perceptual horizon, the other open to a Beauty that, strictly speaking, surpasses the aesthetic.[8] Psellos embraces this double ground in *Letter Five* when he tells us that "I do not therefore write about what I have beheld, but what I have experienced (Γράφω γοῦν οὐχ ὅπερ τεθέαμαι, ἀλλ' ὃ πέπονθα)." For him, the limits of human vision need to be overcome in order for the experience of divine things to take place.

The potential for conflict between these two perceptual modes, the intellectual and the sensible, recurs throughout Psellos' works. It is perhaps most beautifully rendered in his account of a Crucifixion icon, where we find Psellos grappling with the problem of what can and cannot be seen in an icon. He begins by establishing the icon's clarity and accuracy in rendering Christ's human body. This is achieved by emphasizing the naturalistic quality of the painting and using a lengthy and specific evocation of Christ's body to reiterate the precise and tangible qualities of the representation. Hence:

> But there is something more here, or rather this is a very work of nature, so that the picture seems to be the product not of art but of nature. For the belly protrudes a bit from the rest of the body, and its colors make it appear not level with the chest, but it has distended as is reasonable. For the organs within it force out the belly, and the skin itself has been stretched at the navel. The heart, liver, and whatever naturally branches from there, namely, blood vessels and the <membranes> containing the lung or rather both lungs are concealed from the viewer. But if the entry point of the wound in

7. One should note the direct references to Plato's discussions of beauty in the *Phaedrus* and the *Symposium* in the ekphrasis of an *Eros* included in chap. 18 of this collection. See the discussion by Christine Angelidi in the introduction to that text.

8. It is this double aspect of Psellos' aesthetic that raises questions regarding the emphasis upon the Plotinian origins of Byzantine and medieval aesthetics found in Grabar 1945. While the focus upon an anti-naturalistic and intellectual art opens the way towards thinking differently about medieval art (pp. 24–25 esp.), it also underplays the continuing importance of art as an expression of the human horizon.

> his side had not already closed, we would perhaps have observed through it what I mentioned as if through a dilator.[9]

This passage's forensic quality serves to underline the point that one is being invited to see Christ's actual body in the painting. It is a proposition that assumes the possibility of an accurate representation. This point is reiterated in the closely related letter to Konstantinos, the nephew of the Patriarch Keroularios, our *Letter One*, in which Psellos tells us, "For the image in no way differs from its model, so it seems to me at any rate. Thus I have often grasped its colors, as I would a body. And my hand did not belie but confirmed my expectation."[10]

Although Psellos is at pains in his writings on art to establish the accuracy of any given rendering, he also always qualifies this understanding by offering doubts regarding the adequacy of such a rendering for a divine or holy subject. Hence, in *Letter Five* Psellos writes, "Whether it is similar to Her (that supernatural image of beauty), I do not quite know. I know this much and just this much: that the corporal nature has been faithfully imitated by means of the mixing of colors; for Her form remains incomprehensible to me both then visually and now conceptually."[11] Here Psellos tells us that while the icon can offer a depiction of the human nature of its subject, the form (τὸ εἶδος)[12] of this subject remains unclear, being sometimes known to sight and sometimes to the mind. In this way, Psellos indicates that a complete presentation of the subject of the painting remains beyond painting's grasp. For while the icon can present the visual aspects of this subject, other aspects of

9. *Or. hag.* 3B.701–12; Fisher 1994: 52: Ἐνταῦθα δέ τι καὶ πλέον ἐστί, μᾶλλον δὲ αὐτὸ τοῦτο τὸ ἔργον τῆς φύσεως, ἵνα μὴ τέχνῃ ἀλλὰ φύσει ἡ γραφὴ νομισθῇ· ἐπαναβέβηκε γάρ τι τὸ λοιπὸν ἡ γαστὴρ σῶμα καὶ οὐκ ἐξίσωται τοῖς στήθεσιν ὥσπερ ἐν χρώμασιν, ἀλλ' εἰκότως διώγκωτο· ἐξωθεῖ γὰρ αὐτὴν τὰ ὑποκείμενα σπλάγχνα, καὶ αὐτὸ δὲ τὸ σκῦτος τὴν ῥίζαν εὐρύτερον πέπλασται. μήποτε οὖν ὑποκέκρυπται τῷ ὁρωμένῳ καὶ καρδία καὶ ἧπαρ καὶ ὅσα ἐντεῦθεν ἀποφύεται, τὰ μὲν αἵματα, τὰ δὲ περιεκτικὰ πνεύματος ἢ ἀμφοῖν τοῖν μεροῖν. ἀλλ'εἰ μὲν μὴ τοῦ κατὰ τὴν πλευρὰν τραύματος τὸ στόμα ἤδη συμμέμυκεν, ἴσως ἂν ἐκεῖθεν ὥσπερ ἐκ διόπτρας τὸ ὑπονοούμενον διωπτεύσαμεν.

10. K-D 211, 247.19–23; reedited by Stratis Papaioannou; for the Greek text, see below.

11. K-D 194, 220.23–27; reedited; for the Greek text, see below.

12. Psellos is using here this term in its Neoplatonic (i.e., Aristotelian) meaning of internal, intelligible form; see p. 158 above.

this subject can only be grasped by means other than the painting, whose material constraints need to be overcome. This familiar dualism is developed in an extraordinary and beautiful passage in the *Crucifixion* ekphrasis, which speaks of the impossibility of an adequate representation of Christ (*Or. hag.* 3B.843–79):

> But that the painting is exact as regards the accuracy of art "is plain from the complexion," said a philosopher.[13] However, the marvel lies not in this but in the fact that the whole image seems to be living (ἐμψυχῶσθαι) and is not without a share of motions. If one will but direct one's gaze to the parts of the picture one after another, it might seem to him that some might alter, some might increase, some might change, while some <seem> to experience or make a difference, as if presently waxing or waning. Hence the dead body <seems> apparently to be both living and lifeless. The outlines of such a painting might be seen even in images <produced> by the artless—namely, a similar straightening, breaking, or bending <of limbs>, an illusion of life by virtue of blood or of death by virtue of pallor—but these are all, so to speak, imitations of figures and likenesses of likenesses. But here these things do not seem to take their existence from colors, rather the whole thing resembles nature, which is living and artlessly set in motion, and no one is able to discover whence the image has become like this. But, just as beauty exists as a result of the opposition and harmony of limbs and parts, and yet often a woman is extraordinarily radiant as a result of entirely different causes, so it is in this case. While this living painting (ἡ ἔμψυχος αὕτη γραφὴ) exists as a result of component parts combined most felicitously, the entire living form seems to be beyond this, so that life exists in the image from two sources, from art, which makes a likeness, and from grace, which does not liken to anything else. Is this then a comparison of images and shadows? Yet I would not compare this painting to any other paintings, neither those set up by past hands or that represented the archetype accurately, nor those from our own time or from a little before that had made some innovations in form. I declare that this picture to be like my Christ in times past, when a bloodthirsty crowd brought out a vote of con-

13. This is the response by the dying Pherecydes to a question regarding his health asked by Pythagoras (see *Corpus Paroemoegraphorum graecorum* 2 130.17).

> demnation against him to a submissive Pilate. Thus, it seems to me that Christ hangs in the delineated and colored likeness. And I would not dispute that there is oversight that is beyond the painter's hand and that this overseeing mind had returned that painting to its prototype.[14]

This important passage not only describes art's inadequacy, but it also enlarges upon the possible grounds for this failure. Psellos tells us that the "whole image seems to be living (τῷ δοκεῖν ἐμψυχῶσθαι σύμπασαν τὴν εἰκόνα)," and that "But, just as beauty exists as a result of the opposition and harmony of limbs and parts, and yet often a woman is extraordinarily radiant as a result of entirely different causes, so it is in this case (ἀλλ᾽ ὥσπερ τὸ κάλλος ἐξ ἀντιλογίας μέν ἐστι καὶ εὐαρμοστίας μελῶν καὶ μερῶν, πολλάκις δὲ καὶ ἡ ἐκ μὴ οὕτω δοκούντων ἔχειν ὑπερφυῶς ἀπολάμπει, οὕτω δὴ κἀνταῦθα)," and that "while this living painting exists as a result of component parts combined most felicitously, the entire living form seems to be beyond this, so that life

14. Cf. Fisher 1994: 55. The Greek text reads: Ἀλλ᾽ ὅτε μὲν πρὸς ἀκρίβειαν τῆς τέχνης ἠκρίβωται ἡ γραφή, χρῷ δῆλον, ἔφησέ τις σοφός· ἔστι δὲ τὸ θαυμαζόμενον οὐκ ἐντεῦθεν, ἀλλὰ τῷ δοκεῖν ἐμψυχῶσθαι σύμπασαν τὴν εἰκόνα καὶ μηδεμιᾶς ἀμοιρεῖν τῶν κινήσεων. εἰ γοῦν ἐπερείσει τις τοῖς μέρεσιν ἐφεξῆς ταύτης τὰ ὄμματα, τὰ μὲν αὐτῷ ἠλλοιῶσθαι δόξειε, τὰ δὲ ηὐξῆσθαι, τὰ δὲ μεθίστασθαι, τὰ δ᾽ ἄλλο τι πάσχειν ἢ ποιεῖν, ὥσπερ ἄρτι φυόμενα ἢ φθίνοντα, οὕτω καὶ τὸν νεκρὸν αὐτῆς ἔμψυχον καὶ τὸ δοκοῦν οὕτως ἄψυχον ἀκριβῶς· τὰ γάρ τοι τῆς τοιαύτης γραφῆς σχήματα κἂν ταῖς ἀτέχνοις τῶν εἰκόνων ἴδοι τις ἄν, τὸ οὕτως ὀρθοῦσθαι ἢ κεκλάσθαι, τὸ συγκεκάμφθαι, τὸ δοκεῖν αἵματι ζῆν ἢ αὖθις τεθνᾶναι τῷ ὠχριακέναι, ἀλλ᾽ εἰσὶν ἅπαντα τύπων, ὡς ἄν τις εἴποι, μιμήματα καὶ εἰκασμάτων εἰκάσματα. ἐνταῦθα δὲ οὐκ ἐκ χρωμάτων τὰ τοιαῦτα δοκεῖ συνεστάναι, ἀλλ᾽ ἔοικε τὸ σύμπαν ἐμψύχῳ φύσει καὶ ἀτεχνῶς κινουμένῃ, καὶ οὐδὲ δύναταί τις εὑρεῖν ὁπόθεν οὕτω γεγένηται ἡ εἰκών. ἀλλ᾽ ὥσπερ τὸ κάλλος ἐξ ἀντιλογίας μέν ἐστι καὶ εὐαρμοστίας μελῶν καὶ μερῶν, πολλάκις δὲ καὶ ἡ ἐκ μὴ οὕτω δοκούντων ἔχειν ὑπερφυῶς ἀπολάμπει, οὕτω δὴ κἀνταῦθα. ἔστι μὲν ἡ ἔμψυχος αὕτη γραφὴ ἐκ τῶν οἷς σύγκειται συντεθειμένων ὡς ἄριστα, τὸ δ᾽ ὅλον ἔμψυχον εἶδος καὶ ὑπὲρ τοῦτο δοκεῖ, ὡς εἶναι τῇ εἰκόνι διχόθεν τὸ ζῆν, τῷ τε κατὰ τέχνην ἐξωμοιῶσθαι καὶ τῷ κατὰ χάριν ἑτέρῳ μὴ ἐοικέναι. τί τοίνυν καὶ εἰκόνων καὶ σκιῶν ἐστι σύγκρισις; ἀλλ᾽ ἐγὼ ταύτην δὴ τὴν γραφὴν οὐ πρὸς ἑτέρας γραφὰς παραβάλοιμι, οὔτ᾽ εἴ τινες τῶν τῆς ἀρχαίας χειρὸς τοιαύτας ἀνεστηλώκασιν ἢ πρὸς τὸ ἀρχέτυπον ἀκριβῶς ἀπεικόνισαν, οὔτε μὴν εἴ τινες τῶν καθ᾽ ἡμᾶς ἢ τῶν ὀλίγον πρὸ ἡμῶν ἔνιοι τοιαῦτα εἴδη ἐκαινοτόμησαν· αὐτῷ δ᾽ ἐκείνῳ τῷ ἐμῷ Χριστῷ ἀπεοικέναι ταύτην φημί, ὁπηνίκα Πιλάτῳ παραχωρήσαντι ἡ κατ᾽ αὐτοῦ ψῆφος τῷ φονῶντι λαῷ ἐξενήνεκτο. οὕτω γοῦν μοι κἀκεῖνος ἀπῃωρῆσθαι δοκεῖ ἐν ὁμοίῳ τῷ σχήματι, ἐν ὁμοίῳ τῷ χρώματι· καὶ οὐκ ἂν διαμφισβητήσαιμι ὡς κρείττων ἐπιστασία τὴν τοῦ ἐξεικονίσαντος χεῖρα μετὰ καὶ τοῦ ἐπιστατοῦντος νοὸς πρὸς τὴν πρωτότυπον ἐκείνην ἀνήνεγκε γραφήν.

exists in the image from two sources, from art, which makes a likeness, and from grace, which does not liken to anything else (ἔστι μὲν ἡ ἔμψυχος αὕτη γραφὴ ἐκ τῶν οἷς σύγκειται συντεθειμένων ὡς ἄριστα, τὸ δ' ὅλον ἔμψυχον εἶδος καὶ ὑπὲρ τοῦτο δοκεῖ, ὡς εἶναι τῇ εἰκόνι διχόθεν τὸ ζῆν, τῷ τε κατὰ τέχνην ἐξωμοιῶσθαι καὶ τῷ κατὰ Χάριν ἑτέρῳ μὴ ἐοικέναι)." Psellos, while clearly attentive to the play and variety of the parts in the image, argues that these in themselves do not produce the living quality in the painting. Rather, this quality depends upon an understanding of the whole subject.

The relationship between the parts and the whole of a portrayal is a theme that is prevalent in Psellos' accounts of art. For Psellos, it is the orderly arrangement, the symmetry, of these parts, that reveals corporal beauty. But Psellos considers this to be a truly partial account of art's possibility. It reiterates that which can be seen, but Psellos believed, as we have seen, that there should be more. Throughout his writings on art, he considers beauty to lie in the whole form, rather than the shapes that have produced a given image. The basis for Psellos' consideration of this can be found in his *On Intelligible Beauty*, where he writes:

> Those who find fault with this do not see the parts in regard to the wholes, but isolate a particular part of a living being, its hair or nail or bile or phlegm, and then, without considering these in regard to their function, they spit out from the whole the part that disgusts them.[15] But if one were to take and to gather together and to consider their essences and potentialities and actualities as well as their combinations and mixtures and relations with one another, one might be led to believe that this is the first Beauty, by means of which one desires Being, which is a likeness of the Beautiful.[16]

Here Psellos is concerned that one not be too detained by parts, for these do not add up to the whole, which is that which governs beauty, for this—the first beauty—can never be found in the image itself.

15. Plotinos, *Enneads* III 2, 3, 13–16.

16. *Phil. min.* 2.34, 117.2–10: οἱ δὲ μεμφόμενοι τοῦτο οὐκ ἐξ ὅλων ὁρῶσι μερῶν, ἀλλ' οἷον μέρος ζῴου ἀπολαμβάνοντες, τρίχα ἢ ὄνυχα ἢ χολὴν καὶ φλέγμα, καὶ οὐδὲ τοῦτο πρὸς ὃ παρῆκται σκοπήσαντες, ὅπερ τοῦ μέρους δυσχεραίνουσιν ἀποπτύουσι κατὰ τοῦ παντός. εἰ δέ τις ὁμοῦ ≤πάντα≥ λάβῃ τε καὶ συλλάβῃ καὶ γνοίῃ τάς τε οὐσίας αὐτῶν καὶ δυνάμεις καὶ τὰς ἐνεργείας καὶ τὰς πρὸς ἄλλο κράσεις καὶ μίξεις καὶ σχέσεις καὶ ἔτι τὸ πᾶν ἐννοήσειεν, ἀπατηθείη ἂν ἴσως ἐντεῦθεν, ὅτι αὐτὸ τοῦτο τὸ πρώτως καλόν, δι' ὃ καὶ τὸ εἶναι ποθεινόν ἐστιν αὐτῷ, ὅτι ὁμοίωμα τοῦ καλοῦ.

Given Psellos' doubts regarding art's adequate representation of its subject, he needs to examine ways in which these limits may be overcome. In the *Crucifixion* ekphrasis, this is introduced by way of the concept of living painting (ἡ ἔμψυχος γραφή).[17] As the lengthy passage discussed above shows, this was an important quality in this icon. It was also a quality that did not come from the craft of painting alone, rather:

> God inspires with his grace not only creatures who possess reason but also images that lack life; an indication of this fact is the likenesses that often move, speak, and behave with the power of reason towards those who observe them. These likenesses seem to be the product of the human hand, but God actually fashions them without our knowing it, if I may put it thus, and presents them in visible form by using the hand of the craftsman as his vehicle for the picture.[18]

Clearly then it is God's grace that endows an image with this quality. In the case of the *Crucifixion* ekphrasis, it is the artist who mediates the possibility of such presence in the image. For it is thanks to God's guiding the human hand that these images can become animate. This point is returned to at the end of the ekphrasis when Psellos remarks upon the accuracy of the painting and then attributes this quality to an "oversight that is beyond the painter's hand and that this overseeing mind had returned that painting to its prototype."[19] The introduction of this further origin for the work of art allows Psellos to explain the uniqueness of this icon when, in the lengthy passage quoted above, he says, "Yet I would not compare this painting to any other paintings,

17. As implied in Hans Belting's discussion of this concept: Belting 1994: 261–96. An important response to this is to be found in Cormack 2003; Cormack 1997: 156–57 offers a more neutral reading. The concept is also discussed in Pentcheva 2000; Papaioannou 2001; and Barber 2006a.

18. Fisher 1994: 51; *Or. hag.* 3B.644–51: οὐ λογικαῖς μόνον φύσεσιν, ἀλλὰ καὶ ἀψύχοις ἰνδάλμασιν ἐμπνεῖ τὴν χάριν θεός, καὶ σύμβολον τούτου κινούμενα πολλάκις εἰκάσματα καὶ φωνὴν ἀφιέντα καὶ λογικώτερον τοῖς ὁρῶσι διατιθέμενα, καὶ δοκεῖ μὲν ἔργα εἶναι χειρός, λεληθότως δὲ καὶ τεχνουργεῖται τούτοις θεός, εἰ οὕτως εἰπεῖν χρή, καὶ αἰσθητῶς ἐμφαντάζεται, ὀργάνῳ τῇ τοῦ τεχνίτου χειρὶ πρὸς τὴν γραφὴν ἀποχρώμενος.

19. Cf. Fisher 1994: 55; *Or. hag.* 3B.876–79: καὶ οὐκ ἂν διαμφισβητήσαιμι ὡς κρείττων ἐπιστασία τὴν τοῦ ἐξεικονίσαντος χεῖρα μετὰ καὶ τοῦ ἐπιστατοῦντος νοὸς πρὸς τὴν πρωτότυπον ἐκείνην ἀνήνεγκε γραφήν. One might compare these thoughts on an artist's inspiration and invention to the ninth-century discussions in the writings of Patriarch Photios and the Emperor Leo VI; see Barber, forthcoming.

neither those set up by past hands or that represented the archetype accurately, nor those from our own time or from a little before that had made some innovations in form." Thus, for Psellos, this painting, thanks to divine intervention, has escaped both the claims of tradition and the inventiveness of contemporary painters. Furthermore, the presence of this "overseeing mind" helps Psellos to account for his doubled understanding of the icon, one that draws attention to both the seen and the unseen possibilities in painting. This doubled quality is found in Psellos' movement away from the claims to clarity on the part of the icon and towards an altogether more ambiguous account of the image:

> Although this suffering brings him [Christ] in due course to death, the power that moves the hand of the artist also animates the body that has breathed its last. Thus he has been distinguished from those living among the dead, and from the dead who live among the living. For his veiled limbs are somewhat ambiguous, and the visible parts are no less doubtful. Just as art shrouds, it also discloses both the lifeless and the living. This is true of his bloody garments, whether light or dark, as well as of the living dead presented on the cross and clearly suffering an excessive death, now living because of the accuracy of imitation—or rather, then and now in both manners. But there his life is beyond nature and his death is beyond pain. Here both are beyond the art and the grace that has shaped the art.[20]

It seems, then, that even with divine intervention, the image can only offer a partial account of its subject. The icon may allow us to see an accurately rendered subject, but it will also permit us to know that we cannot grasp the whole in the work of art itself.

20. Fisher 1994: 53–54; *Or. hag.* 3B.786–800: Καὶ τὸ μὲν πάθος αὐτίκα τοῦτον ποιεῖ τεθνήξεσθαι, ἡ δὲ τὴν τοῦ ζωγράφου κινήσασα χεῖρα πρὸς τοῦτο δύναμις αὐτὸ μᾶλλον ψυχοῖ τὸ ἐκπεπνευκός· οὕτως αὐτὸν ἐν μὲν νεκροῖς ζῶντα, ἐν δὲ ζῶσι νεκρὸν ἀπειργάσατο· τά τε γὰρ κεκαλυμμένα αὐτῷ τῶν μελῶν οὕτως εἰσὶν ἐπαμφότερα, καὶ τὰ φαινόμενα οὐδὲν ἧττον ἀμφίβολα· ἄμφω γὰρ ἄψυχά τε καὶ ἔμψυχα, ὅσα τε ἡ τέχνη συνέστειλεν καὶ ὅσα ἠνέῳξεν· οὕτως οἱ χιτῶνες τοῦ αἵματος, οὕτως εἴ τι λευκόν, οὕτως εἴ τι τοῦ μέλανος, οὕτω νεκρὸς μὲν ζῶν δὲ καὶ τῷ σταυρῷ παριστάμενος, καὶ τῷ ὑπερβάλλοντι τῶν ἀλγηδόνων ἀκριβῶς τεθνηκώς, ἔμψυχος δὲ νῦν τῷ ἀκριβεῖ τῆς μιμήσεως, ἢ μᾶλλον καὶ τότε ἄμφω καὶ νῦν οὕτως. ἀλλ' ἐκεῖ τὸ μὲν ζῆν παρὰ τὴν φύσιν, τὸ δὲ θανεῖν παρὰ τὴν ὀδύνην· ἐνταῦθα δὲ καὶ τοῦτο κἀκεῖνο παρὰ τὴν τέχνην ἢ τὴν χάριν ἧς ἡ τέχνη τετύχηκε. This point is strongly echoed in this volume's *Letter One* (K-D 211; 247.26–248.17); cf. Cutler and Browning 1992: 23.

Psellos' concern for the visibility of the painting's subject extended beyond the question of its making. He was also very interested in the perception of the work. Once again, he was to argue that the viewer needed assistance in order truly to see the subject of the work of art. The problem of perception can be found throughout *Letter Five*. Even though this letter begins by remarking the fastidious quality of Psellos' viewing, the limitations of this action are soon revealed. This begins when the Marian icon astounds him with its beauty, threatening to disable his senses and his power of judgment. For while her shape is discernible in the icon, her "form remains incomprehensible to me both then visually and now conceptually (τὸ γὰρ εἶδος ἄληπτόν μοι καὶ τότε τῇ ὄψει καὶ νῦν τῇ ἐννοίᾳ καθίσταται)" (K-D 194, 220.24–27). Given this, Psellos chooses not to write of what he has beheld, but of what he has experienced. He thus tells us that he must overcome the sense of sight in order to see more fully. This is not an argument for widening the sensory horizon, it is rather an argument for surpassing it.[21] The experience beyond mere beholding appears to have been one marked by a complete change in the object of vision and thus in the possibilities for vision. Thus Psellos writes of the icon in *Letter Five*: "having completely exchanged its nature, it was transformed into divine-like beauty and surpassed visual perception."[22] The changing quality of the object of vision is crucial for Psellos. We have already noted that Psellos followed Alexander of Aphrodisias' commentary on Aristotle's *De Sensu* in identifying an affective model of vision, in which the thing seen changes the medium of sight. Similarly, for a divine or holy subject to be truly seen, the medium that permits them to be seen also needs to change. Material representation by a human artist could depict the corporal nature of its subject, but it could not, where appropriate, convey the invisible quality of holiness or divinity. For this to become possible, the icon needed to change. This is what occurs in the icon contemplated by Nikolaos of the Beautiful Source, where the icon is transformed into the Mother of God's "entire fleshly nature (μεταβαλοῦσαν ἀθρόως εἰς φύσιν σαρκὸς)" (Psellus 2014: 227, 17.27). Similarly, the Empress Zoe's Christ Antiphonetes icon changes color (*Chronographia* 6.66).

21. Recent writing on Byzantine art and aesthetics has drawn attention to the range of senses that might be engaged by an icon. For example: Peers 2004; James 2004; Barber 2006b; and Pentcheva 2008, 2010. This range of engagement is not what concerns Psellos.

22. K-D 194, 221.1–4. See pp. 374–75 in this volume.

Perhaps most crucially, Psellos is our only witness to a change in the miraculous Marian icon at Blachernai:

> [T]he drapery surrounding the icon lifts all of a sudden, as if some breath of air gently moved it. What happens is unbelievable to those who do not witness it, but for those who do, <it is> wondrous and an overt descent of the Holy Spirit. The form of the handmaiden of the Lord changes simultaneously with what is accomplished, I think, as it receives her animate visitation, thereby visibly signaling the invisible.[23]

This change signals the authentic presence of the Mother of God, thus validating the judicial process and decision brought before her. Later in this discourse, Psellos links this change to Neoplatonic notions of the descent of the divine into the material world:

> Moreover, the divine is similar to itself and not at all subject to change, while everything under the moon is both composed of dissimilar elements and subject to change, and to the degree that the descent <of the divine> proceeds, the change makes its mark. The worse also receives its illuminations from the better, not in the way those <divine beings> possess <illumination> but in the way these <worse ones> are capable <of receiving it>.[24]

The descent thus becomes a condescension to our human nature, but it also introduces an ethical aspect to the process of viewing in that the capacity for the viewer to receive illumination is introduced as a condition of looking.

An ethical aspect to viewing is a consistent presence in Psellos' writings on art. He is interested, in particular, in the beholder's preparedness to see. While this could be an intellectual preparation, it could also be understood in

23. *Or. hag.* 4.132–39: ὁ δὲ περὶ τὴν εἰκόνα πέπλος ἀθρόον μετεωρίζεται ὥσπερ τινὸς αὐτὸν ὑποκινήσαντος πνεύματος, καὶ ἔστι τὸ πρᾶγμα τοῖς μὲν μὴ ἰδοῦσιν ἄπιστον, τοῖς δὲ ἰδοῦσι παράδοξον καὶ τοῦ θείου πνεύματος ἄντικρυς κάθοδος. συνεξαλλάσσεται δὲ τῷ τελουμένῳ καὶ ἡ μορφὴ τῆς θεόπαιδος, οἶμαι, δεχομένη τὴν ἔμψυχον ἐπιδημίαν αὐτῆς καὶ τὸ ἀφανὲς τῷ φαινομένῳ ἐπισημαίνουσα.

24. *Or. hag.* 4.681–85: καὶ τὸ μὲν θεῖον ὅμοιον ἑαυτῷ καὶ ἀπαθέστατον, τὸ δ' ὑπὸ τὴν σελήνην ξύμπαν ἀνόμοιόν τε καὶ παθητόν, καὶ ὅσῳ πρόεισιν ἡ κάθοδος, βαθύνει τὸ πάθος. δέχεται δὲ καὶ τὰ χείρω τὰς ἐλλάμψεις τῶν ὑπερτέρων, οὐχ ὡς ἐκεῖνα ἔχει, ἀλλ' ὡς ταῦτα δύναται.

more broadly ethical terms. Hence, when writing his Blachernai discourse, Psellos notes that an illiterate woman in the crowd could still see the vision, even if she did not know the words of the hymns.[25] Psellos returns elsewhere to the preparation of the one looking. The possibility of ethical ascent is introduced in *On Intelligible Beauty*, where "the beauty in studies and ways of living" (*Phil. min.* 2.34, 115.9–11) are seen as paths to lift one up from visible beauty to the beauty in souls. This point is reiterated in *Letter Three* in which Psellos tells Ioannes Xiphilinos:

> Discourses kindle the intelligible beauty in our souls by the way of earthly beauty; since the former is neither visible nor known in itself, they represent the prototype to us by way of likenesses. If it is then necessary to ascend to that prototype in a systematic way and with proper understanding, let us despise corporal beauty as it is the last echo <of Being> and it is near to matter; let instead beautiful pursuits and beautiful deeds and beautiful discourses raise us up to the first Beauty.[26]

Psellos also insists upon an ethical preparation for looking at icons themselves. Thus in *Letter Two*, Psellos warns his correspondent that a true vision of the Mother of God will not come to those who make frequent visits to the icon, but to those who "first and foremost [succeed] in modeling themselves upon the virtue of the higher ones (τὸ μὲν πρῶτον καὶ μέγιστον ἑαυτοὺς ἀπεικονίσαι πρὸς τὴν ἐν τῷ κρείττονι ἀρετήν)."[27] This point is enlarged upon in his account of Nikolaos of the Beautiful Source, where the abbot is presented as a model of virtue:

> Rather, one should embody the virtue of the man [i.e., Nikolaos] and emulate his dispassion, after which or in which such things are usually achieved—for struggle and exertion last until one has transcended nature, but, once one rises up above, the great toil ceases and one witnesses the divine spectacles. [18.] Thus, when Nikolaos too had reached those heights, he conversed with those on high; sometimes he would contemplate with unerring visions of the

25. *Or. hag.* 4.73–82. Discussed in this light in Barber 2007: 87–90.

26. G 17.55–62 and Maltese 5.55–61, reedited by Stratis Papaioannou; for the Greek text, see p. 367 below.

27. Cf. Cutler and Browning 1992: 26; K-D 124, 148.18–20. See p. 361 in this volume.

mind and sometimes he would even receive the manifestations of the divine through his bodily eyes.[28]

Psellos' interest in the ethical spectator is in part a product of his model of ascent and descent. Ultimately, it is a model that exceeds the limits of painting itself, a fact that Psellos both recognizes and engages. For the icon, as a human product, can be a beautiful thing, appreciated for the skill of its manufacture, and even collected.[29] Yet, for all these qualities, the icon remains limited. As the record of a human perception of the visible world, it cannot embrace the invisible or the supernatural and therefore struggles to provide an adequate description of a divine or holy subject. This might lead Psellos to abandon the work of art as a lowly medium. But he does not. Rather, he embraces the icon as a necessary point of exchange between man and God. The icon remains valuable as an expression of what man might know and as the site for encountering the astounding manner in which divinity, in its excess, can become present and visible in the work of art. It allows him to speak of the preparation of this viewer, but it does not lead Psellos to guarantee that such preparation will lead to a vision. This remains in the gift of the subject seen in and through the painting.

Given the above considerations, it is possible to argue that it is appropriate to speak of both art and aesthetics in regard to Psellos' writings on images. Neither term should be read in terms of their modern usage. Rather both should be read out of Psellos' texts. There, art (τέχνη) is to be understood as an instance of rational human making that is, in these examples, manifest in painted icons. This is a very broad understanding that falls in line with ancient thought. The specific work of these products is to translate human visual perception into artifacts that memorialize this perception by means of imitation. It is in this regard that we can then speak of an aesthetic (related to αἴσθησις). This is not the systematic or disciplinary study of art as an autonomous object of enquiry. Rather, it is a proposition that we can better under-

28. *Or. fun.* I 10.17.33–18.4; ἀλλὰ τυπούσθω πρὸς ἀρετὴν καὶ ζηλούτω τοῦ ἀνδρὸς τὴν ἀπάθειαν, μεθ' ἣν ἢ ἐν ᾗ τὰ τοιαῦτα εἴωθε γίνεσθαι· ὁ γὰρ ἀγὼν καὶ ἡ συντονία, μέχρις ἄν τις ὑπερκύψῃ τῆς φύσεως, ἄνω δὲ γεγονὼς ἵσταταί τε τῆς πολλῆς ἀγωνίας καὶ τὰ θεῖα βλέπει θεάματα. [18.] Ἐκεῖσε οὖν κἀκεῖνος γενόμενος, ὡμίλει τοῖς κρείττοσι, νῦν μὲν ἀπλανέσι θεωρίαις ἐντυγχάνων νοός, νῦν δὲ καὶ σώματος ὄμμασι τὰς ἐμφάσεις τῶν θείων δεχόμενος.

29. As in *Letter Four*: see below; cf. Cutler and Browning 1992: 28–29 and Oikonomides 1991: 36; K-D 129, 152.20–28.

stand Psellos' conception of art by drawing this close to his understanding of the senses.[30] This then leads us to a Plotinian legacy in his account of beauty. For there is a beauty in the work of art itself, but this beauty is but a shadow of the intelligible beauty that exceeds both the work of art and the senses themselves. It would be wrong to interpret Psellos' discussions of art and aesthetics in light of modern conceptions of these terms, but it would be equally wrong to deny the play of these terms in his texts and thereby ignore the possibility of this author's discourse on both art and aesthetics.

30. This appears to be a direction in which James Porter is moving: Porter 2009a: 23–24.

15 *On Perception and Perceptibles*

Translated with introduction and notes
by Charles Barber and David Jenkins

Introduction

Psellos' *On Perception and Perceptibles*[1] offers a somewhat fragmentary series of reflections upon the senses that largely derive from Alexander of Aphrodisias' commentary on Aristotle's *De Sensu*, with some additional references to Aspasios' commentary on the *Nicomachean Ethics* (Aspasios, *Ethica*). Alexander was one of the earliest and most important commentators on Aristotle. He is known to have been active in the years from 198 to 207 CE.[2] Aspasios flourished in the first half of the second century CE. His commentary on the *Nicomachean Ethics* is the earliest to survive. It offers commentary on books 1, 2, 4, 7, and 8.[3] Psellos' text only contains material drawn from book 1 of Alexander's commentary, specifically the section that discusses chapters 2 to 4 of Aristotle's study. He is thus concerned with the relations between the senses themselves, between the senses and the elements, and with the objects of sight and taste.

In the course of his text Psellos reiterates Aristotle's rejection of Plato's understanding of the origins of the senses. Both Aristotle and Plato had grap-

1. In translating the title in this manner, I am following the model found in Towey 2000.

2. Sharples 1987.

3. For further discussion, see the essays in Alberti and Sharples 1999.

pled with the problem of deriving the five senses from the four elements. In the *Timaeus* Plato had argued that sight derives from fire, hearing from the air, taste from water, and touch from the earth. This left Plato with the problem of accounting for the fifth sense, smell. He did this by defining smell as being a mixture of two elements, namely air and water. Aristotle rejected this account. Instead he argued for sight to be from water, hearing from the air, smell from fire and both taste and touch to be derived from earth. Taste and touch are then further distinguished by being linked directly to the heart. Sight, hearing, and smell first passed through the brain. The distinction drawn between these two sets of senses is also present at the end of Psellos' last discussion of vision in this text. Here, Psellos argues that sight is not the same as touch because the eye is not in contact with the thing seen.

The sense of sight dominates this passage. Psellos begins by introducing Aristotle's rejection of Plato's belief that vision was caused by a fire emitted from the eye. Aristotle argued that the shiny surface of the eye offered the illusion of fire, but that it did not in fact consist of fire. Furthermore if sight were mediated by fire, then we would not be able to see in water and we would always be able to see in the dark. Psellos then turns to two other theories of vision that Aristotle repudiated.[4] The first of these extends the rejection of Plato's teaching by further addressing the extramission theory found there. Here Psellos follows the Aristotelian tradition in conflating and to a certain extent misrepresenting the theories of vision espoused by Empedocles (fifth century BCE) and Plato. Accordingly, sight is defined as an emission of a ray of light whose origin is the fire within our eyes. When this ray of fire-produced light is emitted it fuses with daylight in the air and so enables us to see. Then, when this ray touches upon an object, the ray itself is affected and transmits this affect back to the eyes and thence to the soul. Sight is thus presented as something that originates in the eye of the beholder. The sense-data that returns to this eye is borne by the ray that the beholder had emitted and that has now been changed by the sense-object. The second theory of vision rejected in the passage in discussion is one in which the eye is affected by admitting something that has flowed from the things perceived. This notion is associated with the Atomists. Democritus (fifth century BCE) represents this school of thought in our essay. What concerns Aristotle and therefore Psellos

4. For broad introductions to the terms extramission and intromission and their interplay in ancient and medieval accounts of vision, see Lindberg 1976.

is that this theory treated the eye as a form of mirror in which the sense-object is reflected, rather than as a transparent path to the soul.

In proposing an alternative to these theories Aristotle, followed by his commentators, re-focused our attention away from the sense-organ and the sense-object and toward the space between them.[5] This space is brought into play as a medium that both separates and links the one seeing and the thing seen. This medium is called the transparent and is understood to be a material, such as water or air, which has the potential to convey the visible.[6] Aristotle's insistence upon sight's foundation in water rather than fire is linked to this understanding of the transparent.

This mediatory space was crucial for the Aristotelian theory of vision. Its significance is underlined in the passage above, when Psellos makes the parenthetical remark that sight and touch are not the same. One of the foundations of Aristotle's understanding of vision was the notion that contact blinded, by which he meant that if the thing being looked at were to be in touch with the eye, it would be impossible to see it. Aristotle required a gap between subject and object through which vision might take place. Hence, seeing could not be equated with touching.[7]

Having affirmed this opening for vision, Psellos, following Aristotle, was then able to define the process of seeing. This process is marked by a movement or change that is perceived by the one looking and that has originated in the sense-object. This sense-object becomes known to us through its color. For Aristotle, and hence Psellos, color was the visible as such.[8] It is the objective condition that permits a thing to be seen. But in order for this to happen, we need a medium that can convey the color of the thing seen. The medium proposed is light, which is defined as the actuality of the transparent (διαφανής). What brings actuality (light) to this material (air) is the color of the thing seen. It is this color that changes or moves the transparent into becoming light and that thus allows it to convey the sense-data, the material form or shape of the thing seen, from the sense-object to the sense-organ. This transparent medium has a complex role to play in Aristotle's account of vision. Although it is moved or changed by color and conveys this color, it does not become col-

5. The following paragraphs are taken from Barber 2007: 95–96.
6. For the transparent see Vasiliu 1997.
7. Cf. Nelson 2000.
8. For a broad introduction to color in Byzantium, refer to James 1996.

ored. In a similar manner, the eye also remains unchanged or unmoved. The pupil is understood to be a continuity of the transparent medium. As such, the eye itself does not see. Rather the sense-organ is also a medium through which one senses, by which is meant that sense-data is delivered to the heart, the primary organ of sense by means of the passages (πόροι) that link the heart and the various sense organs. Vision thus originates in the object and ends in the heart. These two are not in contact. Rather the perception of the object, visible in its color, is mediated by the actualized transparent, that is, the air and the water of the eye.

The inclusion of the passages from Aspasios' commentary on the first book of the *Nicomachean Ethics* may appear to be an unusual change of source. But if the passages in question are read in relation to the definition of flavor as being that which changes taste from being potential to being actual, then it is possible to suggest that Psellos has found a similar transformation from potential to actual in the process of making. It then follows that the work produced is superior to the activities that produced it and that the higher arts are superior to lower crafts.

Although this text does not always read easily, it does present a strong reiteration of Aristotle's understanding of some of the senses and vision in particular. Whether discussing taste, smell, or sight Psellos presents perception as being caused by the affect of the perceptible upon the perceiving organ. It is the thing seen or tasted or smelled that entirely conditions our perception of that thing, turning our potential for perception into actual perception.[9]

Editions and translations. The latest edition, which has been followed here, is to be found in *Phil. Min.* II 8 (14.21–17.15; pages are indicated in bracketed numbers below). For a complete list of manuscripts, editions, and discussions, see Moore 2005: 278.

9. For a recent and important discussion of Psellos's reading of this text, see Betancourt 2016.

On Perception and Perceptibles

You were certainly at a loss when you said: "if each sense is made out of a single one of the bodily elements, how do five senses come from these four entities? For one must still derive one of them from something else. From what, then, does this have its origin?"[1] It appears to me that you have accepted the arrangement of the senses set forth in Plato's *Timaeus*.[2] For this wise man says there that fire makes sight, air hearing, also water taste, and earth touch,[3] but that smell and the **[15]** genus of smells are intermediate and somehow composite. "For when water changes into air or air into water," he says, "<smells> have come to be in that which is between these." And so smell would be the fifth sense.[4]

Aristotle does not accept this arrangement, nor does he propose that sight is made from fire. Rather he suggests another cause for the flashing of fire when the eye is compressed.[5] He says, "for smooth things naturally shine in the dark."[6] Such is the black, middle part of the eye, which we call the pupil: it is smooth, and because of its smoothness, when the eye is moved, a flash occurs that produces the illusion of fire.[7] Furthermore, this man denies that sight

1. Alexander, *De Sensu* 14, 18–22. He is referring to Aristotle, *De Sensu* 437a18–23. The "quotation" is not a direct quotation from Aristotle's text.

2. Alexander, *De Sensu* 14, 22–23; Plato, *Timaeus* 66d8–67e2.

3. Alexander, *De Sensu* 15, 3–4.

4. Alexander, *De Sensu* 14, 24–15, 3; Plato, *Timaeus* 66d8–67e2.

5. Alexander, *De Sensu* 15, 15–17; Aristotle, *De Sensu* 437a23–24.

6. Alexander, *De Sensu* 16, 4; Aristotle, *De Sensu* 437a31–32.

7. Alexander, *De Sensu* 17, 7–8.

is <caused> by the emission of light.[8] "There could," he says, "be no seeing of things in water. For how can fire and light remain in water and not be extinguished?"[9] And he adds that if vision occurs by means of the emission of light then animals would necessarily see better at night than during the day.[10] In this way Aristotle appears to have confounded the Platonic teachings.

He undermines Empedocles as well. For Empedocles has sometimes stated that the cause of sight is the light that is emitted from the eye and sometimes that <it is caused by> the emanations spreading from the things seen.[11] While he also accepts Democritus' teaching that states that the eye consists of water, he rejects the way in which he says vision comes about.[12] For Democritus says that vision is the reception of the reflection of the thing seen. And this reflection is the reflected form in the pupil. For he believes that images, emanating in some way and in similar shape to that from which they emanate, fall upon the eyes of those looking, and in this way vision occurs.[13] Aristotle says "that it is clear that the pupil through which we see consists of the water from the eyes. For when these are destroyed it appears to be water that flows out from them."[14]

<Aristotle> refutes by means of many counterarguments Plato's teaching on the eye, as he does not want to accept fire as the origin of vision. He says that it is nonsense to say that a body is emitted from one looking, such that this [body] could be extended as far as the stars.[15] He says that rather than saying that the light that is emitted from the eye, once having become external, fuses with the outside light, it is better to say that outside light is fused upon the pupil with the light inside before <this light> is emitted, **[16]** since no emission of light from the eye is necessary, if it did not intend to enclose the thing seen.[16]

Therefore Aristotle maintains that sight is from water, hearing from air, and smell from fire.[17] For he postulates that in actuality smell and that which

8. Alexander, *De Sensu* 20, 18–21.
9. Alexander, *De Sensu* 22, 22–23.
10. Alexander, *De Sensu* 23, 3–4.
11. Alexander, *De Sensu* 23, 6–7.
12. Alexander, *De Sensu* 24, 12–14.
13. Alexander, *De Sensu* 24, 14–21.
14. Alexander, *De Sensu* 27, 7–9; Aristotle, *De Sensu* 438a17–19.
15. Alexander, *De Sensu* 32, 5–6; Aristotle, *De Sensu* 438a25–27.
16. Alexander, *De Sensu* 32, 9–15.
17. Alexander, *De Sensu* 37, 9–10.

can be smelled are the same thing.[18] That which can be smelled and the smell that smelling apprehends are a dry and smoky vapor, a kind of vapor that is fiery and from fire,[19] thence two of the four bodies, touch and taste (for taste is a form of touch), are from earth, sight from water, hearing from air, and smell from fire.[20]

And he says that the perceptive soul is one in number and that it resides in the heart,[21] from which the sensations are transmitted to the brain.[22] For three passages extend thence [from the heart] to the brain, and then from the brain one of them reaches to sight, one to hearing, one to smell. Those of touch and taste extend directly in a straight line from the heart and not by way of the brain.[23]

Light is the actuality of the transparent qua transparent, and, as it were, its color, not simply, but accidently, because the transparent does not receive light passively but relates to it.[24] He says that color is not the limit of the body but is in the limit of the body, not being a limit for the body as such, but <being a limit> for the transparent in so far as it is transparent.[25]

Compared to the teaching of others, the Aristotelian teaching on perception is the following:[26] he says that sight perceives by being affected by the things that are visible, just as each of the other <senses> perceives, not by creating and emitting <something>, and not by receiving something that flows from the things perceived, but, rather, it is affected by the transparent

18. Alexander, *De Sensu* 38, 2–4.

19. Alexander, *De Sensu* 38, 4–6.

20. Alexander, *De Sensu* 39, 22–25.

21. Alexander, *De Sensu* 40, 27–28.

22. Alexander, *De Sensu* 40, 28–41, 2.

23. Alexander, *De Sensu* 41, 3–6.

24. Alexander, *De Sensu* 42, 25–43, 1. The ἀλλὰ κατὰ σχέσιν τὴν πρὸς αὐτό is added by Psellos here. The relational aspect of light is first introduced at Alexander, *De Sensu* 31, 15–18: "It is clear that light is a relation, and is dependent upon a relation between the illuminant and the illuminated, and is not a substance and body, from the fact that <light> does not persist even for a little while when the illuminant has been turned away (trans. Towey 2000: 40). Later at 131, 20–132, 16 Alexander argues that illumination does not arise from movement but is immediate thanks to the relation initiated by the presence of the one illuminating the one being illuminated. This idea can also be found in the *De Anima* 2.7 (418b18–20).

25. Alexander, *De Sensu* 49, 25–27.

26. This teaching summarizes aspects of the discussion already found in Psellos' text and ultimately derives from *De Anima* 2.7, 419a8–24.

medium between the eye and the thing seen, being moved by the things which are visible, that is, the colors (for color moves what is transparent in actuality).[27] For the transparent in actuality, being moved and arranged by the things that are visible, transmits the form <of the thing seen> to the pupil, which is also transparent. And, therefore, since the pupil receives by means of the transparent the intermediate form of the thing seen and transmits this to primary perception, **[17]** vision occurs on account of the intermediate passage full of such a body.[28] This is not caused by emanations, as those before him supposed (for on this view sight would also be touch), but because the transparent medium between that which sees and that which is seen is moved by the things that are visible.[29] The philosopher defines flavor as "the affect produced in what is moist by what is dry in earth, which can alter potential into actual taste."[30]

You have also asked me what politics consists of. It is the care of the citizens for each other, and this is called ethics. Each citizen is a part of the city, and ethics is a part of politics.[31] And where there are ends beyond the activities, such as in the creative arts, the works, that is, the things made, are in these instances better than the activities. But where the activities themselves <are the end>, then nothing is more honorable than these activities.[32] In all arts the ends of the master arts are more virtuous than those below them.[33] It is said that the master arts lead and rule those below them, as for instance the master art <governs that> of the rudder-maker.[34]

27. Alexander, *De Sensu* 59, 1–7.
28. Alexander, *De Sensu* 59, 10–15.
29. Alexander, *De Sensu* 61, 11–13.
30. Alexander, *De Sensu* 75, 1–3; Aristotle, *De Sensu* 441b19–21. The quote is unpacked at Alexander, *De Sensu* 73, 30–76, 21.
31. Aspasios, *Ethica* 6.28–31.
32. Aspasios, *Ethica* 4.21–23.
33. Aristotle, *Nicomachean Ethics* 1094a14–15.
34. Aspasios, *Ethica* 4.28–5.1.

16 *On Beauty* and *On Intelligible Beauty*

Translated with introduction and notes
by Charles Barber and David Jenkins

Introduction

When Psellos discusses the beautiful it is clear that his thinking is much influenced by Plotinos' work in this regard. This section contains translations of two direct discussions of Plotinos' *On Beauty* and *On Intelligible Beauty*.[1] Read together and in light of the works discussed, these passages allow us to consider what it is that Psellos has chosen to take from or to explain about his distinguished predecessor and source.

Psellos' discussion of *On Beauty* is the last part of a text entitled *On Dialectic, Happiness, and Beauty*. The arrangement of the text suggests that it might be understood as a brief summary, perhaps for teaching purposes of tractates 3, 4 and 5, and 6 of Plotinos' First Ennead. The discussion is brief and draws upon relatively few passages from Plotinos' treatise. Psellos opens by stating that sensible beauty is an idol or shadow of a more essential Beauty. This higher Beauty can only be apprehended once the soul has ascended be-

1. A helpful discussion of the relevant texts can be found at O'Meara 1993: 88–99. For a commentary on the text of *On Intelligible Beauty*, see now Mariev 2013: 149–77. Readers should also consult the most recent edition of *On Intelligible Beauty*: Kalligas 2013.

yond the level of the senses. It is only then that the soul will recognize the inherent beauty that has come from Intellect and that becomes more discernible as one ascends to a more intelligible and non-material state of being. It is thanks to this beauty endowed by the Intellect that the Soul is able to shape lesser beings into a likeness to this First Beauty. Psellos is therefore primarily concerned with the mediating role for the soul between the intelligible and the material realms. It is an interest that is much more fully developed in his discussion of *On Intelligible Beauty.*

What is striking about Psellos' account of *On Beauty* is that it does not reflect Plotinos' extended discussion of perceptual beauty that is found in the early sections of the latter's treatise. Psellos begins his account of the tractate at the end of section three, the point at which Plotinos turns from the sensual to the intelligible realm. His focus is then upon a few lines of the sixth section in which an identity between Beauty and Intellect is affirmed. The final sections of the tractate, which discuss the purification and ascent of the Soul to the contemplation of Beauty, are ignored.

Psellos' *On Intelligible Beauty* offers a relatively lengthy and close reading of Plotinos' work *On Intelligible Beauty.* The work is largely dependent upon *Enneads* V.8, including both direct quotations and paraphrases. Notably, at the end of the text Psellos identifies his sources to be both Plotinos and Iamblichos. It is also notable that he excises from his version of Plotinos' teaching all references to the pagan gods and almost all references to cosmological matters.

Psellos opens his text with a statement regarding the hierarchy of Beauty. This places Intellect as the first Beauty, a beauty that exists at the intelligible level. Below this is the psychic beauty found in Souls, which derives from the first Beauty. Soul is then identified as the source for the physical beauty to be seen in Nature. Finally the beauty in Nature is presented as the model and origin for the beauty that is in Art. Psellos now begins to follow the main lines of Plotinos' *On Intelligible Beauty.* He thus begins by noting that the beauty in works of art is there because of the intellectual activity of the artist, who has discerned the beauty that is prior to its material manifestation in the work of art. As this beauty derives from Nature, it follows that natural beauty is superior to the beauty found in works of art. Although Plotinos dwells for a time on the work of art, the role of the artist, and natural beauty—notably in sections one and two of the tractate—Psellos chooses to move quickly on to the beauty that is unseen. This is the beauty found in the Soul and the Intellect and that exists in the intelligible realm. His concern is, therefore, primarily with the Beauty in the Intellect. It is this first Beauty that descends through the Soul to Nature and thence to the work of art. Psellos reiterates the intellectual ground of art, when he emphasizes that the beauty does not reside in the material from which the work is made, but rather in the mind of the artist. It is this mind that returns the work to the first Beauty found in the Intellect. It is this that Psellos elucidates at length. What he wishes to demonstrate is that the intelligible realm, the *there* of the text below, differs from the physical and material realm of the human senses. Discursive or deliberative thought is unnecessary, as knowledge of these higher things does not come from the exercise of human reason but rather is revealed in the immediate flash of the Intellect revealed directly to the Soul. It is the mediation of one's soul that then permits an ascent from the sensible to the intelligible domains.

While this text addresses Beauty *there* in the intelligible domain, it offers little to an aesthetics that might be determined by the sensible and phenomenal human horizon. Instead Psellos, following Plotinos, leads us beyond a phenomenological account to an ethical one. One must raise oneself up beyond visible beauty by means of one's conduct and one's studies. Once risen to that state of being *there*, one does not leave the human or the physical behind, but one may now discern both that which is essential in these and that which is superior to them. It is then that one sees immediately absolutely everything that one has been given to see. Which is to say, one may now see the unified and unifying quality of the Beauty that has descended or flashed forth from the Intellect and that is in everything, no matter how far from this source.

Psellos thus draws our attention to a Beauty that is the origin of the beauty in every beautiful thing. This both draws everything into a relationship and opens the way to an ethical ascent beyond the sensible. Where then does this leave the work of art? Although Psellos does not devote as much space to this as does Plotinos, he references the larger argument when he draws attention to the role that the artist plays in making the work. He makes intellect available for our contemplation by means of the beauty he forms in the material ground of the work of art. This creative act allows one both to enjoy the beauty of the thing itself and to understand that its beauty is a pale shadow of the natural beauty that it imitates and that derived from the beauty inherent in the Soul, which had descended from the Intellect. It is then through the precise imitation of nature that intelligible beauty becomes manifest in the work of art, even as this manifestation is exceeded by the Beauty that is prior to it and superior to it.

These texts suggest that Michael Psellos has used his reading of Plotinos to think through the question of immaterial beauty. This is most tellingly revealed by his relatively limited address to *On Beauty* in which he chooses to set aside much of Plotinos' interest in mundane and perceptible beauty. As such his reading of that text appears to be almost prefatory to his longer and more engaged discussion of the *On Intelligible Beauty* text.

Editions and translations. The latest edition of *On Beauty*, which has been followed here, is to be found in *Phil. min.* I 4.68–83. The latest edition of *On Intelligible Beauty*, which has been followed here, is to be found in *Phil. min.* II 34 (115.1–117.22; bracketed numbers indicate pages). For a complete list of manuscripts, editions, and discussions, see Moore 2005: 234 (*On Beauty*) and 288–89 (*On Intelligible Beauty*).

On Beauty

Perceptible beautiful things, about which you also enquired in your letter, are the images and shadows of the Being of Beauty that somehow have gone forth and entered matter, and have adorned and startled this as they became apparent. Perception is not yet fated to see the more distant beautiful things, but the Soul, without the aid of the senses, gazes upon what <we> should see in <our> ascent, after leaving perception to wait below,[1] for the Soul, cleansed by these <beautiful things>, is a form and a principle and wholly bodiless and intelligible and entirely belonging to the divine. And if the Soul is something Beautiful, it is even more Beautiful when it has been drawn up to the level of Intellect. For Intellect and the things that pertain to <Intellect> are the Soul's proper beauty and not something alien to it, and for this reason it is right to say that the Soul is Good and Beautiful when it has become like the Divine, whence Beauty comes.[2] For Soul is <granted> Beauty by the Intellect, and everything else, when shaped by the Soul, is beautiful in deeds and habits. In fact, Soul also makes bodies <beautiful>, to the extent they are so called; since being a divine thing and a part of Beauty, it makes Beautiful—to the extent that it is possible for them—whatever it touches and holds.[3]

1. Plotinos, *Enneads* I 6, 3, 33–4, 4.
2. Plotinos, *Enneads* I 6, 6, 13–20.
3. Plotinos, *Enneads* I 6, 6, 27–32.

On Intelligible Beauty

The divine and wholly honorable Intellect is the first and intelligible Beauty, and thence the Soul is beautiful, and then Nature is such from the Soul, and Art from Nature.[1] And the visible beauty of form is either from Art or from the thought that conceived it or from that which brought it to be incorporeally.[2] And the beautiful form that is wholly visible has come to that which has come to be from that which made it.[3] Yet if the things made and the materialized forming principle are beautiful, is not <the principle>, which is first and immaterial and not in the material but in the maker, more beautiful?[4] Nature, which produces beautiful things in matter, is far superior to the things <that appear> in matter.[5]

Yet it is necessary to rise up from visible beauty to the beauty in learning and the conduct that follows from this and from this to that which is in souls.[6] For in Nature there is also a principle, which is the archetype of the beauty <found> in a body. But <the principle> that <is> in the Soul is more beautiful than that in Nature, and it is <from this principle> that <the principle> in Nature <derives>. The <principle> in a good Soul is more brilliant and makes

1. Cf. Plotinos, *Enneads* I 6, 6, 16–28 and 8–13.
2. Cf. Plotinos, *Enneads* V 8, 1 14–18.
3. Cf. Plotinos, *Enneads* V 8, 2, 13–15.
4. Plotinos, *Enneads* V 8, 2, 17–19.
5. Plotinos, *Enneads* V 8, 2, 31–32.
6. Plotinos, *Enneads* V 8, 2, 37–38; cf. I 6, 1, 1–6.

one consider what is prior to it [the principle], which no longer comes to be in nor is in anything else, but in itself. Thus it is not the principle itself, but is the creator of the first principle. It is Intellect itself and always Intellect and not just sometimes Intellect, because <Intellect> is not alien to this [the principle].[7] And if one of the entities that is higher than us and ranked below God is both Beautiful and above Nature, it is beautiful on account of Intellect and by means of the presence of Intellect, the first Beauty. This <entity> knows all things, not only human affairs, but also those above Nature, and sees not only those things that have come to be but also those that are essential.[8] For everything is transparent *there* and there is neither darkness nor reflection. All higher things have everything in <Intellect> and it [Intellect] in turn sees everything in the other, and their radiance is infinite. Furthermore, the movement of all these is pure and <their> stillness undisturbed. And <Intellect's> beauty is Beauty itself, because it is not in the beautiful.[9] But I call this "the first Beauty" and this is Intellect itself, which is not in the beautiful, but is the first Beauty itself. There is no weariness or satiety from the sight of both unutterable Beauty and pure pleasure *there*. And there is no differentiation between <higher things> resulting in displeasure on the part of one in regard to that, which is found in the other. Moreover, there is not satiety, in the sense that satiety does entail contempt for that, which created satiety. For, when looking, it sees more, perceiving the infinite itself, and things are seen in accord with its [the Intellect's] own nature. And life holds no weariness when it is pure; how could leading the best life grow wearisome? But the life *there* is a knowledge not supported by the powers of reason. For lacking nothing it would also not need to seek, but is the first and not <derived> from any other.[10] And the vision *there* <is that of> the "exceedingly blessed spectator," whom we have not yet comprehended.[11] And there is neither discourse nor deliberation *there*.[12]

The Greeks were the first to say these things, which, in my opinion, are not completely inappropriate, especially since I have cleaned up anything in

7. Plotinos, *Enneads* V 8, 3, 1–10.
8. Cf. Plotinos, *Enneads* V 8, 3, 18–36.
9. Cf. Plotinos, *Enneads* V 8, 4, 3–15.
10. Plotinos, *Enneads* V 8, 4, 26–38.
11. Cf. Plotinos, *Enneads* V 8, 4, 43–48.
12. Plotinos, *Enneads* V 8, 6, 9.

them that was harsh and repellent. Nevertheless, some of their doctrines should be attributed to them alone. For in proposing to speak of the creation of the visible world, they fashion it as the image of the intelligible world, that is to say of the Ideas and the Self-existent (for they talk about both in the same way), and that, according to their hypotheses, this composite world is without a beginning.[13] For they say that all things are in something else,[14] which is to say that the paradigmatic prototypes of the visible world are set in the Intellect by the first god, whom they say is the Good and beyond Being, sometimes beyond the One, unspeakable and unnameable. They say that no form or image of this can exactly manifest what it is. First, matter is possessed by the elemental forms, and then these forms by other forms, and so on and so on, so that it is difficult to find matter hidden under so many forms, for this [matter] is also a kind of lowest form.[15] For this reason, he [Plotinos] also says that such creation is without toil. And here, one can say why the earth is in the middle, and why it is round, and why the ecliptic slants as it does, while there [one cannot say] that these things are as they should be because they were determined to be this way, but <only> that they are as they are because they are beautiful. For if a conclusion comes prior to a syllogism's logical necessity, then it could not have followed from the premises. For this follows upon neither consequence nor conceptual thought, but is prior to consequence and conceptual thought. For all of these, that is, reasoning and demonstration and persuasion, come later.[16]

[117] Regarding the Beautiful he [Plotinos] says: "if the latter is not more beautiful because of an extraordinary beauty, what then would be more beautiful than this visible <world>?"[17] Those who find fault with this do not see the parts in regard to the wholes, but isolate a particular part of a living being, its hair or nail or bile or phlegm, and then, without considering these in regard to their function, they spit out from the whole the part that disgusts them.[18] But if one were to take and to gather together and to consider their essences and potentialities and actualities as well as their combinations and mixtures and

13. Psellos here references Plato's cosmology: *Timaeus* 28a–31a.
14. Plotinos, *Enneads* V 8, 7, 12–13.
15. Plotinos, *Enneads* V 8, 7, 18–25.
16. Plotinos, *Enneads* V 8, 7, 36–44.
17. Plotinos, *Enneads* V 8, 8, 21–23.
18. Plotinos, *Enneads* III 2, 3, 13–16.

relations with one another, one might be led to believe that this is the first Beauty, by means of which one desires Being, which is a likeness of the Beautiful. Let us reiterate what has been said previously: the first Intellect, as well as the first thoughts, which are the same as this, and which it possesses from the Good, is itself likewise descended from *there*, and first manifests the first Beauty.[19] So that Beauty can appear, the beautiful comes from *there* and is an image of Beauty.[20] While the Soul is beautiful with respect to its nature, it is more beautiful whenever it looks *there*.[21] For if it were beautiful in itself, then it would be wholly beautiful. But Intellect is this very Beauty, and the beautiful things that follow upon this do so either immediately or at a remove. Those that follow immediately are primarily brilliant, while those that proceed through intermediaries do participate in the Beauty *there*, but the further away they are, the fainter their beauty.

The followers of Plotinos and Iamblichos said these things, though not exactly in these words, your holy soul. But I collected and combined all of them here and then cleaned them up for your benefit.

19. Plotinos, *Enneads* I 6, 6, 25–27.
20. Plotinos, *Enneads* V 8, 9, 43–44.
21. Plotinos, *Enneads* V 8, 13, 14–15.

17 *To the Emperor Doukas, Regarding the Inscription*

Translated with introduction and notes by Anthony Kaldellis

Introduction

The reign of Michael VII Doukas (1071–1078) was one of the most disastrous in Byzantine history. By repudiating the emperor Romanos IV Diogenes, who had been defeated at Manzikert (1071) but then came to an agreement with his conqueror Alp Arslan, the Doukas regime in the capital opened the East to Turkish settlement. Michael's reign witnessed rapid loss of territory and multiple rebellions and civil wars. Michael himself was indolent in the face of all this, putting the worse interpretation on the wish that is expressed at the end of this work, namely, that he prove "more peaceful than warlike." He was, inevitably, toppled by a rebel, Nikephoros III Botaneiates (1078–1081), tonsured, and made bishop of Ephesos. The contemporary historian Michael Attaleiates noted with sarcasm that an episcopal position better suited Michael's character, as he was naive, lacking experience in the affairs of life, and disinclined to understand anything regarding imperial matters.[1]

Psellos was on good terms with the Doukas regime, being an advisor of Michael's father, the emperor Konstantinos X Doukas (1059–1068), a personal friend of his uncle Ioannes (the powerful *Kaisar*), and tutor to the young

1. Michael Attaleiates, *History* 303.

prince himself. As such, it was appropriate that Psellos should comment on Michael's intellectual and literary accomplishments, including the composition of iambic verses and allegories (*Chronographia* 7.168). It is for wasting his time with precisely such things under Psellos' direction that the continuator of the historian Ioannes Skylitzes reproached the emperor.[2]

We can form some idea of Michael's occupations from the encyclopedic and introductory works on various topics that Psellos dedicated to him.[3] It seems that he was more inquisitive about such matters than about imperial affairs and the circumstances of his own reign. The work translated here, an explanation of a Greek relief with an accompanying inscription, is likewise cast as a response to an imperial question, and there is no reason to think that this format is only a literary conceit. It is among the first signs in middle Byzantium of a renewed interest in ancient (pagan) Greece, which would culminate in the twelfth-century apogee of rhetorical performance, the revival of ancient genres such as satire and the romance novel, and an obsession with Homer.[4] Psellos was the pioneer of these movements, and we have here an example of how he transmitted his interests to the court, dealing with material culture. We have letters of his that seem to be requesting statues from Greece for his personal collection,[5] though the frieze discussed here was probably not among such items, given that it appears to have been badly preserved and did not excite Psellos' aesthetic sense. It was probably found on the palace grounds or was long embedded in a wall, and the new interest in antiquities sparked the emperor's idle curiosity to ask his philosopher-in-chief.

Medieval Constantinopolitans would often have had occasion to wonder at the content of the hundreds of inscriptions that could be seen in their city. It is often assumed that epigraphy—the study of inscriptions—began with the travels and sketches of Cyriacus of Ancona in the fifteenth century,[6] but there was Byzantine precedent, even after late antiquity (when many inscriptions, actual or forged, made their way into the textual tradition, as oracles or epigrams). In the late ninth century, Gregorios of Kampsa travelled throughout

2. *Continuation of Skylitzes* 171; this continuator was possibly Skylitzes himself.

3. For these works, see D. Polemis 1968: 44–45. That Michael VII was the addressee of the work in question (and not Konstantinos X Doukas, as was believed), see Moore 2005: 354.

4. See now Kaldellis 2007: chap. 5. For the interest in Homer, which pervades Psellos' brief essay, see also Vasilikopoulou-Ioannidou 1971–72.

5. See Papamastorakis 2004.

6. See now Bodnar 2003.

the provinces to gather epigrammatic inscriptions for the collection that would become our *Greek Anthology*.[7]

Psellos' interpretation of the iconography of this inscription has received a mixed reception. Gilbert Dagron suggested that the scene is possibly from a funerary stele for a deceased woman, or a libation.[8] The indistinct object was not the herb moly from the *Odyssey* but perhaps a wreath or branch. The head on the altar was a bust, of course, not the remains of a sacrifice. Little sense can be made today of the inscription. Dagron proposes the restoration ΟΜΟΝΟΙΑΣ, while Psellos reconstructed it as *ide ono(ma) moly*, "behold, the name (of it is) moly," an allusion to the scene in the *Odyssey* between Odysseus and Hermes on the island of Kirke. He then cites and explains the literary context. It is possible that he imagined the sculpted scene as Homeric based solely on his reading of the inscription. This Homeric instinct is not surprising in a man who claimed to have learned the epics by heart as a child.[9] In the *Chronographia* (6.61), he testifies to the workings of the Homeric imagination at the court, where courtiers could be expected to show off passages by heart. This artifact gave Psellos the opportunity to deploy specific textual associations. Růžena Dostálová has related it to the sculpted scenes from Homer depicted on the Tabula Iliacae, substantially defending the likelihood of the philosopher-scholar's interpretation.[10]

At the end of the essay Psellos alludes to alternative interpretations, one from the world of pagan ritual and another that he only hints at and does not disclose, but is probably a kind of Platonizing allegory, a hermeneutical mode that he preferred in many treatises and exposition.[11] These alternative interpretations, it seems, were the only ones that were offered to the emperor in connection with this object. Psellos refers to a prior interpretation by the *magos* Basileios, whom he corrects. This man is not otherwise known, nor is it clear what Psellos means by the word and what position a *magos* could have at the Byzantine court. From Anna Komnene we learn that astrological expertise and various prognosticators (*mathêmatikoi*, etc.) were prized at the court of her father Alexios, only a decade or so after the date of Psellos' treatise.[12]

7. Lauxtermann 2003: 73–74, 184.
8. Dagron 1983: 120.
9. Psellos, *Encomium for His Mother* 359–63; Kaldellis 2006: 62.
10. Dostálová 1986.
11. Kaldellis 2007: chap. 4.
12. Anna Komnene, *Alexiad* 6.7; see Magdalino 2003.

Editions and translations. The latest edition, which has been followed here, is in *Or. min.* 32 (bracketed numbers follow the line numbering of the edition). For a complete list of manuscripts, editions, and discussions, see Moore 2005: 354. A French translation and discussion (in conjunction with the antiquarian and magico-mystical traditions of the Constantinopolitan *Patria*) can be found in Dagron 1983: 118–20.

To the Emperor Doukas, Regarding the Inscription

Translation in collaboration with Demetrios Kritsotakis

[2–3] My holy lord, I reviewed both the inscription and the sculpture on the stone, as you commanded.

[4–25] There is on the left side a man stretching forth a sword with his right hand, pointing with his left hand to some obscure figure; and, on the right part, there is a sculpted throne, on which some image in a foreign style is sitting, bringing its legs together in a straight line and hiding them. The man bearing the sword is Odysseus, the obscure image is Circe. There is a Greek myth according to which Circe was a witch-goddess[1] who bewitched all others and turned them into the forms of animals, but was defeated only by Odysseus.[2] He threatened her by pointing a sword at her. As he himself says in Homer's *Odyssey*: "Drawing the sharp sword from beside my thigh, I rushed at her as though intending to kill her."[3] With his other hand he shows her an herb called moly, which the messenger of the Greek gods, Hermes, gave to him for help. Odysseus himself talks about it like this, in the aforementioned book of Homer:

> And as he spoke, Argeiphontes drew an herb from
> the earth, gave it to me, and showed me its nature.

1. Homer, *Odyssey* 10.276.
2. Homer, *Odyssey* 10.237 ff., 326ff.
3. Homer, *Odyssey* 10.321–22.

It had a black root, but its flower was like milk.
The gods call it moly, and it is difficult to dig up.[4]

So, as I said, Odysseus stretches the sword to Circe with his right hand, while with his left he points to the moly, just as Hermes advised him.[5] Circe's image is not entirely human in form, but is mutated and alien; the sculptor of the stone thereby revealed the unspeakable form of the divine woman.

[26–31] Of the visible letters on the stone, there are three letters above both figures, ο, ν, and ο, and, on the right side, towards the edge of the stone, where Circe is sculpted, we have ι, δ, and ε, while on the left side, where Odysseus is, we have μ and ω, which are being united into one. Behold the name moly, as if Odysseus were saying to Circe, "See the herb and fear it, which is named moly."

[32–40] That is how the inscription seemed to me upon my first attempt. There is a more magical explanation, and I am amazed that the magician Basileios did not know it. For the ancients, when they were making peace-treaties, used to light a fire on an altar and lay upon it victims whose throats they had sliced and who they then cut into small pieces. The throne that appears on the stone is an altar of this kind and the victim on it has its head cut off so that only the neck is visible. He who is drawing the sword is the slayer, and the written words are a libation of peace. The letters are Greek, not foreign or hieroglyphic.

[41–46] I discerned on the stone many other and deeper meanings than these, some more divine, some more pagan. But these are the ones I liked most. The sculpture and the inscription contribute to your power on either explanation. For the bowl of harmony is a symbol of peace, and Odysseus is a hero who overcomes opposing powers. And may you be, in my eyes, more peaceful than warlike.

4. Homer, *Odyssey* 10.302–5.
5. Homer, *Odyssey* 10.287–88.

18 On Ancient Works of Art (*Or. min.* 33 and 34)

Translated with introduction and notes
by Christine Angelidi

Introduction

The two texts presented here offer *ekphraseis* (evocations) of mythological subjects. Both indicate that Michael Psellos had some acquaintance with Philostratos' *Eikones*.[1] The address to a παῖς in "Ekphrasis or Allegory" and to a μειράκιον both hint at the presence of the Philostratian model. In these texts, Psellos reaches beyond this model in that he introduces a strongly interpretative component into his writing, thus playing between evocation and interpretation, as if wrestling with the possibility of truly understanding the work of art. In so doing he not only tests the limits of such a work, but also explores the rhetorical and philosophical limits of the words that attempt to evoke this work for his audience.

In "Ekphrasis or Allegory" Psellos first provides his evocation of Circe's failed attempt to transform Odysseus into a pig, a fate that had already befallen his companions. Psellos' account of this event dwells upon transformation, using different and various terms to introduce this concept by different

1. This brief introductory note should be supplemented by my fuller discussion of these texts in Angelidi 2005.

means (μεταβολή, μεταμόρφωσις, μεταποίησις, μετασχηματισμός, διαλλαγή, ἀλλοίωσις). Having introduced this thread, Psellos not only identifies change as being symptomatic of moral weakness, but also as the very ground of the human condition. In making this point, Psellos assures his young listener that philosophical truths may be found in myths.

The "Ekphrasis of Eros Carved on Stone" is written in a sophisticated style that draws attention to the emotions as it tightly interlaces its evocative passage with their interpretation. Psellos uses the subject of Eros to introduce the correlation of the lower and the higher worlds. Here, Eros serves as a guide who can lead souls in their ascent from perceptible Beauty to the transcendent pleasure that derives from this. This ascent is made possible by the corporal reflections that spiritual Beauty has fashioned of itself. It is these that permit the refined spectator to discern higher things. This process may then be lent support by the intelligent work of the artist. Hence, Psellos tells us that: "The person that molded the stone according to the idea of Eros doesn't seem to me to be unaware either of the highest philosophy or of the differentiation of the souls" (*Or. min.* 34.5–7). Read in these Neoplatonic terms, the work becomes an animate medium linking the world of the senses with the world of the intellect.[2]

Both *ekphraseis* reveal the degree to which Psellos' rhetorical practice was bound to his philosophical interests. Profoundly imbued with Neoplatonic concepts, these texts draw the work of art into an economy that mediates the sensible mundane world with the intelligible and higher domains.

Editions and translations. The latest editions of these texts, which have been followed here, are in *Or. min.* 33 and 34 (bracketed numbers follow the line numbering of the edition). For a complete list of manuscripts, editions, and discussions, see Moore 2005: 354–56.

2. Papaioannou 2006.

Ekphrasis or Allegory

[2–14] Circe intends to transform Odysseus too and to confine him to the pigsty. She prepared the potion and everything necessary for the transmutation. However, she fails when the hero brandishes his sword against her; she is almost dead as you can deduce from her altered figure, whereas he defies her with a terrible gaze. He is concentrated on his own fate and is not yet concerned about his companions. They stand with their deformed faces, artfully represented: one is already transmuted, the other in the process of modification, the third on the verge of transformation. Thus, the first is represented with a long snout and his figure is somehow porcine; the eyes of the next are altered, the face disintegrating, the nose not having yet acquired its final sharp form, while the face of the third is swollen, his transmutation commencing.

[15–22] Why did the potion conquer them, while Odysseus prevailed over it? Listen, my child, to the philosophical explanation and do not reject the disguise of myth, for concealing the mysteries of philosophy under another form is, indeed, a poetic achievement to hide. Thus, you should interpret Circe as the pleasure that stands against us, molding the souls according to the impulse of each of them. The potion is a mixed beverage, precisely as the cup of oblivion. When the souls drink out of it, they forget their own value; hence the inherent reason is driven towards irrationality, and they are impelled to <adopt> a bestial form.

[22–28] Circe is powerful over those souls; she appears to them terrible and, along with her beauty, arrogant and solemn. However, souls that are partly godly, which are moving between the mortal body and the immortal nature, are not afraid of the transformations of Circe or caught by her figure. Instead, by bravely staring at her, they tame her and, eventually, avoid the painful mutation.

Ekphrasis of Eros Carved on Stone

[2–14] Do not wonder, my child, while observing Eros immersed in deep sleep, the wings folded up and the inactive quiver loosely hanging from one hand. The person that molded the stone according to the idea of Eros does not seem to me to be unaware either of the highest philosophy or of the differentiation of the souls. Indeed, some souls are . . . from their creation and Eros does not watch over them, while some others are moving over (mount) his wing and below the latter he . . . the view. . . . Consequently we must cast Eros in the intermediary space, in order to. . . . We should not apprehend his wing nor be afraid of his arrow, because he is not . . . fluttering . . . and does not always hit successfully. Yet, even when his shot is well targeted. . . .

[15–30] If the sculptor had carved the lesser Eros awaken . . ., then he would suggest he was moving toward the best souls. Indeed, there exists, of course, another, higher, and never resting Eros, who does not bring souls down to their corporeal shapes, but guides the intellect in its ascending way toward God. However, if we follow the admirable philosopher—I mean Plato—we should not despise the lesser Eros, because he also leads the souls: he guides them in their ascent from the perceptible Beauty to the transcendent pleasure drawn from it. Furthermore, the spiritual and concealed Beauty forms itself according to its own nature; thus, it creates corporeal reflections that are perceptible to the refined soul that, discerning the trace of the intellectual origin of what can be seen, is spontaneously inspired and violently vibrating. We may therefore conclude that he who beholds the beauty of a body confines himself to the corporeal subject and merely wishes to embrace the reflection may be a lover of bodies, but not a lover of beauty. But he who is able to discern the transcendent origin, then he is the genuine "Platonic lover," ridiculed by those who ignore the significance of the term.

[31–56] There will be in the future another occasion to comment on the higher Eros. Now, let us concentrate on this sculpture and its creator. Observe how naturally harmoniously are displayed the members! I admire the artist even for his choice of stone; he did not use any of the variegated kind of marble—neither the Prokonnesian nor that of the Penteli mountain—but the brightest white, in order to render the color of Eros without the aid of artistry. It gives the impression of frozen milk or of snow before amassed but not yet crystallized. The hair is gently waving around the head and somehow suggests the alertness and the luminosity of the face. He is surrendered to sleep, but the eyes seem to move under the closed eyelids as if in an intermediary stage between wakefulness and sleep. Although he is resting, his arms are active, one supporting the head, the other holding something. Art reveals him and lays him nude without any of the usual clothing. Look how inviting the sculpture is to cuddling. Before you lies one side of the body, and do not wonder if it seems thin and fleshless. Instead, admire the sagacity of art. Indeed, on the opposite part, on which Eros lies, the loose belly draws the skin and is rendered fleshy; on that same side, the buttock meets the thigh and the flesh is abundant. The artist represented the feet departing from the common rule . . ., but crossed one under the other. The wings are folded behind him, . . . but ready to be activated when needed. For he may be reclining and in repose . . . still he is perpetually entrusted with the transcendent. The beloved varies, indeed . . .; it always appears in a different form and each time provokes a novel desire.

19 Ekphrasis of the Crucifixion

Translated with introduction and notes
by Charles Barber and Elizabeth A. Fisher

Introduction

The following ekphrastic account of an icon of the Crucifixion is the last major section of a longer homily on the events of the Crucifixion (*Or. hag.* 3B; the ekphrasis in lines 634–879). The homily begins by discussing the Incarnation, Adam and Eve in Paradise, the Fall, the partial quality of prophetic knowledge of God, and Christ's life and miracles before turning to the Passion and then the Crucifixion itself. The account of the Crucifixion is notable for the variety of perspectives presented, with natural phenomena, the Mother of God, John, the angels, and the thieves all providing different witnesses to these events. Throughout these accounts, Psellos is keen to underline the limits of human learning.[1] Finally, having established the partial quality of human witness, Psellos invites the icon's present audience to become witnesses as well.[2] An experience that is to be achieved by means of an icon of the Crucifixion.[3]

1. A point made at Fisher 1994: 46.

2. Gautier (1991: 10) did not believe that this homily was intended for an actual audience. Fisher argues that aspects of the text do in fact indicate the possibility of an audience (Fisher 1994: 44–45).

3. Reference to the painter (line 1375) underscores the evocation of a made image.

Psellos' ekphrastic account of this icon is conditioned by the paradox inherent in its subject. Christ is understood to be both living and dead on the cross because of his divine and human natures. This understanding then leads to consideration of the limits of a painting's ability to represent this subject. Here Psellos builds from an exacting and physical account of the painting's ability to render Christ's body with great precision. Having established that this is what painting is able to do, Psellos then undermines the apparent clarity and accuracy of this first account by asking us to contemplate that which an icon cannot show. By these means, Psellos demonstrates that the icon remains ensnared within the sensible realm.

As Elizabeth Fisher has noted, this homily should be linked to the letter to the *sakellarios* translated in this volume (*Letter One*). Both texts share the problem of depicting this subject. What is striking is that Psellos neither allows his words nor the image evoked by these words to become adequate to their common subject. This aspect of the text has some bearing on another quality that is in play. Christ's depiction is considered to be "living." Hans Belting and others have drawn attention to this passage and to Psellos' claims for originality in the icon to argue that Psellos offers us an account of a new and more naturalistic style of painting in Byzantium.[4] Before we can accept this possibility, it is important that we consider how the "living" quality is at play in Psellos' text. For Psellos, this introduces a double and ambiguous aspect to painting.[5] For while painting can present a lifelike imitation of its subject, felicitously combined from various parts, the wholeness that brings life to this work is beyond this process. In seeking ways to explain how this limitation can be overcome, Psellos draws attention to the possibility that the artist is inspired. This is playfully linked to the animate aspects of a body that is both living and dead, and again, Psellos uses this to make the point that "life" is beyond art's possibility. He uses the vivid and mobile qualities of an ekphrasis to prepare this possibility, only to remove it. In the end, the ekphrasis of this *Crucifixion* leads Psellos to reaffirm his understanding that painting is primarily a product that is bound by the human and the sensible realm.

4. Belting 1994: 261–96. For further recent discussion, see Pentcheva 2000; Cormack 2003; Barber 2006a; Papaioannou 2006.

5. This discussion is developed in Barber 2007: 61–98.

Editions and translations. The latest edition of the *Discourse on the Crucifixion*, which has been followed here, is to be found in *Or. hag.* 3B.634–879 (bracketed numbers follow this line numbering). For a complete list of manuscripts, editions, and discussions, see Moore 2005: 361–63. An earlier edition, resumé, and partial translation can be found in Gautier 1991. Our translation is based largely on that found in Fisher 1994; certain sections are taken from the translations found in Barber 2007: 72–80.

Ekphrasis of the Crucifixion

[634–51] At any rate, you observe with the discerning eye of your soul that day by day <Christ> is made all things,[1] so that he might make you a participant both in his sufferings and in his glory. Nevertheless you have not entirely relinquished sense perceptions nor have you altogether risen above the body, but you long to gaze upon him with your very eyes and to see, if possible, Christ himself hanging naked upon the tree so that you might rather be nailed up and crucified with him. I shall grant you even this satisfaction, although my claim is astonishing. Now first prepare yourself a little, and in this way I shall show you what you so eagerly desire. God inspires with his grace not only creatures who possess reason but also images that lack life; an indication of this fact is the likenesses that often move, speak, and behave with the power of reason towards those who observe them. These likenesses seem to be the product of the human hand, but God actually fashions them without our knowing it, if I may put it thus, and presents them in visible form by using the hand of the craftsman as his vehicle for the picture.

[651–61] Therefore, since I have made this preliminary statement for you as a sort of beginning for my arguments and some sort of basic premise or commonly held postulation, lo and behold, I am fulfilling my promise to you. Please turn your eyes to the right, and see the Lord himself crucified. Do not marvel if those are absent who smote him, who buffeted him, who spat upon him,[2] for he has already breathed his last, and they have breathed, too —a

1. Cf. 1 Corinthians 9:22.
2. Cf. Matthew 26:67.

sigh of relief in dismissing his body as lifeless. An unpleasant thing to see besides—a man of wrath making a daring display even against the Savior. That is why <God's> grace did not represent those who should be absent, but portrayed as endowed with life those who should be present.

[661–712] The cross, then, has been fitted together as you see. They have fixed its crosspieces firmly on the uprights, and the principle of mutual correspondence brings from unlike elements the harmony of perfect truth and makes pine, cedar, and cypress distinguishable by means of slight variations; for the cross is fashioned and composed from these elements. Moreover, a little hillock of earth has been raised, because the artist's intelligence overlooked not even the slightest detail of the narrative. But the Lord of glory[3] has been crucified upon the cross and represented proportionate to its every dimension. Then, if he had not already died and commended his spirit to his father, you would have seen him in agony, begging for comfort from his father, and you would have heard that divine voice and you would have recognized that this language is not our own, but was drawn from the <psalm> entitled the dawn appeal [Psalm 21/22]. And since he has yielded up the ghost,[4] gaze upon the living dead [Christ]: for the clarity of the likeness is in the body rather than the soul.[5] For since Christ's <body> had by now suffered mortification for some time, the blood had already departed from it, either collecting in the heart or compressed into the concavities of the veins, and for this reason, his complexion is whitish and completely pallid. His head was inclined slightly, not over his breast but to one side, because he died thus, first bowing his head[6] in accordance with <God's> will, and then expiring in this fashion. Now if the inclination of his head were not in acquiescence, <the head> would have fallen upon the chest, since a body, lifeless but possessing natural weight, falls straight downwards. Even so, his eyes are not open in their lids, but they have been carefully drawn closed, although no hand composed them. For the crucified Lord himself suitably made them fast, even as he closed his mouth and composed every <feature> exactly. For only after he had arranged his appearance as is appropriate to him did he thus relinquish

3. 1 Corinthians 2:8.

4. Matthew 27:50.

5. The last part of this sentence has been altered from Fisher's original translation. It now follows Barber's at Barber 2007: 74.

6. John 19:30.

his spirit. For the appearance of his <body's> position and even, I might add, the extension of his arms is neither neat nor graceful, but rather preserves vividness in its irregularity. For nature has not turned our limbs evenly, as if with a lathe, but has destroyed perfect regularity with our buttocks, shoulders, and knee caps, with our belly and flanks, making some <parts of the body> flat and others distended. But there is something more here, or rather this is a very work of nature, so that the picture seems to be a product not of art but of nature. For the belly protrudes a bit from the rest of the body, and its colors make it appear not level with the chest, but it has distended as is reasonable. For the organs within it force out the belly, and the skin itself has been stretched at the navel. Perhaps then the heart, liver, and whatever naturally branches from there, namely, blood vessels and the <membranes> containing the lung or rather, both lungs, <these> are concealed from the viewer. But if the entry point of the wound in his side had not already closed, we would perhaps have observed through it what I mentioned as if through a dilator.

[712–55] But since the wound has been staunched, who then is daring enough to open the recesses of the body? His arms were not stretched out <to their full extension>, and the picture replicated their natural appearance accurately. For the limb from shoulder to knuckles is not <stiff and> without articulation, but the joint at the elbow is not quite straight and is a little relaxed. Moreover, one knee has bent under him, for when the body is upright, the legs do not extend evenly. This is because people controlled by their inborn spirit maintain an even tension <in the body>, but when this spirit is dispersed,[7] the resulting corpse sags upon itself, since the joining of the bones is slightly relaxed. And the ribs can almost be counted, visible beneath the lean flesh. Do you notice how each <rib> ever so gently curves? But the body is still uncared for, and no one has yet dared to wash the blood either from the palms of the hand or the feet. A natural amount of blood remains, according as blood flowed out before his death. For after that, the veins no longer gush blood, but these red streams pour back to their particular source. As for the body elevated <on the cross>, the portions around the feet, knees, flanks, belly, and navel have been spat upon and struck in contrast to the wounds on the head, which have suffered no <further> violence, or rather, remain entirely undisturbed. Thus the beard lies smooth upon the head without standing out <from

7. Plato, *Phaedo* 70b5.

it>, but is drawn into a neat and trim point at the chin. There is nothing extraordinary in this, but it is consonant with the age of the Lord, and both <his age and the appearance of his beard> are consistent with one another. His hair is abundant, but, representative of his race, neither flowing down straight nor standing out <from his head>; rather, it is neat and smooth, curling a little at the ends. Not quite dark, but not yet blond, <his hair> has lost the one color without taking on the other. What a wound in his side <that was>, and if you will, what a blow also, when that insolent fellow thrust his lance in deep![8] If the opening were not such as it is now, but if you wish to return from our time to the time when the actual wounding occurred, you would perceive the wound <to be> many times larger than it now appears <to be>. The streams <issuing> from it, their colors, and their mingling with each other, are flowing now, but not for the first time; one <stream> is of water, one <of> blood, and both flow forth unmixed from the same source. Such, you see, is the Lord's body, so exact, so clear, so endowed with life even in death that it cannot be referred to a model, but serves as a model for all else.

[756–71] As for the mother of the Lord, is she not the life-endowed image of virtues itself? For she suffers pain beyond what humans can bear; her breath suddenly fades in her very nostrils, and her spirit has all but abandoned her. Yet she has not even in her sufferings renounced her dignity; she sighs, but feebly, and she groans, but inwardly and inaudibly. She stands nevertheless strictly restraining herself and bowed down into the depths of her spirit; she neither looks up at her son nor turns her eyes towards him. For she agonizes for him, although her impulse is to look up. She seems to be mediating secret and hidden thoughts. For she fixes her eyes upon thoughts she cannot express, while her spirit within her rehearses what she has experienced early on and with what evils she is now overwhelmed; in a way, she compares these two sets of experiences to one another and conquers <the worse> with the better. All the same, she marvels at <her son's> death and <wonders> how he did not disdain even this.

[772–85] As for the Disciple, just as the blow affected him exceedingly, so the picture graphically represents his sufferings. For he who was beloved beyond the others clung to an equal degree to the one who loved him. Since he was but a young man, not really strong enough to endure catastrophes nor to

8. Cf. John 19:34.

express such an onset or such an excess of grief, he was unable to look at the Lord <hanging> on high, but he has bent in upon himself and clasped his right ear, first deafened, I suppose, by the hammering of the nails, then unable to bear a sound like pealing thunder. With one eye he takes a sidelong glance at the body on high, but the artist's hand does not present this feature in the composition he fashions. The Disciple does not see the body with the other eye, and he does not ever seem to gaze upon it, nor is he astonished at the terrible thing.

[786–800] Although this suffering brings him [Christ] in due course to death, the power that moves the hand of the artist also animates the body that has breathed its last. Thus he has been distinguished from those living among the dead, and from the dead who live among the living. For his veiled limbs are somewhat ambiguous, and the visible parts are no less doubtful. Just as art shrouds, it also discloses both the lifeless and the living. This is true of his bloody garments, whether light or dark, as well as of the living dead presented on the cross and clearly suffering an excessive death, now living because of the accuracy of imitation —or rather, then and now in both manners. But there his life is beyond nature and his death is beyond pain. Here both are beyond the art and the grace that has shaped the art.[9]

[801–35] What then, have my words checked your desire, or do you want to see the angels as well? What sort of appearance do they have, and what do those who are pure in understanding see them doing then? See them in flight above the Lord, in the number that the scriptures from the very beginning have transmitted to those who live on earth, designating and naming these chiefs of the greatest <angelic> hosts. What do differences in appearance mean in their case? For on each side, one of the two comes from either direction; one has prepared himself as if for service and seems to be engaged in some sort of activity, while the other is astonished beyond measure and is all but transfixed at the sight. It seems to me that such things are both forms and symbols of mysteries. For Gabriel has already been trusted to serve the incarnation by bringing the virgin the glad tidings of her ineffable pregnancy and by gaining the first understanding of the secret wonder; <he> does not seem at all amazed here, but performs some service for the Lord, because he has

9. This paragraph is altered from that found in Fisher's original translation. It now follows Barber's at Barber 2007: 74.

been dispatched by the great Father for this purpose. Now Michael, on the other hand, is equal in rank to Gabriel among the Lord's hierarchy and has himself also received enlightenment concerning the mystery; therefore, he has assumed a position equal to Gabriel's. But the rest <of the angels>, who see then for the first time the Lord at once incarnate and crucified, do not know what they should marvel at first, his putting on the garments <of human nature> or his hanging crucified with thieves. But the fact that they do not see the bosom of the Father empty of the only begotten Word increases their wonder. Therefore they both ascend and descend in a manner, observing the Lord complete above and the same below but with something added. Their posture, with neither feet nor wings fully extended, expresses the fact that they are stricken at what they see. Perhaps all this happened long ago, but now the angels marvel exceedingly at the very appearance of his form. If one does not think me oversubtle in such ideas, it seems to me that they deceive <the viewer> in their appearance, and <I think> that they have simply come down at the evident suffering of the Lord, some to serve him, others to marvel.

[835–42] If the Lord had not already died, you would see the lights <of heaven> paradoxically in conjunction, the moon passing in front of the sun at an unnatural time, and the sun exactly eclipsed and depriving the earth of its rays. But these things happened a short time ago, and now the passage of time has drawn apart their conjunction and once again they stand at the extreme of separation from one another.

[843–79] But that the painting is exact as regards the accuracy of art "is plain from the complexion," said a philosopher.[10] However, the marvel lies not in this but in the fact that the whole image seems to be living and is not without a share of motions. If one will but direct one's gaze to the parts of the picture one after another, it might seem to him that some might alter, some might increase, some might change, while some <seem> to experience or make a difference, as if presently waxing or waning. Hence the dead body <seems> apparently to be both living and lifeless. The outlines of such a painting might be seen even in images <produced> by the artless—namely, a similar straightening, breaking, or bending <of limbs>, an illusion of life by virtue of blood or of death by virtue of pallor—but these are all, so to speak,

10. This is the response by the dying Pherecydes to a question regarding his health asked by Pythagoras (see *Clavis patrum graecorum* 2 130,17).

imitations of figures and likenesses of likenesses. But here these things do not seem to take their existence from colors, rather the whole thing resembles nature, which is living and artlessly set in motion, and no one is able to discover whence the image has become like this. But, just as beauty exists as a result of the opposition and harmony of limbs and parts, and yet often a woman is extraordinarily radiant as a result of entirely different causes, so it is in this case. While this living painting exists as a result of component parts combined most felicitously, the entire living form seems to be beyond this, so that life exists in the image from two sources, from art, which makes a likeness, and from grace, which does not liken to anything else. Is this then a comparison of images and shadows? Yet I would not compare this painting to any other paintings, neither those set up by past hands or that represented the archetype accurately, nor those from our own time or from a little before that had made some innovations in form. I declare that this picture to be like my Christ in times past, when a bloodthirsty crowd brought out a vote of condemnation against him to a submissive Pilate. Thus, it seems to me that Christ hangs in the delineated and colored likeness. And I would not dispute that there is oversight that is beyond the painter's hand and that this overseeing mind had returned that painting to its prototype.[11]

11. This paragraph is altered from that found in Fisher's original translation. It now follows Barber's at Barber 2007: 77.

20 *Discourse on the Miracle that Occurred in the Blachernai Church*

Translated with introduction and notes
by Elizabeth A. Fisher

Introduction

Psellos' oration on the miracle at Blachernai is a command performance requested by the Emperor Michael VII Doukas in the summer of 1075 (lines 752–57).[1] Psellos examines a recent legal case at some length and in some detail, dividing his narrative of events into two separate episodes so that he may explore the philosophical and legal questions raised by particular aspects of the court system and of the final court decision. By combining the two episodes, we may reconstruct much of this remarkable case.

As a prologue to his narrative, Psellos describes an inexplicable phenomenon that regularly occurred at the Church of the Blachernai in Constantinople, where a lavishly decorated curtain hung in front of an ancient icon depicting the Virgin (100–163). Every Friday at sunset the church was cleared of all clergy and lay people, who waited in the courtyard while certain unspecified rituals were performed. At the conclusion of these rituals, the doors reopened, and the crowd reentered to observe the miraculous lifting of the curtain in front of the icon. Those present witnessed the form of the Virgin change and

1. Slightly different versions of this introduction and the translation that follows are available at http://chs.harvard.edu/wa/pageR?tn=ArticleWrapper&bdc=12&mn=5478.

appear animate or "ensouled," as Psellos says (138), establishing the real presence of the blessed Virgin at the moment of her miracle. Forestalling skeptical protests that some unknown natural process was the mechanical cause of the phenomenon, Psellos observes that the miracle was unlike a regular and predictable natural event such as an eclipse because the miracle occurred usually and predictably on Friday—but occasionally and unpredictably, it might cease.

Having established the nature and the validity of the Virgin's miracle at Blachernai, Psellos describes how this miracle figured in a court case. At issue was a mill in Thrace and the stream that powered it (164–271). Both the Constantinopolitan Monastery of Kallios and the general Leon Mandalos claimed exclusive rights to the mill, battling one another in a succession of lawsuits without any final and conclusive resolution. At last, the judge of the Thracian *theme* Gabriel Tzirithon delivered a verdict that required the two contending parties to share equally in controlling the property (193–94) and established that neither could control it exclusively. Although Psellos does not describe the rationale behind Tzirithon's decision, his verdict displeased both parties and especially enraged the general, who continued to quarrel bitterly with the monastery until the two opponents managed to reach a paradoxical agreement (210). They agreed to follow the legal precedent for designating a special judge to resolve the case; their judge, however, would be the Virgin, and her verdict would be delivered through the miracle at Blachernai. Under their binding agreement, the two parties would meet at daybreak in the church and individually present their case. If the "usual" miracle occurred at this unusual time, the general would win exclusive rights to the mill; if the miracle did not occur, the monks would be victorious. Not surprisingly, the contenders waited, but the curtain remained in its usual position in front of the icon until the monks ostentatiously began celebrating their victory, and the general surrendered—at which point, the curtain miraculously lifted, and the general triumphed! Reluctantly and with bad grace, the monks accepted defeat. Controversy over the verdict evidently continued, however, for Psellos explores the argument that the Virgin had expressed approval of the monks' position by timing her miracle to coincide with the general's surrender; he rejects this contention because the timing of the miracle had no place in the original agreement about the special court and the special judge (272–323). Before revealing the final episode in this dramatic story, Psellos once again confronts the monks' protest and once again rejects it (612–33), then notes that the judge Ioannes Xeros issued to the general official documents finally and decisively confirming the decision of the Virgin as special judge (643–49). To express his gratitude, the general returned to the Virgin's icon at the Church of Blachernai with his documents and prostrated himself before the icon. In sudden and miraculous confirmation of the general's victory, the icon's curtain lifted yet again and repeated for him the unusual occurrence of the Virgin's "usual" miracle (650–59).

The case of the powerful general and the clever and persistent monks presents compelling moments of confrontation and of suspense as well as a plot enriched by twists worthy of a Euripidean drama, for the Mother of God herself takes the role of the classical *deus ex machina*, resolving a seemingly insoluble dilemma not once but twice. Moreover, the chief actors and supporting cast represent important persons prominent at the highest levels of Byzantine society: the general Leon Mandalos (175), the judge in charge of Thrace, Gabriel Tzirithon (188–89), the final judge in the case, Ioannes Xeros (644–45), and representatives of the wealthy Monastery of Kallios in Constantinople (176). It is not surprising that Emperor Michael VII Doukas heard of this case, found it intriguing, and sought a full account of the matter from Psellos, exploring the particulars of the case and their implications in frequent discussions so detailed that the emperor finally became, as Psellos says, a virtual eyewitness to events. Michael VII then pressed Psellos to explicate the matter fully in what Psellos calls an "extemporaneous" oration (471–81).

Psellos' representation of himself as the close confidant and intellectual mentor of Michael VII Doukas is consistent with the relationship he describes in the work for which he is best known, the *Chronographia,* which concludes with an extraordinarily favorable description of Michael VII (*Chronographia* 7.165–75).[2] Psellos tells us that he served as tutor to Michael, who came to the

2. It is only fair to note that modern historians do not share Psellos' high estimation of Michael VII Doukas (a.k.a. "*Parapinakes,*" or "the market cheat," among his contemporaries because he reduced the quantity of goods sold at a fixed price). In the *ODB* s.v. he is described by Charles Brand and Anthony Cutler as "possibly slow mentally . . . an inactive ruler." The *Continuation of Skylitzes,* contemporary to Psellos, describes the Emperor Michael VII as a foolish dilettante rendered ineffectual by the degenerative influence of Psellos: "<himself> engrossed in trivialities and childish amusements, Michael Psellos, the Chief of the Philosophers, rendered <the Emperor Michael> incompetent and ineffectual as regards every serious pursuit"; ἀθύρμασι τοῦ Μιχαὴλ καὶ παιδιαῖς παιδαριώδεσι προσκειμένου, τοῦ ὑπάτου τῶν φιλοσόφων, τοῦ Ψελλοῦ, πρὸς ἅπαν ἔργον ἀδέξιον καὶ ἄπρακτον αὐτὸν ἀπεργασαμένου (*Continuation of Skylitzes* 156.6–8).

throne in his early twenties and even as emperor continued to look to his intellectual mentor for guidance with deep respect and affection (7.172). Psellos commends his prize student's exceptional personal moderation, political acumen, and humanistic learning, noting in particular his love of literature, sensitivity to style and diction, and mastery of all aspects of philosophy (7.168). One slight reservation, however, creeps into this fawning encomium: "Not having made a special study of legal matters," says Psellos, "he takes a broad view of their interpretation, and passes judgment rather in accordance with the spirit than with the letter of the law" (7.170; translation Sewter 1953: 370). Even in the eyes of a great admirer, therefore, Michael VII Doukas was not competent to assess the legal complexities presented in the case resolved at Blachernai by the Mother of God. For this reason, Psellos quite considerately dedicates substantial attention to an explanation of the laws relevant to the case (495–519, 559–611). Although in this oration Psellos does not mention any particular circumstance motivating Michael's interest in the legal aspects of the case, I would like to suggest the possibility that the emperor anticipated or had already received an appeal of the case from one of the contending parties (probably from the monks), for in Roman law, "The decision of the emperor has the force of law."[3]

At the point in his career when Psellos prepared this oration, both his formal education and his varied and extensive experience in the courts had given him a thorough acquaintance with Byzantine law. He had studied law under Ioannes Xiphilinos, the founder of the law school at Constantinople (1046–47), served first as an assistant to provincial judges and later as a provincial judge himself, taught law to his students, and composed legal documents and speeches for delivery in court.[4]

Byzantine civil law rested upon the *Corpus Iuris Civilis*, a collection of classical Roman legal texts executed under the sponsorship of the Emperor Justinian I in the sixth century and augmented by his own legislation (the *Novels*). Byzantium inherited the Greek version of the *Corpus*, applying and adapting it to the evolving needs of a changing society. At the time of Psellos,

3. *Quod principi placuit, legis habet vigorem* (Justinian, *Digest* I 4.1). This basic legal principle is stated even more forcefully in Byzantium as: "The emperor's decision is law" (Ὅπερ ἀρέσει τῷ βασιλεῖ νόμος ἐστίν, *Basilika* 2.6.2). I am grateful to George Sheets for an illuminating discussion of this aspect of Justinian's legislation.

4. Dennis 1994.

a ninth-century compilation of existing legislation in sixty books represented official and actual Byzantine law; this collection, known as the *Basilika*, eliminated superfluous and anachronistic material from the Justinianic corpus and incorporated more recent legislation.[5] Psellos cites in this oration the sections of the *Basilika* that pertain to the appointment and functions of a special judge, an accommodation to the procedures normally followed in determining the competent judge who had jurisdiction over a particular trial.

At this juncture, a brief excursus on Byzantine trials at the time of Psellos is useful. "Byzantium inherited from Rome a system of trying lawsuits that was based on the principles of a fair trial, a competent judge (πρόσφορος δικαστής), and legality of procedure and judgment—principles that of course had to be adapted to the conditions created by the 'absolute monarchy' of Byzantium."[6] The factors making a judge "competent" in a case like the one discussed by Psellos depended upon two sometimes competing criteria: the place of residence of the defendant and the category of the parties to the suit as defined under the law.[7] Members of the clergy, guilds, and the military, as well as senators, had the right to be tried by the magistrate in authority over them or, in the case of clergy and monks, by an ecclesiastical court. At least seven such magistrates who possessed jurisdiction to judge cases (μεγάλοι or "great" judges) can be identified from legal texts; since their positions were defined by their responsibilities for administration, finance, or the military and their appointments often dependent upon some connection with the emperor, they were not necessarily expert in the law. A great (or competent) judge accordingly sat with his subordinate (μικροί or "small") judges, who had no jurisdiction but were present in court and informed the great judge of relevant points of law in a case; a great judge—and only a great judge—could also delegate temporary jurisdiction in a case to another person. Although he often designated one of his own small judges, the parties in a case were permitted under law to agree upon their own "special judge" (αἱρετὸς δικαστής), as happened in the case decided by the Mother of God at Blachernai.

Under this system civil lawsuits were often protracted and, like the one described by Psellos, dragged on through "a long succession of judges" (187)

5. Cf. *ODB* s.v. "Law, Civil," "Corpus Juris Civilis," and "Basilika."

6. "Trials" s.v. *ODB*.

7. In describing Byzantine courts and judges, I have relied on the "Trials" entry in the *ODB* and primarily on Macrides 1994: 120–21.

because the criteria for determining a competent judge based on one of the parties' place of residence or classification in society could be in competition with the other's. In the case of the general and the monks, one party was in Thrace and the other in Constantinople.[8] In addition, while the general was entitled to trial under a military judge and the monks to trial in an ecclesiastical court, the legal system did not provide an effective procedure for successive appeals, a further factor in prolonging lawsuits.[9]

Aside from the necessity to explain the legal aspects of this case to the emperor, Psellos evidently considered it important to explicate for his imperial pupil the philosophical justification for the Virgin's court at Blachernai. He speaks as a philosopher of broad expertise as he attempts to explicate for Michael VII how the Virgin's actual presence could affect a material object in her miracle at Blachernai. Although the works of Plato are crucial to his thinking, Psellos also cites and paraphrases with comparable frequency the writings of Aristotle on logic, rhetoric, natural science, and ethics, as well as the late antique commentaries on these works by the Neoplatonists Alexander of Aphrodisias, Simplikios, Syrianos, and Ioannes Philoponos.[10]

To establish an appropriately learned tone for such a comprehensive and serious discussion, Psellos followed the usual practice of learned Byzantine authors and studded his prose with allusions to the *realia* and literature of antiquity. To cite but a few of many instances, Psellos refers to Hesiod's *Works and Days* at the beginning of the oration (14–17) and to Homer's *Iliad* in its closing sections (701–2); he makes an ironical comparison between a Byzantine appeals court and the ancient Athenian court of the Areopagos (557) and a metaphorical one between the structure of his oration and an ancient footrace (660–61); and he notes the role of augury in determining whether Romulus or Remus would give his name to Rome at its foundation (434–39). Despite his keen interest in ancient literature and culture, Psellos is also careful to assert the superiority of holy scripture over the writings of the Hellenes, as Byzantium called the pagan authors of classical and late antiquity. Concluding a detailed and very knowledgeable discussion of oracular practice among the Hellenes (356–416), Psellos observes piously, "However, I would be ashamed to compare the nonsense of the ancient Greeks with <oracular matters> that

8. Macrides 1994: 121.
9. *ODB* s.v. "Trials."
10. For Psellos' Neoplatonism, see passim in this volume.

both belong to us and are much superior" (417–18) before he proceeds to describe the oracular use of the Ephod and the Ark of the Covenant by the ancient Hebrews (420–29).

Throughout this long and complex work, Psellos has consistently referred to it as an "oration" (*logos*) and has even indicated at one point that he delivered the oration at the request of the emperor himself (476–78). In closing, Psellos describes his work as representing two distinct and very different genres—it is both a panegyric oration and a ὑπόμνημα, an official court document that explains the judge's rationale for his verdict. Psellos' use of this technical legal term recalls its occurrence earlier in the oration, when he applied it to the document from the court of Gabriel Tzirithon that so displeased both the general and the monks (204–5). Psellos' ὑπόμνημα is also, he claims, a panegyric, or an oration in praise of the Virgin (756–57). In composing his panegyric, Psellos has dared to articulate the ὑπόμνημα on behalf of the Virgin who served as a special judge through the unusual occurrence of her "usual" miracle at Blachernai.[11]

Editions and translations. The text used for this translation is *Or. hag.* 4 (pp. 200–229; bracketed numbers indicate the line numbering); other translations of various passages are indicated in the footnotes. See also the entry in Moore 2005: 363. Unlike practice elsewhere in this volume, words in angle brackets indicate words and phrases that are implied rather than stated in the Greek text.

11. See also Fisher 2012.

Discourse on the Miracle that Occurred in the Blachernai <Church>

[3–31] The court that was constituted <at Blachernai> was not a civil <institution> for investigating matters of civil law, but the place of judgment that resulted from the action of the virginal Mother of God was a mystical and ineffable <institution> for <solving> the problem set before her;[1] the decision it rendered was not human, but the discernment it reached was mystical, not a verdict and sentence pronounced by the lips of judges but a decision and a solution rendered from supernatural signs. She bore her child in an entirely new way (let me say it boldly!) and gave birth to the Word without the presence of man or of pain; it was proper that she also rendered the decree entrusted to her in an entirely new way, decided an ambiguous situation in a quite divine manner, and placed the matter in controversy beyond dispute. The narratives of the poets transport Justice from earth to the heavens and seat <her> in the councils of heaven to prevent all our lives from being deprived of justice and filled with lawlessness.[2] The discourses <belonging to> truth, however, state that the Mother of God descended among us from the very vault of heaven to correct and to better our <earthly> situation or, to put it more correctly, the divine and

1. Psellos adopts terminology ("setting forth a problem"; τοῦ προτεθέντος προβλήματος) used by Aristotle to introduce his logical treatise *Topics* (100a19).

2. According to Hesiod, Justice dwells on earth until she is treated disrespectfully; she then sits with her father Zeus in heaven and reports the offense, leaving him to exact punishment (*Works and Days* 256–62). For related references, see the commentary in West 1978: 221.

blessed nature of the Mother of God did not forsake the role allotted to her in heaven and also did not forget the nature she shares <with us>. But just as the Word born in his essence from her came down to earth without forsaking the thrones of his Father <in heaven>, and by putting on the whole <nature of> man he imparted salvation to the whole of human nature, in the same way she too imitates her Son to the extent possible and is both completely <in heaven> above and descends completely to us. Because she is united to his nature that cannot be circumscribed in a unity that is transcendent and incomprehensible, she herself necessarily surpasses incomparably the nearness to the divine <enjoyed by> the cherubim and also cannot be circumscribed; in every place she is infinite in both her noetic operations and capacities.[3]

[32–82] Her paradoxical <manifestations> occur in great number and in every place; some are apprehensible by the senses and others by the mind, some in physical symbols and others in ineffable thoughts. <They occur> in all cities, among all peoples, in each and every <one>, both collectively and singly. For sometimes she descends to us in visions, and sometimes she acts unseen among us, revealing in signs beyond description what cannot be apprehended by the senses. She fills all earth's boundaries with her own kind favors whenever it is opportune. By no means secondary <in importance> among her great miracles is also the manifestation that now <occurs> paradoxically, which <my> discourse will explain very clearly in due course. As for her identity as guardian and female savior of our people,[4] although no one knows how this is so and what sort of place she now occupies (nor will anyone of us here on earth ever understand, unless some soul transcends all earthly matters and assumes a place and capacity beyond that of the cherubim), nevertheless those of us who express devotion to her in foreshadowings, images, and icons, even in likenesses, one might say, that are unlike <her>,[5] we envision her inimitable nature that cannot be replicated. For we are indeed able on

3. The linkage "noetic operations and capacities" (ταῖς νοεραῖς ἐνεργείαις τε καὶ δυνάμεσι) is distinctive to the anonymous sixth-century mystical author Ps.-Dionysios the Areopagite; see his essay *On Divine Names* 144, line 7; 156, line 16; and 195, line 8.

4. Psellos applies the epithet σώτειρα to the Virgin Mary, using a classical term for the divine female guardian or τύχη of a city. Byzantines believed that the empire and the city of Constantinople were under the special protection of the Virgin, whose icon was taken onto the city walls at times of attack (*ODB* s.v. "Virgin Mary—Theological Perspectives," and s.v. "Virgin Hodegetria").

5. Psellos applies the same phrase "unlike likeness" or "dissimilar similarity" (ἀνόμοιος ὁμοιότης) to religious images also in his *Theol.* I 45.86. It is found frequently in

occasion to see the sun clearly and glance directly <at it> or, if we have poor eyesight, we observe it <reflected> in water or see the air illuminated <by it>,[6] and we judge from such evidence that we see <the sun itself> in some sense. In contrast, no one would see the virgin Mother of God in any place, not in the sky nor in the air, not by looking up nor by gazing upon the basic elements[7] <here> below, but the entities of nature[8] everywhere present do not know her, although she is everywhere.[9] When we portray <her> and produce likenesses <of her>, we apprehend her as revealed by those likenesses, and especially if we make some such <replica> not by <using> colors but by longing <for her> with inexpressible <fervor> and by <entering into> a close relationship with her through virtues.[10] No one could know the celestial paradigms themselves from the stars modeled upon them unless he could derive some small understanding of archetypes from their likenesses.[11] When we depict the Virgin we simultaneously place our heartfelt emotions in the painting, and we then

---

Ps.-Dionysios, who borrows it from Syrianos and Proklos. The concept is that "Symbols serve as analogies not in the sense that they bear similarity to the thing, but rather because they bear images of the divine paradigms, which may themselves be dissimilar" (see Wear and Dillon 2007: 85 with n. 3); for this notion in Psellos, cf. also pp. 136 and 148 above.

6. Psellos borrows this metaphor from Iamblichos' *Life of Pythagoras* (15.67.1–5). In the following discussion he develops the idea of the close relationship between the Virgin and mankind using the Platonic term "sympathy" (line 68, συμπάθεια) and the Stoic term "affinity" (lines 60, 66, οἰκείωσις) as he approaches an explanation of the oracular use of her icon (cf. Ierodiakonou 2006: 109–10, 116).

7. The *stoicheia* were presumably earth, fire, water, and air (cf. Plato *Timaeus* 31b–32b).

8. Aristotle employs the term αἱ φύσεις for natural "entities" such as "fire and earth" in *Metaphysics* 987a17 and in his fragmentary *Protreptikos* fr. 36.1 (see also Iamblichos in his *Protreptikos* 39.5); Psellos also reflects this sense of αἱ φύσεις in *Poem.* 24.200.

9. In the classical world, indications of future events and of the will of the gods were interpreted from natural phenomena such as earthquakes, eclipses, thunder, or exceptional animal behavior (cf. *OCD* s.v. "Portents"). Psellos denies the reliability of such procedures if applied to the Virgin.

10. Psellos commends devotion to the Virgin by emulating her moral qualities also in K-D 124, namely, *Letter Two*, pp. 362–65 below.

11. Psellos recalls the Platonic theory of "Forms," the true realities of things (ἰδέαι) and their visible manifestations (εἴδεα), by using the terms "likenesses" (εἰκάσματα) and "archetypes" (ἀρχέτυποι) here and also in his *Theol.* I 90.43–44; this terminology is particular to Psellos. The locus classicus for "Forms" is of course Plato's myth of the cave (*Republic* 507a–521b, esp. 507b–508d).

perceive her outward appearance with our eyes inasmuch as such things can be perceived, while in our souls we receive her imprint through this experience. Thus we grow into an inexpressibly close relationship with her, and she feels an <even> more ineffable sympathetic affection towards humankind. To put it boldly, God has approached and withdrawn in proportion to the purification of our souls and, in turn, in proportion to our disfigurement by the passions; we are like a mirror of the radiance from God, lustrous when we receive it and dull when deprived of it. However, the compassionate nature of the Mother of God, supernatural in her love for mankind, reveals itself to all alike, both to those whose souls shine brightly and to those whose minds are still <dull and> muddy. A person could see her with his own eyes insofar as it would be possible to see—not only <someone> among those greatest and loftiest in merit, but even some simple, insignificant woman who attends upon the Virgin's icon from the back <of the crowd> and mumbles her hymn incorrectly. <The Virgin> welcomes with approval the most excellent form not of words and phrases but of souls; she finds a close relationship <with us> not in the way one arranges words but in the way one harmoniously conducts oneself.[12]

[83–111] Her precincts are many throughout <Constantinople>, the Queen of Cities, and all are filled with her divine voice; both those <in> priestly orders and those assigned to these <precincts> speak under her inspiration. In some of these she is portrayed high up in the sanctuary, painted among the angelic powers that guard her, while in others she is represented upon the walls, so those who enter can draw near to <her> and be filled with the glory shining from the <walls>. In some places she is represented on materials that are fundamentally different; on occasion some place her likeness on gold, while some engrave silver. In some places a wooden panel contains a representation of her; she does not reject proximate matter as unworthy.[13] To make a comparison, the Son of the Virgin is believed to dwell in every place, and rather above or even beyond everything, that is, in heaven, according to a great number of excellent <sources>; at any rate, we choose to call for his help by immediately raising our hands up to heaven, not because we wish to con-

12. I have benefited from Charles Barber's translation and discussion of this difficult passage; see Barber 2007: 88–90.

13. Psellos apparently expects his audience to appreciate and admire his application to theology of the Aristotelian contention that a form finds its particular realization in "proximate matter" (ἐσχάτη ὕλη). Aristotle illustrates this concept with the example of a bronze ("proximate matter") triangle ("form") in *Metaphysics* 1040b18; see also *Metaphysics* 1035b30.

fine him to that place, but as if to set apart a place that is better for one who is better and to set him apart[14] from the material <world>. In the same way, also the one who bore him is present in a supernatural way and is manifested in each of her divine shrines but is especially acknowledged to dwell at the renowned church in Blachernai, <where> she clearly demonstrates divine signals.[15] Her visitations cannot be circumscribed, however, for some <of these signals are manifested> not at any set time and others within prescribed periods that she does not customarily transgress, unless some inexplicable reason causes her miracle to halt after long periods of time. The <wondrous> miracle and its performance exceed even our capacity to wonder at <them>. And now, to avoid being the sort of person who offers excessive elaborations upon something so well known,[16] I will make a brief comment about this <matter> and cut short the great amount <I could say> about her divine nature.

[112–46] Her icon hangs nicely fitted on the right of the church as one enters facing east. <It is> inimitable in form, incomparable in beauty, unrivalled in potency. A veil of intricately woven <fabric> hangs from the icon, and a cluster of images composed of precious materials encircles the <veil>.[17] The area near her is another sanctuary, where all the <things> prescribed for celebrants and celebrations[18] are reverently dedicated to her—all sorts of hymns, prayers of propitiation, offerings appropriate to a sacred place. The ritual celebrated here on the sixth day of the week (i.e., on Friday) after sunset is extraordinary. At that time, everyone leaves the church, not just the crowd of lay people but also any priests and celebrants,[19] and of these not only the

14. Psellos delights in word play, juxtaposing here two words sharing the same etymological root, ἐξ-αιροῦντες ("reserving, setting apart") and ἀφ-αίρεμα ("something reserved, set apart").

15. This large basilica in the northwestern quarter of Constantinople, built by Justinian in the early sixth century and described by Prokopios (*Buildings* I 3.3), resembled both Qalb Loze in Northern Syria and St. Sophia in Thessalonika; see Papadopoulos 1928: 107–10. See also Moutafov 2008.

16. For the translation of this phrase, see Papaioannou 2001: 183n36.

17. A sheer protective curtain (καταπέτασμα, πέπλος, or ἐγχείριον), often of costly silk decorated with embroidered or woven figures, frequently hung in front of an icon; see Nunn 1986: 76–83. Such a curtain, drawn up to reveal the icon it covered, appears in two images of the fourteenth century; see Evans 2004: 153–55, figs. 77, 78.

18. Stratis Papaioannou suggests that the phrase τοῖς τελοῦσι καὶ τελουμένοις can also be taken in its pagan and Neoplatonic sense, "initiators and initiates."

19. Psellos apparently distinguishes two categories of clergy with the virtually synonymous Greek words θύται (translated here as "priests") and τελεσταί ("celebrants"). τελεσταί is favored by Proklos to designate pagan priests.

ones who are circulating through "the worldly sanctuary"[20] but even any who could pass inside the veil <of the sanctuary> and offer the ineffable <occult>[21] sacrament. What <happens> next? All the entrance gates of the precinct are fastened shut while the crowd stands in the forecourt of the church near the outer entrance. When the officiating priests have completed the regular rituals, it is customary for God's palace to be opened straightaway. Once it is opened, entrance is granted to those standing in front of the church. They enter with commingled fear and joy,[22] while the drapery surrounding the icon lifts all of a sudden, as if some breath of air gently moved it. What happens is unbelievable to those who do not witness it, but for those who do, <it is> wondrous and an overt descent of the Holy Spirit. The form of the handmaiden of the Lord[23] changes simultaneously with what is accomplished,[24] I think, as it receives her animate[25] visitation, thereby visibly signaling the invisible. In fact, the veil of the Temple[26] was torn for her Son and God when he was hanging upon the cross so that he might either manifest the truth concealed in the marks impressed <by his presence> or summon believers into the inner sanctums[27] and destroy the barrier preventing us from a close relationship with God. In contrast, the holy drapery raises itself for the Mother of God in an ineffable fashion so that she may embrace within herself the crowd that enters as if within some new inner sanctum and refuge that cannot be violated.[28]

20. Psellos uses terminology drawn from Hebrews 9:1 to describe the sections of the church open to lay people as "the worldly sanctuary" (τὸ ἅγιον κοσμικόν).

21. Psellos describes the holy sacrament using τελετή, a word with pagan and Neoplatonic connotations; he may be distinguishing priests from deacons, who "circulate" among the laity.

22. Psellos paraphrases the reaction of the women who found Christ's tomb empty (Matthew 28:8).

23. See Luke 1:38.

24. Pentcheva 2010: 188–90 sees in τῷ τελουμένῳ a reference to the operation of the Holy Spirit in the Eucharistic transformation ("transubstantiation") here and in lines 329–30.

25. The meaning of the Greek term ἔμψυχος, which I have translated here as "animate," is the subject of lively scholarly discussion; see, for example, Barber 2007: 80–98.

26. See Matthew 27:51 = Mark 15:38 = Luke 23:45.

27. Psellos combines and paraphrases Hebrews 6:19 and Ephesians 2:14.

28. I have benefited from other translations of this important passage. See Grumel 1931: 136–37; Belting 1994: 511–12; Papaioannou 2001: 184–86; Pentcheva 2000: 46–47; Barber 2007: 80–89.

[147–63] The appropriate time for this miracle has been determined, as I have said. At some point, however, the event halts, and in her case it is like a darkening of the sun, whenever it draws to a halt in the celestial latitudes near one of the ecliptic conjunctions, and the bulk of the moon passes in front of it, blocking the radiance <the sun> sends upon us. Nevertheless, those who are quite learned in the skill of astronomy understand the cause of such a so-called eclipse, and one could cite this as an account of the position <of the sun and the moon>.[29] In contrast, no one would dare cite a <natural> cause for the miracle of the Mother of God "eclipsing." I think that the halting of the miracle is designed to prevent anyone from lighting upon physical causes for what is accomplished. The "eclipse" of the prodigy exists rather as a more exact confirmation of the paradoxical and supernatural <nature of the> event.[30] So the miracle is; it exists like day and night that arrive and depart in succession, and its manner <of occurrence> is as my oration has stated.

[164–86] Based on <that miracle> a yet more wondrous <event> occurred. It originated in <the usual miracle>, but by its untimely occurrence it manifested a miracle in an <even> more timely way. Whatever was it, then? In general for people, and especially for those in the countryside and in villages, it is highly desirable if one of them can have an extremely abundant <supply of> running water and a mill capable of grinding by <waterpower>, so that grain may be easily and conveniently milled at this <mill>.[31] Indeed many have disputed with their rural neighbors over both <water and mill>,

29. In this passage Psellos uses vocabulary particular to learned astronomers (ἐκλειπτικῶν συνδέσμων, "ecliptic conjunctions"; ἐπισκότισις, "darkening"; σχῆμα, "astronomical position"; ἐπέχεται, "halts"; and the related noun ἐποχή, "positioning of a celestial body," which occurs also at line 108), clearly including himself among them; for similar passages, see his *Concise Answers to Various Questions* 128.4 and *Encomiastic Speech about the Most-blessed Patriarch Kyr Keroularios* 312.13 (Sathas IV).

30. Psellos regularly maintains the importance of differentiating between genuine miracles and the unexpected events that occur according to the natural processes described by (pagan) Greek philosophers; see Kaldellis 2007: 202–6.

31. Since watermills represented a form of light industry that could significantly improve the local economy of a region, they were regulated by complex legislation affecting various parties involved in their ownership and operation as early as the seventh–ninth centuries in the *Farmer's Law*. By Psellos' time simple horizontal mills that required little water were built and operated not only by large landowners but also by peasants and small monasteries; disputes over the use of water for mills vs. for crop irrigation were not uncommon. See A. Harvey 1989: 130–34. For a valuable study of the role of mills in the Byzantine economy, see Laiou and Simon 1992: 645–66 or 23–42.

contending with one another; the courts are filled with dispute<s> about these <matters>. Two parties were caught up in such a controversy not long ago, <specifically> the *spatharios*[32] and general Leo, surnamed Mandalos,[33] and the party <representing> the monastery Tou Kalliou.[34] Now the mill was located in the district of Thrace and powered by an abundant water <supply>; each of the two parties registered themselves as indisputable owner of the <rights> awarded now to one, now to the other. They had disputed the <particulars> of the case many times. Each party in turn prevailed and suffered defeat, became victor or vanquished, sometimes according to the documents they presented,[35] sometimes pursuing their own claims in a quite persuasive manner and sometimes, you can be sure, taking in exchange <rights of> ownership and usage with a hand able to give lesser or greater <benefits> in each situation and for every judge.[36]

[187–202] After <coming before> a long succession of judges, the case even reached the *dishypatos* Gabriel Tzirithon, who was at that time responsi-

32. In this period, powerful persons held the purely honorary title *spatharios* that carried no duties, although it originally designated a member of the imperial bodyguard (see *ODB* s.v. "Spatharios").

33. Although the general Leon Mandalos does not seem to be mentioned in any other source, I am grateful to John Nesbitt for bringing to my attention two early eleventh-century seals of Leon Mantoules (an alternative spelling of the surname Mandalos?), whose rank and profession are not identified (see Laurent 1952: 230–31, nos. 456, 457).

34. This Constantinopolitan monastery, identified variously as τοῦ Καλέως, τοῦ Καλλίου, and τοῦ Καυλέα, was closely linked with St. Antony Kauleas, the ninth-century patriarch buried at the monastery who had lived there both as monk and as abbot; its power and influence continued into the mid-fifteenth century, when its abbot accompanied the emperor and the patriarch to the Council of Florence (see Laurent 1965: 80–81). For the biography of Antony Kauleas, his patriarchal seal, and his image on the seal of the monastery and in the Menologion of Basil II (Vat. Gr. 1613), see Cotsonis and Nesbitt 2004. I am grateful to Alice-Mary Talbot for identifying this reference to the monastery and to John Nesbitt for the relevant bibliography.

35. The *Peira*, an eleventh-century collection of secular judicial rulings, provides a valuable if limited insight into judicial proceedings in the Byzantine provinces. Written evidence in one case consisted of a previous agreement between the peasants and a monastery involved in a land dispute, a report from the *epoptes* (the official responsible for recording boundaries in land sales), an imperial chrysobull issued to the monastery, and a document specifying the inexact report of the *epoptes*. See Morris 1986.

36. Before rendering a decision, the judge in a case typically sought advice in writing from respected local figures and officials versed in the particulars of a dispute. Bribery under such a system was not uncommon. See Morris 1986: 138–40.

ble for legal decisions in the district of Thrace.[37] Both he as well as those involved in the ensuing judgment know better <than I> whatever judgment the presiding judge gave. At the conclusion <of the hearing>, the general lost the case by half, for the decision to distribute <rights to the property> was such as to deprive <each party> equally of ownership and of complete loss. For both parties became half owners, as one might say, of the <object of their> contest, themselves contesting legitimate ownership—the general because of what he did not possess but hoped to possess, the party of Tou Kalliou because of what they possessed and thought they would lose. For <they thought> that the general would not remain silent, wronged in every respect, as he saw it, and robbed regarding his property, because the judicial decision in the <matter> in question, I mean, was half in favor of the monastery.

[203–37] Thereupon <the general> refused to accept the verdict but resumed his earlier <wrestler's> grip, as they say.[38] He expressed contempt for the judge's memorandum of the proceedings[39] as half-favorable to the monks and not completely and fully penalizing them. Multiple assertions on multiple occasions were then made in turn by both <parties>, and the details of the judgment were under discussion for some time, but there was not yet agreement on <another> court by those who were still quarrelling after the judge

37. In Psellos' time the title *dishypatos* (literally, "twice-consul") was held by judges as well as by provincial and imperial bureaucrats assigned fiscal and archival responsibilities; see *ODB* s.v. "Dishypatos." The collection of lead seals preserved at Dumbarton Oaks includes a seal of Gabriel Tzirithon dated to 1084; see Nesbitt and Oikonomides 1991: 1:158, no. 71.11. On this seal, Tzirithon is identified as the judge (κριτής) of the Thracian *theme* (θέμα); although the *theme* was originally a territorial unit under a general with both civil and military power, by the eleventh century a civil governor (κριτής) assumed many of the functions formerly assigned to a general (see *ODB* s.v. "Theme").

38. The metaphor of the wrestler's grip applied to the line of argumentation taken by a participant in a dispute originates in Plato's *Phaedrus* 236b9–c1: "Now, my friend, you have given me a fair hold; for you certainly must speak as best you can" (trans. H. N. Fowler, Loeb series, 1938: 441), Περὶ μὲν τούτου, ὦ φίλε, εἰς τὰς ὁμοίας λαβὰς ἐλήλυθας. ῥητέον μὲν γάρ σοι παντὸς μᾶλλον οὕτως ὅπως οἷός τε εἶ.

39. The legal opinion or official memorandum (ὑπόμνημα) was prepared by one of the judges to summarize the arguments presented in a case for discussion by the other judges, who then dated, signed, and sealed the document; the final decision with a brief justification (σημείωμα) was composed on the basis of the official memorandum (Oikonomides 1986: 177). Two such memoranda attributed to Psellos survive (*Or. for.* 4 and 6). For a translation of the first, see Jenkins 2006: 147–56.

delivered his decision. Both parties, however, eventually came together in a compact against all expectations and constituted a special court for themselves that originated from civil laws but in their case did not take its final form based on civil laws. For they did not set up for themselves a court in which they reached mutual agreement upon someone among the judges—a mid-level judge, or a special judge, or one having some other qualifications, since this is the law, and also <it is the law> not to put full confidence in the <judge's> sentences, if he should be a special <judge>. Instead <the two parties> made the Mother of God the arbitrator in the case. How? They did not fly up to heaven, for <this> is not possible, nor did they bring her down here <to earth>,[40] for this is also outside the realm of possibility, but they staked everything upon the decision of the icon's miracle. They undertook a bold initiative that was also contrary to the normal timing of the divine sign, and they each chose a scenario for their own side—whether in a just manner or by the monks' design, I do not know—but they made their choice in this way: that each party would stand together at daybreak in the presence of the icon of her who bore God while holding in their hands the legal documents upon which they were relying for the strength <of their case> and <with which> they were both making storms <of controversy> for one another concerning these <matters>; that they would make this a kind of court that was innovative and reflected the judgment of God, then summon the Virgin in the icon and cry out plaintively <for her> to judge their case with justice and to make a decision by means of the drapery; that if it remained unmoved, the monks would claim victory in the case, but if it was moved, the general would claim the <spoils> of victory and bind <upon his head> another crown <won> against his foes <and> greater than a general's trophy. After this decision was agreed upon, copies were also made of the written documents regarding the provisions of their agreement, such as is customary in the case of special judges.

[238–42] When everything was completed—the entrance into the church, the attendance at the icon, the prayer, the tears, and whatever people usually do in such <circumstances>—they stood still because they <both> feared for their own side and considered valid the <Virgin's> decision <that would be expressed> by the drapery's movement or failure to move.

[243–53] As the time for the sentence they awaited slipped by, the drapery remained yet unmoved. This seemed <to represent> a judgment and deci-

40. Psellos refers to John 3:13 and to Romans 10:6.

sive point. The monks began to boast about their victory and at that point the general lost his case, as if he had received a black pebble[41] regarding culpability in military matters. The other party was applauding, making a din like castanets with their hands, so to speak, and cackling aloud, while the general stood scowling with eyes fixed upon the floor because he had lost his case by a decision that was divine. He then yielded to the monks in the matter they had long disputed and surrendered to them the documents favoring his claim by placing these in <the monks'> hands.

[254–71] What then was your role in these <matters>, you who paid heed to the good news of <the angel> Gabriel,[42] you who conceived the Logos beyond all logic, you who loaned to God flesh from yourself? I hope to avoid conviction on charges of blasphemy <when I ask> if you did not know the means of determining the verdict more exactly? Or did you know, but delay revealing your verdict? Or did you not delay <your verdict>, but reveal it in a way different from the customary one, but with ambiguity, with obscurity, as if by a lapse of attention? No, none of the above! When, however, the general counted out and gave over to the monks the documents favoring his claim as if they were owed like a debt, you immediately raised the fabric dressing[43] your icon, lifted it on high by its cords, and made it rest in midair so that the decisive point would be completely clear. The result was a reversal of emotions <by the two parties>; the ones laughing suddenly scowled and the one wearing a scowl suddenly relaxed with relief, freed <of anxiety> and <his heart> filled with contentment and delight. Even if the monastic party seemed to behave somewhat shamelessly and shamelessly asserted that the sentence came after the time <agreed upon>, nevertheless they eventually acknowledged their defeat and conceded victory to the general.

41. Psellos uses a popular idiomatic expression explained by the tenth-century *Suda* lexicon as "the black pebble, the one that gives sentence against a person, while the white <one> gives sentence in his favor"; Ψῆφος μέλαινα· ἡ καταδικάζουσα· λευκὴ δὲ ἡ δικαιοῦσα (ed. Adler, IV 845.24–25, §85). Using pebbles to vote in a capital trial is an ancient practice referred to frequently in both Greek and Latin literature as early as the fifth century BCE (see Aeschylus, *Eumenides* 674–753). In the first century CE the Roman authors Ovid (*Metamorphoses* XV 42–45) and Pliny (*Epistles* I 2.5) and the Greek author Plutarch refer to the white pebble for acquittal and the black one for condemnation.

42. Psellos refers to the annunciation narrative as it occurs in Luke 1:26–36.

43. Until this point in the narrative, Psellos has referred to the πέπλος ("drapery") of the icon or to its καταπέτασμα ("veil"), but here he uses a word specific to clothing, ἔνδυμα ("garment") and at line 655 the general term περιβόλαιον ("wrap, covering").

[272–97] Some of those who opposed <the verdict> interpreted the sign in favor of their cause and regarded the movement <of the drapery> as a ratification and confirmation of the judgment for themselves because the drapery did not move quickly nor did the symbol of its divine possession occur simultaneously with the <general's> prayer, but <rather> when the general gave over the written judgments in the matter under dispute. This <objection> is insufficient to require a counterargument. For the <two> adversaries did not make an agreement that the movement of the drapery should occur immediately or after a <definite> time. Instead, the general obtained as his lot in the litigation the movement <of the drapery>, while the monks assigned to themselves that the drapery remain motionless. Now if at the time <the drapery> had remained still during the whole <process>, and the contending parties had parted from one another after already leaving the church, and a considerable length of time had elapsed after that, and then the symbol<ic movement> occurred on the same day or later, <the monks'> right of possession would not be in dispute. For the Virgin who was giving the verdict was allowed to determine the proper time for her to announce it, since not even a civil judge would make a decision and announce it immediately, but after determining his decision he delays his sentence until whatever proper time he might wish. Since she decided to delay the movement for a short time, and those who were contending with one another as parties in the case were still standing in the holy precinct, and the divine decree coincided with the <general's> distribution of his documents, and the Virgin in making her decision announced her verdict in a quite innovative manner, what reason is there to oppose it? For they[44] had not associated penalties with the timing of the symbol<ic movement>, but the Virgin knew the right time for the <drapery to> move.

[298–323] "Yes indeed," say <the monks>, "but the <drapery> moved after the surrender of the documents, witnessing as it were to the justice of the surrender." Someone, even someone just chancing upon <the monks>, might say, "But the movement <of the drapery> fell to the lot of the general, and to you its lack of movement. If then it remained still during the entire time, yours <was> the victory. But if it moved, this <victory> is assigned to the side of the general, and, just as you would have won if no movement had occurred, so he has prevailed because it did." I, however, say the movement of the drap-

44. Reading αὐτοῖς for the manuscript's αὐτοί.

ery was not simply an announcement of a verdict, but <an expression> of outright wrath. For the <icon's> garment was shaken at the very moment when you dared to take the documents. Because of what you quite shamelessly did, the Virgin moved <the drapery>, and the symbolic movement represents at once both a sentence favoring the general and a sign of anger against those who already behaved so shamelessly. In this way God is accustomed to sit in judgment and to bring forward His condemnations, not whenever one might wish to transgress, but whenever one might commit or be about to commit the transgression. To Him whom the <divine> mother imitates in loving mankind she likens herself exactly in punishing <mankind>.[45] And the contrast <between love and punishment> is not at all forced, but the logic is both consistent and most true. Thus if someone should not accept the miraculous decree and should not regard what happened with awe but should worry excessively over the miracle, he would all the more be struck by what is opposite <to it>. Just as if someone with weak eyes should dare to stare at the sun where it stands at midday in the season of summer, he would not see <the sun> and would perhaps be deprived of the power of visual perception.

[324–55] This <miracle> could bear no comparison with other <miracles>, but seems to me more astonishing and more miraculous than the usual <miracle at Blachernai>. For that <usual miracle> is customary, and its exact time is known, and <it has> some sort of cycle that is, so to speak, fixed, like the rising of the sun. This however seems to be some sort of prodigy and an innovative action <occurring> now for the first time and a new manifestation[46] of the Spirit and a visitation of the Mother of God that has newly appeared. For through all past history it has never happened in this way, neither based upon such agreements <between parties> nor regarding such decisions. However, even though the risings of the sun are also a paradox, of course it does not shake the very hearts of observers as entirely miraculous when regularly seen—but we are astonished upon hearing <the story of> when the sun

45. Gregory of Nazianzos links God's simultaneous love and punishment of mankind (φιλανθρωπία, τιμωρία); see *On the Theophany* = *Or.* 38.12 and *On Easter* = *Or.* 45.9. This linkage reflects the sense of Hebrews 12:6, "For whom the Lord loveth, he chasteneth, and scourgeth every son whom he receiveth" (ὃν γὰρ ἀγαπᾷ κύριος παιδεύει, μαστιγοῖ δὲ πάντα υἱὸν ὃν παραδέχεται = Proverbs 3:12). See also Proverbs 13:24 and Revelation 3:19.

46. I have followed Cotsonis 1994: 225 in translating ἔμφασις as "manifestation."

stood over against Gabaon and the moon over against the valley <of Aelon> after Joshua son of Naue received from God leadership of the people of Israel.[47] We consider what happened at the cross of the Lord yet more miraculous than this, when midday stood still, and the sun held the very cardinal point of its zenith, and the moon was in the fourteenth day <of its cycle> and at its nadir and then canceled its <normal> courses to appear above the horizon and darken the sun by slipping in front of it.[48] (I omit mentioning also the prodigy concerning Hezekiah, when the sun traveled backward so that he might be assured that years would be added <to his life>.[49]) Accordingly, in this case surely a single <occurrence of the miracle> at an unexpected time is more astonishing than its frequent <manifestations> in a defined manner. Who could know if this might be a pattern for future innovations, and, should human courts come to a standstill after encountering disputed matters and failing repeatedly in their purpose, the Virgin would also decide complex investigations by easily managing <judicial> inquiries as well as announcements of verdicts. Thus would our life be without disputes, and a person would be least likely to devote himself to intentional wrongdoing if he faces immediate conviction by divine symbols.

[356–86] As for the oracular responses of the ancient Greeks—however many <there might be> at Dodona and at Pythian <Delphi>, however many <might> otherwise enjoy a good reputation, and as many as Amphiareus and Amphilochos would deliver in a shrine hidden in the earth—<these> are riddling, oblique, and ambiguous.[50] In addition, "the wooden wall" was contested

47. After designating Joshua as Moses' successor, God granted his request to stop the sun and the moon in their courses for a day so that the Israelites could destroy the Amorite army at Gibeon. See Joshua 1:1–2 and 10:12–13; translation after Brenton 1851.

48. The eclipse that occurred during the crucifixion of Christ is described in Luke 23:44. Psellos' specific reference to the "fourteenth day of the moon" as the date of the Jewish Passover reflects ancient Hebrew practices as discussed by Sozomenos (*Ecclesiastical History* 8.18).

49. God caused the sun to turn back upon its course in order to ratify his promise that Hezekiah's lifespan would be increased by fifteen years; see Isaiah 38:5–8.

50. Eusebios (*Praeparatio evangelica* X 4.7) specifies these same ancient deities as particularly prolific in delivering oracles—Apollo at Pythian Delphi and at Claros in Ionia, Zeus at Dodona, Amphiareus at Oropos, and Amphilochos at Cilician Mallos and in Akarnania. All four oracles relied upon an altered state of human consciousness to convey their messages. In Delphi and at Dodona priestesses went into a mantic trance to deliver the god's words (see Plato, *Phaedrus* 244b), while Amphiareus and Amphilochos appeared in visions or in dreams to suppliants at their shrines (see Clement of Alexandria, *Protreptikos* 2.11.2 and Lucian, *Philopseudes* 38.2).

<regarding its meaning>,[51] and "the great empire that Croesus would destroy by crossing the Halys River" was highly disputed regarding its identity and interpreted in two ways.[52] Also, Bacis and the Sibyl did not shoot forth arrow-straight prophecies relevant to the target set out <by the questioner>, but their prophecies were dispatched consistent with probable inferences.[53] In contrast, what I might call the oracle of the Virgin dispatches no double meaning as sophists might do in the problems they formulate,[54] nor does <her oracle> contradict itself with riddles, but <she gives her response> in accordance with the agreement someone might choose regarding the movement or lack of movement of the drapery, that is, whether it should move immediately or remain in an unmoved state. In Plato's opinion, the priestesses and prophetesses in their frenzied madness were of greater potency than if they had chosen prudent restraint, and he reiterates this frequently in his dialogue with Gorgias.[55] I however would be half-mad if I considered madness better and

51. Herodotus (*Histories* VII 140–44) describes how the Athenians sent a delegation to consult the Delphic oracle regarding Xerxes' imminent invasion of Greece. The oracle's cryptic advice to seek safety behind the wooden wall prompted a debate at Athens; should the population barricade themselves on the Acropolis behind a wooden palisade, or should they trust the wooden hulls of the navy to defend them? The latter interpretation prevailed and resulted in the stunning Athenian victory over the Persian fleet at Salamis.

52. Psellos refers to the famous oracle of Apollo in which the god did not specify to the Lydian king Croesus whether invading Persia by crossing the Halys River would result in the fall of the Persian or of the Lydian Empire; for the full story, see Herodotus *Histories* I 53–55, 90–91. Psellos slightly varies the wording of a frequently quoted formulation of this oracle, "By crossing the Halys, Croesus would destroy a great kingdom" (Κροῖσος Ἅλυν διαβὰς μεγάλην ἀρχὴν καταλύσει), which first occurred in Empedocles (Fr. 25, line 14) and also appears in Aristotle (*Rhetoric* 140a39) and his commentators Ammonios and Elias, as well as in the writings of Diodoros of Sicily, Eusebios, Malalas, Konstantinos VII Porphyrogennetos, et al.

53. "Bacis" and "Sibyl" referred not to individual historical/mythological figures but rather to a category of divinely inspired persons who uttered prophecies (see Aristotle *Problemata* 954a36); the ancient scholion to Aristophanes *Birds* 962.1 identifies three prophets at different locations called "Bacis" and three called "Sibyl." Plutarch attaches to these prophets the proverbial label "good guesser" (ὁ εἰκάζων καλῶς, see Plutarch, *On the Delphic Oracle* 399A4–7), a skepticism reflected by Psellos when he declares that they depended for their prophecies upon Aristotle's "probable inferences" (οἱ ἔνδοξοι συλλογισμοί; see Aristotle, *Sophistical Refutations* 170a40, *Topics* 161b35, etc.).

54. Psellos may be referring obliquely here to the series of judges and courts that had failed to render a consistent decision in the legal case he has described.

55. Psellos has apparently confused Plato's *Gorgias* with his *Phaedrus* here; Plato, *Phaedrus* 244a–d contains his fulsome endorsement of manic prophecy.

superior to prudent restraint, and I would also feel shame if I should ascribe prudent restraint to the Mother of God—if indeed prudent restraint is composure of the soul when the passions have been subdued by her, just as self-control is <composure> of the intellect when it represses the impulses of the soul towards inferiority[56]—in contrast, the Virgin <is> superior to all prudent restraint in surpassing the very summits of the virtues. However, if there should be some oracular sites that are fit for God and of heavenly origin, where the more worthy <supernatural> powers foretell the outcome of events to come and from which and where signs of the future are indicated, the Virgin would possess the best and most truthful <of such oracular sites>, from which her earthly altars are also filled with streams of quite divine illumination.

[387–416] The ancient Greeks pursued empty and frivolous ends by resorting to their particular kinds of oracles and by preparing telestic rites for them that invested certain statues with divine frenzy so they could respond to inquiries.[57] For either the rite they <celebrated> was only half effective and the oracular site of no effect, or the presiding spirit was quite closely attached to the material world and wandered in the realm of things that will happen in the future.[58] Moreover the whirling motion of Hekate's <wheel accomplished> by her ox-hide thong and <accompanied by> the invocation of the Iynxes[59] are

56. Psellos recalls Aristotle *On Virtues and Vices* 1250a6–10 and 1250b11–14, where "prudent restraint" (σωφροσύνη) and "self-control" (ἐγκράτεια) are both described as curbing the desire for base pleasures.

57. Psellos here introduces the dangerous subject of occult practices with an appropriate tone of Christian disdain. He had himself thoroughly studied the now fragmentary Chaldean Oracles, basic to the Neoplatonic doctrines supporting magical rites that were emphatically condemned by the Church. For Psellos' attitude towards magic, see Duffy 1995: 83–90. Psellos' vocabulary in this passage recalls that of the Oracles, i.e., "telestic" or "mystical" (*Oracles* 110, 136, 196) and "speak in a divine frenzy" (*Oracle* 194); citations are to Majercik 1989.

58. The Neoplatonic hierarchy of deities included at the lowest level a triad of divine spirits mediating between the highest gods and the human, material world. Majercik 1989: 1–49 provides a lucid discussion of this complex system; for these Lesser Beings, see Majercik 1989: 8–11. Note that Psellos does not deny the existence of such divinities.

59. Hekate was one of the three chief deities in the Neoplatonic system (Majercik 1989: 7). Chaldean ritual used the whirling motion (στροφάλιγξ, Oracles 12, 49, 87) of Hekate's magical wheel (στρόφαλος) activated by a leather strap to imitate the ceaseless motion of the heavens and to attract for prophetic purposes the lesser spirits called Iynxes (Majercik 1989: 29–30). Psellos gives a detailed description of Hekate's *strophalos* (see *Phil. min.* II 38 133.16–24).

all mere empty words without any effect; even if they should effect something, it <would be> by the action of a malevolent spirit. If however in the opinion of these <ancient Greeks> the more pleasing animals <like> doves and pigeons are filled with divine inspiration, and <if> some bird settles and signals to them by its voice, appearance, or movement what is going to happen,[60] how could the Mother of God not foretell the entire truth to us, especially if a person should fix his hopes upon her and attribute <to her> the decisive point regarding a practical matter as was done in the law case already mentioned. Forget about the daemon of Socrates, then, that prevented <action on the part of> the person it possessed but never promoted <it>.[61] Whatever might this <daemon> be? Was it some echo that cast back <what a person already intended to do>? Or was it some apparition? According to the <system> of <occult> interpretation that we cannot mention, <this> would be the daemon that is assigned to him and watches nearby, which Plato calls the pilot of the mind.[62] The prearranged sign that the Mother of God <used> to promote action is an oracle[63] that is unerring, true, and in existence according to a new way. The statues or rather the idols of the ancient Greeks played games for Chrysanthios and Maximos in the <temple> of Hekate, and the signals they manifested were foreboding; <Maximos>, the more daring of the <two> philosophers, attempted in vain to change <the intention of> that which includes everything within its boundaries[64] so as to come close to more favorable appearances <of the omens>.[65] However, among us <Christians> the symbols of

60. Psellos describes in some detail the process of augury, or determining the will of the gods by the cries and behavior of various birds, in *Phil. min.* I 33.33–56.

61. See Plato, *Apology* 31d2–4.

62. Psellos paraphrases Plato's famous definition of the mind (νόος) as the pilot (κυβερνήτης) of the soul (ψυχή)—see Plato, *Phaedrus* 247c7—and follows the terminology of Proklos (*Comm. on Alcibiades* 1.77.9–11).

63. It is notoriously difficult to translate λόγος, which I have taken to mean "oracle" here. This sense occurs in Plato (e.g., *Phaedrus* 274b, *Apology* 20e) and in a fragment of the Chaldean Oracles quoted by Psellos (*Oracle* 90).

64. Psellos defines the supreme deity as "the boundary of everything" (τὸ θεῖον ὅρος ἐστὶ τοῦ παντός; see *Phil. min.* II 47.10).

65. Psellos conflates two episodes from Eunapios' *Lives of the Sophists* concerning the fourth-century-CE philosophers Maximos and Chrysanthios, both practitioners of magical arts, who were greatly respected by the youthful Emperor Julian. In the first episode set in the temple of Hekate at Ephesos, Maximos magically induced the goddess's statue to smile and the torches she held to burst into flame (*Lives of the Sophists* 44.10–22); in the second episode, Maximos and Chrysanthios were summoned to

the Mother of God are true, and no one would devote attention to changing their appearances or, if he did <try>, he would never be able <to do it>.

[417–44] However, I would be ashamed to compare the nonsense of the ancient Greeks with <oracular matters> that both belong to us and are <much> superior. Did not the shadow of the law have some more forceful overshadowings <of the divine presence>?[66] For there was the oracle of judgment, and stones named "Manifestations" and "Truth," and the garment worn on the breast called in the Hebrew language *ephod*, where these <stones> were inset,[67] indeed, the Propitiatory fitted upon the Ark of the Covenant within the Holy of Holies regularly received flashes of revelation that were quite divine in origin,[68] but even these are of lesser significance than the manifestations and overshadowings of the Mother of God. Those provided guidance that was obscure, and they changed into various colors, but the symbol that appeared was not entirely clear in every respect. Here <at the Blachernai Church> however the movement <of the drapery> for the sake of the truth was a motion that could not be changed, and it was appropriate to the divine in its appearance as well as supernatural in the understanding <it conveyed>. Moreover, it would be a lengthy <task> to relate

---

Constantinople by Julian. Before responding, they consulted the gods and received unfavorable omens. At this, Maximos declared it the duty of learned men to contest with the gods until they granted favorable omens (47.10–27). Maximos eventually suffered extreme torture at the hands of Julian's successors (51.19–52) and was slaughtered (55.6–20).

66. Paul speaks of "the law having the shadow of good things to come" in Hebrews 10:1.

67. *The ephod of the high priest Aaron* was an elaborately embroidered garment with a sack-like breastplate containing two stones called *Urim* and *Thummim*, or "Manifestation" and "Truth," which were used as an oracle of judgment to provide God's answers to questions posed to him. Exodus 28:6–30 provides a detailed description of the *ephod*; Psellos quotes the vocabulary from verse 26. Because Psellos refers to the oracular stones as "inset" (τετύπωται), he may have confused them with the two precious stones set on the shoulder straps of the *ephod* (Exodus 28:9–12). Consultation of the oracular stones is mentioned in scripture (for example Numbers 27:21) without explaining the process used in consulting them. The seventh-century monk Anastasios of Sinai speculated that the high priest put on the *ephod*, held the breastplate in his hands, and formulated a "yes-or-no" question while peering into the breastplate. God indicated affirmation and assent by causing one of the stones to flash (*Quaestiones* 40, PG 89 585A–B).

68. The Propitiatory or Mercy Seat (ἱλαστήριον) set upon the Ark (τῷ κιβωτῷ) was the site of God's pronouncements for Israel (Exodus 25:21–22).

both how many <actual events> are indicated in <scriptural> figures and how many in truths <revealed by dreams and omens>[69] among us, but especially how many the Mother of God indicates. The <colleagues> of Darius the Mede made their decision concerning kingship according to the whinnying of a horse,[70] and the <companions> of Romulus <made their decision> in founding Rome according to the omens delivered by birds. In the one case, the horse belonging to Darius, son of Hytaspes, whinnied because of the clever contrivance of a groom. In the other case, vultures in support of Romulus flew overhead from the left accompanied by a great clamor; <the left is> the direction where the pole of the axis is elevated.[71] However, in the case of the problem and judicial inquiry under discussion here, neither are birds trusted <to reveal> the truth nor a love-crazed horse <to determine> the leadership of the Persians. Indeed, in the vote of the Mother of God a balance between the arguments of each party both hangs <in suspension> and brings a solution with such brilliant clarity that not even those who lost the case can shamelessly refuse <to accept her decision>.

[445–57] The oracular responses provided by the daemons, then, took their impetus from configurations in the heavens, for in this way those who offer interpretations based on natural phenomena determine and confidently affirm <their pronouncements>. When a certain woman who was very close to giving birth asked Apollo whether she would bear a male or a female child, he replied that she would bear[72] not a son but a daughter and cited the

69. Cf. *LSJ* s.v. ἀλήθεια I. 4.

70. Herodotus explains how Darius prevailed in a contest arranged by the claimants to the throne of Persia. Since all agreed that the rider of the first horse to whinny after dawn on the following day would be king, the groom of Darius bred his horse the previous night on a spot where the contestants would pass so that the next day the horse whinnied at the spot and won Darius the throne (Herodotus, *Histories* III 83–86).

71. Psellos conflates two incidents from the *Roman Antiquities* by Dionysios of Halikarnassos. The twins Romulus and Remus agreed to determine which of them should be the founder and namesake of their city according to the flight of auspicious birds; Remus was first to see six vultures flying from the right, but Romulus saw twelve vultures and claimed victory (see *Roman Antiquities* I 86.2–4). After Remus died in the ensuing battle among the brothers' followers, Romulus received divine confirmation of his position as founder of Rome when lightning appeared favorably "on the left," explained by Dionysios as north, the direction of the pole's inclination when the viewer faces east (see *Roman Antiquities* II 5.1–4). Psellos adopts Dionysios' vocabulary for "the pole of the axis is elevated" (μετεωρίζεται . . . ὁ τοῦ ἄξονος πόλος, section 3).

72. Reading τέξεσθαι for the mss. τέξασθαι.

configuration of the stars: "For keen-sighted Phoebe <the moon goddess> caused an act of conception through chaste Cyprian <Aphrodite> who promoted a female offspring." For from the <time of> conception, the <child> to be born was marked <as female> because the moon was approaching Aphrodite.[73] Again using this reasoning, the Pythian <oracle of Apollo at Delphi> explained the source of an appetite for war in a certain man by saying, "He has <the star of> rash Ares, <god of war>, at his birth and <Ares> motivates him."[74]

[458–84] In this way and from that <astrological> source the daemons give their oracles and proclaim future events to those who inquire. The Virgin however, who has accepted the rudders of our lives and steers us from <heaven> above, watches over everything but never raises her eyes towards all the <astrological configurations>. She predicts future events because she is closely attached to God in immediate <bonds of> unity, and from that source she draws the truth and power of her pronouncements. Moreover, when our emperor reads of these <matters> in Holy Scripture, he both understands <them> clearly and acts to interpret and expound things that are quite ineffable to those who do not understand. If his keen nature should gain a spark <of inspiration> by trading <in ideas>[75] with me, even so he would himself still graciously give me leave to speak, or I would myself <give> him the basis for his understanding <of an issue>. For this divine<ly inspired> man would take fire from the flames of my <intelligence> to a greater extent than I myself could ignite <him>. As a result, I assure you, he too became all but an eyewitness of the miracle that took place <in Blachernai> and instigated many lines of reasoning about the quite divine <events>; he both marveled at their fulfillment and elaborated upon it in discourses that he did not write down. He then encouraged me <to provide> a more

73. Interpreting this cryptic oracle requires understanding a double entendre; in modern astrological terminology, "The moon was entering <the house of> Venus (=Aphrodite)." Additionally puzzling is the adjective "chaste" (ἅγνην), usually applied to Artemis, the maiden goddess of the moon, but here referring to the sex-goddess Aphrodite. Psellos quotes this oracle from Porphyrios as it now survives in Eusebios, *Praeparatio evangelica* VI 1.2.3–8.

74. Psellos again quotes Porphyrios (see Eusebios, *Praeparatio evangelica* VI 2.1.2–3).

75. Elaborating upon a Greek pun impossible to convey in English (ἐμπύρευμα: "spark, inspiration"/ ἐμπόρευμα: "merchandise, traffic," lines 468–69), Psellos develops an extended metaphor of ideas kindled in the emperor by discussions with Psellos (lines 471–73).

complete explanation in reverent language, as if assigning to some Pericles the public speech that was significant. Now Pericles was pressed to compose his speech for the virgin <goddess Athena> three days[76] before delivering it in public,[77] while I pronounced mine by improvising it on the spot. If my inspiration derived from that source that moved the drapery of the Virgin, this <work of mine> was also from the Mother of God so that miracle might attach upon miracle, the miracle pertaining to my speech upon the miracle of the drapery.

[485–519] I mentioned in my remarks right at the beginning of this oration that the investigation <of a disagreement> is <characteristic> of civil subject matter for the laws and the courts, but the means of achieving a just resolution <in the present case> is different, beyond everyday laws and in truth transcending them by means of the supernatural.[78] For while a dispute over a civil matter and strife between contending parties over ownership or usufruct belongs to the everyday business of the courts, bringing an investigation to a judgment on the basis of a decisive point that even the law does not understand, while not contrary to the law, is above the law. If someone should wish to force the argument, he is able to say that there is a decisive point that is entirely legal. For in the law codes there are <chapter> titles on judges and on their jurisdictions as well as on coadjutors and on special judges;[79] the

76. Apparently a reference to Thucydides, *History* II 34.2: "Having set up a tent, they put into it the bones of the dead three days before the funeral."

77. Psellos somewhat inaccurately recalls Thucydides' famous account of Pericles' Funeral Oration, which was delivered at the state commemoration of war dead celebrated by Athens, city of the virgin goddess Athena (cf. Thucydides, *History* II 34.1 and 6). I am grateful to Stratis Papaioannou for recognizing this reference as specifically to Pericles' Funeral Oration.

78. My translation of the following section in which Psellos speaks as a lawyer has benefited immeasurably from discussions among the participants in Alice-Mary Talbot's Greek reading group at Dumbarton Oaks (2007–8), especially Diether Roderich Reinsch, Denis Sullivan, and Michael McGann.

79. For a discussion of courts and judges in Byzantium, see Macrides 1994. Macrides describes the three categories of judges mentioned by Psellos: the seven magistrates who served as "competent" judges having jurisdiction, i.e., being "competent" (πρόσφοροι or κύριοι) to hear a case, and two types termed "subordinate" (χαμαιδικασταί). The "coadjutors" (σύμπονοι, Psellos' πάρεδροι) were attached to the courts of the competent judges and had no independent jurisdiction but were well informed in the relevant laws, while the "special" (αἱρετοί) judges were temporarily designated by a competent judge to hear a particular case (Macrides 1994: 120–21).

chapters about these are as follows:[80] "The special court is like a competent court and its <powers> extend to reaching judgments <in a case>" (*Basilika* 7.2.1),[81] and further, "A special judge is one who has received an assignment as judge" (*Basilika* 7.2.13.2, line 7),[82] and again, "Whether just or unjust, the sentence of the special <judge> must stand" (*Basilika* 7.2.27.2), and yet more surprising, "Even should someone serving anywhere at all in the capacity of a special judge be mistaken in casting his vote, he does not correct it; for once he has cast his vote, he ceases to be a judge" (*Basilika* 7.2.20, lines 1–2);[83] other such chapters <also> fall under the title on special judges. The copies of written documents from both parties clearly indicate that the opposing <parties> in the presence of the One Who Bore God chose to have <her> participate in the trial as a special judge, so to speak; the difference in comparison to the special judge as customarily designated under the law <is> that the <law> appoints a man connected with the court or a private person who has been selected as judge by the parties in the trial,[84] while the general and the monks

80. Psellos quotes the opening sentence wholly or in part from the chapter (κεφάλαιον) of the title (ἐπίγραμμα) of the law he wishes to cite; because his audience is expected to understand the full import of each citation, I have supplied additional text in the footnotes when it is necessary for understanding his reference. *Basilika* refers to the ninth-century codification of law under the Emperor Leo VI; the *Ecloga Basilicorum* is a twelfth-century commentary on parts of it (see *ODB* s.v. "Basilika" and "Ecloga Basilicorum"). For a Latin translation of the *Basilika*, see Heimbach 1843; available online at http://www.ledonline.it/rivistadirittoromano/basilici.html.

81. Psellos slightly misquotes the text of the law, substituting the adjective προσφόρῳ ("fitting, suitable") for κυρίῳ ("competent").

82. The text of the law continues, "and has pledged to decide the matter under contention by voting"; καὶ ἐπαγγειλάμενος ψήφῳ τεμεῖν τὸ φιλονεικούμενον.

83. The twelfth-century legal textbook the *Ecloga Basilicorum* expatiates upon this cryptic sentence with an example: "If the special judge once gives his final judgment and makes his decision that 'Peter appeared to me to owe 100 nomismata to Paul, and I judge that he give this <money> to Paul,' he cannot thereafter either change or correct his verdict, even should he perhaps be mistaken, and gave his sentence when he ought not judge against Peter but in his favor. For having once given a judgment, he ceases to be a judge and can no longer cast a vote"; Ὁ αἱρετὸς δικαστής, ἐὰν φθάσῃ δοῦναι ἀπόφασιν τελείαν καὶ διορίσηται, ὅτι "ἐφάνη μοι χρεωστῶν Πέτρος τῷ Παύλῳ ρ´ νομίσματα καὶ ἀποφαίνομαι τοῦτον δοῦναι ταῦτα τῷ Παύλῳ" οὐ δύναται ἔκτοτε τὴν οἰκείαν ψῆφον ἢ ἐναλλάξαι ἢ διορθῶσαι, κἂν ἴσως ἐπλανήθη καὶ μὴ ὀφείλων καταδικάσαι τὸν Πέτρον, ἀλλα δικαιῶσαι κατέκρινε· δοὺς γὰρ ἅπαξ ἀπόφασιν ἐπαύθη εἶναι δικαστὴς καὶ οὐκέτι δύναται διαγινώσκειν (*Ecloga Basilicorum* 72.20, lines 1–7).

84. Only a competent judge who had jurisdiction over a particular case could appoint a special judge to preside in his stead; he often turned to one of the assistant judges in his own court (σύμπονοι); see Macrides 1994: 120–21.

of the monastery Tou Kalliou did not make an appeal to such a <judge>, but to the Mother of God alone. They did not conceive of the decision as <derived> from arguments and laws nor as an oral or written sentence, but they considered that the decisive point and announcement of a verdict in the inquiry would be <something> capable of going either way, <namely>, a symbolic movement or lack of movement <by the drapery>. <Thus> a sort of hybrid court exists, partly civil and partly from a higher sphere.

[520–77] I would make my decision in the matter as follows. <Let us suppose that> the parties in a dispute made a mockery of reasonable arguments and entrusted the decisive point in an ambiguous <case> to some outrageous activity, <such as> to a game of backgammon or the roll of the dice, to birds' flight, their cries, their <manner of> alighting, the number of their movements, or to something else of that sort, <or> to <the outcome of> footraces or wrestling matches of certain <athletes>. Alternatively, <suppose they say that> if someone should throw a discus up beyond the clouds and <someone else> should hurl it as far as six miles,[85] one side will win, the other will lose. If, <as I said> these <opposing parties> were to decide together upon a mutually agreeable means of judging in this way and <if> this was to be the special <court constituted> according to their agreement, I myself would not choose their court nor would I count the choice that settled upon these <criteria> as comparable to the agreements that were determined concerning the special judges. Since the one <choice> is something that is superior to that determined according to laws and the other is inferior, I dismiss the one, inasmuch as it is inferior, into <the category of> illegal <actions>, but the other, inasmuch as it is superior, I pronounce both legal and superior to the law. <It is> legal because the prearranged signal based on a legally observed phenomenon has been acknowledged by both sides, while <it is> superior to the law because <the two parties> have brought <the case> to its conclusion on the basis of a perception mystically <obtained>. For it is not as if one <choice> is deficient and the other excessive, while justice lies as a mean between them, as in the case of someone taking too little or too much, so that the two extremes must be faulted and the median praised, but just as immaterial light is more luminous than material <light> and preferable to it, while darkness is something entirely opposed <to light>, so <in the case> of the special judge, one <choice> is led to an inferior decision that is most strange and contrary to

85. Psellos speaks facetiously in gross exaggerations, using classical terminology for distance; "fifty stades" = ca. six miles, since one stade = 607 feet or an eighth of a mile.

law, as my oration has determined, while the other leads to a superior <decision> that is at once most marvelous and most in compliance with law. If a subordinate <judge> who becomes a special <judge> also confidently passes judgment according to the laws, or even contrary to them on many occasions, would the <Virgin> appear inferior in this case, when she both judged the party in the lawsuit who represented her own place[86] and condemned <them>, just because she resolved the inquiry by means of a novel symbolic <action> that was agreed upon by the contending parties? Far from it! If someone does not understand what has happened and how he would form a judgment <about it> in his bewilderment, will this <miraculous event> be insufficient to function as a decisive point? In no way! Why would someone in present or in future generations even dare to convene a court of appeal[87] for the events that have taken place or, because <a special court> might not conform in every respect to the civil law, <why would someone dare> to nullify as contrary to law that which is better and more noble than this <law> or <dare to> refer the decision to <the pagan court of> the Areopagos?[88] If someone should then opt for a decisive point that is supernatural, he has what he wants here as a shining <example>; if instead he should prefer a sentence under the law, this <example> has both started from the law and the alteration <that resulted> is superior to the law. Now, someone has taken an oath by God, because the law prescribes it or because a judge requires it; there are cases in which he did not obtain a sentence that prevails in a final sense. The law says, when *good cause* is established and new documents *have been discovered*, even the *oath* sworn before the court can be examined in a new trial.[89] Moreover, although every other court's sentence is subject to appeal, as for the decision of the Mother of God, <rendered> in symbols when the parties in the suit so agreed, it will not

86. The monastery Τοῦ Καλλίου was dedicated to the Virgin; see Janin 1969: 40.

87. The right of access to a court of appeal (τὸ ἐφετικὸν δικαστήριον) is described in the *Novellae* of Justinian (Kroll and Schöll 1895: 460, lines 17–20); the sixth-century *Novellae constitutiones* of Athanasios (Simon and Troianos 1989: 3.4, 162, line 1) refers to the appeals courts at Constantinople as having jurisdiction over all cases involving persons under special jurisdictions—military, ecclesiastical, noble, etc. For a description of these special jurisdictions, see Macrides 1994: 117–22.

88. Psellos alludes ironically to the ancient Athenian court of appeal in cases of homicide, wounding, and arson; see *OCD* s.v. "Areopagus."

89. Psellos paraphrases *Basilika* 22.6.4.2–3, which describes the role of the judge in assessing a fine when the plaintiff asserts that he has suffered financial harm by the actions of his opponent. "Only the judge can propose an oath before the court, and it is in <the judge's power> to impose <the oath> and to fix the amount of the claim. He is

be cancelled on the basis of new documents nor referred on appeal.[90] Why? Because there are occasions when civil judges, even if they should reach the pinnacle of legal learning, make errors in their determination, and the one who swears his oath often scorns the Almighty on a selfish impulse and in hope of personal gain. But who in the world would fault the Mother of God when she renders a judgment and discovers the truth, revealing it in a new way? <Who> would dare provide a different verdict?

[578–611] But if someone should not be altogether able to refer to a law the procedure undertaken in this situation, <it would be> nothing new, since one would not even move the *condictio ex lege* with reference to an action limited <to a particular law>. *For this <condictio ex lege> is applicable when legislation introduces a new <sort of> liability and claim without expressly stating by what action it is to be moved.*[91] However, this <citation> is understood as

---

also able even after the oath <has been taken> to lessen <the fine on> the defendant wholly or in part for good cause or if new evidence has later been discovered"; Μόνος ὁ δικαστὴς ἐπάγει τὸν ἔνδικον ὅρκον, καὶ ἐν αὐτῷ ἐστιν ἐπαγαγεῖν αὐτὸν καὶ ταξατεῦσαι· δύναται δὲ καὶ μετὰ τὸν ὅρκον ἐκ μεγάλης αἰτίας ἢ ἀποδείξεων ὕστερον εὑρεθεισῶν ἐν μέρει ἢ εἰς τὸ παντελὲς κουφίσαι τὸν ἐναγόμενον.

Psellos' contemporary the historian and legal writer Michael Attaleiates elaborates upon the general application of the oath before the court (ἔνδικον ὅρκον) in his *Work on the Laws, or Epitome for Lawyers* (Πόνημα νομικὸν ἤτοι σύνοψις πραγματική) 14.59–64: "On the oath before the court. The oath before the court is like this: Whenever someone is convicted of having committed forcible seizure of property or entry into a house or theft or unjust injury, then the party <affected> swears 'So much injury I have suffered and <so much> have I lost as a result of the attack from him by force, theft, or shameless injury,' and he receives this <amount> from his opponent, but not without due examination does he receive all that he swore to, but with a judicial determination of the amount. For the judge decides . . ."; Περὶ ἐνδίκου ὅρκου. Ὁ ἔνδικος ὅρκος τοιοῦτος ἐστίν. Ὅταν τις ἀπελεγχθῇ βιαίαν ἁρπαγὴν ποιησάμενος πραγμάτων ἢ ἐπέλευσιν κατὰ οἰκίας τινός, ἢ κλοπὴν ἢ ζημίαν ἄδικον, τότε ὀμνύει ὁ ἀντίδικος, ὅτι τόσα ἐζημιώθην καὶ ἀπώλεσα ἐν τῇ γενομένῃ κατ' αὐτοῦ ἐπιθέσει ἢ βίᾳ ἢ κλοπῇ ἢ ἀναισχύντῳ ζημίᾳ, καὶ ἀπολαμβάνει ταῦτα εἰς τὸ ἁπλοῦν ἀπὸ τοῦ ἀντιδίκου· πλὴν οὐκ ἀβασανίστως πάντα, ὅσα ὀμόσει, λαμβάνει, ἀλλὰ μετὰ ταξατίωνος. Ὁρίζει γὰρ ὁ δικαστής. . . .

90. I have substituted a period for the question mark in the text.

91. In this passage "action" is used in the technical sense of a legal proceeding established for the judging and enforcing of a claim. Psellos quotes this sentence from his own essay, "Concerning the Disposition of Actions" (Περὶ τῆς τῶν ἀγωγῶν διαιρέσεως in Weiss 1973: 288–91, quotation from lines 102–4). The sentence is preceded by a definition, "There is also a *condictio ex lege*; this is a claim which does not fall under a particular category of action, but is defined under a law," ἔστι καὶ κονδικτ(ίκιος) ἐξ λέγε τουτέστιν ἀπαίτησις μὴ ἔχουσα ἴδιον ἀγωγῆς ὄνομα, ἀλλ' ἐκ νόμου ὁριζομένη (Weiss 1973: 288 lines 102–4).

beside <our> main subject and argued as a parallel, while the procedure <in this case> is itself both conducted under law, if you will, and is brought to its conclusion beyond the law. On both counts, the one who obtains what he justly deserved from the all-holy <Virgin> will have a judgment that is beyond question. Now not in all actions is the role of plaintiff assigned solely to one of the opposing parties and the role of defendant to the other. Sometimes both parties have both roles, and the same <parties> are both plaintiffs and defendants, as in the so-called double trials, such as a case between joint heirs[92] either under a will or without a will, which both is and is termed both *in rem* and *in personam*, (that is, applied to <claims of> property and applied to <claims against> a person). <Another instance is> the <case> concerning land boundaries and so forth—but why should we rehearse everything? If the opposing parties should agree with one another regarding the right to speak first in the action, <that is, regarding> who first enters the court (for both could not be plaintiff with equal rights <to speak first>), and <if> they should assign this <role>, to which they have a common right, by some symbol or in some other manner, and if someone should obtain this by lot, would he not himself be first to bring his accusation, even though this <role> is not assigned to him by law? Would it not be strange, then, if some chance occurrence should prevail regarding the right to speak first and the agreement by both parties should be counted as law, but in the present inquiry, which adopted a previously determined divine sign and praiseworthy compact, the agreement will have some other <status> in comparison to a chance event? For let "chance" be taken in the more common sense <of the word>, even if among the philosophers chance and spontaneity, when enumerated among the causes, possess some distinction <from the others>.[93]

92. Such trials are mentioned in the scholia to the *Basilika* 8.2.15, explaining cases involving two heirs as regulated in *Basilika* 42.2.1.

93. Psellos refers to Aristotle's discussion of the causes (τὰ αἴτια) in the *Physics* where he enumerates four (final, material, efficient, and formal, *Physics* II 3), then notes that chance (ἡ τύχη) and spontaneity (τὸ αὐτόματον) are sometimes considered causes but must be distinguished from the others; see Aristotle, *Physics* II 4-6, esp. 195b32–196a16. The vocabulary used here by Psellos reflects that of the Aristotelian commentator Alexander of Aphrodisias, who speaks of "the distinction of causes" (ἡ τῶν αἰτίων δεικνυμένη διαίρεσις) as quoted by Eusebios (*Praeparatio evangelica* VI 9.3, line 3). The sixth-century Aristotelian commentators Ioannes Philoponos and Simplikios also note the distinction shared by chance and spontaneity.

[612–33] My earnest endeavor in my oration is this, <to establish> that neither did the opposing parties reach an outrageous agreement in resolving their inquiry according to the behavior of the Mother of God's holy drapery nor does the miracle that took place prevail to any lesser degree than a judicial opinion and sentence. Those who lost the case moreover would have no basis for an objection. For in apportioning the sign, they did not assign to the general the symbol that would be his on fair terms, but to him they allotted what was unlikely or what most seldom <occurred>, while to themselves they gave, as I might say, what has no value as a symbol. For the movement of the drapery is <characteristic> of a miracle, while its lack of movement is <characteristic> of its natural state, and the natural state is more <likely to occur> than a wondrous <event>. How then could they claim that the divine signal is not consistent with law? "But you," someone might say to them, "when the prayer took place and the miracle had yet to occur, you had <already> congratulated yourselves as the winners on the basis of the present situation. How then did you lay claim to <victory in> the case with all your might when the miracle had not taken place, then later when <it> did take place, will you again on fair terms make the same claim? Nevertheless, you obviously lost the case both according to the compact you agreed to yourselves and according to the Virgin's decisive point; a person would have his tongue entirely cut out[94] if he opposed the miracle and reckoned the excess of his power <equivalent to> the deficiency of his own persuasive argumentation—as I will say, to avoid calling it 'idle talk.' "[95]

94. Psellos may be speaking metaphorically. However, it is not uncommon to see references to corporal punishment appropriate to a crime that was imposed without the sanction of a specific law; anyone whose speech might threaten the regime was punished by removal of the tongue. Theophanes records four such instances in the seventh and eighth centuries, most famously in the cases of the Empress Martina (*Chronographia* 341.25) and of the Emperor Justinian II (369.26; see also 351.20 and 380.27). Although the law specified removal of the tongue in the case of proven perjury ("once he is discovered, let the perjurer lose his tongue"; ἐπίορκος δὲ μετὰ ταῦτα ἀποδεικνύμενος, γλωσσοκοπείσθω, *Ecloga Basilicorum* 17.2, line 3), the punishment was usually imposed solely at a judge's discretion. The practice found scriptural justification in Matthew 5:29–30: "And if thy right eye offend thee, pluck it out," and "If thy right hand offend thee, cut if off" (KJV). For a discussion of corporal punishment in Byzantium, see Sinogowitz 1956: 19–21, 36.

95. That is, the monks think they should win on the basis of political influence rather than persuasive logic. Psellos gives this hypothetical critic of the monks' position a scriptural tone in his concluding sentence; πιθανολογία ("enticing words" KJV, which I have translated as "persuasive argumentation") occurs in Colossians 2:4, and ματαιολογία ("vain jangling" KJV) in 1 Timothy 1:6.

[634–59] The arguments in my oration have proven that if someone should not only choose to drag us down but should also force <us> from the more heavenly <point of view> into the more mundane one and compel <us> to struggle about the laws, in these <matters> we are not inferior to those who try to oppose us. I, however, shall return to the primary decisive point of my oration, and I both add miracle to miracle, and I would never willingly release my hold upon the wonders belonging to the Mother of God nor retreat from them. But who in the world would not marvel upon hearing of the sequence of miracles <occurring> in this way and the succession of supernatural symbols? The general prevailed in the contest both by virtue of the legal and of the miraculous, and the *prôtoproedros*[96] Ioannes of the Xeros family, who received from the emperor the first position of the service in his ranking,[97] awarded to <the general> the legal documents. Thus <the judgment> was awarded to him both by the authority of the Virgin and by the power of the emperor. Indeed, the general did not depart without paying proper respect to the Virgin from whom he had received a favorable judgment; with the documents he had been given in hand, he approaches the Mother of God, draws near to her icon, and throws himself to the ground in acknowledgment of her every favor. She then, who miraculously decided the case, <even> more miraculously seals anew her verdict. And <what was> the seal? Yet again the covering of her icon is raised, and the holy veil is lifted up; as in the case of the *periodos* and the *kyklos*,[98] which start and end with the same <word>, the

96. The title *prôtoproedros* describes an official who was preeminent in his particular branch of civil or ecclesiastical service; it was awarded quite widely in the eleventh century. In this context it apparently designates a civil "chief judge" (see *ODB* s.v. "Proedros").

97. The Xeros family attained prominence in civil service during the eleventh century, especially as judges; Psellos corresponded with a member of this family who served as judge in the Thrakesian theme of western Anatolia (see *ODB* s.v. "Xeros"). Seibt 1978: 291–92 discusses the career and the surviving lead seals of the "Ioannes Xeros" mentioned by Psellos here, noting that a designation "foremost of the service in his ranking" (πρῶτος τῆς διακονίας ἐν τῇ πρεσβείᾳ) conveyed great honor upon the recipient but had no political significance. Psellos evidently attempts to explain the significance of "protoproedros" with the phrase τὰ πρῶτα τῆς ἐν τῇ πρεσβείᾳ διακονίας, line 645. I am grateful to John Nesbitt for an enlightening discussion of this passage.

98. The rhetorical figure of the *kyklos* (ring composition) can be applied to a *periodos* (sentence) or to an entire narrative, according to "Hermogenes'" influential rhetorical text, *On Invention* 4.8 (see Kennedy 2005: 172–74).

matter she examined comes full circle so that it will be bonded together most securely by two miracles, each like the other.

[660–703] My oration, like a runner that races up and doubles back in a quite new <kind of> race course,[99] also now engages with divine <matters>, then in turn with material substances observable to the senses, and chooses to discuss something yet more sublime and to investigate the possible cause of such divine signs. In fact, often prints of unseen feet or hands are fixed in the ground, and shapes of living beings become visible, like those belonging to the sacred meteors somewhere long ago[100] and <like> scorched marks around stones; certain icons and statues stream with liquid as if perspiring,[101] and movements without a perceptible cause become visible around such things. Also, certain sounds are heard, some from <thin> air, some from wells, some from other <sorts of> springs, and other, stranger things of this sort fall upon the senses. But the truest cause of these <phenomena> God in fact would know and anyone who approaches the nature of the divine; what we then have learned from the more esoteric branch of philosophy, if we could say <this> with modesty, will be sufficient for our audience. Let this first be agreed:[102] some beings are precisely that, "truly beings," both divine and supernatural,

99. Psellos continues the imagery implied by the etymological sense of the word *periodos* (περί: "around" + ὁδός: "way," "track") by comparing the structure of his oration to a racecourse.

100. According to the fifth-century Neoplatonist Damaskios, a lion accompanied a flaming sphere (the *baitylos*) when it appeared in the middle of the night to a man mysteriously summoned to the temple of Athena near Emesa (Syria); upon being questioned, the lion explained the divine origin of the *baitylos* and left the man to be its servant (see Damaskios, *Life of Isidoros* §203, 274–76). For a brief discussion of sacred stones in antiquity, see Faraone 1992: 5. Faraone notes that Philo of Byblos described *baityloi* as "animated stones" in a section of his *Phoenician History* as preserved in Eusebios, *Praeparatio evangelica* I 10.23, lines 4-5: ἐπενόησεν θεὸς Οὐρανὸς βαιτύλια, λίθους ἐμψύχους μηχανησάμενος; "the god Ouranos further invented baetyls, by devising stones endowed with life." Text and translation from Attridge and Oden 1981: 52–53.

101. Classical authors, especially those of the Roman period, not uncommonly mention sweating statues as a divine portent; see, for example, Theophrastos, *On Plants* 5.9.8; Apollonios of Rhodes, *Argonautica* IV 1284–85; Diodoros, *Bibliotheca historica* XVII 10.4; Appian, *Civil War* II 36 and IV 4; Plutarch, *Life of Alexander* 14.8–9 and *Life of Camillus* 6.3, etc. I am grateful to Denis Sullivan for these references.

102. In translating lines 676–89, I have benefited from the translation and discussion in Papaioannou 2001: 186–87, which elucidates the sense of the Neoplatonic terminology drawn by Psellos from Proklos' commentaries on Plato's *Parmenides* and *Timaeus*.

while others are inferior to them; their abasement descends even to sense perception and to matter itself, and their bodies here <on earth> receive certain reflections and disclosures of the superior things, for the inferior partake of the superior. Moreover, the divine is similar to itself and not at all subject to change, while everything under the moon is both composed of dissimilar elements and subject to change, and to the degree that the descent <of the divine> proceeds, the change makes its mark. The worse also receives its illuminations from the better, not in the way those <divine beings> possess <illumination> but in the way these <worse ones> are capable <of receiving it>.[103] Divinity then is unmoved, but wherever illumination might advance from those <divine beings> to the <material> body, this <body> is moved, for it does not receive reflection and disclosure without being subject to change, nor can it. The creating force is also without form, while that which is susceptible to change receives some sort of form and transformation. Colors[104] are also the symbols of things to come, for the whites <symbolize> the brilliance of future events, while the blacks <belong to> the obscure and indefinite, and the <colors> that are between these are worse to the degree they are darker, better to the degree they are lighter, and mixed at the midpoint; an example <is> grey, which participates equally in the extremes of <black and white>. The scorched marks indicate some more violent movement to come and the worst sort of reversal <in fortune>; mysterious handprints <are evidence> of the touch of a superior nature, but footprints, of a sudden movement in future events. Upon experiencing reflection and disclosure of the divine, air and water produce a <sound> discordant to its hearers because they would not be able to experience <the divine> without being subject to change. Also the poet says, "Loudly did the oaken axle creak," not because the superior <na-

103. Psellos paraphrases the statement of Proklos "And in fact each thing participates in the better things to the extent of its natural capacity, but not as those <better things truly> are"; καὶ γὰρ ἕκαστον, ὡς πέφυκεν, οὕτω μετέχει τῶν κρειττόνων, ἀλλ' οὐχ ὡς ἐκεῖνα ἔστιν, *The Elements of Theology* 173.5–6. For a discussion of this passage in relation to Psellos' understanding of the process of human vision, see Barber 2007: 90.

104. In translating lines 689–94, I have benefited from the translation and discussion by Barber 2007: 85. For a different interpretation of χρῶμα in this passage as a reference to brightness or intensity rather than to hue, see Pentcheva 2010: 189. For the spiritual significance of color in Byzantine theology, see James 2003.

ture>, being subject to change, was burdened with matter, but because matter in its normal state received reflection and disclosure.[105]

[704–16] <I spoke of> these <matters> in a cursory fashion and in a spirited manner as a teacher of rhetoric would concerning inferior responses to questions being raised.[106] However, this much must be said at this point regarding the evocation of God by souls:[107] since we are composed of faculties that differ from one another—superior and inferior, loftier and more humble (I am speaking of intellect, of discursive thought, of imagination, and of the others)[108]—whenever the soul is inspired as a whole and the intellect is first to receive the illumination, the other <faculties> are set in motion as <the intellect's> instrument, since they are restricted in the life that is theirs; this is why <the intellect> as it sees God is then also unaware of itself.[109] If in contrast the <faculty of> discursive thought or the spirit of the imagination has been set in motion by evoking God, the intellect, which is placed above these <faculties>, would recognize the divine movements and interpret them, without being subject to change.

[717–33] Thanks <be> to the Mother of God, who has provided us through the miracle with resources to interpret inspiration <from> superior

105. Psellos quotes and paraphrases *Iliad* 5.838–39: "Loudly did the oaken axle creak beneath its burden, for it bare a dread goddess and a peerless warrior" (trans. Samuel Butler), μέγα δ' ἔβραχε φήγινος ἄξων βριθοσύνῃ· δεινὴν γὰρ ἄγεν θεὸν ἄνδρά τ' ἄριστον.

106. I am grateful to Börje Bydén for illuminating suggestions on translating the following complex Neoplatonic passage.

107. In his *Accusation* against the Patriarch Kerularios, Psellos uses similar Neoplatonic reasoning to explain the process by which divine possession affected the Delphic oracle and sometimes drove her out of her senses (*Or. fun.* 1.322–332). The two passages share some vocabulary: "evocation of God" (θεαγωγία), "be inspired," "inspiration" (ἐπιπνέηται, ἐπίπνοια), "discursive thought" (διάνοια), and "(not) being conscious" ([ἀ]παρακολουθ-).

108. Psellos mentions here three of the five faculties of the soul (δυνάμεις τῆς ψυχῆς) that are enumerated in a poem attributed to him: "Every soul has by nature five faculties: intellect, perception, discursive thought, judgment, and imagination"; ψυχὴ γὰρ πᾶσα πέφυκε δυνάμεις ἔχειν πέντε, / νοῦν, αἴσθησιν, διάνοιαν, δόξαν καὶ φαντασίαν (*Poem.* 54: 141–42). This is a traditional list found in late antique commentators such as John Philoponos, John of Damascus, Olympiodoros, Elias, and David.

109. For the sense of ἀπαρακολουθήτως . . . πρὸς ἑαυτὸν, see Plotinos, *Enneads* I 4.5 μηδ' ἑαυτῷ παρακολουθοῖ; "suspends consciousness."

<things>. I indeed know that a dearth of wisdom existing[110] in the portion of time allotted to me has made the souls of many <people> immovable and implacable in matters of the supernatural. However, just because many <people> remain unmoved regarding superior <things>, we who love them passionately need not join these <people> in becoming like an <unthinking> tree or a stone and like <someone> living the life of a plant uprooted from the soil when we interpret these <superior matters> especially in a manner more spiritual but not Aristotelian, so that we gain from them understanding of what the words concerning the <Old Testament> prophets were and what sort of things the headings and the *Selah* in the Psalms are.[111] For all these matters belong to the understanding of superior things. If we must set forth propositions and draw conclusions by means of <Aristotelian> syllogisms, we would collect axiomatic principles concerning each genus that are more divinely appropriate to the underlying <subjects> and completely irrefutable; the Logos sees the essential attributes of <each genus>.[112]

[734–49] May this improvised oration suffice at one and the same time both to praise the miracle and to confirm the matter in dispute for anyone who happens upon <this> judicial decision, while for me may <this> oration come to its conclusion in a novel kind of prayer. May <Christ our> God judge our <efforts> (as he will indeed judge them!) by taking (or by already having taken) his decisions from the Father on the occasion of his Second Coming, and may the one who bore Him also share in the decision with Him so that a compassionate Mother who renders a joint verdict alongside <her> compassionate child might not observe an exacting standard in measuring our deeds nor weigh <them> in the balance in such a way that she strikes thought with

110. Psellos adopts a phrase from Plato's *Meno* here (ὥσπερ αὐχμός τις τῆς σοφίας γέγονεν, 70c4) and uses it again in a similar context in one of his orations on miscellaneous subjects ("So great a dearth of wisdom existed during our lifetime"; τοσοῦτος γὰρ αὐχμὸς σοφίας ἐπὶ τοῦ καθ' ἡμᾶς βίου ἐγένετο, *Or. min.* 24.61).

111. In three of his poems (*Poem.* 1, 53, 54) and in his essay "On the Psalms," Psellos discusses the various meanings assigned to the Hebrew word *Selah*, termed in Greek τὸ διάψαλμα. In *Poem* 1.269–92 he notes that some interpret the word as signifying a change in rhythm, in harmonic type, in melody, etc., and himself favors a Neoplatonic interpretation, bolstering his argument by citing Gregory of Nyssa.

112. In suggesting that he could use the principles of Aristotelian logic to analyze this case, Psellos reflects the vocabulary of Aristotle's *Posterior Analytics* 75a42–b2 and 76a13–14 (ἀξιώματα: "axioms"; γένος: "genus"; καθ' αὑτὰ τὰ πάθη: "the essential attributes"; ὑποκειμένοις: "underlying <things>" or *subjecta* in Latin).

thought and examines deed with deed,[113] but may she assess our <deeds> with a more sympathetic turn of the scale. For in this way either would we all receive salvation not corresponding to the good deeds the majority of us have done but <corresponding> to the remission of our sins—or at least we shall fall not into the midst of Hell<'s eternal punishment> but be seated somewhere far from its flames.

[750–57] These <documents> have been signed and sealed in regard both to spiritual and at the same time to civil <considerations>. They have been delivered to the general who prevailed in the case thanks to the Mother of God. <This took place> in the month of July in the thirteenth year of the indiction,[114] when the miracle happened to be performed and made known during the reign of his Excellency Michael Doukas. By him the honorable monk Michael was urged to write an oration that <belongs to the category> of an official memorandum and simultaneously of a panegyric type,[115] when the year 6583 was already waning.[116]

113. Psellos adopts and adapts a phrase from the essay of Gregory of Nazianzos *On His Father's Silence* ("striking thought with thought and examining action with action"; λογισμῷ λογισμὸν πλήσσων, καὶ πράξει πρᾶξιν εὐθύνων, *Or.* 16.8); he uses this same phrase again in his essay *On "Lord, Have Mercy"* (*Theol.* I 13.90).

114. An indiction was a cycle of fifteen years, each running from September to August, regularly used to mark a date in Byzantium even though it was not precise, since the indiction cycles were never marked in a sequence (see *ODB* s.v. "Indiction").

115. For Psellos' view of the panegyric, see p. 306 (cf. also p. 120) above. Psellos apparently uses the technical term "official memorandum" (ὑπόμνημα) to describe the form and content of his oration but not its function; for a similar use of the term in his writings, see Jenkins 2006: 139–40.

116. The year 6583 (͵ςφπγ´ in the manuscripts) is 1075 CE in modern notation, a designation also supplied in the margin of the chief manuscript; in Psellos' time, the year was reckoned from the creation of the world dated to 5508 BCE (see *ODB* s.v. "Chronology"). Since the Byzantine year began in September, this oration was delivered sometime in late July or August.

21 A Miraculous Icon of the Mother of God

Translated with introduction and notes
by Charles Barber, David Jenkins,
and Stratis Papaioannou

Introduction

Michael Psellos composed a lengthy encomium in praise of Nikolaos at some point after the abbot's death. Neither the date of death nor the date of composition is known. The abbot may have died in 1054, and the encomium might have been written during Psellos' brief residency within the Monastery of the Beautiful Source in the first months of 1055, but we cannot be certain (Gautier 1974). As an encomium, the text offers a praise-filled account of Nikolaos' life, a story replete with comparisons to a range of biblical and monastic forebears. The speech has also provided Psellos with an occasion to project his own conception of an intellectually rigorous spiritual life on to that of Nikolaos. It was a model that perhaps offered an alternative to the more mystical spiritualism espoused by Symeon the New Theologian and his followers (Weiss 1977: 283–91; cf. also Papaioannou 2013: 173–74).

The passage translated below falls at the mid-point of the encomium. It follows upon the death of Nikolaos' parents and subsequent arrival on Mt. Olympos (Mt. Uludağ) above Prousa (Bursa) in northwestern Turkey. This was a major monastic center, especially during the middle Byzantine period.

Psellos weaves Nikolaos into the spiritual landscape of the mountain. He then turns to Nikolaos' devotion to the Mother of God, a devotion that will later lead to the foundation of the Monastery of the Beautiful Source.[1] Nikolaos' relation to the Mother of God is introduced by way of his devotion to an icon of hers. Psellos begins by noting that it is not just Nikolaos' prayers but also his song that prompts the Mother of God to speak to him. Interestingly, even before this miracle, the icon is presented as a medium through which one can both see the Mother of God and be seen by her. But it is the advent of the miracle, manifest when the Mother of God again assumes her fleshly nature in the icon, that allows Nikolaos to say that he sees her. Psellos is then led to propose that an ethical preparation has made this manifestation possible, and he invites his audience to model themselves after Nikolaos. A similar point is made in *Letters Two* and *Three* of this volume. It is this spiritual ascent that will then allow one to see the "divine visibles (τὰ θεῖα . . . θεάματα)," that is, the things that have become visible to those who have become able to look upon divinity. This vision is described as being received by the one looking. This sense of direction reiterates one of Psellos' key themes, namely, that the divine subject controls the possibility and limits of human vision. Psellos then discusses the manner in which vision may be contested. Man is both intellectual and material. It is important that his vision be directed by the mind towards God or else the dangerous spirits that lurk in matter might deceive him. This point is possibly directed against the followers of Symeon the New Theologian. When Psellos points out that, "ignorant of our fall, we might perhaps see light, but replete with deceptions and trickery," he may be directly addressing their mystical spirituality and denouncing it as being potentially misleading because it was based in ignorance. This argument is developed more fully in his 1058 *Accusation* against the Patriarch Michael I Keroularios (*Or. for.* 1).

This passage, therefore, develops a number of themes that resonate throughout Psellos' aesthetics. The icon is a potential portal between the human and the divine. The one looking at the image may prepare himself to see, ascending towards the possibility of both seeing and being with the divine. This possibility can, however, only be realized when that divine being lets itself extraordinarily to be seen. This use of the miraculous is also to be

1. *Or. fun.* I 10.21. Having seen the Mother of God in a vision, Nikolaos chooses to name his church the Beautiful Source in honor of her.

found in Psellos' account of the regular miracle at the Blachernai (also in this volume).

Editions and translations. We have used the text in the new edition by Polemis (2014: *Or. fun.* I 10); cf. also the earlier edition by Gautier (1974). A German translation can be found at Weiss 1977: 221–322.

From An Encomium for a Monk Nikolaos, Who Became Abbot of the Beautiful Source Monastery on Olympos[1]

[17.] Nikolaos used to converse with the Mother of God with propitiatory prayers as if she were both watching him and being seen by him; and when at times he also used chants in order to offer Her thanks and praises, he calmly addressed her in his soul[2] and directed all of his desire toward her. Therefore, on one occasion, when he set up her icon before him and looked at it intently, speaking to her with the words of the Archangel, saying now this, then that "Hail," and adding melody and rhythm to his praise,[3] he saw that the divine icon (trembling and astonishment are seizing me!) had changed completely into her fleshly nature; then, when She first gazed upon him graciously with Her eyes (O awesome countenance and voice!), whispering softly through her lips, She said: "Hail you as well, father!"; and he, with a calm soul, responded: "Indeed, I rejoice, since I see you, the cause of joy!"[4]

1. *Or. fun.* I 10.17.19–18.23. Gautier's French paraphrase of this passage can be found on pages 27–28 of the article (1974). A full German translation can be found at: Weiss 1977: 245–47.

2. Reading "τῇ ψυχῇ," following Polemis' suggestion in his app. crit.

3. Weiss (1977: 246n17) asks whether this song might not be the *Akathistos Hymn*, which was marked by the use of the "Hail" found in our passage, while Gautier (1974: 51n494) simply links the "Hail" to the Archangel's greeting addressed to Mary at Luke 1:28; however, Nikolaos' chanting (as well as allusion; see next n.) suggests that he may be singing from the relevant *kanôn.*

4. Χαρᾶς αἰτίαν: as noted by Polemis, the phrase echoes (if not cites) Joseph the Hymnographer, *Kanôn on the Mother of God, for the Saturday of the Akathistos Hymn* 117 (ed. Christ and Paranikas 1871: 249).

If someone does not believe these things, I will not argue. But, if one might be disposed to accept this account, he should not stop at this acceptance. Rather, he should embody the virtue of the man and emulate his dispassion, after which or in which such things are usually achieved—for struggle and exertion last until one has transcended nature,[5] but, once one rises up above, the great toil ceases and one witnesses the divine spectacles.

[18.] Thus, when Nikolaos too had reached those heights, he conversed with those on high; sometimes he would contemplate with unerring visions of the mind and sometimes he would even receive the manifestations of the divine through his bodily eyes.[6] Though exerting himself in contemplation, however, he still did not neglect action. After all, contemplation divorced from action fails to reach distinction;[7] for spirits embedded in matter fear nothing more than one's separation from matter and this separation is the effect of action; hence, the demons assume the darkness of matter entirely and thus both approach and affect us. As long as we are in the flesh and thus are in the middle of the two extremes (namely, matter and intellect), we are neither purely intellectual nor purely material; for, as we are proximate to both, we acquire something from each of these. For this reason, even when we become intellectual, we still require action in accordance with God, mixed as we are still with matter. If we refrain from action, then we will not achieve the city of the living God,[8] but shall be cast into the valley of weeping;[9] and then, ignorant of our fall, we might perhaps see light, but replete with deceptions and trickery. Rather, may we be in divine darkness where the light without dissimulation and the truth shine.[10] As for the fact that the intellect, which is still in the body, casts away entirely neither nature nor matter (since these burdens are united with it, like stalks, husks, and beards are united with the corn), it is the demonic assaults that prove this—for the devil does not stay away from a contemplative intellect, as he knows that it is still in matter, namely, in that from which he gains his power.

5. ὑπερκύψῃ τῆς φύσεως: from Synesios, *On Dreams* 4.4 (ed. Lamoureux).

6. Cf. Gregory Nazianzos, *Apologêtikos* = *Or.* 2.7 with Papaioannou 2013: 172–74. See also Synesios, *On Boldness* 7.1 (ed. Lamoureux), as noted by Polemis.

7. Cf. Maximos the Confessor, *On Difficulties in the Bible, to Thalassios* 58.65–69, as noted by Polemis.

8. Cf. Hebrews 12:22.

9. Cf. Psalms 83:7.

10. Cf. Exodus 20:21 with Psellos, *Theol.* I 94.34, as noted by Polemis.

22 The Empress Zoe and Christ Antiphonêtês

Translated with introduction and notes
by Charles Barber

Introduction

Although the following passage is brief (*Chronographia* 6.66), it has become one of the more discussed texts concerning an icon written by Michael Psellos.[1] The text was probably written before 1063 and certainly refers to the years before 1050, when the Empress Zoe died. Zoe had been the key to the imperial throne in the years that followed upon the death of her father Constantine VIII in 1028. She had been married to Romanos III, Michael IV, and Constantine IX Monomachos, and in 1042 she had ruled the empire without a consort, but with her sister Theodora.[2]

This passage is part of an account of Zoe's qualities. It is found in the section of the *Chronographia* devoted to Constantine IX's reign (1042–55). Psellos has just praised Zoe's devotion to God when he offers the example of her veneration of her *Christ Antiphonêtês* (the Guarantor) to illustrate this quality.

1. Recent essays include: Mango 1959: 142–48; James 1996: 83–85; Duffy 1995: 88–90; Magdalino 1998; Barber 2007: 83–85.

2. There are numerous accounts of Zoe's life. Perhaps the most nuanced is that found in Hill 1999.

This icon has been made to order for the Empress. It must therefore be understood as a version of one of the major Constantinopolitan icons, the *Christ Antiphonêtês*, which was kept in a chapel attached to the church of the Theotokos at Chalkoprateia.[3] As further evidence of Zoe's devotion to this cult, we know that she refurbished this chapel and chose to be buried there.[4] Her icon is described as being highly accurate (ἀκριβέστερον) and embellished with shining matter (λαμπροτέρᾳ ὕλῃ ποικίλασα). This might imply an icon covered with a metal revetment or perhaps an enamel icon. Psellos is most concerned to tell us about the oracular qualities of this icon. For Zoe not only speaks to the icon and contemplates it and embraces it and weeps before it, she also uses it to foretell the future. If in answer to a question the icon's color becomes pale, then she expects bad things to happen. Should the icon's coloring become fiery and radiant, it would appear that this was good news and worthy of reporting to the emperor.

It is striking to see that this man-made thing could become an oracular medium. It is also worth noting that this is not an isolated instance in Psellos' writings. In his account of the icon at Blachernai (*Or. hag.* 4.689–94; see this volume), he goes to great lengths in comparing it to ancient oracles and even speaks of the predictive value of colors.[5] Zoe's *Christ Antiphonetes* should not therefore be seen as an exceptional item, rather, for Psellos, it is an apt means of illustrating her piety.

Editions and translations. Among the numerous English translations of this passage one may note those at: Sewter 1966: 188 and Papamastorakis 2003: 505. For a complete list of manuscripts, editions, and discussions, see Moore 2005: 445–57. We would like to thank Professor Roderich Reinsch who kindly allowed us to consult, before its publication, his new edition of Psellos' *Chronographia* for the translation of this passage.

3. Magdalino 1998.

4. Papamastorakis 2003: 497–511. Anna Komnene is our witness for Zoe's burial in the chapel (*Alexiad* 6.3 = p. 173.63–67).

5. Discussed in Barber 2007: 83–93.

From The Chronographia (6.66)

I should mention also *her* (to say it thus) Jesus, whom she had had shaped most accurately and embellished with the most brilliant material, an icon which was made for her as if it were almost alive; for it responded to questions with its colors, and its appearance revealed the future. She thus foretold many things concerning the future from that thing. Indeed, whether something pleasant had happened or whether something unfortunate had occurred, she would immediately go to the icon, either to express gratitude or to make atonement. I myself have often seen her at more difficult times, now embracing and contemplating this sacred icon, both speaking to it as if it were alive and addressing it with the best of names, and now lying on the ground with tears washing the earth and beating and tearing at her breasts. If she saw Him turn pale, she would go away crestfallen, but if He became fiery and luminous with the most splendid radiance, she would immediately notify the emperor about this and would announce the future.

23 Select Letters on Art and Aesthetics

Charles Barber

Introduction

The following section offers translations of five examples drawn from the extensive corpus of letters produced by Michael Psellos.[1] Few of these letters betray their date of composition, nor can the recipient of the letter always be identified; nonetheless each letter offers some remarks regarding icons, art, or aesthetics. While some of these remarks appear to be illustrative of other points within the letters, others form the substance of the letter itself. Each instance given here indicates that it is possible to identify points in common between these brief reflections and those in Psellos' more extended discussions found elsewhere in this volume. As such, these letters reveal that Psellos deployed his more theoretical considerations in other contexts, implying some continuity in his thought, regardless of the medium in which it was exposed.

When Anthony Cutler and Robert Browning drew attention to the art-historical value of Michael Psellos' letters, they argued that these brief texts offered their readers perceptions of Byzantine icons that had generally been marginalized. They rightly pointed out that an overemphasis upon the more orthodox and theological views found in the proceedings of church councils

1. The selection made here draws upon the letters identified in Cutler and Browning 1992.

and similar sources might limit our understanding of the life of the icon in Byzantium.[2] This led them to conclude that sources such as Psellos' letters allow us to witness a multiplicity of roles for and responses to such works and to suggest that this understanding ought to take a more central place in our conception of the Byzantine icon.[3]

The following selection of letters does not include all those that pertain to icons or visual aesthetics in general.[4] Our translations will not only provide the entire letter that remains to us, but sets these letters alongside many of Psellos' other essays on icons and aesthetics. These will inform and extend our reading of these letters and will, as already mentioned, demonstrate that the perceptions found in these letters belong within the wider horizon of Psellos' thought. As such, they remain firmly embedded within his philosophical purview.

The first letter was written to Konstantinos, the nephew of the Patriarch Keroularios, who in the letter's inscription is identified as "sakellarios"—a high position with financial responsibilities in the imperial or patriarchal administration.[5] In seeking to praise the recipient of this letter, Psellos has used a lengthy discussion of an icon owned by the *sakellarios* to introduce the *topos* of the inadequacy of his own words regarding the praise owed his audience.

The icon's subject is not specifically identified in the letter, but in speaking of "the blood from the wound," "the living mortification of the face and the living death," it is probably reasonable to assume that the image showed a Crucifixion.[6] As such, this letter invites comparison with the *ekphrasis* of a Crucifixion found at the end of Psellos' sermon on the Crucifixion (see

2. Cutler and Browning 1992: 21–22.

3. Cutler and Browning 1992: 31–32.

4. For example, we have not included all the letters pertaining to Psellos' habits as collector of art objects (icons: S 184; ancient statues: S 141); see also Papaioannou 2013: 179 and p. 6 above.

5. For the identification with Konstantinos, cf. Psellos' letters S 45 and 46, as well as S 174, which precedes our letter in two of the manuscripts that transmit it: Vat. gr. 1912 f. 145v and Athen. Mus. Benaki TA 250 (93) f. 47r. On Konstantinos (and his brother Nikephoros), see the bibliography in Papaioannou 2013: 10 and, further, Wassiliou-Seibt 2011, as well as the forthcoming dissertation by Nepheli Mauche (Université Paris-Sorbonne [Paris IV]). See also p. 5 above.

6. Other possibilities include the deposed Christ (Cutler and Browning 1992: 23) or perhaps a very early example of a Byzantine *Man of Sorrows* image.

introduction to text 19 in this volume). In both cases Psellos is intrigued by the possibilities for paradox in the crucifixion itself and its representation. Christ is understood to be both living and dead. Psellos feigns doubt regarding the possibility that discourse could match this subject, while marveling at the icon's ability to repudiate nature. In setting up this contrast, Psellos makes a number of interesting points regarding the work of art. To begin with, we are told that an image "in no way differs from its model." This point is startlingly underlined by the description of Psellos touching the painted icon as if it were Christ's body. It is an identity between the painting and the painted that is conveyed by the icon itself. This proceeds from the depiction of Christ's head, body, and blood from the wound to the contemplation of the paradoxical quality of what is seen there, namely, "the living mortification of the face and the living death" of Christ. This paradox then leads Psellos to contemplate the novelty of the icon, suggesting that its ability to depict this subject has changed the rules for both the work and its assessment: "once something novel has happened, how can it be repeated successfully? For if the icon is simply the result of the power of art or of mixing of colors, then perhaps the art of versification too would not give up competing against the lower craft <of painting>." This possibility leads Psellos to reconsider his verbal art—likely referring to an epigram commissioned for the icon—noting how a discordant play of words might bring one closer to the truth of the subject that is Christ.

The second letter was written to a *kritês* (governor/judge) of the Aegean theme,[7] Psellos' close friend Nikolaos Skleros.[8] Psellos writes requesting support for the monastery of the *Acheiropoietos* found outside the walls of Constantinople near the Golden Gate, and owned by Psellos (see K-D 250-1, and perhaps also K-D 77).[9] As the image of the Mother of God found there was of miraculous origin, that is, not-made-by-human-hands, it has brought her to be ineffably and invisibly there in the church. Interestingly, the seeming paradox of an invisible presence mediated by a visual object appears to fuel a discussion that is reluctant to grant too great an importance to the object itself. For Psellos suggests that the judge should not only reverence the icon but also the invisible shadows of the Mother of God. This line of thought is reiterated when Psellos argues that faith in the Mother of God does not de-

7. On the *Aigaion thema*, see Koder 1998: 78–81.

8. On Nikolaos Skleros, see Seibt 1976: 93–97.

9. Correctly identified as the monastery of the Abramites (Janin 1969: 4–6 and 1975: 441) in Cutler and Browning 1992: 26n6. See also Külzer 2008: 680–81.

rive from standing before her icon nor from frequently embracing this; rather he proposes a more ethical model for the development of such faith. As such he invites the judge to model himself upon the virtues of the higher powers and thence to give to the church that houses the image. In drawing the reader to this ethical point, Psellos both recognizes the power of the miraculous icon while at the same time circumscribing its value as an object.

The third letter is addressed to John Xiphilinos and also touches upon the relation between an image and an ethical life.[10] Xiphilinos was an old friend of Psellos. He had been the head of legal education in Constantinople; however, following tensions with the emperor Constantine X Monomachos in the mid-eleventh century, he had chosen to become a monk and to retire to Mount Olympos. Psellos had also, briefly, undertaken to follow this same path. This letter might date to 1054 and follows upon Psellos' return to Constantinople. Unlike Psellos, Xiphilinos appears to have taken well to the monastic life and was to serve as patriarch of Constantinople from 1064 until 1075. Our third letter praises Xiphilinos' spirituality while excusing Psellos' return to Constantinople. In so doing, he offers perhaps backhanded praise for Xiphilinos' greater disposition for the spiritual life. As such Psellos presents Xiphilinos as one who has already achieved an elevated spiritual status. This is contrasted with his own difficulties in balancing his human and his spiritual/intellectual disposition. In order to illustrate this point Psellos leaves behind the lengthy sailing metaphor that burdens this letter and offers the example of an ascent to spiritual beauty as a model for his own potential journey. For Psellos, intelligible beauty is neither visible nor knowable in itself and so can only become known to us by means of a likeness. This likeness may be found in material things, but it is necessary that one ascend beyond these by using other means, such as beautiful ways of being, beautiful deeds, and beautiful words, in order to achieve a proper spiritual disposition. This understanding closely parallels Psellos' reading of Plotinos' teaching on intelligible beauty found elsewhere in this volume. Like *Letter Two* above, the icon itself is placed at a relatively low level in the path to spiritual ascent.

The fourth letter was written to a metropolitan of Chalkedon. The reference in the letter to the impoverished dress of newly appointed senators allowed Oikonomides to date this brief note to the mid-1050s (though this dating

10. Xiphilinos was to be patriarch of Constantinople from 1064 until 1075. Our best introduction to him is Michael Psellos' funeral oration for his old friend: *Or. fun.* I 3, trans. in Kaldellis and Polemis 2015: 177–228. See also Bonis 1937a.

is far from certain), a period that, under Constantine IX Monomachos, witnessed the broadening of access to the Senate.[11] Oikonomides interprets the letter to be written in response to the metropolitan's rejection of the gift of an icon. Psellos appears to be making a rather extraordinary argument in favor of the metropolitan accepting the proffered gift, as it appears that Psellos might be offering him stolen goods. Psellos suggests that he is content both to steal icons from churches and to give them away without any pangs of guilt. Both propositions imply a certain indifference to the material value of these icons. Yet, it is his motive for both purloining and retaining the icons that is of interest. He explains that it is because these faint images were "formed by the painter's art" that he holds on to them, even though, lacking gold or silver covers, their monetary value is not high. The letter thus presents the existence of a collection of small icons that are valued for their artistic qualities alone.

The fifth letter was written to an unknown recipient. It reports on Psellos' experience with a miraculous image of the Mother of God owned by a monastery of Ta Kathara.[12] As argued in the introduction to part 2 of this volume, this letter summarizes Psellos' understanding of the image. In its consideration of the impact of an image upon its viewer, it bears some points of resemblance to Psellos' accounts of miraculous icons.[13] Psellos begins by identifying himself as "a most fastidious viewer of icons." This claim to attentiveness would appear to strengthen the implications of a connoisseurial attitude in *Letter Three*. It is striking then to find that, having introduced this quality, Psellos shows that it is overwhelmed by another possibility. This icon has "astonished (ἐκπλήξασα)" him with its indescribable beauty and now threatens both his senses and his judgment. Rather than reading these phrases as expressions of a "purely aesthetic" judgment, one should first consider the degree to which they enhance a position found in several of Psellos' texts that seeks to embrace both a sensible and an intellectual relation with the icon.[14]

11. Oikonomides 1991: 36.

12. For this Bithynian monastery, see Janin 1975: 158–60. The monastery was owned by Psellos (cf. S 77 and K-D 200 with Papaioannou 2013: 10). For the possible existence of a monastery with the same name also in Constantinople, see Janin 1969: 3:273.

13. For example the discussions of the icon in the *An Encomium for a Monk Nikolaos, Who Became Abbot of the Beautiful Source Monastery on Olympos*, the account of the miraculous icon at Blachernai, and the *Antiphonetes* text found in this volume.

14. We are here arguing against the interpretation offered at Cutler and Browning 1992: 28.

Thus while his fastidious eyes may see the colors that have presented the Mother of God's corporal nature, her actual form is only partly rendered by these means, requiring a further intervention to make the whole available to Psellos. For this to happen, Psellos enlarges his perception of the icon beyond the visual alone. His argument for doing so rests in his understanding that the icon needs to address more than a likeness to the Mother of God's body. It must also grasp the divine beauty into which her body has been transformed. This lies beyond the senses themselves. As such the fastidious vision that might find beauty in a strand of hair is inadequate. Her astounding us in and through the icon overwhelms our ability to see the shape of the Mother of God. This reading of the perception of the icon gives a privileged role to the thing seen as that which determines how we see it. Nonetheless, Psellos remains interested in the part that the beholder can play. He thus notes the formation of a more privileged beholder, who, thanks to their performance of the usual prayers is able to become witness to Christ in the icon. It is a model of miraculous intervention and change that can also be found in Psellos' account of other Marian icons, such as those at Blachernai and at the Monastery of the Beautiful Source (see elsewhere in this volume).

These five letters show that Psellos' discourse on icons and visual aesthetics in his letters echoes that to be found in his other works. These five pieces reveal a correspondent who is willing to express pleasure in and care for works of art. Rather than reading these as an echo of our own modernist aesthetics, one can find traces of the eleventh-century intellectual concerns that have shaped his attitudes to these works. Psellos' aesthetics are shaped by a philosophy that was profoundly concerned with the boundaries that distinguished the human sensible knowledge mediated by icons and the intelligible and superior knowledge that existed beyond these material things and perceptions. His own pleasure in painting could thereby be surpassed by an astonishing and miraculous experience of the subject mediated by such painting.

Editions and translations. The letters are offered here in a new critical edition in anticipation of the new edition of Psellos' letters by Papaioannou (where more details on editorial technique, etc.); information on the earlier editions and manuscripts is offered in the first note of the Greek text of each letter, followed by notes that record variant readings. Citations and allusions are in the notes to the translations. Partial translations may be found at Cutler and Browning 1992.

Letters

Critical edition by Stratis Papaioannou

Translation with notes by Charles Barber, David Jenkins, and Stratis Papaioannou

Abbreviations

Manuscripts

A	Athen. Mus. Benaki TA 250 (93), 16th/17th c.
E	Scorial. Y I 9 (248), 16th c. (a copy of M)
L	Laur. Plut. gr. 57.40, late 11th c. or early 12th c.
M	Marc. gr. 524, late 13th c.
O	Oxon. Barocc. gr. 131, 13th c., second half (produced in the circle of Manuel Holobolos?)
U	Vat. gr. 1912, 12th c., first third
a^1	Ambros. M 84 sup, 16th c. (a likely copy of e)
e	Scorial. Φ III 1 (220), 16th c. (a likely copy of E)
m^2	Monac. gr. 98, 16th c. (a likely copy of e)

Editions

G	Gautier, P. "Quelques lettres de Psellos inédites ou déjà éditées." *Revue des Études Byzantines* 44 (1986): 111–97.

K-D Kurtz, E., and F. Drexl, eds. *Michael Psellus: Scripta minora magnam partem adhuc inedita II, Epistulae.* Orbis romanus, biblioteca del testi medievali a cura dell' Università cattolica del Sacro cuore 5.2. Milan: Società editrice "Vita e pensiero," 1941.

Maltese Maltese, E. V. "Epistole inedite di Michele Psello." *Studi Italiani di Filologia Classica* III 5 (1987): 82–98 and 214–23; 6 (1988): 110–34.

S Sathas, K. N., ed. Μεσαιωνικὴ Βιβλιοθήκη: Συλλογὴ ἀνεκδότων μνημείων τῆς Ἑλληνικῆς ἱστορίας V; Μιχαὴλ Ψελλοῦ ἱστορικοὶ λόγοι, ἐπιστολαὶ καὶ ἄλλα ἀνέκδοτα. Venice: Phoinix, 1876 = Paris: Libraires-Éditeurs, 1876. Repr. Athens: Γρηγοριάδης, 1972.

Letter One

Τῷ σακελλαρίῳ[1] <Κωνσταντίνῳ>

Ὥσπερ εἴ τι δ' ἂν πρὸς σὲ ὑπὲρ σοῦ φθεγξαίμην, συνέσεως καὶ εὐφυΐας ἔμψυχον ἄγαλμα, ἔλαττόν ἐστι τῆς ἐμφύτου μοι πρός σε διαθέσεως, κἀνταῦθα μόνον ἡ γλῶττα τῆς γνώμης ἀπολιμπάνεται, οὕτω δὴ καὶ τῆς σῆς εἰκόνος (λεγέσθω γὰρ οὕτως, εἰ βούλει·[2] εἰ δὲ τὸ ἀληθὲς ἀκούειν ἐθέλεις[3]: τοῦ πρώτου καὶ ἀκριβοῦς παραδείγματος) τὸ ἐν τοῖς λόγοις μέτρον[4] μᾶλλον ὑστέρησεν, ἢ ὅσον ἐστὶν ὃ λέγεται· τὸ γάρ τοι μέτρον, αὐτὸ τοῦτο ὅπερ ἐστί, κανών, πρὸς ἃ[5] παραμεμέτρηται, λέγεται· ἐνταῦθα δὲ τοσούτου δεῖν αὐτὸ ἥγημαι, ὥστε τυχεῖν τοῦ ὀνόματος, ὁπόσου ητύχηκεν.[6]

Ἡ μὲν γὰρ εἰκὼν οὐδὲν τοῦ παραδείγματος διενήνοχεν, ὥς γέ μοι[7] δοκεῖ. Ἔγωγ' οὖν[8] καὶ ὡς σώματος πολλάκις ἡψάμην τοῦ χρώματος· καί μοι ἡ χεὶρ οὐκ ἐψεύσατο, ἀλλὰ τῇ δόξῃ συνηκολούθησεν. Οὕτως ἡ βάσις· οὕτως ἡ τάσις· οὕτω τὸ σχῆμα τῆς κεφαλῆς· οὕτω τοῦ τραύματος ὁ ἰχώρ, καὶ ἡ ζῶσα τοῦ προσώπου νέκρωσις, καὶ ὁ ἔμψυχος θάνατος![9]

1. K-D 211 (based only on ms. O); U 145v (des. mut.), O 287v–288r (= O[1]) et 348v (= O[2]), A 47r (des. mut.); tit. scripsi: τῷ σακελλαρίῳ U O[1] A K-D τοῦ ὑπερτίμου Ψελλοῦ O[2]
2. εἰ βούλει, οὕτως O[1]
3. ἀκριβὲς ἐθέλεις ἀκούειν O[2]
4. μέτρον om. A
5. πρὸς ὃ K-D
6. ἠτύχηκεν U O[2] A: ηὐτύχηκεν O[1] K-D
7. γ' ἐμοὶ A
8. ἐγὼ γοῦν A
9. θάνατος des. U (post θάνατος folia ceciderunt) et A, itaque epistulae finis deest in U et A

To <Konstantinos>, the Sakellarios[1]

Just as whatever I might say to you about yourself, the living image[2] of sagacity and good nature, is less than my innate disposition towards you and, only in your case, my tongue lags behind my intention, so too, in regard to your icon (let me call it that, if you like; but if you wish to hear the truth, <let me call it> the icon of the first and exact model [i.e., Christ]), the meter [i.e., *metron* = measure/meter] of my verses is rather inferior—as much as meter is what we call it; for in its very essence measure [*metron*] is said to be a rule [*kanôn*] in relation to things against which it is measured; yet in this case, I consider that it is so much lacking as much as it has failed.[3]

For the image in no way differs from its model [i.e., Christ]—so it seems to me at any rate. Thus I have often grasped its colors, as I would a body; and my hand did not belie but confirmed my impression. Such was the lower part of the body, such the stretching out <of the hands>, such the pose of the head, such the blood from the wound, the living mortification of the face, and the living death!

1. A partial translation of this text together with a commentary can be found in Cutler and Browning 1992. Moore 2005: 142 (*Ep.* 523). For the addressee, see p. 349 above.

2. For this metaphor, see Papaioannou 2013: 179–91.

3. The references to *metron* throughout the letter as well as to *stichoi* (verses) below suggest that Psellos wrote a poem about, or an inscription for, an icon of Konstantinos. This letter is thus a rare case of a Byzantine who reflects on the composition of poetry for icons, a ubiquitous art; see also Psellos' S 184 (also to Konstantinos, most likely) with a similar topic.

Τίς δ' ἂν εἴη[10] τῷ παραδείγματι λόγος προσόμοιος, πρὸς ὃ ἡ εἰκὼν τὴν φύσιν ἠρνήσατο; Πῶς δ' ἂν[11] τὸ μέτρον συσχηματισθείη τῇ ἀληθείᾳ, καὶ συναποθάνοι ἡ λέξις τῷ Λόγῳ νεκρῷ;[12] Πῶς δ' ἂν ὁ νοῦς τὴν ἐκπνοὴν μιμήσαιτο τῆς ψυχῆς; Ἅπαξ δὲ καινοτομηθέντος τοῦ πράγματος, πῶς τὸ πολλάκις γινόμενον ἔσται ἐπιτυχές; Εἰ μὲν γὰρ τέχνης δύναμις ἡ εἰκών, εἰ χρωμάτων κράσις,[13] τάχ' ἂν καὶ ἡ τοῦ μέτρου τέχνη οὐκ ἀπείρηκε[14] πρὸς τὴν βάναυσον.[15] Ἐπεὶ δὲ τὸ πᾶν ἐκμαγεῖόν ἐστι τῆς ἀληθοῦς φύσεως, τίνι τρόπῳ ὁ λόγος τὸ ὑπὲρ φύσιν χαρακτηρίσειεν; Ἔπειτα ἔκθαμβος εὐθὺς[16] ὁ νοῦς γινόμενος, καὶ κατὰ τὴν πρώτην ἐπιβολὴν ἐκπλαγεὶς ὥσπερ οἱ φοιβόληπτοι, ἰλίγγου καὶ σκοτοδίνης καὶ τὸν ὑπηρέτην λόγον πληροῖ. Καὶ ὥσπερ ἵππος ἁρμάτειος οὗτος,[17] τὸν ἐφεστηκότα[18] νοῦν ἀποβεβληκώς, οἴχεται περιφερόμενος[19] πάσαις πλάναις καὶ πάσαις περιφοραῖς. Καὶ τό γε χαλεπώτερον ἐναντίωμα, ὅτι χείρων τῆς πλάνης ἡ ἐπιστροφή· ὅτε γὰρ ἐρεῖσαι τὸν νοῦν πρὸς τὸν τύπον βουλήσομαι, τότε ταράττομαι, ὥσπερ οἱ ναυτιῶντες προσκεκυφότες τοῖς κύμασι.

Γενοῦ οὖν αὐτὸς μέτρον ἀμφοῖν, τῷ τε ἐμῷ φημι[20] λόγῳ καὶ τῷ σῷ παραδείγματι (οὕτω γὰρ εἰπεῖν κάλλιον), τὸ μὲν ὑπὲρ φύσιν τιθείς, τὸ δὲ ἐμὸν φύσεως εὕρημα. Κἂν εἰ τοσοῦτον ἡμάρτηκα τῆς πρωτοτύπου μορφῆς, μήτε μοι μέμφου, μήτε με θαύμαζε, πῶς, ἐν ἄλλοις κρεῖττον μετρῶν, ἐνταῦθα ἧττον[21] ἑάλωκα· οὐ γάρ ἐστιν ὅμοιον, ἀλλὰ καὶ πάντῃ ἀνόμοιον: τοῖς μὲν γὰρ ἄλλοις ὁ λόγος διαιτᾷ τὸ κατάλληλον, διαιτᾶσθαι δὲ παρὰ τοῦ κρείττονος εὐτύχημα ἥγηται.

Ἡδέως δ' ἄν σου πυθοίμην: εἴ με ἑώρακας σκιᾶς τινος σώματος τοῖς δακτύλοις περιδραξάμενον, οὐκ ἂν ἐξεπλάγης, καὶ «ἀποτρόπαιε»[22] πολλάκις

10. εἴη om. O[1]
11. δ' ἂν om. O[2]
12. τῷ ζῶντι νεκρῷ O[1]
13. κράσεις O[2] K-D
14. ἡ τοῦ μέτρου βάσις ἀπείρηκε O[2]
15. βάσανον O[2] K-D
16. εὐθὺς om. O[1]
17. οὕτως O[2]
18. ἀφεστηκότα O[1]
19. φερόμενος O[1]
20. φημι om. O[2]
21. ἥττων O[2]
22. ἀποτρόπαιον O[1]

Yet what discourse could resemble the model [i.e., Christ] with respect of whom the icon has repudiated its nature? How could meter conform to the truth and diction share in the death of the Word? How could the sense <of my verses> imitate the death of the soul? Once this novel event has occurred, how can meter that repeats itself many times be successful? For if the icon is simply the result of the power of art or of mixing of colors, then perhaps the art of versification too would not give up competing against the lower craft <of painting>. But since the entire thing [i.e., the icon] is an impression of the true nature,[4] how is discourse to portray the supernatural? At this the mind becomes terrified and panic-stricken during the first attempt, and, like those possessed by Phoebus,[5] it fills its servant discourse with dizziness and vertigo. And like a chariot horse that has cast off mind, its driver,[6] discourse rushes off into all kinds of digressions and circumvolutions. And the most difficult obstacle is that the journey of return is worse than the digression. For when I wish to fix my mind on the figure, I then become confused, like seasick voyagers who lean towards the waves.[7]

You yourself should therefore become the "measure" of both, that is to say, of both my poem and your model (for it is better to say it this way), considering that the latter is supernatural and my poem is the offspring of natural talent. And if I have failed so much in regard to the form of the prototype, neither chastise me nor wonder how is it that I, who uses meter in the best way in other cases, am here caught using it in the worst manner. For this situation is not similar; in fact it is utterly dissimilar: for while discourse might govern its correspondent in other instances, <in this instance> it considers <itself> fortunate to be governed by that which is superior.

I would now like to learn from you: if you had seen me grasping the shadows of some body with my fingers, would you not have been frightened and

4. Wording that echoes Plato, *Timaeus* 50c: ἐκμαγεῖον γὰρ φύσει παντὶ κεῖται.

5. That is, Apollo. Psellos likely borrows the term φοιβόληπτοι from Proklos (cf., e.g., *Platonic Theology* 5.131.25); see also Psellos, *Theol.* I 74.84–85.

6. See Plato, *Phaedrus* 246a6–b4 and 253d1–254e9; see also *Phil. min.* II 7.

7. For a similar image, see Psellos' *Encomium of Gregory of Nazianzos' Style* § 6: 46–53 (above pp. 127–28).

εἴρηκας, ὥσπερ ἀποτροπιαζόμενος τὴν καινοτομίαν τοῦ πράγματος; Πόσῳ οὖν ἐστι μᾶλλον τοῦ σκιὰν κατασχεῖν τὸ λόγῳ[23] συλλαβεῖν ποσῶς τὴν ἀλήθειαν; Τοῦτο δέ ἐστι τὸ μὴ πόρρω γενέσθαι τοῦ τῆς σῆς εἰκόνος μορφώματος. Καὶ εἴ μοι τοῖς στίχοις προσέξεις τὸν νοῦν, καὶ τὴν κατάλληλον ἀκαταλληλίαν τῶν λέξεων ἐννοήσειας, καὶ τὴν ἔμψυχον ἀπορίαν, καὶ τὴν μονοειδῆ διχόνοιαν, τάχ' ἂν σκιὰν ἐρεῖς καὶ τὸν λόγον τοῦ χρώματος.

Ἀλλ' ἐγὼ μὲν ἐλάττων τῆς ἀληθείας ἐλήλυθα· ἀνομολογήσομαι[24] δὲ καὶ τῶν σῶν ἐπαίνων ἐλλείπειν, ὦ μόνος σὺ μετά γε τὸν μέγιστον αὐτοκράτορα ἡμῶν τοῦτον τὸν λόγον[25] ἀκηκοὼς παρ' ἐμοῦ,[26] καὶ ταῦτα ἐν γράμμασιν, ἵν' ἔχῃς τῆς μαρτυρίας τὸ ἀσφαλές. Ἀλλὰ μὴ οὕτω σὺ πρὸς ἡμᾶς ἔν γε τῇ διαμείψει τοῦ σηρικοῦ, ἀλλὰ καλλίω φάνηθι διδοὺς ἢ οἰόμενος, κάλλιστε πάντων ἐμοί, καὶ μαργάρων, καὶ ὑφασμάτων, καὶ τῆς λοιπῆς εὐδαιμονίας τε καὶ λαμπρότητος.[27]

23. τῷ λόγῳ O[2]
24. ἀνωμολόγημαι O[1]
25. αὐτοκράτορα τὸν λόγον τοῦτον O[2] K-D
26. παρ' ἡμῶν O[2]
27. εὐδαιμονίας καὶ τῆς λαμπρότητος O[2]

said repeatedly, "Be gone," as if baffled by the strangeness of my action? How much more difficult is it to grasp the truth with discourse than to grasp a shadow? This is what has happened to <my> not being too far off from your icon. And indeed if you pay close attention to my verses and realize the appropriate inappropriateness of my words, the animate difficulty, and the singular discord, you might also call my text a shadow of the colors.

But I have arrived at that which is less than the truth, and I shall also admit to having failed in your praises, O you who alone, after our greatest ruler,[8] has heard these words from me, and this in a letter, so that you might have the assurance of its witness. But do not appear similarly inferior to us in the exchange of silk, rather appear giving better than what you think, <you who are> to me the most precious in comparison to anything, whether pearls, or fabrics, or any other fortune and brilliance.

8. This is most likely emperor Isaakios Komnenos (r. 1057–1059); cf. letters S 73 and S 49.

Letter Two

Τῷ αὐτῷ (scil. τῷ κριτῇ τοῦ Αἰγαίου Νικολάῳ τῷ Σκληρῷ)[1]

Εἰ βούλει πᾶσαν ἐν ταὐτῷ συλλέξασθαι ἀρετὴν καὶ ἀφορμὴν τῆς πρὸς τὰ κρείττω ἀναγωγῆς, τῇ θεοτόκῳ μάλιστα πρόσκεισο· καὶ ταύτης, μὴ τὰς εἰκόνας μόνον, ἀλλὰ καὶ τὰς ἀφανεῖς σέβου σκιάς, ὥσπερ δὴ καὶ ποιεῖν εἴωθας. Εἰ δέ που χειρὸς ἀνθρωπίνης χωρὶς ἐμπεφάνισται καὶ οἱονεὶ γέγραπται, ἐκεῖσε ταύτην οἴου ἀρρήτως ἐφεστάναι καὶ ἀθεάτως· ὥσπερ ἐν τῇ πρὸ τῶν τειχῶν τῆς βασιλίδος πόλεως μονῇ ὦπται τοῖς πᾶσιν ἐπέκεινα θαύματος, ἣν δὴ καὶ τῆς Ἀχειροποιήτου ἐντεῦθεν κατονομάζουσι.

Δείγματα[2] δὲ φιλοθεΐας, φιλοσοφωτάτη ψυχή, καὶ τῆς πρὸς τὴν μητέρα τοῦ θεοῦ διαθέσεως οὐ τὸ ταῖς εἰκόσι προσιέναι οὐδὲ τὸ πολλάκις καταπτύξασθαι τὸ ὁμοίωμα. Ἀλλὰ τί ποτε; Τὸ μὲν πρῶτον καὶ μέγιστον: ἑαυτοὺς ἀπεικονίσαι πρὸς τὴν ἐν τῷ κρείττονι ἀρετήν· εἶτα καὶ τοῦ νεὼ ποιήσασθαι ἐπιμέλειαν[3], ἐν ᾧ τὸ θεῖον τετίμηται, ἢ αὐτὸν καλλύνοντας, ἢ τῶν ὑπ' αὐτὸν ἀντεχομένους[4] κτημάτων. Ὅπερ δή σε νῦν ἡ ἀχειροποίητος θεοτόκος εἰσπράττεται δι' ἐμοῦ μεσίτου.

Καὶ εἴ γε[5] μοι πείθοιο, ὁ πάντοτε μέν μοι πειθόμενος καὶ τῶν ἐμῶν ἐξαρτώμενος λόγων καὶ βουλόμενος ὡς πρὸς παράδειγμα βλέπειν ἐμέ, νῦν δὲ μηδὲ γράμματι ὁμιλῶν μηδ' ἐρωτῶν ὅπως ἂν τῶν καλλίστων ἰχνῶν ἔχοιο

1. K-D 124; L 60v–61r; tit. scripsi: τῷ αὐτῷ L K-D.
2. δείγματα prop. Polemis: δόγματα L K-D
3. τοῦ ναοῦ ἀντέχεσθαι ἐπιμελῶς K-D
4. ἀντέχεσθαι K-D
5. γε om. K-D

To the same (the *kritês* of the Aegean theme, Nikolaos Skleros)[1]

If you wish to gather together in one place every virtue and means of ascending to higher things, devote yourself above all to the Mother of God; and revere not only her icons but also her invisible shadows, as indeed you are wont to do. And if she has become manifest somewhere and, as it were, painted without human hand, think that she has appeared there ineffably and invisibly, as for instance she has been seen by all beyond marvel in the monastery before the walls of the imperial city, which as a result they call the monastery of the *Acheiropoietos*.[2]

Most philosophical soul, signs of one's love of God and one's disposition towards the Mother of God lie neither in coming before her icons nor in frequently embracing her likeness. But then in what do these lie? First and foremost in modeling ourselves upon the virtue of the higher one, and next in attending carefully to the church in which the divinity is honored, either beautifying it or caring for the possessions belonging to it. This is what the Theotokos *Acheiropoietos* is now exacting from you by way of my mediation.

And if you might be persuaded by me (you who have always been persuaded by me and have been dependent upon my words, wishing to see me as an example, yet now neither converse by letter nor ask how to follow the most

1. A partial translation of this text together with a commentary can be found in Cutler and Browning 1992: 26–27. Moore 2005: 41 (*Ep.* 97). For the addressee, see p. 350 above.

2. On this monastery, see p. 350 above.

ἣν διέπεις ἀρχήν, ἀρχὴν ποίησον καὶ τῆς πρὸς τὸ θεῖον ἀκριβοῦς διαθέσεως, καὶ πρὸς τοὺς ἀκριβεστέρους τῶν φίλων τοῦ φιλίου καθήκοντος. Κἂν εἰ πάντων καταφρονήσειας, ἀλλὰ τῆς γε Ἀχειροποιήτου ἐπιμελήθητι, τῶν κτημάτων αὐτῆς ὡς οἰκειοτάτων ἀντεχόμενος κτήσεων.

Ἐμοὶ δὲ οὐ μέλει περὶ τῶν ἐμῶν (οἶδα γάρ, ὡς πεφρόντικας τούτων, εἰ καὶ μὴ τοσοῦτον ὅσον βεβουλήμεθα), ἀλλὰ περὶ ἐμοῦ, ὅτι οὐδέπω[6] καὶ τήμερόν μοι γεγράφηκας.

6. οὐδέπω scripsi (cf. app. font.): οὐδέποτε L K-D

beautiful traces in administering your authority), begin now both the proper disposition towards divinity and the obligation of friendship toward your best friends. And even if you neglected all else, do care for the *Acheiropoietos* by protecting her possessions as your very own.

I am not concerned about my own property (for I know that you have cared about it, even if not as much as we have wanted), but about myself, since to this day[3] you have not written to me.

3. The relevant Greek phrase, οὐδέπω καὶ τήμερον, originates in Demosthenic discourse (e.g., *Against Meidias* 81, 91, and 157), echoed, among others, in Gregory of Nazianzos' *Letters* (145.4 and 248.1) and in Psellos himself (see *Or. hag.* 7.344 and p. 216 above).

Letter Three

Τῷ μοναχῷ Ἰωάννῃ τῷ Ξιφιλίνῳ[1]

Μετεστράφης ποτέ, πρὸς οὓς ἀπεστράφης ὀψέ, φιλτάτη καὶ ἡγιασμένη ψυχή, ὥστε καὶ λόγον δοῦναι, καὶ βούλεσθαι τὸν ἴσον λαβεῖν, καὶ τὴν ἐντεῦθεν κοινωνίαν ἡμῖν προτρέψασθαι. Πότερον οὖν ἡμεῖς ἐξανθρωπίζομέν σε, ἢ αὐτὸς ἀποθεοῖς[2] ἡμᾶς; Καὶ πότερόν σοι[3] τὸ πρᾶγμα κατάβασις, ἢ ἡμετέρα ὁ[4] λόγος ἀνάβασις; Καί, εἰ μή τί σὴ δυσχερὲς δόγμα παρὰ φιλοσοφίας λαβεῖν, οἱ ἀκριβέστερον τῶν ἄλλων φιλοσοφήσαντες οὐ πάσαις ταῖς κρείττοσι φύσεσι τὴν αὐτὴν φύσιν διδόασιν. Ἀλλ' αἱ μὲν αὐτοῖς νεύσασαι πρὸς τὰ τῇδε τὴν ἄνω θεωρίαν ἀπολελοίπασιν· αἱ δέ, καὶ καταβᾶσαι καὶ πρὸς τοὺς ἥττους ταῖς προνοίαις ἐπιστραφεῖσαι, ἐν ταῖς πρώταις εἰσὶν ἐλλάμψεσι. Καί μοι τούτων εἴης αὐτός, ἵνα καὶ ἡμῖν ἀνθρωπικῶς ὁμιλῇς, καὶ τῆς θειοτέρας ἔχῃ σιγῆς, καὶ ἑκατέρωθεν ἐρανίζῃ τὰ πρόσφορα: παρὰ θεοῦ μὲν τὴν τοῦ ὄντος κατάληψιν, παρ' ἡμῶν δὲ ἡμᾶς, τὸ κάλλιστόν σοι[5] ἀγώγιμον.

1. G 17, Maltese 5; U 182r–183v (τῷ μοναχῷ Ἰωάννῃ τῷ Ξιφιλλίνῳ), M 159r–v (τῷ Ξιφιλίνῳ), E 220v–222v (τῷ Ξιφιλίνῳ), a[1] 143v–145r (τῷ Ξιφιλίνῳ), e 89r–90r (τῷ Ξιφιλίνῳ), m[2] 397v–399r (τῷ Ξιφιλίνῳ).
2. ἀποθειοῖς U
3. σοι G
4. ὁ om. E a[1] m[2]
5. σοι om. E a[1] m[2]

To the monk John Xiphilinos[1]

You have finally turned back to those whom you lately repudiated, o beloved and holy soul, so as to give an explanation,[2] expect the same <from me>, and urge us toward association from now on. So, do *we* humanize you or do *you* make us divine? Is this exchange a descent for you or an ascent for us? And if it does not irk you to learn something from philosophy, <know that> the more scrupulous among the philosophers do not attribute the same nature to all of the superior natures. Rather, while some natures, having been drawn to the things here, have abandoned contemplation of that which is above, while others, even though they have descended and turned to those who are inferior in foreknowledge, are among the foremost of the enlightened.[3] May you be one of the latter for me, so that you might both speak on a more human level with us and continue your more divine silence and so gather the offerings from both: from God, the understanding of Being, and from us, ourselves, the best commodity you can carry.

1. The letter dates likely in 1054 when Psellos went through a period of indecision as to whether he should join the monastic life together with his friend Xiphilinos on Mt. Olympos in Bithynia. In defending his secular way of life, Psellos puts forward, among other things, a manifesto about the value of discourses (their *aesthetics* included).

2. Alternatively, "give your word" or, simply, "send us a word."

3. See Ps.-Dionysios the Areopagite, *On the Divine Names* 4.8 (p. 153.4–9) καὶ κινεῖσθαι μὲν οἱ θεῖοι λέγονται νόες κυκλικῶς μὲν ἑνούμενοι ταῖς ἀνάρχοις καὶ ἀτελευτήτοις ἐλλάμψεσι τοῦ καλοῦ καὶ ἀγαθοῦ, κατ' εὐθεῖαν δέ, ὁπόταν προΐασιν εἰς τὴν τῶν ὑφειμένων πρόνοιαν εὐθείᾳ τὰ πάντα περαίνοντες, ἑλικοειδῶς δέ, ὅτι καὶ προνοοῦντες τῶν καταδεεστέρων ἀνεκφοιτήτως μένουσιν ἐν ταὐτότητι περὶ τὸ τῆς ταὐτότητος αἴτιον καλὸν καὶ ἀγαθὸν ἀκαταλήκτως περιχορεύοντες. See also, e.g., Proklos, *Comm. on the Republic* I 136.10–14 with Synesios of Kyrene, *Dion* 5.2.

Σὺ μὲν γάρ, τὸ ἱστίον τοῦ νοῦ πετάσας πρὸς οὐρανόν, ὑπὸ τοῖς ἄνω πυρσοῖς πρὸς τοὺς θείους[6] κατῆρας λιμένας· καὶ τῆς ἀρχαίας ἡμῶν πατρίδος πᾶσι τέρπῃ τοῖς κάλλεσιν. Ἡμεῖς δὲ[7] ἀπαίρειν μὲν ἐπηγγείλαμεν, καί που δὴ καὶ σκάφους ἐπιβάντες ἀνήχθημεν· τὸ δὲ πνεῦμα, βραχύ τι τὴν ἄγουσαν ὦσαν ὁλκάδα, ἀπέλιπε. Διὰ ταῦτα τῆς σῆς δεόμεθα τεχνικῆς κυβερνήσεως. Φασὶ δὲ ὑμᾶς[8] τοὺς πνευματικοὺς οἰακοστρόφους, μὴ μόνον κυβερνᾶν τὴν ναῦν δύνασθαι, ἀλλὰ καὶ κορυφούμενα κύματα[9] καταστέλλειν, καὶ θάλασσαν οἰδοῦσαν εὐνάζειν, καὶ πνεῦμα ἐπεγείρειν οἷος ὁ Ζέφυρος, ἡδὺς ὁμοῦ καὶ λεῖος καὶ παραπέμπων σὺν εὐμενείᾳ τὸ σκάφος. Ἀλλὰ καὶ ἕτερόν τι πρόσεστιν ὑμῖν ὥσπερ ἀκήκοα: ὅτι καὶ καταδῦσαν ὁλκάδα, εἴτε μυριοφόρον, εἴτε νῦν πρώτως καθελκυσθεῖσαν εἰς πέλαγος, ἀνιμᾶν δύνασθε,[10] καὶ αὖθις ἐπὶ τῆς θαλάσσης ἱστᾶν, οὐ τὴν χεῖρα κινοῦντες, ἀλλὰ τὴν γλῶσσαν.

Ὁπότε οὖν σοι τοσαῦτα τῷ ἐμοὶ φιλτάτῳ ἀνδρὶ ὡς κυβερνήτῃ πνευματικῷ μεμαρτύρηται, ἐπὶ κούφης αὐτὸς ἐλπίδος εἰμὶ καὶ πτερούμενος, καὶ τοῦ ἱστίου στερούμενος· πτερώσεις γὰρ αὖθις καὶ τοῖς ἀνέμοις ἐπιτάξεις, εἰ βούλοιο ἀπαγαγεῖν ἡμᾶς ὅπῃ σοι θελητόν. Οὐ τοίνυν ἀπογνώσομαι οὔτε τὴν εὔπλοιαν, οὔτε τοὺς λιμένας ἐφ' ὧν αὐτὸς ἐγκαθώρμισαι· σὺ μὲν γὰρ καὶ βούλοιο ἅμα καὶ δύναιο· ἐγὼ δὲ βουλοίμην (μέν καὶ μάρτυς ἐπὶ τῷ λόγῳ θεός), δυναίμην δ' οὐ πάνυ, ἀλλ' ἔλαττον ἢ βουλοίμην· εἰ δὲ γενναίως βουλοίμην, πάντως δ' ἂν καὶ δυναίμην.

Ἀλλ' οὐκ οἶδ' ὅπως ἂν περὶ τῶν ὀνομάτων τούτων φιλοσοφήσω· ὁρῶ γὰρ ὅτι μὴ πάντα τῆς ἡμετέρας προαιρέσεως ἤρτηται, ἀλλ' ἔστι τι καὶ τῶν παρὰ ταύτην καὶ βουλημιγές[11] τι ὡς ἀληθῶς χρῆμα ὁ ἄνθρωπος, πείσμασιν οἷον ἐντεταμένος πολλοῖς, μᾶλλον δὲ ὕσπληξι, τοῖς μὲν ἔσωθεν, τοῖς δ' ἔξωθεν, ὥστε καὶ προνοίας ἀπῃωρῆσθαι ἡμᾶς, καὶ ἀνάγκης, καὶ προαιρέσεως.

Εἴπερ γὰρ ἦν σοι ὥσπερ τι τῶν ὁρωμένων τὴν ἡμετέραν γνώμην περὶ τούτου[12] ἰδεῖν, ἐθαύμασας ἂν[13] ὑπὸ τοιούτῳ πνεύματι μὴ κινούμενον.[14] Ἀλλ'

6. θείου U
7. δὲ om. e a[1] m[2]
8. ἡμᾶς E a[1] e m[2]
9. τὰ κύματα M E a[1] e m[2] Maltese
10. δύνασθαι U
11. βουλημιγές U Maltese: βουλυμιγές M E a[1] e m[2]: πουλυμιγές G (cf. Plato, *Epigrammata* 24 = *AP* 9.823)
12. περὶ τούτου U G: περὶ τοῦτο M Maltese: τε τοῦτο E a[1] e m[2]
13. ἂν om. M E a[1] e m[2] Maltese
14. κινουμένην prop. in app. crit. G

Having directed the broad sail of your mind toward heaven, guided by the lights above, *you* have reached the divine harbors;[4] and you now enjoy the beautiful things of our primordial fatherland.[5] On the other hand, *I* promised that I would depart, I even boarded a ship, and began the trip. But after a short while the wind pushing my vessel has died away. Therefore, I need your expertise at the helm.

They say that you, the spiritual helmsmen, can not only steer the ship but can also diminish the high waves and calm the swollen sea and awaken a wind like, for instance, the pleasant and gentle westerly one[6] that calmly conveys the ship. But, as I have heard, you possess also another quality: you are able to bail out a ship that is swamped, whether a large, much travelled merchant ship[7] or a ship launched for the first time on to the high seas, and to set it aright upon the sea, not by using your hands but your tongue.

Therefore since such things are attested about you as a spiritual helmsman, my dearest friend among men, I become buoyantly hopeful[8] and take wing, even though I am without a sail. For you will provide me with wings and, should you so wish, command the winds to carry us wherever you want. So, I will despair neither the smooth sailing nor the harbors to which you yourself have anchored; for you might be able both to will this and to do it. And I too might want this (God is my witness); but I am not quite able to do it as much as I would have wanted; if I had wanted it in a high-minded manner, I should definitely be able to do this.[9]

I do not know how to philosophize regarding these terms. For I see that not everything depends on our free will, rather there are things that happen

4. A similar image and wording also in Gregory of Nyssa, *On the Inscriptions of the Psalms* 60.18–20; see also S 167 (426.8–10) and K-D 43 (72.1–2).

5. A commonplace, referring to paradise and the heavenly kingdom; see, e.g., *Or. hag.* 1a 8–9 and 65.

6. For the "westerly wind" (Ζέφυρος), see the relevant entry in the *Suda* zeta.41: Ζεφυρία πνοή: . . . Ζέφυρος γὰρ λεῖος ἄνεμος.

7. ὁλκάδα . . . μυριοφόρον: a common phrase; see, e.g., Heliodoros, *Aethiopian Tale* 4.16.6.3.

8. ἐπὶ κούφης αὐτὸς ἐλπίδος εἰμὶ; see Isaiah 19:1: ἐπὶ νεφέλης κούφης

9. In juxtaposing will with power, Psellos echoes a phrase in Synesios of Kyrene, *Letter* 95.62–63: οὐδ' ἂν εἰ δυναίμην βουλοίμην, πάντως δὲ οὐδ' ἂν εἰ βουλοίμην δυναίμην.

ἔχει καὶ οὕτως[15] ἡμᾶς ἡ πέδη, τοῦ σώματος μὲν ἴσως ἔλαττον,[16] ἑτέρα δὲ ἐκ προφάσεως[17] οὐ φαύλης εἰς οὐ καλὸν καταλήγουσα. Μὴ γάρ με οἰηθῇς, φίλτατε ἀδελφέ, καί μοι μηδὲν ἀχθεσθῇς λέγοντι ὅτι ἄρκυσι[18] δόξης ἑάλωκα, ἢ πλούτου θηράτροις τεθήραμαι, ἢ ὅτι ζηλῶ ἐπὶ ταῖς βασιλείαις[19] αὐλαῖς, ἢ ἐπ' ἄλλῳ τῳ τῶν ἐνταῦθα καλῶν. Μενοῦνγε καὶ διαπτύω πᾶν τὸ φαινόμενον· καὶ μάλιστα ἡνίκα τί μοι σχολάσει[20] πρὸς ἑαυτὴν ἡ ψυχή. Εἰ δὲ βούλει τἀληθὲς ἀκοῦσαι, πολλάκις τοῖς περιττοῖς ναυτιῶν, ἀπεμέσαι καὶ τἀναντία βεβούλημαι· οὕτω πᾶσαν ἐβδελυξάμην τὴν ἐνταῦθα ζωήν.

Μᾶλλον δὲ τῆς προτέρας τὸ πᾶν σχεδὸν ἀπεπτύσθη[21] μοι· Τὸ γὰρ περὶ τοὺς λόγους καὶ τὴν ἐν τούτοις ἀγλαΐαν οὐ μόνον οὐκ ἀπωσάμην, ἀλλ' ἔτι ζητῶ,[22] καὶ μάλιστα ὁπόσον φιλοσοφία δίδωσιν ἐκ τῶν ἄνωθεν ἀπεικονισαμένη μορφῶν, ἢ μάλιστα τὸ ἀνείδεον, μέχρις[23] ἡμῶν καταγαγοῦσα,[24] εἰς εἶδος ἀπετυπώσατο. Ἀλλὰ τὴν περὶ τοὺς λόγους σχέσιν ἔστι καὶ πρὸς ἡμᾶς διαβιβάσαι· καὶ οὐ πάνυ ἐμαυτῷ μέμφομαι, καὶ τούτου τοῦ κάλλους ἐρῶντι. Καί, εἰ μὴ φορτικῶς πάλιν ἀκούεις τῶν ἔξω σοφῶν μηδέ γε βούλοιο τῷ ἐκείνων ἐλαίῳ πιαίνεσθαι, τὸ νοητὸν κάλλος ἐκεῖνοι[25] ἀπὸ τοῦ τῇδε κάλλους ἀνάπτουσι[26] ταῖς ψυχαῖς· ἐπεὶ γὰρ μή ἐστιν ἐκεῖνο ὁρατὸν ἀφ'[27] ἑαυτοῦ καὶ γνωστόν, ἀπὸ τῶν εἰκασμάτων τὸ πρωτότυπον ἡμῖν εἰκονίζουσιν. Εἰ τοίνυν δεῖ σὺν ἐπιστήμῃ πρὸς ἐκεῖνο ἀνιέναι, τοῦ μὲν ἐν σώματι κάλλους καταφρονήσωμεν,[28] ὡς ἀπηχήματος τελευταίου καὶ τῇ ὕλῃ προσεγγίζοντος· ἐπιτηδεύματα δὲ καλὰ καὶ πράξεις καλαὶ καὶ λόγοι καλοὶ ἀναγέτωσαν ἡμᾶς εἰς τὸ πρῶτον καλόν. Κἂν μὲν ἐκείνου γενναιότερον ἀντιλάβοιμεν, ὥστε μὴ μετεστράφθαι,[29] ῥείτωσαν τἆλλα ἡμῖν καὶ ὑποχωρείτωσαν· εἰ δὲ ἡ ἐπίκηρος

15. οὗτος U
16. ἐλάττων corr. G
17. προφάσεως U: προαιρέσεως M E a[1] e m[2] G Maltese
18. ἄρκυσι M E a[1] e m[2] Maltese
19. βασιλείοις U G sed cf. Psel. Or. min. 18.34: βασιλείαις αὐλαῖς
20. σχολάζει Maltese
21. ἀπεπτύσθητί e a[1] m[2]
22. ζηλῶ Maltese
23. μέχρις U: μέρος M E a[1] e m[2] G Maltese
24. κατάγουσα M E a[1] e m[2]
25. ἐκείνου U
26. ἀνάπτου U
27. ἐφ' M E a[1] e m[2] Maltese
28. καταφρονήσομεν U G
29. μεταστρέφθαι e a[1] m[2]

despite our will, and man is truly of mixed will, as if stretched by many cables, or rather snares,[10] some from within, others from without, so that we are suspended between providence, necessity, and free will.

If indeed it were really possible for you to see our intention about this as if it were some other visible thing, you would have marveled at me not being moved by a wind such as yours. But shackles bind us, not so much of the body, but others that derive from a good motive, which ends up in something bad. O most beloved brother, neither think about me nor be vexed by me when I speak, that I have perhaps been seized by the nets of vainglory or caught in the snares of wealth or yearn for the imperial halls or some other worldly pleasures. On the contrary, I spit upon all visible things, especially when my soul finds respite in itself. For if you wish to hear the truth, I have often wanted to vomit everything out thanks to the nausea born of excess. This is how much I have come to loathe this worldly life.[11]

Or, rather, I have rejected *nearly* everything of my former life. For I have not only *not* rejected discourses as well as their adornment, but still seek them out, and especially what philosophy provides reflecting higher forms, philosophy that has brought down to us what is formless and gave it form.[12] But it is possible to transfer the relation of <higher things> with discoures also to us; so I do not blame myself much for desiring also this kind of beauty. And, to continue (unless you listen again with difficulty to pagan philosophers and would not wish to be fattened by their oil), discourses kindle the intelligible beauty in our souls by way of earthly beauty;[13] since the former is neither visible nor known in itself, they represent the prototype to us by way of likenesses. If it is then necessary to ascend to that prototype in a systemic way and with proper understanding, let us despise corporal beauty as it is the last

10. πείσμασιν – ὕσπληξι; from Plutarch, *On the Daimonion of Socrates* 588f7–8: ψυχὴ δ' ἀνθρώπου μυρίαις ὁρμαῖς οἷον ὕσπληξιν ἐντεταμένη.

11. Similar thoughts and wording appear in another letter of Psellos to Xiphilinos; see K-D 191 (218.5–7).

12. Similar wording may be found also in Psellos, *Theol.* I 104.55–59.

13. τὸ νοητὸν κάλλος ἐκεῖνοι ἀπὸ τοῦ τῇδε κάλλους ἀνάπτουσι ταῖς ψυχαῖς; Psellos' phrasing is inspired by Plato, *Phaedrus* 249d5–6: τὸ τῇδέ τις ὁρῶν κάλλος, τοῦ ἀληθοῦς ἀναμιμνῃσκόμενος. See also the relevant Neoplatonic commentary by Hermeias (179.15–18). Psellos returns to similar notions in S 1 (220.15–18), this time as his defense for intending to join an engagement party: καίτοι γε καὶ τὸ ὁρώμενον κάλλος εἰς τὸ νοητὸν τὸν φιλόσοφον ἀντιπεριάγειν κάλλος δεδύνηται, καὶ ἡ ἐμφανὴς ἁρμονία τοῦ ἀφανοῦς ἀνάμνησις γίνεται.

φύσις ἀνθέλκοι, ἐκ τοῦ σχεδὸν ἡμᾶς ὁ λόγος καταβάντας[30] ὑποδεχέσθω, καὶ πάλιν τῷ ἑαυτοῦ κάλλει πρὸς ἀνάμνησιν ἐκείνου τὴν ψυχὴν κεντριζέτω. Καί, ἵνα τἆλλα ἐάσω, ἴσθι, πνευματικὲ ἀδελφέ, ὅτι ὑπὸ βραχεῖ μίτῳ ἐνταῦθα πεπέδημαι· κἂν τμηθῇ, θαυμάσεις οἵας κατεῖχε τὸ ἀράχνιον πτέρυγας.

Ἀλλ' ἐπλήσθης[31] τῆς ἅλμης; Σαυτὸν αἰτιῶ· αὐτὸς γάρ μοι προετρέψω τοῦτο δὴ τὸ θαλάττιον πόμα κεράσαι σοι.[32]

30. καταβάντος U G
31. ἐπεπλήσθης M E a[1] e m[2] Maltese
32. μοι E a[1] m[2]

echo <of Being> and is near to matter;[14] let instead beautiful pursuits and beautiful deeds and beautiful words raise us up to the first Beauty.[15] And if we should take hold of it in a nobler fashion so that we can not turn away from it, let everything else flow away and recede from us; but if mortal nature[16] should draw us in the opposite direction, let discourse receive us by its side as we descend and may it in turn, by means of its beauty, stimulate the soul to the remembrance of that first Beauty.[17] Leaving aside all else, know, o most spiritual brother, that I have been bound here below by a thread. And if it were cut, you would marvel at what sort of wings the spider's net was holding back.

Have you perhaps been filled with brine? You have yourself to blame; for it was you who urged me to treat you with this salty brew.[18]

14. The ideas presented here are of Neoplatonic origin; they echo, e.g., Synesios of Kyrene, *Dion* 5.4. See also Proklos, *Platonic Theology* 1.116.7–8 and Psellos, *Theol.* I 26.49–51. Always ready to change tune, Psellos elsewhere defends corporal beauty for the very reasons that he rejects it here; see his "Ekphrasis of Eros Carved on Stone" (*Or. min.* 34.19–26; translated above, p. 288). On Psellos' views on bodily beauty, see further Papaioannou 2013: 139–40, 144, 155–58, and 184–91.

15. From Plato, *Symposium* 210a4–211d1; see also Plotinos, *Enneads* 1, 6, 1.

16. ἡ ἐπίκηρος φύσις: see Synesios of Kyrene, *Dion* 7.2; a phrase often used in Psellos.

17. This entire passage evokes passages from a favorite Psellian text, Synesios of Kyrene, *Dion* (6.4 and 8.2–3) and its defense of the value of discourses. Similar usage of these parts of the *Dion* may be found in two other letters by Psellos to Xiphilinos: K-D 191 and Criscuolo 1990 (these references may also be added to Kaldellis' translations of these letters: Kaldellis and Polemis 2015: 163–76).

18. brine . . . salty brew: a metaphor for Hellenic (non-Christian) discourse often used by Psellos; see further Duffy 2000.

Letter Four

Τῷ Χαλκηδόνος[1]

Οὐδὲ εἰκόνας; Καὶ διὰ τί, ὁ θειότατος τῷ ὄντι δεσπότης μου;

Ἐγὼ δὲ καὶ ἱεροσυλῶ ταύτας, νὴ τὴν ἱεράν σου ψυχήν· καὶ κέκλοφά γε πολλὰς ἀπὸ τῶν ἀδύτων· καὶ ὑπαγκαλισάμενος, τότε μὲν διέλαθον, ὕστερον δὲ ὑποπτευθείς, αὐτίκα ἀπωμοσάμην. Προστέτηκα δὲ μᾶλλον ταῖς ἀμυδραῖς ταύταις γραφαῖς, ὅτι τὴν τέχνην τοῦ γραφέως ἐξεικονίζουσι. Καί μοι συνῆκται τοιαῦτα σανίδια πλείω ἄχρυσα καὶ ἀνάργυρα, ὥσπερ ἔνιοι τῶν νέων συγκλητικῶν ἄσταυροί τε καὶ ἄβλαττοι. Ἐγὼ δὲ διδοὺς οὐκ ἀλγῶ.

1. K-D 129; L 62r–v.

To the Metropolitan of Chalkedon[1]

Not even icons? And why so, my most divine Lord? On your holy soul, I actually rob them from churches. Indeed, I have stolen many from sanctuaries and at first I escaped everyone's notice, leaving with them clasped in my arms, but later on, when I came under suspicion, I immediately denied it on oath. But I have clung on to these faint pictures, because they represent the painter's art. I have a collection of such boards, mostly without gold or silver, resembling some of the new senators, who have neither crosses nor robes. Yet I do not suffer when I give them away.

1. Translations of this text together with commentary can be found in Oikonomides 1991: 36 and Cutler and Browning 1992: 28–29. Moore 2005: 97 (*Ep.* 331).

Letter Five[1]

Εἰκόνων ἐγὼ θεατὴς ἀκριβέστατος. Ἀλλά με μία, κάλλει ἀφάτῳ ἐκπλήξασα, καὶ οἷον ἀστραπῆς βολῇ τὰς αἰσθήσεις πηρώσασα, ἀφείλετό μου τὴν περὶ τὸ πρᾶγμα δύναμίν τε καὶ σύνεσιν. Εἶχε δὲ παράδειγμα αὕτη τὴν θεομήτορα καὶ πρὸς ἐκείνην ἐγέγραπτο. Ἀλλ' εἰ μὲν ἐμφερὴς ἐκείνῳ τῷ ὑπερφυεῖ καθειστήκει ἀγάλματι, οὐ πάνυ τι οἶδα. Ὅτι δὲ συγκραθέντα τὰ χρώματα σαρκὸς φύσιν ἀπεμιμήσαντο, τοῦτο καὶ τοσοῦτον ἐπίσταμαι· τὸ γὰρ εἶδος ἄληπτόν μοι καὶ τότε τῇ ὄψει, καὶ νῦν τῇ ἐννοίᾳ καθίσταται.

Γράφω γοῦν, οὐχ ὅπερ τεθέαμαι, ἀλλ' ὃ πέπονθα· ἔοικε γάρ, μεταβεβλημένη τὴν φύσιν παντάπασι, καὶ πρὸς τὸ θεοειδὲς μεταμορφωθῆναι κάλλος, καὶ τὴν ἐκ τῶν ὀφθαλμῶν αἴσθησιν ὑπερβαίνουσα. Ἀλλ' οὔτε βλοσυρά τίς ἐστιν ἐντεῦθεν, οὔτ' αὖθις ἐνικῷ κάλλει κομᾷ. Ἀλλ' ὑπὲρ ἄμφω τὰ μέτρα ἐστί, καὶ τοσοῦτον εἰς γνῶσιν καταβᾶσα, ὅσον μὴ γινώσκεσθαι τὴν μορφήν, ἀλλ' ἐκπλήττειν τὸν θεατήν.

Πεποίηται μὲν οὖν πρεσβείαν ποιουμένη πρὸς τὸν υἱόν, καὶ τοῖς ἀνθρώποις ἐκκαλουμένη τὸν ἔλεον· τοῦτο δὴ τὸ σύνηθες ἔν τε ἀληθείᾳ καὶ σχήμασιν. Οὐκ ἐπιδοιάζει δὲ πρὸς τὴν ἱκετείαν, οὐδ' οἷον ἐπιθρηνεῖ πρὸς τὴν δέησιν, ἀλλ' ἠρέμα τὰς χεῖρας ἐκτείνουσα, ὡς αὐτόθεν ληψομένη τὴν χάριν, θαρρεῖ τὴν εὐχήν. Αἱ δὲ τῶν ὀμμάτων βολαί, ἁπανταχῇ τὸ θαυμάσιον· μερίζεται γὰρ οὐρανῷ καὶ γῇ, ἵν' ἄμφω ἔχῃ, ᾧ τε πρόσεισι, καὶ ὑπὲρ ὧν τοῦτο πεποίηται.

1. K-D 194; O 199v.

[Unknown recipient][1]

I am a most fastidious viewer of icons; but one astonished me by its indescribable beauty and like a bolt of lightning it disabled my senses and deprived me of my power of judgment in this matter. It has the Mother of God as its model and has been painted in Her likeness. Whether it is similar to Her (that supernatural image of beauty), I do not quite know. I know this much and just this much: that the corporal nature has been faithfully imitated by means of the mixing of colors; for Her form remains incomprehensble to me both then visuall and now conceptually.

I do not therefore write about what I have beheld, but what I have experienced. For it seems that having completely exchanged its nature, it was transformed into divine-like beauty and surpassed visual perception. Yet, because of this, she neither looks stern nor is she again decked out in a monotonous beauty; rather she is beyond both these measures and descends into knowledge only so much that, while her shape is not known, she astounds the viewer.

She has been depicted interceding with the Son and eliciting mercy for humankinds, as is customary in both truth and images. Moreover, she entertains no doubts in her supplication nor does it appear that she laments over her request; rather, she calmly extends her hands in anticipation of receiving His

1. A partial translation of this text together with a commentary can be found in Cutler and Browning 1992: 27–28. Moore 2005: 43–44 (*Ep.* 108).

Τοῦτο γοῦν τὴν πρώτην ἰδών, ἥρπασα· τὸ δὲ λοιπὸν πλῆξαν τοὺς ὀφθαλμούς ὑπερβέβηκεν. Ἐντεῦθεν οὖν εὐδαίμων ἡ μονὴ τῶν Καθαρῶν, ἣ τῇ Ἐδὲμ ἡ ξύμπασα γῆ.

favor and is confident in her prayer. The bolts from her eyes[2] are miraculous in every direction. For she is divided between heaven and earth so that she might have both: both the one (i.e., Christ) whom she approaches and the people for whom she supplicates.

At any rate seeing this the first time, I <would/could have> snatched <the icon>;[3] however, the rest <of the image> astounded my sight, and thus surpassed me. Because of this icon, the monastery of ta Kathara is fortunate;[4] more so than the earth is fortunate because of Eden.

2. The phrase "bolts from her eyes" is reminiscent of an often evoked Homeric line (*Odyssey* 4.150).

3. We chose to take ἥρπασα literally here, as it seems reminiscent of Psellos' proclivity to steal icons as presented (somewhat playfully) in our previous letter (K-D 129); indeed, perhaps a word like ἄν should be added after ἥρπασα in the Greek text. A figurative meaning is possible as well; it would give the following translation: "At any rate this is what I grasped seeing the icon for the first time."

4. For this Bithynian monastery, see p. 352 above.

List of Rhetorical Terms

The following list includes only a selection of some of the most frequent, important, or particular terms. Hermogenian *forms* are set in italics.

Greek to English

ἀκμή	*vigor*
ἀληθινὸς λόγος	*sincerity*
ἀνάγνωσις	reading
ἀνάπαυσις	cadence
ἀναστροφή	repetition
ἀντιπαράστασις	counter-rejoinder
ἀντίστασις	counterstance
ἀντιστροφή	counterturn
τὸ ἀντίθετον	opposition
ἀξίωμα	dignity
τὸ ἀπαριθμητικόν	the enumerative figure
ἁπλοῦς	simple
ἀπόδειξις	demonstration
ἀπόστασις	employment of detached phrases
τὸ ἀσύνδετον	lack of connectives
αὔξησις	augmentation
ἀφέλεια	*simplicity*
βάρος, *βαρύτης*	*sternness*
βάσις	rhythm
γλυκύτης	*sweetness*
γλῶττα	eloquence, tongue
γνωμολογίαι	maxims
γοργότης	*rapidity*
τὸ δεικτικόν	deictics
δεινότης	*force*
δέσις	complication
διάνοια	thought
διασκευή	embellishment
διήγησις	narration
δικανικός	judicial
διλήμματον	dilemma
δριμύτης	*pungency*
εἶδος	kind/genre (in reference to the three genres of rhetoric), species (Aristotelian, as opposed to γένος), beauty, form (Aristotelian, as opposed to matter)
τὰ εἰκότα	plausibilities
ἐπεισόδιον	additional narrative
ἐμψυχία	animation
ἔμψυχος	animated

ἐνάργεια	vividness
ἐναργής	vivid
ἐνδιάσκευος	highly wrought
ἐνθύμημα	enthymeme
ἔννοια	thought
ἔνστασις	objection
ἔξοδος	exit ode
ἐπαναφορά, ἡ κατὰ κῶλα	repetition of a word at the beginning of a colon
ἐπιείκεια	*moderation*
ἐπικρίσεις	judgments
ἐπίλογος	peroration
ἐπιστροφαί	interruptions
ἐπιφώνημα	remark
ἐργασία	elaboration
εὐκρίνεια	*distinctness*
εὕρεσις	invention
εὐστομία	euphony
ἡδονή	pleasure
ἦθος	*character*
θεατρικός	spectacular, theatrical
θεωρία	contemplative meaning
ἰδέα, ἰδέαι	form/forms (Platonic, Hermogenian, and Neoplatonic), style
ἱστορία	story, narrative, literal meaning
καθαρότης	*purity*
καιρός	opportune moment
κάλλος, τὸ καλόν	*beauty*
τὸ κατ᾽ ὀρθότητα	the simple sentence
κατασκευή	logical elaboration, confirmation
κεφάλαιον	main point, heading
κινήσεις	gestures
κλῖμαξ	climax
κύκλος	circle
κῶλον	colon
λαμπρότης	*brilliance*
λελυμένος	loose
λέξις	diction, speech, style
λύσις	resolution
μαλακός	effeminate
μεγαλοπρέπεια	magnificence
μέγεθος	*grandeur*
μέθοδος	method
μελοποιία	composition (in music)
μέλος	melody
μερισμός	partition
μεταβολή	variety
νοῦς	intellect
ὄγκος	gravity
οἰκονομία	disposition, handling
ὄργανον	instrument
ὄψις	spectacle
πάθος	emotion, suffering
πανηγυρικός	panegyrical
παράδειγμα	example
παρήχησις	echo
παρισώσεις	clauses with an equal number of syllables
πάροδος	entrance ode
τὸ ἐκ παρονομασίας	use of puns
περιβολή	*amplification*
περίοδος	period
τὸ πιθανόν	persuasiveness
πλαγιασμός	subordination
πνεῦμα	period delivered in a single breath
ποικιλία	variety
πολιτικὸς λόγος	civic discourse

πράγματα	actions
τὸ πρέπον	appropriateness
πρόβλημα τῶν ἐσχηματισμένων	figured kind of problem
προοίμιον	preface
προκατάστασις	preliminary statement
πρόσωπον	persons
ῥυθμός	rhythm
σαφήνεια	*clarity*
σεμνότης	*solemnity*
σημεῖον	indication
στάσις	issue
στοιχεῖον	element of proof, phoneme
συμβουλή	advisory (genre)
συμπλοκαί	interweaving
σύνθεσις	composition
συνθήκη	composition, arrangement
σύμφρασις	context
σφοδρότης	*vehemence*
σχῆμα	figure
τάξις	arrangement
τεκμήριον	proof
τεχνικὸς λόγος	rhetoric
τόνοι	modes
τόποι	settings
τραχύτης	*asperity*
τροπή	metaphor
ὑπόθεσις	case, subject matter
ὑπόκρισις	delivery
φράσις	expression
χαρακτήρ	style
χάρις	charm, grace
ᾠδή	song
ὥρα	elegance

English to Greek

actions	πράγματα
additional narrative	ἐπεισόδιον
advisory (genre)	συμβουλή
amplification	*περιβολή*
animated	ἔμψυχος
animation	ἐμψυχία
appropriateness	τὸ πρέπον
arrangement	τάξις, συνθήκη
asperity	*τραχύτης*
augmentation	αὔξησις
beauty	*κάλλος*, τὸ καλόν, εἶδος
brilliance	*λαμπρότης*
cadence	ἀνάπαυσις
case	ὑπόθεσις
character	*ἦθος*
charm	χάρις
circle	κύκλος
civic discourse	πολιτικὸς λόγος
clarity	*σαφήνεια*
clauses with an equal number of syllables	παρισώσεις
climax	κλῖμαξ
colon	κῶλον
complication	δέσις
composition	συνθήκη, σύνθεσις
composition (in music)	μελοποιία
confirmation	κατασκευή
contemplative meaning	θεωρία
context	σύμφρασις
counter-rejoinder	ἀντιπαράστασις
counterstance	ἀντίστασις
counterturn	ἀντιστροφή
deictics	τὸ δεικτικόν
delivery	ὑπόκρισις
demonstration	ἀπόδειξις
detached phrases, employment of	ἀποστάσεις

diction	λέξις
dignity	ἀξίωμα
dilemma	διλήμματον
disposition	οἰκονομία
distinctness	*εὐκρίνεια*
echo	παρήχησις
effeminate	μαλακός
elaboration	ἐργασία
elegance	ὥρα
element of proof	στοιχεῖον
eloquence	γλῶττα
embellishment	διασκευή
emotion	πάθος
enthymeme	ἐνθύμημα
entrance ode	πάροδος
the enumerative figure	τὸ ἀπαριθμητικόν
euphony	εὐστομία
example	παράδειγμα
exit ode	ἔξοδος
expression	φράσις
figure	σχῆμα
figured kind of problem	πρόβλημα τῶν ἐσχηματισμένων
force	*δεινότης*
form, forms (Platonic, Hermogenian, and Neoplatonic)	ἰδέα, ἰδέαι
form (Aristotelian and Neoplatonic)	εἶδος
genre	εἶδος
gestures	κινήσεις
grace	χάρις
grandeur	*μέγεθος*
gravity	ὄγκος
handling	οἰκονομία
heading	κεφάλαιον
indication	σημεῖον
instrument	ὄργανον
intellect	νοῦς
interruptions	ἐπιστροφαί
interweaving	συμπλοκαί
invention	εὕρεσις
issue	*στάσις*
judgments	ἐπικρίσεις
judicial	δικανικός
lack of connectives	τὸ ἀσύνδετον
literal meaning	ἱστορία
logical elaboration	κατασκευή
loose	λελυμένος
magnificence	μεγαλοπρέπεια
magnitude	μέγεθος
main point	κεφάλαιον
maxims	γνωμολογίαι
melody	μέλος
metaphor	τροπή
method	μέθοδος
moderation	*ἐπιείκεια*
modes	τόνοι
narration	διήγησις
narrative	ἱστορία
objection	ἔνστασις
opportune moment	καιρός
opposition	ἀντίθετον
panegyrical	πανηγυρικός
partition	μερισμός
period	περίοδος
period delivered in a single breath	πνεῦμα
peroration	ἐπίλογος
person	πρόσωπον
persuasiveness	τὸ πιθανόν
phoneme	στοιχεῖον
plausibilities	τὰ εἰκότα
pleasure	ἡδονή
preface	προοίμιον
preliminary statement	προκατάστασις
proof	τεκμήριον
pungency	*δριμύτης*
use of puns	τὸ ἐκ παρονομασίας
purity	*καθαρότης*

rapidity	*γοργότης*
reading	ἀνάγνωσις
remark	ἐπιφώνημα
repetition	ἀναστροφή
repetition of a word at the beginning of a colon	ἡ κατὰ κῶλα ἐπαναφορά
resolution	λύσις
rhetoric	τεχνικὸς λόγος
rhythm	ῥυθμός, βάσις
settings	τόποι
simple	ἁπλοῦς
simple sentence	τὸ κατ᾽ ὀρθότητα
simplicity	*ἀφέλεια*
sincerity	*ἀληθινὸς λόγος*
solemnity	*σεμνότης*
song	ᾠδή
species	εἶδος
spectacle	ὄψις
spectacular	θεατρικός
speech	λέξις
sternness	βάρος, *βαρύτης*
story	ἱστορία
style	ἰδέα, χαρακτήρ, λέξις
subject matter	ὑπόθεσις
subordination	πλαγιασμός
suffering	πάθος
sweetness	*γλυκύτης*
theatrical	θεατρικός
thought	διάνοια, ἔννοια
tongue	γλῶττα
variety	ποικιλία, μεταβολή
vehemence	*σφοδρότης*
vigor	*ἀκμή*
vivid	ἐναργής
vividness	ἐνάργεια
highly wrought	ἐνδιάσκευος

Bibliography

Primary Sources

With few exceptions, citations are offered here for editions of only those texts that date after the sixth century CE.

Alexandros of Aphrodisias. *De Sensu*. Edited by P. Wendland, *Alexandri in Librum De Sensu Commentarium*. Commentaria in Aristotelem Graeca 3.1. Berlin: Reimer, 1901.

Ammonios. *Comm. On Aristotle's Categories*. Edited by A. Busse, *Ammonius in Aristotelis categorias commentarius*. Commentaria in Aristotelem Graeca 4.4. Berlin: Reimer, 1895.

———. *Comm. on Aristotle's On Interpretation*. Edited by A. Busse, *Ammonius in Aristotelis de interpretatione commentaries*. Commentaria in Aristotelem Graeca 4.5. Berlin: Reimer, 1897.

Anna Komnene. *Alexiad*. Edited by D.R. Reinsch and A. Kambylis, *Annae Comnenae Alexias*. Corpus Fontium Historiae Byzantinae 40. Berlin: De Gruyter, 2001.

Anonymous. *Comm. on Aristotle's Rhetoric*. Edited by H. Rabe, *Anonymi et Stephani in artem rhetoricam commentarium*, 1–262. Commentaria in Aristotelem Graeca 21.2. Berlin: Reimer, 1896.

Anonymous. *On the Figures of Speech*. Edited by L. Spengel, *Rhetores Graeci*, 3:174–88. Leipzig: Teubner, 1856; repr. 1966.

Anonymous. *On the Four Parts of the Perfect Speech*. Edited by W. Hörandner, "Pseudo-Gregorios Korinthios, Über die vier Teile der perfekten Rede." *Medioevo Greco* 12 (2012): 87–131.

Anonymous. *On the Tropes of Poetry*. Edited by L. Spengel, *Rhetores Graeci*, 3:207–14. Leipzig: Teubner, 1856; repr. 1966.

Anonymous. *Prolegomena to Aphthonios' Progymnasmata*. Edited by C. Walz, *Rhetores Graeci*, 2:1–68. Stuttgart: J.G. Cottae, 1835.

Anonymous. *Prolegomena to a Comm. on Hermogenes' On Invention*. Edited by C. Walz, *Rhetores Graeci*, vol. 7. Stuttgart: J.G. Cottae, 1836.

Anonymous. *Prolegomena to Hermogenes' On Issues.* Edited by H. Rabe, *Prolegomenon sylloge,* 183–228. Rhetores Graeci 14. Leipzig: Teubner, 1931.

Anonymous. *Prolegomena to Platonic Philosophy.* Edited by L. G. Westerink, *Anonymous Prolegomena to Platonic Philosophy.* Amsterdam: North Holland Publishing, 1962.

Anonymous. *Synopses of the On Forms.* Edited by M. Patillon, *Corpus rhetoricum, Tome IV: Prolégomènes au De Ideis —Hermogène, Les catégories stylistiques du discours (De Ideis) —Synopse des exposés sur les Ideai,* 235–54. Paris: Les Belles Lettres, 2012.

Aphthonios. *Progymnasmata.* Edited by M. Patillon, *Corpus rhetoricum Tome I: Anonyme, Préambule à la rhetoric; Aphthonios, Progymnasmata; Pseudo-Hermogène, Progymnasmata.* Paris: Les Belles Lettres, 2008.

Arethas. *Scholia on Lucian.* Edited by H. Rabe, *Scholia in Lucianum.* Leipzig: Teubner, 1906; repr. Stuttgart, 1971.

Aspasios. *Ethica.* Edited by G. Heylbut, *Aspasii in Ethica Nicomachea quae supersunt commentaria.* Commentaria in Aristotelem Graeca 19.1. Berlin: Reimer, 1889.

Attaleiates, Michael. *History.* Edited by E. T. Tsolakis, *Michaelis Attaliatae Historia.* Corpus Fontium Historiae Byzantinae 50. Athens: Ἀκαδημία Ἀθηνῶν, 2011.

Basilika. Edited by H. Sheltema, N. van der Wal, and D. Holwerda, *Basilicorum libri LX.* 8 vols. Groningen: J. B. Wolters, 1955–88.

Codices Chrysostomici Graeci. Paris: Éditions du Centre National de la Recherché Scientifique,1968–.

Continuation of Skylitzes. Edited by E. T. Tsolakes, Ἡ συνέχεια τῆς χρονογραφίας τοῦ Ἰωάννου Σκυλίτση. Ἵδρυμα Μελετῶν Χερσονήσου τοῦ Αἵμου 105. Thessalonike: Ἑταιρεία Μακεδονικῶν Σπουδῶν, 1968.

Damaskios. *Life of Isidoros.* Edited by C. Zintzen, *Damascii Vitae Isidori reliquiae.* Hildesheim: Olms, 1967.

Dionysios the Areopagite. *On Divine Names.* Edited by B. R. Suchla, *Pseudo-Dionysius Areopagita, Corpus Dionysiacum.* Patristische Texte und Studien 33. Berlin: De Gruyter, 1990.

Doxapatres, Ioannes. *Rhetorical Homilies on Aphthonios' Progymnasmata.* Edited by C. Walz, *Rhetores Graeci,* vol. 2. Stuttgart: J. G. Cottae, 1835; and edited by H. Rabe, *Prolegomenon sylloge.* Rhetores Graeci 14, 80–155. Leipzig: Teubner, 1931.

———. *Prolegomena* to his *Comm. on Hermogenes' On Form.* Edited by H. Rabe, *Prolegomenon sylloge.* Rhetores Graeci 14, 420–26. Leipzig: Teubner, 1931.

Ecloga Basilicorum. Edited by L. Burgmann, *Ecloga Basilicorum.* Frankfurt: Löwenklau-Gesellschaft, 1988.

Elias or David. *Commentary on the Ten Categories of Philosophy.* Edited by A. Busse, *Eliae in Porphyrii isagogen et Aristotelis categorias commentaria.* Commentaria in Aristotelem Graeca 18.1. Berlin: Reimer, 1900.

Eustathios of Thessalonike. *Parekbolai on the Iliad.* Edited by M. van der Valk, *Eustathii archiepiscopi Thessalonicensis commentarii ad Homeri Iliadem pertinentes,* vols. 1-4. Leiden: Brill, 1971–87.

———. *Preface on his Comm. on Pindar.* Edited by Athanasios Kambylis, *Proemium Commentariorum Pindaricorum.* Veröffentlichung de Joachim Junguis-Gessellschaft der Wissenschaften Hamburg, NR 65. Göttingen: Vanderhoeck and Ruprecht, 1991.

Geometres, Ioannes. *Progymnasmata.* Edited by A. R. Littlewood, *The Progymnasmata of Ioannes Geometres.* Amsterdam: Adolf M. Hakkert, 1972.

Hermeias. *Scholia on Plato's Phaedrus.* Edited by P. Couvreur, *Hermeias von Alexandrien: In Platonis Phaedrum scholia.* Paris: Bouillon, 1901; repr. Hildesheim: Olms, 1971.

Hermogenes. *On Forms.* Edited by M. Patillon, *Corpus rhetoricum, Tome IV: Prolégomènes au De Ideis—Hermogène, Les catégories stylistiques du discours (De Ideis)—Synopse des exposés sur les Ideai.* Paris: Les Belles Lettres, 2012.

"Hermogenes." *On Invention.* Edited by M. Patillon, *Corpus rhetoricum, Tome III, 1re partie: Pseudo-Hermogène, L'Invention —Synopse des exordes. Tome III, 2e partie: Anonyme, Scolies au traité sur l'Invention du Pseudo-Hermogène.* Paris: Les Belles Lettres, 2012.

Ioannes of Sardeis. *Comm. on Aphthonios' progymnasmata.* Edited by H. Rabe, *Ioannis Sardiani Commentarium in Aphthonii Progymnasmata.* Leipzig: Teubner, 1928.

Longinos. *Art of Rhetoric.* Edited by M. Patillon and L. Brisson, *Longin: Fragments; Art Rhétorique; Rufus: Art Rhétorique*, 48, 189–208. Paris: Les Belles Lettres, 2001.

Mauropous, Ioannes. *Discourse on the Three Holy Fathers and Teachers.* Edited by de P. Lagarde, *Joannis Euchaitorum Metropolitae quae in codice Vaticano Graeco 676 supersunt.* Abhandlungen der Historisch-Philologische Classe der Königlichen Gesellschaft der Wissenschaften zu Göttingen Bd. 28. Göttingen: 1882; repr. Amsterdam: Hakkert, 1979.

———. *Letters.* Edited by A. Karpozilos, *The Letters of Ioannes Mauropous Metropolitan of Euchaita.* Corpus Fontium Historiae Byzantinae. Series Thessalonicensis 34. Thessalonike: Association for Byzantine Research, 1990.

Melampous the Grammarian (or Diomedes). *Comm. on the Art of Dionysios of Thrace.* Edited by A. Hilgard. *Scholia in Dionysii Thracis. Graeci Grammatici*, vol. 3. Leipzig: Teubner, 1901.

Nemesios. *On the Nature of Man.* Edited by M. Morani, *Nemesii Emeseni de natura hominis.* Leipzig: Teubner, 1987.

Niketas David Paphlagon. *Encomium in Honor of Gregory.* Edited by J. J. Rizzo, *The Encomium of Gregory Nazianzen.* Subsidia Hagiographica 58. Brussels: Société des Bollandistes, 1976.

Nikolaos I, patriarch. *Letters.* Edited by R. Jenkins and L. Westerink. *Nicholas I, Patriarch of Constantinople: Letters.* Corpus Fontium Historiae Byzantinae 6. Washington, D.C.: Dumbarton Oaks Center for Byzantine Studies, 1973.

Ps.-Nonnos. *Commentaries.* Edited by J. Nimmo Smith, *Pseudo-Nonniani in IV orationes Gregorii Nazianzeni Commentarii: Collationibus, versionum Syriacarum a Sebastian Brock, versionisque Armeniacae a Bernard Coulie additis.* Corpus Christianorum, Series Graeca 27, Corpus Nazianzenum 2. Turnhout: Brepols, 1992.

Pardos, Gregorios. *Comm. on Hermogenes' On the Method of Forceful Style.* Edited by C. Walz, *Rhetores Graeci,* vol. 7. Stuttgart: J. G. Cottae, 1832–36.

Photios. *Bibliothêkê.* Edited by R. Henry, *Photius: Bibliothèque*, 8 vols. Paris: Les Belles Lettres, 1959–77.

———. *Homilies.* Edited by B. Laourdas, Φωτίου ὁμιλίαι*: Ἑλληνικά 12* Παράρτημα. Thessalonike: Ἑταιρεία Μακεδονικῶν Σπουδῶν, 1959.

———. *Letters* and *Amphilochia*. Edited by B. Laourdas and L. G. Westerink, *Photii Patriarchae Constantinopolitani Epistulae et Amphilochia*. Leipzig: Teubner, 1983–88.

Scholia on Demosthenes. Edited by M. R. Dilts, *Scholia Demosthenica*, 2 vols. Leipzig: Teubner, 1983–86.

Sikeliotes, Ioannes. *Comm. on the Forms of Hermogenes*. Edited by C. Walz, *Rhetores Graeci*, 6:80–504. Stuttgart: J. G. Cottae, 1834.

———. *Prolegomena* to his *Comm. on Hermogenes*. Edited by H. Rabe, *Prolegomenon sylloge*. Rhetores Graeci 14, 393–420. Leipzig: Teubner, 1931.

Skylitzes, Stephanos. *Comm. on Aristotle's Rhetoric*. Edited by H. Rabe, *Anonymi et Stephani in artem rhetoricam commentarium*. Commentaria in Aristotelem Graeca 21.2, 263–322. Berlin: Reimer, 1896.

Stephanos. *Commentary on Hippocrates' Prognosticon*. Edited by J. Duffy, "*Stephanus: Commentary on Hippocrates' Prognosticon*." Ph.D. diss., State University of New York, Buffalo, 1975.

Suda. Edited by A. Adler, *Suidae lexicon*, 4 vols. Leipzig: Teubner, 1928–35.

Theophanes the Confessor. *Chronographia*. Edited by C. De Boor, *Theophanis: Chronographia*, vol. 1. Leipzig: Teubner 1883; repr. Hildesheim: Olms, 1963.

Tzetzes, Ioannes. *On Tragic Poetry*. Edited by G. Pace, *Giovanni Tzetzes, La poesia tragica: Edizione critica, traduzione e comment*. Speculum 27. Naples: M. D'Auria, 2011.

Secondary Literature

Periodicals are abbreviated as in *Dumbarton Oaks Papers* and *L'Année philologique*.

Aerts, W. J. 1990. *Michaelis Pselli Historia Syntomos*. Corpus Fontium Historiae Byzantinae, Series Berolinensis 30. Berlin: De Gruyter.

Afinogenov, D. E. 1995. "Patriarch Photius as Literary Theorist: Aspects of Innovation." *BSl* 56:339–45.

Agapitos, P. A. 1998. "Narrative, Rhetoric, and 'Drama' Rediscovered: Scholars and Poets in Byzantium Interpret Heliodoros." In *Studies in Heliodorus*, edited by R. Hunter, 125–56. Cambridge: Cambridge University Press.

———. 2008. "Literary Criticism." In *Oxford Handbook of Byzantine Studies*, edited by E. Jeffreys, J. F. Haldon, and R. Cormack, 77–85. Oxford: Oxford University Press.

Agapitos, P. A., and M. Hinterberger. 2006. *Εἰκὼν καὶ λόγος: ἕξι περιγραφὲς ἔργων τέχνης*. Athens: Agra.

Alberti, A., and R. W. Sharples, eds. 1999. *Aspasios: The Earliest Extant Commentary on Aristotle's Ethics*. Berlin: De Gruyter.

Allen, W. S. 1987. *Vox Graeca*, 3rd ed. Cambridge: Cambridge University Press.

Angelidi, C. 2005. "Observing, Describing and Interpreting: Michael Psellos on Works of Ancient Art." *Νέα Ῥώμη: Rivista di ricerche bizantinistiche* 2:227–42 (= Ἀμπελοκήπιον: *Studi di amici e colleghi in onore di Vera von Falkenhausen*).

Antonopoulou, T. 1997. *The Homilies of the Emperor Leo VI*. Leiden: Brill.

Athanassiadi, P. 1999. *Damascius: The Philosophical History; Text with Translation and Notes*. Athens: Apamea Cultural Association.

Attridge, H., and R. Oden. 1981. *Philo of Byblos, the Phoenician History: Introduction, Critical Text, Notes*. Washington, D.C.: Catholic Biblical Association of America.

Aujac, G. 1974. "Recherches sur la tradition du *peri syntheseôs onomatôn* de Denys d'Halicarnasse." *Revue de l'Institut d'Histoire des Textes* 4:1–44.

———. 1975. "Michel Psellos et Denys d' Halicarnasse: Le traité sur la composition des éléments du langage." *Revue des Études Byzantines* 33:257–75.

———, ed. 1978. *Denys d'Halicarnasse: Opuscules rhétoriques I; Les orateurs antiques*. Paris: Les Belles Lettres.

Bady, G. 2010. "Les figures du Théologien: Les citations de Grégoire de Nazianze dans les manuels byzantins de figures rhétoriques." In *Studia nazianzenica II*, edited by A. Schmidt, 257–322. Turnhout: Brepols.

Bake, J. 1849. *Apsinis et Longini Rhetorica*. Oxford.

Baldi, D. 2011. "Nuova luce sul Riccardiano 46." *Medioevo Greco* 11:13–22.

Barber, C. 2002. *Figure and Likeness: On the Limits of Representation in Byzantine Iconoclasm*. Princeton: Princeton University Press.

———. 2006a. "Living Painting, or the Limits of Pointing? Glancing at Icons with Michael Psellos." In *Reading Michael Psellos*, edited by C. Barber and D. Jenkins, 117–30. Leiden: Brill.

———. 2006b. "Icons, Prayer, and Vision in the Eleventh Century." In *Byzantine Christianity: A People's History of Christianity*, edited by Derek Krueger, 149–63. Minneapolis: Augsburg Fortress, 2006.

———. 2007. *Contesting the Logic of Painting: Art and Understanding in Eleventh-Century Byzantium*. Leiden: Brill.

———. Forthcoming. "On the Origin of the Work of Art: Tradition, Inspiration and Invention in the Post-Iconoclastic Era." In *L'icône dans la pensée et dans l'art: Constitutions, contestations, reinventions de la notion d'image divine en context chrétien*, edited by Kristina Mitalaité and Anca Vasiliu. Turnhout: Brepols.

Barber, C., and D. Jenkins, eds. 2006. *Reading Michael Psellos*. Leiden: Brill.

———. 2009. *Medieval Greek Commentaries on the Nicomachean Ethics*. Leiden: Brill.

Battisti, D. G. 1997. *Dionigi d'Alicarnasso, Sull'Imitazione: Edizione critica, traduzione e commento*. Pisa-Rome: Istituti Editoriali e Poligrafici Internazionali.

Beaton, R. 1980. *Folk Poetry of Modern Greece*. Cambridge: Cambridge University Press.

Beck, H. G. 1959. *Kirche und theologische Literatur im Byzantinischen Reich*. Munich: Beck.

Belting, H. 1994. *Likeness and Presence: A History of the Image before the Era of Art*. Chicago: University of Chicago Press.

Berger, F. 2005. *Die Textgeschichte der Historia Animalium des Aristoteles*. Wiesbaden: Reichert.

Bernard, F. 2014. *Writing and Reading Byzantine Secular Poetry, 1025–1081*. Oxford: Oxford University Press.

Betancourt, R. 2016. "Tempted to Touch: Tactility, Ritual, and Mediation in Byzantine Visuality." *Speculum* 91:660–89.

Bodnar, E. D., ed. and trans. 2003. *Cyriac of Ancona, Later Travels*. Cambridge, MA: Harvard University Press.

Boissonade, J. F. 1838. *Michael Psellus de operatione daemonum cum notis Gaulmini: Accedunt inedita opuscula Pselli*. Nürnberg.

Bompaire, J. 1981. "Photius et la Seconde Sophistique, d'apres la Bibliotheque." *TM* 8:79–86.

Bonis, K. G. 1937a. *Ἰωάννης ὁ Ξιφιλῖνος: ὁ νομοφύλαξ, ὁ μοναχός, ὁ πατριάρχης καὶ ἡ ἐποχὴ αὐτοῦ*. Athens: Verlag der "Byzantinish-neugrechischen Jahrbücher."

———. 1937b. *Προλεγόμενα εἰς τὰς "ἑρμηνευτικὰς Διδασκαλίας" τοῦ Ἰωάννου VIII: Ξιφιλίνου πατριάρχου Κωνσταντινουπόλεως [2 Ἰαν. 1064–2 Αὐγ. 1075]*; Συμβολὴ εἰς μίαν νέαν ἔκδοσιν. Athens.

Bonner, S. F. 1939. *The Literary Treatises of Dionysius of Halicarnassus: A Study in the Development of Critical Method.* Cambridge: Cambridge University Press.

Bossina, L., and F. Fatti. 2004. "Gregorio a due voci." *Medioevo Greco* 4:65–93.

Brenton, L. 1851. *The Septuagint Version of the Old Testament, according to the Vatican Text, Translated into English.* London: S. Bagster and Sons.

Browning, R. 1963. "A Byzantine Treatise on Tragedy." In Γέρας: Studies Presented to G. Thomson, 67–81. Acta Universitatis Carolinae philosophica et historica, Graecolatina Pragensia 1; Prague; repr. in *Studies on Byzantine History, Literature and Education*, no. XI. London: Variorum Reprints, 1977.

Bychkov, V. 1983. *L'estetica bizantina: Problemi teorici.* Bari: Congedo Editore.

———. 2001. *2000 Jahre Philosophie der Kunst im christlichen Osten: Alte Kirche, Byzanz, Russland.* Würzburg: Augustinus-Verlag.

Cameron, A. 2011. *The Last Pagans of Rome*. New York: Oxford University Press.

Cantone, V., and S. Pedone, eds. 2013. *Phantazontes: Visioni dell'arte bizantina.* Padua: CLEUP.

Carruthers, M. 1998. *The Craft of Thought: Meditation, Rhetoric, and the Making of Images, 400–1200.* Cambridge: Cambridge University Press.

Cavallo, G. 2006. *Lire à Byzance*. Paris: Les Belles Lettres.

Cesaretti, P. 1991. *Allegoristi di Omero a Bisanzio: Richerche ermeneutiche (XI–XII secolo).* Milan: Guerini studio.

Chiron, P. 2010. "La figure *d'hyperbate*." In *Rhetorica philosophans:* Mélanges offerts à Michel Patillon, edited by L. Brisson and P. Chiron, 311–35. Paris: Vrin.

Christ, W., and M. Paranikas. 1871. Anthologia graeca carminum. Leipzig: Teubner.

Chrysostallis, A. 2012. *Recherches sur la tradition manuscrite du Contra Eusebium de Nicéphore de Constantinople*. Paris: CNRS Éditions.

Colonna, A. 1953. "Michaelis Pselli de Euripide et Georgio Pisida iudicium." *Studi Bizantini e Neoellenici* 7:16–21.

Conley, T. M. 2003. "Demosthenes Dethroned: Gregory Nazianzus in John Sikeliotes' Commentary on Hermogenes' *Peri ideôn*." *ICS* 27/28: 145–52.

———. 2004. "John Italos' *Methodos Rhetorikê*: Text and Commentary." *Greek, Roman, and Byzantine Studies* 44:411–37.

———. 2009. "Byzantine Criticism and the Uses of Literature." In *The Cambridge History of Literary Criticism,* vol. 2, *The Middle Ages*, edited by A. Minnis, 669–92. Cambridge: Cambridge University Press.

Cormack, R. 1997. *Painting the Soul: Icons, Death Masks and Shrouds.* London: Reaktion Books.

———. 2003. "Living Painting." In *Rhetoric in Byzantium*, edited by E. Jeffreys, 235–53. Aldershot: Ashgate.

Cotsonis, J. 1994. "The Virgin with the 'Tongues of Fire' on Byzantine Lead Seals." *Dumbarton Oaks Papers* 48:221–27.

Cotsonis, J., and J. Nesbitt. 2004. "An 11th-Century Seal with a Representation of Patriarch Antony II Kauleas." *Byzantion* 74:517–26.

Criscuolo, U. 1976. "Note filologiche." *Bollettino della Badia greca di Grottaferrata*, ns. 30:59–63.

Cutler, A., and R. Browning. 1992. "In the Margins of Byzantium? Some Icons in Michael Psellos." *Byzantine and Modern Greek Studies* 16:21–32.

Dagron, G. 1983. "Psellos épigraphiste." *Harvard Ukrainian Studies* 7:117–24.

Davies, W., and P. Fouracre, eds. 1986. *The Settlement of Disputes in Early Medieval Europe*. Cambridge: Cambridge University Press.

Dawson, D. 1992. *Allegorical Readers and Cultural Revision in Ancient Alexandria*. Berkeley: University of California Press.

de Jonge, C. C. 2008. *Between Grammar and Rhetoric: Dionysius of Halicarnassus on Language, Linguistics, and Literature*. Leiden: Brill.

Demoen, K. 2001. "Classicizing Elements in John Geometres' Letters about his Garden." In *Πρακτικά ΙΑ' Διεθνοῦς Συνεδρίου Κλασικῶν Σπουδῶν: Καβάλα, Αὔγουστος 1999*, 1:215–30. Athens.

Dennis, G. 1994. "A Rhetorician Practices Law: Michael Psellos." In *Law and Society in Byzantium: Ninth–Twelfth Centuries*, edited by A. Laiou and D. Simon, 187–97. Washington, D.C.: Dumbarton Oaks Research Library and Collection.

Dostálová, R. 1986. "Tabula Iliaca (Odysseaca) Ducaena." *BSl* 47:28–33.

Dubel, S. 1997. "Ekphrasis et enargeia: La description antique comme parcours." In *Dire l'évidence: Philosophie et rhétorique antiques*, ed. by C. Lévy and L. Pernot, 249–64. Paris: L'Harmattan.

Duffy, J. 1992. *Michael Psellus: Philosophica Minora* I. Stuttgart: Teubner.

———. 1995. "Reactions of Two Byzantine Intellectuals to the Theory and Practice of Magic: Michael Psellos and Michael Italikos." In *Byzantine Magic*, edited by H. Maguire, 83–95. Washington, D.C.: Dumbarton Oaks.

———. 2000. "Bitter Brine and Sweet Fresh Water: The Anatomy of a Metaphor in Psellos." In *Novum Millennium: Studies on Byzantine History and Culture Dedicated to Paul Speck, 19 December 1999*, edited by C. Sode and S. Takács, 89–96. Ashgate: Aldershot.

Duffy, J., and S. Papaioannou. 2003. "Michael Psellos and the Authorship of the *Historia Syntomos*: Final Considerations." In *Byzantium, State and Society: In Memory of Nikos Oikonomides*, edited by A. Abramea, A. Laiou, and E. Chrysos, 219–29. Athens: Hellenic National Research Foundation.

Dugan, J. 2005. *Making a New Man: Ciceronian Self-fashioning in the Rhetorical Works*. Oxford: Oxford University Press.

Dyck, A. 1986. *Michael Psellus, The Essays on Euripides and George of Pisidia and on Heliodorus and Achilles Tatius*. Vienna: Verlag der Österreichischen Akademie der Wissenschaften.

Ehrhard, A. 1937–52. Überlieferung und Bestand der hagiographischen und homiletischen Literatur der griechischen Kirche von den Anfängen bis zum Ende des 16. Jahrhunderts. 3 vols. Leipzig: Hinrichs.

Evans, H., ed. 2004. *Byzantium: Faith and Power (1261–1557)*. New Haven: Yale University Press.

Faraone, C. 1992. *Talismans and Trojan Horses: Guardian Statues in Ancient Greek Myth and Ritual*. Oxford: Oxford University Press.

Fisher, E. A. 1994. "Image and Ekphrasis in Michael Psellos' Sermon on the Crucifixion." *BSl* 55:44–55.

———. 2006. "Michael Psellos in a Hagiographical Landscape: The Life of St. Auxentios and the Encomion of Symeon the Metaphrast." In *Reading Michael Psellos*, edited by C. Barber and D. Jenkins, 57–71. Leiden: Brill.

———. 2012. "Michael Psellos on the 'Usual' Miracle at Blachernae, the Law, and Neoplatonism." In *Byzantine Religious Culture: Studies in Honor of Alice-Mary Talbot*, edited by D. Sullivan, E. Fisher, and S. Papaioannou, 187–204. Leiden: Brill.

Flinterman, J.-J. 2000–2001. "'. . . Largely Fictions . . .': Aelius Aristides on Plato's Dialogues." *Ancient Narrative* 1:32–54.

Flusin, B., and J. Paramelle. 1984. "La Vie métaphrastique de Pélagie BHG 1479." In *Pélagie la pénitente: Métamorphoses d'une légende*, vol. 2, *La survie dans les littératures européennes*, edited by P. Petitmengin, 15–45. Paris: Études augustiniennes.

Gaisford, T. 1848. *Etymologicum magnum*. Oxford: Oxford University Press.

Gaul, N. 2010. "The Manuscript Tradition." In *A Companion to the Ancient Greek Language*, edited by E. J. Bakker, 69–81. Malden, MA: Wiley-Blackwell.

Gautier, P. 1972. *Michel Italikos: Lettres et Discours*. Paris: Institut Français d'Études Byzantines.

———.1974. "Eloge funèbre de Nicolas de la Belle Source par Michel Psellos moine à l'Olympe." *Byzantina* 6:11–69.

———. 1980–82. "Éloge inédit du lecteur Jean Kroustoulas par Michel Psellos." *RSBN* 17–19:119–47.

———. 1986. "Deux manuscrits pselliens: Le Parisinus Graecus 1182 et le Laurentianus Graecus 57-40." *REB* 44:45–110.

———. 1991. "Un discours inédit de Michel Psellos sur la Crucifixion." *REB* 49:5–66.

Gill, C. 1984. "The *êthos/pathos* Distinction." *CQ* 34:149–66.

Glucker, J. 1968. "Notes on the Byzantine Treatise on Tragedy." *Byzantion* 38:267–72.

Grabar, A. 1945: "Plotin et les origines de l'esthétique médiévale." *Cahiers archéologiques* 1:15–36.

Greene, W.C. 1938. *Scholia Platonica*. Haverford, PA: American Philological Association.

Grumel, V. 1931. "Le 'miracle habituel' de Notre-Dame des Blachernes à Constantinople." *Échos d'Orient* 30:129–46.

Guilland, R. 1976. *Titres et fonctions de l'Empire byzantin*. London: Variorum Reprints.

Haidacher, S. 1902. *Studien über Chrysostomus-Eklogen*. Vienna: C. Gerold's Sohn.

Halliwell, S., ed. and trans. 1995. "Aristotle, Poetics." In *Aristotle, Poetics, edited and translated by S. Halliwell; Longinus, On the Sublime, edited and translated by W. H. Fyfe, revised by D. Russell; Demetrius, On Style, edited and translated by D. C. Innes, based on W. Rhys Roberts*, 27–141. Cambridge, MA: Harvard University Press.

Harkins, P., trans. 1982. *Saint John Chrysostom: On the Incomprehensible Nature of God*. Washington, D.C.: Catholic University of America Press.

Harlfinger, D., and D. Reinsch. 1970. "Die Aristotelica des Parisinus Gr. 1741." *Philologus* 114:28–50.

Harsting, P., and S. Ekman, eds. 2002. *Ten Nordic Studies in the History of Rhetoric*. Copenhagen: Nordisk Netværk for Retorikkens Historie.

Harvey, A. 1989. *Economic Expansion in the Byzantine Empire, 900–1200*. Cambridge: Cambridge University Press.

Harvey, S. 2006. *Scenting Salvation: Ancient Christianity and the Olfactory Imagination*. Berkeley: University of California Press.

Heath, M. 1995. *Hermogenes, On Issues: Strategies of Argument in Later Greek Rhetoric.* Oxford: Clarendon Press.

———. 2002. Review of Patillon and Brisson 2001. *Classical Review* 52:276–74.

———. 2003. "Pseudo-Dionysius' *Art of Rhetoric* 8-11: Figured Speech, Declamation and Criticism." *AJP* 124:81–105.

———. 2004. *Menander: A Rhetor in Context.* Oxford: Oxford University Press.

Heimbach, C. G. E., ed. 1843. *Basilicorum Libri LX,* vol. I. Leipzig: Teubner.

Hennessy, C. 2012. "The Chapel of Saint Jacob at the Church of the Theotokos Chalkoprateia in Istanbul." In *Proceedings of 7th International Congress on the Archaeology of the Ancient Near East, 12 April–16 April 2010, the British Museum and UCL, London,* vol. 2, *Ancient and Modern Issues in Cultural Heritage; Colour and Light in Architecture; Art and Material Culture; Islamic Archaeology,* edited by J. Curtis, R. Matthews, A. Fletcher, C. Gatz, M. Seymour, St J. Simpson, and J. N. Tubb, 351–66. Wiesbaden: Harrassowitz.

Hexter, R. J. 2012. "Canonicity." In *The Oxford Handbook of Medieval Latin Literature,* edited by R. J. Hexter and D. Townsend, 25–45. Oxford: Oxford University Press.

Hilgard, A. 1901. *Grammatici Graeci,* vol. 1.3. Leipzig: Teubner.

Hill, B. 1999. *Imperial Women in Byzantium 1025–1204: Power, Patronage and Ideology.* Harlow: Longman.

Hoche, R. 1866. *Nicomachi Geraseni Pythagorei introductionis arithmeticae libri ii.* Leipzig: Teubner.

Hoffmann, P. 2006. "What was Commentary in Late Antiquity? The Example of the Neoplatonic Commentators." In *A Companion to Ancient Philosophy,* edited by M. L. Gill and P. Pellegrin, 598–622. Malden, MA: Blackwell Pub.

Høgel, C. ed. 1996. *Metaphrasis: Redactions and Audiences in Middle Byzantine Hagiography.* Oslo: The Research Council of Norway.

———. 2002a. *Symeon Metaphrastes: Rewriting and Canonization.* Copenhagen: Museum Tusculanum Press.

———. 2002b. "Metaphrasis and the Rewriting of Saints' Lives in Byzantium." In *Nordic Studies in the History of Rhetoric,* vol. 1, edited by P. Harsting and S. Ekman, 27–38. Copenhagen: Nordisk Netvaerk for Retorikkens Historie.

———. 2003. "Hagiography under the Macedonians: The Two Recensions of the Metaphrastic Menologion." In *Byzantium in the Year 1000,* edited by P. Magdalino, 217–32. Leiden: Brill.

———. 2004. "Psellos Hagiographicus: Contradictio in Adjecto?" In *Les Vies des saints à Byzance: Genre littéraire ou biographie historique? Actes du IIe colloque international "EPMHNEIA," Paris, 6-7-8 juin 2002,* edited by P. Odorico and P. A. Agapitos, 191–200. Dossiers byzantins 4. Paris: Centre d'études byzantines, néohelléniques et sud-est européennes.

Hörandner, W. 1995. "Beobachtungen zur Literarästhetik der Byzantiner: Einige byzantinische Zeugnisse zu Metrik und Rhythmik." *BSl* 56:279–90.

———. 1995–96. "Literary Criticism in 11th-Century Byzantium: Views of Michael Psellos on John Chrysostom's Style." *IJCT* 2:336–44.

———. 2007. "Der Aristoteles-Kommentator Stephanos in seiner Zeit." In *Byzantina Mediterranea: Festschrift für Johannes Koder zum 65. Geburtstag,* edited by K. Belke, E. Kislinger, A. Külzer, and M. A. Stassinopoulou, 257–67. Vienna: Böhlau.

———. 2012. "Pseudo-Gregorios Korinthios, Über die vier Teile der perfekten Rede." *Medioevo greco* 12:87–131.

Hunger, H., et al., eds. 1961. *Geschichte der Textüberlieferung der antiken und mittelalterlichen Literatur* I. Zurich: Atlantis Verlag.

Ierodiakonou, K. 2006. "The Greek Concept of *Sympatheia* and Its Byzantine Appropriation in Michael Psellos." In *The Occult Sciences in Byzatium*, edited by P. Magdalino and M. Mavroudi, 97–117. Sofia: La Pomme D'or.

Irigoin, J. 1997. *Tradition et critique des textes grecs.* Paris: Les Belles Lettres.

James, L. 1996. *Light and Colour in Byzantine Art.* Oxford: Clarendon Press.

———. 2003. "Color and Meaning in Byzantium." *Journal of Early Christian Studies* 11:223–33.

———. 2004. "Senses and Sensibility in Byzantium." *Art History* 27:522–37.

Janin, R. 1969. *La géographie ecclésiastique de l'Empire byzantine: Première partie, Le siège de Constantinople et le patriarcat œcuménique.* 2nd ed. Paris: Institut français d'études byzantines.

———. 1975. *Les églises et les monastères des grands centres byzantins.* Paris: Institut français d'études byzantines.

Jeffreys, M. 1974. "The Nature and Origins of the Political Verse." *Dumbarton Oaks Papers* 28:143–95.

Jenkins, D. 2006. "The Court Memorandum (*Hypomnema*) Regarding the Engagement of his Daughter." In *Mothers and Sons, Fathers and Daughters: The Byzantine Family of Michael Psellos,* edited by A. Kaldellis, 139–56. Michael Psellos in Translation. Notre Dame, IN: University of Notre Dame Press.

Jordan, R. H. 2000–2005. *The Synaxarion of the Monastery of the Theotokos Evergetis: Text and Translation.* Belfast: Belfast Byzantine Enterprises, the Institute of Byzantine Studies, the Queen's University of Belfast.

Jordan, R. H., and R. Morris. 2012. *The Hypotyposis of the Monastery of the Theotokos Evergetis, Constantinople (11th–12th Centuries): Introduction, Translation and Commentary.* Farnham: Ashgate.

Kaldellis, A. 1999. *The Argument of Psellos' Chronographia.* Leiden: Brill.

———, ed. and trans. 2006. *Mothers and Sons, Fathers and Daughters: The Byzantine Family of Michael Psellos.* Michael Psellos in Translation. Notre Dame, IN: University of Notre Dame Press.

———. 2007. *Hellenism in Byzantium: The Transformations of Greek Identity and the Reception of the Classical Tradition.* Cambridge: Cambridge University Press.

Kaldellis, A., and I. Polemis, trans. 2015. *Psellos and the Patriarchs: Letters and Funeral Orations for Keroullarios, Leichoudes, and Xiphilinos.* Michael Psellos in Translation. Notre Dame, IN: University of Notre Dame Press.

Kalligas, P. 2013. *Πλωτίνου, Εννεάς Πέμπτη: Αρχαίο κείμενο, μετ'φραση, σχόλια.* Athens: Βιβλιοθήκη Α. Μανούση.

Kambylis, A. 1978. "Epiphyllides: Neunzig kritische Bemerkungen zu byzantinischen Prosatexten." In *Kyklos: Griechisches und Byzantinisches. Rudolf Keydell zum neunzigsten Geburtstag,* edited by H. G. Beck, A. Kambylis, and P. Moraux, 137–38. Berlin: De Gruyter.

———. 1994. "Michael Psellos' Schrift über Euripides und Pisides. Probleme der Textkonstitution." *JÖB* 44:203–15.

———. 2006. "Michael Psellos' Schrift Τίς ἐστίχιζε κρεῖττον ὁ Εὐριπίδης ἢ ὁ Πισίδης: Textkritische Bemerkungen." *JÖB* 56:135–49.

Kannicht, R. 2004. *Tragicorum Graecorum Fragmenta,* 5.1, *Euripides*. Göttingen: Vandenhoeck and Ruprecht.

Karahan, A. 2010. *Byzantine Holy Images: Transcendence and Immanence; The Theological Background of the Iconography and Aesthetics of the Chora Church.* Leuven: Peeters.

Karamanolis, G. 2007. "Porphyry's Notion of Empsychia." In *Studies on Porphyry*, edited by G. Karamanolis and A. Sheppard, 91–109. London: Institute of Classical Studies, School of Advanced Study, University of London.

Karpozilos, A. 2009. *Βυζαντινοὶ ἱστορικοὶ καὶ χρονογράφοι: Τόμος Γ' (11ος–12ος αἰ.).* Athens: Kanake.

Kavrus-Hoffmann, N. 2010a. "Catalogue of Greek Medieval and Renaissance Manuscripts in the Collections of the United States of America. Part V.1: Harvard University, The Houghton Library." *Manuscripta* 54.1:64–147.

———. 2010b. "From *Pre-bouletée* to *Bouletée*: Scribe Epiphanios and the Codices Mosq. Synod. gr. 103 and Vat. gr. 90." In *The Legacy of Bernard de Montfaucon: Three Hundred Years of Studies on Greek Handwriting. Proceedings of the Seventh International Colloquium of Greek Palaeography (Madrid–Salamanca, 15–20 September 2008)*, 55–66 and 693–700. Bibliologia 31. Turnhout: Brepols.

Kayser, C.L. 1844. *Flavii Philostrati quae supersunt: Philostrati junioris Imagines, Callistrati Descriptiones.* Zurich: Meyeri et Zelleri.

Kazhdan, A.P. 1983. "Hagiographical Notes, 3. An Attempt at Hagio-autobiography: The Pseudo-Life of "Saint" Psellus?" *Byzantion* 53:546–56.

Keil, B. 1904. "Schriftzeugnis über Pheidias." *Mitteilungen des Deutschen Archäologischen Instituts* 29:383–84.

Kemp, J.A. 1986. "The *Tekhne Grammatike* of Dionysius Thrax." *Historiographia Linguistica* 13.2–3:343–63.

Kennedy, G.A. 2003. *Progymnasmata: Greek Textbooks of Prose Composition and Rhetoric.* Writings from the Greco-Roman World 10. Atlanta: Society of Biblical Literature, Leiden: Brill.

———. 2005. *Invention and Method: Two Rhetorical Treatises from the Hermogenic Corpus.* Writings from the Greco-Roman World 15. Atlanta: Society of Biblical Literature, Leiden: Brill.

Kinneavy, J.L. 1986. "Kairos: A Neglected Concept in Classical Rhetoric, in Rhetoric and Praxis." In *The Contribution of Classical Rhetoric to Practical Reasoning,* edited by J. Dietz Moss, 79–105. Washington, D.C.: Catholic University of America Press.

Koder, J. 1998. *Aigaion Pelagos (Die nördliche Ägäis).* Vienna: Verlag der Österreichischen Akademie der Wissenschaften.

Komines, A.D. 1968. *Πίνακες χρονολογημένων Πατμιακῶν κωδίκων.* Athens: Βασιλικὸν Ἵδρυμα Ἐρευνῶν, Κέντρον Βυζαντινῶν Ἐρευνῶν.

Krausmüller, D. 2011. "Making the Most of Mary: The Cult of the Virgin in the Chalkoprateia from Late Antiquity to the Tenth Century." In *The Cult of the Mother of God in Byzantium: Texts and Images,* edited by M. Cunningham and L. Brubaker, 219–46. Burlington, VT: Ashgate.

Kristeller, P. O. 1951. "The Modern System of the Arts: A Study in the History of Aesthetics (I)." *Journal of the History of Ideas* 12:496–527.

———. 1952. "The Modern System of the Arts: A Study in the History of Aesthetics (II)." *Journal of the History of Ideas* 13:17–46.

Kroll, W., and R. Schöll. 1895. *Justinian: Novellae*. Vol. 3 of *Corpus iuris civilis*, edited by P. Krueger et al. Berlin.

Külzer, A. 2008. *Ostthrakien (Eurōpē)*. Vienna: Verlag der Österreichischen Akademie der Wissenschaften.

Kustas, G. L. 1961–62. "Photian Methods in Philology." *GOTR* 7:78–91.

———. 1962. "The Literary Criticism of Photius: A Christian Definition of Style," *Hellenika* 17:132–69.

———. 1973. *Studies in Byzantine Rhetoric*. Thessalonike: Πατριαρχικὸν Ἵδρυμα Πατερικῶν Μελετῶν.

Laiou, A. 1996. "Life of St. Mary the Younger." In *Holy Women of Byzantium: Ten Saints' Lives in English Translation*, edited by A.-M. Talbot, 239–89. Washington, D.C.: Dumbarton Oaks Research Library and Collection.

Laiou, A., and D. Simon. 1992. "Eine Geschichte von Mühlen und Mönchen: Der Fall der Mühlen von Chantax." *Bullettino dell' Istituto di Diritto Romano,* 3rd ser., 30: 619–76. Trans. 2013. "Of Mills and Monks: The Case of the Mill of Chantax." In *Economic Thought and Economic Life in Byzantium*, edited by C. Morrisson and R. Dorin. Farnham: Ashgate Variorum.

Lapatin, K. D. S. 2001. *Chryselephantine Statuary in the Ancient Mediterranean World*. Oxford: Oxford University Press.

Laurent, V. 1952. *Documents de sigillographie byzantine: La collection C. Orghidan*. Paris: Presses Universitaires de France.

———. 1965. *Le corpus des sceaux de l'empire byzantine*, vol. 5.2.1, *L'eglise*. Paris: Ed. du Centre National de la Recherche Scientifique.

Lauritzen, F. 2013. *The Depiction of Character in the Chronographia of Michael Psellos*. Turnhout: Brepols.

Lauxtermann, M. D. 1998. "What is an Epideictic Epigram?" *Mnemosyne* 51:525–37.

———. 1999. *The Spring of Rhythm: An Essay on the Political Verse and Other Byzantine Metres*. Vienna: Verlag der Österreichischen Akademie der Wissenschaften.

———. 2003. *Byzantine Poetry from Pisides to Geometres*. Wiener Byzantinische Studien 24. Vienna: Verlag der Österreichischen Akademie der Wissenschaften.

Lemerle, P. 1971. *Le premier humanism byzantin: Notes et remarques sur enseignement et culture à Byzance des origines au Xe siècle*. Paris: Presses universiatires de France.

Levy, P. 1912. *Michael Psellus: De Gregorii Theologi charactere iudicium, accedit eiusdem de Ioannis Chrisostomi charactere iudicium ineditum*. Diss. Straßburg. Leipzig: R. Noske.

Lilie, R.-J., C. Ludwig, T. Pratsch, and B. Zielke. 2013. *Prosopographie der mittelbyzantinischen Zeit. 2 Abt. 6. Bd. Sinko (#27089)–Zuhayr (#28522): Herausgegeben von der Berlin-Brandenburgischen Akademie der Wissenschaften; nach Vorarbeiten F. Winkelmanns; unter Mitarbeit von H. Lichlmeier, B. Krönung, D. Fŏller; sowie A. Beihammer, G. Prinzing.* Berlin: De Gruyter.

Lindberg, D. 1976. *Theories of Vision from Al-Kindi to Kepler*. Chicago: University of Chicago Press.

Littlewood, A. R. 1988. "A Statistical Survey of the Incidence of Repeated Quotations in Selected Byzantine Letter-Writers." In *Gonimos: Neoplatonic and Byzantine Studies Presented to Leendert G. Westerink at 75*, edited by J. Duffy and J. Peradotto, 147–54. Buffalo: Arethusa.

———. 2005. "Literature." In *Palgrave Advances in Byzantine History*, edited by J. Harris, 133–46. New York: Palgrave Macmillan.

Ljubarskij, J. N. 1975. "Literaturno-estetičeskije vzgljady Michaila Psella." In *Antičnost' i Vizantija*, edited by L. A. Freiberg, 114–39. Moscow: Nauka.

———. 2001. *Michail Psell: Licnost i tvorcestvo; k istorii vizantijskovo predgumanisma*, 183–542. St. Petersburg: Aleteia; updated ed., 1978, *Michail Psell: Licnost i tvorcestvo; k istorii vizantijskovo predgumanisma*. Moscow: Nauka; updated modern Greek trans., 2004, *Η προσωπικότητα και το έργο του Μιχαήλ Ψελλού: Συνεισφορά στην ιστορία του βυζαντινού ουμανισμού*, trans. by A. Tzelesi. Athens: Kanake.

Longo, O., ed. 1971. *Scholia Byzantina in Sophoclis Oedipum tyrannum*. Padua: Antenore.

Macrides, R. 1994. "The Competent Court." In *Law and Society in Byzantium: Ninth–Twelfth Centuries*, edited by A. Laiou and D. Simon, 117–29. Washington, D.C.: Dumbarton Oaks Research Library and Collection.

Magdalino, P. 1998. "Constantinopolitana." In *Aetos: Studies in Honour of Cyril Mango*, edited by I. Ševčenko and I. Hutter, 220–27. Stuttgart: Teubner.

———. 2003. "The Porphyrogenita and the Astrologers: A Commentary on *Alexiad* VI.7.1–7." In *Porphyrogenita: Essays on the History and Literature of Byzantium and the Latin East in Honour of Julian Chrysostomides*, edited by C. Dendrinos et al., 15–31. Aldershot: Ashgate.

———. Forthcoming. "John Geometres, the Church of ta Kyrou, and the Kyriotai." In *Reading Byzantium*, edited by N. Gaul, T. Shawcross, and I. Toth. Oxford: Oxford University Press.

Maguire, H., ed. 1995. *Byzantine Magic*. Washington, D.C.: Dumbarton Oaks Research Library and Collection.

Majercik, R. 1989. *The Chaldean Oracles: Text, Translation and Commentary*. Leiden: Brill.

Mango, C. 1959. *The Brazen House: A Study of the Vestibule of the Imperial Palace in Constantinople*. Copenhagen: I kommission hos Munksgaard.

Mariev, S. 2013. "Ästhetische Theorien in Byzanz." Habilitationsschrift for the Fakultät für Kulturwissenschaften der Ludwig-Maximilians-Universität München.

Mariev, S., and W.-M. Stock, eds. 2013. *Aesthetics and Theurgy in Byzantium*. Byzantinisches Archiv 25. Boston: De Gruyter.

Mathew, G. 1964. *Byzantine Aesthetics*. New York: Viking Press.

Mayer, A. 1911. "Psellos' Rede über den rhetorischen Charakter des Gregorios von Nazianz." *BZ* 20:27–100.

Mazzucchi, P. 1990. "Longino in Giovanni di Sicilia." *Aevum* 6:183–98.

Mensching, G., ed. 2007. *De usu rationis: Vernunft und Offenbarung im Mittelalter*. Würzburg: Königshausen and Neumann.

Messis, C. 2006. "La mémoire du 'je' souffrant: Construire et écrire la mémoire personelle dans les récits de captivité." In *L'écriture de la mémoire: La littérarité de l'historiographie; Actes du colloque international sur la Littérature Byzantine,*

Nicosie 6–8 mai 2004, edited by P. Odorico, P. A. Agapitos, and M. Hinterberger, 107–46. Paris: Centre d'études byzantines, néo-helléniques et sud-est européennes, École des Hautes Études en Sciences Sociales.

———. 2014. *Les Eunuches à Byzance, entre réalité et imaginaire*. Dossiers byzantins 14. Paris: Centre d'études byzantines, néo-helleniques et sud-est européennes, École des Hautes Études en Sciences Sociales.

Messis, C., and S. Papaioannou. Forthcoming. "Orality (and Textuality)." In *The Oxford Handbook of Byzantine Literature*, edited by S. Papaioannou. Oxford: Oxford University Press.

Michelis, P. 1955. *An Aesthetic Approach to Byzantine Art*. London: Batsford.

Milazzo, A. M. 2002. *Un dialogo difficile: La retorica in conflitto nei Discorsi Platonici di Elio Aristide*. New York: G. Olms Verlag.

Miller, T. A. 1975. "Michail Psell i Dionisij Galikarnasskij." In *Antičnost' i Vizantija*, edited by L. A. Freiberg, 140–74. Moscow: Nauka.

Milovanović, Č. 1979. "Mihajlo Psel kao književni teoretičar." Ph.D. dissertation, University of Belgrade.

Minnis, A. J., and A. B. Scott. 1991. *Medieval Literary Theory and Criticism, c. 1100–c. 1375*. Oxford: Clarendon Press.

Moore, P. 2005. *Iter Psellianum: A Detailed Listing of Manuscript Sources for All Works Attributed to Michael Psellos*. Toronto: Pontifical Institute of Mediaeval Studies.

Morris, R. 1986. "Dispute Settlement in the Byzantine Provinces in the Tenth Century." In *The Settlement of Disputes in Early Medieval Europe*, edited by W. Davies and P. Fouracre, 129–35. Cambridge: Cambridge University Press.

Morrow, G. R., and J. M. Dillon, trans. 1987. *Proclus' Commentary on Plato's Parmenides*. Princeton: Princeton University Press.

Mossay, J., and L. Hoffmann. 1996. *Repertorium Nazianzenum: Orationes; Textus Graecus*. 5 Codices Civitatis Vaticanae. Paderborn: F. Schöningh.

Moutafov, E. 2008. "Blachernai, Basilica of the Virgin Mary." *Encyclopaedia of the Hellenic World, Constantinople*. Available at http://www.ehw.gr/l.aspx?id=11778.

Nelson, R. S. 2000. "To Say and to See: Ekphrasis and Vision in Byzantium." In *Visuality Before and Beyond the Renaissance*, edited by R. S. Nelson, 143–68. Cambridge: Cambridge University Press.

Nesbitt, J., and N. Oikonomides, eds. 1991. *The Catalogue of Seals at Dumbarton Oaks and in the Fogg Museum of Art*. Washington, D.C.: Dumbarton Oaks Research Library and Collection.

Nunn, V. 1986. "The Encheirion as Adjunct to the Icon in the Middle Byzantine Period." *Byzantine and Modern Greek Studies* 10:73–102.

Oikonomides, N. 1973. "Two Seals of Symeon Metaphrastes." *Dumbarton Oaks Papers* 27:323–26.

———. 1986. "The 'Peira' of Eustathios Rhomaios: An Abortive Attempt to Innovate in Byzantine Law." In *Fontes Minores 7*, edited by D. Simon, 169–92. Frankfurt: Löwenklau Gesellschaft.

———. 1991. "The Holy Icon as Asset." *Dumbarton Oaks Papers* 45:35–44 [= *Society, Culture, and Politics in Byzantium* (Aldershot: Ashgate, 2005) XIII].

O'Meara, D. 1989. *Pythagoras Revised: Mathematics and Philosophy in Late Antiquity*. Oxford: Clarendon Press.

———. 1993. *Plotinus: An Introduction to the Enneads*. Oxford: Clarendon Press.

Overbeck, J. 1868. *Die antiken Schriftquellen zur Geschichte der bildenden Künste bei den Griechen.* Leipzig: W. Engelmann.

Pace, G., ed. and trans. 2011. *Giovanni Tzetzes: La poesia tragica; Edizione critica, traduzione e comment.* Speculum 27. Naples: M. D'Auria editore.

Penella, R. 2000. "The Rhetoric of Praise in the Private Orations of Themistius." In *Greek Biography and Panegyric in Late Antiquity*, edited by T. Hägg and P. Rousseau, 194–208. Berkeley: University of California Press.

Papadopoulos, I. 1928. *Les palais et les églises des Blachernes.* Thessaloniki: Imp. de la Société commerciale & industrielle de Macédoine.

Papaioannou, S. 2001. "The 'Usual Miracle' and an Unusual Image: Psellos and the Icons of Blachernai." *Jahrbuch der Österreichischen Byzantinistik* 51:177–88.

———. 2004. "Der Glasort des Textes: Selbstheit und Ontotypologie im byzantinischen Briefschreiben (10. und 11. Jh.)." In *Wiener Byzantinistik und Neogräzistik: Beiträge zum Symposion Vierzig Jahre Institut für Byzantinistik und Neogräzistik der Universität Wien; Im Gedenken an Herbert Hunger (Wien, 4.–7. Dezember 2002)*, edited by W. Hörandner, J. Koder, and M. Stassinopoulou, 324–36. Byzantina et Neograeca Vindobonensia 24. Vienna: Verlag der österreichischen Akademie der Wissenschaften.

———. 2006. "Animate Statues: Aesthetics and Movement." In *Reading Michael Psellos*, edited by C. Barber and D. Jenkins, 95–116. The Medieval Mediterranean 61. Leiden: Brill.

———. 2010. "The Aesthetics of History: From Theophanes to Eustathios." In *History as Literature in Byzantium: Papers from the Fortieth Spring Symposium of Byzantine Studies, The Centre for Byzantine, Ottoman and Modern Greek Studies of the University of Birmingham April 2007*, edited by R. Macrides, 3–21. Aldershot: Ashgate Variorum.

———. 2011. "Byzantine *Enargeia* and Theories of Representation." In *Ekphrasis: La représentation des monuments dans les littératures byzantine et byzantino-slaves—Réalités et imaginaires = BSl* 69:48–60.

———. 2012. "Rhetoric and the Philosopher in Byzantium." In *Essays in Byzantine Philosophy*, edited by K. Ierodiakonou and B. Bydén, 171–97. Athens: The Norwegian Institute at Athens.

———. 2013. *Michael Psellos: Rhetoric and Authorship in Byzantium.* Cambridge: Cambridge University Press.

———. 2014a. "Byzantine *Historia.*" In *Thinking, Recording, and Writing History in the Ancient World*, edited by K. Raaflaub, 297–313. Malden, MA: Wiley-Blackwell.

———. 2014b. "Voice, Signature, Mask: The Byzantine Author." In *The Author in Middle Byzantine Literature*, edited by A. Pizzone, 21–49. Byzantinisches Archiv 28. Berlin: De Gruyter.

———. 2015. "Sicily, Constantinople, Miletos: The Life of a Eunuch and the History of Byzantine Humanism." In *Myriobiblos: Essays on Byzantine Literature and Culture*, edited by Th. Antonopoulou, S. Kotzabassi, and M. Loukaki, 261–84. Berlin: De Gruyter.

———. 2017. *Christian Novels from the Menologion of Symeon Metaphrastes.* Dumbarton Oaks Medieval Library. Cambridge, MA: Harvard University Press.

———. Forthcoming. "Aesthetics." In *The Oxford Handbook of Byzantine Literature*, edited by S. Papaioannou. Oxford: Oxford University Press.

———. Forthcoming. *Christian Novels from the Menologion of Symeon Metaphrastes.* Dumbarton Oaks Medieval Library. Cambridge, MA: Harvard University Press.

———. In preparation. "A Performance in the Church of the Virgin at Chalkoprateia."

Papamastorakis, T. 2002. "The Display of Accumulated Wealth in Luxury Icons: Gift-Giving from the Byzantine Aristocracy to God in the Twelfth Century." In *Byzantine Icons: Art, Technique, and Technology,* edited by M. Vassilaki, 35–49. Heraklion: Crete University Press.

———. 2003. "The Empress Zoe's Tomb." In *The Empire in Crisis? Byzantium in the 11th Century, 1025–1081,* edited by V. Vlyssidou, 497–511. Athens: National Hellenic Research Foundation.

———. 2004. "The Discreet Charm of the Visible." In *Byzantium Matures: Choices, Sensitivities, and Modes of Expression (Eleventh to Fifteenth Centuries),* edited by C. G. Angelidi, 111–27. Athens: National Hellenic Research Foundation.

Parry, K. 1996. *Depicting the Word: Byzantine Iconophile Thought of the Eighth and Ninth Centuries.* Leiden: Brill.

Patillon, M. 1988. *La théorie du discours chez Hermogène le Rhéteur.* Paris: Les Belles Lettres.

———, trans. 1997. *Hermogène: L'Art rhétorique.* Paris: L'Âge d'Homme.

———. 2008–12. *Corpus rhetoricum.* 4 vols in 6 parts. Paris: Les Belles Lettres.

Patillon, M., and L. Brisson. 2001. *Longin: Fragments; Art Rhétorique; Rufus: Art Rhétorique.* Paris: Les Belles Lettres.

Patterson Ševčenko, N. 1990. *Illustrated Manuscripts of the Metaphrastian Menologion.* Chicago: University of Chicago Press.

Peers, G. 2004. *Sacred Shock: Framing Visual Experience in Byzantium.* University Park: Pennsylvania State University Press.

Pentcheva, B. 2000. "Rhetorical Images of the Virgin: The Icon of the 'Usual Miracle' at Blachernai." *RES* 38:34–55.

———. 2008. "The Performative Icon." *Art Bulletin* 88:631–55.

———. 2010. *The Sensual Icon: Space, Ritual and the Senses in Byzantium.* University Park: Pennsylvania State University Press.

Pérez Martín, I. 2012. "The Transmission of Some Writings by Psellos in Thirteenth-Century Constantinople." In *Theologica minora: The Minor Genres of Byzantine Theological Literature,* edited by A. Rigo in collaboration with P. Ermilov and M. Trizio, 159–74 and 180–85. Turnhout: Brepols.

Perusino, F., ed. 1993. *Anonimo (Michele Psello?) La tragedia greca: Edizione critica, traduzione e commento.* Urbino: QuattroVenti.

Pickard-Cambridge, A. 1968. *The Dramatic Festivals of Athens.* 2nd ed., revised by J. Gould and D. M. Lewis. Oxford: Oxford University Press.

Pizzone, A., ed. 2014. *The Author in Middle Byzantine Literature.* Byzantinisches Archiv 28. Berlin: De Gruyter.

Pöhlmann, E., ed. 1994–2003. *Einführung in die Überlieferungsgeschichte und in die Textkritik der antiken Literatur.* 2 vols. Darmstadt: Wissenschaftliche Buchgesellschaft.

Polemis, D. I. 1968. *The Doukai: A Contribution to Byzantine Prosopography.* University of London Historical Studies 22. London: Athlone.

Polemis, I. D. 1991. "Φιλολογικὲς παρατηρήσεις σὲ κείμενα τοῦ Μιχαὴλ Ψελλοῦ." Παρνασσὸς 33:306–14.

Pontikos, I. 1992. *Anonymi Miscellanea Philosophica: A Miscellany in the Tradition of Michael Psellos (Codex Baroccianus Graecus 131); Critical Edition and Introduction.* Athens, Paris, and Brussels: The Academy of Athens, Librairie J. Vrin, Éditions Ousia.

Porter, J. I. 2009a. "Is Art Modern? Kristeller's 'Modern System of the Arts' Reconsidered." *British Journal of Aesthetics* 49:1–24.

———. 2009b. "Reply to Shiner." *British Journal of Aesthetics* 49:171–78.

———. 2010. *The Origins of Aesthetic Thought in Ancient Greece: Matter, Sensation, and Experience.* Cambridge: Cambridge University Press.

Pratsch, T. 2005. *Der hagiographische Topos.* Berlin: De Gruyter.

Probert, P. 2006. *Ancient Greek Accentuation: Synchronic Patterns, Frequency Effects, and Prehistory.* Oxford: Oxford University Press.

Psellus, M. 2014. *Orationes Funebres*, vol. 1, edited by I. Polemis. Berlin: De Gruyter.

Rabe, H. 1907. "Aus Rhetoren-Handschriften, 3: Die Quellen des Doxapatres in den Homilien zu Aphthonius." *Rheinisches Museum* 62:559–86.

———. 1913. *Hermogenis opera.* Leipzig: Teubner.

———. 1931. *Prolegomenon sylloge.* Rhetores Graeci 14. Leipzig: Teubner.

Radt, S., ed. 1977. *Tragicorum Graecorum fragmenta*, vol. 4. Göttingen: Vandenhoeck & Ruprecht.

Reinsch, D. R. 2013. "Wer waren die Leser und Hörer der Chronographia des Michael Psellos?" *Zbornik Radova Vizantoloshkog Instituta* 50:389–98.

———. 2014. *Michaelis Pselli Chronographia.* Berlin: De Gruyter.

———. 2015. *Leben der byzantinischen Kaiser (976–1075): Chronographia; griechisch-deutsch / Michael Psellos; eingeleitet, herausgegeben, übersetzt und mit Anmerkungen versehen; in Zusammenarbeit mit L. H. Reinsch-Werner.* Berlin: De Gruyter.

Riginos, A. S. 1976. *Platonica: The Anecdotes Concerning the Life and Writings of Plato.* Leiden: Brill.

Rosenqvist, J. 1986. *The Life of St. Irene, Abbess of Chrysobalanton: A Critical Edition with Introduction, Translation, Notes and Indices.* Uppsala: Upsalla University Press.

Russo, G. 2011. *Contestazione e conservazione Luciano nell'esegesi di Areta.* Berlin: De Gruyter.

Sajdak, J. 1914. *Historia critica scholiastarum et commentatorum Gregorii Nazianzeni, Pars 1.* Meletemata patristica 1. Krakow: G. Gebethner.

Seibt, W. 1976. *Die Skleroi: Eine prosopographisch-sigillographische Studie.* Vienna: Verlag der Österreichischen Akademie der Wissenschaften.

———. 1978. *Die byzantinischen Bleisiegel in Österreich.* Vienna: Verlag der Österreichischen Akademie der Wissenschaften.

Ševčenko, I. 1981. "Levels of Style in Byzantine Prose." *Jahrbuch der Österreichischen Byzantinistik* 31.1:289–312.

Sewter, E. R. A., trans. 1966. *Fourteen Byzantine Rulers: The Chronographia of Michael Psellus.* Baltimore: Penguin Books.

Sharples, R. W. 1987. "Alexander of Aphrodisias: Scholasticism and Innovation." *Aufstieg und Niedergang der römischen Welt* II 36.2:1176–1243.

Shiner, L. 2009. "Continuity and Discontinuity in the Concept of Art." *British Journal of Aesthetics* 49:159–69.

Simon, D., ed. 1986. *Fontes Minores 7.* Frankfurt: Löwenklau Gesellschaft.

Simon, D., and S. Troianos. 1989. *Das Novellensyntagma des Athanasios von Emesa.* Forschungen zur byzantinischen Rechtsgeschichte 16. Frankfurt: Löwenklau-Gesellschaft.

Sinogowitz, B. 1956. *Studien zum Strafrecht der Ekloge.* Athens: Ἀκαδημία Ἀθηνῶν.

Siorvanes, L. 1996. *Proclus: Neo-Platonic Philosophy and Science.* Edinburgh: Edinburgh University Press.

Smith, R. M. 1992. "Photius on the Ten Orators." *GRBS* 33:159–89.

Solomon, J. 2000. *Ptolemy Harmonics: Translation and Commentary.* Leiden: Brill.

Somers-Auwers, V. 2002. "Les collections byzantines de XVI discours de Grégoire de Nazianze." *BZ* 95:102–35.

Sophocles, E. A. 1887. *Greek Lexicon of the Roman and Byzantine Periods.* New York: Scribner's.

Steel, C. 2005. "Theology as First Philosophy: The Neoplatonic Concept of Metaphysics." *Quaestio* 5:3–21.

Steiner, D. T. 2001. *Images in Mind: Statues in Archaic and Classical Greek Literature and Thought.* Princeton: Princeton University Press.

Sternbach, L. 1893. *De Georgio Pisida Nonni sectatore.* Krakow.

Stornajolo, C. 1895. *Codices urbinates graeci Bibliothecae Vaticanae.* Rome: Typographeo vaticano.

Sturz, F. W. 1818. *Etymologicum Graecae linguae Gudianum et alia grammaticorum scripta e codicibus manuscriptis nunc primum edita.* Leipzig: Weigel.

Sullivan, D. F., A.-M. Talbot, and S. McGrath. 2014. *The Life of Saint Basil the Younger: Critical Edition and Annotated Translation of the Moscow Version.* Washington, D.C.: Dumbarton Oaks Research Library and Collection.

Tacchi-Venturi, P. 1893. "De Ioanne Geometra eiusque in S. Gregorium Nazianzenum inedita laudatione in Cod. Vaticano-Palatino 402 adservata." *Studi e documenti di storia e diritto* 14:133–62.

Tarán, L., and D. Gutas. 2012. *Aristotle Poetics: Editio Maior of the Greek text with Historical Introductions and Philological Commentaries.* Mnemosyne supplements: Monographs on Greek and Latin language and literature 338. Leiden: Brill.

Todorov, T. 1973. "The Notion of Literature." *New Literary History* 5.1 = *What Is Literature?* 5–16.

Towey, A., trans. 2000. *Alexander of Aphrodisias: On Aristotle's "On Sense Perception."* Ithaca: Cornell University Press.

Tsakiridou, C. A. 2013. *Icons in Time, Persons in Eternity: Orthodox Theology and the Aesthetics of the Christian Image.* Farnham: Ashgate.

Valiavitcharska, V. 2013. *Rhetoric and Rhythm in Byzantium: The Sound of Persuasion.* Cambridge: Cambridge University Press.

———. Forthcoming. "Rhetorical Figures." In *The Oxford Handbook of Byzantine Literature,* edited by S. Papaioannou. Oxford: Oxford University Press.

Vasilikopoulou-Ioannidou, A. 1971–72. Ἡ ἀναγέννησις τῶν γραμμάτων κατὰ τὸν 12ον αἰῶνα εἰς τὸ Βυζάντιον καὶ ὁ Ὅμηρος. Athens: Kapodistrian University of Athens, School of Philosophy.

Vasiliu, A. 1997. *Du diaphane: Image, milieu, lumière dans la pensée antique et medieval*. Paris: Librairie philosophique J. Vrin.
Volk, R. 1990. *Der medizinische Inhalt der Schriften des Michael Psellos*. Munich: Institut für Byzantinistik und Neugriechische Philologie der Universität.
Wahlgren, S., ed. 2006. *Symeonis Magistri et Logothetae Chronicon*. Berlin: De Gruyter.
Walker, J. 2000. *Rhetoric and Poetics in Antiquity*. Oxford: Oxford University Press.
———. 2001. "Michael Psellos on Rhetoric: A Translation and Commentary on Psellos' Synopsis of Hermogenes." *Rhetoric Society Quarterly* 31:5–40.
Wallraff, M., and R. Brändle, eds. 2008. *Chrysostomosbilder in 1600 Jahren: Facetten der Wirkungsgeschichte eines Kirchenvaters*. Berlin: de Gruyter.
Walz, C. 1833. *Rhetores Graeci*, vol. 5. Stuttgart: J. G. Cottae.
———. 1834. *Rhetores Graeci*, vol. 6. Stuttgart: J. G. Cottae.
———. 1835. *Rhetores Graeci*, vol. 2. Stuttgart: J. G. Cottae.
Wassiliou-Seibt, A.-K. 2011. "Die Neffen des Patriarchen Michael I. Kerullarios (1043–1058) und ihre Siegel. Ikonographie als Ausdrucksmittel der Verwandtschaft." *Bulgaria Mediaevalis* 2:145–57.
Wear, S., and J. Dillon. 2007. *Dionysius the Areopagite and the Neoplatonist Tradition: Despoiling the Hellenes*. Aldershot: Ashgate.
Webb, R. 1997. "Mémoire et imagination: Les limites de l'*enargeia* dans la théorie rhétorique grecque." In *Dire L'evidence: (Philosophie et rhétorique antiques)*, edited by C. Levy and L. Pernot, 229–48. Paris: L'Harmattan.
———. 2008. *Demons and Dancers: Performance in Late Antiquity*. Cambridge, MA: Harvard University Press.
Weiss, G. 1973. *Oströmische Beamte im Spiegel der Schriften des Michael Psellos*. Munich: Institut für Byzantinistik und neugriechische Philologie.
———. 1977. "Die Leichenrede des Michael Psellos auf den Abt Nikolaos vom Kloster von der Schönen Quelle." *Byzantina* 9:221–322.
West, M. 1978. *Hesiod: Works and Days*. Oxford: Oxford University Press.
———. 1992. *Ancient Greek Music*. Oxford: Oxford University Press.
Westerink, L. G., ed. 1948. *Michael Psellus, De omnifaria doctrina*. Utrecht: J. L. Beijers.
———. ed. 1962. *Anonymous Prolegomena to Platonic Philosophy*. Amsterdam: North Holland Publishing.
———. ed. 1992. *Michaeli Pselli Poemata*. Stuttgart: Teubner.
Wiater, N. 2011. *The Ideology of Classicism: Language, History, and Identity in Dionysius of Halicarnassus*. Berlin: De Gruyter.
Wilson, N. G. 1978. "A Byzantine Miscellany: MS. Barocci 131 Described." *JÖB* 27:157–79.
———. 1983. *Scholars of Byzantium*. Baltimore: Johns Hopkins University Press.
———. "Symeon Metaphrastes at Work." Νέα Ῥώμη 11:105–7.
Wooten, C. W., trans. 1987. *Hermogenes' On Types of Style*. Chapel Hill: University of North Carolina Press.
Xenofontos, S. 2013. "Imagery and Education in Plutarch." *Classical Philology* 108:126–38.
Zucker, F. 1963. "Ἀνηθοποίητος: Eine semasiologische Untersuchung aus der antiken Rhetorik und Ethik." In *Semantica, Rhetorica, Ethica*, edited by F. Zucker, 33–47. Akademie der Wissenschaften, Berlin, Sektion für Altertumswissenschaft, Schriften 38. Berlin: Akademie Verlag.

Contributors

Christine Angelidi is research director emerita at the Institute for Historical Studies of the National Hellenic Research Foundation (Athens). She has written on hagiography, literature, and cultural history. She also published on icons and cult, dreams, and has collaborated in A. Kazhdan, *A History of Byzantine Literature*, vols. 1–2 (Athens, 1999, 2006).

Charles Barber is a professor of early Christian, Byzantine, and post-Byzantine art in the Department of Art and Archaeology at Princeton University. He has published widely on theoretical issues in Byzantine art. His books include: *Contesting the Logic of Painting: Art and Understanding in Eleventh-Century Byzantium* (Brill, 2007) and *Figure and Likeness: On the Limits of Representation in Byzantine Iconoclasm* (Princeton University Press, 2002).

Elizabeth A. Fisher (Ph.D. Harvard) is professor of classical languages and literatures at George Washington University in Washington, D.C. Her scholarship focuses upon Greek texts of the middle and late Byzantine periods that continue and complement the classical tradition. Her publications include an edition of Psellos' hagiographical orations (Teubner, 1994) and an annotated translation with introduction of Ignatios' "Life of the Patriarch Nikephoros" in *Byzantine Defenders of Images* (ed. A.-M. Talbot, Dumbarton Oaks, 1998). She continues publishing articles on the prefaces accompanying Byzantine translations of works in Latin and Arabic.

Christopher Geadrities graduated with a B.A. in classics from the University of Scranton, an M.A. from the University of Pittsburgh, and is completing doctoral work at Brown University in classics on a thesis titled "Einhard Vita Karoli Magni: Introduction, Text, Translation, and Commentary." His interests include late antiquity, reception of the classics, textual criticism and ancient scholarship.

David Jenkins was the Byzantine studies librarian at the University of Notre Dame from 1999 to 2009 and is currently the librarian for classics, Hellenic studies, and linguistics at Princeton University. He maintains the database of Modern Language Translations of Byzantine Sources and is interested in the high register of Byzantine prose, Byzantine philosophy and science, and in particular the life and work of Michael Psellos.

Anthony Kaldellis, professor of classics, Ohio State University, has written extensively on many aspects of Byzantine history, literature, and culture. His work has focused on the reception of the classical tradition, including texts, identities (*Hellenism in Byzantium*), and monuments (*The Christian Parthenon*). He has recently begun to explore how the Byzantines perceived foreign peoples (*Ethnography After Antiquity*), and has offered Roman interpretation of the Byzantine political sphere (*The Byzantine Republic: People and Power at New Rome*). Professor Kaldellis has also translated many Byzantine texts into English, most recently the historians Prokopios, Michael Attaleiates, and Laonikos Chalkokondyles.

Demetrios Kritsotakis (College Year in Athens) holds a Ph.D. in Roman history from Ohio State University. Since 2001 he has been employed by the Center for Epigraphical and Palaeographical Studies of the Ohio State University and conducts research for the Epigraphic Project of the Packard Humanities Institute (PHI). His research interests include the history of Greece during the period of the Roman Empire with special emphasis on the reign of Hadrian, the political propaganda of the Roman emperors, and Greek epigraphy and paleography.

Antony Littlewood was educated at the Universities of Leeds and Oxford before spending his entire active career at the University of Western Ontario, of which institution he is now Professor Emeritus. For fifteen years he was the president of the Canadian Committee of Byzantinists. He is a permanent Visiting Fellow at the Research Centre for Late Antique and Byzantine Studies at the University of Reading, and was recently a Fellow at the Swedish Collegium for Advanced Study in Uppsala. His publications are all on aspects of Byzantine secular literature, Byzantine originality, Byzantine (and Roman) gardens and, recently, cricket history. On Psellos specifically he has written four articles and edited the polymath's *Oratoria Minora* for Teubner.

Stratis Papaioannou, associate professor of classics and director of the Medieval Studies Program, Brown University, works on Byzantine literature, with a focus on the rhetorical tradition. He has published a monograph on Michael Psellos (*Michael Psellos: Rhetoric and Authorship in Byzantium*, Cambridge, 2013) and several articles on different aspects of the Byzantine discursive culture. Recent work includes: a critical edition and translation of texts from the menologion of Symeon Metaphrastes (for the *Dumbarton Oaks Medieval Library,* to appear in 2017), the preparation of *The Oxford Handbook of Byzantine Literature,* and the critical edition of Psellos' letter-collection for the Teubner series.

Jeffrey Walker is professor and chair of the Department of Rhetoric and Writing at the University of Texas at Austin. His interests include the theory and history of rhetoric, ancient and Byzantine rhetoric, rhetoric and poetics, and rhetorical education. His publications include *The Genuine Teachers of This Art: Rhetorical Education in Antiquity* (2011); *Rhetoric and Poetics in Antiquity* (2000); *Bardic Ethos and the American Epic Poem* (1989); *Rhetorical Analysis: A Brief Guide for Writers* (with Mark Longaker, 2011); *Investigating Arguments: Readings for College Writing* (with Glen McClish, 1991); and articles, book chapters, and translations.

Index